When should I travel to get the best airfare?
Where do I go for answers to my travel questions?
What's the best and easiest way to plan and book my trip?

frommers.travelocity.com

Frommer's, the travel guide leader, has teamed up with **Travelocity.com**, the leader in online travel, to bring you an in-depth, easy-to-use resource designed to help you plan and book your trip online.

At **frommers.travelocity.com**, you'll find free online updates about your destination from the experts at Frommer's plus the outstanding travel planning and purchasing features of Travelocity.com. Travelocity.com provides reservations capabilities for 95 percent of all airline seats sold, more than 47,000 hotels, and over 50 car rental companies. In addition, Travelocity.com offers more than 2,000 exciting vacation and cruise packages. Travelocity.com puts you in complete control of your travel planning with these and other great features:

> **Expert travel guidance from Frommer's** - over 150 writers reporting from around the world!
>
> **Best Fare Finder** - an interactive calendar tells you when to travel to get the best airfare
>
> **Fare Watcher** - we'll track airfare changes to your favorite destinations
>
> **Dream Maps** - a mapping feature that suggests travel opportunities based on your budget
>
> **Shop Safe Guarantee** - 24 hours a day / 7 days a week live customer service, and more!

Whether traveling on a tight budget, looking for a quick weekend getaway, or planning the trip of a lifetime, Frommer's guides and Travelocity.com will make your travel dreams a reality. You've bought the book, now book the trip!

Other Great Guides for Your Trip:

Frommer's Europe

Frommer's Scandinavia

Frommer's Denmark

Jean Max
582-5759

Here's what the critics say about Frommer's:

"Amazingly easy to use. Very portable, very complete."
—*Booklist*

♦

"The only mainstream guide to list specific prices. The Walter Cronkite of guidebooks—with all that implies."
—*Travel & Leisure*

♦

"Complete, concise, and filled with useful information."
—*New York Daily News*

♦

"Hotel information is close to encyclopedic."
—*Des Moines Sunday Register*

Sweden

2nd Edition

by Darwin Porter & Danforth Prince

HUNGRY MINDS, INC.

New York, NY • Cleveland, OH • Indianapolis, IN

ABOUT THE AUTHORS

Co-authors **Darwin Porter** and **Danforth Prince** have written numerous best-selling Frommer's guides, notably to England, France, the Caribbean, Italy, and Germany. Porter was a bureau chief for the *Miami Herald* when he was 21, and Prince was formerly with the Paris bureau of *The New York Times*. They are also the authors of two other Scandinavia titles: one devoted to Denmark, another to all of Scandinavia.

Published by:

HUNGRY MINDS, INC.

909 Third Ave.
New York, NY 10022
www.frommers.com

ISBN 0-7645-6352-1
ISSN 1098-1543

Editor: Christine Ryan
Production Editors: Todd Siesky, Stephanie Lucas
Design by Michele Laseau
Cartographer: Elizabeth Puhl
Photo Editor: Richard Fox
Production by Hungry Minds Indianapolis Production Department

SPECIAL SALES

For general information on Hungry Minds' products and services please contact our Customer Care department; within the U.S. at 800-762-2974, outside the U.S. at 317-572-3993 or fax 317-572-4002. For sales inquiries and reseller information, including discounts, bulk sales, customized editions, and premium sales, please contact our Customer Care department at 800-434-3422.

Manufactured in the United States of America

5 4 3 2 1

Contents

List of Maps

AN INVITATION TO THE READER

In researching this book, we discovered many wonderful places—hotels, restaurants, shops, and more. We're sure you'll find others. Please tell us about them, so we can share the information with your fellow travelers in upcoming editions. If you were disappointed with a recommendation, we'd love to know that, too. Please write to:

Frommer's Sweden, 2nd Edition
Hungry Minds, Inc.
909 Third Avenue
New York, NY 10022

AN ADDITIONAL NOTE

Please be advised that travel information is subject to change at any time—and this is especially true of prices. We therefore suggest that you write or call ahead for confirmation when making your travel plans. The authors, editors, and publisher cannot be held responsible for the experiences of readers while traveling. Your safety is important to us, however, so we encourage you to stay alert and be aware of your surroundings. Keep a close eye on cameras, purses, and wallets, all favorite targets of thieves and pickpockets.

WHAT THE SYMBOLS MEAN

✪ Frommer's Favorites

Our favorite places and experiences—outstanding for quality, value, or both.

The following abbreviations are used for credit cards:

AE	American Express	EC	Eurocard
CB	Carte Blanche	JCB	Japan Credit Bank
DC	Diners Club	MC	MasterCard
DISC	Discover	V	Visa
ER	EnRoute		

FIND FROMMER'S ONLINE

www.frommers.com offers up-to-the-minute listings on almost 200 cities around the globe—including the latest bargains and candid, personal articles updated daily by Arthur Frommer himself. No other Web site offers such comprehensive and timely coverage of the world of travel.

The Best of Sweden

Sweden presents visitors with an embarrassment of riches, everything from sophisticated cities to medieval towns to Europe's last untamed wilderness. To help you decide how best to spend your time in Sweden, we've compiled a list of our favorite experiences and discoveries. In the following pages you'll find the kind of candid advice we'd give our close friends.

1 The Best Travel Experiences

- **Shopping in the Kingdom of Crystal:** Many visitors come to Sweden to go shopping—for glass, that is. In the Kingdom of Crystal, which stretches some 70 miles between the port city of Kalmar and the town of Växjö in Småland province, some of the world's most prestigious glassmakers, including Kosta Boda and Orrefors, showcase their wares. At least 16 major glassworks are spread across this area, welcoming visitors, many of whom pick up cut-rate discounts by purchasing "seconds," goods containing flaws hardly noticeable except to the most carefully trained eye. Visitors can see glass being blown and crystal being etched by the land's most skilled craftspeople. See chapter 7.
- **Exploring the High Coast:** The Höga Kusten is the most panoramic stretch of the Bothnian Coast along the northern regions of eastern Sweden. It stretches between the towns of Härnösand and Örnsköldsvik, a land of rolling mountains and forested valleys that seem at times to plunge into the Gulf of Bothnia itself. Along the coast you can cross Höga Kusten Bridge, the seventh longest in the world, spanning the Ångermanalv River, and encounter dramatic coastal scenery in every direction. In America, only the coasts of Maine and northern California compete in general magnificence. See chapter 11.
- **Viewing the Awe-Inspiring Northern Lights:** In the darkest of winter in the north of Sweden (called Lapland or Norrbotten), you can view the shimmering phenomenon of the northern lights on many clear nights, usually from early evening until around midnight. The sun and solar winds create this amazing light show when electrons from the sun collide with atmospheric atoms and molecules. See chapter 12.
- **Touring the Land of the Midnight Sun:** Above the Arctic Circle, where the summer sun never dips below the horizon, you

have endless hours to enjoy the beauty of the region and the activities that go with it—from hiking to white-water rafting. After shopping for distinctive wooden and silver handcrafts, you can dine on fillet of reindeer served with cloudberries. You can even pan for gold with real-life pioneers in Lannavaara, or climb rocks and glaciers in Sarek's National Park. See chapter 12.

2   The Best Active Vacations

- **Fishing:** Sweden offers some of the world's best fishing—its pristine lakes and streams are crystal clear, and many of them are extremely well stocked. Many varieties of fresh- and saltwater fish are available in Sweden's waters. See especially chapters 5, 9, 11, and 12.
- **Golfing:** Many Swedes are obsessed with golf. Most courses are open to the public, from the periphery of Stockholm to Björkliden (above the Arctic Circle), where enthusiasts play under the Midnight Sun. Halland, south of Gothenburg, is called the Swedish Riviera, and it's the golf capital of the country. Båstad is the most fashionable resort in Halland, and you can play a game of golf here at two prestigious courses: the **Båstad Golf Club** at Boarp (☎ 0431/731-36) and the **Bjäre Golf Club** at Solomonhög (☎ 0431/36-10-53), both located right outside the center of Båstad. See chapter 5.
- **White-Water Rafting:** Sweden has some of Europe's best white-water rafting. Trips run the gamut from a short and comfortable ride through a peaceful landscape to fast-running rivers. In Dalarna, the best white-water rafting is on the Västerdalälven River rapids, which are rated moderately difficult. In northern Värmland, 3 miles south of Höljes, you can take easy white-water trips in paddle boats. See chapter 10.
- **Hiking:** The Kungsleden (Royal Trail) may provide the hike of a lifetime, as it takes you through the mountains of Lapland, including Kebnekaise, which, at 6,965 feet, is the highest mountain in Sweden. This 500-kilometer trail cuts through the mountains of Abisko National Park to Riksgränsen on the Norwegian frontier. See chapter 12.
- **Skiing:** In Lapland, you can enjoy both downhill and cross-country skiing year-round. In Kiruna, serious skiers head for the Kebnekaise mountain station, where skiing can be combined with dogsledding and other winter sports. South of the city of Gällivare, you arrive at Dundret, or "Thunder Mountain," for some of the finest skiing in the north. The hotel to stay at here also is called **Dundret** (☎ 0970/145-60), and its staff possesses all the expertise needed to link you up with both cross-country skiing and skiing on the downhill slopes. Inaugurated in 1955, its chairlift to the top of the slopes was the first of its kind in Sweden. See chapter 12.

3   The Best Ways to Spend Time on the Water

- **Exploring the "Garden of Skerries" Around Stockholm:** Few cities enjoy Stockholm's dramatic marine-scape, surrounded by some 24,000 "islands" (some no more than skerries or rocks jutting out of the water), and dotted by colorful yachts. You can easily explore the archipelago in summer, using the car ferries and bridges that connect it. The highlight of the journey is taking a boat trip from the center of Stockholm to the town of Sandhamn, a ride that will introduce you to the scenic highlights of a place many Stockholmers call home in summer. See chapter 4.

- **Riding Along the Göta Canal:** This canal, known as Sweden's blue ribbon, links Stockholm in the east with Gothenberg in the west, and is one of Scandinavia's major tourist attractions. As boats travel along the canal, some of the most beautiful panoramas in Sweden unfold. The canal dates from 1810 and covers 350 miles of scenic beauty. Artificial canals, lakes, and rivers are linked by a series of 65 locks, some of them rising 300 feet above sea level. Any travel agent can book you on this trip. See chapter 9.
- **Angling on the Göta Älv:** The southwestern sector of Lake Vänern, which is part of the Göta Canal (see the preceding), has been called an angler's El Dorado, especially in the valley of the River Göta. The Göta Älv's well-stocked trout waters make for some of Scandinavia's finest spinning and fly-fishing. There are more than 30 different species of fish in Lake Vänern, especially perch, pike, and different types of carp. Some 35,000 young salmon and trout are released annually to keep the waters well-stocked. See chapter 9.
- **Sailing the Gustaf Wasa:** The best way to go between the lakeside resorts of Mora and Leksand in Dalarna, the folkloric province of Sweden, is by boat. This way you can see and experience this most traditional of Swedish provinces from a seascape, as the scenery along the shoreline unfolds before you. Leksand itself is the doorway to the province's most scenic lake, Siljan. No less an authority than Hans Christian Andersen pronounced this trip idyllic. After a panoramic trip you arrive in Mora, a provincial town in Upper Dalarna, where passengers disembark to see the Santa complex (Santa's house and factory). See chapter 10.
- **Viewing the Hudiksvall Archipelago:** The islands around the small town of Hudiksvall along the Bothnian Coast are the most beautiful in the north of Sweden. At one time there were 50 fishing villages and harbors in this archipelago, but today what formerly were fishers' homes serve as summer cottages for vacationers, and you can wander and explore at your leisure in this naturalist's paradise. It has such unique species of flora and fauna that it was made a nature reserve and is protected by the government. See chapter 11.

4 The Most Scenic Towns & Villages

- **Sigtuna:** Sweden's oldest town, founded at the beginning of the 11th century, stands on the shores of Lake Mälaren, northwest of Stockholm. Walk High Street; with its low-timbered buildings it is believed to be the oldest street in Sweden. Traces of Sigtuna's Viking and early Christian heritage can be seen throughout the town. See chapter 4.
- **Uppsala:** Located northwest of Stockhom, Uppsala is Sweden's major university city and boasts a celebrated 15th-century cathedral. Nearby Gamla Uppsala also is intriguing, built on the site of Viking burial grounds where both humans and animals were sacrificed. See chapter 4.
- **Lund:** This town, situated 11 miles northeast of Malmö, rivals Uppsala as a university town. It, too, is ancient, having been founded by Canute the Great in 1020. The town is filled with centuries-old buildings, winding passages, and cobblestone streets; a major attraction is its ancient cathedral, one of the finest expressions of Romanesque architecture in northern Europe. See chapter 6.
- **Visby:** On the island of Gotland, this once was a great medieval European city and former Viking stronghold. For 8 days in August, this sleepy Hanseatic town awakens for the annual Medieval Week, which features fire-eaters, belly dancers, and tournaments. Visby's ruins of 13th- and 14th-century churches and memories of a more prosperous period are intriguing in any season. See chapter 8.

- **Rättvik:** This is a great resort bordering Lake Siljan in the heart of Dalarna, a province known for its regional painting, handcrafts, and folk dancing. Timbered houses reflect Dalarna's old-style architecture, and on summer nights fiddle music evokes the long-ago past. See chapter 10.
- **Jokkmokk:** Located just north of the Arctic Circle, this is the best center for absorbing Lapp (or Sami) culture. The Lapps hold their famous "Great Winter Market" here in early February, a tradition that is 4 centuries old. You can visit a museum devoted to Sami culture in the center of town and then go salmon fishing in the town's central lake. See chapter 12.

5   The Best Places to Go Back in Time

- **Gamla Uppsala** (Uppsala): Gamla Uppsala, 3 miles north of the center of the university city, is one of the most revered historic spots in Sweden. Some 1,500 years ago, the Kingdom of the Svea (Swedes) was ruled from a spot outside the modern university city of Uppsala, north of Stockholm. Here Viking life dominated, and both animals and humans were sacrificed to pagan gods. It is suspected, although not authenticated, that three Swedish kings dating from the 6th century were entombed here. See chapter 4.
- **Skansen** (Djurgården, Stockholm): Called "Old Sweden in a Nutshell," this is the best open-air museum in all of Sweden in terms of numbers of dwellings and authenticity. Some 150 structures were moved from places ranging from the château country in southwest Sweden to as far north as Lapland. From manor houses to windmills, they're all here, giving visitors an idea of how Sweden used to look. This is an especially valuable stop for visitors who see only Stockholm and don't have time to visit the rest of the country. Folk dancing and concerts enliven the atmosphere, and young Swedes demonstrate the creation of handcrafts from the 17th and 18th centuries. See chapter 4.
- **Kivik Tomb** (Bredaror): In the château country of Sweden, the Kivik Tomb was discovered in 1748 north of the coastal town of Simrishamn. It immediately became the most important Bronze Age discovery in the country. One of the former members of the discovery team compared it to being "invited into the living room of a Bronze Age family." Not only were the usual bronze fragments uncovered, but also some grave carvings and, most notably, tomb furniture. A total of eight runic slabs depict scenes from everyday life, including horses and a sleigh, plus what appears to be a troupe of dancing seals (a bit of prehistoric humor). See chapter 6.
- **Eketorp Ring-Fort** (Öland): This prehistoric fortified village is the most important of more than a dozen prehistoric forts known to have existed on Öland in prerecorded times. It appears that the heavily protected village was inhabited by various settlers from A.D. 300 to 1300. Swedish archaeologists have filled the settlement with the Iron Age–style houses that once existed here, and they have reconstructed a massive wall along its edges. Although it is a reconstruction, it is believed to be an authentic replica of what the ring fort and village once looked like, giving an amazing insight into life in the Sweden of ages ago, when prehistoric people fought to survive in an inhospitable terrain. See chapter 8.
- **A Visit to Gamlia** (Umeå): Along the Bothnian Coast, Umeå is called "the city of birch trees," because hundreds of these trees grow here. In this leafy setting lies a museum complex called Gamlia, half a mile northeast of the city center, but centuries into the past. At the original museum, Friluftsmuseet, you can view 20 old-fashioned buildings, many of them dating from the 17th century. Guides

dressed up in clothing like that worn 200 or 300 years ago will show you around while answering questions about how the people lived and worked. On the same site is the Västerbottens Museum, with a repository of artifacts, some prehistoric, discovered in the area. See chapter 11.

6 The Best Museums

- **Millesgården** (Lidingö, outside Stockholm): Sweden's foremost sculptor, Carl Milles (1875–1955), lived here and created a sculpture garden by the sea that now has been turned into a museum. Milles relied heavily on mythological themes in his work, and many of his best-known pieces are displayed here. See chapter 4.
- **National Museet (National Museum of Art)** (Stockholm): One of the oldest museums in the world (it celebrated its 200th birthday in 1992), the National Museum houses Sweden's treasure trove of rare paintings and sculpture. From Rembrandt to Rubens, from Bellini to van Gogh, a panoply of European art unfolds before your eyes. In addition to paintings, you'll find everything from porcelain to antiques. See chapter 4.
- **Vasamuseet (Royal Warship *Vasa*)** (Stockholm): In the Djurgården, this 17th-century man-of-war—now a museum—is a popular tourist attraction, and deservedly so. The *Vasa* is the world's oldest known complete ship. It capsized and sank on its maiden voyage in 1628 before horrified onlookers. The ship was salvaged in 1961 and has been carefully restored; 97% of its 700 original sculptures were retrieved. See chapter 4.
- **Göteborgs Konstmuseum** (Gothenburg): This is the city's leading art museum, a repository of modern paintings that's strong on French impressionists, including van Gogh and Bonnard. Modern artists such as Picasso and Edvard Munch also are represented, as are sculptures by Milles. See chapter 5.
- **Ájtte** (Jokkmokk): In true Lapp country, this is the best repository of artifacts of the Sami culture. Integrating nature with culture, the museum is the largest of its kind in the world. It depicts how the Lapps lived and struggled for survival in a harsh terrain—the houses they lived in and the animals and weapons needed for their livelihood. See chapter 12.

7 The Best Castles & Palaces

- **Drottningholm Palace and Theater** (Drottningholm): Lying 7 miles from Stockholm on an island in Lake Mälaren, Drottningholm, or "Queen's Island," has been dubbed the Versailles of Sweden. It is a magnificent royal residence, a gem of baroque architecture with a palace, gardens, a Chinese pavilion and one of the most remarkable court theaters in Europe. Since 1981, Sweden's royal family has occupied the south wing. See chapter 4.
- **Kungliga Slottet** (Stockholm): One of the few official residences of the royal family that is open to the public, this palace has stood in Gamla Stan (Stockholm's Old Town) for 700 years. Encompassing 608 rooms, today it is used by the Swedish king and his family mainly for ceremonial occasions. The 18th-century Royal Apartments with their painted ceilings, glittering chandeliers, and heirloom tapestries are the highlight of any visit. See chapter 4.
- **Castle of Bosjökloster** (Lund): The origins of this former Benedictine convent date from 1080. Closed in the 1500s, at the time of the Reformation, it fell into disrepair but has since been restored to some of its former glory. Situated on the

shores of Lake Ringsjö, today the castle is surrounded by a recreation area with beautiful gardens. The great courtyard here is high drama, with thousands of flowers and exotic shrubs. You can bring along a picnic lunch to enjoy on the grounds. See chapter 6.

- **Kalmar Slott** (Kalmar): Once called "the key to Sweden," this historic castle was the setting for the Kalmar Union that temporarily united the thrones of Denmark, Norway, and Sweden in 1397. The original keep dates from the 12th century, but in the 16th century King Gustav Vasa rebuilt the castle; his sons eventually transformed it into a Renaissance palace. The castle is the major sight in this port city in southern Sweden, which also makes a good base for exploring the "kingdom of crystal," the greatest concentration of glassworks in Sweden (with lots of bargains). See chapter 7.

- **Läckö Slott** (Lidköping): Lying in the vicinity of the pleasant little town of Lidköping, this castle on the waters of Lake Vänern often has been likened to a "fairy-tale setting." Between 1298 and 1681, 250 rooms were built, many quite large; only the royal palace in Stockholm is larger than Läckö. As you approach from a distance, its distinctive white walls, towers, and turrets seem to rise out of the water. The palace furnishings eventually were carted off and the rooms left bare, but over the years many of the original furnishings have been reclaimed and returned. A visit here and a walk through the once royal grounds is a highlight of any trip to the waters of Lake Vänern. See chapter 9.

8   The Best Cathedrals & Abbeys

- **Riddarholm Church** (Stockholm): Evoking pre-Reformation Sweden, this is one of the best-preserved Franciscan churches left in northern Europe. After being consecrated at the dawn of the 14th century, it served for centuries as the mausoleum for Swedish royalty. The church's cast-iron steeple, which dates from 1841, remains one of the most distinctive landmarks on the Stockholm skyline. The interior is especially impressive; coats of arms of knights of the Order of Seraphim, founded in 1336, cover the walls. The floor is paved with gravestones. After you visit the church, you can walk through Stockholm's Gamla Stan, or Old Town. See chapter 4.

- **Uppsala Domkyrka** (Uppsala): This twin-spired Gothic structure, nearly 400 feet tall, was constructed in the 13th century. Today, the silhouette of this largest cathedral in Scandinavia dominates the landscape, affording Uppsala the status of ecclesiastical capital of Sweden. With a remarkably simple layout compared to other major European cathedrals, its high Gothic aura is nevertheless impressive. In one of the chapels on the south aisle, you can visit the tomb of the philosopher Emanuel Swedenborg (1688–1772). See chapter 4.

- **Domkyrkan (Cathedral of Lund)** (Lund): The apex of Romanesque architecture in Sweden, this imposing twin-towered gray sandstone cathedral is one of the most ancient in Sweden. It was consecrated in 1145, although actually launched sometime in the 1080s by King Canute II. Some of the sculptural details of its architecture evoke Lombardy or other parts of Italy. This is especially evident in its apse, which dates from the 1130s. See chapter 6.

- **Vadstena Abbey** (Vadstena): Sweden's greatest abbey is dedicated to its patron saint, St. Birgitta, who has brought lasting fame to this charming little town on the shores of Lake Vättern. In the Middle Ages, the abbey was at the center of a pilgrimage, which earned it the appellation of "Rome of the North." One of the most important stopovers for those taking the Göta Canal trip, Vadstena is dominated by its Klosterkyrkan, or Abbey Church, built between the mid-14th and -15th centuries to the specifications of its founder, St. Birgitta herself. This Gothic church is rich in art and relics from the Middle Ages. See chapter 7.

- **Kiruna Kyrka** (Kirvna): This church in the far north of Sweden in the midst of Lapland would hardly make it in the grand cathedral circuit of northern Europe. However, it is one of the most unusual churches in the world and causes a lot of raised eyebrows at first sight. It was constructed in 1912 like a stylized Sami tent, with an origami design of rafters and wood beams. In Lapland it is hailed as "the Shrine of the Nomadic people." A free-standing bell tower in front is supported by props and the tombstone of the founder of Kiruna. The only incongruous note is that the altarpiece has a scene representing Paradise as a Tuscan, not Lappish, landscape. See chapter 12.

9 The Best Hotels

- **Grand Hotel** (Stockholm; ☎ 800/223-5652 in the U.S., or 08/679-35-00): Opposite the Royal Palace, this is the most prestigious hotel in Sweden; many well-known people have stayed here, from Sarah Bernhardt to Nobel Prize winners. Set on the waterfront, it dates from 1874 but is continuously renovated to keep it in state-of-the-art condition. The rooms have been luxuriously redecorated, and the bathrooms are made of Italian marble with underfloor heating. See chapter 3.
- **Victory Hotel** (Stockholm; ☎ 08/506-400-00): In the Old Town, this small but stylish hotel ranks among the top in Sweden. Famous for the treasure once buried here (part of which can be seen at the Stockholm City Museum), the hotel originally was built in 1642. The well-furnished bedrooms with modern beds typically have exposed beams and pine floors. On a small rooftop terrace, tables are arranged around a fountain. See chapter 3.
- **Radisson SAS Park Avenue Hotel** (Gothenburg; ☎ 800/221-2350 in the U.S., or 031/758-40-00): Since its opening in 1950, Gothenburg's premier hotel has hosted everybody from the Beatles to David Rockefeller. Located on Gothenburg's attractive main boulevard, near the cultural center, it's a cosmopolitan hotel with a fresh and contemporary ambience. The best double rooms are quite spacious and decorated in a semi-modern, sleek style; about a quarter of the guest rooms are equipped with balconies. See chapter 5.
- **Marina Plaza** (Helsingborg; ☎ 800/528-1234 in the U.S., or 042/19-21-00): This is the most innovative hotel in this port city, which faces the eastern coast of Denmark across from "Hamlet's Castle." A nautical decor prevails, and large glass windows are typical of the sleek contemporary architecture of Sweden. With its rock gardens, abundant flowers, and fountains, it is a lovely place to spend the night in grand comfort and style. See chapter 6.
- **Calmar Stadhotell** (Kalmar; ☎ 0480/496-900): With very reasonably priced rooms, at times less than $100 a night in a double, this is an exceptional choice for lodgings in this historic port city in southeastern Sweden. A landmark hotel constructed in 1906, but completely modernized in 1999, it still retains its look of romanticized architecture, with gables and a bell tower. Many art nouveau embellishments remain, including cut-glass chandeliers and an Edwardian-style library. Its bedrooms are the largest and most comfortable in town. See chapter 7.
- **Halltops Gästgiveri** (Borgholm; ☎ 0485/850-00): On the Baltic Island of Öland, you can stay in an inn whose origins date from 1850. It has been a restaurant longer than it has been a hotel, but it is an ideal place to stay on this historic

island. Bedrooms are light and airy and are frequently renovated, ensuring a good night's sleep in comfort and style. Its restaurant, Bakfickan, or "hip pocket" in English, is one of Öland's best. See chapter 8.

- **Ronnums Herrgård** (Vargön; ☎ 0521/22-32-70): One of the most idyllic stopovers along the Göta Canal is in Vargön, which a poet once labeled "Little Paris." In this setting of charm and grace, you can enjoy life in a restored 18th-century manor house with yellow clapboards and a red roof, standing in its own parklike grounds. Among the 19th-century antiques, you can enjoy life as it was lived in old Sweden, all at a very reasonable price. See chapter 9.
- **Stadshotellet** (Karlstad; ☎ 800/528-1234 in the U.S., or 054/21-52-20): In the heart of the folkloric province of Värmland, this hotel, behind its neo-baroque façade, is one of the most impressive of the nineteenth-century hotels remaining in Sweden. If you like old-fashioned style but modern comfort, this is for you. From its British-inspired pub to its gourmet restaurant, it's a winner. See chapter 10.
- **The Ice Hotel** (Jukkasjärvi; ☎ 980/668-00): Surely there is no hotel in all of Europe as curious as this one deep in the heart of Swedish Lapland. Every winter the hotel is carved out of the ice at a point 125 miles north of the Arctic Circle. Come spring, this igloo-shaped hotel literally melts away. In its hyper-glacial setting, guests can check in for an icy night—hopefully with a good bed partner. If you've ever dreamed of living like an Eskimo, here is your wintry chance. See chapter 12.

10 The Best Restaurants

- **Paul & Norbert** (Stockholm; ☎ 08/663-81-83): With only eight tables on the fashionable Strandvägen, this exclusive restaurant is set in a patrician residence dating from 1873. The most innovative restaurant in Stockholm, it's the culinary domain of German owners Paul Beck and Norbert Lang. In winter, the Swedish game served here is without equal in the country—try the pigeon with Calvados sauce. And you can always count on something tempting and unusual; sautéed sweetbreads in nettle sauce, anyone? See chapter 3.
- **Gripsholms Värdshus Restaurant** (Mariefred; ☎ 0159/34750): If you're seeking traditional Swedish food with French overtones, this is the best dining choice on the periphery of the capital. Local game dishes, including wild grouse, are featured in autumn, and marinated salmon with a mild mustard sauce is a year-round favorite. Tastings also can be arranged in the wine cellar. See chapter 4.
- **Sjömagasinet** (Gothenburg; ☎ 031/773-59-20): By far the most intriguing and interesting restaurant in town, this is one of the finest places to go for seafood on the west coast of Sweden. Lying in the western suburb of Klippan, this converted 1775 warehouse serves an array of fresh fish whose flavor never diminishes regardless of the sauce or preparation. The fish and shellfish pot-au-feu with a chive-flavored crème fraîche is worth the trek. See chapter 5.
- **Anna Kock** (Helsingborg; ☎ 042/18-13-00): "Anna the Cook" was known all over this port city across the eastern coast from Denmark. She's gone now, but her relatives carry on, offering inexpensive Swedish food with style and flair. In this cozy enclave, feast on such dishes as fillet of reindeer with lingonberry sauce or breast of wild duck with rhubarb chutney. See chapter 6.
- **Kalmar Hamn Krog** (Kalmar; ☎ 0480/411-020): Since it was established in 1988 in this historic port city in southeastern Sweden, this international restaurant has quickly moved to the front of the line. Hailed as the best in town, it

prepares reasonably priced food with flair, using only market-fresh ingredients deftly handled by a trained kitchen staff. The chefs borrow freely from the world's larders, using spices or ingredients from any country where their culinary imaginations wander. See chapter 7.

- **Halltops Gästigiveri** (Borgholm; ☎ 0485/850-00): On the historic Baltic island of Öland, this dining room serving Swedish food takes you back to the good old days. Here you can feast on the dishes beloved by your great-grandparents—provided they came from Sweden. Herbs and vegetables come from suppliers who grow them right on the island, and the local fishers bring in their catch of the day. The place is charming, a bit stylish, and occupies one of the oldest manor houses on the island. See chapter 8.

- **Stek Huset** (Karlstad; ☎ 054/56-00-80): Deep in the heart of the province of Värmland, made famous by the great international writer Selma Lagerlöf, you can dine on refined Swedish and international cuisine, some of the best in the area. Patrons arrive from miles around to enjoy the fare, all for a reasonable price. Fresh fish and steaks often are flambéed at the table with high drama. See chapter 10.

- **Restaurant Kriti** (Skellefteå; ☎ 0910/77-95-35): Along the Bothnian coast of eastern Sweden, across from Finland, this restaurant in a port city of the far north is acclaimed for its Greek food. A taste of the Mediterranean cheers devoted local diners during the long, dark, Swedish winter nights of snow and ice. Dig into their stuffed vine leaves, souvlaki, or moussaka, and you'll think you're looking at the Acropolis instead of a wintry landscape. Their pizzas also are known as the best along the coast. See chapter 11.

2

Planning a Trip to Sweden

In the pages that follow, we've compiled everything you need to know about how to handle the practical details of planning your trip in advance—airlines, a calendar of events, details on currency, and more.

1 The Regions in Brief

GÖTALAND The southern part of Sweden takes its name from the ancient Goths. Some historians believe they settled in this region, which is similar in climate and architecture to parts of northern Europe, especially Germany. This is the most populated part of Sweden, and includes eight provinces—Östergötland, Småland (the kingdom of crystal), Västergötland, Skåne, Dalsland, Bohuslän, Halland, and Blekinge—plus the islands of Öland and Gotland. The Göta Canal cuts through this district. **Gothenburg** is the most important port in the west, and **Stockholm,** the capital, the chief port in the east. Aside from Stockholm, **Skåne,** the château district, is the most heavily visited area. It's often compared to the Danish countryside. There are many seaside resorts on both the west and east coasts.

SVEALAND The central region encompasses the folkloric province of **Dalarna** (Dalecarlia in English) and **Värmland** (immortalized in the novels of Selma Lagerlöf). These districts are the ones most frequented by visitors. Other provinces include Våstmanland, Uppland, Södermanland, and Nårke. Ancient Svealand often is called the cultural heart of Sweden. Some 20,000 islands lie along its eastern coast.

NORRLAND Northern Sweden makes up Norrland, which lies above the 61st parallel and includes about 50% of the land mass. It's inhabited by only about 15% of the population, including Lapps and Finns. Norrland consists of 24 provinces, of which **Lapland** is the most popular with tourists. It's a land of thick forests, fast-flowing (and cold) rivers, and towering mountain peaks. Lapland, the home of the Lapp reindeer herds, consists of tundra. **Kiruna** is one of Norrland's most important cities because of its iron-ore deposits.

2 Visitor Information & Entry Requirements

VISITOR INFORMATION

In the **United States,** contact the **Scandinavian Tourist Board,** 655 Third Ave., 18th floor, New York, NY 10017 (☎ 212/885-9700), at

Sweden

least 3 months in advance for maps, sightseeing information, ferry schedules, and other advice and tips.

In the **United Kingdom,** contact the **Swedish Travel & Tourism Council,** 11 Montague Pl., London W1H 2AL (☎ 020/7870-5600).

You also can try the Web site **www.visit-sweden.com**.

If you get in touch with a travel agent, make sure the agent is a member of the **American Society of Travel Agents (ASTA).** If a problem arises, you can complain to the society's Consumer Affairs Department at 1101 King St., Suite 200, Alexandria, VA 22314 (☎ **703/739-8739**).

ENTRY REQUIREMENTS

American, Canadian, Irish, Australian, and **New Zealand** citizens; and **British** subjects need only a valid passport to enter Norway. You need a visa only if you want to stay more than 3 months. A British Visitor's Passport also is valid for a holiday or some business trips of less than 3 months. The passport can include your spouse, and it's valid for 1 year. Apply in person at a main post office in the British Isles, and the passport will be issued that day.

In the **United States,** you can apply for a passport by mail or in person at 1 of 13 regional offices. To apply, you need a passport application form, available at U.S. post offices and federal court offices, and proof of citizenship, such as a birth certificate or naturalization papers; an expired passport also is accepted. Two identical passport-size (2"×2") photographs are required. First-time applicants for passports pay $60 ($40 if under 15 years of age). Persons 18 or older who have an expired passport that is not more than 12 years old can reapply by mail. The old passport must be submitted along with new photographs and a pink renewal form (DSP-82). The fee is $40. For an additional $35 a passport can be renewed within 3 business days. Call ☎ **202/647-0518** any time for information. Information also can be obtained on the Internet at **travel.state.gov** or by calling the **National Passport Information Center (NPIC)** at ☎ **900/225-5674.** The cost is 35¢ per minute for 24-hour automated service, or $1.05 per minute from 9am to 3pm for live operator service. You also can write to Passport Service, Office of Correspondence, Department of State, 1111 19th St. NW, Suite 510, Washington, DC 20522-1075.

In **Canada,** citizens can go to one of 28 regional offices, or mail an application to the **Passport Office,** External Affairs and International Trade Canada, Ottawa ON K1A 0GE (☎ **613/996-8885**). Applicants residing in a city where a passport office is located are requested to submit their applications in person. Passport applications are available at passport offices, post offices, and most travel agencies. All requirements for obtaining a passport are outlined on the application form. The fee is Can$60. Passports are valid for 5 years. For travel information, call ☎ **800/567-6868,** or 819/994-3500 for general information.

In **Great Britain,** British subjects may travel to Sweden with only an identity card. A passport is not necessary. British visitors who wish to own a passport can do so at a cost of £28 for a 10-year passport. Basic documentation is available at any post office in Great Britain. For more information regarding fees, documentation requirements, or to ask for an emergency passport, telephone the London Passport office at ☎ **0990/210410**.

In **Australia,** citizens can apply at the nearest post office. Provincial capitals and other major cities have passport offices. Application fees are subject to review every 3 months. Call ☎ **02/13-12-32** for the latest information. An adult's passport is valid for 10 years; for people under 18, a passport is valid for 5 years.

In **New Zealand,** citizens should contact the nearest consulate or passport office to obtain an application. One can file in person or by mail. Proof of citizenship is required and the passport is good for 10 years. Passports are processed at the **New Zealand Passport Office,** Documents of National Identity Division, Department of Internal Affairs, P.O. Box 10-526, Wellington (☎ **0800/22-50-50**). The fee is NZ$80.

In **Ireland,** write in advance to the Passport Office, Molesworth Street, Dublin 2, Ireland (☎ **01/671-16-33**). The cost is IR£45. Applications are sent by mail. Irish citizens living in North America can contact the **Irish Embassy,** 2234 Massachusetts Ave. NW, Washington, DC 20008 (☎ **202/462-3939**). The embassy can issue a new passport or direct you to one of the three North American consulates that have jurisdiction over a particular region; the charge is $75 to $81 depending on the consulate.

In **South Africa,** citizens can apply for a passport at any Home Affairs office. Passports issued are valid for 10 years, costing R80. For children under 16, passports are valid for only 5 years for a fee of R60. For further information, contact your nearest Department of Home Affairs office.

3 Money

THE SWEDISH KRONA   Sweden's basic unit of currency is the **krona** (or SEK). Note that the Swedes spell the plural kronor with an *o* instead of an *e* as in the kroner of Denmark and Norway. One krona is divided into 100 **öre.** Banknotes are issued in denominations of 20, 50, 100, 500, 1,000, and 10,000 SEK. Silver coins are issued in denominations of 50 öre and 1 and 5 SEK.

TRAVELER'S CHECKS   Although regarded as old fashioned by today's ATM users, traditionalists still like to carry traveler's checks as a safe means of carrying cash abroad. Most banks will give you a better exchange rate for traveler's checks than for cash. Checks denominated in U.S. dollars or British pounds are accepted virtually anywhere; sometimes you also can get these checks in a local currency.

Each of the agencies in the following list will refund checks if lost or stolen, provided that you produce documentation. When purchasing checks, ask about refund hotlines. American Express has the largest number of offices around the world.

Issuers sometimes have agreements with groups to sell traveler's checks commission free. For example, the American Automobile Association (AAA) clubs sell American Express checks in several currencies without commission.

American Express (☎ 800/221-7282 in the U.S. and Canada) is one of the largest and most immediately recognized issuers of traveler's checks. No commission is charged to members of the American Automobile Association and holders of certain types of American Express cards. For questions or problems arising outside the United States or Canada, contact any of the company's many regional representatives. We'll list locations throughout this guide.

Citicorp (☎ 800/645-6556 in the U.S. and Canada, or 813/623-7300, collect, from anywhere else in the world) issues checks in several different currencies.

Thomas Cook (☎ 800/223-7373 in the U.S. and Canada, or 609/987-7300, collect, from anywhere else in the world) issues MasterCard traveler's checks denominated in several currencies; not all currencies are available at every outlet.

Visa Travelers Checks (☎ 800/221-2426 in the U.S. and Canada, or 212/858-8500, collect, from most other parts of the world) sells Visa checks denominated in several major currencies.

CREDIT & CHARGE CARDS   American Express, Diners Club, and Visa are widely recognized throughout Sweden. Discover cards are not accepted. If you see a

What Things Cost in Stockholm	in U.S.$
Taxi from the airport to the city center	38.50
Basic bus or subway fare	1.75
Local telephone call	.30
Double room at the Grand Hotel (very expensive)	351.45
Double room at the Adlon Hotel (moderate)	146.30
Double room at the Hotell Kom (inexpensive)	102.85
Lunch for one at Eriks Bakfica (moderate)	31.90
Lunch for one at Cattelin Restaurant (inexpensive)	7.15
Dinner for one, without wine, at Operakällaren (very expensive)	52.80
Dinner for one, without wine, at Prinsens (moderate)	37.20
Dinner for one, without wine, at Tennstopet (inexpensive)	22.00
Pint of beer (draft pilsner) in a bar	4.30
Coca-Cola in a cafe	3.50
Cup of coffee in a cafe	3.10
Admission to Drottningholm Palace	5.50
Movie ticket	10.50
Budget theater ticket	12.10

Eurocard or Access sign, it means that the establishment accepts MasterCard. With an American Express, MasterCard, or Visa card, you also can withdraw currency from cash machines (ATMs) at various locations. Always check with your credit or charge card company about this before leaving home.

ATM NETWORKS   Plus, Cirrus, and other networks connect with automated teller machines throughout Scandinavia. If your credit card has been programmed with a PIN (personal identification number), you probably can use your card at Scandinavian ATMs to withdraw money as a cash advance on your card. Always determine the frequency limits for withdrawals and check to see if your PIN code must be reprogrammed for usage on your trip abroad. Also, be aware that most likely you will be able to access only your checking account from overseas ATM machines. For **Cirrus** locations abroad, call ☎ **800/424-7787; www.mastercard.com**. For **Plus** usage abroad, check the Plus site on the Web at **www.visa.com** or call ☎ **800/843-7587**.

4 When to Go

THE CLIMATE   Sweden's climate is hard to classify because temperatures, aided by the Gulf Stream, vary considerably from the fields of Skåne to the wilderness of Lapland (the upper tenth of Sweden lies north of the Arctic Circle).

The Midnight Sun

In summer, the sun never fully sets in northern Sweden; even in the south, daylight can last until 11pm and then the sun rises around 3am.

In Sweden the best vantage points and dates when you can see the thrilling spectacle of the midnight sun are as follows: **Björkliden,** May 26 to July 19; **Abisko,** June 12 to July 4; **Kiruna,** May 31 to July 14; and **Gällivare,** June 2 to July 12. All these places can be reached by public transportation.

Remember that although the sun may be shining brightly at midnight, it's not as strong as at midday. Bring along a warm jacket or sweater.

The country as a whole has many sunny days in summer, but it's not super-hot. July is the warmest month, with temperatures in both Stockholm and Gothenburg averaging around 64°F. February is the coldest month, when the temperature in Stockholm averages around 26°F (Gothenburg is a few degrees warmer).

It's not always true that the farther north you go the cooler it becomes. During summer the northern parts of the country—from Halsingland to northern Lapland—may suddenly have the warmest weather and the bluest skies. Check the weather forecasts on television and in the newspapers. (Swedes claim these forecasts are 99% reliable.)

SUMMER   Regarding weather, the ideal time to visit Sweden is from June to August. At this time all its cafes and attractions, including open-air museums, are open and thousands flock to the north of Sweden to enjoy the midnight sun. Bad weather can close attractions at other times of the year. However, summer also is the most expensive time to fly to Sweden, as airlines charge their highest fares then. To compensate, hotels sometimes grant summer discounts (it pays to ask).

SPRING & FALL   Almost prettier than a Swedish summer are the months of spring and autumn, notably May through June and the month of September. When spring comes to the Swedish countryside and wild flowers burst into bloom after a long dark winter, it is a joyous celebration in the country.

WINTER   Scandinavia's off-season is winter (from about November 1 to March 21). Many visitors, except those on business, prefer to avoid Sweden in winter. The cold weather sets in by October, and you'll need to keep bundled up heavily until long past April. However, other, more adventurous tourists do go to Sweden in the winter. The students have returned to such university cities as Stockholm and Lund, and life seems more vibrant then. Also, there are more cultural activities. Except for special festivals and folkloric presentations, the major cultural venues in Sweden, including opera, dance, ballet, and theater, shut down in summer. Skiers also go to Sweden in winter, but we don't recommend it. It is pitch dark in winter in the north of Sweden, and the slopes have to be artificially lit. You'd be better off soaking up the alpine sun in Germany, Switzerland, or Austria.

Of course, one of the most eerie and fascinating experiences available in Europe is to see the shimmering northern lights, which can be viewed only in winter.

Sweden's Average Daytime Temperatures (°F)

	Jan	Feb	Mar	Apr	May	June	July	Aug	Sept	Oct	Nov	Dec
Stockholm	27	26	31	40	50	59	64	62	54	45	37	32
Karesuando	6	5	12	23	39	54	59	51	44	31	9	5
Karlstad	33	30	28	37	53	63	62	59	54	41	29	26
Lund	38	36	34	43	57	63	64	61	57	47	37	37

HOLIDAYS   Sweden celebrates the following public holidays: New Year's Day (January 1); Epiphany (January 6); Good Friday, Easter Sunday, Easter Monday; Labor Day (May 1); Ascension Day (mid-May); Whitsunday and Whitmonday (late May); Midsummer Day (June 21); All Saints' Day (November 1); and Christmas Eve, Christmas Day, and Boxing Day (December 24, 25, and 26). Inquire at a tourist bureau for the actual dates of the holidays that vary from year to year.

Sweden Calendar of Events

The dates given here may in some cases be only approximations. Be sure to check with the tourist office before you make plans to attend a specific event. For information on Walpurgis night and midsummer celebrations, call the local tourist offices in the town where you plan to stay. (See individual chapters for the phone numbers.)

April

- **Walpurgis Night,** nationwide. Celebrations with bonfires, songs, and speeches welcoming the advent of spring. These are especially lively celebrations among university students at Uppsala, Lund, Stockholm, Gothenburg, and Umeå. April 30.

May

- ✪ **Drottningholm Court Theater.** Some 30 opera and ballet performances, from baroque to early romantic, are presented in the unique 1766 Drottningholm Court Theater, Drottningholm, with original decorative paintings and stage mechanisms. Call ☎ **08/660-82-24** for tickets. Take the T-bana to Brommaplan, then bus no. 301 or 323. A steamboat runs in the summer; call ☎ **08/411-7023** for information. Late May to late September.

June

- **Midsummer,** nationwide. Swedes celebrate Midsummer Eve all over the country. Maypole dances to the sound of the fiddle and accordion are the typical festive events of the day. Dalarna observes the most traditional celebrations. June 21 to 23.

July

- ✪ **Falun Folk Musical Festival.** International folk musicians gather to participate in and attend concerts, seminars, lectures, exhibitions, and films on folk music. Events are conducted at various venues; contact the **Falun Folk Music Festival,** S-791 28 Falun (☎ **023/83-637**), for more information. Mid-July.
- **Around Gotland Race,** Sandhamn. The biggest and most exciting open-water Scandinavian sailing race starts and finishes at Sandhamn in the Stockholm archipelago. About 450 boats, mainly from Nordic countries, take part. Call the Stockholm tourist office for information. Two days in mid-July.
- **Rättviksdansen** (International Festival of Folk Dance and Music), Rättvik. Every other year for some 20 years, around 1,000 folk dancers and musicians from all over the world have gathered to participate in this folkloric tradition. Last week in July, 2001.

August

- **Medieval Week,** Gotland. Numerous events are held throughout the island of Gotland—tours, concerts, medieval plays, festivities, and shows. For more information, contact the Tourist Office, Hamngatan 4, S-621 25 Visby (☎ **0498/20-17-00**). August 4 to 11.

- **Stockholm Waterfestival.** A tradition since 1989, this weeklong festival around the city's shores offers entertainment such as fireworks, competitions, and concerts, as well as information about the care and preservation of water. An award of $150,000 is given to an individual or organization that has made an outstanding contribution to water preservation. Call the Stockholm tourist office for information. August 4 to 18.
- **Minnesota Day,** Utvandra Hus, Växjö (Småland). Swedish-American relations are celebrated at the House of Emigrants with speeches, music, singing, and dancing; climaxing in the election of the Swedish-American of the year. Call ☎ 0470/201-20 for information. Second Sunday in August.

December

✪ **Nobel Day,** Stockholm. The king, members of the royal family, and invited guests attend the Nobel Prize ceremony for literature, physics, chemistry, medicine, physiology, and economics. Attendance is by invitation only. The ceremony is held at the concert hall and followed by a banquet at City Hall. December 10.

- **Lucia, the Festival of Lights,** nationwide. To celebrate the shortest day and longest night of the year, young girls called "Lucias" appear in restaurants, offices, schools, and factories, wearing floor-length white gowns and special headdresses, each holding a lighted candle. They are accompanied by "star boys"—young men in white with wizard hats covered with gold stars, each holding a wand with a large golden star at the top. One of these "Lucias" eventually is crowned queen. In olden days, Lucia was known as "Little Christmas." December 13.

This observed nationwide. Actual planned events change from year to year and vary from community to community The best place for tourists to observe this event is at the open-air museum at Skansen in Stockholm.

5 The Active Vacation Planner

BIKING Much of Sweden is flat, which makes it ideal for cycling tours. Bicycles can be rented all over the country, and country hotels sometimes make them available free of charge. A typical rental is 200 SEK ($22) per day. For more detailed information, contact the **Svenska Turist-förening** (Swedish Touring Club), P.O. Box 25, Amiralitetshuset 1, Flagmansvägen 8, S101 20 Stockholm (☎ 08-463-21-00).

FISHING In Stockholm, within view of the king's palace, you can cast a line for what are some of the finest salmon in the world. Ever since Queen Christina issued a decree in 1636, Swedes have had the right to fish in waters adjoining the palace. Throughout the country, fishing is an everyday affair; it has been estimated that one of every three Swedes is an angler.

But if you'd like to fish elsewhere in Sweden, you'll need a license; the cost varies from region to region. Local tourist offices in any district can give you information about this. Pike, pike-perch, eel, and perch are found in the heartland and the southern parts of the country.

GOLFING After Scotland, Sweden may have more golf enthusiasts than any other country in Europe. There are about 400 courses, and they're rarely crowded. Visitors often are granted local membership cards and greens fees vary, depending on the club. Many golfers fly from Stockholm to Boden in the far north in the summer months to play by the light of the midnight sun at the **Björkliden Arctic Golf Course,** which opened in 1989 some 150 miles north of the Arctic Circle. It's not only the world's northernmost golf course, but it's one of the most panoramic anywhere, set against a backdrop of snow-capped peaks, green valleys, and crystal lakes. The narrow fairways and small greens of this nine-hole, par-36 course offer multiple challenges. For details, contact the **Björkliden Arctic Golf Club,** Kvarnbacksvägen 28, Bromma S-168 74 (☎ 08/28-94-30). For general information on courses in Sweden, contact the **Svenska Golfförbundet,** P.O. Box 84, Daneered S-182 11 (☎ 08/622-15-00).

HIKING   Sarek, in the far north, is one of Europe's last real wilderness areas; Swedes come here to hike in the mountains, pick mushrooms, gather berries, and fish. The **Svenska Turist-förening (Swedish Touring Club),** P.O. Box 25, Amiralitetshuset 1, Flagmansvägen 8, S101 20 Stockholm (☎ 08/463-21-00), provides accommodations in the area in mountain huts with 10 to 30 beds. The staff knows the northern part of Sweden very well, and can advise you about marked tracks, rowboats, the best excursions, the problems you're likely to encounter, communications, and transportation. The company also sells trail and mountain maps.

HORSEBACK RIDING   There are numerous opportunities for overnight horseback pack trips in such wilderness areas as the forests of Värmland or Norrbotten, where reindeer, musk oxen, and other creatures roam. The most popular overnight horseback trips start just north of the city of Karlstad in Värmland. There also are covered-wagon trips with overnight stopovers. A typical horseback trip begins in the lakeside village of Torsby and follows a forested trail up a mountain. An average of 4 hours a day is spent on the horse, with meals cooked over an open fire.

In northern Sweden, two popular starting points are Funäsdalen, close to the Norwegian border, and Ammarnäs, not far from the Arctic Circle and the midnight sun. These trips begin in June. Local tourist offices can provide further information.

Sweden also has many riding stables and riding schools. Ask about them at local tourist offices. One of the most popular excursions is a pony trek through the region of Sweden's highest mountain, Knebnekaise.

In sites convenient to Stockholm, you might try a ride or two around the rinks at **Djurgärdens ridskola,** Kaknäs, Djurgårend (☎ 08/6602111), or a bit farther afield at **Bögs Gård AB,** in Sollentuna (☎ 08/96-79-71), which maintains a complement of Icelandic ponies which seem to thrive throughout the region's frigid winters. Both sites can help arrange overnight treks through the surrounding fields and forests, even though most of their business derives from rink riding and improvement of equestrian forms.

One more unusual choice is exploring the Orsa (outback) by horse and covered wagon. In the province of Dalarna, you can rent a horse and wagon with space for up to five people. The outback is an almost unpopulated area of wild beauty, and the route goes past beautiful summer pastures, small forest lakes, and panoramic views. Rides are available June through August. Clients cover about 10 miles a day, sleeping in or beside the covered wagon, following a pre-selected itinerary, usually overnighting beside lakes or rivers. For more information, contact **Häst och Vagn,** Torsmo 1646, S-794 91 Orsa (☎ 2505/530-14).

If you prefer to make your horseback riding arrangements before your departure from the United States, perhaps as part of an organized bus, rail, or self-drive tour, **Passage Tours of Scandinavia,** 239 Commercial Blvd., Fort Lauderdale, FL 33308 (☎ 800/548-5960), can custom design a suitable tour for you, usually configured with visits to Sweden's cultural, architectural, or historical highlights en route.

RAFTING   White-water rafting and river rafting are the two major forms of this sport. For white-water rafting, you go in a fast river boat, the trip made all the more exciting by a series of rapids. Throughout the country there are both short trips and those lasting a week or so. In Värmland, contact **Branäs Sport AB,** Branäs Fritidsanläggnin, P.O. Box 28, S-680 60 Syssleback (☎ 564/352-09).

River rafting is much tamer, because you go gently down a slow-moving river in Sweden's heartland. For information about the best river rafting in Sweden, contact **Kukkolaforsen-Turist & Konferens,** P.O. Box 184, S-593 91 Haparanda (☎ **922/ 310-00**). If you want to try log-rafting, we recommend a lazy trip down the Klarälven River, winding through beautiful and unspoiled valleys between high mountains, with sandy beaches where you can swim if temperatures and river conditions allow. There also is excellent fishing for pike and grayling. You will travel through northern Värmland at a speed of 1¼ miles per hour from the mouth of the Vingümngssjön Lake in the north to Ekshärad in the south, a distance of 68 miles in 6 days. Overnight accommodations are arranged either on the moored raft or ashore. Each raft can accommodate between two and five people, and the trips are available from May to August. For a 6-day tour, adults pay 1,860 SEK ($204.60); for a 3-day tour, 1,530 SEK ($168.30). Rental of a tent and kitchen equipment costs an additional 350 SEK ($38.50) per person. Participants supply their own food and fishing equipment. Contact **Sverigeflotten,** Transtrand 20, S-680 63 Likenäs (☎ **564/402-27;** www.tordata.se/bf).

SAILING & CANOEING   Canoes and sailing boats can be rented all over the country; you can obtain information about this from the local tourist office. Often hotels situated near water-sports areas have canoes for rent.

SWIMMING   If you don't mind swimming in rather cool water, Sweden has one of the world's longest coastlines—plus some 100,000 lakes—in which you can take the plunge. The best bathing beaches are on the west coast. Both the islands of Öland and Gotland have popular summer seaside resorts. Beaches in Sweden generally are open to the public, and nude bathing is allowed on certain designated beaches. Topless bathing for women is prevalent everywhere. If a Swedish lake is suitable for swimming, it's always signposted.

WALKING & JOGGING   Sweden is ideal for either activity. Local tourist offices can provide details and sometimes even supply you with free maps of the best trails or jogging paths. In Stockholm, hotel reception desks often can tell you the best places to go jogging nearby.

6 Special-Interest Vacations

ADVENTURE TOURS   In the U.S.   For overall adventure travel, including skiing, hiking, and biking, the best bet is **Borton Overseas,** 5412 Lyndale Avenue South, Minneapolis, MN 55419 (☎ **800/843-0602** or 612/822-4640; www. bortonoverseas.com), which offers sea kayaking and backpacking expeditions in Sweden. Tours really should be arranged before you go. **Backroad Travel in Sweden, Inc.,** 18 Lake Shore Drive, Arlington, MA 02474 (☎ **888/648-3522** or 781/646-2955; www.backroadtravel.com), offers bicycle and walking tours off the beaten paths in Sweden, especially in Gotland and the Stockholm archipelago.

In the U.K.   The oldest travel agency in Britain, **Cox & Kings,** Gordon House 10, Greencoat Place, London SW1P 1PH (☎ **020/7873-5006;** www. coxandkings. co.uk), was established in 1758; at that time, the company served as the paymasters and transport directors for the British armed forces in India. Today, the company sends large numbers of travelers from Britain throughout the rest of the world, specializing in unusual—if pricey—holidays. Its offerings in Scandinavia include cruises through the region's spectacular fjords and waterways, bus and rail tours through sites of historic and aesthetic interest, and visits to the region's best-known handcraft centers, Viking burial sites, and historic churches. The company's staff is noted for its focus on tours of ecological and environmental interest.

Those who would like to cycle their way through the splendors of Scandinavia should join Britain's oldest and largest association of bicycle riders, the **Cyclists' Touring Club,** 69 Meadrow, Godalming, Surrey GU7 3HS (☎ **01483/417-217;** www. ctc.org.uk). Founded in 1878, it charges £25 ($40) a year for membership, which includes information, maps, a subscription to a newsletter packed with practical information and morale boosters, plus recommended cycling routes through virtually every country in Europe. The organization's information bank on scenic routes through Scandinavia is especially comprehensive. Membership can be arranged over the phone with an appropriate credit card (such as MasterCard, Visa, Access, or Barclaycard).

In Sweden   Swedish outfitter **30,000 Oar,** Fågelbrouhus, S-139 60 Värmdö (☎ **08/ 571-401-78**), specializes in tours and adventures which can be booked locally.

LEARNING VACATIONS   An international series of programs for persons over 50 who are interested in combining travel and learning is offered by **Interhostel,** developed by the University of New Hampshire. Each program lasts 2 weeks, is led by a university faculty or staff member, and is arranged in conjunction with a host college, university, or cultural institution. Participants may stay longer if they wish. Interhostel offers programs consisting of cultural and intellectual activities and includes field trips to museums and other centers of interest. For information, contact the **University of New Hampshire,** Division of Continuing Education, 6 Garrison Ave., Durham, NH 03824 (☎ **800/733-9753** or 603/862-1147; www.learn.unh.org).

Another good source of information about courses in Sweden is the **American Institute for Foreign Study (AIFS),** River Plaza, 9 W. Broad St., Stamford, CT 06902 (☎ **800/727-2437** or 203/399-5000; www.aifs.org). This organization can set up transportation and arrange for summer courses, with room and board included.

The biggest organization dealing with higher education in Europe is the **Institute of International Education (IIE),** 809 United Nations Plaza, New York, NY 10017 (☎ **800/445-0443** or 212/883-8200). A few of its booklets are free, but for $39.95, plus $6 for postage, you can purchase the more definitive *Vacation Study Abroad.* Visitors to New York can use the resources of its Information Center, which is open to the public Tuesday through Thursday from 11am to 4pm. The institute is closed on major holidays.

One well-recommended clearinghouse for academic programs throughout the world is the **National Registration Center for Study Abroad (NRCSA),** 823 N. 2nd St., P.O. Box 1393, Milwaukee, WI 53201 (☎ **414/278-0631;** www.nrcsa.com). The organization maintains language study programs throughout Europe.

HOME STAYS   Friendship Force International (FFI), 34 Peachtree St., Suite 900, Atlanta, GA 30303 (☎ **404/522-9490;** www.friendship-force.org), is a nonprofit organization that fosters and encourages friendships among people worldwide. Dozens of branch offices throughout North America arrange en masse visits, usually once a year. Because of group bookings, the airfare to the host country usually is less than the cost of individual APEX tickets. Each participant spends 2 weeks in the host country, one as a guest in the home of a family and the second traveling in the host country.

Servas, 11 St. John St., Room 407, New York, NY 10038 (☎ **212/267-0252;** www.usservas.org), is an international nonprofit, nongovernmental, interfaith network of travelers and hosts whose goal is to help promote world peace, goodwill, and understanding. (Its name means "to serve" in Esperanto.) Servas hosts offer travelers hospitality for 2 days. Travelers pay a $65 annual fee and a $25 list deposit after filling out an application and being approved by an interviewer (interviewers are located across the United States). They then receive Servas directories listing the names and addresses of Servas hosts.

HOME EXCHANGES   One of the most exciting breakthroughs in modern tourism is the home exchange. Home exchanges cut costs. You don't pay hotel bills and you also can save money by shopping in markets and eating in. Sometimes even the family car is included. Of course, you must be comfortable with the idea of having strangers in your home, and you must be content to spend your vacation in one place. Also, you may not get a home in the area you request.

Intervac, U.S., 30 Corte San Fernando, Tiburon, CA 94159 (☎ 800/756-HOME or 415/435-3497; www.intervacus), is part of the largest worldwide exchange network. It publishes four catalogs a year, containing more than 10,000 homes in more than 36 countries. Members contact each other directly. The cost is $65 plus postage, which includes the purchase of three of the company's catalogs (which will be mailed to you), plus the inclusion of your own listing in whichever one of the three catalogs you select. A fourth catalog costs an extra $21. If you want to publish a photograph of your home, there is an additional charge of $11.

The Invented City, 41 Sutter St., Suite 1090, San Francisco, CA 94104 (☎ 800/788-CITY or 415/252-1141; www.invented-city.com), publishes home exchange listings three times per year. For the $75 membership fee, you can list your home with your own written descriptive summary.

Home Link, P.O. Box 650, Key West, FL 33041 (☎ 800/638-3841 or 305/294-7766; www.homelink.org), will send you five directories per year—one of which contains your listing—for $98.

PEOPLE TO PEOPLE   Established in 1971, **Friends Overseas** places American visitors to Scandinavia in touch with Scandinavians, including Swedes, who would like to meet those with similar interests and backgrounds. Names and addresses are given to each applicant, and letters must be written before the visitors depart; Scandinavians may not meet visitors unless they have ample time to plan. For more information, write to Friends Overseas, 68–04 Dartmouth St., Forest Hills, NY 11375 (☎ 718/544-5660; www.nordbalt.com). Send a self-addressed, stamped, business-size envelope including your age, occupation or occupational goals, approximate dates of your visit, and whom you will be traveling with. A fee of $25 is charged for this   service.

7 Health & Insurance

Sweden's national health care program does not cover U.S. or Canadian visitors or nationals of other countries. Any medical expenses that arise must be paid in cash. (Medical costs in Sweden, however, generally are more reasonable than elsewhere in western Europe.)

STAYING HEALTHY

You will encounter few health problems while traveling in Sweden. The water is safe to drink, the milk is pasteurized, and the health services are excellent. Occasionally, a change in diet might cause minor diarrhea, so you may want to take some anti-diarrhea medicine along. In summer, arrive at buffets early so that your smörgåsbord or salads made with mayonnaise are fresh.

Put all your essential medicines in your carry-on luggage, and bring enough of any prescription medications to last during your stay. Bring along copies of your prescriptions written in generic form.

If you need a doctor, your hotel will find one. You also can obtain a list of English-speaking doctors from the **International Association for Medical Assistance to**

Traveler's Tips

Remember, **Medicare** covers U.S. citizens traveling in Mexico and Canada only. Also note that to submit any claim to any insurance carrier, you must always have complete documentation including all receipts, police reports, medical records, or other data.

Travelers (IAMAT), 417 Center St., Lewiston, NY 14092 (☎ **716/754-4883**), or in Canada, Regal Rd., Guelph, ON N1K 1B5 (☎ **519/836-0102**).

If you suffer from a chronic illness, talk to your doctor before taking the trip. For conditions such as heart trouble, epilepsy, or diabetes, wear a Medic Alert identification tag, which will immediately alert any doctor to your condition. The tag also provides Medic Alert's 24-hour hot line number so that a foreign doctor can obtain your medical records. The initial membership costs $35, plus a $15 yearly fee. Contact the **Medic Alert Foundation,** 2323 Colorado Ave., Turlock, CA 95381-1009 (☎ **800/825-3785**).

INSURANCE

Before purchasing any additional insurance, check your homeowner's, automobile, and medical insurance policies as well as the insurance provided by credit- and charge-card companies and auto and travel clubs. If you're prepaying for your vacation or are taking a charter or any other flight that imposes high cancellation penalties, consider getting cancellation insurance.

One final note: The restrictions tied to most of these policies are sweeping, vast, and somewhat unforgiving. Check the restrictions very carefully. Chances are you won't be covered if you're injured in an activity that could even remotely be deemed "athletic." Also, check with your local insurance agent to see if you already have a policy that would cover what these policies would cover.

The following companies can provide helpful information:

Travel Guard International, 1145 Clark St., Stevens Point, WI 54481 (☎ **800/826-1300** or 715/345-0505; www.noelgroup.com), offers comprehensive insurance programs starting as low as $44. The program covers basically everything, including emergency assistance, accidental death, trip cancellation and interruption, medical coverage abroad, and lost luggage. There are restrictions, however, that you should understand before you purchase the coverage.

Travelers Insured International Inc., P.O. Box 280568, Hartford, CT 06128-0568 (☎ **800/243-3174** in the U.S. or 860/528-7663 outside the U.S. between 7:45am and 7pm EST; www.travelinsured.com), provides trip cancellation and emergency evacuation policies costing $5.50 for each $100 of coverage. Travel accident and illness policies start from $10 for 6 to 10 days; $500 worth of coverage for lost, damaged, or delayed baggage costs $20 for 6 to 10 days; and trip cancellation goes for $5.50 per $100 worth of coverage (written approval is necessary for cancellation coverage above $10,000).

Travelex, 11717 Burt St., Suite 202, Omaha, NE 68175 (☎ **800/228-9792** in the U.S.; www.travelex-insurance.com), offers insurance packages based on the age of the traveler as well as the cost of the trip per person. Included in the packages are travel-assistance services and financial protection against trip cancellation, trip interruption, flight and baggage delays, accident-related medical costs, accidental death and dismemberment, and medical evacuation.

Healthcare Abroad, c/o Wallach & Co., 107 W. Federal St., Middleburg, VA 20118 (☎ **800/237-6615;** www.wallach.com), offers $250,000 of comprehensive medical expense protection, plus the multilingual services of a worldwide travelers' assistance network. Any U.S. resident under the age of 85 traveling outside the country is eligible to participate. Provisions for trip cancellation also can be written into the policy for a nominal cost.

Access America, 6600 W. Broad St., Richmond, VA 23230 (☎ **800/284-8300** in the U.S.; www.accessamerica.com), offers comprehensive travel insurance and assistance packages, including medical expenses, on-the-spot hospital payments, medical transportation, baggage insurance, trip-cancellation/interruption insurance, and collision-damage insurance for a car rental. Its 24-hour hotline connects you to multilingual coordinators who can offer advice and help on medical, legal, and travel problems. Varying coverage levels are available.

Travel Assistance International by Worldwide Assistance Services, Inc., 9200 Keystone Crossing, Suite 300, Indianapolis, IN 46240 (☎ **800/821-2828** in the U.S., or 202/331-1596; www.specialtyrisk.com), is another option. It offers on-the-spot medical-payment coverage up to $15,000, $30,000, or $60,000 for emergency care practically anywhere in the world, as well as unlimited medical evacuation or repatriation coverage back to the United States if necessary. For an additional fee you can be covered for trip cancellation or disruption, lost or delayed luggage, and accidental death and dismemberment. Fees are based on the length of your trip and the coverage you select. Prices begin at $65 per person ($95 per family) for a 1- to 8-day trip.

INSURANCE FOR BRITISH TRAVELERS   Most big travel agencies offer their own insurance and probably will try to sell you their package when you book a holiday trip. Think before you sign up. Britain's Consumers Association recommends that you insist on seeing the policy and reading the fine print before you buy travel insurance.

You also should shop around for better deals. You might contact **Columbus Travel Insurance Ltd.** (☎ **020/7375-0011** in London) or, for students, **Usit Campus Travel** (☎ **0870/240-1010** in London; www.usitcampus.co.uk).

8 Tips for Travelers with Special Needs

There are a number of resources and organizations in both North America and Britain to assist travelers with special needs in planning their trips to Sweden.

FOR TRAVELERS WITH DISABILITIES

IN THE UNITED STATES   You may want to contact an agency that can provide advance planning information. One is the **Travel Information Service** at the Moss-Rehab Hospital in Philadelphia (☎ **215/456-9603,** or 215/456-9602 TTY; www. mossresourcenet.org), which provides information to telephone callers only.

For a $35 annual fee, you can join **Mobility International USA,** P.O. Box 10767, Eugene, OR 97440 (☎ **541/343-1284;** www.miusa.org). Aside from answering questions on various destinations, it offers discounts on videos, publications, and programs it sponsors. One of the best organizations serving the needs of persons with disabilities is **Flying Wheels Travel,** 143 W. Bridge St. (P.O. Box 382), Owatonna, MN 55060 (☎ **800/535-6790** or 507/451-5005; www.flyingwheelstravel.com); it offers various international escorted tours and cruises.

You also may want to take an organized tour that's geared toward travelers with disabilities. You can obtain the names and addresses of such tour operators and miscellaneous travel information by writing to the **Society for the Advancement of Travel for the Handicapped,** 347 Fifth Ave., New York, NY 10016 (☎ **212/ 447-7248;** www.sath.org). Annual membership dues are $45, or $30 for senior citizens and students. Send a stamped, self-addressed envelope.

For the blind or visually impaired, the best source of information is the **American Foundation for the Blind,** 11 Penn Plaza, Suite 300, New York, NY 10001 (☎ 800/232-5463 or 212/502-7600). It offers information on travel and various requirements for the transport and border formalities for seeing-eye dogs.

IN BRITAIN British travelers with disabilities can contact **RADAR (Royal Association for Disability and Rehabilitation),** Unit 12, City Forum, 250 City Rd., London EC1V 8AF (☎ 020/7250-3222; www.radar.org.uk), for useful annual holiday guides. *Holidays and Travel Abroad* costs £5, *Holidays in the British Isles* goes for £7, and *Long Haul Holidays and Travel* is £5. RADAR also provides holiday information packets on such subjects as sports and outdoor holidays, insurance, and financial arrangements for people with disabilities. Each of these fact sheets is available for £2. All publications can be mailed outside the United Kingdom for a nominal fee.

Another good British service is the **Holiday Care,** 2nd Floor Imperial Buildings, Victoria Road, Horley, Surrey RH6 7PZ (☎ 01293/774-535; fax 01293/784-647), which advises on accessible accommodations. Annual membership costs £30 and includes a newsletter and access to a free reservations network for hotels throughout Britain and, to a lesser degree, Europe and the rest of the world.

If you're flying around Europe, the airline and ground staff can help you on and off planes and reserve seats for you with sufficient leg room, but you *must* arrange for this assistance *in advance* by contacting the airline.

IN SWEDEN About two million people in Sweden have a disability; as a result, Sweden is especially conscious of their special needs. In general, trains, airlines, ferries, and department stores and malls are accessible. For information about wheelchair access, ferry and air travel, parking, and other matters, your best bet is to contact the Scandinavian Tourist Board (see "Visitor Information & Entry Requirements," earlier in this chapter). For information on youth hostels with special rooms for those with disabilities, contact **STF (Swedish Touring Club),** P.O. Box 25, S-101 20 Stockholm (☎ 08/463-21-00).

FOR GAY MEN & LESBIANS

IN THE UNITED STATES To learn about gay and lesbian travel throughout Scandinavia in advance, you can obtain publications or join data-dispensing organizations. Men can order *Spartacus,* the international gay guide ($32.95), or *Odysseus 2001, The International Gay Travel Planner,* a guide to international gay accommodations ($29). Both lesbians and gay men may want to pick up a copy of *Gay Travel A to Z,* a Ferrari guide ($16), which focuses on general information, while listing bars, hotels, restaurants, and places of interest for gay travelers throughout the world. These and other books are available from **Giovanni's Room,** 345 S. 12 St., Philadelphia, PA 19107 (☎ 215/923-2960; fax 215/023-0813; www.giovannisroom.com).

The magazine *Our World,* 1104 N. Nova Rd., Suite 251, Daytona Beach, FL 32117 (☎ 904/441-5367; www.ourworldmag.com), covers options and bargains for gay and lesbian travel worldwide. It costs $35 for 10 issues. *Out and About,* 657 Harrison St., San Francisco, CA 94107 (☎ 800/929-2268 or 415/229-1793; www.outandabout.com), has been hailed for its "straight" reporting about gay travel. It profiles the best gay or gay-friendly hotels, gyms, clubs, and other places at destinations throughout the world. It costs $49 for 10 information-packed issues.

International Gay Travel Association (IGTA), 4331 N. Federal, Suite 304, Fort Lauderdale, FL 33308 (☎ 800/448-8550 for voice mail, or 954/776-2626; www.iglta.com), encourages gay and lesbian travel worldwide. With around 1,200 member agencies, it specializes in putting travelers in touch with appropriate gay-friendly service organizations or tour specialists. It offers a quarterly newsletter, marketing mailings, and a membership directory (updated four times a year). Travel agents who are IGTA members are included in this organization's vast information resources.

IN SWEDEN   Sweden is not as openly liberal as Denmark (where gay marriages have the same legal status as heterosexual marriages), but it has enacted an anti-discrimination law, and many gay and lesbian organizations in Stockholm welcome visitors from abroad.

Foremost among these is the **Federation for Gay and Lesbian Rights (RFSL),** Sveavägen 57 (Box 45090), S-104 30 Stockholm (☎ **08/736-02-12**), open Monday through Friday from 9am to 5pm. Established in 1950, the group's headquarters are located on the upper floors of the biggest gay nightlife center in Stockholm. Meetings are held weekly—a Wednesday 3pm meeting for gay men over 60 and a twice-monthly meeting of "Golden Ladies" (yes, they use the English expression) for lesbians over 50, plus a Monday night youth session for those 18 to 21. They also operate a **Gay Switchboard** (☎ **08736-02-12**), staffed with volunteers; call daily from 8 to 11pm for information. The **Rosa Rummet Bookstore** (☎ **08/736-02-15**), on the same premises, is a nonprofit bookstore specializing in gay and lesbian literature and information. It's open Monday through Friday from noon to 9pm and on Saturday and Sunday from noon to 3pm. The biggest event of the year is **Gay Pride Week,** usually held the first week in August. Call or write the RFSL for information.

FOR SENIORS

IN THE UNITED STATES   Many senior discounts are available, but some may require you to be a member of a particular association (such as the AARP). For information before you go, try to obtain a copy of the free booklet *101 Tips for the Mature Traveler,* available from **Grand Circle Travel,** 347 Congress St., Suite 3A, Boston, MA 02210 (☎ **800/221-2610** or 617/350-7500).

SAGA International Holidays, 222 Berkeley St., Boston, MA 02116 (☎ **800/ 343-0273**), organizes all-inclusive tours for seniors, specifically for those 50 years of age or older. Insurance is included in the net price of the tours.

The **American Association of Retired Persons (AARP),** 601 E. St. NW, Washington, DC 20049 (☎ **800/424-3410** or 202/434-AARP; www.aarp.org), is the best U.S. organization for seniors. It offers discounts on car rentals and hotels.

Information also is available from the **National Council of Senior Citizens,** 8403 Colesville Rd., Suite 1200, Silver Spring, MD 20910 (☎ **301/578-8800**), which charges $13 per person or per couple, for which you receive a bimonthly magazine, part of which is devoted to travel tips. Discounts on hotels and auto rentals are available.

Sears Mature Outlook, P.O. Box 9390, Des Moines, IA 50306 (☎ **800/336-6330;** fax 847/286-5024), is a travel organization for people over 50. Members are offered discounts at ITC-member hotels and a bimonthly magazine. The annual membership fee of $39.95 entitles members to coupons for discounts at Sears, Roebuck & Co.

Elderhostel, 75 Federal St., Boston, MA 02110-1941 (☎ **877/426-8056** or 617/426-8056; www.elderhostel.org), offers an array of university-based educational programs for senior citizens throughout the world, including Scandinavia. Most courses abroad last about 3 weeks and offer remarkable value considering the modest cost includes airfare, accommodations in student dormitories or modest inns, all meals, and tuition. The courses, which require no homework, tend to be in the liberal arts. Participants must be at least 55 years old; spouses of any age may attend, but companions must be at least 50. Meals consist of the basic, no-frills fare found in education institutions worldwide. Elderhostel programs provide a safe and congenial environment for older single women, who comprise about 67% of the enrollment.

Interhostel offers international educational and cultural programs for those over 50 who want to combine travel and education. Developed by the University of New Hampshire, Division of Continuing Education, 6 Garrison Ave., Durham, NH 03824 (☎ 800/733-9753 in the U.S., or 603/862-1147; www.learn.unh.org), each program lasts 2 weeks, is led by a university faculty or staff member, and is arranged in conjunction with a host college, university, or cultural institution. Participants may stay longer if they wish.

Uniworld, 16000 Ventura Blvd., Encino, CA 91436 (☎ 800/733-7820 or 818/382-7820), specializes in single tours for the mature person. It arranges for you to share an accommodation with another single person or gets you a low-priced single supplement. Uniworld specializes in travel to certain districts of England, France, Spain, Italy, and Scandinavia, including Denmark.

IN SWEDEN   Visitors over age 65 can obtain 30% off first- and second-class train travel (except Friday and Sunday) on the Swedish State Railways. There also are discounts on the ferries crossing from Denmark to Sweden, and on certain attractions and performances. However, you may have to belong to a seniors organization to qualify for certain discounts. **In Stockholm,** there are discounts on transportation, concert, theater, and opera tickets.

FOR FAMILIES

Family Travel Times newsletter costs $40 (online only—www.familytraveltimes.com), and it's updated every 2 weeks. Subscribers also can call in with travel questions, but only on Wednesday from 10am to 1pm Eastern Standard Time. Contact Family Travel times, 40 5th Ave., New York, NY 10011 (☎ 888/822-4322 or 212/477-5524).

The best deals for **British families** often are package tours put together by some of the giants of the British travel industry. Foremost among these is **Thomsons Tour Operators.** Through its subsidiary, **Skytours** (☎ 020/7387-9321), it offers dozens of air/land packages that have a pre-designated number of airline seats reserved for free use by children under 18 who accompany their parents. To qualify, parents must book airfare and hotel accommodations lasting 2 weeks or more, and book as far in advance as possible. Savings for families with children can be substantial.

FOR SINGLES

Unfortunately for the 85 million or so single Americans, the travel industry is far more geared toward couples, and so singles often wind up paying the penalty. It pays to travel with someone. One company that resolves this problem is **Travel Companion Exchange,** which matches single travelers with like-minded companions. It's headed by Jens Jurgen, who charges $159 for an annual listing in his well-publicized records. People seeking travel companions fill out forms stating their preferences and needs and receive a listing of potential travel partners. Companions of the same or opposite sex can be requested. For $48 you can get a bimonthly newsletter averaging 70 large pages, which also gives numerous money-saving travel tips of special interest to solo travelers. A sample copy is available for $6. For an application and more information, contact Jens Jurgen at **Travel Companion Exchange,** P.O. Box P-833, Amityville, NY 11701 (☎ 800/392-1256 or 613/454-0880; fax 631/454-0170; www.whytravelalone.com).

Because single supplements on tours carry a hefty price tag, some tour companies will arrange for you to share a room with another single traveler of the same gender. One such company that offers a "guaranteed-share plan" is **Cosmos.** Book through your travel agent or call ☎ 800/221-0090.

In the **United Kingdom,** a tour operator whose groups usually are composed of at least 50% of unattached persons is **Explore Worldwide, Ltd.,** 1 Frederick St., Aldershot, Hampshire GU11 1LQ (☎ **01252/344-161;** www.explore.co.uk), which has a well-justified reputation of assembling offbeat tours. Groups rarely include more than 20 participants, and children under 14 are not allowed.

FOR STUDENTS

IN THE UNITED STATES   A subsidiary of the Council on International Educational Exchange, **Council Travel** is America's largest student, youth, and budget travel group, with more than 60 offices worldwide. The main office is at 205 E. 42nd St., New York, NY 10017 (☎ **212/822-2600;** fax 212/822-2699). **International Student Identity Cards,** issued to all bona-fide students for $19, entitle the holder to generous travel and other discounts. Discounted international and domestic air tickets are available.

Other offices of Council Travel are at 844 E. Lancaster Ave., Bryn Mawr, PA 19010 (☎ **610/527-6272**); 565 Melville, University City, MO 63130 (☎ **314/721-7779**), and Franklin House Suite 102, 480 E. Broad St., Athens, GA (☎ **706/543-9600**).

Eurotrain rail passes, YHA passes, weekend packages, overland safaris, and hostel/hotel accommodations also are bookable. Council Travel sells a number of publications for young people, including *Work, Study, Travel Abroad: The Whole World Handbook; Volunteer: The Comprehensive Guide to Voluntary Service in the U.S. and Abroad;* and *Going Places: The High School Student's Guide to Study, Travel, and Adventure Abroad.*

For real budget travelers, it's worth joining **Hostelling International/IYHF** (International Youth Hostel Federation). For information, contact Hostelling Information/American Youth Hostels (HI-AYH), 733 15th St. NW, Suite 840, Washington, DC 20005 (☎ **202/783-6161;** www.hiayah.org). Membership costs $25 annually; those under 18 are free, and those over 54 pay $15.

IN BRITAIN   **Usit Campus Travel,** 52 Grosvenor Gardens, London SW1W 0AG (☎ **0870/240-1010;** www.usitcampus.co.uk), open 7 days a week, is Britain's leading specialist in student and youth travel worldwide. Founded to meet the needs of students and young people, it provides a comprehensive travel service specializing in low-cost rail, sea, and air transportation, holiday breaks, travel insurance, and student discount cards. No matter what kind of trip you have in mind, the experienced staff at Usit Campus Travel can assist you.

9 Getting There

BY PLANE

Flying in winter, Scandinavia's off-season, is cheapest; summer is the most expensive. Spring and fall are in between. In any season, midweek fares (Monday through Thursday) are the lowest.

THE MAJOR AIRLINES

Travelers from the U.S. East Coast usually choose **SAS** (☎ **800/221-2350** in the U.S.; www.flysas.com) or **TWA** (☎ **800/221-2000** in the U.S.; www.twa.com), both of which fly every day from the New York/Newark area to Stockholm. Their major competitor is **American Airlines** (☎ **800/443-7300** in the U.S.; www.americanair.com), which offers daily flights to Stockholm from Chicago, and excellent connections through Chicago from American's vast North American network. Between November and March (excluding the Christmas holidays), American offers round-trip fares as low as $500 for weekday departures from Chicago. There's a supplemental charge of $49 for travel on a Friday, Saturday, or Sunday. This fare, matched for the most part by SAS, requires a stay abroad of between 7 and 60 days, as well as several other restrictions. Although these fares probably will have changed by the time you make your vacation plans, the new prices are likely to be somewhat similar. Travelers from Seattle usually fly SAS to Copenhagen, then connect to one of the airline's frequent shuttle flights into Stockholm. Likewise, **Delta** (☎ 800/ 241-4141 in the U.S.; www.delta-air.com) offers daily nonstop flights to Stockholm from JFK in New York, usually at prices comparable to those offered by SAS, TWA, and American.

Other airlines fly to gateway European cities and then connect to other flights into Stockholm. **British Airways** (☎ 800/247-9297 in the U.S.; www.british-airways.com), for example, flies from almost 20 North American cities to London/ Heathrow, and then connects with onward flights to Stockholm. **Northwest** (☎ 800/ 325-1999 in the U.S.; www.nwa.com), **Delta,** and **TWA** also fly at frequent intervals to London, from which ongoing flights to Stockholm are available on either SAS or British Airways. Finally, **Icelandair** (☎ 800/223-5500 in the U.S.; www. icelandair.is) has proved to be an excellent choice for travel to Stockholm, thanks to connections through its home port of Reykjavik. It often offers great deals.

People traveling **from Britain** can fly **SAS** (☎ 020/7734-4020 in London) from London's Heathrow to Stockholm on any of five daily nonstop flights. Flying time is about 2½ hours each way. Likewise, SAS flies daily to Stockholm from Manchester, making a brief stop in Copenhagen en route. Flight time from Manchester to Stockholm is about 3½ hours each way.

DISCOUNTED AIRFARES

Currently the most popular discount fare is the **APEX** (advance-purchase excursion), which usually carries restrictions—advance-purchase requirements, minimum and maximum stays abroad—and cancellation or change-of-date penalties. In addition, airlines often introduce special promotional **discount fares.** Always check the travel sections of your local newspapers for such advertisements.

BUCKET SHOPS   More politely referred to as consolidators, these agencies purchase large blocks of unsold seats from the airlines and sell them to the public often at dramatic discounts (from 20% to 35% off regular fares). The terms of payment may vary from the last minute to 45 days in advance. Here are some recommendations to get you started:

In New York, try **TFI Tours International,** 34 W. 32nd St., 12th Floor, New York, NY 10001 (☎ 212/736-1140 in New York State or 800/745-8000 elsewhere in the U.S.). This tour company offers service to 177 cities worldwide.

Headquartered in the Midwest is **Travel Avenue,** 10 S. Riverside Plaza, Suite 1404, Chicago, IL 60606 (☎ 800/333-3335; www.travelavenue.com), a national agency. Its tickets often are cheaper than those sold by most shops.

All Travel (☎ 800/300-4567 or 310/312-3368) recognizes that its clients collect information on the Web, but offers a person to talk to about personal vacation plans, and also assists you with options for making the right decision. It usually features at least 14 "hot deals" of the week, including some off-the-beaten-path treks as well as eco-adventures.

One of the biggest U.S. consolidators is **Travac,** 989 Sixth Ave., New York, NY 10018 (☎ 800/TRAV-800 or 212/563-3303). It offers discounted seats from points throughout the United States to most cities in Europe on TWA, United, Delta, and other major airlines.

UniTravel, 1177 N. Warson Rd., St. Louis, MO 63132 (☎ **800/325-2222**), offers tickets to Europe at prices that may be lower than what airlines charge if you order tickets directly from them. UniTravel is best suited for providing discounts to passengers who want (or need) to get to Europe on short notice.

Another option, suitable for clients with flexible travel plans, is available through **Airhitch,** 2641 Broadway, 3rd Floor, Suite 100, New York, NY 10025 (☎ **212/864-2000**). You let Airhitch know which 5 consecutive days you're available to fly to Europe, and Airhitch agrees to fly you there within those 5 days. It arranges for departures from the East or West Coast, the Midwest, and the Southeast, and tries, but cannot guarantee, to fly you from and to the cities of your choice.

You also can try **800-FLY-4-LESS,** a discount domestic and international airline ticketing service. Travelers unable to buy their tickets 3 weeks in advance can utilize this service to obtain low discounted fares with no advance purchase requirements. 800-FLY-4-LESS is a nationwide airline reservation and ticketing service that specializes in finding only the lowest rates.

CHARTER FLIGHTS   Strictly speaking, a charter is a one-time-only flight between two predetermined points, for which the aircraft is reserved months in advance. Before you pay for a charter, check the restrictions on your ticket or contract. You may be asked to purchase a tour package and pay for it far in advance, and there will be a stiff penalty (or ticket forfeit) if you cancel. Some charter ticket sellers offer an insurance policy for a legitimate cancellation (such as hospitalization or a death in the family). Be aware that a charter may be canceled if the plane cannot be filled.

Some charter companies have proved to be unreliable in the past. Recommended charter flight operators include **Council Charter,** a subsidiary of the Council on International Educational Exchange, 205 E. 42nd St., New York, NY 10017 (☎ **888/2-COUNCIL**). It can arrange charter seats to most major European cities on regularly scheduled aircraft.

REBATORS   Rebators are firms that pass along to a passenger part of their commission, although many assess a fee for their services. They are not the same as travel agents, but sometimes can offer similar services. Most rebators offer discounts averaging from 10% to 25%, plus a $25 handling charge. **Travel Avenue,** 10 S. Riverside Plaza, Suite 1404, Chicago, IL 60606 (☎ **800/333-3335;** www.travelavenue.com), is one of the oldest agencies of its kind. It offers up-front cash rebates on every airfare over $300 it sells. The agency does not offer travel counseling; instead, it sells airline tickets to independent travelers who have already worked out their travel plans. Also available are tour and cruise fares, plus hotel reservations, usually at prices less expensive than if you had reserved them on your own.

TRAVEL CLUBS   Travel clubs are another possibility for low-cost air travel, offering discounts usually in the range of 20% to 60%. After you pay an annual fee, you're given a hotline number to call to find out what discounts are available. Of course, you're limited to what's available, so you have to be fairly flexible. Two travel clubs are **Moment's Notice,** 7301 New Utrecht Ave., Brooklyn, NY 11204 (☎ **718/234-6295;** www.moments-notice.com), which charges $25 per year for membership and is geared for impulse purchases and last-minute getaways; and **Sears Mature Outlook,** 3033 S. Parker Rd., Suite 1000, Aurora, CO 80014 (☎ **800/336-6330** in the U.S.), which, for a $39.95 annual membership fee, offers members a quarterly catalog, maps, discounts at select hotels, and a limited guarantee that equivalent packages will not be undersold by any other travel organization.

Encore Travel Club, 4501 Forbes Blvd., Lanham, MD 20706 (☎ **800/638-8976**), charges $59.95 per year for membership and offers up to a 50% discount at more than 4,000 hotels, sometimes during off-peak periods; it also offers substantial discounts on airfare, cruises, and car rentals through its volume-purchase plans. Membership includes a travel package outlining the company's many services and use of a toll-free telephone number for advice and information.

GOING AS A COURIER   Couriers are hired by overnight air-freight firms hoping to skirt the often tedious customs delays that regular cargo faces at the other end. For the service, the courier pays the firm a fee much lower than the cost of the ticket, and sometimes can fly free. Don't worry—the service is legal. You won't be asked to handle any contraband. Also, you don't actually carry the merchandise you're "transporting;" you just carry a shipping invoice to present at customs when you arrive.

This cost-saving approach is not for everyone—there are lots of restrictions, and courier opportunities are hard to come by. You're allowed only one piece of carry-on luggage; your checked baggage allowance is used by the courier firm to transport its cargo. Also, you must fly alone.

For more information, try **Now Voyager,** 74 Varick St., Suite 307, New York, NY 10013 (☎ **212/431-1616;** www.nowvoyager.com), Monday through Friday from 10am to 5:30pm, Saturday from noon to 4:30pm. An automatic telephone answering system announces last-minute specials and the firm's fees for the round trip. Courier services also are listed in the yellow pages or in advertisements in newspaper travel sections.

For a $45 annual membership fee, the **International Association of Air Travel Couriers,** P.O. Box 1349, Lake Worth, FL 33460 (☎ **516/582-8320**), will send you six issues of its newsletter, *Shoestring Traveler,* and about a half dozen issues of *Air Courier Bulletin,* a directory of air-courier bargains around the world. The fee also includes access to their 24-hour "Fax-on-Demand" update of last-minute courier flights available for those who can travel on short notice.

A NOTE FOR BRITISH TRAVELERS   Because regular airfares from the United Kingdom to Scandinavia tend to be rather high, savvy Brits usually call a travel agent for a "deal"—either a charter flight or some special air travel promotion. These so-called deals often are available because of Scandinavia's popularity as a tourist destination. If you can't get one, the next best choice is an APEX ticket. Although these tickets must be reserved in advance, they offer a discount without the usual booking restrictions. You also can inquire about a **Eurobudget ticket,** which carries restrictions or length-of-stay requirements.

British newspapers typically carry lots of classified advertisements touting "slashed" fares from London to other parts of the world. One good source is *Time Out,* a magazine published in London. London's *Evening Standard* has a daily travel section, and the Sunday editions of almost all British newspapers run ads. Although competition is fierce, one well-recommended company that consolidates bulk ticket purchases and then passes the savings on to its customers is **Trailfinders** (☎ **020/7937-5400** in London). It offers tickets on such carriers as SAS, British Airways, and KLM. You can fly from London's Heathrow or Gatwick airports to Copenhagen, Oslo, Stockholm, and Helsinki.

In London, there are many bucket shops around Victoria Station and Earl's Court that offer low fares. Make sure the company you deal with is a member of the IATA, ABTA, or ATOL. These umbrella organizations will help you out if anything goes wrong.

CEEFAX, a British television information service (included on many home and hotel TVs), runs details of package holidays and flights to Europe and beyond. Just switch to your CEEFAX channel and you'll find a menu of listings that includes travel information.

Make sure that you understand the bottom line on any special deal you purchase—that is, ask if all surcharges, including airport taxes and other hidden costs, are

Surfing for Bargains

Savvy travelers can find excellent deals on vacation packages by searching the Internet. Increasingly, travel agencies and companies use the Web to offer everything from vacations to plane reservations to budget airline tickets on major carriers. Many travel sites maintained by services and agencies offer basically the same service as the airlines' sites (listed under "The Major Airlines," earlier in this chapter), but on a much wider and larger scale. Although their exact configuration and specific offerings change as fast as the Internet itself, a good place to start is with your favorite search engine. Check for tips on narrowing your search, because a simple scan of "travel" could yield 10 million matches. To save you time and effort, we have found some sites that may be useful:

- **www.yahoo.com** is a no-nonsense site that gets the job done efficiently and quickly, offering links to Web sites and search engines all over the globe.

- **www.travelcom.es** allows you to search travel destinations and offers links to travel agencies all over the world and in all 50 states.

- **www.previewtravel.com** is the foremost of these sites. Featured prominently on America Online, it offers vacation, airline, and hotel deals, and updates its offerings daily. The most user friendly of the travel sites, Preview Travel even lets you book your vacation on its site.

- **www.moments-notice.com** promotes itself as a travel service, not an agency, providing a vacation bargain hunter's dream. Deals are updated daily, and many are snapped up by the end of the day. A drawback is that many of these vacations require you to drop everything and go almost immediately.

- **www.1800hotel.com** offers budget reservations at prestigious hotels all over the world. Prices for many accommodations are up to 65% off, and you can book online instead of through a travel agent.

- **America Online** (www.aol.com) has areas devoted to many of these businesses and can be customized to investigate a particular region of the world you otherwise may have trouble finding.

- **www.qixo.com** is a site that allows you to view results from several Internet fare finders (such as Expedia and LowestFare) simultaneously.

indicated before you commit yourself to purchase it. Upon investigation, people often find that some of these "deals" are not as attractive as advertised. Also, make sure you understand what the penalties are if you're forced to cancel at the last minute.

BY CAR

FROM GERMANY   You can drive to the northern German port of Travemünde and catch the 7½-hour ferry to the Swedish port of Trelleborg, a short drive south of Malmö. This route saves many hours by avoiding transit through Denmark. If you want to visit Denmark before Sweden, you can take the 3-hour car ferry from Travemünde to Gedser in southern Denmark. From Gedser, the E64 and the E4 express highways head north to Copenhagen. After a visit here, you can take the Øresund Bridge from Copenhagen to Malmö.

FROM NORWAY   From Oslo, E18 goes east through Karlstad all the way to Stockholm. This is a long but scenic drive.

BY TRAIN

Copenhagen is the main rail hub between the other Scandinavian countries and the rest of Europe. There are seven daily trains from Copenhagen to Stockholm, and six from Copenhagen to Gothenburg. All connect with the Danish ferries that operate to Sweden via Helsingør or Frederikshavn.

There are at least three trains a day from Oslo to Stockholm (travel time: about 6½ hours). One of the trains leaves Oslo about 11pm. There are also three trains a day from Oslo to Gothenburg (travel time: about 4 hours).

RAIL PASSES FOR NORTH AMERICAN TRAVELERS

If you plan to travel extensively on the European and/or British railroads, it would be worthwhile for you to get a copy of the latest edition of the *Thomas Cook European Timetable of Railroads*. It's available exclusively in North America from **Forsyth Travel Library,** 226 Westchester Ave., White Plains, NY 10604 (☎ **800/FORSYTH**), at a cost of $27.95, plus $4.50 priority shipping in the States and $5 (U.S.) for airmail shipments to Canada.

EURAILPASS   If you plan to travel extensively in Europe, the **Eurailpass** may be a good bet. It's valid for first-class rail travel in 17 European countries. With one ticket, you travel whenever and wherever you please; more than 100,000 rail miles are at your disposal. Here's how it works: The pass is sold only in North America. A Eurailpass good for 15 days costs $554, a pass for 21 days is $718, a 1-month pass costs $890, a 2-month pass is $1,260, and a 3-month pass goes for $1,558. Children under 4 travel free if they don't occupy a seat; all children under 12 who take up a seat are charged half-price. If you're under 26, you can buy a **Eurail Youthpass,** which entitles you to unlimited second-class travel for 15 days ($388), 21 days ($499), 1 month ($623), 2 months ($882) or 3 months ($1,089). Travelers considering buying a 15-day or 1-month pass should estimate rail distance before deciding whether a pass is worthwhile. To take full advantage of the tickets for 15 days or a month, you'd have to spend a great deal of time on the train. Eurailpass holders are entitled to substantial discounts on certain buses and ferries as well. Travel agents in all towns and railway agents in such major cities as New York, Montréal, and Los Angeles, sell all of these tickets. For information on Eurailpasses, and other European train data, call RailEurope at ☎ **800/438-7245,** or visit them on the Web at **www.raileurope.com**.

Eurail Saverpass offers 15% discounts to groups of three or more people traveling together between April and September, or two people traveling together between October and March. The price of a Saverpass, valid all over Europe for first class only, is $715 for 15 days, $928 for 21 days, $1,150 for 1 month, $1,630 for 2 months, and $2,013 for 3 months. Even more freedom is offered by the **Saver Flexipass,** which is similar to the Eurail Saverpass, except that you are not confined to consecutive-day travel. For travel over any 10 days within 2 months, the fare is $556; any 15 days over 2 months, the fare is $732.

Eurail Flexipass allows even greater flexibility. It's valid in first class and offers the same privileges as the Eurailpass. However, it provides a number of individual travel days over a much longer period of consecutive days. Using this pass makes it possible to stay longer in one city and not lose a single day of travel. There are two Flexipasses: 10 days of travel within 2 months for $654, and 15 days of travel within 2 months for $862.

With many of the same qualifications and restrictions as the Eurail Flexipass, the **Eurail Youth Flexipass** is sold only to travelers under age 25. It allows 10 days of travel within 2 months for $458 and 15 days of travel within 2 months for $599.

SCANRAIL PASS   If your visit to Europe will be primarily in Scandinavia, the Scanrail pass may be better and cheaper than the Eurailpass. This pass allows its owner a designated number of days of free rail travel within a larger time block. (Presumably, this allows for days devoted to sightseeing scattered among days of rail transfers between cities or sites of interest.) You can choose a total of any 5 days of unlimited rail travel during a 15-day period, 10 days of rail travel within a 1-month period, or 1 month of unlimited rail travel. The pass, which is valid on all lines of the state railways of Denmark, Finland, Norway, and Sweden, offers discounts or free travel on some (but not all) of the region's ferry lines as well. The pass can be purchased only in North America. It's available from any office of **RailEurope** (☎ **800/361-RAIL**) or **ScanAm World Tours,** 933 Highway 23, Pompton Plains, NJ 07444 (☎ **800/545-2204**).

Depending on whether you choose first- or second-class rail transport, 5 days out of 2 months ranges from $200 to $270, 10 days out of 2 months ranges from $310 to $420, and 21 consecutive days of unlimited travel ranges from $360 to $486. Seniors get an 11% discount; students a 25% discount.

RAIL PASSES FOR BRITISH TRAVELERS

If you plan to do a lot of exploring, you may prefer one of the three rail passes designed for unlimited train travel within a designated region during a predetermined number of days. These passes are sold in Britain and several other European countries.

An **InterRail Pass** is available to passengers of any nationality, with some restrictions—they must be under age 26 and able to prove residency in a European or North African country (Morocco, Algeria, and Tunisia) for at least 6 months before buying the pass. It allows unlimited travel through Europe, except Albania and the republics of the former Soviet Union. Prices are complicated and vary depending on the countries you want to include. For pricing purposes, Europe is divided into eight zones; the cost depends on the number of zones you include. The most expensive option (£219) allows 1 month of unlimited travel in all eight zones and is known to BritRail staff as a "global." The least expensive option (£129) allows 22 days of travel within only one zone.

Passengers over 25 can buy an **InterRail 26-Plus Pass** which, unfortunately, is severely limited geographically. Many countries—including France, Belgium, Switzerland, Spain, Portugal, and Italy—do not honor this pass. It is, however, accepted for travel throughout Denmark, Finland, Norway, and Sweden. Second-class travel with the pass costs £179 for 22 days or £235 for 1 month. Passengers must meet the same residency requirements that apply to the InterRail Pass (described above).

For information on buying individual rail tickets or any of the just-mentioned passes, contact **British Rail International,** Victoria Station, London (☎ **0990/ 848-848** or 0845/748-4950). Tickets and passes also are available at any of the larger railway stations as well as selected travel agencies throughout Britain and the rest of Europe.

BY SHIP & FERRY

FROM DENMARK   From Copenhagen, you can go to Malmö, Sweden, by **hydrofoil** (known locally as the "Flyvebadene;" call ☎ 33-12-80-88 in Copenhagen for information). This is the fastest way for pedestrians to travel from Copenhagen to Sweden. (The hydrofoil doesn't transport cars.) Travel time is 45 minutes each way. A one-way ticket from Copenhagen to Malmö costs 35 DKK ($4.40). A business-class ticket without restrictions costs 80 DKK ($10). Hydrofoils depart from a terminal directly on Copenhagen's waterfront, at the corner of Havnegade and Nyhavn. Departures are daily, every hour on the hour, from 6am to 9pm and 11pm to 1am.

Between 9 and 11pm, hydrofoils depart every half-hour in both directions. In mid-summer, it's a good idea to reserve passage in advance (there's no extra charge).

Another boat route—this one by ferry—is the brief trip between Helsingør, a short drive north of Copenhagen, and Helsingborg, Sweden, just across the narrow channel that separates the countries. The 25-minute trip on a conventional ferry (not a catamaran) begins at 20- to 40-minute intervals, 24 hours a day. Operated by **Scandlines** (☎ **32-53-15-85** in Copenhagen), it's one of the most popular ferry routes in Europe. Round-trip passage costs 510 SEK ($56.10) for a car with up to nine passengers; the ticket is valid for up to 2 months. If you return to Denmark the same day, round-trip passage for a car and up to five passengers costs 245 to 345 SEK ($26.95 to $37.95). Pedestrians pay 40 SEK ($4.40) round-trip, regardless of when they return.

FROM ENGLAND   Two English ports, Harwich (year-round) and Newcastle upon Tyne (summer only), offer ferry service to Sweden. Harwich to Gothenburg takes 23 to 25 hours; Newcastle to Gothenburg, 27 hours. Boats on both routes offer overnight accommodations and the option of transporting cars. Prices are lower for passengers who book in advance through the company's U.S. agent. For details, call **DFDS Seaways,** Cypress Creek Business Park, 6555 NW Ninth Ave., Suite 207, Fort Lauderdale, FL 33309 (☎ **800/533-3755** in the U.S. or 020/7616-1400 in the U.K.; www.scansea.com).

FROM GERMANY   Stena Line Ferries (☎ **800/688-3876** in the U.S., or 031/704-00-00) sails daily from Kiel to Gothenburg. The trip takes 14 hours and costs 840 SEK ($92.40) for a one-way passage.

10 Getting Around

BY PLANE

WITHIN SWEDEN   For transatlantic flights coming from North America, Stockholm is Sweden's major gateway for Scandinavia's best-known airline, **SAS (Scandinavian Airlines System).** For flights arriving from other parts of Europe, the airport at Gothenburg supplements Stockholm's airport by funneling traffic into the Swedish heartland. In the mid-1990's, SAS acquired **LIN Airlines (Linjeflyg);** thus it now has access to small and medium-size airports throughout Sweden, including such remote but scenic outposts as Kiruna in Swedish Lapland. Among the larger Swedish cities serviced by SAS are Malmö, capital of Sweden's château country; Karlstad, center of the verdant and folklore-rich district of Värmland; and Kalmar, a good base for exploring the glassworks district.

During the summer, SAS offers a number of promotional "minifares," which enable one to travel round-trip between two destinations for just slightly more than the price of a conventional one-way ticket on the same route. Children 11 and under travel free during the summer, and up to two children 12 to 17 can travel with a parent at significantly reduced rates. Airfares tend to be most reduced during July, with promotions almost as attractive during most of June and August. A minimum 3-night stopover at the destination is required for these minifares, and it must include a Friday or a Saturday night. When buying your tickets, always ask the airline or travel agency about special promotions and corresponding restrictions.

Those under 26 can take advantage of SAS's special **standby fares,** and senior citizens over 65 can apply for additional discounts, depending on the destination.

WITHIN SCANDINAVIA   The best way to get around the whole of Scandinavia is to take advantage of the air passes that apply to the whole region or, if you're traveling extensively in Europe, to use the special European passes. The vast distances of Scandinavia encourage air travel between some of its most far-flung points. One of the most worthwhile promotions is SAS's **Visit Scandinavia Pass.** This pass, available only to travelers who fly SAS across the Atlantic, includes up to six coupons, each of which is valid for any SAS flight within or between Denmark, Norway, and Sweden. Each coupon costs $85, a price that's especially appealing when you consider that an economy-class ticket between Copenhagen and Stockholm can cost as much as $250 each way. The pass is especially valuable if you plan to travel to the far northern frontiers of Sweden; in that case, the savings over the price of a regular economy-class ticket can be substantial. For information on purchasing the pass, call **SAS** (☎ **800/221-2350**).

BY TRAIN

The Swedish word for train is *tåg,* and the national system is the Statens Järnvägar, the Swedish State Railways.

Swedish trains follow tight schedules. Trains leave Malmö, Helsingborg, and Gothenburg for Stockholm every hour throughout the day, Monday through Friday. There are trains every hour, or every other hour, to and from most big Swedish towns. On *expresståg* runs, seats must be reserved.

Children under 12 travel free when accompanied by an adult, and those up to age 18 are eligible for discounts.

BY BUS

Rail lines cover only some of Sweden's vast distances. Where the train tracks end, a bus usually serves as the link with remote villages. Buses usually are equipped with toilets, adjustable seats, reading lights, and a telephone. Fares depend on the distance traveled; for example, the one-way fare for the 326-mile trip from Stockholm to Gothenburg is 315 SEK ($34.65). **Swebus** (☎ **08/655-90-00**), the country's largest bus company, provides information at the bus or railway stations in most cities. For travelers who don't buy a special rail pass (such as Eurail or ScanRail), bus travel between cities sometimes can be cheaper than traveling the same distances by rail. It's a lot less convenient and frequent, however—except in the far north, where there isn't any alternative.

BY CAR FERRY

Considering that Sweden has some 100,000 lakes and one of the world's longest coastlines, ferries play a surprisingly small part in the transportation network.

After the car ferry crossings from northern Germany and Denmark, the most popular route is from the mainland to the island of Gotland, in the Baltic. Service is available from Oskarshamn and Nynäshamn (call ☎ **08/20-10-20** for more information). The famous "white boats" of the Waxholm Steamship Company (☎ **08/679-58-30**) also travel to many destinations in the Stockholm archipelago.

BY CAR

As one of the best-developed industrialized nations in Europe, Sweden maintains an excellent network of roads and highways, particularly in the southern provinces and in the central lake district. Major highways in the far north are kept clear of snow by heavy equipment that's in place virtually year-round. If you rent a car at any bona-fide rental agency, you'll be given the appropriate legal documents, including proof of adequate insurance (in the form of a "Green Card") as specified by your car rental agreement. Current driver's licenses from Canada, the United Kingdom, New Zealand, Australia, and the United States are acceptable in Sweden.

Drop-Off Charges

Some travelers prefer to begin and end their trip to Sweden at different points, perhaps landing in Stockholm but departing by ferryboat elsewhere. For an additional fee, often car rental companies will allow you to drop off your rented car elsewhere, but only if you tell them of your plans when you first pick up the car. Otherwise, you may be in for an unpleasant surprise at the end of your trip.

RENTALS   The major U.S.-based car rental firms are represented throughout Sweden, both at airports and in urban centers. The companies' rates are aggressively competitive, although periodic sales promotions will favor one company over the others from time to time. Prior to your departure from North America, it would be advantageous to phone around to find out about the lowest available rates. Membership in AAA or another auto club may enable you to get a moderate discount. Be aware that you may avoid a supplemental airport tax by picking your car up at a central location rather than at the airport.

Avis (☎ **800/331-1084** in the U.S. and Canada; www.avis.com) offers a wide variety of cars. If you pay before you leave North America, the least expensive, a VW Polo, rents for around $191 a week. Avis's most expensive car, a Swedish-made Saab 903, goes for around $374 a week.

If you pay before your departure from the United States, **Hertz** (☎ **800/654-3001** in the U.S. and Canada) offers a Ford Fiesta for $245 a week.

Budget (☎ **800/527-0700** in the U.S. and Canada; www.budgetrentacar.com) charges $246 a week for its cheapest car, a VW polo, and $305 for the somewhat roomier Ford Mondeo. Many people upgrade to an Opel Vectra, at $355. For families with lots of luggage or camping equipment, Budget also offers a Vectra station wagon for about $517. These prices are for rentals paid for in North America before your departure. Any change in pickup date or type of vehicle costs an additional $25. Drop-offs can be made at any Budget office in Sweden for about $30 extra. Dropping off outside of Sweden—if allowed at all—is more expensive.

INSURANCE   All of these U.S. car rental companies include a basic amount of automatic liability insurance in their rates. Nevertheless, most renters feel more comfortable arranging for additional insurance to protect them from financial liability in the event of theft or damage to the car. A collision-damage waiver (CDW) is an optional insurance policy that can be purchased when you sign a rental agreement. For a fee of around $10 a day or more, depending on the value of the car, the rental agency will eliminate all but a token amount of your financial responsibility for collision damage in case of an accident. If you don't have a CDW and you have an accident, you'll usually have to pay the full cost of repairing the vehicle. Exact figures, penalties, and deductibles vary from company to company.

Some credit and charge card companies (including American Express, MasterCard, Visa, and Diners Club) will reimburse card users for the deductible in the event of an accident. Because of that, many renters waive the cost of the extra CDW. However, although the card issuer usually will reimburse the renter for the cost of damages (several weeks after the accident), sometimes payments have been delayed with such coverage until after the filing of certain legal and insurance-related documents. Unless there's a large line of credit associated with a particular card, some car renters involved in an accident could have to pay a large amount of cash on the spot. Considering that you're in a foreign country, if you have any doubt whatsoever—even at the risk of "double coverage"—it's usually best to purchase the CDW, if only for your own peace of mind.

11 Organized Tours

Sweden's various regions, especially Dalarna and Lapland, offer such a variety of sights and activities that you may want to take an organized tour. The following tours are just a small sample of what's available. Contact your travel agent to learn about tours of interest to you or to design a special one for you.

ScanAm World Tours (☎ **800/545-2204**) offers a tour of the Dalarna folklore region by rail. "Mora and the Folklore District" includes round-trip train fare from Stockholm to Mora and 2 nights at the Hotel Siljan. The 3-day tour is available May through September; prices start at $275 per person. The company also offers a "Kalmar and the Swedish Glass District" rail tour. The 3-day excursion includes round-trip train fare from Stockholm to Kalmar and 2 nights at the Kalmarsund Hotel. Prices start at $285 per person. The tour is available from May through September.

Scantours, Inc. (☎ **800/223-7226**), offers a 3-day tour of Sweden's folklore district. Participants travel from Oslo to Stockholm in a car with an English-speaking driver-guide. Along the way, it stops in Arvika, Mora, and Lake Siljan. "Kingdom of Folklore" tours include accommodations in first-class hotels and breakfast. Itineraries can be altered.

"Gotland Island and the City of Roses," offered by ScanAm World Tours (see the preceding), is a cruise on the Gotland Line from Stockholm to Nynäshamn or from Oskarshamn to Visby, including 2 nights at the Visby Hotel. The 4-day cruise is available May through September.

For the more adventurous, Sweden's rugged north offers endless opportunities to achieve an adrenaline rush. On the "Midnight Sun Skiing" package offered by **Passage Tours** (☎ **800/548-5960**), you can ski in shorts. Offered from May to June, the tour has additional options, including a reindeer sleigh safari and Stockholm lodging packages. This company also offers hiking tours that include a trip through the mountains; the views are panoramic. Prices vary according to the season.

Suggested Itineraries

If You Have 1 Week

Day 1   Settle into Stockholm and relieve your jet lag.

Days 2 and 3   Explore Stockholm's attractions, including the raised royal flagship *Vasa*. One afternoon should be reserved for a boat trip through the archipelago and another for exploring Drottningholm Palace, on an island in Lake Mälaren.

Day 4   Take a day trip north to Sweden's oldest town, Sigtuna, on the shores of Lake Mälaren, and to the nearby 17th-century Skokloster Castle, which houses one of the most interesting baroque museums in Europe. Then it's on to the university city of Uppsala, and also to the neighboring Gamla (old) Uppsala to see Viking burial mounds.

Day 5   Begin a fast 3-day excursion through the most interesting folkloric provinces of Sweden: Dalarna and Värmland. Arrive first at the mining town of Falun to visit the Falun Copper Mine and the home of Carl Larsson, the famous Swedish painter. Spend the night here or in one of the smaller resort towns such as Tällberg, Rättvik, Mora, or Leksand.

Day 6   Visit the Lake Siljan towns just mentioned. This blue glacial lake, ringed by lush forests, is one of the most beautiful in Europe. Take a boat tour leaving from Rättvik. On the outskirts of town you can visit Gammelgården, an old farmstead, for a glimpse into the past; stay overnight again in one of the lakeside villages or towns.

Day 7   From Falun, Route 60 heads south to Karlstad. You'll pass through the heart of Selma Lagerlöf country (Sweden's most famous novelist). Have lunch at Filipstad, the birthplace of John Ericsson, who designed the U.S. Civil War ironclad ship *Monitor*. Spend the night in Karlstad.

If You Have 2 Weeks

Days 1–7   Spend the first week as described above. But instead of cutting short your trip in Karlstad, extend it another night and then use the following itinerary.

Day 8   Spend another night in Karlstad, exploring its attractions and branching out into the environs, including Rottneros Manor.

Day 9   In the morning, head south along the eastern shore of Lake Vänern. After lunch in charming lakeside Lidköping, head for Gothenburg, Sweden's second-largest city.

Day 10   Explore Gothenburg and make a side trip to such places as Kungälv or Marstrand, a former royal resort.

Days 11–13   From Gothenburg, take the Göta Canal excursion, a distance of 350 miles to Stockholm. As you pass through 58 locks, you'll have a chance to see the "essence" of Sweden.

Day 14   Arrive in Stockholm and prepare for your return flight.

If You Have 3 Weeks

Days 1–14   In addition to the 2-week itinerary outlined above, you may want to explore Sweden's southern region.

Days 15 and 16   Head south (by air or ferry) to Sweden's largest island, Gotland, whose capital is Visby. Spend the next day exploring the island's attractions.

Day 17   Return to the mainland and continue south to the old city of Kalmar, where you can explore Kalmar Castle and other attractions.

Day 18   Visit the glassworks district, which is centered at Växjö. Within less than an hour's drive from Växjö are several glassworks, including Orrefors and Kosta Boda, both of which offer guided tours. You can purchase "seconds" in their workshops.

Days 19–21   Explore Skåne, Sweden's southernmost region, which often is called the "château district." Malmö, Sweden's third-largest city, makes an ideal base because of its many hotels and attractions. The university city of Lund, northeast of Malmö, also is a good bet, and Ystad is a favorite stop along the southern coastline. From Helsingborg, north of Malmö, you can cross into Denmark and see Hamlet's Castle.

Fast Facts: Sweden

Area Code   The international country code for Sweden is **46.** The local city (area) codes are given for all phone numbers in the Sweden chapters.

Business Hours   Generally, **banks** are open Monday through Friday from 9:30am to 3pm. In some larger cities banks extend their hours, usually on Thursday or Friday, until 5:30 or 6pm. Most **offices** are open Monday through Friday from 8:30 or 9am to 5pm (sometimes to 3 or 4pm in the summer); on Saturday, offices and factories are closed, or open for only a half day. Most **stores and shops** are open Monday through Friday between 9:30am and 6pm, and on Saturday from 9:30am to somewhere between 1 and 4pm. Once a week, usually on Monday or Friday, some of the larger stores are open from 9:30am to 7pm (during July and August, to 6pm).

Camera & Film   Cameras (especially the famed Hasselblad), film, projectors, and enlarging equipment are good values in Sweden. Practically all the world's brands are found here. Photographic shops give excellent service, often developing and printing in 1 day.

Customs   The government allows visitors aged 16 and older to bring in 200 cigarettes or 50 cigars duty-free. If you're over 21, you also are allowed 1 liter of liquor, 2 liters of wine, gifts totaling 600 SEK ($66), and what the Swedes call a "reasonable" amount of perfume. There's no limit on the amount of currency you can bring in or take out of the country.

Dentists   For emergency dental services, ask your hotel or host for the location of the nearest dentist. Nearly all dentists in Sweden speak English.

Doctors   Hotel desks usually can refer you to a local doctor, nearly all of whom speak English. If you need emergency treatment, your hotel also should be able to direct you to the nearest facility. In case of an accident or injury away from the hotel, call the nearest police station.

Drug Laws   Sweden imposes severe penalties for the possession, use, purchase, sale, or manufacture of illegal drugs. Penalties often (but not always) are based on quantity. Possession of a small amount of drugs, either hard or soft, can lead to a heavy fine and deportation. Possession of a large amount of drugs can entail imprisonment from 3 months to 15 years, depending on the circumstances and the presiding judge.

Drugstores   Called *apotek* in Swedish, drugstores generally are open Monday to Friday from 9am to 6pm and on Saturday from 9am to 1pm. In larger cities, one drugstore in every neighborhood stays open until 7pm. All drugstores post a list of the names and addresses of these stores (called *nattapotek*) in their windows.

Electricity   In Sweden, the electricity is 220 volts AC (50 cycles). To operate North American hair dryers and other electrical appliances, you'll need an electrical transformer (sometimes erroneously called a converter) and plugs that fit the two-pin round continental electrical outlets that are standard in Sweden. Transformers can be bought at hardware stores. Before using any American-made appliance, always ask about it at your hotel desk.

Embassies & Consulates   All embassies are in Stockholm. The Embassy of the **United States** is at Strandvägen 101, S-115 89 Stockholm (☎ 08/783-53-00); **United Kingdom,** Skarpögatan 6–8, S-115 27 Stockholm (☎ 08/671-30-00); **Canada,** Tegelbacken 4, S-101 23 Stockholm (☎ 08/453-30-00); **Australia,** Sergels Torg 12, S-103 27 Stockholm (☎ 08/613-29-00). **New Zealand** does not maintain an embassy in Sweden.

Emergencies   Call ☎ 90-000 from anywhere in Sweden if you need an ambulance, the police, or the fire department (*brandlarm*).

Language   The national language is Swedish, a Germanic tongue, and there are many regional dialects. Some minority groups speak Norwegian and Finnish. English is a required course of study in school and is commonly spoken, even in the hinterlands, and especially among young people.

Liquor Laws   Most restaurants, pubs, and bars in Sweden are licensed to serve liquor, wine, and beer. Some places are licensed only for wine and beer. Purchases of wine, liquor, and export beer are available only through the government-controlled monopoly, Systembolaget. Branch stores, spread throughout the country, usually are open Monday through Friday from 9am to 6pm. The minimum age for buying alcoholic beverages in Sweden is 21.

Mail   Post offices in Sweden usually are open Monday through Friday from 9am to 6pm and on Saturday from 9am to noon. To send a postcard to North America costs 6.50 SEK (85¢) by surface mail, 8 SEK ($1) by airmail. Letters weighing not more than 20 grams (⁷⁄₁₀ oz.) cost the same. Mailboxes can easily be recognized—they carry a yellow post horn on a blue background. You also can buy stamps in most tobacco shops and stationers.

Maps   Many tourist offices supply routine maps of their districts free of charge, and you also can contact one of the Swedish automobile clubs. Bookstores throughout Sweden also sell detailed maps of the country and of such major cities as Gothenburg and Stockholm. The most reliable country maps are published by Hallweg. The best and most detailed city maps are those issued by Falk, which have a particularly good and properly indexed map to Stockholm.

Newspapers & Magazines   In big cities such as Stockholm and Gothenburg, English-language newspapers, including the latest editions of the *International Herald Tribune* and *USA Today,* usually are available. American newspapers are not commonly available, but in Stockholm and Gothenburg you can purchase such London newspapers as *The Times.* At kiosks or newsstands in major cities, you also can purchase the European editions of *Time* and *Newsweek.*

Police   In an emergency, dial ☎ **90-000** anywhere in the country.

Radio & TV   In summer, Radio Stockholm broadcasts a special program for English-speaking tourists, "T-T-T-Tourist Time," on 103.3 MHz (FM) from 6 to 7pm daily. Swedish radio transmits P1 on 92.4 MHz (FM) and P2 on 96.2 MHz (FM) in the Stockholm area. P3 is transmitted on 103.3 MHz (102.9 MHz in southern Stockholm), a wavelength shared by Radio Stockholm and local programs.

The two most important TV channels, STV1 and STV2, are nonprofit. There are three major privately operated stations—Channel 4, TV3, and TV5, as well as several minor stations.

Rest Rooms   The word for toilet in Swedish is *toalett,* and public facilities are found in department stores, rail and air terminals, and subway (T-bana) stations. They're also located along some of the major streets, parks, and squares. DAMER means women and HERRAR means men. Sometimes the sign is abbreviated to D or H, and often the toilet is marked WC. Most toilets are free, although a few have attendants to offer towels and soap. In an emergency you also can use the toilets in most hotels and restaurants, although in principle they're reserved for guests.

Shoe Repairs   Shoe-repair shops rarely accommodate you while you wait. In summer, especially in July, many shops close, but the larger stores in the center of Stockholm have their own repair departments. If all you need is a new heel, look for something called *klackbar* in the stores or shoe departments of department stores. They'll make repairs while you wait.

Taxes   Sweden imposes a "value-added tax," called MOMS, on most goods and services. Visitors from North America can beat the tax, however, by shopping in stores with the yellow-and-blue tax-free shopping sign. There are more than 15,000 of these stores in Sweden. To get a refund, your total purchase must cost a minimum of 200 SEK ($22). Tax refunds range from 14% to 18%, depending on the amount purchased. MOMS begins at 19% on food items, but is 25% for most goods and services. The tax is part of the purchase price, but you can get a tax-refund voucher before you leave the store. When you leave Sweden, take the voucher to a tax-free customs desk at the airport or train station you're leaving from. They will give you your MOMS refund (minus a small service charge) before you wing off to your next non-Swedish destination. Two requirements: You cannot use your purchase in Sweden (it should be sealed in its original packaging), and it must be taken out of the country within 1 month after purchase. For tax-free shopping information in Sweden, phone ☎ 024/74-17-41.

Telephone, Telex & Fax   Information on these facilities in Stockholm will be found in "Fast Facts: Stockholm," in chapter 3. The same rules apply to calling from public phones elsewhere in the country. Avoid placing long-distance calls from your hotel, where the charge may be doubled or tripled when you get your final bill.

Time   Sweden is on central European time—Greenwich mean time plus 1 hour or eastern standard time plus 6 hours. The clocks are advanced 1 hour in summer.

Tipping   Hotels include a 15% service charge in your bill. Restaurants, depending on their class, add 13% to 15% to your tab. Taxi drivers are entitled to 8% of the fare, and cloakroom attendants usually get 6 SEK (65¢).

Water   The water is safe to drink all over Sweden. However, don't drink water from lakes, rivers, or streams, regardless of how clear and pure it appears.

3

Settling into Stockholm

Stockholm, a city of 1.4 million people, is built on 14 islands in Lake Mälaren, which marks the beginning of an archipelago of 24,000 islands, skerries, and islets stretching all the way to the Baltic Sea. A city of bridges and islands, towers and steeples, cobblestone squares and broad boulevards, Renaissance splendor and steel-and-glass skyscrapers, Stockholm also has access to nature just a short distance away. You can even go fishing in the downtown waterways, thanks to a long-standing decree signed by Queen Christina.

Although the city was founded more than 7 centuries ago, it did not become the official capital of Sweden until the mid-17th century. Today it reigns over a modern welfare state. The medieval walls of the Old Town (Gamla Stan) no longer remain, but the old winding streets have been preserved.

1 Orientation

ARRIVING

BY PLANE   You'll arrive at **Stockholm Arlanda Airport** (☎ 08/797-61-00 for information on flights), about 28 miles north of the city on the E4 highway. A long, covered walkway connects the international and domestic terminals.

A bus outside the terminal building will take you to the **City Terminal,** on Klarabergsviadukten, about a 40-minute trip, for 60 SEK ($6.60).

A taxi to or from the airport is expensive, costing 350 to 400 SEK ($38.50 to $44) or more. (See "Getting Around," later in this chapter, for the name of a reputable taxi company.)

BY TRAIN   Trains arrive at Stockholm's **Centralstationen** (Central Station) on Vasagatan, in the city center (☎ 020/75-75-75 in Sweden or 08/696-75-09 from abroad), where connections can be made to Stockholm's subway, the T-bana. Follow the tunnelbana sign.

Virtually every part of Sweden can be reached by rail from Stockholm's Centralstationen.

BY BUS   Buses also arrive at the Centralstationen city terminal, and from here you can catch the T-bana (subway) to your final Stockholm destination. For bus information or reservations, check with the bus system's **ticket offices** at the station (☎ 08/440-85-70). Offices in the station labeled "bus stop" sell bus tickets.

Don't Get Taken for a Ride

There has been a recent influx of smaller taxi companies that might charge you up to 650 SEK ($71.50) for the same taxi ride that normally would cost around 350 SEK ($38.50). To avoid any unpleasant surprises, be sure to ask in advance what the price will be for transport to your destination.

BY CAR   Getting into Stockholm by car is relatively easy because the major national expressway from the south, E4, joins with the national expressway, E3, coming in from the west, and leads right into the heart of the city. Stay on the highway until you see the turnoff for Central Stockholm (or Centrum).

Parking in Stockholm is extremely difficult unless your hotel has a garage. Call your hotel in advance and find out what the parking situation is. Most hotels do not offer parking. However, if you're driving into the city, often you can park long enough to unload your luggage; then a member of the hotel staff will direct you to the nearest parking garage.

BY FERRY   Large ships, including those of the **Silja Line,** Kungsgatan 2 (☎ 08/22-21-40), and the **Viking Line,** Centralstationen (☎ 08/452-40-00), arrive at specially constructed berths jutting seaward from a point near the junction of Södermalm and Gamla Stan. This neighborhood is called Stadsgården, and the avenue that runs along the adjacent waterfront is known as Stadsgårdshamnen. The nearest T-bana stop is Slussen, a 3-minute walk from the Old Town. Holders of a valid Eurailpass can ride the Silja ferries to Helsinki and Turku at a reduced rate.

Other ferries arrive from Gotland (whose capital is Visby), but these boats dock at Nynäshamn, south of Stockholm. Take a Nynäshamn-bound bus from the Central Station in Stockholm or the SL commuter train to reach the ferry terminal at Nynäshamn.

VISITOR INFORMATION

The **Tourist Center,** Sweden House, Hamngatan 27, off Kungsträdgården (Box 7542), S-103 93 Stockholm (☎ 08/789-24-95 or 08/789-24-90), is open June through August, Monday through Friday, from 9am to 7pm and Saturday and Sunday from 9am to 5pm; September through May, Monday through Friday, from 9am to 6pm and Saturday and Sunday from 10am to 3pm. Maps and other free materials are available.

The largest organization of its kind in all of Sweden is the **Kulturhuset,** Sergels Torg 3 (☎ 08/508-31-400). It was built in 1974 by the city of Stockholm as a showcase for Swedish and international art and theater. There are no permanent exhibits; instead, the various spaces inside are allocated to a changing array of paintings, sculpture, photographs, and live performance groups. Kulturhuset also serves as the focal point for information about other cultural activities and organizations throughout Sweden and the rest of Europe. Inside are a snack bar, a library (which has newspapers in several languages), a reading room, a collection of recordings, and a somewhat bureaucratic openness to new art forms. Admission is 30 SEK ($3.30) for adults, 20 SEK ($2.20) for children 12 to 18. Those 11 and under are admitted free. Open Tuesday through Thursday 11am to 7pm, Friday 11am to 6pm, Saturday 11am to 4pm, and Sunday noon to 4pm.

CITY LAYOUT

MAIN STREETS & ARTERIES   Stockholm's major streets—**Kungsgatan** (the main shopping street), **Birger Jarlsgatan,** and **Strandvägen** (which leads to

Stockholm Orientation

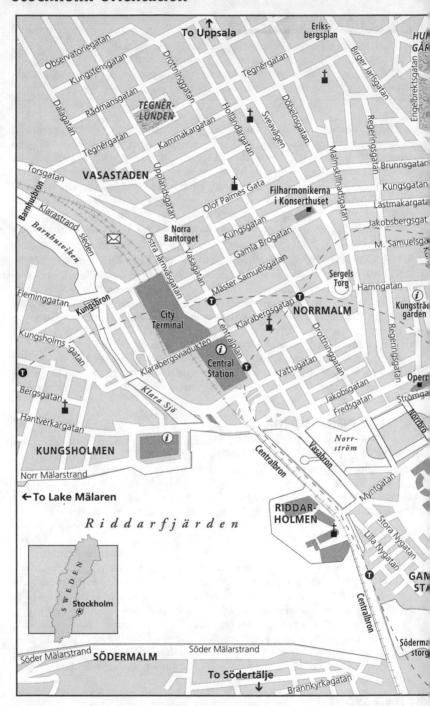

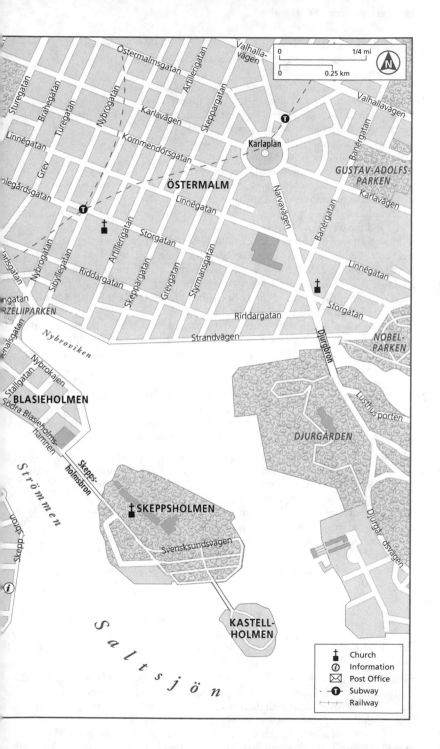

0

1/4 mi

0

0.25 km

N

Sturegatan
Brahegatan
Turegatan
Grev
nlegårdsgatan
Linnégatan
Östermalmsgatan
Nybrogatan
Artillerigatan
Valhalla-
vägen
Valhallavägen
Karlavägen
Kommendörsgatan
Skeppargatan
Karlaplan
Banérgatan
GUSTAV-ADOLFS-
PARKEN
Karlavägen
T
ÖSTERMALM
Narvavägen
Linnégatan
Banérgatan
†
Linnégatan
Storgatan
Nybrogatan
Sibyllegatan
Riddargatan
Artillerigatan
Skeppargatan
Grevgatan
Styrmansgatan
Linnégatan
†
Storgatan
ngatan
RZELIIPARKEN
alsgatan
Nybroviken
Riddargatan
Strandvägen
Djurgbron
NOBEL-
PARKEN
Nybrokajen
Stallgatan
Södra Blasieholms-
BLASIEHOLMEN
hamnen
Södra Blasieholms-
Skepps-
holmsbron
S t r ö m m e n
Skepps bron
† SKEPPSHOLMEN
DJURGÅRDEN
Lusthusporten
Djurgår dsvägen
Svensksundsvägen
KASTELL-
HOLMEN
S a l t s j ö n
i

† Church
■ Church
ⓘ Information
⊠ Post Office
- T Subway
┼┼┼ Railway

45

Djurgården)—are on Norrmalm (north of the Old Town). **Stureplan,** which lies at the junction of the major avenues Kungsgatan and Birger Jarlsgatan, is the commercial hub of the city.

About 4 blocks east of Stureplan rises **Hötorget City,** a landmark of modern urban planning, which includes five 18-story skyscrapers. Its main traffic-free artery is **Sergelgatan,** a 3-block shopper's promenade that eventually leads to the modern sculptures at the center of Sergels Torg.

About 9 blocks south of Stureplan, at **Gustav Adolfs Torg,** are both the Royal Dramatic Theater and the Royal Opera House.

A block east of the flaming torches of the opera house is the verdant north-to-south stretch of **Kungsträdgården**—part avenue, part public park—which serves as a popular gathering place for students and a resting spot for shoppers.

Three blocks to the southeast, on a famous promontory, are the landmark Grand Hotel and the National Museum.

Most visitors to Stockholm arrive at either the SAS Airport Bus Terminal, the Central Station, or Stockholm's Central (Public) Bus Station. Each of these is in the heart of the city, on the harbor front, about 7 blocks due west of the opera house. **Kungsholmen** (King's Island) lies across a narrow canal from the rest of the city, a short walk west from the Central Station. It's visited chiefly by those who want to tour Stockholm's elegant Stadshuset (City Hall).

South of **Gamla Stan** (Old Town), and separated from it by a narrow but much-navigated stretch of water, is **Södermalm,** the southern district of Stockholm. Quieter than its northern counterpart, it's an important residential area with a distinctive flavor of its own.

To the east of Gamla Stan, on a large and forested island completely surrounded by the complicated waterways of Stockholm, is **Djurgården** (Deer Park). The summer pleasure ground of Stockholm is the site of many of its most popular attractions: the open-air museums of Skansen, the *Vasa* man-of-war, Gröna Lund's Tivoli, the Waldemarsudde estate of the "painting prince" Eugen, and the Nordic Museum.

FINDING AN ADDRESS All even numbers are on one side of the street and all odd numbers are on the opposite side. Buildings are listed in numerical order, but often will have an A, B, or C after the number. In the very center of town, numbered addresses start from Sergels Torg.

MAPS Free maps of Stockholm are available at the tourist office, but if you want to explore the narrow old streets of Gamla Stan, you'll need a more detailed map. The best, published by **Falk,** is a pocket-size map with a street index that can be opened and folded like a wallet. It's sold at most newsstands in central Stockholm and at major bookstores, including **Akademibokhandeln,** Mäster Samuelsgatan 32 (☎ 08/613-61-00).

Neighborhoods in Brief

Any city spread across 14 major islands in an archipelago has many neighborhoods, but those of concern to the average visitor lie in central Stockholm.

Gamla Stan (Old Town) The "cradle" of Stockholm, Gamla Stan lies at the entrance to Lake Mälaren on the Baltic. Its oldest city wall dates from the 13th century. The Old Town, along with the *Vasa,* is the most popular attraction in Stockholm. This is our favorite place to spend our nights in Stockholm. The hotels here are in general the most evocative in Stockholm, built in romantic architectural styles. The downside of this area is that there are few hotels, and they tend to be expensive; but there are dozens of restaurants. Gamla Stan's major shopping street is Västerlånggatan, but many artisans' galleries and antique stores abound on its small lanes. Its main square, and the heart of the ancient city, is Stortorget.

Norrmalm   North of Gamla Stan, this is the cultural and commercial heart of modern Stockholm. Once it was a city suburb, but now it virtually is the city. Chances are your hotel will be in this district, as the area is generously endowed with hotels in all price ranges; it's also the most convenient location for most visits, as it encompasses the City Terminal and the Central Station. Hotels here are not the most romantic in town, but they're generally modern, up-to-date, and well run.

The most famous park in Stockholm, Kungsträdgården (King's Garden), also is in Norrmalm. In summer, this park is a major rendezvous point. Norrmalm also embraces the important squares of Sergels Torg and Hötorget, the latter a modern shopping complex. Norrmalm's major pedestrian shopping street is Drottninggatan, which starts at the bridge to the Old Town.

Vasastaden   As Norrmalm pushed ever northward, the new district of Vasastaden was created. It's split by a trio of main arteries: S:t Eriksgatan, Sveavägen, and Odengatan. The area around S:t Eriksplan now is called "the Off-Broadway of Stockholm" because it has so many theaters. Increasingly, this district has attracted fashionable restaurants and bars and has become a popular residential area for young Stockholmers in fields such as journalism, television, and advertising.

Vasastaden is slightly more removed from the scene of the action, but it's still a good bet for hotels. In New York City terms, Norrmalm would be like staying in the Times Square area, whereas Vasastaden would be equivalent to staying up in the 60th or 70th Street areas. Hotels in Vasastaden come in a wide range of price categories.

Kungsholmen   Once known as "Grey Friars Farm," today Kungsholmen (King's Island), to the west of Gamla Stan, is the site of City Hall. Established by Charles XI in the 17th century as a zone for industry and artisans, the island now has been gentrified. One of its major arteries is Fleminggatan. Along Norrmälarstrand, old Baltic cutters tie up to the banks. Stockholm's newspapers' headquarters are at Marieberg on the southwestern tip of the island.

Södermalm   South of Gamla Stan, Södermalm (where Greta Garbo was born) is the largest and most populated district of Stockholm. Once synonymous with poverty, today this working-class area is becoming more fashionable, especially with artists, writers, and young people. If you don't come here to stay in one of the moderately priced hotels or to dine in one of its restaurants, you might want to take the Katarina elevator for a good view of Stockholm and its harbor.

Östermalm   In central Stockholm, east of Birger Jarlsgatan, the main artery, lies Östermalm. In the Middle Ages, the royal family used to keep its horses, and even its armies, here. Today it's the site of the Army Museum. There are wide, straight streets, and it also is home to one of the city's biggest parks, Humlegården, dating from the 17th century.

This is another area of Stockholm that's a hotel district. Östermalm doesn't have quite the convenience of Norrmalm and Vasastaden, but it still is not so far removed from the action as to be called inconvenient. In summer, when visitors from all over the world are in town, this is a good place to hunt for a room. Because Norrmalm and Vasastaden are located close to the Central Station, hotels in those neighborhoods tend to fill up very quickly.

Djurgården   To the east of Gamla Stan (Old Town) is Djurgården (Deer Park), a lake-encircled forested island that's the summer recreation area of Stockholm. Here you can visit the open-air folk museums of Skansen, the *Vasa* man-of-war, Gröna

Lund's Tivoli (Stockholm's own version of the Tivoli), the Waldemarsudde estate and gardens of the "painting prince" Eugen, and the Nordic Museum. The fastest way to get here is over the bridge at Strandvägen/Narvavägen.

Skeppsholmen   On its own little island, and reached by crossing Skeppsholmsbron, a bridge from the Blasieholmen district, Skeppsholmen is like a world apart from the rest of bustling Stockholm. Although it makes for a pleasant stroll, most people visit it to see the exhibits at the Moderna Museet (see Chapter 4, "Discovering Stockholm"). Skeppsholmen also is home of af *Chapman,* Sweden's most famous youth hostel, a gallant tall ship that, with its fully rigged masts, is a Stockholm landmark.

2 Getting Around

BY PUBLIC TRANSPORTATION

You can travel throughout Stockholm county by bus, local train, subway (T-bana), and trams, going from Singö in the north to Nynäshamn in the south. The routes are divided into zones, and one ticket is valid for all types of public transportation in the same zone within 1 hour of the time the ticket is stamped.

REGULAR FARES   The basic fare for public transportation (in Stockholm this means subway, tram/streetcar, or bus) requires tickets purchased from the agent in the toll booth on the subway platform, not from a vending machine. Each ticket costs 16 SEK ($1.75). To travel within most of urban Stockholm, all the way to the borders of the inner city, requires only two tickets. The maximum ride, to the outermost suburbs, requires five tickets. You can transfer (or double back and return to your starting point) within 1 hour of your departure free of charge.

SPECIAL DISCOUNT TICKETS   Your best transportation bet is to purchase a **tourist season ticket.** A 1-day card, costing 60 SEK ($6.60), is valid for 24 hours of unlimited travel by T-bana, bus, and commuter train within Stockholm. It also includes passage on the ferry to Djurgården. Most visitors probably will prefer the 3-day card for 135 SEK ($14.85), valid for 72 hours in both Stockholm and the adjacent county. The 3-day card also is valid for admission to Skansen, Kaknästornet, and Gröna Lund. Children 8 to 17 are charged 70 to 80 SEK ($7.70 to $8.80) and kids up to 7 years of age can travel free with an adult. These tickets are available at tourist information offices, in subway stations, and at most news vendors. Call ☎ **08/ 689-10-00** for more information.

Stockholmskortet (**Stockholm Card**) is a personal discount card that allows unlimited travel by bus, subway, and local trains throughout the city and county of Stockholm (except on airport buses). You can take a sightseeing tour with City Sightseeing, where you can get on and off as often as you please. These tours are available daily mid-June through mid-August. In addition, the card enables you to take a boat trip to the Royal Palace of Drottningholm for half price. Admission to 70 attractions also is included in the package.

You can purchase the card at several places in the city, including the Tourist Center in Sweden House, HotellCentralen, the Central Station, the tourist information desk in City Hall (in summer), the Kaknäs TV tower, SL-Center Sergels Torg (subway entrance level), and Pressbyrån newsstands. The cards are stamped with the date and time at the first point of usage. A 24-hour card costs 199 SEK ($21.90) for adults and 25 SEK ($2.75) for children 7 to 17.

BY T-BANA (SUBWAY)   Before entering the subway, passengers tell the ticket seller the destination, then purchase tickets. Subway entrances are marked with a blue T

Subway Art

In 1950 two women came up with the idea of commissioning artists to decorate the subway stations of Stockholm. Some of the country's finest artists were asked to participate; their work now is displayed in "the longest and deepest art gallery in the world," some 100 stations stretching all the way from the center of Stockholm to the suburbs.

on a white background. For information about schedules, routes, and fares, phone ☎ **08/686-10-00.**

BY BUS Where the subway line ends, the bus begins; therefore, if a subway connection doesn't conveniently cover a particular area of Stockholm, a bus will. The two systems have been coordinated to complement each other. Many visitors use a bus to reach Djurgården (although you can walk), because the T-bana doesn't go there. For a list of bus routes, purchase the *SL Stockholmskartan* booklet (10 SEK or $1.10) which is sold at the Tourist Center at Sweden House, Hamngatan 27, off Kungsträdgården (☎ **08/789-24-95**).

BY CAR

If you're driving around the Swedish capital, you'll find several parking garages in the city center as well as on the outskirts. In general, you can park at marked spaces Monday through Friday from 8am to 6pm. Exceptions or rules for specific areas are indicated on signs in the area. At Djurgården, parking is always prohibited, and from April to mid-September it's closed to traffic Friday through Sunday.

BY TAXI

Taxis are expensive—in fact, the most expensive in the world—with the meter starting at 28 SEK ($3.10). A short ride can easily cost 80 SEK ($8.80). Those that display the sign LEDIG can be hailed, or you can order one by phone. **Taxi Stockholm** (☎ **08/15-00-00** or 08/15-04-00) is one of the city's larger, more reputable companies.

BY FERRY

Ferries from Skeppsbron on Gamla Stan (near the bridge to Södermalm) will take you to Djurgården if you don't want to walk or go by bus. They leave every 20 minutes Monday through Saturday, and about every 15 minutes on Sunday, from 9am to 6pm, charging 20 SEK ($2.20) for adults and 10 SEK ($1.10) for senior citizens and children 7 to 12; passage is free for children 6 and under.

BY BICYCLE

The best place to go cycling is on Djurgården. You can rent bicycles from **Skepp o Hoj,** Djurgårdsbron (☎ **08/660-57-57**), for about 150 SEK ($16.50) per day. It's open May through August, daily from 9am to 9pm.

Fast Facts: Stockholm

American Express American Express is at Norrlandsgatan 21 (☎ **08/ 411-05-40**) , open Monday through Friday from 9am to 6pm (until 5pm in winter) and Saturday from 10am to 3pm (until 1pm in winter).

Area Code The international country code for Sweden is 46; the city code for Stockholm is **08** (if you're calling Stockholm from abroad, drop the zero). You do not need to dial 8 within Stockholm; only if you're outside the city.

Baby-Sitters   Stockholm hotels maintain lists of competent baby-sitters. Nearly all of them speak English. There is no official agency; rather, it's a word-of-mouth system. Your hotel reception desk can assist you.

Bookstores   For a good selection of English-language books, including maps and touring guides, try **Akademibokhandeln,** Mäster Samuelsgatan 32 (☎ 08/ 613-61-00), open Monday through Friday from 9:30am to 6pm and Saturday from 10am to 4pm.

Car Rentals   See "Getting Around," in chapter 2. In Stockholm, some of the big car rental companies include **Avis,** Ringvägen 90 (☎ 08/644-99-80), and **Hertz,** Vasagatan 24 (☎ 08/24-07-20).

Currency Exchange   There's a currency exchange office, **Forex,** at the Central Station (☎ 08/411-67-34), open daily from 7am to 9pm. It's fully approved by both the Bank of Sweden and the Swedish tourist authorities, offers some of the best exchange rates in town, and takes some of the lowest commissions for cashing traveler's checks. Several other offices are scattered throughout the city.

Dentists   Emergency dental treatment is offered at **Sct. Eriks Hospital,** Fleminggatan 22 (☎ 08/654-11-17), open daily from 8am to 8pm.

Doctors   If you need 24-hour emergency medical care, check with **Medical Care Information** (☎ 08/672-10-00). There's also a private clinic, **City Akuten,** at Apelberg Sq. 481, 4th floor (☎ 08/412-29-61).

Drugstores   A pharmacy that remains open 24 hours a day is **C. W. Scheele,** Klarabergsgatan 64 (☎ 08/454-81-00).

Embassies & Consulates   See "Fast Facts: Sweden," in chapter 2.

Emergencies   Call ☎ 112 for the police, ambulance service, or the fire department.

Eyeglasses   **The Nordiska Kompaniet,** Hamngatan 18-20 (☎ 08/762-80-00), a leading Stockholm department store, has a registered optician on duty at its ground-floor service center. The optician performs vision tests, stocks a large selection of frames, and makes emergency repairs.

Hospitals   Call **Medical Care Information** at ☎ 08/672-21-00 and an English-speaking operator will inform you of the hospital closest to you 24 hours a day.

Internet Café   One of the most central places for receiving e-mail or checking messages is **Café Nine,** Odengatan 44 (☎ 08/673-67-97; e-mail: info@ ninestudios.com). It charges only 1 krone (10¢) per minute, and is open Monday through Friday 10am to 1am and Saturday and Sunday 11am to 1am. T-Bana: Odenplan.

Laundry & Dry Cleaning   **City Kemtvatt,** Drottningholmsvägen 9 (☎ 08/ 654-95-34), does dry cleaning and also laundry by the kilo for same-day delivery if it's brought in before 10am. It's open Monday through Friday from 7am to 6pm and Saturday 10am to 2pm. Note that the system of coin-operated launderettes is pretty much outmoded in Sweden. The cost for doing laundry is 55 SEK ($6.05) per kilo (2.2 lb.). Your clothes will be neatly folded for you as part of the price.

Libraries   **The Stockholms Stadsbibliotek,** Sveavägen 73 (☎ 08/508-31-00), is the biggest municipal library in Sweden, with 2.5 million books (many in English) and audiovisual materials. It also subscribes to 1,500 newspapers and periodicals (again, many in English). It's open Monday through Thursday from 10am to 8:30pm, Friday from 10am to 6pm, and Saturday and Sunday from noon to 4pm.

Lost Property   If you've lost something on the train, go to the Lost and Found office in the Central Station, lower concourse (☎ **08/762-25-50**). The police also have such an office at the police station at Bergsgatan 39 (☎ **08/ 401-07-88**). The Stockholm Transit Company (SL) keeps its recovered articles at the Rådmansgatan T-bana station (☎ **08/736-07-80**), and Vaxholmsbolaget has one at Nybrokajen 2 (☎ **08/679-58-30**).

Luggage Storage & Lockers   Facilities are available at the Central Station on Vasagatan, lower concourse (☎ **08/762-25-50**). Lockers also can be rented at the ferry stations at Värtan and Tegelvikshamnen, at the Viking Line terminal, and at the Central Station.

Photographic Needs   Photo shops are plentiful in Stockholm. One of the most centrally located is the **Kodak Image Center,** at Hamngatan 16 (☎ **08/ 21-40-42**). Open Monday through Friday 8am to 6pm, and Saturday from 10am to 2pm.

Police   Call ☎ **112** in an emergency.

Post Office   The main post office is at Vasagatan 28–34 (☎ **08/781-20-00**), open Monday through Friday from 8am to 6pm and Saturday from 9am to 1pm. If you want to pick up letters while you're abroad, they should be addressed to your name, C/o Post Restante, C/o Postens Huyudkontor (main post office), Vasagatan 28–34, S-10 430 Stockholm, Sweden.

Radio & TV   Sweden has two TV channels and three national radio stations, plus a local station for Stockholm, broadcasting on 103.3 MHz (FM). Many hotels are equipped to receive English-language TV programs broadcast from England, and many of the more expensive hotels have 24-hour CNN news broadcasts in English.

Rest Rooms   Public facilities are found in the Central Station, in all subway stations, and in department stores, as well as along some of the major streets, parks, and squares. In an emergency, you also can use the toilets in most hotels and restaurants, although in principle they're reserved for patrons.

Shoe Repair   In the basement of **Nordiska Kompaniet,** Hamngatan 18–20 (☎ **08/762-80-00**), a leading Stockholm department store, there is a shoe repair place, which also may be able to repair broken luggage.

Taxis   See "Getting Around," earlier in this chapter.

Telephone, Telex & Fax   Instructions in English are posted in public phone boxes, which can be found on street corners. Very few phones in Sweden are coin operated; most require a phone card, which can be purchased at most newspaper stands and tobacco shops. You can send a telegram by phoning ☎ **00-21** anytime.

Post offices throughout Stockholm now offer phone, fax, and telegram services. Of course, most guests ask their hotels to send a fax. All but the smallest boarding houses in Stockholm today have fax services.

Transit Information   For information on all services, including buses and subways (Tunnelbana), and suburban trains (pendeltåg), call ☎ **08/689-10-00.** Or, visit the SL Center, on the lower level of Sergels Torg. It provides information about transportation and also sells a map of the city's system, as well as tickets and special discount passes. Open in summer, Monday through Thursday from

9am to 6pm, on Friday from 9am to 5:30pm, on Saturday from 9am to 4pm, and on Sunday from 10am to 3pm; the rest of the year, open only Monday through Friday.

3 Where to Stay

By the standards of many U.S. or Canadian cities, hotels in Stockholm are very expensive. If these high prices make you want to cancel your trip, read on. Dozens of hotels in Stockholm offer reduced rates on weekends all year, and daily from around mid-June to mid-August. For further information, inquire at a travel agency or the tourist center (see "Orientation," above). In summer it's best to make reservations in advance just to be on the safe side.

Most of the medium-priced hotels are in Norrmalm, north of the Old Town, and many of the least expensive lodgings are near the Central Station. There are comparably priced inexpensive accommodations within 10 to 20 minutes of the city, easily reached by subway, streetcar, or bus. We'll suggest a few hotels in the Old Town, but these choices are limited and more expensive.

Note: In most cases, a service charge ranging from 10% to 15% is added to the bill, plus the inevitable 21% MOMS (value-added tax). Unless otherwise indicated, all of our recommended accommodations come with a private bath.

BOOKING SERVICES   HotellCentralen, Vasagatan (☎ **08/789-24-56**), on the lower level of the Central Station, is the city's official housing bureau; it can arrange accommodations in hotels, pensions (boarding houses), and youth hostels—but not in private homes. There's a 40 SEK ($4.40) service fee. It's open June through August, daily from 7am to 9pm; in May and September, daily from 8am to 7pm; and October through April, daily from 9am to 6pm. Credit cards are accepted.

The least expensive accommodations in Stockholm are rooms in a private home. The best way to get booked into a private home is by going to the **Hotell Tjänst AB,** Vasagatan 15–17 (☎ **08/10-44-37** or 08/10-44-57; fax 08/21-37-16). As you leave the Central Station, turn left on Vasagatan and proceed to this address, which is on the fourth floor of an older building. Here, Mr. Gustavsson and his staff will book you into a double, private room, without breakfast, from 450 SEK ($49.50) including the reservation fee. From June 15 through August 15 this agency also can book you into Stockholm's major hotels at a big discount.

Mr. Gustavsson asks that you avail yourself of these bargains only upon your arrival in Stockholm. He's confident of booking you into a room because of his long "secret" list of private addresses; he doesn't answer letters requesting reservations. Hotel Tj[um]nst is open Monday through Friday from 9am to noon and 1 to 5pm. Advance booking is rarely accepted; however, if you're going to arrive in Stockholm on a weekend, when the office is closed, call or fax the office and maybe Mr. Gustavsson will bend the rules.

IN NORRMALM (THE CENTER)
VERY EXPENSIVE

Berns' Hotel. Näckströmsgatan 8, S-111 47 Stockholm. ☎ **08/614-07-00.** Fax 08/ 566-32-201. www.berns.se. E-mail:hotelberns@bernshotel.se. 68 units. A/C MINIBAR TV TEL. 2,495–2,995 SEK ($274.45–$329.45) double; 3,795–5,500 SEK ($417.45–$605) suite. Rates include breakfast. AE, DC, MC, V. T-bana: Östermalmstorg.

During its 19th-century heyday, this was the most elegant hotel in Sweden, with a lush and ornate Gilded Age interior that was the setting for many legendary rendezvous'.

In 1989, following years of neglect, its premises were rebuilt in their original style and the restaurant facilities upgraded for modern tastes. Although the establishment's dining and drinking areas usually are crowded with young disco lovers and bar patrons, the upstairs bedrooms are calm, soundproofed, and comfortably isolated from the activities downstairs. Each room has a satellite TV, CD player, and a good-size bathroom (with hair dryer) sheathed in Italian marble. Some units are no-smoking and accessible to those in wheelchairs.

Dining/Diversions: The Red Room, once used as a breakfast room, is the setting and namesake of one of Stringberg's most trenchant novels (Röda Rummet). The hotel also has a bar.

Amenities: Baby-sitting, dry cleaning and laundry service, car rental desk, access to nearby health club.

✪ **Grand Hotel.** Södra Blaisieholmshamnen 8, S-103 27 Stockholm. ☎ **800/223-5652** in the U.S. and Canada, or 08/679-35-00. Fax 08/611-86-86. www.grandhotel.se. E-mail: guest@grandhotel.se. 320 units. MINIBAR TV TEL. 3,195–3,995 SEK ($351.45–$439.45) double; from 4,895 SEK ($538.45) suite. Rates include breakfast. AE, DC, MC, V. Parking 340 SEK ($37.40). T-bana: Kungsträdgården. Bus: 46, 55, 62, or 76.

Opposite the Royal Palace, this hotel is the finest in Sweden. A favorite of everybody from Sarah Bernhardt to Nobel Prize winners, the Grand Hotel is a bastion of elite hospitality. Built in 1874, it has seen continuous renovations (the last in 1996), but its old-world style has always triumphed. The bedrooms come in all shapes and sizes, but each is elegantly appointed with traditional styling; some feature air conditioning. Pale blue fabrics and light woods predominate. The bathrooms are decorated with Italian marble and tiles and have heated floors and hair dryers. The most expensive rooms overlook the water. The hotel's ballroom is an exact copy of Louis XIV's Hall of Mirrors at Versailles.

Dining/Diversions: The Grand Veranda specializes in traditional food served from a buffet, and the Franska Matsalen is the gourmet restaurant of the hotel. The Cadier Bar is one of the most sophisticated rendezvous spots in Stockholm.

Amenities: Room service (24 hours), same-day laundry and dry cleaning, ticket-securing concierge, house doctor, shoeshine service, valet parking, limousine service, sauna, hairstylist, newsstand, florist, gift shop, fitness center.

Scandic Sergel Plaza. Brunkebergstorg 9, S-103 27 Stockholm. ☎ **800/THE-OMNI** in the U.S., or 08/22-66-00. Fax 08/21-50-70. www.scandic-hotels.com. E-mail: sergel.plaza.hotel@provobis.se. 418 units. A/C TV TEL. 2,200–3,200 SEK ($242–$352) double; from 7,000 SEK ($770) suite. Rates include breakfast. AE, DC, MC, V. Parking 210 SEK ($23.10). T-bana: Centralen. Bus: 47, 52, or 69.

Originally designed as living quarters for members of the Swedish parliament in Stockholm, this hotel, built in 1984 at the entrance to Drottninggatan, the main shopping street, has been improved to such an extent that today it's one of the city's best. The elegant decor includes 18th-century artwork and antiques. All units contain firm mattresses, good double glazing, and air conditioning. The average-size tiled bathrooms also have hair dryers. Maintenance is first rate, and some accommodations are no-smoking and wheelchair accessible. A special executive floor offers enhanced amenities and several electronic extras.

Dining/Diversions: The Anna Rella, the gourmet restaurant, offers both Swedish and international specialties. There's also a lobby and piano bar.

Amenities: Concierge, room service (24 hours), laundry, baby-sitting, saunas, solariums, Jacuzzis.

Stockholm Accommodations

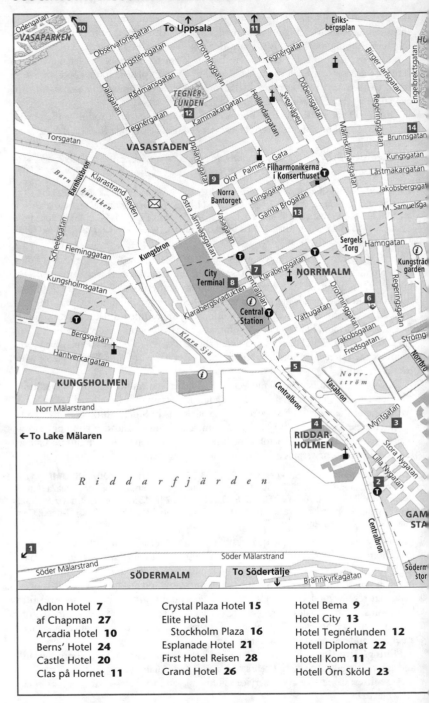

Adlon Hotel **7**	Crystal Plaza Hotel **15**	Hotel Bema **9**
af Chapman **27**	Elite Hotel	Hotel City **13**
Arcadia Hotel **10**	Stockholm Plaza **16**	Hotel Tegnérlunden **12**
Berns' Hotel **24**	Esplanade Hotel **21**	Hotell Diplomat **22**
Castle Hotel **20**	First Hotel Reisen **28**	Hotell Kom **11**
Clas på Hornet **11**	Grand Hotel **26**	Hotell Örn Sköld **23**

Kung Carl Hotel **14**	Radisson SAS Royal Viking Hotel **8**
Lady Hamilton Hotel **3**	Radisson SAS Strand Hotel **25**
Långholmen Hotel **1**	Radisson SAS SkyCity Hotel **10**
Lydmar Hotel **17**	Scandic Sergel Plaza **6**
Mälardrottningen **4**	Sheraton Stockholm & Towers **5**
Mornington Hotel **18**	Victory Hotel **2**

EXPENSIVE

Hotell Diplomat. Strandvagen 7C, Ostermalm, S-104-40 Stockholm. ☎ **08/663-5800.** Fax 08/783-6634. 128 units. MINIBAR TV TEL. Mon–Thurs 2,495 SEK ($274.45) double; Fri–Sun 1,395–2,495 SEK ($153.45–$274.45) double; all week 3,295–3,495 SEK ($362.45–$384.45) suite. AE, DC, MC, V. Rates include breakfast. T-bana: Storeplan.

Well managed, discreet, and solid, this hotel offers dignified and conservative premises and knows how to handle business clients and corporate conventions. Originally built in 1911, it retains hints of its original art nouveau styling within its bay-windowed facade. Public areas are less nostalgic; they were streamlined in recent times into a seamless kind of international modern styling. Bedrooms are outfitted in tones of green, blue, or yellow, with most electronic amenities, such as TVs and minibars, concealed within well-crafted furniture or built-in cupboards. Many contain bay windows overlooking the harbor; less expensive options face a quiet inner courtyard. Rooms come in a wide variety of sizes ranging from cramped singles to spacious doubles with sitting areas. All have good beds, plus average-size bathrooms with tiled vanities and both mounted and hand-held showers. At least once bypass the birdcage-style elevator in favor of the circular stairs for views from the hotel's antique stained-glass windows.

Dining/Diversions: The Tea Room restaurant has potted palms, wicker furnishings, decor inspired by colonial Asia, and views over Stockholm's harbor. A bar on the hotel's second floor carries the men's club theme even further, thanks to varnished paneling and sink-into-them chairs.

Amenities: Sauna, meeting rooms, room service daily 7am to midnight.

Lydmar Hotel. Sturegatan 10, S-114 36 Stockholm. ☎ **98/566-11-300.** Fax 08/566-11-301. www.lydmar.se. E-mail: info@lydmar.se. 63 units. MINIBAR TV TEL. 2,200–3,750 SEK ($242–$412.50) double; 7,500 SEK ($825) junior suite. Rates include buffet breakfast. AE, DC, MC, V. Parking 250 SEK ($27.50). T-bana: Östermalmstorg. Bus: 41, 46, 56, or 91.

Located opposite the garden of the King's Library, in what looks like an office building, the Lydmar opened in 1930 and for most of its life was known as the Eden Terrace. It offers a large dining room and a rooftop terrace where guests can enjoy drinks in the summer. The bedrooms are cozy and traditionally furnished, and come in many shapes and sizes. Although the rooms aren't large, they are exceptionally well maintained; mattresses are firm and bathrooms are state of the art. The hotel offers a large dining room and a rooftop terrace where guests can enjoy drinks in the summer. Don't overlook the possibility of dining here. The restaurant in the past year or so has become ever-so-chic. The pan-fried scallops with citrus risotto are scrumptious. You can listen to a Swedish jazz trio several nights a week. There's also a popular lobby bar with live jazz and soul music.

Radisson SAS Royal Viking Hotel. Vasagatan 1, S-101 23 Stockholm. ☎ **800/333-3333** in the U.S., or 08/14-10-00. Fax 08/10-81-80. www.radisson.com. E-mail: guest@ stozs. rdsas. com. 319 units. A/C MINIBAR TV TEL. 1,300–1,800 SEK ($143–$198) double; 2,950–3,450 SEK ($324.50–$379.50) suite. Rates include breakfast. AE, DC, MC, V. Parking 250 SEK ($27.50). T-bana: Centralen.

Built as a nine-story tower in 1984, this airline-affiliated hotel is located in a commercial neighborhood near the railway station and the Stockholm World Trade Center. Part of its interior has a soaring atrium filled with plants, offering a streamlined, sunny, modern ambience. Especially popular in summertime with organized tours and conventioneers, it offers rooms decorated in vivid yellows, reds, and blues with stylized modern furniture, including good, firm beds, and such amenities as trouser presses. Bathrooms are smallish but big enough for hair dryers, phones, and adequate shelf space. Some rooms are no-smoking; other units are wheelchair accessible. The hotel also provides a large number of mini-suites, each of which are well accessorized with electronic extras.

Dining/Diversions: Breakfast and lunch are served in a separate part of the atrium lobby, near what becomes a bar in the evening. (Sometimes a live pianist performs at brief interludes during the cocktail hour.) The main dining outlet is Stockholm Fisk, open for dinner. Light suppers are served on the ninth floor in the Sky Bar, which offers glass-sided elevators and a sweeping view over Stockholm.

Amenities: Room service; laundry; office services; SAS check-in desk (Euro-Class only); indoor swimming pool with saunas, solarium, and Jacuzzi.

Radisson SAS Strand Hotel. Nybrokajen 9, S-103 27 Stockholm. ☎ **800/333-3333** in the U.S., or 08/678-78-00. Fax 08/611-2436. www.radisson.com. E-mail: Strand@stockholm. mail.telia.com. 149 units. A/C MINIBAR TV TEL. Mon–Thurs 2,589–2,889 SEK ($284.80–$317.80) double; from 3,499 SEK ($384.90) suite. Fri–Sun 1,499–1,990 SEK ($164.90–$218.90) double; from 2,390 SEK ($262.90) suite. Rates include breakfast. AE, DC, MC, V. Parking 290 SEK ($31.90) per night. T-bana: Kungsträdgården.

In stark contrast to the angular modernity of many other SAS hotels in Scandinavia, this one has a traditional and charming exterior. Originally built in 1912 with a hint of art nouveau styling, it lies at the edge of a complicated network of canals and waterways, in a prosperous and conservative neighborhood near the Royal Palace. As part of hotel renovation and modernization in the early 1980s, all the antique detailing was ripped out and replaced with a blandly international modernism. Much of the hotel's clientele consists of business travelers from other parts of northern Europe. The bedrooms are outfitted with solid furniture and light pastel colors, with appliances such as hair dryers and trouser presses. Rooms are available in a wide range of sizes, with those at the lowest end of the spectrum being rather small, and containing smallish, not particularly comfortable beds. The more expensive rooms are considerably larger, plusher, and have the larger beds more suited to North American tastes.

Dining/Diversions: The Piazza is the in-house restaurant, featuring a glassed-over roof, lots of plants, and a greenhouse-like setting. Nearby is a friendly bar, the Piazza Bar.

Amenities: 24-hour room service, business center, access to a nearby (independent) health club with its own swimming pool and sauna.

Sheraton Stockholm & Towers. Tegelbacken 6, S-101 23 Stockholm. ☎ **800/325-3535** in the U.S. and Canada, or 08/412-34-00. Fax 08/412-34-09. www.sheratonstockholm.com. E-mail: sheraton-stockholm@ittsheraton.com. 461 units. A/C MINIBAR TV TEL. 1,200–2,800 SEK ($132–$308) double; from 4,300 SEK ($473) suite. Rates include breakfast. AE, DC, MC, V. Parking 200 SEK ($22). T-bana: Centralen.

Originally built in 1971 and sheathed with Swedish granite, this eight-story hostelry is located within view of Stockholm's City Hall (Rådhuset). Short on Swedish charm, it's excellent by chain hotel standards, attracting many business travelers. The bedrooms are the largest in the city, decorated in shades of yellow or pink. Mirrored closets, one king or two double beds (good, firm mattresses) with bedside controls, and medium-size tile bathrooms with such amenities as hair dryers, add to the allure. Some units have bidets and all enjoy heated racks with plenty of fluffy towels. Most units enjoy sweeping views over the city, many over Gamla Stan.

Dining/Diversions: Le Bistro specializes in game, fish, meats, and fresh vegetables and fruits. Snacks and quick meals also are served at Le Bistro. The hotel has a casino and the Lobby Lounge features live piano music nightly. Die Ecke is a German beer hall serving traditional Bavarian dishes.

Amenities: Room service (24 hours), laundry and valet service, business center, same-day laundry and dry cleaning, sauna, wheelchairs upon request, physician on call.

MODERATE

Adlon Hotel. Vasagatan 42, S-111 20 Stockholm. ☎ **08/402-65-00.** Fax 08/20-86-10. www.adlon.se. E-mail: hotel@adlon.se. 72 units. TV TEL. 525–1,330 SEK ($57.75–$146.30) double. Rates include breakfast. AE, DC, MC, V. T-bana: Centralen.

This 1890s building was redesigned by brothers Axel and Hjalmar Jumlin in the 1920s. Upgraded and improved many times since, it lies near the Central Station (and the subway) and is convenient to buses to and from Arlanda Airport. All the rather small rooms have been renovated and are comfortably furnished, and 70% of them are designated for nonsmokers. The small bathrooms have hair dryers.

Castle Hotel. Riddargatan 14, S-114 35 Stockholm. ☎ **08/679-57-00.** Fax 08/611-20-22. www.castle/hotel.se. E-mail: receptionen@castle/hotel.se. 49 units. TV TEL. 875–1,700 SEK ($96.25–$187) double; 2,400 SEK ($264) suite. Rates include breakfast. AE, DC, MC, V. T-bana: Östermalmstorg.

In an expensive neighborhood a short walk east of the center, this house originally was built in 1920 as a private apartment building. In the late 1980s it was renovated as a hotel. It has a gray marble floor in the lobby, and the good-size bedrooms are adorned with gilded accents and art deco accessories to match the original construction of the building. Discounts are offered on various weekends throughout the year.

Clas på Hornet. Surbrunnsgatan 20, S-113 48 Stockholm. ☎ **08/16-51-36.** Fax 08/612-53-15. 10 units. MINIBAR TV TEL. Mon–Thurs 1,545 SEK ($169.95) double; 1,445 SEK ($158.95) suite. Fri–Sun 1,345 SEK ($147.95) double; 1,445 SEK ($158.95) suite. Rates include breakfast. Parking 200 SEK ($22). Bus: 46, 53.

Small and choice, this is an upscale, very charming inn that occupies what was built in the 1730s as a private house, about a half mile north of the commercial heart of Stockholm. Its attention to period detail—whose installation was supervised by the curators of the Stockholm City Museum—gives a distinctive country-inn ambience that's enhanced with bedrooms outfitted in the late 18th-century style of Gustavus III. Each of the bedrooms is outfitted in a different color scheme and motif, usually with cheerful colors, wide floorboards, antiques, and all the electronic amenities you'd expect from a well-managed and intimate hotel, including good beds and medium-size bathrooms with hair dryers. Many have four-poster beds. The in-house restaurant, Clas på Hornet (Clas on the Corner), is recommended separately under "Where to Dine."

Crystal Plaza Hotel. Birger Jarlsgatan 35, S0111 45 Stockholm. ☎ **08/406-8800.** Fax 08/24-15-11. E-mail: central@crystalplazahotel.se. 105 units. TV TEL. Sun–Thurs 1,845–2,048 SEK ($202.95–$225.30) double; 998 SEK ($109.80) double for "cabins." Fri–Sat 1,048–1,148 SEK ($115.30–$126.30) double; 848 SEK ($93.30) double for "cabins." Rates include breakfast. AE, DC, MC, V. Parking 200 SEK ($22). T-bana: Östermalmstorg. Bus: 46.

In the 1990s, a charming, richly detailed, turn-of-the-century hotel, the Karelia, was transformed after several large-scale renovations. Many aspects of the building's original grandeur were retained, including the soaring Romanesque entranceway, the decorative double staircase, and the copper-capped tower. Renovations improved the bedrooms with renewed bathrooms and firm mattresses, but retained some of the old-fashioned touches, including the high, ornate ceilings and some of the old-world detailing. A noteworthy exception to this is the basement-level "cabins," as they're called, which are bargains and immensely popular. They are small and have no windows, but they're comfortable, well ventilated, and well maintained.

Elite Hotel Stockholm Plaza. Birger Jarlsgatan 29, S103 95 Stockholm. ☎ **08/566-22-000.** Fax 08/566-22-020. www.elite.se. E-mail: info@stoplaza.elite.se. 151 units.

ⓘ Family-Friendly Hotels

af _Chapman_ _(see p. 64)_   Although there are no family rooms, kids delight in staying in one of the staterooms (two to eight beds) aboard an authentic three-masted schooner.

Hotel Tegnérlunden _(see p. 60)_   Twenty big, airy rooms are ideal for families on a budget.

Sheraton Stockholm & Towers _(see p. 57)_   This well-run chain has always pampered children. The spacious rooms are comfortably shared with parents.

TV TEL. 1,290–2,095 SEK ($141.90–$230.45) double; 2,495–3,495 SEK ($274.45–$384.45) suite. Rates include breakfast. AE, DC, MC, V. Parking 220 SEK ($24.20). T-bana: Hötorget or Östermalmstorg.

Built on a triangular lot that may remind some visitors of New York's Flatiron Building, this first-class hotel is a well-run and inviting choice in the city center. Since its construction a century ago, the building has had many uses: a run-down rooming house, private apartments, and offices. In 1984 it was radically upgraded into a hotel. The light, fresh guest rooms have firm beds, tiled bathrooms, and hair dryers. The elegant restaurant, the Plaza Grill, serves French and Swedish specialties. Below the restaurant is a stylish disco, the Penny Lane. To be admitted, guests must appear to be mature and reasonably well dressed. The music is dance tunes from the 1960s and 1970s. The disco is open Wednesday to Saturday from 8:30pm to 2am. Admission is free for hotel guests, 75 SEK ($8.25) for others.

Esplanade Hotel. Strandvägen 7A, S-114 56 Stockholm. ☎ **08/663-07-40.** Fax 08/662-59-92. E-mail: hotel@esplanadesto.se. 34 units. TV TEL. 1,495–1,995 SEK ($164.45–$219.45) double. Rates include breakfast. AE, DC, MC, V. Parking 200 SEK ($22). T-bana: Östermalmstorg. Bus: 47 or 69.

This informal hotel, next to the more expensive Diplomat, attracts diplomats from the nearby embassies and others who like its atmosphere. Originally constructed in 1910, it was transformed into a family-style hotel in 1954. Many rooms have minibars, and each is furnished in an old-fashioned style. The single rooms are minuscule, but doubles, for the most part, have double glazing, trouser presses, extra-long beds, and decent-size tile bathrooms that are well maintained. Four rooms provide a water view, and the English lounge features a balcony with a view of Djurgården. Breakfast is the only meal served.

Kung Carl Hotel. Birger Jarlsgatan 23, S-11145 Stockholm. ☎ **08/463-50-00.** Fax 08/463-50-50. www.hkchotels.se. E-mail: kungcarl@hkchotels.se. 110 units. MINIBAR TV TEL. 1,850–2,450 SEK ($203.50–$269.50) double; 4,000 SEK ($440) suite. Rates include breakfast. AE, DC, MC, V. Parking 200 SEK ($22). T-bana: Östermalmstorg.

Discreet, tasteful, and quietly glamorous, this four-star hotel in the heart of Stockholm originally was built in the mid-1800s by a religious group that offered lodgings to women newly arrived in Stockholm from the countryside. Transformed into a hotel in the 1870s and elevated to four-star status thanks to many improvements, it retains many examples of old-fashioned charm. It's one of the oldest continuously operated hotels in Stockholm. Public areas contain a scattering of antiques, and following an expansion and renovation that occurred in 1998, bedrooms are freshly outfitted with conservative furnishings and pale colors. The beds have firm mattresses and the bathrooms, although small, are well maintained. There's no restaurant on the premises, but the lobby bar serves pizzas and sandwiches.

INEXPENSIVE

Hotel Bema. Upplandsgatan 13, S-11123 Stockholm. ☎ **08/23-26-75.** Fax 08/20-53-38. E-mail: hotell.bema@stockholm.mail.telia.com. 12 units. TV TEL. Mon–Thurs 880 SEK ($96.80) double; Fri–Sun 680 SEK ($74.80) double. Rates include breakfast. AE, DC, MC, V. Parking 120 SEK ($13.20) in nearby garage. Bus: 69.

Set on the street floor of what was built a century ago as an apartment house, within a 10-minute walk north of Stockholm's railway station, this hotel is small, cozy, intimate, and just battered enough to relieve the inhibitions of anyone who fears formality. The decor and amenities date from 1987, when the owners radically upgraded the place in a contemporary style. Most of the clients here are backpackers, students, and cyclists who appreciate the youthful ambience and the good-natured reception. The mattresses on the beds are a bit skimpy and the towels a bit thin, but this is one of the city's better deals. Housekeeping generally is adequate despite the functional, no-frills atmosphere.

Hotel City. Slöjdgatan 7 (at Hötorget), S-111 81 Stockholm. ☎ **08/723-72-00.** Fax 08/ 723-72-09. www.rica.cityhotel.se. 292 units. TV TEL. 1,125–1,740 SEK ($123.75–$191.40) double. Rates include breakfast. AE, DC, MC, V. Parking 175–250 SEK ($19.25–$27.50). T-bana: Hötorget.

Clean and functional, Hotel City consists of two sections; one built as late as the 1980s. In a desirable location between two of Stockholm's biggest department stores, PUB and @hléns, the hotel has small but comfortable bedrooms that have been elegantly refurbished using combinations of mirrors, hardwood trim, carpeting, and tilework. Although the hotel doesn't serve alcohol of any kind, it maintains a clean, simple lunch-only restaurant that's open Monday to Friday from 11am to 3pm. If you're feeling tense, you can luxuriate in the hotel's sauna.

Hotell Kom. 17 Böbelnsgatan, S-11140 Stockholm. ☎ **08/412-23-00.** Fax 08/412-23-10. E-mail: dymling@komhotell.se. 90 units. MINIBAR TV TEL. Mon–Thurs 1,450–1,550 SEK ($159.50–$170.50) double; Fri–Sun 965 SEK ($106.15) double. Rates include breakfast. Parking 120 SEK ($13.20). T-bana: Rådmansgatan.

Originally built in 1972 as a youth hostel, this hotel was upgraded and renovated in 1978. It stands on steeply sloping land overlooking a residential neighborhood scattered with stores and private apartments. Hotell Kom is appropriate for extended stays in Stockholm, as each unit has a small kitchenette, creating an ambience more like that of a private apartment than that of a hotel. The rooms are clean and decent, with reasonably comfortable beds, and rather small but immaculate baths. However, don't expect too much—stay here mainly for the price. There's an exercise room and health club on the premises, and a solarium. Other than breakfast, no meals are served.

Hotell Örn Sköld. Nybrogatan 6, S-11434 Stockholm. ☎ **08/667-02-85.** Fax 08/ 667-69-91. 27 units. MINIBAR TV TEL. 1,175–1,275 SEK ($129.25–$140.25) double; 300 SEK ($33) discount on selected weekends (Fri–Sat). Rates include breakfast. AE, MC, V. Parking 100 SEK ($11) in a nearby public garage. T-bana: Östermalmstorg.

The five-story building that contains this hotel originally was built in 1910, and today most of it is used for storage of props and for housing of staff members who work at the nearby Royal Dramatic Theater. However, the floor above street level contains the hotel's rooms. Each is clean; high ceilinged; outfitted with simple, contemporary furnishings; and the more expensive rooms are big enough to allow the setup of extra beds if they're needed.

Hotel Tegnérlunden. Tegnérlunden 8, S-113 59 Stockholm. ☎ **08/5454-5550.** Fax 08/ 5454-5551. E-mail: info.tegener@swedenhotels.se. 103 units. TV TEL. 990–1,460 SEK

($108.90–$160.60) double. Rates include breakfast. AE, DC, MC, V. Parking 140 SEK ($15.40) at a nearby garage. Bus: 47, 53, or 69.

In a 19th-century building at the edge of a city park, this hotel has a few public rooms, a lobby, and a bar. The hotel's best feature is its tasteful rooms, each blissfully quiet, especially those opening onto the rear. The rooms come in a variety of sizes and shapes; all those we inspected were well maintained, but furnished in a somewhat functional way. There's comfort here, but not a lot of style, and the bathrooms are small. There is, however, a sauna.

Mornington Hotel. Nybrogatan 53, S-102 44 Stockholm. ☎ **800/528-1234** in the U.S., or 08/8507-33-000. Fax 08/8507-33-039. www.mornington.se. E-mail: Stockholm@ mornington. se. 141 units. TV TEL. June 26–Aug 9, 800 SEK ($88) double; Aug 10–June 25, 1,595–1,770 SEK ($175.45–$194.70) double; year-round, 3,250 SEK ($357.50) suite. Rates include breakfast. AE, DC, MC, V. T-bana: Östermalmstorg. Bus: 49, 54, or 62.

Proud of its image as an English-inspired hotel, this efficiently modern establishment has a concrete exterior brightened with rows of flower boxes. It was built in 1956 and has been renovated several times since; most recently in 1997. Most rooms, many quite small, feature a standard decor using exposed wood and pastel color schemes. The lobby is enhanced with a small rock garden and modern versions of Chesterfield armchairs. The hotel offers no-smoking rooms and rooms for guests with disabilities, and its sauna and Turkish bath are free. Its Restaurant Eleonora serves both international and Swedish cuisine, and there's a library bar.

Sandströms Hotell. 75 S:t Eriksgatan, S-113 32 Stockholm. ☎ **08/30-83-32.** 7 units, 4 with bathroom. TV. 600 SEK ($66) double without bathroom; 900 SEK ($99) double with bathroom. AE, MC, V. Parking 100 SEK ($11) at a nearby public garage. T-bana: S:t Eriksplan.

This hotel occupies the fifth floor (there is an elevator) of what originally was built around 1900 as an apartment house, and whose lower floors for the most part are still functioning as private homes. Enjoying views that sweep out over large neighborhoods of Stockholm, it has been a hotel since 1925. A kindly, well-mannered staff has spent great effort decorating each of the seven small bedrooms in a style that corresponds to an individual era. Examples include a 1970s room in tones of orange and avocado green, a 1950s room (painted violet and filled with nostalgic reminders of the age of Sputnik), and a 1940s room in yellow-beige. Beds are firm, bathrooms are a bit cramped, but in high-priced Stockholm this is not a place to overlook. This is one of the smallest and most intimate hotels in town, with a loyal clientele that tends to return for more than one visit.

Wellington. Storgatan 6, S-11451 Stockholm. ☎ **08/667-09-10.** Fax 08/667-12-54. www.wellington.se. E-mail: info@wellington.se. 60 units. Fall, winter, spring, Sun–Thurs 1,795 SEK ($197.45) double; summer and Fri–Sat year-round, 1,245 SEK ($136.95) double. Rates include breakfast. AE, DC, MC, V. T-bana: Östermalmstorg.

A long-enduring favorite with the frugal traveler, the Wellington sounds like something you'd find in London. Built in the late 1950s, it still maintains some English decorative touches and lies in a quiet but convenient neighborhood about a half mile east of Stockholm's commercial core. The public rooms are filled with engravings of English hunting scenes and leather-covered chairs. Some of the small but stylish bedrooms overlook a flower-filled courtyard. Rooms on the top floor have panoramic views. Beds are firm and the bathrooms, though small, are well equipped with hair dryers. Two floors of accommodations are reserved for nonsmokers. The hotel has an excellent sauna where you may want to linger. Its breakfast room is inviting and the fare is good, although no other meals are served.

ON GAMLA STAN (OLD TOWN)
EXPENSIVE

First Hotel Reisen. Skeppsbron 12–14, S-111 30 Stockholm. ☎ **08/22-32-60.** Fax 08/
20-15-59. www.firsthotels.com. E-mail:info@firsthotels.se. 144 units. MINIBAR TV TEL.
2,299–2,899 SEK ($252.90–$318.90) double; 3,800–4,800 SEK ($418–$528) suite. Rates
include breakfast. AE, DC, MC, V. Parking 275 SEK ($30.25). Bus: 43, 46, 55, 59, or 76.

In Stockholm's Old Town, facing the water, this hotel is located just three alleyways
from the Royal Palace. Dating from the 17th century, the three-building structure
attractively combines the old and the new. A former coffeehouse that stood here was
mentioned in the writings of the national poet Carl Michael Bellman. The rooms are
comfortably furnished in a stylishly modern way, but inspired by traditional designs.
Light florals and pastel colors are used. Mattresses are frequently replaced, and the
bathrooms are excellent, with such amenities as massaging showerheads, scales, marble floors, heated towel racks, and phones. Some no-smoking units are available, and
the top-floor accommodations open onto small balconies.

   Dining/Diversions: The hotel's specialty restaurant, Ciao Ciao, serves a refined
international and Italian cuisine, and the Clipper Club specializes in grills. There's also
a library bar and Clipper Club Piano Bar, with live entertainers Monday through
Saturday.

   Amenities: Room service (7am to 11pm), laundry service, guide services in summer, indoor pool, sauna, Jacuzzis in some suites.

✪ **Lady Hamilton Hotel.** Storkyrkobrinken 5, S-111 28 Stockholm. ☎ **08/23-46-80.**
Fax 08/411-11-48. www.lady-hamilton.se. E-mail: info@lady-hamilton.se. 34 units, some with
shower only. MINIBAR TV TEL. 1,590–2,570 SEK ($174.90–$282.70) double. Rates include
breakfast. AE, DC, MC, V. Parking 250 SEK ($27.50). T-bana: Gamla Stan. Bus: 48.

This nicely located hotel, consisting of three connected buildings, stands on a quiet
street in the Old Town, surrounded by antique shops and restaurants. Dozens of
antiques are scattered among the well-furnished bedrooms. Most of the rooms rest
under beamed ceilings, with wood floors or carpeting. The beds, either queen or double, are of a high standard. Bathrooms are tiled and come in a variety of sizes, ranging
from spacious to cramped; however, all of them have heated towel racks, heated floors,
and hair dryers, although only some have complete tub baths (the rest offer showers).
If you'd like to get away from it all, opt for a top-floor room with skylights and memorable views over the Old Town. Some no-smoking rooms are available. You'll get a
sense of the 1470 origins of this hotel when you use the luxurious sauna, which encompasses the stone-rimmed well that formerly supplied the building's water. Extra touches
include 18th-century paintings, an ivory ship model (probably made by French prisoners in the 1700s), and several carved figureheads from old sailing vessels. The ornate
staircase wraps around a large model of a clipper ship suspended from the ceiling.

✪ **Victory Hotel.** Lilla Nygatan 3–5, S-111 28 Stockholm. ☎ **08/506-400-00.** Fax 08/
20-21-77. www.victory-hotel.se. E-mail: info@victory-hotel.se. 48 units, some with shower
only. A/C MINIBAR TV TEL. 1,750–2,750 SEK ($192.50–$302.50) double; 3,590–4,890 SEK
($394.90–$537.90) suite. Rates include breakfast. AE, DC, MC, V. T-bana: Gamla Stan. Bus: 48.

A small but stylish hotel, the Victory opened in 1980 on the foundations of a 1382
fortified tower. In the 1700s, those who owned the building buried a massive treasure
of silver under its basement floor (today the treasure is housed in the Stockholm City
Museum). There's a shiny brass elevator, but if you take the stairs you'll see one of Sweden's largest collections of 18th-century nautical needlepoints, many created by the
sailors themselves during their long sea voyages. The warm and inviting rooms, each
named after a prominent sea captain, have a pleasing combination of exposed wood,

carpeting, antiques, and 19th-century memorabilia. Many of the rooms are smoke-free, and all of the beds are comfortable, with firm mattresses. The average-size bathrooms are tiled and come with heated floors, hair dryers, robes, and phones, but only the suites offer tub baths (the rest have showers).

Dining/Diversions: The Restaurant Leijontornet specializes in fish, fowl, and game. A bistro, the Lohe Room, named after the 18th-century family that lived in the building, serves Swedish home cooking in a cozy, informal atmosphere.

Amenities: Room service (7am to 11pm), same-day laundry and dry cleaning, a complete travel and concierge desk, safe-deposit boxes, heated bathroom floors and towel racks, saunas.

MODERATE

Mälardrottningen. Riddarholmen, S-11128 Stockholm. ☎ **08/545-187-80.** Fax 08/24-36-76. www.malardrottningen.se. E-mail:receptionen@malardrottningen.se. 60 units. A/C TV TEL. Mon–Thurs 1,020–1,460 SEK ($112.20–$160.60) double; Fri–Sun 860–1,360 SEK ($94.60–$149.60) double. Rates include breakfast. AE, DC, MC, V. Parking 15 SEK ($1.65) per hour. T-bana: Gamla Stan.

During its heyday, this was the most famous yacht in the world, the subject of gossip columns everywhere, thanks to the complicated friendships that developed among the passengers and, in some cases, the crew. It was built in 1924 by millionaire C.K.G. Billings as the largest (240 feet long) motor yacht in the world, and was later acquired by the Woolworth heiress Barbara Hutton. Its below-deck space originally contained only seven suites, but after its transformation in the early 1980s into a hotel, it was permanently moored beside a satellite island of Stockholm's Old Town, and subdivided into 59 cramped and somewhat claustrophobic cabins. Space within the wood-trimmed, blue-and-white cabins definitely is limited, and most of the cabins have bunk-style twin beds, which you may or may not find enchanting. Bathrooms aren't really rooms but extremely small cubicles that are even more claustrophobic than the bedrooms. Of course, this was typical of many cabins on ships back then. But considering the novelty of this hotel, its role as a conversation piece, and its proximity to the Old Town, it may be worth an overnight stay. There's a sauna within the ship, and a lounge and TV room that are separated with a glass panel from the gleaming brass of what used to be the engine room.

Mälardrottningen also is one of the most upscale floating restaurants in Sweden. (See "Where to Dine" in the following section for a full review.)

ON LANG HOLMEN
INEXPENSIVE

Långholmen Hotel. Kronohåktet, S-101 72 Stockholm. ☎ **08/668-05-00.** Fax 08/720-85-75. www.langholmen.com/hotellang.html. E-mail: hotel@langholmen.com. 102 units. TV TEL. Sun–Thurs 1,255 SEK ($138.05) double; Fri–Sat 925 SEK ($101.75) double. Extra bed 205 SEK ($22.55) per person. AE, MC, V. Rates include breakfast. T-bana: Hornstul. Bus: 4, 40, and 66.

In 1724 it was a state penitentiary on the little island of Lang Holmen detaining women charged with "loose living." The last prisoner was released in 1972. Today it's a newly restored and reasonably priced accommodation which, in addition to comfortable but small rooms, also houses a museum of Sweden's prison history and one of the best restaurants in the country—so you certainly won't have to eat bread and water for dinner, as did the former occupants. Cells have been transformed into cramped but mostly serviceable rooms equipped with such modern amenities as phones, radios, cable TVs, and even small showers and toilets. The accommodations were carved out of 200 prison cells.

Ten of the bedrooms are suitable for persons with disabilities and 91 are reserved for nonsmokers. This is one of the best hotels in Stockholm for the single visitor on a budget, as 89 rooms are rented only to solo travelers. Just 13 rooms are large enough to accommodate two persons. Instead of a prison induction area, you get the hotel's reception area and a 24-hour snack bar.

ON SKEPPSHOLMEN
INEXPENSIVE

af Chapman. Västra Brobänken, Skeppsholmen, S-111 49 Stockholm. ☎ **08/679-50-15.** Fax 08/611-98-75. www.stfchapman.com. E-mail: info@chapman.stfturist.se. 136 beds in 33 cabins, none with bathroom. Members, 145 SEK ($15.95) per adult, 65 SEK ($7.15) per child; nonmembers, 190 SEK ($20.90) per adult, 95 SEK ($10.45) per child. MC, V. Closed Dec 16–Apr 1. Bus: 65.

Moored off Skeppsholmen, this authentic three-masted full-rigger has been converted into a youth hostel. Its staterooms have two, four, six, or eight beds, but there are no single cabins. One section is reserved for men; another for women. Each section has showers and washrooms. Personal lockers are available. The gangplank goes up at 2am—with no exceptions—and there's a 5-day maximum stay. The rooms are closed from 11am to 3pm. No cigarette smoking is allowed. A summer cafe operates on the ship's deck. Breakfast, at an extra charge, is available in the self-service coffee bar and dining room. International Youth Hostel Association cards can be obtained at the af *Chapman*.

NORTH OF THE CENTER
INEXPENSIVE

Arcadia Hotel. Kärnbärsvagen 1, S-114 89 Stockholm. ☎ **08/16-01-95.** Fax 08/16-62-24. 84 units. TV TEL. Sun–Thurs 1,195 SEK ($131.45) double; Fri–Sat 845 SEK ($92.95) double. Rates include breakfast. AE, DC, MC, V. Parking in nearby public lot 12 SEK ($1.30) per hour 9am–5pm; free parking 5pm–9am. T-bana: Tekniska Högskolan.

This angular-looking five-story hotel has gone through several administrations and name changes since its original construction as a student dormitory in the 1960s. Its present role as an uncomplicated, unpretentious tourist-class hotel began in 1975 when it was renovated and upgraded. In 1998, bedrooms on the second floor were renovated as part of a process that eventually will encompass most of the rooms in the hotel. Its location is upon a tree-lined boulevard, on a hillside with a good view, a 5-minute walk from the railway station. The hotel has a restaurant, Babylon, serving Swedish and international food, and there's an outdoor terrace for sunbathing and reading. Be warned in advance that bedrooms here are not particularly plush, but they are clean and well maintained with good beds and small but adequate bathrooms.

NEAR THE AIRPORT
EXPENSIVE

Radisson SAS SkyCity Hotel. SkyCity, P.O. Box 82, S-19045 Stockholm-Arlanda. ☎ **08/ 590-77300.** Fax 08/50-67-40-01. E-mail: mlh@stozr.rdsas.com. 230 units. A/C MINIBAR TV TEL. 2,179–2,419 SEK ($239.70–$266.10) double; 3,299 SEK ($362.90) suite. Rates include breakfast. AE, DC, MC, V. Parking 230 SEK ($25.30). Airport bus departing at 10-minute intervals for city center, 60 SEK ($6.60) each way.

This three-story hotel lies at Stockholm's Arlanda airport, 24 miles north of the city. Built in 1993, it's a part of the sprawling SkyCity airport complex that includes banks, travel agencies, restaurants, cafes, souvenir shops, and the busiest of the airport's terminals (numbers 4 and 5). Bedrooms are outfitted in one of three distinct styles: Scandinavian modern, Oriental/Chinese, and business class units with slightly upgraded

Bar Food

One tip to save you a little inconvenience: Don't rush into a bar in Stockholm for a pick-me-up martini. "Bars" in Stockholm are self-service cafeterias, and the strongest drink that many of them offer is apple cider.

---

amenities. The staff is multilingual, well trained, and hardworking, contributing to the successful day-to-day administration of this mini-city where visitors wing in at all times of the day and night from practically everywhere.

Dining/Diversions: The hotel's SkyCity Bar and Restaurant is the best within the airport complex, with formal service and views of takeoffs and landings at the airport.

Amenities: Room service (24 hours), sauna, health club, business center, underground convention center with 38 separate meeting spaces.

4 Where to Dine

Increasingly, visitors are viewing Sweden as a culinary citadel of renown. Part of this derives from the legendary freshness of Swedish game and produce; part derives from the success of Sweden's culinary team at cooking contests everywhere. Some social pundits claim that the fame of Sweden's culinary team now rivals that of its national hockey team. There are today an estimated 1,500 restaurants and bars in Stockholm alone.

Food is expensive in Stockholm, but those on a budget can stick to self-service cafeterias. At all restaurants other than cafeterias, a 12% to 15% service charge is added to the bill to cover tipping, and the 21% value-added tax also is included in the bill. Wine and beer can be lethal to your final check, so proceed carefully. For good value, try ordering the *dagens ratt* (daily special), also referred to as dagens lunch or dagens menu, if available.

IN THE CENTER
VERY EXPENSIVE

✪ **Operakällaren.** Operahuset, Kungsträdgården. ☎ **08/676-58-00.** Reservations required. Main courses 300–400 SEK ($33–$44); 3-course fixed-price menu 480 SEK ($52.80); 4-course fixed-price menu 800 SEK ($88); 7-course menu dégustation 1,250 SEK ($137.50). AE, DC, MC, V. Daily 5–10pm. Closed July. T-bana: Kungsträdgarden. FRENCH/SWEDISH.

Opposite the Royal Palace, this is the most famous and unashamedly luxurious restaurant in all of Sweden. Its elegant, classic decor and style are reminiscent of a royal court banquet at the turn of the century. Its Paris equivalent would be Le Grand Véfour. Dress formally to enjoy its impeccable service and house specialties. Many come here for the elaborate fixed-price menus; others prefer the classic Swedish dishes or the modern French ones. A house specialty—and worth the trip here—is the platter of northern delicacies, which includes everything from smoked eel to smoked reindeer along with Swedish red caviar. Salmon and game, including grouse from the northern forests, both are prepared in various ways. Recent changes include a new cigar room.

✪ **Paul & Norbert.** Strandvägen 9. ☎ **08/663-81-83.** Reservations required. Main courses 150–296 SEK ($16.50–$32.55); 8-course grand menu de frivolité 1,300 SEK ($143). AE, DC, MC, V. Mid-Aug to June, Tues–Fri noon–3pm; Mon–Sat 5:30–10:30pm. July to mid-Aug, Mon–Sat 5:30–10:30pm. Closed Dec 24–Jan 6. T-bana: Östermalmstorg. CONTINENTAL.

In a patrician residence dating from 1873, adjacent to the Hotell Diplomat, this is the finest and most innovative restaurant in Stockholm. Seating only 30 people, it has a vaguely art deco decor, beamed ceilings, and dark paneling. Paul Beck and Norbert

Stockholm Dining

Akvarium **1**

Bakfickan **2**

Berns' Salonger **20**

Cattelin Restaurant **6**

Clas på Hornet **15**

Den Gyldene Freden **29**

Djurgårdsbrunns

Wärdshus **25**

Edsbacka Krog **14**

Eriks Bakfica **24**

Fem Små Hus **30**

Franska Matsalen **33**

Garlic & Shots **10**

Gondolen **9**

Grand Veranda **32**

Hannas Krog **10**

KB Restaurant **19**

Leijontornet **7**

Lisa Elmquist **23**

Långholmen Restaurant **11**

Magnus Ladulås **28**

Mälardrottningen **5**
Noilo **4**
Operakällaren **3**
Paul & Norbert **35**
Pontus in the
  Green House **31**
Prinsens **21**

Restaurangen **17**
Solliden **27**
Stadshuskällaren **12**
Stortorgskallären **8**
Sturehof **18**
Teatergrillen **22**
Tennstopet **13**

Ulla Winbladh **26**
Ulriksdals Wärdshus **16**
Wedholms Fisk **34**

Church
Information
Post Office
Subway
Railway

Lang worked in many top European restaurants before opening this establishment. (Beck has since passed away, and Lang's new partner is Rudolf Hanenkammer.) To start, they prepare a tantalizing terrine of scallops in saffron sauce. The foie gras is the finest in town. Perfectly prepared main dishes include sautéed medallion of fjord salmon, scallops, and scampi in a lobster sauce, crisp breast of duck with a caramelized orange sauce, and juniper-stuffed noisettes of reindeer immersed in a caraway sauce with portobella mushrooms.

EXPENSIVE

Franska Matsalen (French Dining Room). In the Grand Hotel, Södra Blasieholmshamnen 8. ☎ **08/679-35-84.** Reservations required. Main courses 225–315 SEK ($24.75–$34.65); 5-course fixed-price menu 685 SEK ($75.35). AE, DC, MC, V. Mon–Fri 6–11pm. Closed July. T-bana: Kungsträdgården. Bus: 46, 55, 62, or 76. FRENCH.

Widely acclaimed as one of the greatest restaurants in Stockholm, this elegant establishment is on the street level of the city's most deluxe hotel. The dining room is one of the most imperial in Sweden, featuring an ensemble of polished mahogany, ormolu, and gilt accents—all placed under a richly ornate plaster ceiling. Tables on the enclosed veranda permit a view of the Royal Palace and the Old Town. Begin with a cannelloni of foie gras with flap mushrooms, or perhaps the mousseline of scallops with Sevruga caviar. Main dishes include seared sweetbreads served with artichokes, langoustines, and frog's legs with broad beans, and a tartar of veal served with caviar. Fresh Swedish salmon also is featured. The chefs are highly trained professionals who secure only the finest ingredients. Over the years they have pleased some of the more demanding palates of Europe.

Restaurangen. Oxtorgsgatan 14. ☎ **08/220-952.** Reservations recommended. 3-course fixed-price menu 200 SEK ($22); 5-course fixed-price menu 300 SEK ($33); 7-course fixed-price menu 400 SEK ($44). AE, DC, MC, V. Mon–Fri 11:30am–2pm; Mon–Sat 5–11pm. T-Banen: Hörtorget. INTERNATIONAL.

Come here for a high-ceilinged decor whose angularity may remind you of an SAS airport lounge, and for combinations of cuisine that many cosmopolitan Swedes have found absolutely fascinating. Owner and chef Malker Andersson divides his menu into "fields of flavor" defined by unexpected categories. These include, among others, lemon-flavored themes or coriander-flavored themes, which can be consumed in any order you prefer. If you want a "taste of the lemon," for example, it may appear flavoring fresh asparagus and new potatoes. Freshly chopped coriander is used to flavor a delectable shellfish ceviche. The chef roams the world and, instead of duplicating classical international dishes, takes the flavor of one country and combines its traditional dish with the time-honored dish of another country. An amazing and very tasty example of this is tacos from Mexico combined with French foie gras and Russian caviar. Because none of the portions are overly large, some diners interpret a meal here like something akin to a series of tapas, each permeated with flavors that linger on your palate after you consume them.

Wedholms Fisk. Nybrokajen 17. ☎ **08/611-78-74.** Reservations required. Lunch main courses 110–260 SEK ($12.10–$28.60); dinner main courses 255–450 SEK ($28.05–$49.50). AE, DC, MC, V. Mon–Sat 5–11pm. Closed July. T-bana: Östermalmstorg. SWEDISH/FRENCH.

This is one of the classic—and one of the best—restaurants in Stockholm. Housed in an old Swedish building whose decor has been stripped down to its basics, it has no curtains in the windows and no carpets, but the display of modern paintings by Swedish artists is riveting. You might begin with marinated herring with garlic and bleak roe, or tartare of salmon with salmon roe. The chef has reason to be proud of such dishes as perch poached with clams and saffron sauce, prawns marinated in herbs and served with Dijon hollandaise, and grilled filet of sole with a Beaujolais sauce. For dessert, try the homemade vanilla ice cream with cloudberries. The menu offers both innovative and traditional choices. How many places today would prepare a chèvre mousse to accompany a simple tomato salad? On the other hand, they also serve Grandmother's favorite: cream-stewed potatoes.

MODERATE

Akvarium. Kungsträdgården. ☎ **08/100-626.** Reservations recommended. Main courses 150–175 SEK ($16.50–$19.25); fixed-price lunches 55–110 SEK ($6.05–$12.10). AE, DC, MC, V. Mon–Fri 11:30am–2:30pm and 5pm–midnight, Sat–Sun 11:30am–midnight. T-bana: Kungsträdgården. CONTINENTAL.

Don't expect bubbling fish tanks as a background for this hip and stylish restaurant: Its name derives from its former incarnation as a seafood restaurant, not from any aquariums it contains. Amid lime-green and lemon-yellow walls and lots of stainless steel, you'll find a bustling kitchen that's open to view, a bar dotted with colored lamps, and a big veranda that accommodates diners who appreciate the heat and light of midsummer. Menu items include a "duck espresso," breast of duck with port wine sauce and plums; veal saltimbocca (with ham); tagliatelle with mussels, clams, and squid ink; grilled butterfish with pesto sauce; and an all-vegetarian version of ravioli stuffed with porcini mushrooms. Despite this establishment's allure as a restaurant, don't overlook its appeal as a bar as well.

✪ **Bakfickan.** Jakobs Torg 12. ☎ **08/676-58-09.** Reservations not accepted. Main courses 87–169 SEK ($9.55–$18.60). AE, DC, MC, V. July, Mon–Fri 5–11:30pm; Aug–June, Mon–Sat 11:30am–11:30pm. T-bana: Kungsträdgården. SWEDISH.

Tucked away in the back of the Operakällaren, the "Back Pocket" is a chic place to eat for a moderate price. Its food is from the same kitchen as the very glamorous (and previously recommended) Operakällaren, but its prices are more bearable. Main dishes are likely to include several varieties of salmon, including boiled with hollandaise and salmon roe. You also might try beef Rydberg (thin-sliced tenderloin). In season, order reindeer and elk. In summer, there is nothing finer than the rich ice cream with a sauce made of Arctic cloudberries. Many patrons prefer to sit at the horseshoe-shaped bar, enjoying their food and drink there.

Berns' Salonger. Näckströmsgatan 8. ☎ **08/614-05-50.** Reservations recommended. Main courses 130–250 SEK ($14.30–$27.50). AE, DC, MC, V. Mon–Sat 11:30am–3pm and 5pm–1am. T-bana: Östermalmstorg. SWEDISH.

Built in 1860, this "pleasure palace" was once one of the most famous restaurants and nighttime venues in Stockholm. It was dramatically renovated in 1989 and is now one of the most atmospheric choices for dining in the capital. The main hall is adorned with galleries, mirrors, and wooden paneling, and lit by a trio of monumental chandeliers. The Red Room was frequented by August Strindberg, who described it in his novel of the same name. It's still there—plush furniture and all—and is used by guests at Berns' Hotel. Each day a different Swedish specialty is featured, including fried filet of suckling pig with fresh asparagus. You also might try calves' liver with garlic and bacon, or grilled tournedos. Newer and more innovative main dishes include cuttlefish with black pasta and tomato sauce or filet of ostrich with mushroom cannelloni and Marsala sauce. More and more exotic dishes are appearing on the menu— tandoori-marinated lamb with mango, curry sauce, and couscous, for example.

Clas på Hornet. Surbrunnsgatan 20. ☎ **08/15-51-30.** Reservations recommended. Main courses 195–255 SEK ($21.45–$28.05). AE, DC, MC, V. Mon–Fri 11:30am–10pm, Sat–Sun 5–10pm. Bus 46, 53. SWEDISH/CONTINENTAL.

Authentic to the decorative traditions of the late 1700s, and contained within five cream-colored dining rooms within the previously recommended hotel, this restaurant is owned by the entrepreneur who made Nils Emil (also recommended) into one of the capital's most acclaimed restaurants. Homage to the place has even appeared in the poetic verse of one of Sweden's most valued poets, Carl Michael Bellman, so if you opt for a meal here, it won't occur without illustrious previous references. There's a sometimes crowded bar area that many clients visit regularly, in some cases even those who have no interest in dining. No one will mind if you come just for a drink, but the true value of the place emerges only at a table. Here, menu items change with the seasons, but are likely to include an "Archipelago Platter," named after the islands near Stockholm that provided many of its ingredients. It contains assorted preparations of herring, a medley of Swedish cheeses, and homemade bread. Other delectable foodstuff includes blinis stuffed with bleak roe, trout roe, and onions; cream of wild-mushroom soup with strips of reindeer; grilled char served with hollandaise sauce enriched with fish roe; baked turbot in horseradish sauce; and roasted venison with a timbale of chanterelles.

✪ **Eriks Bakfica.** Fredrikshovsgatan 4. ☎ **08/660-15-99.** Reservations recommended. Main courses 145–245 SEK ($15.95–$26.95); 5-course entrecôte dinner 345 SEK ($37.95). AE, DC, MC, V. Mon–Fri 11:30am–11pm, Sat 4–10pm, Sun 5–11pm. Bus: 47. SWEDISH.

Although there are other restaurants in Stockholm bearing the name Erik's (see "On Gamla Stan," below), this one is relatively inexpensive and offers particularly good value. Established in 1979, it features a handful of Swedish dishes from the tradition of husmanskost (wholesome home cooking). A favorite opener is toast Skagen, with shrimp, dill-flavored mayonnaise, spices, and bleak roe. There's also a daily choice of herring appetizers. Try the tantalizing "archipelago stew," a ragoût of fish prepared with tomatoes and served with garlic mayonnaise. Marinated salmon is served with hollandaise sauce. You also might try Erik's cheeseburger with a secret sauce, but you'll have to ask for it—the secret specialty is not on the menu.

Grand Veranda. In the Grand Hotel, Södra Blasieholmshamnen 8. ☎ **08/679-35-00.** Reservations required. Main courses 135–225 SEK ($14.85–$24.75); Swedish buffet 245 SEK ($26.95). AE, DC, MC, V. Mon–Sat 11am–3pm; daily 6–9:30pm. T-bana: Kungsträdgården. Bus: 46, 55, 62, or 76. SWEDISH.

On the ground floor of Stockholm's most prestigious hotel, and fronted with enormous sheets of glass, this restaurant opens onto a stunning view of the harbor and the Royal Palace. The Veranda is famous for its daily buffets. Occasionally these are upgraded to include a medley of shellfish, including all the shrimp and lobster you want. Try such à la carte dishes as filet of reindeer marinated in red wine or braised wild duck and deep-fried root vegetables served with an apple-cider sauce. Here is your chance to sample the offerings of the most famous hotel in Sweden, to enjoy wonderful food, and to have one of the best views in town—all for a reasonable price.

KB Restaurant. Smålandsgatan 7. ☎ **08/679-60-32.** Reservations recommended. Main courses 195–310 SEK ($21.45–$34.10); fixed-price lunch 265–325 SEK ($29.15–$35.75); fixed-price dinner 365–470 SEK ($40.15–$51.70). AE, DC, MC, V. Mon–Fri 11:30am–11:30pm, Sat 5–11:30pm. Closed June 23–Aug 7. T-bana: Östermalmstorg. SWEDISH/CONTINENTAL.

A traditional artists' rendezvous in the center of town, KB Restaurant features good Swedish cooking as well as continental dishes. Fish dishes are especially recommended. You might begin with salmon trout roe and Russian caviar, followed by boiled turbot or lamb roast with stuffed zucchini in a thyme-flavored bouillon. Dishes usually are accompanied by an aromatic, freshly baked sourdough bread. Desserts include sorbets with fresh fruits and berries and a heavenly lime soufflé with orange-blossom honey. There's also a relaxed and informal bar.

Lisa Elmquist. Östermalms Saluhall, Nybrogatan 31. ☎ **08/660-92-32.** Reservations recommended. Main courses 100–350 SEK ($11–$38.50). AE, DC, MC, V. Mon–Thurs 10am–6pm, Fri 10am–6:30pm, Sat 9am–4pm. T-bana: Östermalmstorg. SEAFOOD.

Under the soaring roof and amid the food stalls of Stockholm's produce market (the Östermalms Saluhall), you'll find this likable cafe and oyster bar. It's owned by one of the city's largest fish distributors, so its menu varies according to the catch. Some patrons come just to order a serving of shrimp with bread and butter for 85 to 115 SEK ($9.35 to $12.65). Typical dishes include fish soup, salmon cutlets, and sautéed filet of lemon sole. It's not the most refined cuisine in town, but it offers an authentic "taste of Sweden," and does so exceedingly well. The establishment looks like a pleasant bistro under a tent at a country fair.

Noilo. Gustav Adolfs Torg 20. ☎ **08/10-27-57.** Reservations recommended. Main courses 175–220 SEK ($19.25–$24.20); fixed-price lunch 195 SEK ($21.45). AE, DC, MC, V. Mon–Fri 11:30am–3pm, Sat 7pm–3am. T-bana: Kungsträdgården. SWEDISH.

Located at the corner of this landmark square at the opera, this restaurant overlooks the Royal Palace. It has rustic, old-fashioned charm and satisfies different tastes and pocketbooks. You might begin with a selection of herring washed down with a glass of aquavit or smoked salmon with Swedish red caviar. Seafood selections include filet of perch-pike with basil, fresh asparagus, and lobster sauce; or such meat dishes as filet of beef with potato hash. If you're arriving late, you might prefer the late-night menu, whose offerings range from cheeseburgers to a chicken drumstick with potato salad. Although a lunch-only place during the week, on Saturday this becomes your best bet for late-night dining in the capital.

Prinsens. Mäster Samuelsgatan 4. ☎ **08/611-13-31.** Reservations recommended. Main courses 169–245 SEK ($18.60–$26.95); fixed-price lunch 99–250 SEK ($10.90–$27.50). AE, DC, MC, V. Mon–Fri 11:30am–10:30pm, Sat 1–10:30pm, Sun 5–9:30pm. T-bana: Östermalmstorg. SWEDISH.

A 2-minute walk from Stureplan, this is a favorite haunt of artists and has become increasingly popular with foreign visitors. It has been serving people since 1897. Diners are seated on one of two levels, and in summer some tables are placed outside. The cuisine, which is fresh and flavorful, includes such traditional Swedish dishes as veal patty with homemade lingonberry preserves, sautéed fjord salmon, and roulades of beef. For dessert, try the homemade vanilla ice cream. Basically, the menu lists Swedish food prepared in a conservative French style. Later in the evening, the restaurant becomes something of a drinking club.

Sturehof. Stureplan 2. ☎ **08/440-57-30.** Main courses 100–350 SEK ($11–$38.50). AE, DC, MC, V. Mon–Fri 11am–2am, Sat noon–2am, Sun 1pm–2am. T-bana: Östermalmstorg. SWEDISH.

This long-enduring seafood restaurant in the center of town was founded in 1897. Tasty and carefully prepared specialties include Swedish or Canadian lobsters and oysters, fried plaice, boiled salmon with hollandaise, and fresh shrimp. A daily changing menu of genuine Swedish *husmanskost* (home cooking) is a bargain. For example, try the boiled salted veal tongue or potato and beet soup with sour cream. You also might order the famous sotare (grilled small Baltic herring served with boiled potatoes) if you want to sample a local favorite. In fact, many patrons, including us, often come here to make an entire meal from the various types of herring—everything from tomato herring to curry herring.

ⓘ   Family-Friendly Restaurants

Djurgårdsbrunns Wärdshus *(see p. 76)*   At this restaurant set in the Royal Deer Park, about 2 miles east of the center, families can either dine inexpensively in a cafeteria or enjoy more elaborate food in the formal inn dating from the early 19th century.

Lisa Elmquist *(see p. 71)*   Because this restaurant is found in the produce market, Östermalms Saluhall, having lunch here is a colorful adventure. One favorite food item is a portion of shrimp with bread and butter. Families can dine under a tent, which evokes a country fair setting.

Solliden   Near the top of the Skansen compound, a Williamsburg-type park dating from 1891, Solliden (☎ **08/662-93-03**) is a cluster of restaurants set in a sprawling building. This all-purpose dining emporium has an array of dining facilities, which is attractive to families. Solliden offers a lunch smörgåsbord.

Teatergrillen. Nybrogatan 3. ☎ **08/611-70-44.** Reservations recommended. Main courses 160–300 SEK ($17.60–$33). AE, DC, MC, V. Mon–Fri 11:30am–2:30pm and 5–11:30pm, Sat 5–11:30pm. Closed July. T-bana: Östermalmstorg. Bus: 46. SWEDISH/FRENCH.

A great place for theater buffs, this restaurant, decorated with theatrical memorabilia, is near the Royal Dramatic Theater on Nybroplan, where Ingmar Bergman once was arrested for a tax investigation. Many home-style Swedish dishes are offered at lunch. Each day at noon a different specialty is featured—perhaps sautéed fish in a tarragon sauce with rice or pork schnitzel and thyme-flavored fried potatoes. At dinner the cuisine is considerably upgraded with the likes of halibut with chanterelles in a curry sauce or pike-perch appearing with mussels in a citrus-flavored tomato broth. A classic is the Swedish beefsteak with red onion. Increasingly, the chefs have become more innovative, offering such appetizers as deep-fried chicken in peanut sauce accompanied by a coriander and mint salad. Marinated duck appears with pickled shiitake mushrooms and soba noodles. The dessert chef advises that you save room for some of his more daring experiments—everything from mango yogurt ice cream to cashewnut dumplings. The Teatergrillen shares its kitchen with the century-old Restaurant Riche, a nightclub/dining emporium whose entrance is on the far side of the building.

ON GAMLA STAN (OLD TOWN)
VERY EXPENSIVE

✪ **Pontus in the Green House.** Österlånggatan 17. ☎ **08/23-85-00.** Reservations recommended. Main courses 350–500 SEK ($38.50–$55); 8-course fixed-price menu 985 SEK ($108.35). AE, DC, MC, V. Mon–Fri 11:30am–3pm and 6–11pm, Sat noon–4pm and 5:30–11pm. T-bana: Gamla Stan. FRENCH/SWEDISH/ASIAN.

Set within a building whose foundations date to the 16th century, this is a well-orchestrated and elegant restaurant that has attracted some of the most powerful figures in modern Stockholm. Your dining experience will begin with a drink or apéritif in the ground-floor bar and cocktail lounge, where a staff member will explain the menu and record your choices. You'll then be ushered upstairs to a gold-and-green dining room with high, arched windows where there's an undeniable sense of respect for food and its presentation. The chef here, Pontus Frithiof, was inspired by some of the grand francophile chefs of England, Marco Pierre White and Gordon Ramsay, as shown by dishes that include garlic-sautéed turbot with sweetbreads; tender veal tongue with Jerusalem artichokes; steamed turbot with horseradish, prawns, and brown butter; and citrus-glazed

Challonais duck breast that's served with foie gras, shiitake mushrooms, spring onions, and teriyaki sauce. In our view, his herring with vinegar and onion marmalade is Old Town's tastiest. It's worth the trek across town to sample the creamy Roquefort made from the first milk the nursing cows produce. After tasting this cheese, you'll never go back—except with regret—to that store-bought stuff again.

EXPENSIVE

Den Gyldene Freden. Österlånggatan 51. ☎ **08/24-97-60.** Reservations recommended. Main courses 110–265 SEK ($12.10–$29.15). AE, DC, MC, V. Mon–Fri 6–11pm, Sat 1–11pm. Closed July 2–Aug 2. T-bana: Gamla Stan. SWEDISH.

The "Golden Peace" (its English name) is said to be Stockholm's oldest tavern. The restaurant opened in 1722 in a structure that had been built only the year before. The building is owned by the Swedish Academy, and members frequent the place on Thursday nights. Inside, various cozy dining rooms are named for Swedish historical figures who were long-ago patrons. Today, artists, lawyers, and poets still patronize this establishment. You get good, traditional Swedish cookery here, especially fresh Baltic fish and game from the forests of Sweden. Herring is a favorite appetizer. Chefs tempt you with a variety of other more imaginative appetizers, including a creamy soup of regular artichokes and Jerusalem artichokes with a dollop of caviar, and an especially intriguing consommé of oxtail with tiny ravioli stuffed with breast of quail. From here, proceed to the main courses, especially the fried breast of wild duck in a Calvados sauce or the roast of reindeer in a juniper berry sauce. A particular delight to the palate is their homemade duck sausage with three different kinds of mushrooms in a black pepper sauce. Want something different for dessert? How about the warm rose hip soup with vanilla ice cream? Of course, if you order that, you'd be denying yourself the privilege of their "symphony" of lingonberries or a longtime favorite: Stockholm's best chocolate cake.

Fem Små Hus. Nygränd 10. ☎ **08/10-87-75.** Reservations required. Main courses 195–245 SEK ($21.45–$26.95). AE, DC, MC, V. Tues–Sat 5pm–midnight, Sun–Mon 5–11pm. T-bana: Gamla Stan. SWEDISH/FRENCH.

This historic restaurant, whose cellars date from the 17th century, is furnished like the interior of a private castle, with European antiques and oil paintings. After being shown to a candlelit table somewhere in the nine rooms of the labyrinthine interior, you can order assorted herring, slices of fresh salmon in chablis, braised scallops with saffron sauce, terrine of duckling with goose liver and truffles, filet of beef with herb sauce, and sorbets with seasonal fruits and berries. The best indigenous ingredients from Sweden's forests and shorelines appear on the menu here. The cuisine and staff are worthy of the restaurant's hallowed reputation.

Leijontornet. In the Victory Hotel, Lilla Nygatan 5. ☎ **08/14-23-55.** Reservations required. Main courses 145–315 SEK ($15.95–$34.65); fixed-price dinner 420 SEK ($46.20). AE, DC, MC, V. Mon–Sat 5pm–midnight. Closed July and bank holidays. T-bana: Gamla Stan. SWEDISH/INTERNATIONAL.

This is one of the Old Town's most stylish and fashionable restaurants, noted for its fine food and the quality of its service. From the small, street-level bar where you can order a before-dinner drink, patrons descend into the intimately lit cellar (the restaurant was built around a medieval defense tower). To reach this restaurant, you need to negotiate a labyrinth of brick passageways through the Victory Hotel.

You might begin with grilled, marinated calamari with eggplant and paprika cream, or a salad with roast deer and curry dressing, or perhaps a potato crêpe with bleak roe vinaigrette and fried herring. Main courses include roast lamb with moussaka and basil; grilled salmon with tomato, spinach, and lime taglierini; and risotto with pumpkin and flap mushrooms. Dishes often arrive at your table looking like works of art, and some of the country's finest produce appears on the menus here.

MODERATE

Gondolen. 13 Stadtsgården. ☎ **08/641-7090.** Reservations recommended. Main courses 200–300 SEK ($22–$33); fixed-price lunch 95 SEK ($10.45). AE, DC, MC, V. Mon–Fri 11:30am–4pm and 4–11pm, Sat 1–4pm and 4:30–11pm. T-bana: Slussen. SWEDISH/ FRENCH.

For a view that's more panoramic than that from virtually any other restaurant in Stockholm, consider a meal at this unusual monument from the 1930s. Partially suspended beneath a pedestrian footbridge that connects the island of Gamla Stan with the island of Södermalm, it requires access through a (free) private elevator from the Stadtsgården. That elevator will haul you and your party the equivalent of 11 stories up to a decor that hasn't changed much since it was built as an engineering oddity in 1935.

There's a cozy bar on the premises and a well-managed and very popular dining room that attracts a crowd of diners whose menfolk usually wear jackets and ties. Menu items reflect a mixture of French and Swedish cuisine. Examples include smoked salmon served with Iranian caviar, whitebait roe, and potato crêpes; and a ballotine of chicken with a lobster, morels, and champagne vinaigrette. There's also grilled Dover sole stuffed with lobster and scallops, served with a lobster and potato terrine; and scalloped veal with truffle-and-lobster sausages and champagne sauce. The talent of the kitchen keeps local habitués returning, and hotel concierges often recommend this restaurant to guests seeking excellent fare at a reasonable price.

Mälardrottningen. Riddarholmen. ☎ **08/24-36-00.** Reservations recommended. Main courses 105–225 SEK ($11.55–$24.75). AE, DC, MC, V. Mon–Fri 11am–2pm and 3–10pm, Sat 5–10pm. T-bana: Gamla Stan. INTERNATIONAL.

This is one of the most upscale floating restaurants in Sweden, with historic antecedents associated with the Jazz Age and the Woolworth heiress Barbara Hutton. It occupies the showplace deck of what was the largest and most opulent motor yacht in the world when it was built by industrialist C.K.G. Billings in 1924. Today, it's permanently moored to a satellite island of the Old Town, and most of its premises is devoted to a hotel which is separately recommended in "Where to Stay," in the preceding section. Admittedly, a lot of its allure derives from its role as a novelty and conversation piece, but food is well prepared with some of the flair associated with the ship's heyday. Menu items change with the seasons, but may include salmon-filet spring roll with a pepper-garlic vinaigrette; pear-and-goat-cheese salad with thyme-flavored honey; and skewered scampi served with parmesan cheese and chutney sauce made from pesto and bananas. This cuisine, we suspect, is far better and more imaginative than that consumed by Cary Grant during his ill-fated marriage to the heiress when Hollywood dubbed them "Cash & Cary."

Stortorgskällaren. Stortorget 7. ☎ **08/10-55-33.** Reservations required. Main courses 150–220 SEK ($16.50–$24.20); 3-course fixed-price dinner 216 SEK ($23.75). AE, DC, MC, V. Mon–Fri 11am–11pm, Sat noon–11pm, Sun noon–10pm. T-bana: Gamla Stan. SWEDISH.

Set beside a charming square opposite the Stock Exchange in the Old Town, this restaurant was created in medieval wine cellars whose vaulted ceilings date from the 15th century. Old walls and chandeliers are combined with plush carpeting and subtle lighting. This medieval cellar is a cold-weather venue; in summer it's closed and patrons use the outdoor terrace or the street-level dining room.

The menu changes often. You might begin with pâté of wild game with blackberry chutney and pickled carrots, or cured salmon and white bleak roe served with crème fraîche and onions. There's also fried salmon with mushroom sauce. Another specialty is a casserole of Baltic fish seasoned with saffron. After you've sampled some of these dishes, you'll know why Stockholmers have long cited this restaurant as one of their most reliable kitchens. You don't get fireworks, but you do get a cheerful atmosphere, lots of flavor in the food, and a hearty menu.

INEXPENSIVE

✪ **Cattelin Restaurant.** Storkyrkobrinken 9. ☎ **08/20-18-18.** Reservations recommended. Main courses 95–195 SEK ($10.45–$21.45); *dagens menu* 65 SEK ($7.15). AE, DC, MC, V. Mon–Fri 11am–10pm, Sat–Sun noon–10pm. T-bana: Gamla Stan. SWEDISH.

Set on a historic street in Gamla Stan, this restaurant opened in 1897 and continues to serve fish and meat in a boisterous and bustling kind of conviviality. Don't expect genteel service rituals here—the clattering of china can sometimes be almost deafening, but few of the regular patrons seem to mind. Menu choices include various preparations of beef, salmon, trout, veal, and chicken, which frequently comprise the daily specials, often preferred by lunch patrons. Because this restaurant has survived various wars and disasters, as well as changing food tastes, it must be doing something right. It remains a sentimental and nostalgic favorite. But don't go here just for the memories; the kitchen remains first rate and the Cattelin has always been known as one of the more reasonably priced restaurants in a city where people have been known to faint when presented with their dining tabs. We can't say that Greta Garbo actually dined here, but we spotted her one wintry day staring in the window. When our table motioned for her to come in to join us, she fled into the snowy night. The fixed-price lunch is served only Monday through Friday from 11am to 2pm.

Magnus Ladulås. Österlånggatan 26. ☎ **08/21-19-57.** Reservations recommended. Main courses 138–179 SEK ($15.20–$19.70). AE, DC, MC, V. Mon–Fri 11am–midnight, Sat–Sun 4pm–midnight. Closed lunch in July. T-bana: Gamla Stan. SWEDISH/INTERNATIONAL.

This is a pleasant restaurant converted from a vaulted inner room of a 12th-century weaving factory. You can enjoy a drink at the bar before your meal, which might include a mixed seafood plate with lobster sauce, fresh salmon from Lapland, or filet of beef in puff pastry with a deviled sauce. A specialty is steak cooked as you like it on a hot stone placed on your table. The cookery is first rate, and the quality of the ingredients remains high. It's a local favorite, and deservedly so.

ON KUNGSHOLMEN
MODERATE

✪ **Stadshuskällaren.** Stadshuset. ☎ **08/650-54-54.** Main courses 170–225 SEK ($18.70–$24.75); 2-course fixed-price lunch 300 SEK ($33); 3-course fixed-price dinner 360 SEK ($39.60). AE, DC, MC, V. Skänken, Mon–Fri 11:30am–11pm. Stora Matsalen, Mon–Fri 11:30am–11pm, Sat 2–11pm. T-bana: Rådhuset. Bus: 48 or 62. SWEDISH/INTERNATIONAL.

Two dignified restaurants are located in the basement of the City Hall, near the harbor (look for the beautiful, carved wooden doorway). The chefs here prepare the annual banquet for the Nobel Prize winners, and they'll even arrange a banquet with a Nobel menu for you. The interior is divided into two sections: the Skänken, which serves only at lunchtime, and the Stora Matsalen. Dining here is like taking a culinary trip through Sweden. We can't say that eating the food will lead to any Nobel Prizes for yourself, but at least you'll get a sample of what these geniuses feast on. To go truly local, you should try the elk or reindeer dishes if they're in season. Swedish salmon is our all-time favorite, and here it's prepared with consummate skill by the highly trained chefs. Lately the chefs have become more imaginative, preparing such dishes as marinated filet of chicken breasts with avocado pesto (yes, avocado pesto), and almond-fried catfish with olives and mushrooms. Our vote for the finest dish offered

Picnic Fare & Where to Eat It

Fast-food eateries and fresh food markets abound in Stockholm, especially in the center of the city, around Hötorget. Here you can visit **Hötorgs Hallen,** a fresh food market where you can buy the makings of an elegant picnic. Recently arrived immigrants sell many Turkish food products here, including stuffed pita bread.

For the most elegant fare of all, however, go to **Östermalms Hallen** at the corner of Humlegårdsgatan and Nybrogatan, east of the center. Here, stall after stall sells picnic fare, including fresh shrimp and precooked items that will be wrapped carefully for you.

With your picnic fixings in hand, head for **Skansen** or the wooded peninsula of **Djurgården.** If you like to picnic with lots of people around, go to **Kungsträdgården,** "the summer living room of Stockholm," in the center of town.

to Nobel prize winners recently: Roast pigeon breast with a cèpe (flap mushrooms) and pigeon meat ragoût, flavored with tart raspberry vinegar and accompanied by an onion and potato compote.

ON DJURGÅRDEN
MODERATE

Djurgårdsbrunns Wärdshus. Djurgårdsbrunnsvägen 68. ☎ **08/667-90-95.** Main courses 166–200 SEK ($18.25–$22). AE, DC, MC, V. Summer, daily 11:30am–9pm. Off-season, Mon–Fri 11:30am–3pm, Sat–Sun 11:30am–5pm. Bus: 69. SWEDISH.

This establishment occupies a cluster of antique and modern buildings in the Royal Deer Park, about 2 miles east of Stockholm's center. Although there's a simple cafeteria on the premises, most diners prefer the more formal restaurant, an intimate place in what originally was built as an inn in the early 1800s. Menu choices include grilled salmon with morel-butter sauce, noisettes of venison with fresh vegetables, roast beef with horseradish, and fried trout with almonds. Come here to get good, honest cooking with flavor but little flair. Ingredients are well chosen, and the recipes have stood the test of time. The prices also are quite fair. You might opt for a drink in a small bar either before or after your meal.

Ulla Winbladh. Rosendalsvägen 8. ☎ **08/663-05-71.** Reservations required. Main courses 95–270 SEK ($10.45–$29.70). AE, DC, MC, V. Mon 11:30am–10pm, Tues–Fri 11:30am–11pm, Sat 1pm–11pm, Sun 1pm–10pm. Bus: 47. SWEDISH.

Since it opened early in 1994, this Djurgården restaurant has enjoyed an explosion of publicity, which has impressed even the most jaded of Stockholm's restaurant aficionados. It's located in a white stone structure, built originally as part of Stockholm's International Exposition of 1897. There's a large, pale-colored dining room decorated with the works of various Swedish artists and a summer-only outdoor terrace laced with flowering plants. The menu focuses on conservative Swedish cuisine, but everything is impeccably prepared. (Patrons who agree with this assessment include members of the Swedish royal family and a bevy of well-known TV, theater, and art-world personalities.) In 1996, the king presented a medal to chef Emel Ahalen for his proficiency in preparing Swedish cuisine. Menu choices include tender steak with artichokes, a perfectly prepared rack of Swedish lamb flavored with bacon, platters of herring (marinated and fried), whitefish or pike-perch in white-wine sauce, a divine turbot with saffron sauce, the inevitable salmon with dill sauce, and others that vary with the season.

NEAR VASAPARKEN
INEXPENSIVE

Tennstopet (Pewter Tankard). Dalagatan 50. ☎ **08/32-25-18.** Reservations recommended. Main courses 82–240 SEK ($9–$26.40); 2-course fixed-price menu 200 SEK ($22). AE, DC, MC, V. Mon–Fri 4pm–1am, Sat–Sun 1pm–1am. T-bana: Odenplan. Bus: 54. SWEDISH.

A well-known pub and restaurant, Tennstopet is located in the northern part of town, near the Hotel Oden. It's the oldest pub in Sweden, adjacent to a classical Swedish dining room. Main dishes might include a ragoût of fish and shellfish, salmon schnitzel, and plank steak. For lunch, you can dine on pork chops, vegetables, bread, butter, and coffee—or just order a draft beer, toss some darts, and admire the setting. This is the type of food that accompanies heavy drinking—it's good, hearty, and filling—nothing more. The place prides itself on serving genuine English pints. A pint of lager costs 48 SEK ($5.30).

AT SOÅDERMALM
INEXPENSIVE

Garlic & Shots. Folkungagatan 84. ☎ **08/640-84-46.** Reservations recommended. Main courses 85–190 SEK ($9.35–$20.90). MC, V. Daily 5–11pm. T-bana: Medborgarplatsen. CONTINENTAL.

This is a theme restaurant that follows two strong, overriding ideas: that everyone needs a shot of garlic every day, and everything tastes better if it's doctored with a dose of the Mediterranean's most potent herb. The setting is artfully Spartan, with no frills of any kind, and bare wooden tables that have hosted an unexpectedly high percentage of rock stars. Expect garlic in virtually everything that's served, from soups (garlic-ginger with clam soup) to such main courses as beefsteak covered with fried minced garlic and Transylvania-style vampire steak, drenched in a horseradish, tomato, and garlic sauce. Dessert might be a slice of garlic-laced cheese or garlic-honey ice cream garnished with honey-marinated cloves of garlic. An appropriate foil for all these flavors? You can try some garlic ale or garlic beer, if you're up to it.

Hannas Krog. Skånegatan 80. ☎ **08/643-82-25.** Reservations recommended. Main courses 98–189 SEK ($10.80–$20.80). AE, DC, MC, V. Mon–Fri 11:30am–3pm; daily 5pm–midnight. T-bana: Medborgarplatsen. INTERNATIONAL.

One of the most appealing neighborhood restaurants in Södermalm is this bustling and, in its own way, fashionable bistro whose decor may remind you of a Swedish version of a British pub. Amid paneled walls and such artfully rustic touches as a collection of cuckoo clocks, it serves a medley of globally inspired food. You might begin with a slice of pie made from Swedish cheddar cheese, then move on to marinated and baked salmon wrapped in Italian pancetta ham; Provençale-style lamb; or grilled butterfish with tiger prawns wrapped in wontons and served with a crayfish consommé. Trendy Stockholmers, who used to avoid Södermalm like the plague, are increasingly showing up at this address to sample the good fare, excellent service, and inviting ambience.

ON LANG HOLMEN
MODERATE

Långholmen Restaurant. Kronohäktet. ☎ **08/720-85-50.** Reservations recommended. Main courses 158–250 SEK ($17.40–$27.50). AE, DC, MC, V. Mon–Fri 11:30am–5pm and 5–11pm, Sat noon–midnight, Sun noon–8pm. T-bana: Hornstul. Bus: 4, 40, and 66. INTERNATIONAL.

This is the premier dining venue within a hotel, restaurant, and convention facility that occupies what originally was built in the 1600s as a brewery. From around 1700

Cheap Eats

While touring Djurgårdsvagen, you can enjoy lunch at **Café Blå Porten,** Djurgårdsvagen 64 (☎ **08/663-8759**), a cafe/cafeteria that often draws patrons of the Lilijevalch art gallery next door. Soups, salads, sandwiches, and hot meals are served. Take the ferry from Slussen or Gamla Stan. At Nybrogatan, **College Restaurant,** Smalandsgatan 2 (☎ **08/611-31-95**), lies in the vicinity of the Royal Dramatic Theater. Its extensive 40 SEK ($4.40) buffet served from 6:30 to 9:30pm nightly is one of Stockholm's best food values. Take the T-bana to Östermalmstorg.

Also at Östermalmstorg, you can patronize the well-known **Örtagården,** Nybroatan 31 (☎ **08/662-17-28**). This eatery on the second floor of the Östermalms food hall allows you to help yourself to a small smörgåsbord of both hot and cold Swedish fare. It is increasingly rare to find the typical Swedish smörgåsbord in Stockholm these days, and Örtagården is a holdout of the old culinary tradition at a bargain price.

until 1975, it functioned as a women's prison, and from the windows of the old-fashioned dining room, you can still see the high brick walls. Paintings on the walls, many in gentle pastels, depict the workhouse drudgery that used to prevail here. Come here for an unusual insight into the hardships of the 19th century and menu items that change with the seasons. Examples include a carpaccio of shellfish; smoked breast of duck with a walnut-cranberry vinaigrette; a combination of lobster and turbot stewed with vegetables in shellfish bouillon; and tournedos of venison with juniper-berries, smoked ham, pepper sauce, and Swedish potatoes. This is hardly prison food—in fact, the most dedicated devotees of the restaurant hail it as one of the finest in Stockholm. There is a dedication here to using only the freshest and best of ingredients available in the market on any given day.

Ulriksdals Wärdshus. Ulriksdals Royal Park, S-170 79 Solna. ☎ **08/85-08-15.** Reservations required. Main courses 280–350 SEK ($30.80–$38.50); smörgåsbord 250 SEK ($27.50); fixed-price menus 375–500 SEK ($41.25–$55). AE, DC, MC, V. Mon–Fri noon–10pm, Sat 12:30–10pm, Sun 12:30–6:30pm. Closed Dec 24–26. Take Sveavägen toward Arlanda Airport (Exit E18), 3 miles north of Stockholm. SWEDISH.

This out-of-town establishment serves the best smörgåsbord in Sweden. On the grounds of Ulriksdal's Royal Palace on Edviken Bay, you can dine in the all-glass Queen Silvia Pavilion, which opens onto gardens owned by the king and queen. The smörgåsbord, featuring 86 delicacies (both shellfish and meat), is accompanied by beer or aquavit. Most people eat the smörgåsbord in five courses, beginning with herring (20 varieties), followed first by salmon and then meat dishes, including fridadeller (meatballs) or perhaps reindeer, then a choice of cheese, and finally dessert. Some dishes are based on old farm-style recipes, including Lansson's Temptation, which blends anchovies, heavy cream, potatoes, and onions. Over the Christmas season, the buffet is expanded to almost twice its normal size, is lavishly decorated in a seasonal theme, and is priced at 450 SEK ($49.50) per person.

AT SOLLENTUNA
EXPENSIVE

Edsbacka Krog. Sollentunavägen 220, Sollentuna. ☎ **08/96-33-00.** Reservations recommended. Main courses 255–360 SEK ($28.05–$39.60); fixed-price menus 575–1,295 SEK ($63.25–$142.45). AE, DC, MC, V. Mon 5:30pm–midnight, Tues–Fri 11:30am–2:30pm and 5:30pm–midnight, Sat 2pm–midnight. T-bana: Sollentuna. SWEDISH/FRENCH.

Set within an historic, thick-walled building dating from 1626, a 10-minute taxi ride from the town center, this was the first licensed inn in Stockholm. Inside, you'll find dining rooms outfitted in soft tones of green and orange, 19th-century antiques, and exposed beams, all of which contribute to an atmosphere of upscale country living in the city. Menu items include the kinds of combinations that you're not likely to find in many other restaurants: Examples include whitebait roe with marinated halibut and avocado; boiled lobster in a vegetable terrine; scallops with smoked cod in a duck liver sauce; a terrine of duck liver served with fried sweetbreads; and a platter that combines oxtail and beef tongue with duck liver and duck liver sauce. Christer Lindström is the chef whose dishes inspire visits from around the district. He is dedicated to his cuisine, offering a judicious combination of sturdy continental cookery with immaculate taste.

4

Discovering Stockholm

Regardless of your age, interests, or the time of year, Stockholm is loaded with interesting sights and activities. If the Vasa Ship Museum doesn't pique your interest, perhaps the changing of the guard at the Royal Palace or the Gröna Lunds Tivoli amusement park will. Even window shopping for beautifully designed Swedish crafts can be an enjoyable way to spend an afternoon. And after dark, Stockholm becomes one of the livelier cities in the north of Europe.

Suggested Itineraries

If You Have 1 Day

It's far too short, but take a ferry to Djurgården and visit the _Vasa_ Ship Museum, Stockholm's most famous attraction, and explore the open-air Skansen folk museum. In the afternoon, take our walking tour of Gamla Stan (Old Town) (see below) and have dinner at one of its restaurants.

If You Have 2 Days

On your first day, follow the suggestions above.

On Day 2, get up early and visit the Kaknästornet television tower for a panoramic view of the city and its archipelago. Go to the Museum of Nordic History for a review of 5 centuries of life in Sweden. After lunch, visit the Millesgården of Lidingö, the sculpture garden, and former home of Carl Milles.

If You Have 3 Days

For the first 2 days follow the itinerary given above.

On the third morning take our "Walking Tour 2" (see below). At noon (1pm on Sunday), return to Gamla Stan to see the changing of the guard at the Royal Palace. View this French-inspired building that has been the residence of Swedish kings for more than 700 years. In the afternoon visit the National Museum.

If You Have 4 or 5 Days

For Days 1 to 3, follow the suggestions given above.

On Day 4, take one of the many available tours of the Stockholm archipelago. Return to Stockholm and spend the evening at the Gröna Lunds Tivoli amusement park on Djurgården.

For your last day, visit Drottningholm Palace and its 18th-century theater. In the afternoon go to Uppsala, which is easily reached by public transportation (see "Side Trips from Stockholm," later in this chapter).

1 Seeing the Sights

THE TOP ATTRACTIONS

GAMLA STAN & NEIGHBORING ISLANDS

✪ **Kungliga Slottet (Royal Palace) & Museums.** Kungliga Husgerådskammaren. ☎ **08/ 402-61-32** for Royal Apartments & Treasury, 08/402-61-34 for the Skattkammaren, 08/ 666-44-75 for Royal Armory, or 08/402-61-30 for Museum of Antiquities. Royal Apartments 50 SEK ($5.50) adults, 25 SEK ($2.75) students, free for children under 7. Royal Armory 50 SEK ($5.50) adults, 30 SEK ($3.30) seniors and students, 15 SEK ($1.65) children, free for children under 7. Museum of Antiquities 50 SEK ($5.50) adults, 25 SEK ($2.75) seniors and students, free for children under 7. Treasury 50 SEK ($5.50) adults, 25 SEK ($2.75) seniors and students, free for children under 7. Combination ticket to all parts of palace 100 SEK ($11) adults, 70 SEK ($7.70) students and children. Apartments and Treasury Sept–June, Tues–Sun noon–3pm; July–Aug, daily 10am–4pm; closed during government receptions. Royal Armory Sept–Apr, Tues–Sun 11am–4pm; May–Aug, daily 11am–4pm. Museum of Antiquities Sept–Apr, daily noon–3pm; May–Aug, daily 10am–4pm. T-bana: Gamla Stan. Bus: 43, 46, 59, or 76.

Severely dignified, even cold-looking on the outside, with a lavish interior designed in the Italian baroque style and built between 1691 and 1754, Kungliga Slotta is one of the few residences of a European monarch that's open to the public. Although the Swedish king and queen prefer to live at Drottningholm, this massive 608-room showcase remains their official address.

Visitors may walk through the **Council Chamber** where the king and his ministers meet several times a year. The **State Apartments,** with three magnificent baroque ceilings and fine tapestries, the **Bernadotte Apartment,** and the **Guest Apartment** also are on view. They're beautifully furnished in Swedish rococo, Louis XVI, and Empire style.

In the cellar, the **Skattkammaren (Treasury),** exhibiting one of the most celebrated collections of crown jewels in Europe, is worth a visit. You'll see a dozen crowns, scepters, and orbs, along with pieces of antique jewelry. Nearly all visitors want to see the **Royal Armory,** Slottsbacken 3, also housed in the cellars of the palace. Kings used to ride in these elegant gilded coaches. In addition, you'll see coronation costumes from the 16th century, weapons, and armor.

Gustav III's collection of sculpture from the days of the Roman Empire can be viewed in the **Antikmuseum** (Museum of Antiquities).

Changing of the Royal Guard: In summer you can watch the parade of the military guard daily; in winter it takes place on Wednesday and Sunday (on the other days there's no parade—just the changing of the guard). The parade route on weekdays begins at Sergels Torg and proceeds along Hamngatan, Kungsträdgårdsgatan, Strömgatan, Gustav Adolfs Torg, Norrbro, Skeppsbron, and Slottsbacken. On Sunday the guard departs from the Army Museum, going along Riddargatan, Artillerigatan, Strandvägen, Hamngatan, Kungsträdgårdsgatan, Strömgatan, Gustav Adolfs Torg, Norrbro, Skeppsbron, and Slottsbacken. For information on the time of the march, ask at the Tourist Center in Sweden House. The actual changing of the guard takes place at noon Monday through Saturday and at 1pm on Sunday in front of the Royal Palace.

ON NORRMALM

Nationalmuseum (National Museum of Art). Södra Blasieholmshamnen. ☎ **08/ 519-54-300.** www.nationalmuseum.se/enindex.shtml. Admission 75 SEK ($8.25) adults, 60 SEK ($6.60) seniors and students, free for children under 16. Tues 11am–8pm, Wed–Sun 11am–5pm. T-bana: Kungsträdgården. Bus: 46, 62, 65, or 76.

At the tip of a peninsula, a short walk from the **Royal Opera House** and the Grand Hotel, is Sweden's state treasure house of paintings and sculpture. One of the oldest

Stockholm Attractions

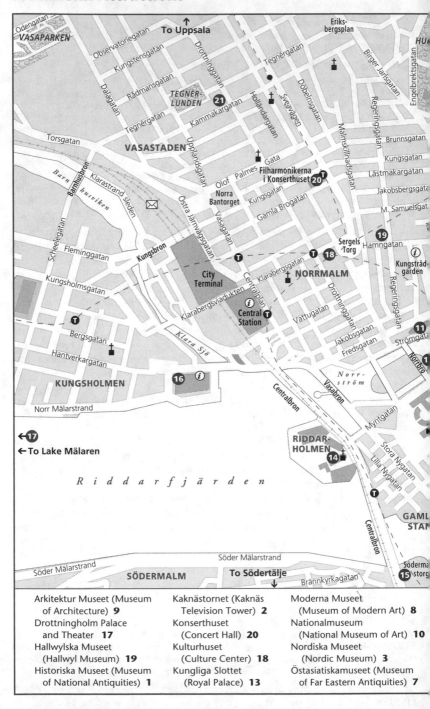

Arkitektur Museet (Museum of Architecture) **9**

Drottningholm Palace and Theater **17**

Hallwylska Museet (Hallwyl Museum) **19**

Historiska Museet (Museum of National Antiquities) **1**

Kaknästornet (Kaknäs Television Tower) **2**

Konserthuset (Concert Hall) **20**

Kulturhuset (Culture Center) **18**

Kungliga Slottet (Royal Palace) **13**

Moderna Museet (Museum of Modern Art) **8**

Nationalmuseum (National Museum of Art) **10**

Nordiska Museet (Nordic Museum) **3**

Östasiatiskamuseet (Museum of Far Eastern Antiquities) **7**

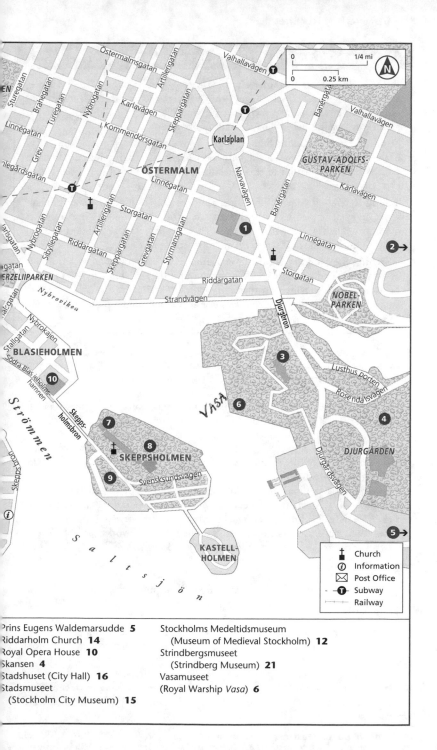

Östermalmsgatan
Artillerigatan
Valhallavägen
1/4 mi
0   0.25 km
Valhallavägen

Sturegatan
Brahegatan
Turegatan
Nybrogatan
Skeppargatan
Karlavägen
Kommendörsgatan
Karlaplan
GUSTAV-ADOLFS-
PARKEN

Linnégatan
Grev
Karlavägen

egårdsgatan
ÖSTERMALM
Linnégatan
Narvavägen
Banérgatan

T
Storgatan
Artillerigatan
Nybrogatan
Sibyllegatan
Riddargatan
Skeppargatan
Greygatan
Styrmansgatan
Linnégatan

1
Storgatan

ERZELIIPARKEN
Riddargatan
NOBEL-
PARKEN

gatan
Nybroviken
Strandvägen
Djurgården

Nybrokajen
Stallgatan
Södra Blasieholms
hammen
BLASIEHOLMEN
3
Lusthus porten

10
Rosendalsvägen

Strömmen
Skepps-
holmsbron
7
Vasa
6
4

8
SKEPPSHOLMEN
DJURGÅRDEN

9
Svensksundsvägen
Djurgårdsvägen

5

KASTELL-
HOLMEN
Saltsjön

† Church
ⓘ Information
✉ Post Office
-Ⓣ Subway
Railway

✪ Frommer's Favorite Stockholm Experiences

Experiencing Skansen. Butter churning or folk dancing, there's always something to intrigue people of all ages here. Wander at leisure through the world's oldest open-air museum (which covers about 75 acres of parkland), getting a glimpse of Swedish life in the long-ago countryside.

Strolling Through Gamla Stan at Night. To walk the narrow cobblestone alleys of the Old Town on foot at night, with special lighting, is like going back in time. It takes little imagination to envision what everyday life must have been like in this "city between the bridges."

Taking the Baths. Swedes, both men and women, are fond of roasting themselves on wooden platforms like chickens on a grill, then plunging into a shower of Arctic-chilled water. After this experience, bathers emerge lighthearted and lightheaded into the northern fresh air, fortified for an evening of revelry.

Watching the Summer Dawn. In midsummer at 3am, you can get out of bed, as many Swedes do, and sit on a balcony to watch the eerie blue sky—pure, crystal, exquisite. Gradually it's bathed in peach as the early dawn of a summer day approaches. Swedes don't like to miss a minute of their summer, even if they have to get up early to enjoy it.

---

museums in the world, it celebrated its 200th anniversary in 1992. Its collections include a wide assortment of masterpieces by such artists as Rembrandt and Rubens (*Sacrifices to Venus*).

The first floor focuses on applied arts (silverware, handcrafts, porcelain, Empire furnishings, and the like), but first-time visitors, if pressed for time, may want to head directly to the second floor. Here, among the paintings from northern Europe, is Lucas Cranach's most amusing *Venus and Cupid*. Also displayed is a rare collection of Russian icons, most of them—such as *St. George and the Dragon*—from the Moscow School of the mid-16th century.

On view is an exceptional number of excellent paintings by such masters as Perugino (*St. Sebastian*), Ribera (his oft-rendered *Martyrdom of Bartolomé*), El Greco (*Peter and Paul*), Giovanni Bellini (*Portrait of Christ*), Lotto (*Portrait of a Man*), and Poussin (*Bacchus*). The gallery contains some outstanding Flemish works, notably Rubens's *Bacchanal at Andros* and *Worship of Venus*, and Jan Brueghel's *Jesus Preaching from the Boat*.

Perhaps the most important room in the entire museum has one whole wall featuring the works of Rembrandt—*Portrait of an Old Man* and *Portrait of an Old Woman*, along with his *Kitchen Maid* (one of the more famous works in Stockholm). Here also is *The Oath of the Batavians*.

In yet another room is Watteau's *Lesson in Love*, and another room is noted for its Venetian works by Guardi and Canaletto, as well as English portraits by Gainsborough and Reynolds.

Modern works include Manet's *Parisienne*; Degas's dancers; a nude male by Rodin (*Copper Age*) and his bust of Victor Hugo; van Gogh's *Light Movements in Green*; landscapes by Cézanne, Gauguin, and Pissarro; and paintings by Renoir, notably *La Grenouillère*.

Moderna Museet (Museum of Modern Art). Skeppsholmen. ☎ **08/519-55-200.** www.modernamuseet.se/eng/start/. Admission 60 SEK ($6.60) adults, 40 SEK ($4.40) seniors and students, free for children under 17. Tues–Thurs 11am–10pm, Fri–Sun 11am–6pm. T-bana: Kungsträdgården. Bus: 65.

After residing at Birger Jarlsgatan since its inception, the museum moved to a new home better fitting a museum of modern art. The new museum building, designed by renowned contemporary Spanish architect Rafael Moneo, reopened at its new location on Skeppsholmen on Valentine's Day 1998. The museum focuses on contemporary works by Swedish and international artists, including kinetic sculptures. Highlights include a small but good collection of cubist art by Picasso, Braque, and Léger; Matisse's *Apollo* découpage; the famous *Enigma of William Tell* by Salvador Dalí; and works by Brancusi, Max Ernst, Giacometti, and Arp, among others. There's also a collection of pop art—from Rauschenberg's *Monogram,* through Oldenburg, to Andy Warhol. Among 1960s works by prominent New York artists are the 12-foot-high *Geometric Mouse* by Claes Oldenburg; *Fox Trot,* an early Warhol; and *Total Totality All,* a large sculpture by Louise Nevelson.

Museum activities include a children's workshop, concerts, films, discussions, and theater. There's a bookshop with posters, cards, books, and reproductions, plus a cafe, a restaurant, and a pub.

AT DJURGÅRDEN ✗

○ **Vasamuseet (Royal Warship *Vasa*).** Galärvarvsvägen, Djurgården. ☎ 08/ **666 18 00.** www.vasamuseet.se/indexeng.html. Admission 60 SEK ($6.60) adults, 40 SEK ($4.40) seniors and students, 10 SEK ($1.10) children 7–15, free for children under 7. June 10–Aug 20, daily 9:30am–7pm; Aug 21–June 9, Wed 10am–8pm, Thurs–Tues 10am–5pm. Closed Jan 1, May 1, Dec 24–26 and 31. Bus: 44 or 47. Ferry from Slussen year-round, from Nybroplan in summer only.

This 17th-century man-of-war is the number-one sightseeing attraction in Scandinavia—and for good reason. Housed in a museum specially constructed for it at Djurgården (near Skansen), the *Vasa* is the world's oldest identified and complete ship.

In 1628, on its maiden voyage and in front of thousands of horrified onlookers, the Royal Warship *Vasa* capsized and sank almost instantly to the bottom of Stockholm harbor. In a feat that was an engineering triumph, it was salvaged in 1961. On board were found more than 4,000 coins, carpenter's tools, sailor's pants (in a color known as Lübeck gray), fish bones, and other items of archaeological interest. Best of all, 97% of the ship's 700 original sculptures were found. Carefully restored and impregnated with preservatives, they now are back aboard the ship, which looks stunning as it once again carries its grotesque faces, lion masks, fish-shaped bodies, and other carvings; some still covered with the original paint and gilt.

A full-scale model of half of the *Vasa's* upper gun deck has been rebuilt, along with the admiral's cabin and the steering compartment. Several carved wooden figures represent the crew. By walking through the "gun deck" and the exhibit of original objects (including medical equipment, preserved clothes, and a backgammon board), you can get an idea of everyday life aboard the ship.

Another exhibit tells the story of naval warfare in the *Vasa's* (brief) heyday. A diorama shows a battle fought by the Swedish and Polish navies in 1627. The ships, sculpted in copper, are positioned on a large cupola. Inside the cupola, a film illustrates the horrors of war at sea.

○ **Skansen.** Djurgården 49–51. ☎ 08/442-80-00. www.skansen.se/eng/. Admission 30–60 SEK ($3.30–$6.60) adults, depending on time of day, day of the week, and season; 10 SEK ($1.10) children 6–15; free for children 5 and under. Historic buildings, May–Aug, daily 11am–5pm; Sept–Apr, daily 11am–3pm. Bus: 47 from central Stockholm. Ferry from Slussen.

Often called "Old Sweden in a Nutshell," this open-air museum lies on Djurgården, near Gröna Lunds Tivoli. More than 150 dwellings from Lapland to Skåne, most from the 18th and 19th centuries, have been reassembled on some 75 acres of parkland.

The exhibits range from a windmill to a manor house to a complete town quarter. Browsers can explore the old workshops and see where the early book publishers, silversmiths, and druggists plied their trade. Many handcrafts for which Swedes later became noted (glassblowing, for example) are demonstrated here, along with such traditional peasant crafts as weaving and churning. For a tour of the buildings, arrive no later than 4pm. Folk dancing and open-air symphonic concerts also are featured. In summer, international stars perform at Skansen; check the tourist center for these special events. In addition, there's much to do on summer nights here (see "Stockholm After Dark," later in this chapter), and many places to eat.

ON KUNGSHOLMEN

Stadshuset (Stockholm City Hall). Hantverksgatan 1. ☎ **08/508-290-59.** Admission 50 SEK ($5.50), free for children under 12. Tower, May–Sept, daily 10am–4pm. City Hall tours (subject to change), June–Sept, daily at 10am, 11am, noon, and 2pm; Oct–Apr, daily at 10am and noon. T-bana: Centralen or Rådhuset. Bus: 3 or 62.

Built in what is called the "National Romantic Style," the Stockholm City Hall (Stadhuset), on the island of Kungsholmen, is one of the finest examples of modern architecture in Europe. Designed by Ragnar Ostberg, it was completed in 1923. The redbrick structure is dominated by a lofty square tower 348 feet high, topped by three gilt crowns, the symbol of Sweden, and the national coat-of-arms. There are two courts: the open civic court and the interior covered court. The Blue Hall is used for banquets and other festive occasions, including the Nobel Prize banquet. About 18 million pieces of gold and colored mosaics made of special glass cover the walls, and the southern gallery contains murals by Prince Eugen, the painter prince. The 101 City Council members meet in the council chamber.

NEAR STOCKHOLM

✪ **Drottningholm Palace and Theater.** Ekerö, Drottningholm. ☎ **08/402-62-80.** www.royalcourt.se/drottningholm/eng/index.html. Palace, 50 SEK ($5.50) adults, 25 SEK ($2.75) students and persons under 26; theater, guided tour 50 SEK ($5.50) adults, 20 SEK ($2.20) students and persons under 26; Chinese Pavilion, 50 SEK ($5.50) adults, 25 SEK ($2.75) students and persons under 26. All free for children under 16. Palace, Oct–Apr Sat–Sun noon–3:30pm; May–Aug, daily 10am–4:30pm; Sept, daily noon–3:30pm. Theater, guided tours in English, May, daily 12:30pm, 1:30pm, 2:30pm, 3:30pm, and 4:15pm; June–Aug, daily 11:30am, 12:30pm, 1:30pm, 2:30pm, 3:30pm, and 4:15pm; Sept, daily 1:30pm, 2:30pm, 3:30pm. Chinese Pavilion, Apr and Oct, daily 1–3:30pm, May–Aug, daily 11am–4:30pm, Sept, daily noon–3:30pm. T-bana: Brommaplan, then bus no. 301 or 323 to Drottningholm. Ferry from the dock near City Hall.

What originally was conceived as the centerpiece of Sweden's royal court, this regal complex of stately buildings sits on an island in Lake Mälaren. Dubbed the Versailles of Sweden, Drottningholm (Queen's Island) lies about 7 miles west of Stockholm. The palace, loaded as it is with courtly art and furnishings, is surrounded by fountains and parks, and still functions as one of the official residences of the country's royal family.

On the grounds is one of the most perfectly preserved 18th-century theaters in the world, **Drottningholm Court Theater** (☎ **08/759-04-06**), whose 30 annual performances are held only between June and August. Devoted almost exclusively to a repertoire of 18th-century operas, and with seats for only 450 spectators at a time, many of which are sold out long in advance to season ticket holders, it provides one of the most unusual performance experiences in Sweden. The theater can be visited only as part of a guided tour, an experience that focuses on the original sets and stage mechanisms. For tickets to the evening performances, which are priced from 150 to 545 SEK ($16.50 to $59.95) each, call ☎ 08/660-82-25.

◯ Millesgården. Carl Milles Väg 2, Lidingö. ☎ **08/446-75-90.** Admission 70 SEK ($7.70) adults, 50 SEK ($5.50) seniors and students, 20 SEK ($2.20) children 7–16, free for children under 7. May–Sept, daily 10am–5pm; Oct–Apr, Tues–Sun noon–4pm. T-bana: Ropsten, then bus to Torsviks Torg or train to Norsvik.

On the island of Lingingö, northeast of Stockholm, is the former villa and sculpture garden of Carl Milles (1875–1955), the country's foremost sculptor. Although it takes time to reach the villa from the center of Stockholm, it is worth the trip. Some of the artist's most important works are found here, including his monumental and much-reproduced sculpture *Hands of God*. Sculptures sit atop columns on terraces in this garden of almost magical proportions set high above the harbor and the city landscape. These are copies of his most famous works; the originals are found all over Sweden and also in the United States. In his early works you can see how much he was influenced by the French sculptor Auguste Rodin (1840–1917), and also by art nouveau. But in his later works his sculpture took on a more simplified quality that was both dramatic and expressive. As you wander about, you are immediately overcome by how strongly Milles relied on mythological themes. The site also includes his personal collection of works by other leading sculptors. The villa displays a unique collection of art from both the Middle Ages and the Renaissance, plus rare artifacts excavated in the ruins of ancient Rome and Greece.

MORE TO EXPLORE
GAMLA STAN & NEIGHBORING ISLANDS

◯ Riddarholm Church. Riddarholmen. ☎ **08/402-61-30.** Admission 20 SEK ($2.20) adults, 10 SEK ($1.10) students and children. June–Aug, daily 11am–4pm; May and Sept, Wed and Sat–Sun noon–3pm. Closed Oct–Apr. T-bana: Gamla Stan.

The second-oldest church in Stockholm is located on the tiny island of Riddarholmen, next to Gamla Stan. It was founded in the 13th century as a Franciscan monastery. Almost all the royal heads of state are entombed here, except Christina, who is buried in Rome.

There are three principal royal chapels including one, the Bernadotte wing, which belongs to the present ruling family. Karl XIV Johan, the first king of the Bernadotte dynasty, is buried here in a large marble sarcophagus.

Stockholms Medeltidsmuseum (Museum of Medieval Stockholm). Strömparterren, Norrbro. ☎ **08/508-31-790.** Admission 40 SEK ($4.40) adults, 5 SEK (55¢) children. July–Aug, Tues–Thurs 11am–6pm, Fri–Mon 11am–4pm; Sept–June, Tues and Thurs–Sun 11am–4pm, Wed 11am–6pm. Bus: 43.

Built around archaeological excavations, including parts of the old city wall dating from 1530 (discovered 1978–80), this museum traces the city's founding and development during the Middle Ages. In essence, it is an excavated peepshow into the Middle Ages. Objects tell us about children's games, women's work, monastic life, and so on. The museum also houses the Riddarsholmship, leather goods, ceramics, and metal articles.

Östasiatiskamuseet (Museum of Far Eastern Antiquities). Skeppsholmen. ☎ **08/ 519-55-750.** Admission 50 SEK ($5.50), free for children under 16. Tues noon–8pm, Wed–Sun noon–5pm. T-bana: Kungsträdgården. Bus: 65 to Karl XII Torg; 7-minute walk.

This small, intimate museum was opened in 1963 in an old building erected in 1699–1700 as stables for Charles (Karl) XII's bodyguard. It's about a 7-minute walk from Karl XII Torg. The permanent exhibit consists of archaeological objects, fine arts, and handcrafts from China, Japan, Korea, and India. The collection is one of the finest and most important of its kind outside Asia. Among the outstanding displays are Chinese Neolithic painted pottery, ritual bronze vessels, archaic jades, wood carvings, ivory, lacquerwork, enamelware, Chinese glass, Buddhist sculpture, Chinese painting and calligraphy, T'ang tomb pottery figurines, Sung classical stoneware (such as celadon and temmoku), Ming blue-and-white wares, and Ch'ing porcelain made for both the Chinese and the European market.

ON NORRMALM

✪ **Hallwylska Museet (Hallwyl Museum).** Hamngatan 4. ☎ **08/666-44-99.** Guided tours 60 SEK ($6.60), 25 SEK ($2.75) students, free for children under 8. Guided tours July–Aug, weekdays on the hour 11am–3pm; Sept–June, Tues–Sun at noon, 1pm, 2pm, and 3pm. T-bana: Kungsträdgården.

Sweden has never seen a collector to compare with Countess Wilhelmina von Hallwyl. She spent nearly three-quarters of a century collecting "things," most of them of rare value. And not only did she collect them, she also carefully catalogued them (in a whopping 78 volumes) and left them to the state upon her death. Today, this most eccentric and esoteric of Stockholm's museums is housed in a turn-of-the-century residence of great splendor. Sandwiched between a restaurant and a cafe, her former home evokes different epochs in decoration. The house itself is a fine example of the skilled craftsmanship of its day. Open to the public since 1938, the collection includes priceless paintings, rare tapestries, silver, armor, weapons, antique musical instruments, glassware, even umbrellas and buttons (but only the finest ones made). The aristocratic Hallwyl family occupied this townhouse from 1898 to 1930. Of the three Hallwyl daughters, one became a sculptor, studying with the great Carl Milles. As you're taken around on the tour, you learn historical tidbits; for example, this house had a modern bathroom even before the royal palace. If you're in Stockholm in summer, ask about summer evening concerts presented in the central courtyard.

Kaknästornet (Kaknäs Television Tower). Mörkakroken. ☎ **08/789-24-35.** Admission 25 SEK ($2.75) adults, 15 SEK ($1.65) children 7–15, free for children under 7. May–Aug, daily 9am–10pm; Sept–Apr, daily 10am–9pm. Closed Dec 24–25. Bus: 69.

Situated in the northern district of Djurgården is the tallest structure in Scandinavia— a radio and television tower that stands 508 feet high. Two elevators take visitors to an observation platform, where you can see everything from the cobblestone streets of Gamla Stan (Old Town) to the city's modern concrete-and-glass structures and the archipelago beyond. A moderately priced restaurant, serving classic Swedish cuisine, also awaits you at the top of the tower.

Historiska Museet (Museum of National Antiquities). Narvavägen 13–17. ☎ **08/519-556-00.** Admission 60 SEK ($6.60) adults, 50 SEK ($5.50) seniors and students, 35 SEK ($3.85) children 7–15, free for children under 7, family ticket 140 SEK ($15.40). Apr–Sept, Tues–Sun 11am–5pm; Oct–Mar, Tues–Wed and Fri–Sun 11am–5pm, Thurs 11am–8pm. T-bana: Karlaplan or Östermalmstorg. Bus: 44, 47, or 54.

If you're interested in Swedish history, especially the Viking era, this museum is the nation's finest repository of relics left by those legendary conquerors who once terrorized Europe. Many relics have been unearthed from ancient burial sites. The collection of artifacts ranges from prehistoric to medieval times, including Viking stone inscriptions and coins minted in the 10th century. In 1994, in the presence of King Carl XVI Gustaf and Queen Silvia, a Gold Room was inaugurated. It features authentic Viking silver and gold jewelry, large ornate charms, elaborate bracelet designs found nowhere else in the world, and a unique neck collar from Färjestaden. Because the exhibits displayed are literally worth their weight in gold, the treasury is underground along long corridors and behind solid security doors.

AT DJURGÅRDEN ✕

Nordiska Museet (Nordic Museum). Djurgårdsvägen 6–16, Djurgården. ☎ 08/5195-6000. www.nordm.se/index-e.html. Admission 60 SEK ($6.60) adults, 50 SEK ($5.50) seniors, 30 SEK ($3.30) students, 20 SEK ($2.20) ages 7–12, free for children under 7. Tues and Thurs 2–8pm, Wed and Fri–Sun 2–5pm. Bus: 44, 47, or 69.

This is the most outstanding museum of national life in Scandinavia and contains more than a million objects, costumes, and furnishings of Swedish life from the 1500s to the present. Highlights include dining tables and period costumes ranging from matching garters and ties for men to purple flowerpot hats from the 1890s. In the basement is an extensive exhibit of the tools of the Swedish fishing trade, plus relics from nomadic Lapps.

Prins Eugens Waldemarsudde. Prins Eugens Väg 6. ☎ 08/545-837-00. Admission 60 SEK ($6.60) adults, 40 SEK ($4.40) seniors and students, free for children under 17. June–Aug, Tues and Thurs 11am–8pm, Wed and Fri–Sun 11am–5pm; Sept–May, Tues–Sun 11am–4pm. Bus: 47 to the end of the line.

This once-royal residence of the "painting prince" functions today as an art gallery and a memorial to one of the most famous royal artists in recent history, Prince Eugen (1865–1947). The youngest of Oscar II's four children (all sons), he was credited with making innovative contributions to the techniques of Swedish landscape painting, specializing in depictions of his favorite regions in central Sweden. Among his most publicly visible works are the murals on the inner walls of the city hall.

Built between 1903 and 1904, and set directly on the water, the house is surrounded by a flower and sculpture garden. Eugen's private collection of paintings, which includes works by Edvard Munch, Carl Larsson, and Anders Zorn, is one of the most rewarding aspects of a visit here. The house and its contents were willed to the Swedish government after the prince's death, and opened to the public for the first time in 1948.

The house and art gallery are furnished as the prince left them. While at Waldemarsudde, make sure to see the old mill, built in the 1780s.

Thielska Galleriet (Thiel Gallery). Sjötullsbacken 6–8, Djurgården. ☎ 08/662-58-84. Admission 50 SEK ($5.50) adults, 30 SEK ($3.30) seniors and students, free for children under 12. Mon–Sat noon–4pm, Sun 1–4pm. Bus: 69.

At the tip of Djurgården, this gallery houses one of Sweden's major art collections, surpassing, many feel, that of Waldemarsudde. The sculptures and canvases here were acquired by Mr. Thiel, a financier and banker who eventually went bankrupt. The collection was acquired by the Swedish government in 1924.

Some of the big names in Scandinavian art are here, including Norway's Edvard Munch and Sweden's Anders Zorn (see his nude, *In Dreams*). Gustav Fjaestad's furniture also is displayed. You'll also see a portrait of Nietzsche, whom Thiel greatly admired. Works by Manet, Rodin, and Toulouse-Lautrec, among others, round out the collection. Thiel is buried on the grounds beneath Rodin's statue *Shadow.*

ON SÖDERMALM

Stadsmuseet (Stockholm City Museum). Ryssgården, Slussen. ☎ 08/508-31-600. Admission 40 SEK ($4.40), free for children under 17. June–Aug, Tues–Wed and Fri–Sun 11am–5pm, Thurs 5–7pm; Sept–May, Tues–Wed and Fri–Sun 11am–5pm, Thurs 11am–9pm. T-bana: Slussen. Bus: 43 or 46.

Housed in a building dating from 1684, the Stadsmuseet depicts the history of Stockholm and its citizens. Various exhibits portray life in this industrial city throughout the past few centuries. Daily at 1pm, a 30-minute slide show is presented in English documenting Stockholm from the 16th century to the present.

ESPECIALLY FOR KIDS

The open-air park, Skansen (see above), on Djurgården, offers **Lill-Skansen,** the children's own "Little Skansen." There's a petting zoo with lots of child-friendly animals, including pigs, goats, and horses. Lill-Skansen offers a break from the dizzying (and often tantrum-inducing) excitement frequently generated by a commercial amusement park. A miniature train ride through the park is about as wild as it gets. Lill-Skansen is open daily in summer from 10:30am to 4pm.

Kids can spend a day or several at Skansen and not get bored. Before going to Skansen, stop off at the **Vasa Museum,** which many youngsters find an epic adventure. The evening can be capped by a visit to **Gröna Lunds Tivoli** (see "Stockholm After Dark," below), which also is on Djurgården.

A LITERARY LANDMARK

Strindbergsmuseet (Strindberg Museum). Drottninggatan 85. ☎ **08/411-53-54.** Admission 35 SEK ($3.85) adults, 25 SEK ($2.75) students, free for children. Tues noon–7pm (June–Aug 11am–4pm), Fri 11am–4pm, Sat–Sun noon–4pm. T-bana: Rådmansgatan.

This building, popularly known as "The Blue Tower," is where August Strindberg, the dramatist and novelist, spent his last 4 years (1908–12). It contains a library; three rooms with his furnishings; and books, articles, and letters representing the last 20 years of his life. The library is a typical working author's library, with fiction and non-fiction works, including encyclopedias in Swedish, German, English, and French. Many of the volumes are full of pen and pencil markings—comments on the contents, heavily marked deletions of points he did not approve of, and underlinings indicating his diligent research into matters that concerned him.

Of special interest to those familiar with Strindberg's plays is that he furnished his rooms like stage sets from his plays, with color schemes as he visualized them. The dining room contains sculptures, casts of busts, and masks evoking, for the writer, people and events that were important to him.

ARCHITECTURAL HIGHLIGHTS

In Stockholm, architects or architecture buffs often are captivated by such grand buildings as Drottningholm Palace and Riddarholm Church. But many of the expanding suburb "cities" of Stockholm also are worth seeing for their urban planning and architecture, which in Stockholm is among the most advanced in the world.

One of these model developments is **Farsta,** completed in 1960, although much altered since then. It lies 6 miles from the heart of Stockholm, and can be reached by the Farsta train departing from the Central Station, or by taking bus no. 18 to the end of the line. With its traffic-free shopping mall, bright and airy modern apartment houses, and contemporary stores and restaurants, this makes a pleasant afternoon tour.

Arkitektur Museet (Museum of Architecture). Skeppsholmen. ☎ **08/587-27-000.** Admission 60 SEK ($6.60) adults, 30 SEK ($3.30) students and seniors. Tues–Thurs 11am–8pm, Fri–Sun 11am–6pm; archive and library Tues 4–8pm, Wed–Fri noon–4pm. Bus: 65.

Founded in 1962 in a building created by the famous Spanish architect Rafael Moneo, this museum illustrates the art of architecture combined with social planning. The exhibition displays copies of rooms, buildings, places, and cities from different eras, covering 1,000 years of Swedish architecture. The history of the buildings is divided into chronologically arranged sections. The collection consists of some two million sketches, drawings, and documents, plus some half million photographs and approximately 1,000 architectural models. The library alone has some 25,000 volumes, most of which were donations from Swedish architects. The library is dedicated to the memory of Raoul Wallenberg, known for his humanitarian efforts in Hungary in 1944 and 1945. A lesser-known fact is that Wallenberg was a trained architect; his few existing drawings—mainly from his student days in the United States—are in the museum's archives.

Walking Tour 1: Gamla Stan (Old Town)

Start: Gustav Adolfs Torg.

Finish: Slussplan.

Time: 3 hours.

Best Times: Any day it's not raining.

Worst Times: Rush hours (Monday through Friday from 8 to 9:30am and 5:30 to 7pm).

Begin at:

1. **Gustav Adolfs Torg,** facing the Royal Palace, with the Royal Opera on your left. Gustavus III, patron of the arts, was assassinated here at a masked ball in 1792.

   Walk across Norrbro (North Bridge) heading toward the Royal Palace, passing on your right the:

2. **Swedish Parliament,** at Helgeandsholmen. The Parliament building dates from 1897, when its foundation stone was laid. It can be visited only on guided tours.

   Along the bridge on your left are stairs leading to the:

3. **Medeltidsmuseet** (Museum of Medieval Stockholm), Strömparterren, with objects and settings from medieval Stockholm, including the Riddarholmship and parts of the old city wall.

   ☕**TAKE A BREAK**   One of the hidden cafes of Stockholm, **Café Strömparterren,** Helgeandsholmen (☎ **08/21-95-45**), also is one of the most centrally located—just next door to the Medeltidsmuseet. Many Stockholmers come here for a morning cup of coffee and a stunning view of the waterfront. In summer, tables are placed outside; the interior of the cafe is built into the walls under Norrbro.

   After leaving the museum, turn to the right and walk back to the bridge until you come to Slottskajen. Here, directly in front of the Royal Palace, make a right turn and head to Mynttorget, site of the **Kanslihuset,** a government office building erected in the 1930s. The neoclassical, columned facade remains from the Royal Mint of 1790.

   Continue straight along Myntgatan until you reach Riddarhustorget. On your right is the:

4. **Riddarhuset,** the 17th-century House of Nobles, where the Swedish aristocracy met during the Parliament of the Four Estates (1665–68).

Continue straight across Riddarholmsbron (bridge) until you come to the little island of:

5. **Riddarholmen,** called "the island of the knights." It's closely linked to the Old Town; its chief landmark, which you'll see immediately, is the **Riddarholmskyrkan** (church) with its cast-iron spire. Founded as an abbey in the 13th century, it has been the burial place of Swedish kings for 4 centuries.

Walk along the right side of the church until you reach Birger Jarls Torg. From there, take the 1-block-long Wrangelska Backen to the water. Then go left and walk along Södra Riddarholmshamnen.

Veer left by the railroad tracks, climb some steps, and go along Hebbes Trappor until you return to Riddarholmskyrkan. From here, cross over Riddarholmsbron and return to Riddarhustorget.

Cross Stora Nygatan and take the next right onto Storkyrkobrinken, passing the landmark Cattelin Restaurant on your right. Continue along this street, past the Lady Hamilton Hotel, turning right onto Trångsund, which leads to:

6. **Stortorget** (Great Square), where you'll find park benches for resting. This plaza was the site of the Stockholm Blood Bath of 1520 when Christian II of Denmark beheaded 80 Swedish noblemen and displayed a "pyramid" of their heads in the square. The Börsen on this square is the Swedish Stock Exchange, a building dating from 1776. This is where the Swedish Academy meets every year to choose the Nobel Prize winners in literature.

At the northeast corner of the square, take Källargränd north to view the entrance to the:

7. **Royal Palace,** opening onto Slottsbacken. The present palace dates mainly from 1760 after a previous one was destroyed by fire. The changing of the guard takes place here on this square, which also is the site of the:

8. **Storkyrkan,** on your right. This church was founded in the mid-1200s but has been rebuilt many times since. It's the site of coronations and royal weddings; kings are also christened here. The most celebrated sculpture here is *St. George and the Dragon,* a huge work dating from 1489. The royal pews have been used for 3 centuries, and the altar, mainly in ebony and silver, dates from 1652. This is still a functioning church, so it's best to visit when services are not in progress. It's open Monday through Saturday from 9am to 7pm and on Sunday from 9am to 5:30pm; admission is free.

Continue right along Slottsbacken, either visiting the palace now or saving it for later. Go right as you reach Bollshusgränd, a cobblestone street of old houses leading to one of the most charming squares of the Old Town:

9. **Köpmantorget,** with its famous copy of the *St. George and the Dragon* statue. From the square, take Köpmanbrinken, which runs for 1 block before turning into:

10. **Österlånggatan,** once the Old Town's harbor street, and site of many restaurants and antiques shops. Continue along Österlånggatan, but take the first left under an arch, leading into:

11. **Stora Hoparegränd,** one of the darkest and narrowest of Gamla Stan streets. Some buildings along this dank street date from the mid-1600s. Walk down the alley toward the water, emerging at Skeppsbron (bridge). Turn right for 2 blocks until you reach Ferkens Gränd. Go right again up Ferkens Gränd until you return to Österlånggatan. Go left on Österlånggatan until you come to Tullgränd. Take the street on your right, Prästgatan, named after the priests who used to live here.

Walking Tour: Gamla Stan (Old Town)

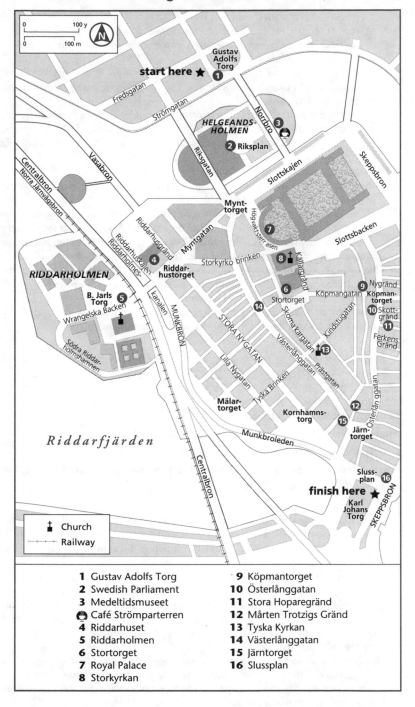

start here ★

finish here ★

✝ Church
┼┼┼┼ Railway

1 Gustav Adolfs Torg
2 Swedish Parliament
3 Medeltidsmuseet
☕ Café Strömparterren
4 Riddarhuset
5 Riddarholmen
6 Stortorget
7 Royal Palace
8 Storkyrkan

9 Köpmantorget
10 Österlånggatan
11 Stora Hoparegränd
12 Mårten Trotzigs Gränd
13 Tyska Kyrkan
14 Västerlånggatan
15 Järntorget
16 Slussplan

As you climb this street, note on your left:

12. **Mårten Trotzigs Gränd,** a street of steps that's the narrowest in Gamla Stan.

Continue along Prästgatan, passing a playground on your right. Turn right onto Tyska Brinken until you come to:

13. **Tyska Kyrkan** on your right. Since the beginning of the 17th century, this has been the German church of Stockholm. The church has a baroque interior and is exquisitely decorated.

After you leave the church, the street in front of you will be Skomakargatan. Head up this street until you come to Stortorget once again. From Stortorget, take a little street, Kåkbrinken, at the southwest corner of the square, until you reach:

14. **Västerlånggatan,** where you should turn left. This pedestrian street is the main shopping artery of Gamla Stan, and the best place to purchase gifts and souvenirs of Sweden. The street leads to:

15. **Järntorget,** which used to be known as Korntorget when it was the center of the copper and iron trade in the 16th and 17th centuries. At times in its long history it has been the place of punishment for "wrongdoers." The most unusual statue in Stockholm stands here—a **statue of Evert Taube,** the troubadour and Swedish national poet of the early 1900s. He's carrying a newspaper under his arm, his coat draped nonchalantly, his sunglasses pushed up high on his forehead.

From the square, take Järntorgsgatan to:

16. **Slussplan** and the water. Here you can catch a bus to return to the central city or you can board a ferry to Djurgården and its many museums.

Walking Tour 2: Along the Harbor

Start: Stadshuset.

Finish: Museum of Architecture.

Time: 3 hours.

Best Times: Any day it's not raining.

Worst Times: Rush hours (Monday through Friday from 8 to 9:30am and 5:30 to 7pm).

Start at the:

1. **Stadshuset** (Stockholm City Hall), Hantverkargatan 1, on Kungsholmen. This island has some of the loveliest and most varied waterfront walks in the city. It took 12 years, 8 million bricks, and 19 million gilded mosaic tiles to erect this city hall, which can be visited on a guided tour.

Go inside the courtyard on your own and admire the architecture. After exploring the building, exit and turn right, walking across Stadshusbron (City Hall Bridge) to Norrmalm. You'll see the Sheraton Hotel coming up on your left, and on your right is the Stadshuscafeet, where sightseeing boats depart on canal cruises in summer. Walk past the boats and go under an underpass (watch out for fast-riding bicyclists).

Continue along the canal until you reach Tegelbacken, a waterfront square. At the entrance to the Vasabron (bridge), cross the street and continue along Fredsgatan. Veer right at the intersection, hugging the canal. This will take you to Rosenbad, a little triangular park.

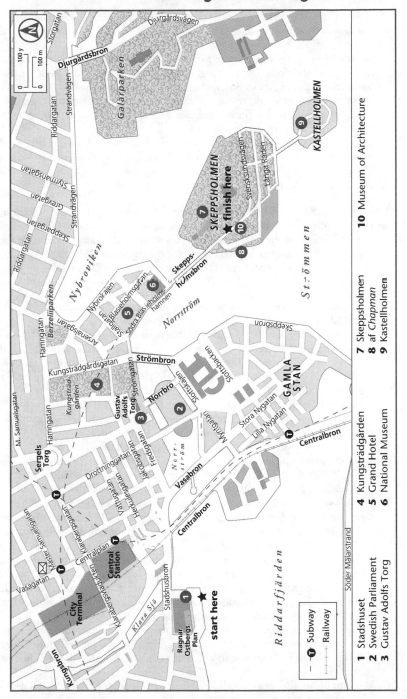

1 Stadshuset
2 Swedish Parliament
3 Gustav Adolfs Torg

4 Kungsträdgården
5 Grand Hotel
6 National Museum

7 Skeppsholmen
8 af *Chapman*
9 Kastellholmen

10 Museum of Architecture

At the canal-bordering Strömgatan, the building on your right will be the:

2. **Swedish Parliament,** which can be visited on a guided tour. Upon your arrival at:

3. **Gustav Adolfs Torg,** you'll have a panoramic view of the Royal Palace across the canal and of the Royal Opera straight ahead. This is one of the most famous landmark squares of Stockholm, and the most scenically located.

Strömgatan resumes at the corner of the Opera House, site of the Operakällaren, for many years the finest restaurant in Stockholm. Continue along until you reach the southern tier of the:

4. **Kungsträdgården,** which is the summer living room of Stockholm. These royal gardens reach from Hamngatan on the north side down to the water. Established in the 1500s as a pleasure garden for the court, now they are open to all, with cafes, open-air restaurants, and refreshment kiosks.

TAKE A BREAK Since the late 1800s, the **Café Victoria,** Kungsträdgården (☎ **08/10-10-85**), in the center of Stockholm, has attracted crowds. It's an ideal spot for a refreshing drink or snack at any time during the day or evening. It's open Monday through Saturday from 11:30am to 3am and on Sunday from noon to 11pm. (See "Stockholm After Dark," following, for more information.)

Continue along the waterfront, past Strömbron, a bridge leading to Gamla Stan, and emerge onto Södra Blasieholmshamnen, site of the:

5. **Grand Hotel,** at no. 8. For decades this has been the prestige address of Stockholm, attracting Nobel Prize winners as well as most visiting dignitaries and movie stars. On your right, any number of sightseeing boats depart in summer for tours of the Stockholm archipelago. From this vantage point, you'll have a good view of the Royal Palace and Gamla Stan.

Continue along this street until you reach (on your right) the:

6. **National Museum,** Södra Blasieholmshamnen, which is the repository of the state's art treasures—everything from Renoir to Rembrandt.

Cross the Skeppsholmsbron (bridge) leading to the little island of:

7. **Skeppsholmen,** which has a number of attractions (see "Gamla Stan & Neighboring Islands" under "The Top Attractions," above). After crossing the bridge, turn right along Västra Brobänken. On your right you'll pass the:

8. **af** *Chapman,* a "tall ship" with fully rigged masts that once sailed the seas under three different flags before being permanently anchored in 1949 as a youth hostel.

Turn left onto Flaggmansvägen. Continue along Holmamiralens Torg, passing the Nordiska Institute on your right. Cut right toward the water at Södra Brobänken. Take a right turn and cross the bridge leading to the small island of:

9. **Kastellholmen,** one of the most charming, but least visited, islands in Stockholm. Head right along the water, going around Kastellholmskajen. Circle around and turn left at the end of Kastelleton. Walk back along Örlogsvägen, which runs through the center of the small island.

Cross the Kastellholmsbron (bridge) and return to the larger island of Skeppsholmen. This time go straight along Amiralsvägen, turning left onto Långa Raden. Cut right and continue to walk along Långa Raden. The first building on your left is the:

10. **Museum of Architecture,** which has slides and thousands of architectural drawings and sketches from the last 100 years.

From this point at the end of the walking tour, you can catch bus 65 to take you back to the heart of Stockholm.

2 Organized Tours

CITY TOURS   The quickest and most convenient way to see the highlights of Stockholm is to take one of the bus tours that leave from Karl XII Torg, near the Kungsträdgården.

Stockholm Sightseeing, Skeppsbron 22 (☎ **08/587-140-20**), offers a variety of tours, mostly in summer. The 3-hour "Royal Stockholm" tour visits the Royal Palace or the Treasury and the Vasa Museum, with daily departures mid-April to mid-October from Gustav Adolfs Torg, by the Royal Opera House. They cost 240 SEK ($26.40). The quickest and least expensive tour—but also the most superficial—is the regular 1-hour "City Tour," for 130 SEK ($14.30). It leaves daily year-round from Gustav Adolfs Torg. "Under the Bridges" takes 2 hours and goes through two locks and two bodies of water. Departures are from Stromkajen (near the Grand Hotel), daily from mid-April through mid-September. The cost is 140 SEK ($15.40). "Sightseeing Anno 1935" is in an open-topped wooden boat, with a captain in period uniform. The tour explores the Stockholm harbor for 1 hour, and costs 110 SEK ($12.10). Daily departures, early July through mid-August, are from the statue of Gustavus III by the Royal Palace.

OLD TOWN STROLLS   Authorized guides lead 1½-hour walking tours of the medieval lanes of Stockholm's Old Town. These walks are conducted daily from the first of June until mid-August, departing from the Royal Opera House at Gustav Adolfs Torg. The cost is 75 SEK ($8.25). Tickets and times of departure are available from **Stockholm Sightseeing,** Skeppsbron 22 (☎ **08/587-140-20**).

CANAL CRUISES   **Stockholm Sightseeing** (☎ **08/587-140-20**) offers the "Royal Canal Tour," May through September, daily, every half hour on the hour. Tours cost 90 SEK ($9.90) for adults and 45 SEK ($4.95) for children. Visitors are ferried around the canals of Djurgården.

3 Spectator Sports

Soccer and **ice hockey** are the two most popular spectator sports in Sweden, and Stockholm is the home of world-class teams in both. The most important venue for any spectator sport in the capital, the **Stockholm Globe Arena** (Globen), lies less than 4 miles south of central Stockholm. Built in 1989, it's believed to be the biggest round building in the world, with a seating capacity of 16,000. It offers everything from political rallies, motorcycle competitions, and sales conventions to basketball games, tennis, ice hockey, and rock concerts. Its ticket office (☎ **08/600-34-00**) also sells tickets Monday through Friday from 9am to 4pm for most of Stockholm's soccer games, which are played in an open-air stadium nearby. The Globen complex lies in the suburb of Johnneshov (T-bana: Globen).

Another popular pastime is watching and betting on **trotting races.** These races usually take place on Wednesday at 6:30pm and on an occasional Saturday at 12:30pm in both summer and winter. (In winter an attempt is made to clear snow and ice from the racecourse; slippery conditions sometimes lead to unpredictable results.) Admission to **Solvalla Stadium** (☎ **08/635-90-00**), which lies about 4 miles north of the city center, is 20 SEK ($2.20). From Stockholm, take the bus marked SOLVALLA.

For schedules and ticket information, inquire at your hotel or the city's tourist office, or buy a copy of *Stockholm This Week* from a newspaper kiosk.

4 Active Pursuits

GOLF   For those who want to play golf at the "top of Europe," there is the **Bromma Golf Course,** Kvarnbacksvägen 303, 16874 Bromma (☎ **08/289-430**), lying 3 miles west of the center of Stockholm. It's a nine-hole golf course with well-maintained greens. Greens fees are 130 SEK ($14.30), and golf clubs can be rented.

HORSEBACK RIDING (VIKING STYLE)   Iceland horses—gentle and small—can be ridden at the **Haniwnge Iceland Horse Center** at Hemfosa, 23 miles south of Stockholm (☎ **08/500-481-81**), at a cost of 400 SEK ($44) per person for 2½ hours, including a picnic lunch. Aside from walking, galloping, trotting, and cantering, the horses have another gait, the *tölt,* a kind of equine speed walk that has no English translation.

SAUNA & SWIMMING   A combination sauna, outdoor heated pool, and children's paddling pool, **Vilda Vanadis** is at Vanadislunden (☎ **08/30-12-11**), near the northern terminus of Sveavägen, within easy walking distance of the Oden Hotel and the city center. This really is an adventure park, with a variety of attractions, as well as a sauna and a restaurant. The entrance fee is 60 SEK ($6.60), but once you're inside, the attractions are free. It's open from early May until the end of August, daily from 10am to 6pm.

TENNIS, SQUASH & WEIGHTLIFTING   Aside from tennis at the **Royal Tennis Hall,** Lidingövägen 75 (☎ **08/459-15-00** for reservations), you also can lift weights and enjoy a sauna and solarium. The center has 16 indoor courts, 5 outdoor clay courts, and 8 squash courts. Tennis courts cost 170 to 200 SEK ($18.70 to $22) per hour; squash courts, 70 to 95 SEK ($7.70 to $10.45) for a 30-minute session; the weight room entrance fee is 30 SEK ($3.30). The center is open Monday through Thursday from 7am to 11pm, Friday from 7am to 9pm, and Saturday and Sunday from 8am to 9pm.

5 Shopping

THE SHOPPING SCENE

Stockholm is filled with shop after shop of dazzling merchandise—often at dazzling prices that reflect the high esteem in which Swedish craftspeople are held.

Bargain shoppers should proceed with caution. There are some good buys, but it takes a lot of searching. If you're a casual shopper, you may want to confine your purchases to handsome souvenirs and gifts.

Swedish glass, of course, is world famous. Swedish wooden items are outstanding, and many people love Swedish functional furniture in blond pine or birch. Other items to look for include play suits for children, silver necklaces, reindeer gloves, stainless-steel utensils, hand-woven neckties and skirts, sweaters and mittens in Nordic patterns, Swedish clogs, and colorful handcrafts from the provinces. The most famous souvenir to buy is the Dala horse from Dalarna.

SHOPPING STREETS & DISTRICTS   Everybody's favorite shopping area in Stockholm is **Gamla Stan** (Old Town). Site of the Royal Palace, it even attracts such shoppers as the Queen. The main street for browsing is **Västerlånggatan.** Many antique stores are found here, but don't expect low prices.

In summer, **Skansen** is an interesting area to explore because many craftspeople display their goods here. There are gift shops (some selling "Skansen glass") as well as individuals who offer their handmade goods on temporary stands.

Avoiding Mr. Taxman

The value-added tax in Sweden, called MOMS, is imposed on all products and services, but you can avoid MOMS if you spend a total of at least 200 SEK ($22). Just give the store your name, address, and passport number and ask for a tax-free check. Don't unwrap your purchase until after you've left Sweden. The customs official will want to see both the tax-free check and your purchase; you'll be given a cash refund, minus a small commission, on the spot. If you're departing by plane, hold onto your luggage until after you've received your refund, and then you can pack your purchase in your bag and check it (or carry the purchase with you, if it's not too big). At the **Tourist Center,** Hamngatan 27 (☎ **08/789-24-95**), you can pick up a pamphlet about tax-free shopping in Sweden; additional information is available by calling ☎ **0410/613-01.** (For more information, see "Taxes" in "Fast Facts: Sweden," in chapter 2.)

In the **Sergels Torg** area, the main shopping street is **Hamngatan,** site of the famous shopping center Gallerian, at the corner of Hamngatan and Sergels Torg, and crossing the northern rim of Kungsträdgården at Sweden House. Big department stores, such as NK and Åhléns, are located nearby.

The **Kungsgatan** area is another major district for shopping, stretching from Hötorget to the intersection of Kungsgatan and Vasagatan. **Drottninggatan** is one long pedestrian mall, flanked with shops. Many side streets branching off from it also are filled with shops. Hötorget, home to the PUB department store, is another major shopping district.

SHOPPING HOURS Stockholm shops are open Monday through Friday from 10am to 6pm and on Saturday from 10am to somewhere between 1 and 4pm. Once a week, usually on Monday or Friday, some of the larger stores are open from 9:30am to 7pm (during July and August, to 6pm).

SHOPPING A TO Z
ART GALLERIES
Gallerie Nordenhake. 12 Fredsgatan. ☎ **08/211-892.** T-bana: T-centralen.

This prestigious, high-profile art gallery may remind you of a spare loft in New York's meat-packing district. Pale Nordic light streams into some of the display areas from arched, 19th-century windows, flooding the minimalist displays with light.

AN AUCTION
Stockholms Auktionsverket (Stockholm Auction Chambers). In Gallerian, Hamngatan 37. ☎ **08/453-67-00.** T-bana: Kungsträdgården.

The oldest auction company in the world (dating from 1674), this auction house now is centrally located in the Gallerian mall, just up Hamngatan from Sweden House. Auctions are held 3 days per week from noon to "whenever," and you're allowed two viewings: on Friday from 11am to 5pm and on Saturday from 10am to 4pm. It's estimated that some 150,000 lots per year are auctioned off here with the pound of a gavel—everything from ceramics to Picassos.

BOOKS & MAPS
Akademibokhandeln. Mäster Samuelsgatan 32. ☎ **08/613-61-00.** T-bana: Hötorget.

The biggest bookstore in Sweden, this outlet has more than 100,000 titles. A wide range of fiction and nonfiction in English is available. Many travel-related materials, such as maps, also are sold.

Sverige Bokhandeln (Sweden Bookshop). Sweden House (Sverige-Huset). Kungsträdgården. ☎ **08/789-21-31.** T-bana: Kungsträdgården.

Whatever is available in English about Sweden can be found at this bookstore in Sweden House on the second floor (above the tourist center). The store has many rare items for sale, including records of Swedish music.

CERAMICS

Blås & Knåda. Hornsgatan 26. ☎ **08/642-77-67.** T-bana: Slussen.

This store sells the best products made by members of a cooperative of 50 Swedish ceramic artists and glassmakers.

Keramiskt Centrum Gustavsberg. Värmdö Island. ☎ **08/570-356-58.** Bus: 422 or 440.

Bone china, stoneware dinner services, and other fine table and decorative ware are made at the Gustavsberg Ceramics Center, on Värmdö Island, about 13 miles east of Stockholm. A museum at the center displays historic pieces such as Parian (a kind of plaster of paris or porcelain) statues based on the work of the famous Danish sculptor Torvaldsen and other artists, hand-painted vases, Toby jugs, majolica, and willow ware. There also are examples of Pyro (the first ovenware produced), dinner services made for royalty, and sculptures by modern artists.

Year-round, visitors to the center can watch potters at work and see artists handpainting designs. You can even decorate a mug or plate yourself if you wish. There's a shop at the center where you can purchase Gustavsberg ware, including seconds.

DEPARTMENT STORES

Åhléns City. Klarabergsgatan 50. ☎ **08/676-60-00.** T-bana: Centralen.

This department store, the largest in Sweden, has a gift shop, a restaurant, and a renowned food department. Also seek out the fine collection of home textiles and both Orrefors and Kosta Boda crystal ware. The pewter with genuine Swedish ornaments makes a fine gift item.

Nordiska Kompaniet (NK). Hamngatan 18–20. ☎ **08/762-80-00.** T-bana: Kungsträdgården.

NK has been a high-quality department store since 1902. Most of the big names in Swedish glass are displayed at NK, including Orrefors and Kosta. Thousands of Swedish handcrafted items can be found in the basement. Stainless steel, also a good buy in Sweden, is ubiquitous. Nordiska Kompaniet is open Monday through Friday from 10am to 7pm, Saturday from 10am to 5pm, and Sunday from noon to 5pm.

PUB. Hötorget 13. ☎ **08/23-99-15.** T-bana: Hötorget.

Greta Garbo once worked here in the millinery department. Today it's one of the most popular department stores in Stockholm; the boutiques and departments sell midrange clothing and good-quality housewares without the international designer names of the more prestigious (and more expensive) NK. Massive and bustling, with an emphasis on traditional and conservative Swedish clothing, it offers virtually anything you'd need to stock a Scandinavian home. There's also a restaurant on the premises.

A FLEA MARKET

Loppmarknaden i Skärholmen (Skärholmen Shopping Center). Skärholmen. ☎ **08/710-00-60.** Bus: 13 or 23 to Skärholmen, a 20-minute ride.

At the biggest flea market in northern Europe, you might find a pleasing item that came from an attic in Värmland. Indeed you might find anything. Try to go on

Saturday or Sunday (the earlier the better) when the market is at its peak. Admission is 10 SEK ($1.30) for adults, free for children.

GEMS & MINERALS

Geocity. Tysta Marigången 5, Tegélbacken. ☎ **08/411-11-40.** T-bana: Centralen.

Geocity offers exotic mineral crystals, jewelry, Scandinavian gems, Baltic amber, and lapidary equipment. The staff includes two certified gemologists who will cut and set any gem you select and also appraise jewelry you already own. The inventory includes stones from Scandinavia and around the world.

GIFTS & SOUVENIRS

Slottsbodarna (Royal Gift Shop). In the south wing of the Royal Palace, Slottsbacken. ☎ **08/402-61-48.** T-bana: Gamla Stan.

This unusual outlet sells products related to or copied from the collections in the Royal Palace. Items are re-created in silver, gold, brass, pewter, textiles, and glass. Every item is made in Sweden.

GLASS & CRYSTAL

Rosenthal Studio-Haus. Birger Jarlsgatan 6. ☎ **08/611-66-01.** T-bana: Östermalmstorg.

This is the largest outlet in Sweden for the delicate German-made porcelain of Rosenthal. Inside, you'll find mostly modern patterns of crystal, porcelain, glass, and upscale stainless steel.

✪ **Svenskt Glas.** Karlavägen 61. ☎ **08/679-79-09.** T-bana: Östermalmstorg.

Royal families patronize this establishment, but Swedish-made glass at every price level is featured. Orrefors and Kosta Boda glass are displayed here in stemware, candlesticks, flower-shaped bowls in full lead crystal, bar sets, vases, wine glasses, pitchers, and perfume bottles. Worldwide shipping is available.

HANDCRAFTS & GIFTS

Brinken Konsthantverk. Storkyrkobrinken 1. ☎ **08/411-59-54.** T-bana: Gamla Stan.

On the lower floor of a building near the Royal Palace in the Old Town, this rather elegant purveyor of gift items will ship handcrafted brass, pewter, wrought iron, or crystal anywhere in the world. About 95% of the articles sold are made in Scandinavia.

✪ **DesignTorget.** In the Kulturhuset, Sergels Torg 3. ☎ **08/508-31-400.** T-bana: Centralen.

In 1994, faced with a decreasing number of visitors to its rather impersonal, bureaucratic-looking premises, the government-owned **Kulturhuset** (Swedish Culture House) invited one of Stockholm's most influential designers and decorators, Jerry Hellsrtöm, to organize an avant-garde art gallery (Swedes modestly refer to it as a "shop"). Set within a large room in Kulturhuset's cellar, you'll find a display of handcrafts created by between 150 and 200 craftspeople whose work must be approved by a jury of connoisseurs before being offered for sale to the public. The merchandise includes some of the best pottery, furniture, textiles, clothing, pewter, and crystal in Sweden, at prices that range from 20 to 20,000 SEK ($2.55 to $2,560) per object. The most expensive object in the gallery at the time of this writing was a magnificently proportioned bathtub assembled from glued and laminated strips of wood in a style you might have expected in a boatyard, and then polyurethaned to a high-gloss sheen. Almost as impressive were a series of ergonomically designed computer workstations. The organization maintains a second branch in southern Stockholm, **Design Torget Mode,** Götgatan 31 (☎ **08/462-35-20**), that stocks furniture and a wider inventory of clothing for men, women, and children, with less emphasis on ceramics and handcrafts.

Duka. Kungsgatan 41. ☎ **08/20-60-41.** T-bana: Hötorget.

A large selection of crystal, porcelain, and gifts is available in this shop near the Konserthuset (Concert Hall). It offers tax-free shopping and shipping.

Gunnarssons Träfigurer. Drottninggatan 77. ☎ **08/21-67-17.** T-bana: Rådmansgatan.

One of the city's most interesting collections of Swedish carved wooden figures includes World War II figures such as Winston Churchill, and most of the U.S. presidents. All the figures are carved by Urban Gunnarsson, a second-generation master carver. The figures also include a host of mythical and historical European personalities.

Konsthantverkarna. Mäster Samuelsgaten 2. ☎ **08/611-96-60.** T-bana: Östermalmstorg.

Created by a group of artisans, this store has an unusual selection of some of the best Swedish handcrafts, all of which have passed scrutiny by a strict jury before they're offered for sale. Choose from glass, sculpture, ceramics, wall textiles, clothes, jewelry, silver, brass, and wood and leather work. Each item is handmade and original. Ask about the tax-free service.

Svensk Hemslojd (Society for Swedish Handcrafts). Sveavägen 44. ☎ **08/23-21-15.** T-bana: Hötorget.

Svensk Hemslojd offers a wide selection of glass, pottery, gifts, and wooden and metal handcrafts—the work of some of Sweden's best artisans. You'll also be shown a display of hand-woven carpets, upholstery fabrics, hand-painted materials, tapestries, lace, and embroidered items. You also can find beautiful yarns for weaving and embroidery.

HOME FURNISHINGS

Nordiska Galleriet. Nybrogatan 11. ☎ **08/442-83-60.** T-bana: Östermalmstorg.

This store features the finest in European furniture design, including the best from Scandinavian countries. Situated on two floors are the latest designs in contemporary furniture. The store can arrange shipment for any of your purchases.

✪ **Svenskt Tenn.** Strandvägen 5. ☎ **08/670-16-00.** T-bana: Östermalmstorg.

Along "embassy row," Swedish Pewter (its English name) has, since 1924, been the most prominent store in Sweden for home furnishings. In spite of its name, pewter is no longer king, and the shop now sells the best selection of home furnishings in Scandinavia—furniture, printed textiles, lamps, glassware, china, and gifts. The inventory is stylish, and although there aren't a lot of bargains, it's an excellent place to see the newest trends in Scandinavian design. It carries an exclusive collection of Josef Frank's hand-printed designs on linen and cotton. For your convenience, it will pack, insure, and ship your purchases to anywhere in the world.

LINENS ✗

Solgården. Karlavägen 58. ☎ **08/663-9360.** T-bana: Rådmansgatan.

For the dwindling few who really care about luxury linens and elegant lace and embroideries, this shop is the finest of its kind in Scandinavia. It was conceived by its owner, Marianne von Kantzow Ridderstad, as a tribute to Gustav III, the king who is said to have launched the neoclassical style in Sweden. Ridderstad designed her shop like a country house with rough-hewn wood and whimsical furnishings. Each of her linens is virtually a work of art. The tablecloths are heirloom pieces, and the work is cherished for its originality as much as its loveliness.

A Market

Östermalms Saluhall. Nybrogatan 31. No central phone. T-bana: Östermalmstorg.

This is one of the most colorful indoor markets anywhere in Scandinavia and features cheese, meat, vegetable, and fish merchants who supply food for much of the area. You may want to have a snack or a meal at one of the restaurants here.

Shopping Malls

Gallerian Arcade. Hamngatan 37. No central phone. T-bana: Kungsträdgården.

A short walk from Sweden House at Kunådgården, this modern two-story shopping complex is, to many, the best place in Sweden to go shopping. Merchandise in most of the individually managed stores is designed to appeal to local shoppers, not the tourist market, although in summer that changes a bit as more souvenir and gift items appear.

○ **Sturegallerian.** Stureplan. ☎ **08/611-46-06.** T-bana: Östermalmstorg.

In 1990, a year after this mall opened in the center of Stockholm, it was proclaimed "Shopping Center of the Year in Europe" by the International Council of Shopping Centers. Store after store (about 50, all told) displays a dazzling array of merchandise, both foreign and domestic. The merchandise changes seasonally, with summer seeing more displays of Swedish souvenirs and gift items. There are various restaurants and cafes here, too.

Textiles

Handarbetets Vänner. Djurgårdsslatten 82–84. ☎ **08/667-10-26.** Bus: 47.

This is one of the oldest and most prestigious textile houses in Stockholm, with art weaving and embroidery items also sold.

JOBS. Stora Nygatan 19. ☎ **08/20-98-16.** T-bana: Gamla Stan.

Hand-painted fabrics from the JOBS family workshops in Dalarna are sought out for their quality and the beauty of their design. Patterns are inspired by the all-too-short Swedish summer and by rural traditions. If you plan to be in Dalarna, you may enjoy visiting the **JOBS factory** in Leksand, at Västanvik 201 (☎ **0247/122-22**). Other items available here include tablecloths, handbags, and children's clothing.

Toys

Bulleribock (Toys). Sveavägen 104. ☎ **08/673-61-21.** T-bana: Rådmansgatan.

Since it opened in the 1960s, this store has made it a point to carry only traditional (non-computerized) toys made of wood, metal, or paper (no plastics of any kind). There are no commando-tactic war games that pacifist parents find objectionable. Many of these toys are undeniably charming, and suitable for children from newborns up to age 10. "As many as possible" are made in Sweden, with wood from Swedish forests.

6 Stockholm After Dark

Djurgården remains the favorite spot for both indoor and outdoor events on a summer evening. Although the more sophisticated may find it corny, this is your best early evening bet. Afterward, you can make the rounds of jazz and disco clubs, some of which stay open until 3 or 4 in the morning.

Pick up a copy of *Stockholm This Week,* distributed at the Tourist Center at Sweden House (see chapter 3) to see what's on. To buy tickets to theater, music, and other cultural events in Stockholm before you leave home, contact **Globaltickets** (www.globaltickets.com). They have member offices around the world, including the U.S. and Canada (☎ **800/223-6108**), England (☎ **207/734-4555**), Australia (☎ **2/9327-7599**), New Zealand (☎ **09/525-2360**), and Denmark (☎ **7010-2014**).

THE PERFORMING ARTS

All the major opera, theater, and concert seasons begin in the fall, except for special summer festival performances. Fortunately, most of the major opera and theatrical performances are funded by the state, which keeps ticket prices reasonable.

CONCERT HALLS

Berwaldhallen (Berwald Concert Hall). Strandvägen 69. ☎ **08/784-18-00.** Tickets 50–355 SEK ($5.50–$39.05). T-bana: Karaplan.

This hexagonal concert hall is Swedish Radio's big music studio. The Radio Symphonic Orchestra performs here, and there are other musical programs as well, such as lieder and chamber music recitals. The hall has excellent acoustics. The box office is open Monday through Friday from 11am to 6pm and always 2 hours before a concert.

☉ Filharmonikerna i Konserthuset (Concert Hall). Hötorget 8. ☎ **08/10-21-10** or 08/457-02-11. Tickets 110–200 SEK ($12.10–$22). T-bana: Hötorget.

Home of the Stockholm Philharmonic Orchestra, this is the principal place to hear classical music in Sweden. The Nobel Prizes also are awarded here. Originally constructed in 1920, the building houses two concert halls—one, seating 1,600, better suited for major orchestras; the other, seating 450, suitable for chamber music groups. Aside from local orchestras, the hall features visiting ensembles, such as the Chicago Symphony Orchestra. Some series are entirely sold out in advance to subscription ticket holders; others are less heavily attended and visitors can get tickets easily. Sales begin 2 weeks before a concert and continue up until the concert begins. Concerts usually start at 7:30pm, although occasionally a lunchtime or "happy hour" concert may be scheduled for either noon or 5:30pm. The box office is open Monday through Friday from 10am to 6pm and Saturday from 10am to 1pm. The concert hall is closed in July and early August, but if you miss your usual roster of classical music, most of the organization's performances are broadcast regularly on Stockholm's main classical music station, 107.5 FM.

OPERA & BALLET

☉ Drottningholms Slottsteater. Drottningholm. ☎ **08/660-82-25.** Tickets 150–545 SEK ($16.50–$59.95). T-bana: Brommaplan, then transfer to bus no. 301 or 323; or take the boat that departs from the City Hall in Stockholm.

Founded by Gustavus III in 1766, this unique theater is on an island in Lake Mälaren, 7 miles from Stockholm. It stages operas and ballets with full 18th-century regalia, complete with period costumes and wigs. Its machinery and some 30 or more complete theater sets are still intact and used today. The theater, a short walk from the royal residence, seats only 450, which makes it difficult to get tickets. The season is May through September, and most performances begin at 7:30pm, lasting 2½ to 4 hours. To order tickets in advance, phone the number above and give your American Express card number (only American Express is accepted).

☉ Operan (Opera House). Gustav Adolfs Torg. ☎ **08/24-82-40.** Tickets 100–400 SEK ($11–$44); discounts of 10% to 30% for seniors and students. T-bana: Kungsträdgården.

Founded in 1773 by Gustavus III (who later was assassinated here at a masked ball), the Opera House is the home of the Royal Swedish Opera and the Royal Swedish

Ballet. The present building dates from 1898. Performances are traditionally given Monday through Saturday at 7:30pm (closed mid-June through August). The box office is open Monday through Friday from noon to 7:30pm (closes at 6pm if no performance is scheduled) and Saturday from noon to 3pm.

THEATER

At most theaters, the season begins in mid-August and lasts until mid-June.

Kungliga Dramatiska Teatern (Royal Dramatic Theater). Nybroplan. ☎ **08/ 667-06-80.** Tickets 100–300 SEK ($11–$33); student discounts available; Sun tickets reduced for seniors. T-bana: Östermalmstorg.

This is where Greta Garbo got her start in acting and where Ingmar Bergman stages two productions a year. The theater presents the latest experimental plays and the classics, but in Swedish only. The theater is open all year (with a slight slowdown in July), and performances are scheduled Tuesday through Saturday at 7pm and on Sunday at 4pm. The box office is open Monday through Saturday from 10am to 6pm.

Oscars Teatern. Kungsgatan 63. ☎ **08/20-50-00.** Tickets 240–375 SEK ($26.40–$41.25). T-bana: Hötorget.

Oscars is the flagship of Stockholm's musical entertainment world—the home of classic operetta and musical theater since the turn of the century. Known for its extravagant staging of traditional operettas, it was one of the first theaters in Europe to produce such hits as *A Chorus Line* in Swedish. The box office is open Monday to Saturday from 9am to 5pm.

Regina Theater. Drottninggatan 71A. ☎ **081/411-63-20.** Tickets 185–395 SEK ($20.35–$43.45). T-bana: Hötorget.

This is the only permanent English-language theater in Sweden, although its yearly repertoire is not always in English—you'll have to check to see what's playing at the time of your visit. Originally built in 1911 as a cinema, the building was converted for drama in 1960. The Regina Theater Company, established in 1980, presents everything from Victorian thrillers to Dickensian Christmas musicals. Its London-style theater pub is unique in Sweden. Open Tuesday through Saturday from noon to 8pm. American Express cardholders can reserve by phone.

LOCAL CULTURAL ENTERTAINMENT

Skansen. Djurgården 49–51. ☎ **08/442-80-00.** Admission 30–60 SEK ($3.30–$6.60) adults, 10 SEK ($1.10) children 6–15, free for children 5 and under. Bus: 44 or 47. Ferry from Nybroplan.

Skansen arranges traditional seasonal festivities, various special events, autumn market days, and a Christmas Fair. In summer there are concerts, singalongs, and guest performances. Folk dancing performances are staged from June through August, Monday through Saturday at 7pm and again on Sunday at 2:30 and 4pm. From June to August, dance performances are held outdoors with live music Monday through Friday from 8:30 to 11:30pm.

AN AMUSEMENT PARK

Gröna Lunds Tivoli. Djurgården. ☎ **08/587-501-00.** Admission 45 SEK ($4.95) adults, free for children 12 and under. Bus: 44 or 47. Djurgården ferry from Nybroplan.

Unlike its Copenhagen namesake, this is an amusement park, not a fantasyland. One of the big thrills of Tivoli is to go up to the revolving tower for an after-dark view of Stockholm.

The Capital of Gay Scandinavia

Copenhagen thrived for many years as a refreshingly raunchy city with few inhibitions and fewer restrictions on alternative sexuality. But beginning in the mid-1990s, Stockholm—Copenhagen's more imperial and, in many ways, more staid competitor—witnessed an eruption of new gay bars, discos, and roaming nightclubs that made the legendary permissiveness of the Danes look a bit weak in the knees. Today, thanks partly to a huge influence on Stockholm from the ever-so-jaded gay subcultures of London, no other city in Scandinavia offers gay-friendly nightlife options that are as broad and diverse as Stockholm's.

Some of the new crop of gay bars and clubs maintain hours and addresses that remain constant throughout the week. Others are roving parties whose addresses change constantly. The widely acknowledged king of the gay underground is Swedish-born entrepreneur Ulrik Bermsio, who has been compared to the legendary Steve Rubell, impresario behind New York's once-majestic Studio 54. His entertainment venues, as well as those promoted by his competitors, appear regularly in the Swedish- and English-language gay magazine *QX*, which is widely available at news kiosks throughout Stockholm. Alternatively, before your trip, you can check out its Web site at **www.qx.se**, which lists the various late-night gay venues in Stockholm. Also, don't overlook **www.rfsl.se**, maintained by RFSL, an organization devoted to equal rights for gays within Sweden. Its Web site will tell you even more about the who, what, where, and how of gay nightlife in Stockholm.

One of our favorite places is **The Disco,** Torsgatan 1 (☎ 08/22-51-70; T-bana: Centralen), which, along with its attractively permissive restaurant, Las Vegas, is open every Wednesday, Friday, and Saturday at 7pm, with the music finally shutting down at 3am. Unless you opt to dine here before your dance fest, you'll pay an entrance fee of 60 SEK ($6.60). It seems like a high-energy gay disco in New York or Los Angeles; Fridays are the best nights.

Looking for a basic bar peopled with regular guys who happen to be gay? Consider slugging back a round or two at **Sidetrack,** Wollmar Yxkullsgatan 7 (☎ 08/641-1688; T-bana: Mariatorget), sort of a Swedish version of a bar and lounge at your local bowling alley where everyone happens to be into same-sex encounters. Small and deliberately not trendy, it was named after its founder's favorite gay bar in Chicago. It's open every night from 6pm to 1am; Tuesdays here seem to be something of an institution, but other nights are fine, as well.

The park is open from the end of April to August daily, usually from noon to 11pm or midnight, but you'll have to call for exact hours, as they're subject to weekly changes.

THE CLUB & MUSIC SCENE
NIGHTCLUBS/CABARET

✪ **Café Opera.** Operahauset, Kungsträdgården. ☎ **08/676-58-07.** Cover 80 SEK ($8.80) after 10pm. T-bana: Kungsträdgården.

The cafe—Swedish beaux arts at its best—functions as a bistro, brasserie, and tearoom during the day and as one of the most crowded nightclubs in Stockholm in the evening. Visitors have the best chance of getting in around noon when a daily special lunch is offered for 120 SEK ($13.20). This establishment is not to be confused with the opera's main, and far more expensive, dining room, the Operakällaren, whose

Are you looking for a Viking, or Viking wannabe, in leather? Head for **SLM** (**"Scandinavian Leather Men"**), Wollmar Yxkullsgatan 18 (☎ **08/643-3100;** T-bana: Mariatorget). Technically, this is a private club, but if you look hot, wear just a hint (or even a lot) of cowhide, rawhide, or whatever, or if you just happen to have spent the last 6 months felling timber in Montana, you stand a very good chance of getting in. Wednesday and Friday, from 10pm to 2am, the place is Stockholm's premier leather bar, with lots of manly men on the street level and a handful of toys and restrictive accoutrements in the cellar-level dungeon. On Saturday, from 10pm to 2am, there's a DJ spinning highly danceable music. It's closed the other days of the week.

If you need a caffeine fix and a slice of chocolate cake before all that leather and latex, you may want to drop into Stockholm's most appealing, best-managed gay cafe, **Chokladkoppen,** Stortorget (☎ **08/203170;** T-bana: Gamla Stan). Open daily from 11am to 11pm, it specializes in sandwiches, pastries, and all manner of chocolate confections. The pastries are gorgeous, the staff is charming, and the clientele is more gay than not.

There are gay parties that are held only on specific nights of the week, and which often change locations. Examples include **Häcktet ("The Jail"),** Hornsgatan 82 (no phone; T-bana: Mariatorget). Most of the week, the clientele is straight, but every Wednesday and Friday, from 7pm till around 1am, the place becomes definitely gay, with a heavy percentage of lesbians. Disco music energizes a too-small dance floor; otherwise, people just drink. There's no cover charge. In summer, a barbecue pit does an active business in an outside courtyard.

Then, there's **Patricia,** Stadsgårdskajen 152 (☎ **08/743-0570;** T-bana: Slussen), a site that's straight most of the week, and avowedly gay every Sunday between 7pm and 5am. Sprawling and labyrinthine, with three bars and a good sound system, it attracts gay folk of all walks of life and income levels. It's most crowded on Sundays during the summer months; much less so during winter. There's a restaurant on the premises as well.

Lesbians appreciate the freedom afforded by a roving party held at a series of rented catering halls throughout Stockholm. **The Bitch Girl Club** takes place on the second Saturday of every month. The usual admission price is 75 SEK ($8.25). For information, consult *QX* magazine or either of the Web sites mentioned above.

entrance is through a different door. Near the entrance of the cafe is a stairway leading to one of the Opera House's most beautiful corners, the clublike Operabaren (Opera Bar), which is likely to be as crowded as the cafe. It's a monumental but historically charming place to have a drink; beer costs 53 SEK ($5.85). After 10pm there is less emphasis on food and more on disco activities. Open Monday to Saturday from 11:30am to 3am and Sunday from 1pm to 3am. At night, long lines of patrons form outside waiting to get in.

DANCE CLUBS/DISCOS

The Daily News. In Sverigehuset, at Kungsträdgården. ☎ **08/21-56-55.** Cover 60–90 SEK ($6.60–$9.90), depending on the night. T-bana: Kungsträdgården.

This is one of the capital's most enduring entertainment emporiums, a place that has flourished despite dozens of venue changes over the years. Currently there's a disco and a pub in the cellar, a somewhat smaller dance floor and a bar on the street level, and a street-level restaurant serving platters of Swedish and international food. On weekends there's sometimes a line outside as patrons wait to enter a setting where dancing, drinking, and eating all flow into one high-energy labyrinth. Platters of food begin at around 70 SEK ($7.70); full dinners, at around 200 SEK ($22). Beer costs 38 to 42 SEK ($4.20 to $4.60). The place is open every night from 11pm to between 4 and 5am, depending on business.

Göta Källare. In the Medborgplatsen subway station, Södermalm. ☎ **08/642-08-28.** Cover 70 SEK ($7.70) before 9:30pm; 90 SEK ($9.90) after 9:30pm. T-bana: Medborgplatsen.

This is the largest and most successful supper club–style dance hall in Stockholm, with a long list of clients who have met here and subsequently fallen in love and gotten married. Large, echoing, and paneled with lots of wood in a pseudo-Spanish style, it has a large terrace that surrounds an enormous tree and a restaurant that serves platters of food priced at 80 to 200 SEK ($8.80 to $22) each. Menu items include tournedos, fish, chicken, and veal. Expect an ambience similar to the old days at Roseland in New York City, a crowd aged 45 and older, and music from a live orchestra every night that performs *Strangers in the Night* a bit too frequently. The place is open every night from 8:30pm.

ROCK/JAZZ CLUBS

Fasching. Kungsgatan 63. ☎ **08/21-62-67.** Cover 90–200 SEK ($9.90–$22), depending on the act that's presented. T-bana: Centralen.

This is the premier venue in Sweden for the presentation of live jazz, with a roster of artists who have appeared here that reads like a who's who of the entertainment industry. It originated around the turn of the century as a cafe that served drinks to patrons of a nearby theater, but today its smoke-filled premises rocks and rolls with a crowd that's a lot less sedate than it was in the old days. Monday through Thursday, doors open at 6pm, with the main act beginning at 8pm. Friday and Saturday, doors open at 8pm, with the main act beginning at 9pm. On Friday and Saturday between midnight and 4am, the site is transformed into a salsa or soul club, depending on the whim of the management. Patrons already in the club don't pay any extra cover charge; those straggling in after midnight are charged 60 SEK ($6.60) each. An on-site restaurant will serve meals with main courses priced at around 100 SEK ($11) each.

Hard Rock Café. Sveavägen 75. ☎ **08/16-03-50.** No cover.

The Swedish branch of this chain is fun and gregarious. Sometimes an American, British, or Scandinavian rock 'n' roll band presents a live concert; otherwise it's a rock blast on the sound system. Club sandwiches, hamburgers, T-bone steaks, and barbecued spareribs are available. Burgers cost 95 SEK ($10.45), steaks are 150 to 192 SEK ($16.50 to $21.10), and a beer goes for 39 SEK ($4.30). Open Sunday through Thursday from 11am to 1am and Friday and Saturday from 11am to 3am.

Pub Engelen/Nightclub Kolingen. Kornhamnstorg 59B. ☎ **08/20-10-92.** No cover before 8pm, 40–60 SEK ($4.40–$6.60) after 9pm. T-bana: Gamla Stan.

Located in Gamla Stan, this three-in-one combination consists of the Engelen Pub, the Restaurant Engelen, and the Nightclub Kolingen in the cellar. The restaurant, which serves some of the best steaks in town, is open Sunday through Thursday from 5 to 11:30pm and Friday and Saturday from 5pm to 1:30am, with plates priced at 80 to 198 SEK ($8.80 to $21.80). Live performances, mostly Swedish groups, are offered in the pub daily from 8:30pm to midnight—usually soul, funk, and rock. The pub is open Tuesday through Thursday from 4pm to 1am, Friday and Saturday from 4pm to

2am, and Sunday from 5pm to 1am. Beer begins at 34 SEK ($3.75), and items on the bar menu range from 30 to 70 SEK ($3.30 to $7.70). In the cellar (which dates from the 15th century), the Nightclub Kolingen is a disco nightly from 10pm to about 3am. It charges the same prices for food and drink as the pub, and you must be at least 23 to enter.

Stampen. Stora Nygatan 5. ☎ **08/20-57-93.** Cover 100 SEK ($11). T-bana: Gamla Stan.

This fun-loving pub attracts crowds of jazz lovers in their thirties and forties. Guests crowd in to enjoy live Dixieland, New Orleans, mainstream, and swing music from the 1920s, 1930s, and 1940s. On Tuesday it's rock 'n' roll from the 1950s and 1960s. A menagerie of stuffed animals and lots of old, whimsical antiques are suspended from the high ceiling. It's open Monday to Wednesday from 8pm to 1am, and Thursday to Saturday from 8pm to 2am. In summer, an outdoor veranda also is open during regular hours when the weather permits. The club has two stages, offering dancing downstairs almost every night.

THE BAR SCENE

Akvarium. Kungsträdgården. ☎ **08/100-626.** No cover. T-bana: Kungsträdgården.

Most of the business at this hip, bustling place comes from its restaurant. But even if you don't want to dine, you can still enjoy its bar, which has a social energy and life of its own. The crowd tends to be attractive and hip. American-style drinks are popular here. The bar is open daily from 11:30am to midnight.

Cadier Bar. In the Grand Hotel, Södra Blasieholmshamnen 8. ☎ **08/679-35-00.** T-bana: Kungsträdgården.

Named after the original builder of this deluxe hotel—one of the most famous in Europe—the bar permits a view of the harbor and the Royal Palace. It's one of the most sophisticated places for a rendezvous in Stockholm. You also can enjoy light meals—open-faced sandwiches and smoked salmon—at any time of the day in the extension overlooking the waterfront. Drinks run 96 to 120 SEK ($10.55 to $13.20); imported beer is 45 SEK ($4.95). Open Monday through Saturday from noon to 2am and Sunday from noon to 12:30am; a piano player performs Monday through Saturday from 9:30pm to 1:30am.

Café Victoria. Kungsträdgården. ☎ **08/10-10-85.** T-bana: Kungsträdgården.

This place, the most central cafe in Stockholm, becomes crowded after 9pm in winter (7pm in summer) because it attracts a varied crowd. Many people come here just to drink; but if you're hungry, you can have lunch or dinner in an interior section beyond the lively bar area. Light snacks cost 80 to 130 SEK ($8.80 to $14.30), with main dishes priced at 120 to 230 SEK ($13.20 to $25.30). A bottle of beer will set you back 46 SEK ($5.05). Open Monday through Saturday from noon to 3am, and Sunday from 1pm to 3am.

Gondolen. Stadsgården 13. ☎ **08/641-70-90.** T-bana: Slussen.

You might come here for the engineering triumph this place represents as much as you do for the view. Part of it is suspended beneath a pedestrian footbridge that soars 11 stories above the narrow channel that separates the island of Gamla Stan from the island of Södermalm, about a mile south of City Hall. The structure you'll see today was built in 1935. At that time, what had been a steam-powered elevator was converted into a more modern, electric device. Today, the bar maintains its own elevator, which hauls customers (without charge) from its lowest point, at 13 Stadsgården, up the equivalent of 11 stories to the restaurant above. Within a decor entirely based on the most sophisticated styles of the 1940s, you'll admire a view that encompasses Lake Malar, the open sea, and huge areas of downtown Stockholm. It is open Monday through Friday 11:30am to 1am; Saturday 1pm to 1am.

Sturehof. Stureplan 2. ☎ **08/440-57-30.** T-bana: Hötorget.

Since 1897, this pub and restaurant has been one of the major hangouts for drinking and dining in Stockholm. This establishment in the exact center of Stockholm has been engulfed in urban restoration and now is incorporated in a covered arcade of other restaurants and shops. It remains a pleasant refuge from the city's congestion, and is popular as both an after-work bar and a restaurant. It's open daily from 11am to 1am; beer costs 46 SEK ($5.05).

Tiger Bar/Havana Bar. 18 Kungsgatan. ☎ **08/244-700.** Cover 50 SEK ($5.50) Wed, 60 SEK ($6.60) Thurs, 100 SEK ($11) Fri–Sat. T-bana: Östermalmstorg.

One of the hippest, most talked-about bars in Stockholm recently has attracted a bevy of supermodels and TV actors from all over. It's divided into a street-level site (the Tiger Bar) that's outfitted in black leather upholstery and a postmodern kind of cool, and a basement-level recreation of pre-Castro Cuba (the Havana Bar) that's outfitted with artificial palms and the deliberately garish colors associated with Old Havana's most raunchy 1950s-era excesses. On both levels, everybody's favorite drink seems to be Russian-inspired *caprinoshka,* concocted from vodka and limes. Depending on where you happen to be within the two venues, you're likely to hear anything from recorded disco (every Friday and Saturday beginning at midnight) to live salsa and merengue (every Wednesday from 9pm to 5am). The place is open Wednesday and Thursday from 7pm to 3am, and Friday and Saturday from 7pm to 4am. Incidentally, no one will object if you light up a cigar—the salsa and all that black leather seem to encourage it.

7 Side Trips from Stockholm

Some of Sweden's best-known attractions are clustered around Lake Mälaren— centuries-old villages and castles (Uppsala and Gripsholm) that revive the pomp and glory of the 16th-century Vasa dynasty.

You can spend a very busy day exploring Sigtuna, Skokloster Castle, Uppsala, and Gamla Uppsala, staying overnight in Sigtuna or Uppsala where there are good hotels. Another easy day trip is to Gripsholm Castle in Mariefred or Tullgarn Palace.

A popular route is to take the boat from Klara Mälarstrand in Stockholm at 9:45am, going along the beautiful waterway, Mälaren, and the Fyris River to Sigtuna for a 2-hour stop before arriving at Uppsala at 5pm. Here you can visit the cathedral and other interesting sights, dine, and return by train, a 45-minute trip. Trains run every hour until 11pm.

✪ SIGTUNA

Founded at the beginning of the 11th century, Sigtuna, on the shores of Lake Mälaren, northwest of Stockholm, is Sweden's oldest town. Its **High Street (Stora Gatan),** with its low timbered buildings, is believed to be the oldest street in Sweden that still follows its original route. Traces of Sigtuna's Viking and early Christian heritage can be seen throughout the town.

Sigtuna has many church ruins, mostly from the 12th century. Chief among them is **S:t Per's,** Sweden's first cathedral. The 13th-century **Monastery of St. Maria** is open to the public daily. The well-preserved **Town Hall** dates from the 18th century.

Side Trips from Stockholm

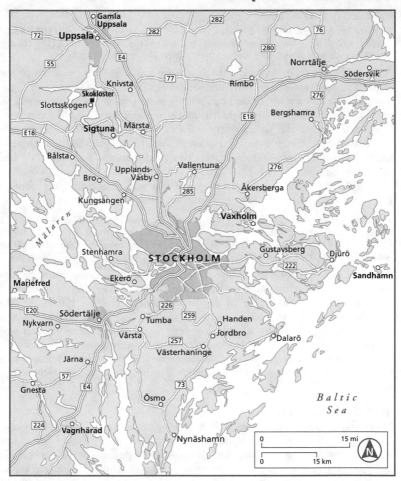

Wander the narrow streets and, if you have time, visit the **Sigtuna Museum,** Storogatan (☎ **08/592-510-18**), the archaeological museum where artifacts found in the surrounding area that date from the early medieval period can be viewed. You'll see gold rings, runic inscriptions, and coins, as well as exclusive objects from Russia and Byzantium. Admission is 20 SEK ($2.20); free 16 and under. Hours are June through August, daily, noon to 4pm; September through May, Tuesday through Sunday, noon to 4pm.

One of the reasons for Sigtuna's resurgence is the **Sigtuna Foundation,** a Lutheran retreat and cultural center founded near the turn of the century and often frequented by writers. It's open to the public daily from 1 to 3pm.

Daily buses and trains connect Stockholm to Sigtuna and Uppsala. From Stockholm take a train to Märsta, then a bus for the 10-minute ride to Sigtuna. In summer boats run from Klara Mälarstrand Pier in Stockholm and from Uppsala to Sigtuna.

WHERE TO STAY & DINE

Sigtuna Foundation. Manfred Björkquists Allé 2–4, S-193 31 Sigtuna. ☎ **08/592-589-00.** Fax 08/592-589-99. E-mail: bokninken@sigtunastiftelsen.se. 55 units. 880 SEK ($96.80) double. Rates include breakfast. MC, V. Free parking. Bus: 570 or 575.

A stay within the solid 1917 walls of this massive building may provide one of your most memorable stopovers in Sweden. Intended as a center where various sociological and philosophical viewpoints could be aired, it's more a way of life than a hotel. Over the years, guest lecturers have included the Dalai Lama, various Indian gurus, and many of the leading theologians of postwar Europe. The establishment functions as both a conference center and a guest house, and still holds guest lectures. There are secluded courtyards, lush rose and herb gardens, and fountains. Recently all the bedrooms were refurbished in a blandly modern style and modern bathrooms were added. The management would like visitors to phone or wire in advance so that a room can be guaranteed. The foundation is less than a mile from the town center.

Sigtuna Stadshotell. Stora Nygatan 3, S-193 00 Sigtuna. ☎ **08/592-501-00.** Fax 08/592-515-87. www.sigtunastadshotell.se. E-mail: info@sigtunastadshotell.se. 24 units. TV TEL. 950–1,450 SEK ($104.50–$159.50) double; 1,520 SEK ($167.20) suite. Rates include breakfast. MC, V. Free parking. Bus: 570 or 575.

This Victorian-style hotel in the town center is a traditional choice, with the most comfortable accommodations in town. The old-fashioned rooms are well kept, clean, and inviting. Full meals are served daily, with dinners going for 150 to 245 SEK ($16.50 to $26.95) à la carte. These might include Gorgonzola-flavored cream of morel soup, scallop of salmon with vermouth sauce, medallions of reindeer with juniper berries, and braised snow grouse in cream sauce with apples and Calvados. For dessert, there's warm cloudberry jam with strawberry ice cream. In winter the restaurant is open from 11:30am to 11pm daily; during the summer months only evening meals are served.

SKOKLOSTER CASTLE

Skokloster, S-746 96 Sklokloster (☎ **018/38-60-77**), is a splendid 17th-century castle and one of the most interesting baroque museums in Europe. It's located next to Lake Mälaren, 40 miles from Stockholm and 31 miles from Uppsala. The castle is noted for its original interiors as well as its extensive collections of paintings, furniture, applied art, tapestries, arms, and books. Admission is 65 SEK ($7.15) for adults, 50 SEK ($5.50) for seniors, and 30 SEK ($3.30) for students and children. Guided tours are conducted May through August, daily on the hour from 11am to 4pm; in September, Monday through Friday at 1pm and on Saturday and Sunday at 1, 2, and 3pm; closed off-season.

Skokloster Motor Museum (☎ **018/38-61-06**), on the palace grounds, houses the largest collection of vintage automobiles and motorcycles in the country. One of the most notable cars is a 1905 eight-horsepower De Dion Bouton. Unlike the castle, the museum is open all year. It costs 40 SEK ($4.40) for adults, 10 SEK ($1.10) for children 7 to 14, and is free for children 6 and under. Open May through September, daily from 11am to 5pm; October to April, Saturday and Sunday from 11am to 5pm. Take bus no. 894 from Bålsta, which is connected by rail to Stockholm.

♡ UPPSALA

The major university city of Sweden, Uppsala, 42 miles northwest of Stockholm, is the most popular destination of day-trippers from Stockholm—and for good reason. Uppsala has not only a great university, but also a celebrated 15th-century cathedral.

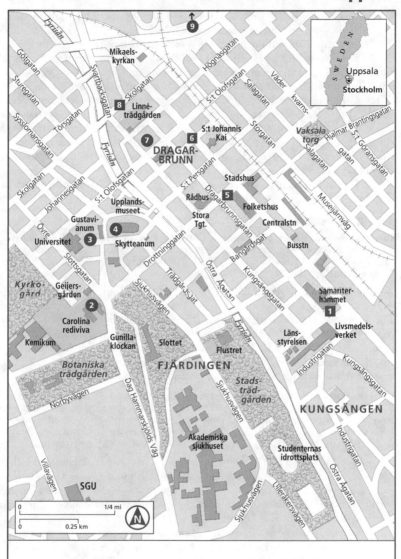

ATTRACTIONS ●

Carolina Rediviva
 (University Library) **2**
Gamla Uppsala **9**
Linnaeus Garden and Museum **7**
Museum Gustavianum **3**
Uppsala Domkyrka **4**

ACCOMMODATIONS ■

Diakonistiftelsen
 Samariterhemmet **1**
First Hotel Linné **8**
Hotel Uplandia **5**
Sara Hotel Gillet **6**

Even in the Viking period, Uppsala was a religious center; later it became a center of royalty as well. Queen Christina occasionally held court here. The church is still the seat of the archbishop, and the first Swedish university was founded here in 1477.

The best time to visit Uppsala is on April 30, Walpurgis Eve, when academics celebrate the rebirth of spring with a torchlight parade and rollicking festivities lasting until dawn throughout the 13 student "nations" (residential halls).

The town is easily reached by train—about 45 minutes from Stockholm's Central Station. Trains leave about every hour during the peak daylight hours. Boats from Stockholm to Uppsala (or vice versa) also stop at Skokloster and Sigtuna. For details, check with the tourist office in any of these towns. Some visitors prefer to spend the day in Uppsala and return to Stockholm on the commuter train in the late afternoon. If you have a Eurail pass, you ride free.

The **Tourist Information Office** is at Fyris Torg 8 (☎ **018/27-48-00**), open Monday through Friday from 10am to 6pm and Saturday from 10am to 3pm.

SEEING THE SIGHTS

Carolina Rediviva (University Library). Drottninggatan. ☎ **018/471-39-00.** Admission 20 SEK ($2.20), free children under 12. Exhibit room, June 18–Aug 17, Mon–Fri 9am–5pm, Sat 10am–4pm, Sun 11am–4pm; June 2–17 and Aug 18–Sept 15, Sun 1–3:30pm. Closed Sept 16–June 1. Bus: 6, 7, or 22.

At the end of Drottninggatan is the Carolina Rediviva, with its more than 5 million volumes and 40,000 manuscripts, including many rare works from the Middle Ages. The manuscript that interests most visitors is in the exhibit room—the *Codex Argenteus* (Silver Bible), translated into the old Gothic language in the middle of the 3rd century and copied in about A.D. 525. It's the only book extant in old Gothic script. Also worth seeing is *Carta Marina*, the earliest known map in Sweden (1539), and a fairly accurate rendering of Sweden and its neighboring countries.

Linnaeus Garden & Museum. Svartbäcksgatan 27. ☎ **018/13-65-40** for the museum or 018/10-94-90 for the garden. Museum, 25 SEK ($2.75) adults; gardens, donation suggested. Both free for children. Museum, June to mid-Sept, Tues–Sun noon–4pm. Closed mid-Sept to May. Gardens, May–Aug, daily 9am–9pm; Sept, daily 9am–7pm. Closed Oct–Apr. Walk straight from the train station to Kungsgatan, turn right, and walk about 10 minutes.

The garden and former home of Swedish botanist Carl von Linné, known as Carolus Linnaeus, who developed a classification system for the world's plants and flowers, are located on the spot where he restored Uppsala University's botanical garden. Linnaeus left detailed sketches and descriptions of the garden (which resembles a miniature baroque garden), which have been followed faithfully.

Linnaeus was professor of theoretical medicine, including botany, pharmacology, and zoology, at Uppsala University. His house, which has been restored to its original design, may be visited. A summer art gallery exhibits the works of contemporary local artists.

✪ **Uppsala Domkyrka.** Domkyrkoplan 2. ☎ **018/18-72-01.** Free admission to cathedral; museum 20 SEK ($2.20) adults, 15 SEK ($1.65) seniors and students, 10 SEK ($1.10) children 7–15, free for children under 7. Cathedral: daily 8am–6pm. Museum: Apr–Aug, daily 10am–5pm; Sept–Mar, Sat 10am–5pm, Sun 12:30–5pm. Bus: 1.

The largest cathedral in Scandinavia, this twin-spired Gothic structure, nearly 400 feet tall, was founded in the 13th century. It was severely damaged in 1702 in a disastrous fire that swept over Uppsala, then was restored near the turn of this century. Among the regal figures buried in the crypt is Gustavus Vasa. The remains of St. Erik, patron saint of Sweden, are entombed in a silver shrine. The botanist Linnaeus and the philosopher-theologian Swedenborg also are buried here. A small museum displays ecclesiastical relics of Uppsala.

Museum Gustavianum. Akademigatan 3. ☎ **018/471-75-71.** Admission 40 SEK ($4.40) adults, 20 SEK ($2.20) students, free for children under 12. Mid-May to mid-Sept, daily 11am–4pm (until 9pm Thurs). Off-season, Wed–Sun 11am–4pm (until 9pm Thurs). Bus: 1, 2, 51, or 53.

Gustavianum is Uppsala University's oldest preserved building. Here you can see a number of attractions, including an Anatomical Theatre, the Augsburg Art Cabinet, and an exhibition about the history of the university itself. The museum also includes archeological exhibitions, from Swedish prehistory to the Middle Ages. Some of the rarer pieces are from the Mediterranean and the Nile Valley, including the sarcophagus of a priest, Khonsumes, from the 21st dynasty. In the historical exhibition on the ground floor you can see everything from student lecture notes from the first term in 1477, the year the university was founded, to the development of the institution over the years as a seat of learning.

✪ GAMLA UPPSALA

About 15 centuries ago Gamla Uppsala was the capital of the Svea kingdom. In its midst was a sacrificial grove where both human and animal sacrifices were made. It's believed that three Viking kings were buried here in the 6th century.

Nearby, on the site of the old pagan temple, is a 12th-century **parish church,** once badly damaged by fire and never properly restored. Indeed, some people describe it as a stave church that was turned into stone. Before Uppsala Cathedral was built, Swedish kings were crowned here.

Across from the church is the **Stiftelsen Upplandsmuseet,** Sankt Eriksgränd 6 (☎ **018/16-91-00**), an open-air museum with reassembled buildings, depicting peasant life in Uppland. It's open from mid-May until the end of August, daily from noon to 5pm. Tours are conducted Monday through Friday at 1 and 2pm and on Saturday and Sunday every hour on the hour from noon to 4pm. Admission is free.

Gamla Uppsala, about 3 miles north of the commercial heart of Uppsala, is easily reached by bus no. 2 or 24, which leaves frequently from the Central Station.

WHERE TO STAY

Diakonistiftelsen Samariterhemmet. Samaritegränd 2, S-753 19 Uppsala. ☎ **018/10-34-00.** Fax 018/10-83-75. 25 units, 12 with bathroom. 670 SEK ($73.70) double without bathroom, 770 SEK ($84.70) double with bathroom. Rates include breakfast. V. Bus: 1.

One of the best bargains in town, this large guest house has spotlessly maintained rooms, most resembling those found in a college dormitory, and you can use a kitchenette with a refrigerator. The beds are comfortable; the housekeeping is spotless. It's run by a Christian charity, and was founded in 1882 by Miss Ebba Boström. The house has a TV lounge; smoking is not permitted.

First Hotel Linné. Skolgatan 45, S-75332 Uppsala. ☎ **018/10-20-00.** Fax 018/13-75-97. www.firsthotels.com. E-mail: linne@firsthotels.se. 116 units. MINIBAR TV TEL. Sun–Thurs 1,449–1,549 SEK ($159.40–$170.40) double; 1,569–1,749 SEK ($172.60–$192.40) suite. Fri–Sat 799–849 SEK ($87.90–$93.40) double; 899–999 SEK ($98.90–$109.90) suite. Rates include breakfast. AE, DC, MC, V. Parking 30 SEK ($3.30). Bus: 1.

This hotel at the edge of Linnaeus Garden is one of the best managed in town. You'll probably be able to see Carl von Linnaeus's lovely garden from your bedroom window. The rooms feature modern furniture and plumbing, and each has a refrigerator or minibar that you stock yourself. It's a good-value hotel; one drawback is that the less expensive doubles are a bit cramped. One floor of 36 rooms is reserved for nonsmokers. The hotel has a bar and a sauna.

Hotel Uplandia. Dragarbrunnsgatan 32, S-751 40 Uppsala. ☎ **800/528-1234** in the U.S., or 018/10-21-60. Fax 018/69-61-32. www.provobis.se. E-mail: hoteluplandia@provobis.se. 133 units. MINIBAR TV TEL. 1,395–1,580 SEK ($153.45–$173.80) double. Rates include breakfast. AE, DC, MC, V. Bus: 1.

This hotel, located next to the bus terminal, is the best in town. It was constructed in two stages, in the 1960s and early 1980s, in two connected buildings rising three to six floors each. During the final enlargement, all rooms in the older section were brought up to modern standards. The year 1996 saw a complete overhaul of all its bathrooms. The hotel offers comfortably furnished bedrooms with such extras as a trouser press. There's a sauna on the premises.

On the lobby level are an elegant cocktail lounge and a spacious restaurant. The menu might include a mousse of shrimp and salmon, noisettes of veal, Alsatian sauerkraut, and a selection of all-vegetarian platters.

Sara Hotel Gillet. Dragarbrunnsgatan 23, S-751 42 Uppsala. ☎ **018/15-53-60.** Fax 018/15-33-80. E-mail: info@gillet.softwarehotels.se. 160 units. TV TEL. 900–1,850 SEK ($99–$203.50) double; 2,000–3,500 SEK ($220–$385) suite. Rates include breakfast. AE, DC, MC, V. Parking 95 SEK ($10.45). Bus: 801.

This attractively designed first-class hotel, built in 1972, offers well-furnished bedrooms, a breakfast room, cozy cocktail bar and lounge, swimming pool, and sauna. Medium-size bedrooms in Nordic pastels have good beds, modern furnishings, and excellent housekeeping. With its two restaurants, it's also one of the major dining venues for Uppsala. The East West Bistro serves dinner Monday through Saturday and the more upscale Gillet Restaurant offers both lunch and dinner, also Monday through Saturday.

WHERE TO DINE

Domtrappkällaren. Sankt Eriksgränd 15. ☎ **018/13-09-55.** Reservations recommended. Main courses 145–230 SEK ($15.95–$25.30). AE, DC, MC, V. Mon–Sat 11:30am–11pm, Sun 5–9pm. Closed Dec 24–26. Bus: 1. SWEDISH.

No other restaurant in Uppsala can compete with this one for charm and atmosphere—it was built in the town center on the ruins of 12th-century cathedral buildings. The vaulted ceilings and copies of Jacobean paintings in the main dining room are complemented by the low-ceilinged, sun-flooded intimacy of the upper floors. If you request it, you can dine in a narrow room that imprisoned unruly students in the Middle Ages, or in another that served as a classroom in the 17th century. The restaurant serves delicious salmon and reindeer and specializes in game. Salads often are exotic, including one with breast of pigeon and roasted nuts.

Restaurant Flustret. Svandammen. ☎ **018/13-01-14.** Reservations recommended. Main courses 120–150 SEK ($13.20–$16.50). AE, DC, MC, V. Mon–Fri 11am–2pm and 4–9pm, Sat–Sun 11am–10pm. Bus: 24. FRENCH.

In a riverside setting near the castle, this pavilion is an exact replica of its predecessor, a long-ago-demolished Victorian building. Its spacious ground-floor dining room serves tasty meals, which might include lobster soup, salmon "boathouse style," veal steak Oscar, pheasant Véonique, and bananas flambé. A disco on the second floor is open Saturday from 9pm to 2am. Admission is free before 9pm, 60 SEK ($6.60) after 9pm.

Restaurant Odinsborg. Near the burial grounds, Gamla Uppsala. ☎ **018/323-525.** Main courses 110–180 SEK ($12.10–$19.80); Sun smörgåsbord 205 SEK ($22.55). AE, DC, MC, V. Daily noon–6pm. Bus: 2 or 24. SWEDISH.

In a century-old building that once was a private house, this restaurant serves strictly old-fashioned Swedish food in a dining room decorated in a Viking theme. The culinary highlight of the week involves the Sunday smörgåsbord, when a traditional roster of foods like those you'd find at a family celebration is laboriously prepared and laid out. The rest of the week, menu items include traditional preparations of fried herring, marinated salmon, smoked eel, whitefish with a dill-flavored butter sauce, roasted lamb, chicken fillets, and steaks. Street addresses aren't used in Gamla Uppsala, but the restaurant is easy to spot; it's near the burial grounds.

✪ GRIPSHOLM CASTLE

On an island in Lake Mälaren, Gripsholm Castle (☎ 0159/101-94)—the fortress built by Gustavus Vasa in the late 1530s—is one of the best-preserved castles in Sweden. The castle is 42 miles southwest of Stockholm, easily reached by driving along E20 south. You also can take the Eskilstuna bus from Stockholm. In Stockholm, boats also leave mid-May through September at 10am from Stadshuset, the Klara Malarstrand Pier. The castle is a 5-minute walk from the center of Mariefred, an idyllic small town known for its vintage narrow-gauge railroad.

During the reign of the 18th-century actor-king Gustavus III, a theater was built at Gripsholm, but the outstanding feature of the castle is its large collection of portrait paintings.

Even though Gripsholm was last occupied by royalty in 1864 (Charles XV), it's still a royal castle. It's open May through August, daily from 10am to 4pm; in April and September, Tuesday to Friday from 10am to 3pm and Saturday and Sunday from 10am to 3pm; October to March, only on Saturday and Sunday from noon to 3pm. Admission is 50 SEK ($5.50) for adults and 25 SEK ($2.75) for children.

WHERE TO STAY

✪ **Gripsholms Värdshus & Hotel.** Kyrkogatan 1, S-647 23 Mariefred. ☎ **0159/34750.** Fax 0159/34777. www.gripsholms-vardshus.se. 45 units. A/C MINIBAR TV TEL. 1,690–1,960 SEK ($185.90–$215.60) double; suites require a supplement of between 500–2,500 SEK ($55–$275), depending on the unit and the season. Rates include breakfast. AE, DC, MC, V.

Originally built as an inn in 1609 (making it among the oldest in Sweden), this building was restored and reopened in 1989, and is now the most stylish and charming hotel in the region. It's a few steps from the village church, in the center of Mariefred, a 10-minute walk from the castle. Each bedroom is individually decorated and furnished with a mixture of antiques and contemporary pieces. The walls and ceiling decors are painted in the style of the 17th century. Amenities include such thoughtful extras as hair dryers and bathrooms with heated floors and towel racks.

Dining/Diversions: The hotel has the best restaurant in the region (see "Where to Dine," below), as well as a pub for less formal meals. It keeps the same hours as the restaurant and serves ample platters of homemade Swedish food.

Amenities: Room service, massage, laundry, solarium, recreation center, sauna, copper tub for ice baths, public bar, billiard room.

WHERE TO DINE

✪ **Gripsholms Värdshus Restaurant.** Kyrkogatan 1. ☎ **0159/34750.** Reservations recommended. Main courses 195–235 SEK ($21.45–$25.85); 2-course fixed-price lunch 210 SEK ($23.10). AE, DC, MC, V. Midsummer, daily noon–10pm; rest of year, Mon–Fri noon–2pm, Sat noon–4pm, Mon–Sat 6–10pm. FRENCH/SWEDISH.

Traditional Swedish food and local game dishes are served along with international cuisine at this elegantly appointed restaurant. The main dining room has an adjoining veranda opening onto Gripsholm Bay. Tastings can be arranged in the wine cellar. The menu changes every season, but is likely to include such dishes as baked saddle of venison with herbs and mushroom pastry, grilled halibut accompanied by a red paprika cream and basil ratatouille, and lamb cutlets smothered in Dijon mustard and shallots. For dessert, try the raspberry mousse parfait.

TULLGARN PALACE

The royal palace of Tullgarn, in Vagnhärad (☎ 08/551-720-11), built starting in 1719 in a panoramic setting on a bay of the Baltic Sea, was the favorite of Gustavus V (1858–1950), the great-grandfather of Sweden's present king. The well-kept interiors date from the late 18th century. Admission is 50 SEK ($5.50) for adults, 25 SEK ($2.75) for students and children. The palace is open to the public on weekends from early May through early September. Guided tours leave the main entrance every hour from 11am to 4pm.

The castle lies 37 miles south of Stockholm; if you're driving, take E4 south about 37 miles and follow the sign to the right directing you to Tullgarns Slott, near Vagnhärad. It's another quarter of a mile to the palace. Or take the Blue Train from the Central Station in Stockholm to Södertälje Södra (about 20 minutes) and catch a bus to Trosa.

WHERE TO STAY

Romantik Stadtshotell Trosa. Västra Langgatan 19, S-61921 Trosa. ☎ **0156/17070.** Fax 0156/16696. E-mail: info@trosastadtshtell.se. 44 units. TV TEL. Mid-June to mid-Aug and Fri–Sat year-round, 980 SEK ($107.80) double; rest of year, 1,300 SEK ($143) double. AE, DC, MC, V.

The most charming and historically evocative hotel in the region lies in the heart of Trosa, a quiet hamlet 4½ miles south of Tullgarns Castle. Built in 1867 of yellow-tinged bricks and set in the center of the town, it was enlarged and modernized in the early 1990s. Today, it provides cozy, clean rooms with a hint of the aesthetics of yesteryear; wooden floors and a scattering of antique accessories, always coupled with color schemes of yellow and green. Bathrooms are modern and up-to-date, in most cases added (or upgraded) in the mid-1980s. There's a restaurant on the premises that's open every day, year-round, for lunch and dinner; a bar, a sauna, and a Jacuzzi.

WHERE TO DINE

Tullgarns Värdshus. In Tullgarn Palace, in Vagnhärad. ☎ **08/551-720-26.** Reservations recommended. Main courses 180–197 SEK ($19.80–$21.65). MC, V. May 15–Sept 8, Mon–Fri noon–2:30pm and 5–7pm, Sat–Sun noon–7pm. Closed Sept 9–May 14. SWEDISH/FRENCH.

Located in a wing of Tullgarn Palace, this inn offers three-course lunches or dinners. You can sample such dishes as salted salmon with creamed potatoes, an old Swedish specialty, or perhaps pâté of wild boar. You also can order breast of wild duck with a mousse of chicken liver or poached fillet of salmon with a chive-flavored butter sauce.

If you prefer your dining al fresco, order a picnic lunch to go, and eat in the royal park. Picnics of cold chicken or roast beef, with beer or coffee (in a take-out container), or a cup of coffee with a sandwich, can be ordered at the inn daily from 11am to 5pm.

SANDHAMN, VAXHOLM & THE ARCHIPELAGO OF STOCKHOLM

Stockholm is in what the Swedes call a garden of skerries, more than 24,000 islands (including some rocks jutting out of the water). The islands nearest to Stockholm have become part of the suburbs, thickly populated and connected to the mainland by car-ferries or bridges, but many are still wild and largely deserted, attracting those who can boat out to them for picnics and swimming. Summer homes dot some of the islands; July is the peak vacation month, when yachts crowd the waters.

You can see the islands by taking a boat trip from Stockholm harbor. For a stopover at one of the resorts, consider **Sandhamn,** where you'll find shops and restaurants. The entire island takes about an hour to explore on foot. The beaches at the eastern tip are the best in the archipelago. **Vaxholm,** a bathing resort known as "the gateway to the northern archipelago" with full tourist facilities, also makes a nice stopover. Artists and writers have traditionally been drawn to Vaxholm, and some hold exhibits during the summer when the population quadruples as tourists throng into town. The west harbor and the main sea route north are filled with pleasure craft.

Throughout the year (but more often in summer), boats operated by several different companies depart from the front of the Grand Hotel at Södra Blasieholm-shåmnen. Most of them say VAXHOLM, although boats often continue to Sandhamn after a stopover in Vaxholm. Be sure to ask before boarding.

The trip from Stockholm through the archipelago to Sandhamn takes 3½ hours each way and costs 95 SEK ($10.45). Traveling by ferryboat to Vaxholm from Stockholm takes less than 40 minutes and costs 60 SEK ($6.60). If you plan on doing a lot of traveling around the archipelago, consider buying an Inter-Skerries Card, priced at 300 SEK ($33). This card allows you 16 days of unlimited travel anywhere within the Stockholm archipelago. Vaxholm-bound boats depart every hour during the summer (about five times a day in winter) from the Strömkagen, the piers outside the Grand Hotel. For information, call the Vaxholm steamship company, **Vaxholmes Belaget** (☎ **08/679-5830**).

Buses to Vaxholm (no. 670, 671, 672, and 673) often (but not always) go on to Sandhamn. They depart from the East Railway Station every 30 minutes beginning at 6am. The last bus from Vaxholm leaves at 1am.

Strömma Kanal Steamship (☎ **08/541-314-80**) offers a guided cruise in English to Sandhamn. Ships sail through canals and bays to reach the sailing city. Tours last 8 hours and depart June to August at 10am. The "Canal Cruise to Sandhamn" begins at 185 SEK ($20.35); free for children under 12. This company also offers the "Thousand Island Cruise" through the Stockholm archipelago. The 11-hour guided tour includes lunch, dinner, and a stopover on four islands. Tours are available in July and August.

WHERE TO STAY

Vaxholm Hotel. Hamngatan 2, S-185 00 Vaxholm. ☎ **08/541-301-50.** Fax 08/541-313-76. www.vaxholmhotel.se. E-mail: info@vaxholmhotel.se. 32 units. TV TEL. 930–1,240 SEK ($102.30–$136.40) double. Rates include breakfast. AE, DC, MC, V. Closed Dec 24–Jan 1. Free parking.

Built in 1902, this stone hotel, painted bright yellow, is situated right at the pier where the ferryboats from Stockholm dock. It offers modern but rather bland bedrooms. Its summer disco is open Friday and Saturday from 9pm to 2am, charging a cover of 80 SEK ($8.80). An informal pub, Kabyssen, is located at street level. One floor above, with a view overlooking the water, is the Vaxholm Hotel Restaurant.

WHERE TO DINE

In Vaxholm

Vaxholm Hotel Restaurant. Hamngatan 2. ☎ **08/541-301-50.** Reservations required in summer. Main courses 87–245 SEK ($9.55–$26.95). AE, DC, MC, V. Summer, daily noon–11pm; off-season, daily noon–9pm. Closed Dec 24–Jan 1. SEAFOOD.

This restaurant, offering a view of the water at the pier where the ferryboats from Stockholm dock, is the best place to dine in Vaxholm. When queried, the chef said that his specialties are "fish, fish, fish." The uncompromising house specialty (and the best buy) is a platter of pan-fried Swedish herring served with mashed potatoes. Other notable dishes are smoked reindeer with horseradish, tender tournedos stuffed with herbs and served with a mustard sauce, and poached fillet of sole with a white wine sauce. In summer, the chef prepares desserts with locally grown berries and fruits, including rhubarb pie, elderberry sorbet, and lingonberries with an almond flan.

In Sandhamn

Sandhamns Värdshus. Harbourfront. ☎ **08/571-53-051.** Reservations required Sat–Sun. Main courses 145–239 SEK ($15.95–$26.30); 3-course fixed-price menu 260 SEK ($28.60). AE, DC, MC, V. Sun–Thurs noon–9pm, Fri–Sat noon–10:30pm. SWEDISH.

This local favorite, established in 1672, offers a view of the moored boats at the harbor front. You can rely on a good, reasonably priced meal by selecting one of the fish dishes or the local choice, steak with red onions.

Gothenburg & Beyond

Called the gateway to northern Europe, Gothenburg (Göteborg in Swedish) is the country's chief port and second-largest city. Swedes often say that Gothenburg is a more welcoming town than Stockholm, and in fact, a recent opinion poll showed that half the Swedish population would be happy to move to Gothenburg because of its friendly atmosphere. Canals, parks, and flower gardens enhance its appeal, as do a large number of museums (featuring everything from the world's only stuffed blue whale to modern art) and the largest amusement park in northern Europe. Gothenburg also is a convenient center for excursions to the fishing villages and lovely vacation resorts north of the city.

Gothenburg received its city charter from Gustavus Adolphus II in 1621. The port contains a shipyard, Cityvarvet, and a manufacturer of platforms for oil rigs, Götaverken/Arendal. The city also is the home of Volvo, the car manufacturer (whose plant is about a 15-minute drive from the city center), and of the Hasselblad space camera. Despite this heavy industry, Gothenburg's environmental programs have made it a European leader in developing new products and procedures for dealing with waste.

A walk down Kungsportsavenyn, known as *Avenyn* (The Avenue) is a Gothenburg tradition, even in winter, when the street is heated by underground pipes so that the snow melts quickly. There are many outdoor cafes from which to watch the passing action on this wide, pedestrian thoroughfare.

1 Orientation

ARRIVING

BY PLANE SAS (☎ 800/221-2350 in the U.S.; www.flysas.com) operates 8 to 10 daily flights from Copenhagen to Gothenburg (most of them nonstop) between 7:30am and 11:05pm. (Many Swedes who live on the west coast of Sweden consider Copenhagen a more convenient airport than the one in Stockholm.) SAS also operates 10 to 20 daily flights between Stockholm and Gothenburg, beginning about 7am and continuing until early evening.

Planes arrive at **Landvetter Airport** (☎ 031/94-10-00), 16 miles east of Gothenburg. An airport bus (Flygbuss) departs every 30 minutes for the 30-minute ride to the central bus terminal, just behind Gothenburg's main railway station. Buses run daily between 5am and 11:15pm. A one-way trip costs 50 SEK ($5.50).

BY TRAIN   The Oslo–Copenhagen express train runs through Gothenburg and Helsingborg. Trains run frequently on a north-south route between Gothenburg and Helsingborg/Malmö in the south. The most traveled rail route is between Gothenburg and Stockholm, with trains leaving hourly in both directions; the trip takes 4⅔ hours.

Trains arrive at the **Central Station,** on one side of Drottningtorget. Inside the station is a currency exchange bureau and an office of the Swedish National Railroad Authority (SJ), which sells rail and bus tickets for connections to nearby areas. For information, call **020/75-75-75.**

BY BUS   There are several buses from Gothenburg to Helsingborg/Malmö (and vice versa) daily. Trip time from Gothenburg to Helsingborg is 3½ hours; Gothenburg to Malmö, 4½ hours. Several buses connect Stockholm and Gothenburg daily. The trip takes 7 to 8 hours. Gothenburg's bus station, at Nils Ericson Gate, is located behind the railway station. For information in Gothenburg, call **Swebus,** Sweden's largest bus company (☎ **031/10-38-00**).

BY FERRY   The **Stena Line** (☎ **031/704-00-00**) has six crossings per day in summer from North Jutland (a 3-hour trip); call for information on specific departure times, which vary seasonally. The vessels have excellent dining rooms.

Stena offers twice-weekly ferry service between Harwich (England) and Gothenburg, taking 24 hours. From June to mid-August, there's also service from Newcastle upon Tyne (England) to Gothenburg once a week, also taking 24 hours. This service is operated by **Scandinavian Seaways** (☎ **031/65-06-50** for information). There's no railpass discount on the England–Sweden crossings.

BY CAR   From either Malmö or Helsingborg, the two major "gateways" to Sweden on the west coast, take E6 north. Gothenburg is 173 miles north of Malmö and 141 miles north of Helsingborg. From Stockholm, take E4 west to Jonköping and continue west the rest of the way through Borås to Gothenburg, a distance of 292 miles.

VISITOR INFORMATION

Gothenburg Tourist Office is at Kungsportsplatsen 2 (☎ **031/10-07-40;** www. goteborg.com), open June through August, daily from 9am to 8pm; September through May, Monday through Friday from 9am to 5pm and Saturday from 10am to 2pm.

CITY LAYOUT

The layout of Gothenburg, with its network of streets separated by canals, is reminiscent of Amsterdam—not surprisingly, as it was designed by Dutch architects in the 17th century. Its wealth of parks and open spaces has given it a reputation as Sweden's greenest city.

Some of the old canals have been filled in, but you can explore the major remaining waterway and the busy harbor by taking one of the city's famous **Paddan sightseeing boats** (☎ **031/60-96-70**). *Paddan* is the Swedish word for "toad," and the allusion is to the squat shape of the boats that enables them to navigate under the many low bridges. A Paddan service takes you from the point of embarkation, Drottningtorget (near the Central Station), direct to the Liseberg amusement park. The park is the most popular visitor attraction in the area, attracting some 3 million visitors annually.

The best place to start sightseeing on foot is **Kungsportsavenyn (The Avenyn),** a wide, tree-lined boulevard with many sidewalk cafes. (Take a look at the Gothenburg Attractions map later in this chapter.) Avenyn leads to **Götaplatsen,** a square that's the

Fun Fact

Spanning the Göta River, Älvsborg Bridge (the longest suspension bridge in Sweden) is almost 3,000 feet long and built high enough to allow ocean liners to pass underneath.

city's artistic and historic center. Its centerpiece is a huge bronze fountain with a statue of the sea god Poseidon, sculpted by Carl Milles.

Gothenburg's old commercial section lies on either side of the central canal. At the central canal is **Gustav Adolfs Torg,** dominated by a statue of Gustav himself. Facing the canal is the **Börshuset** (Stock Exchange building). On the western side is the **Rådhuset** (Town Hall), originally constructed in 1672. Around the corner, moving toward the river, is the **Kronhuset** (off Kronhusgatan), a 17th-century Dutch-designed building—the oldest in Gothenburg.

Gothenburg is dominated by its **harbor,** which is best viewed from one of the Padden boats. The major attraction here is the **Maritime Center** (see "Seeing the Sights," below). The shipyards, whose spidery forms look as if they were made from an Erector Set, are dominated by the IBM building and other industries. Part of the harbor is connected by an overhead walkway to the shopping mall of **Nordstan.**

2 Getting Around

Visitors usually find that the cheapest way to explore Gothenburg (except on foot) is to buy a **Göteborgskortet (Gothenburg Card).** Available at hotels, newspaper kiosks, and the city's tourist office, it entitles you to unlimited travel on local trams, buses, and ferryboats; certain sightseeing tours; either free or discounted admission to the city's major museums and sightseeing attractions; discounts at certain shops; free parking in certain centrally located parking lots; and several other extras that usually make the card worthwhile. A ticket valid for 24 hours costs 90 SEK ($9.90) for adults and 60 SEK ($6.60) for children, a 48-hour ticket is 180 SEK ($19.80) for adults and 90 SEK ($9.90) for children, and a 72-hour ticket goes for 270 SEK ($29.70) for adults and 135 SEK ($14.85) for children.

BY PUBLIC TRANSPORTATION (TRAM)   A single tram ticket costs 20 SEK ($2.20); a 24-hour travel pass goes for 60 SEK ($6.60). If you don't have an advance ticket, board the first car of the tram and buy one from the driver. One-way tram tickets are stamped by the driver who sells them to you. Previously purchased tickets must be stamped in the automatic machine as soon as you board the tram.

BY TAXI   Taxis are not as plentiful as you might like. However, you can always find one by going to the Central Station. **To call a taxi,** dial ☎ **031/27-27-27.** A taxi traveling within the city limits now costs 155 to 275 SEK ($17.05 to $30.25). With the Gothenburg Card, you get a 10% reduction.

BY CAR   Because of parking problems, a car is not a practical vehicle for touring Gothenburg. You may need a car to tour the surrounding area, but there is good public transportation within the city, as well as to many sights. **Avis** (☎ 031/80-57-80) has a rental office at the Central Station and another at the airport (☎ 031/94-60-30). **Hertz** has an office at the center of town at Spannmålsgatan 16 (☎ 031/80-37-30) and one at the airport (☎ 031/94-60-20). Compare rates and make sure you understand the insurance coverage before you sign a contract.

Fast Facts: Gothenburg

Area Code   The international country code for Sweden is **46;** the city code for Gothenburg is **031** (if you're calling Gothenburg from abroad, drop the zero; within Gothenburg, drop the 031).

Bookstores   The biggest and most central is Akademi Bokhandeln, Norra Hamngatan 32 (☎ **031/61-70-80**).

Business Hours   Generally, **shops** are open Monday through Friday from 9am to 6pm and on Saturday from 9am to 2pm; **banks,** Monday through Friday from 9:30am to 3pm; and **offices,** Monday through Friday from 9am to 5pm.

Currency Exchange   Currency can be exchanged at **Forex,** in the Central Station (☎ **031/15-65-16**). There's also a currency exchange desk at Landvetter Airport, open daily from 8am to 9pm.

Dentists   Call the referral agency, Akuttandkliniken (☎ **031/80-78-00**), daily from 8am to 8pm.

Doctors   If it's not an emergency, your hotel can call a local doctor and arrange an appointment. If it's an emergency, go to City Akuten, Drottninggatan 45 (☎ **031/10-10-10**).

Drugstores   A good pharmacy is Apoteket Vasen, Götgatan 12, Nordstan (☎ **031/80-44-10**), open daily from 8am to 10pm.

Embassies & Consulates   There is no U.S. consulate in Gothenburg; Americans and citizens of Australia, Ireland, and New Zealand, must contact their embassies in Stockholm. The **British Consulate** is at Götgatan 15 (☎ **031/ 13-13-27**), open Monday through Friday from 9am to 1pm and 2 to 4pm.

Emergencies   The number to call for nearly all emergencies (fire, police, medical) is ☎ **112.**

Eyeglasses   Go to Wasa Optik, Vasaplatsen 7 (☎ **031/711-05-35**). It's open Monday through Friday from 9am to 6pm.

Hairdressers & Barbers   A good one is Salong Noblesse, Södra Larmgatan 6 (☎ **031/711-71-30**), open Monday through Friday from 9am to 7pm and Saturday from 9am to 3pm.

Internet   The city library, Stadsbibliotek, Götaplatsen (☎ **031/61-65-00**), has free internet access. Open Monday through Thursday 10am to 8pm, Friday 10am to 6pm, and Saturday and Sunday 11am to 4pm. There's also an internet cafe with at least a dozen internet terminals at **Game Station,** Kungstorget 1 (☎ **031/711-05-95**).

Laundry & Dry Cleaning   Laundries are hard to find. There's one at Kärralund Camping, Olbersgatan (☎ **031/25-27-61**). For dry cleaning, go to Express Kem, Drottninggatan 57 (☎ **031/711-22-22**).

Liquor Laws   You must be 18 to consume alcohol in a restaurant, but 20 to purchase alcohol in liquor stores. No alcohol can be served before noon. Most pubs stop serving liquor at 3am, except special nightclubs with a license to stay open later. Liquor can be purchased at state-owned liquor shops known as Systembolag, but only Monday through Friday from 9am to 6pm.

Lost Property   Go to the police station (see "Police," below).

Luggage Storage & Lockers   You can store luggage and rent lockers at the Central Station (☎ **031/10-44-64**). It's open Monday through Saturday 8am to 8pm.

Photographic Supplies   An excellent store is Arkadens Fotoexpert, Arkaden 9 (☎ 031/80-20-70), open Monday through Friday from 10am to 6pm and Saturday from 10am to 2pm.

Police   The main police station is Polismyndigheten, Skånegatan 5 (☎ 031/61-80-00).

Post Office   The main post office is at Nordstan (☎ 031/62-33-36), next to the Central Station. It's open Monday through Friday from 10am to 6pm.

Radio & TV   Gothenburg has Swedish-language TV broadcasts on TV1, TV2, TV3, and TV4, and receives such foreign channels as Super Sky and BBC broadcasts from London. National radio stations include P1, P2, P3, and P4; Radio Gothenburg broadcasts on 101.9 MHz (FM).

Shoe Repair   Try Norrdvan's Klackbar, Nyagatan (☎ 031/215-91-02). Repairs are made while you wait.

Taxes   Gothenburg imposes no special city taxes other than the value-added tax (MOMS), which applies nationwide.

Telegrams, Telex & Fax   Go to Telebutiken, V. Hamngatan 15 (☎ 031/771-81-10), open Monday through Friday from 9:30am to 6pm and Saturday from 10am to 2pm.

Transit Information   For tram and bus information, call **031/80-12-35**; for train information, call **031/10-44-45.**

3 Where to Stay

Reservations are important, but if you need a place to stay on the spur of the moment, try the **Gothenburg Tourist Office,** at Kungsportsplatsen 2 (☎ 031/10-07-40; www.goteborg.com). It lists the city's hotels and boarding houses and reserves rooms in private homes. Reservations can be made in advance, by letter or phone. The tourist office charges a booking fee of 60 SEK ($6.60). Double rooms in private homes start at 475 SEK ($52.25). Breakfast is always extra.

The hotels listed in the following as "expensive" actually become "moderate" in price on Friday and Saturday and during midsummer.

EXPENSIVE

Hotel Europa. Köpmansgatan 38, P.O. Box 11444, S-404 29 Göteborg. ☎ **031/80-12-80.** Fax 031/15-47-55. 460 units. MINIBAR TV TEL. Sun–Thurs 1,350–1,590 SEK ($148.50–$174.90) double; Fri–Sat 890–952 SEK ($97.90–$104.70) double; all week long from 2,000 SEK ($220) suite. Rates include breakfast. AE, DC, MC, V. Parking 150 SEK ($16.50). Trams: 1, 5.

This is one of the largest hotels in Scandinavia; a big, bustling, blockbuster of a building that rises eight bulky stories across from Gothenburg's railway station. Built in 1972 of concrete and glass, thousands of slabs of russet-colored marble were added during a massive renovation that ended in 1994. Today, it's a member of one of Scandinavia's most upscale chains, Proverbis, and the well-trained staff includes dozens of young graduates from hotel training schools. Bedrooms are outfitted in monochromatic tones of either autumn-inspired browns or pale Nordic tones of blue, and have comfortable beds, conservative, modern furniture, and up-to-date bathrooms. The largest, most plush, and most recently renovated rooms lie on the hotel's sixth floor.

Dining/Diversions: Most upscale of the hotel's dining facilities is the French-inspired Le Boeuf, which serves thick, juicy steaks in your choice of sizes. A slightly less expensive alternative, with an emphasis on continental and international food, is the Restaurant Europa. Both are open Monday to Saturday at lunch and dinner. On Sunday, guests dine on platters served within the hotel's bar.

Amenities: There's a limited number of convention facilities here, but not anything approaching the state-of-the-art sophistication of the convention facilities at the Hotel Gothia (reviewed below). There's also a sauna and exercise facilities; laundry facilities, and a concierge. Room service is available every day from 6:30am to 10:30pm.

Hotel Gothia. Mässans gata 24, S-402 26 Göteborg. ☎ **031/75-08-800.** Fax 031 /18-98-04. www.hotel-gothia.se. E-mail: hotelbok@hotel-gothia.se. 292 units. MINIBAR TV TEL. Mon–Thurs 1,690–1,795 SEK ($185.90–$197.45) double; Fri–Sun 1,140–1,320 SEK ($125.40–$145.20) double; all week long 3,500–4,600 SEK ($385–$506) suite. AE, DC, MC, V. Tram: 4 or 5.

This well-respected four-star hotel, which rises 18 mirror-plated stories above Sweden's largest convention center, was the tallest building in Gothenburg until the late 1990s. Inaugurated in 1985 and renovated in the mid-1990s, it is permeated with an international kind of modernism and brisk, friendly service that's equivalent to the best business-oriented hotels of Scandinavia. Bedrooms are comfortable, contemporary, tasteful, and have enough touches of wood, particularly as part of the hardwood floors, to take the edge off any sense of cookie-cutter standardization. Bathrooms are spacious, with lots of fluffy towels and steaming hot water. Rooms on the uppermost three floors are more plush, with enhanced amenities and services.

Dining/Diversions: The "18th floor restaurant" serves lunch and dinner daily. Adjacent is a panoramic pub whose old-time paneling contrasts with big-windowed aerial views over the city.

Amenities: Sauna, health club, business center, laundry service, and a concierge to arrange virtually anything in and around Gothenburg. Room service is available daily from 7am to 11pm. The city's convention center—the largest in Sweden—is accessible by covered passageway directly from the hotel.

✪ Radisson SAS Park Avenue Hotel. Kungsportsavenyn 36–38, S-400 16 Göteborg. ☎ **800/221-2350** in the U.S., or 031/758-40-00. Fax 031/16-95-68. www.radissonsas.com. 329 units. MINIBAR TV TEL. June 22–Aug 22, 1,455 SEK ($160.05) double; 3,150 SEK ($346.50) suite. Aug 23–June 21, 1,455–2,225 SEK ($160.05–$244.75) double; 3,150 SEK ($346.50) suite. Rates include buffet breakfast. AE, DC, MC, V. Parking 250 SEK ($27.50). Tram: 1, 4, 5, or 6. Bus: 40.

Constructed in 1950 and renovated in 1992, this modern hotel stands on Gothenburg's major boulevard. Everyone from Henry Kissinger and David Rockefeller to the Beatles and the Rolling Stones has stayed here. The hotel has 10 floors, with attractively designed bedrooms. Those on the upper floors enjoy excellent views of the city. The rooms are equipped with work desk, cable TV, and trouser press. Bathrooms are a bit small but are well-maintained and are equipped with robes, hair dryers, and good towels.

Dining/Diversions: The Parkbaren serves lunch, dinner, and light meals throughout the day. The hotel's gourmet dining room, Belle Avenue, is one of the best known in Gothenburg, specializing in game and fresh fish from the Atlantic. The hotel's famous nightclub, Park Lane, is recommended separately (see "Gothenburg After Dark," later in this chapter).

Amenities: Room service, SAS Euroclass check-in, valet parking, same-day laundry and dry cleaning, garage, beauty salon, sauna, solarium, newsstand, business service center, Royal Club with separate breakfast lounge.

Gothenburg

ATTRACTIONS ●

Botaniska Trädgården
(Botanical Garden) **11**
Drottning Kristinas Jaktslott
(Queen Christina's
Hunting Lodge) **16**
East India House
(Museum of
Gothenburg) **17**
Feskekörka
(Fish Church) **15**
Göteborg Maritimecenter **20**
Göteborgs Konstmuseum **8**
Göteborgsoperan
(Gothenburg
Opera House) **19**
Guldhedens Våttentorn
(Water Tower) **10**
Kronhusbodarna **18**
Liseberg Park **4**
Röhsska Museum of
Arts and Crafts **28**
Slottsskogen **12**
Stadsbibliotek (Library) **7**
Stadsteatern (Theater) **6**
Trägårdsföreningen **26**

ACCOMMODATIONS ■

Hotel Best Western
Eggers **23**
Hotel Europa **24**
Hotel Gothia **3**
Hotel Royal **25**
Hotel Onyxen **2**
Hotel Opera **22**
Hotel Örgyte **1**
Hotel Winn **21**
Novotel Göteborg **13**
Panorama Hotel **5**
Radisson SAS
Park Ave Hotel **27**
Radisson SAS
Scandinavia **9**
Tidbloms Hotel **14**

✪ Radisson SAS Scandinavia. Södra Hamngatan 59–65, S-401 24 Göteborg. ☎ **800/ 221-2350** in the U.S., or 031/80-60-00. Fax 031/15-98-88. www.radissonsas.com. 344 units. A/C MINIBAR TV TEL. 1,890–2,125 SEK ($207.90–$233.75) double; 2,800–4,800 SEK ($308–$528) suite. Rates include breakfast. AE, DC, MC, V. Parking 215 SEK ($23.65). Tram: 1, 2, 3, 4, 5, or 7. Bus: 40.

This unusual deluxe hotel opposite the railroad station is one of the best-run and -equipped hotels in Sweden. Opened in 1986 and built around a large atrium, the hotel offers the finest bedrooms in town; the rooms are large with good beds and are luxuriously appointed (some are suitable for people with disabilities). The uppermost floor of the hotel (the fifth) is reserved for the Sheraton Towers, the most exclusive accommodations. Bathrooms are small but have excellent towels and hair dryers.

Dining/Diversions: In the atrium lobby is a restaurant called Frascati, which serves international cuisine. There's also a piano bar and a small casino in the lobby, open Monday to Saturday from 7pm to 1am.

Amenities: Room service (24 hours), laundry, baby-sitting, health club, large swimming pool, Jacuzzi, saunas, solariums, indoor garage.

MODERATE

✪ Hotel Best Western Eggers. Drottningtorget, S-401 25 Göteborg. ☎ **800/528-1234** in the U.S. and Canada, or 031/80-60-70. Fax 031/15-42-43. E-mail: hotel.eggers@mailbox. swipnet.se. 79 units. TV TEL. June 29–Aug 6 and Fri–Sat year-round, 925–1,255 SEK ($101.75–$138.05) double; rest of year, 1,640–1,890 SEK ($180.40–$207.90) double. Rates include breakfast. AE, DC, MC, V. Parking 110 SEK ($12.10). Tram: 1, 2, 3, 4, 5, 6, 7, 8, or 9. Bus: 40.

The second-oldest hotel in Gothenburg was built in 1859, predating the Swedish use of the word "hotel" to describe a building with rooms for travelers. Many emigrants to the New World spent their last nights in the old country at the Hotel Eggers, and during World War II the Germans and the Allies met here for secret negotiations. Today it's better than ever, with stained-glass windows, ornate staircases, and wood paneling. All rooms are individually furnished and beautifully appointed, often with large bathrooms. Only the superior doubles have hair dryers. The room sizes vary. In the hotel dining room gilt leather tapestry and polished mahogany evoke the 19th century.

Hotel Onyxen. Sten Sturegatan 23, S-412 52 Göteborg. ☎ **031/81-08-45.** Fax 0321/ 16-56-72. www.hotelonyxen.com. 34 units. TV TEL. July–Aug and Fri–Sat year-round, 850 SEK ($93.50) double; rest of year, 1,190–1,240 SEK ($130.90–$136.40) double. Extra bed set up in room, 200 SEK ($22). Rates include breakfast. AE, DC, MC, V. Tram: 4, 5.

Clean, decent, and family managed, this hotel occupies the dignified, stone-fronted premises of what originally was built around 1900 as a many-balconied apartment house. In the 1980s, its interior was extensively reconfigured into the streamlined and efficiently decorated hotel you see today. Bedrooms are high-ceilinged, with comfortable beds and, in most cases, a color scheme of white and pale blue. Bathrooms are small but well cared for. There's a pub and cocktail lounge near the lobby, but the only meal served is breakfast.

Hotel Opera. Norra Hamngatan 38, S-411 06 Göteborg. ☎ **031/80-50-80.** Fax 031/ 80-58-17. www.hotelopera.se. 146 units. TV TEL. June 22–Aug 19 and Fri–Sat year-round, 850 SEK ($93.50) double; rest of year, 1,050–1,200 SEK ($115.50–$132) double. Rates include breakfast. AE, DC, MC, V. Parking 115 SEK ($12.65). Tram: 1, 4, 5, 6, 7, 8, or 9.

In July 1994 the Hotel Ekoxen joined forces (and facilities) with another hotel to become the Hotel Opera. It's an up-to-date and well-run hotel that often attracts business travelers, although summer visitors gravitate to it as well. Originally built in

1885, it was remodeled in the 1980s. All rooms are individually designed and tastefully furnished, and beds have firm mattresses. Amenities include such conveniences as a trouser press and plenty of thick towels. The hotel also offers a sauna and Jacuzzi.

Novotel Göteborg. Klippan 1, S-414 51 Göteborg. ☎ **800/221-4542** in the U.S., or 031/14-90-00. Fax 031/42-22-32. www.novotel.com. E-mail: hotel.got@novotel.se. 152 units. A/C TV TEL. June 26–Aug 10 and Fri–Sat year-round, 700 SEK ($77) double; 1,190 SEK ($130.90) suite. Rest of year, 1,440 SEK ($158.40) double; 1,790 SEK ($196.90) suite. Rates include breakfast. AE, DC, MC, V. Free parking. From Gothenburg, follow the signs on E20 to Frederikshavn, then the signs to Kiel; exit at Klippan, where signs direct you to the hotel. Tram: 3 or 9. Bus: 91 or 92.

This converted harbor-front brewery 2½ miles west of the center is a stylish hotel run by the French hotel conglomerate Accor. Each plushly carpeted room offers panoramic views of the industrial landscape. The room styling is Swedish modern with many built-in pieces, good-size closets, and firm sofa beds. The small bathrooms have hair dryers, but only adequate towels. A well-accessorized sauna and laundry facilities are available. The hotel restaurant, Carnegie Kaj (open until midnight), serves well-prepared food with French accents. In summer, snacks and light meals are served on the terrace. Guests rendezvous at the Carnegie Porter Pub, named after the beer that was produced on this site for 160 years.

Panorama Hotel. Eklandagatan 5153, S-400 22 Göteborg. ☎ **800/528-1234** in the U.S. and Canada, or 031/767-70-00. Fax 031/767-70-70. www.panorama.se. E-mail: info@panorama.se. 338 units, some with shower only. TV TEL. June 20–Aug 10 and Fri–Sat year-round, 890 SEK ($97.90) double; 1,260 SEK ($138.60) suite. Rest of year, 1,490 SEK ($163.90) double; 1,600 SEK ($176) suite. Rates include breakfast. AE, DC, MC, V. Free parking. Closed Dec 21–Jan 7. Tram: 4 or 5. Bus: 40 or 51.

This spacious, dramatic hotel is a 10-minute walk west of the center of town. At 13 stories, it's one of the tallest buildings in Gothenburg. Built in 1984, its plant-filled lobby has a skylight piano bar and balcony-level restaurant. The bedrooms provide stylish furnishings and soft lighting. Extra room amenities include electronic locks, double glazing, and wood floors. Bathrooms tend to be small, mostly without tubs, and only those in the superior rooms contain hair dryers. The finest accommodations are found on floors 7 through 13. On the premises is a whirlpool, along with a sauna and solarium.

INEXPENSIVE

Hotel Örgyte. Danska Vägen 68–70, S-416 59 Göteborg. ☎ **031/707-89-00.** Fax 031/707-89-99. www.hotelorgryte.se. E-mail: info@hotelorgryte.se. 70 units. TV TEL. Sun–Thurs 1,200–1,290 SEK ($132–$141.90) double; Fri–Sat 700 SEK ($77) double; all week long 1,470–1,670 SEK ($161.70–$183.70) suite. Rates include breakfast. AE, DC, MC, V. Parking 85 SEK ($9.35). Bus: 60 or 62.

Named after the leafy residential district of Örgyte, this hotel lies a mile east of the commercial core of Göteborg. It originally was built around 1960, and has been renovated many times since, most recently in the mid-1990s. Rooms are outfitted with pastel-colored upholsteries and streamlined, uncomplicated furniture that makes use of birch-veneer woods. Rooms are medium-sized, often big enough to contain a sitting area; mattresses are firm but a bit thin; and bathrooms are rather cramped. Both the exterior and the public areas are clean but not particularly inspired in their design; but overall, the place provides decent, safe accommodations at a relatively reasonable price. On the premises is a restaurant that serves full-meal platters for 75 SEK ($8.25) at lunchtime and 100 SEK ($11) at dinner.

Hotel Royal. Drottninggatan 67, S-411 07 Göteborg. ☎ **031/700-11-70.** Fax 031/ 700-11-79. www.hotel-royal.com. E-mail: info@hotel-royal.com. 81 units. TV TEL. June 22– Aug 14 and Fri and Sat year-round, 760–910 SEK ($83.60–$100.10) double; 1,200 SEK ($132) suite. Rest of year, 1,200–1,300 SEK ($132–$143) double; 1,695 SEK ($186.45) suite. Rates include buffet breakfast. AE, DC, MC, V. Parking 100 SEK ($11). Tram: 1, 2, 3, 4, 5, or 6. Bus: 60.

A quarter mile from the railroad station (all major bus and tram lines pass close by), the Hotel Royal is the oldest operating hotel in Gothenburg. The hotel was completely renovated in 1989 and again in 1993. It's decorated in a typical 19th-century style, with wrought-iron banisters and heavy cast-bronze lamps at the stairs. In the reception area is a unique hand-painted glass ceiling. The rooms are individually designed and modernized, with firm mattresses plus ample bathrooms and towels. The breakfast buffet included in the price is generous. The hotel serves a light evening meal and sandwiches are always available.

Hotel Winn. Gamla Tingstadsgatan 1, S-402 76 Göteborg. ☎ **031/750-1900.** Fax 031/ 51-21-00. www.winnhotel.com. E-mail: info@winnhotel.com 121 units. MINIBAR TV TEL. June 15–Aug 15 and Fri–Sat year-round, 840 SEK ($92.40) double; rest of year, 1,140 SEK ($125.40) double. Rates include breakfast. AE, DC, MC, V. Free parking. Bus: 40.

Named after the mythical explorer who circumnavigated the globe in 80 days, this four-story hotel is about 2 miles north of Gothenburg's ferryboat terminal. Its functional, modern bedrooms are more comfortable than you might imagine from their uninspired, pastel appearance. The Broken Dreams bar is frequented by business travelers, and the Hotel Winn Restaurant serves regional and continental food. Facilities include a swimming pool, sauna, and solarium.

✪ **Tidbloms Hotel.** Olskroksgatan 23, S-416 66 Göteborg. ☎ **031/707-50-00.** Fax 031/707-50-99. www.tidblomshotel.com. E-mail: info.tidbloms@swedenhotels.se. 42 units. MINIBAR TV TEL. Sun–Thurs 1,090–1,400 SEK ($119.90–$154) double; Fri–Sat 890 SEK ($97.90) double. Rates include breakfast. AE, DC, MC, V. Free parking. Tram: 1, 3, or 6.

This cozy, charming, well-accessorized hotel is 2 miles east of Gothenburg's center, in a residential neighborhood filled with other Victorian buildings. Originally built in 1897 as a dormitory for Scottish craftsmen imported to work at the nearby lumber mill, the building is graced with a conical tower, fancy brickwork, and architectural adornments. After stints as a warehouse, a delicatessen, and a low-rent hotel, the building was upgraded in 1987. Bedrooms with good, firm beds and ample bathrooms have more flair and character than you'll find at many larger, more anonymous hotels in Gothenburg's center, and often contain appealing contrasts of patterns in the upholstery and hardwood floors. On the premises is a restaurant, which is recommended separately in the following section (see "Where to Dine"), and a sauna whose wall paintings and recordings of waves and sea birds were inspired by the sights and sounds of the archipelago. The hotel also contains a scattering of convention facilities for business meetings and reunions. The most dramatic of these lies under the soaring cone-shaped roof of the building's tower.

4 Where to Dine

EXPENSIVE

Bistro Mannerström. Archivgatan 7. ☎ **031/16-03-33.** Reservations recommended. Main courses 250–300 SEK ($27.50–$33); fixed-price menus 245–270 SEK ($26.95–$29.70). AE, DC, MC, V. Mon–Sat 5–11pm. Closed July. Tram: 4 or 5. SWEDISH.

This place's appeal is due in part to the way in which it celebrates old-fashioned Swedish wholesomeness and *husmanskost* (home cooking), with a sophisticated and often upscale flair. Bistro Mannerström calls itself a simple neighborhood restaurant, despite the fact that its culinary aspirations are far higher than that. You'll be seated within one or two white-walled dining rooms whose only color derives from the varnished light-grained woods that permeate the place. Elegant versions of traditional Swedish dishes might include poached halibut with a turbot and scallop mousseline; broiled cutlets of turbot with glazed carrots and a sauce concocted from red wine, butter, lemon, and rosemary; breast of wild Swedish duck served with a confit of bacon-flavored puree of potatoes served in a cabbage shell; or grilled and cured brisket of beef with chanterelles, bacon, and spring onions. Expect a clientele of entrepreneurs and corporate leaders, many of whom combine business with their meals.

Fiskekrogen. Lilla Torget 1. ☎ **031/10-10-05.** Reservations recommended. Main courses 225–325 SEK ($24.75–$35.75); fixed-price small menu 595 SEK ($65.45); fixed-price big menu 795 SEK ($87.45); vegetarian menu 395 SEK ($43.45). AE, MC, V. Mon–Fri 11:30am–11pm, Sat 1–11pm. Tram: 2 or 5. SEAFOOD.

Situated across the canal from the Stadtsmuseum, Fiskekrogen is one of the most appealing seafood restaurants in Gothenburg. It prides itself on a medley of seafood that's fresh, artfully displayed, and prepared with a zest that has made it a preferred venue for loyal clients throughout the city. One of the most appealing aspects of the place is a richly accessorized seafood bar, from which heaping platters of oysters, lobster, crayfish, clams, and mussels are gracefully arranged on crushed ice and presented usually with a flourish, at your table. More conventional seafood dishes include poached fillets of cod with beetroot marmalade and a horseradish-butter sauce; and grilled halibut with a ragoût of baby scallops, bacon, onions, mushrooms, and Zinfandel.

Restaurang Räkan/Yellow Submarine. Lorensbergsgatan 16. ☎ **031/16-98-39.** Reservations recommended. Main courses 175–265 SEK ($19.25–$29.15). AE, DC, MC, V. Tram: 1, 4, 5, or 6. Bus: 40. SEAFOOD.

One of the best seafood restaurants in Gothenburg, Restaurang Räkan has (naturally) a nautical decor with buoy lamps, wooden-plank tables typical of the Swedish west coast, and a shallow-bottomed re-creation of a Swedish lake. Your seafood platter will arrive on a battery-powered boat with you directing the controls. You can order various combinations of crayfish (in season), along with prawns, poached sole, mussels, lobster, fillet of gray sole, and fresh crabs. If you don't want fish, chicken and beef dishes also are available. Attached to the restaurant is a popular pub, Yellow Submarine, named for the Beatles song by the same name.

Restaurant 28+. Götabergsgatan 28. ☎ **031/20-21-61.** Reservations recommended. Main courses 245–325 SEK ($26.95–$35.75); fixed-price menus 655–755 SEK ($72.05–$83.05). AE, DC, MC, V. Mon–Wed 6–10pm, Thurs–Sat 6–11pm. INTERNATIONAL.

Cozy, intimate, and reeking of old-world charm, this is a chic and stylish restaurant whose trio of dining rooms are lit with flickering candles and capped with soaring masonry ceiling vaults. It's one of the city's more hip and with-it culinary venues, featuring main courses that include cooked crayfish with a fennel-flavored *nage;* smoke filet of char in a red wine and butter sauce; grilled breast of pigeon, or saddle of reindeer with Jerusalem artichokes and blackberry vinaigrette. We have consistently found that the finest cuisine in Gothenburg is served here, as well as the most imaginative. It's as if the chef personally goes to the market demanding only perfect produce for his sumptuous meals. And it's lip-smacking good. The items taste fabulously fresh, and the food is handled faultlessly in the kitchen and delicately seasoned. The service is the city's best, and the sommelier will offer expert guidance, although the tax on wine is so high you'll feel like you're putting his kid through school. The most demanding palates in Gothenburg come here and leave satisfied.

✪ **Sjömagasinet.** Klippans Kulturreservat. ☎ **031/775-59-20.** Reservations recommended. Main courses 265–345 SEK ($29.15–$37.95); 1-course fixed-price lunch 105 SEK ($11.55); 3-course fixed-price dinner 410–545 SEK ($45.10–$59.95). AE, DC, MC, V. Mon–Fri 11:30am–11pm, Sat 5–11pm, Sun 2–9pm. From the town center, head west on E3, following the signs to Frederikshavn and then to Kiel; exit at Klippan and then follow the signs for the Novotel. Tram: 3 or 9. SEAFOOD.

By far the most interesting and intriguing restaurant in town, Sjömagasinet is located near the Novotel in the western suburb of Klippan, about 2½ miles from the center. The building, erected in 1775, originally was a warehouse. Before dinner, you can enjoy a drink in the cozy English colonial bar or in the second bar upstairs.

Very fresh seafood is served here: shrimp-stuffed crepes with dill, shellfish with curry sauce, baked fillet of beef and lobster, poached fillets of sole with crayfish, and turbot béarnaise. Two specialties are pot-au-feu of fish and shellfish, served with a chive-flavored crème fraîche, and poached fillet of halibut with warm cabbage salad and potato salad.

MODERATE

A Hereford Beefstouw. Linnégatan. ☎ **031/775-04-41.** Reservations recommended. Main courses 115–285 SEK ($12.65–$31.35); salad bar as a main course 80 SEK ($8.80). AE, DC, MC, V. Mon–Fri 11:30am–2pm and 5–10pm, Sat 4–11pm, Sun 3–9pm. Tram: 1, 3, 4, or 9. STEAKS.

This is the most appealing and best-recommended steakhouse in Gothenburg, with a reputation for well-prepared Australian beef and a salad bar that's one of the largest and most varied in town. Inside, you'll find three separate dining rooms (one of which is smoke free), each outfitted with thick-topped wooden tables, lots of varnished pine, and touches of African oak. The only sauces available to accompany your beef are béarnaise-butter, parsley butter, or garlic butter (management clearly believes in allowing the meat to speak for itself). The largest platter available is a 500-gram (17½-ounce) T-bone steak, a portion so large that you should consume all of it only at your own risk. Other platters, such as fillet steaks, veal sirloins, or tenderloins, are more reasonably sized. A full list of wines and beers is available.

Brasserie Lipp. Kungsportsavenyn 8. ☎ **031/711-50-58.** Reservations required. Main courses 155–198 SEK ($17.05–$21.80); daily platters 85 SEK ($9.35). AE, DC, MC, V. Daily 11:30am–11:30pm. Tram: 1, 4, 5, or 6. Bus: 40. SWEDISH/FRENCH.

Located on Gothenburg's busiest avenue, this brasserie is inspired by the legendary bistro of the same name in Paris, with palate adjustments for Swedish tastes. It's a culinary melting pot that produces such dishes as Lipp's Skagen toast (piled high with shrimp), Swedish entrecôte of beef with Dijon mustard sauce, grilled halibut with garlic-tomato sauce, carpaccio of beef, and Thai chicken. There's also *choucroute garni* (sauerkraut with sausage and pork, the most famous dish served at its Paris namesake), and many different kinds of fish, most caught in the waters near Gothenburg.

La Gondola. Kungsportsavenyn 4. ☎ **031/711-68-28.** Reservations recommended. Main courses 85–210 SEK ($9.35–$23.10); dagens (daily) lunch 70–80 SEK ($7.70–$8.80). AE, DC, MC, V. Daily 11:30am–11pm. Tram: 1, 4, 5, or 6. Bus: 38 or 75. ITALIAN.

You'll find the best pizzas in town here, as well as many classic Italian dishes. With its striped poles, sidewalk awnings, and summer outdoor cafe, this restaurant evokes Venice. The spaghetti Gondola is very good, and the saltimbocca ("jump in your mouth") alla romana, a veal-and-ham dish, is tasty. You also might try one of the grilled specialties, or fried scampi or plank steak. The minestrone is freshly made and filling; and a velvety-smooth ice cream is served for dessert. Every day there's a different lunch specialty, and an à la carte dinner is served.

Picnic Fare

Go to **Saluhallen,** Kungstorget, for the makings of an elegant picnic. This colorful indoor market was built in 1888 and sells meat, fruit, vegetables, delicatessen products, and everything in between. You can find quail, moose, and reindeer; fruits and vegetables from all over the world; and bread, coffee, olives, pâtés, and more. Much of the food is already cooked and will be packaged for you to take out. If you don't feel like venturing outside, there are four restaurants and a coffee bar in the building. The hall is open Monday through Thursday from 8:30am to 6pm, Friday from 8am to 6pm, and Saturday from 8am to 1pm. Take tram no. 1, 4, 5, or 6 to Kungsportsplatsen.

Once you've packed your picnic basket with goodies, go to any of Gothenburg's major parks (see "Parks & Gardens" in "Seeing the Sights," later in this chapter). Especially recommended is **Trädgårdsföreningen,** across from the Central Station, although there's a 10 SEK ($1.10) entrance fee.

Lilla London. Avenyn/Vasagatan 41. ☎ **031/18-40-62.** Reservations recommended. Main courses 100–210 SEK ($11–$23.10). AE, DC, MC, V. Daily 5pm–midnight. Tram: 1, 4, 5, or 6. Bus: 40. SWEDISH/FRENCH.

This is good standard fare prepared with fresh ingredients and selling for a fair price— nothing more. The restaurant, down a flight of steps, is dark and attractively designed, with illuminated paintings of clipper ships and nautical accents. Full meals might include grilled chicken with morels, beef and lamb fillet in a mustard-flavored cream sauce, filet mignon, and broiled salmon with fresh asparagus. Less expensive light meals also are available. The quiet, pub-like bar, which sells about 10 different kinds of beer, is a local favorite.

Restaurang Gillestugan. Järntorget 6. ☎ **031/24-00-50.** Reservations recommended. Main courses 82–185 SEK ($9–$20.35); fixed-price menus 250–275 SEK ($27.50–$30.25). AE, DC, MC, V. Daily 11:30am–2pm and 5–11:30pm. Bar, Sun–Thurs 11am–1am, Fri–Sat 11am–3am. Entertainment 9–11pm. Tram: 1, 3, 4, and 9. SWEDISH/INTERNATIONAL.

Local entrepreneurs put a new spin on one of Gothenburg's most nostalgic restaurants in the mid-1990s when they transformed its antique-looking premises into the city's busiest and most creative cabaret and supper club. Throughout most of the day, you can drop in for a meal and a drink and be entertained only by whomever you happen to be dining with and the good-natured, hardworking staff.

One floor above street level, every evening beginning at 9pm, a small stage is the site of a revolving series of musical, theatrical, or poetic events. Recent examples have included folk singers whose repertoire is in both Swedish and English, and an Elvis impersonator whose act, *The Burning Star,* drew rave reviews from local residents who insisted that he was better than the real thing. Because some of the entertainment involves Swedish-language satire that you'll need a strong linguistic ability to understand, we advise that you phone in advance so you can avoid any production that's too esoteric.

Food is well prepared and served in generous portions, and there's no cover charge for the entertainment. Menu items include salmon tartare with horseradish sauce and fried onions; a mushroom and apple terrine with air-dried ham and spicy oil; a rather odd Vietnamese dish defined as braised oilfish with a lukewarm salad of marinated potatoes and vegetables and a lime-leaf cream sauce; and fillet of lamb with tomato and feta cheese sauce and sliced, fried potatoes.

There's additional seating within the street-level bar, the Tullen Pub, whose wood panels haven't changed much since they were originally installed in 1892, but there's no view of the cabaret from here.

INEXPENSIVE

Froken Olssons Café. Östra Larmgatan 14. ☎ **031/13-81-93.** Coffee 16 SEK ($1.75); dagens (daily) menu 58 SEK ($6.40); hot pies with salad 50 SEK ($5.50); sandwiches 20–50 SEK ($2.20–$5.50). MC, V. Mon–Thurs 9am–10pm, Fri 9am–1am. Tram: 1, 4, 5, or 6. Bus: 40. SWEDISH.

This local favorite features light cafe dining, with homemade soups and such main courses as entrecôte. It's a popular spot, less than 2 blocks from the Avenyn, that tends to be crowded and noisy at lunchtime. Even though there's a large interior, the scene overflows onto an outdoor terrace in summer. At night, hot pies with a salad are featured along with an array of baguette sandwiches filled with ingredients such as shrimp or ham and cheese. Light beer is served, but no wine or liquor.

Solrosen (Sunflower). Kaponjärgatan 4. ☎ **031/711-66-97.** Main courses 50–110 SEK ($5.50–$12.10). AE, DC, MC, V. Mon–Fri 11:30am–1am, Sat 2pm–1am. Tram: 1, 3, or 4. VEGETARIAN.

Situated in the Haga district, a low-rise neighborhood of 18th- and early 19th-century buildings, this is the best vegetarian restaurant in Gothenburg. The food is dispensed from a self-service counter, with an all-you-can eat salad bar that accompanies any main dish. There's unlimited coffee and second helpings. Beer and wine are available.

Tapas Bar & Brasserie. Kungsgatan 8. ☎ **031/711-3077.** Reservations recommended on weekends. Main courses 60–130 SEK ($6.60–$14.30). AE, MC, V. Daily 5–11pm. Bar stays open till 1am. Tram: 1, 4, or 5. INTERNATIONAL.

Many of the clients who drop in here don't ever move on to a table, remaining instead at the bar, which can get busy with the singles crowd as the night progresses. But if you do get hungry, the blue-and-white dining room will present a relatively inexpensive and unpretentious roster of well-prepared dishes that include a tomato and onion salad garnished with shrimp and scallops, sea bass in teriyaki sauce, chicken breast with chili sauce, and well-prepared steaks.

✪ Tidbloms Restaurang. Olskroksgatan 23. ☎ **031/707-50-00.** Main courses 149–199 SEK ($16.40–$21.90); fixed-price menus 80–190 SEK ($8.80–$20.90). AE, DC, MC, V. Mon–Fri 11:30am–1:30pm and 6–10pm, Sat 4–10pm, Sun 1–8pm. Tram: 1, 3, or 6. INTERNATIONAL.

Set near the lobby of the previously recommended hotel, this restaurant is particularly charming, thanks to origins stretching from the late 19th century and a staff that works hard to keep things personal. Within a dining room sheathed with wooden paneling and hints of the Victorian age, you can order items that include cream of chanterelle soup; seafood medley on toast; African-style beef in a piquant peanut sauce, served with rice; salmon in a saffron-flavored cream sauce; and a combination of pork with beef prepared Provençal style with red wine and Lyonnais potatoes.

5 Seeing the Sights

As with any new destination, often the problem is having too much to do. Following the itineraries below will help you plan your time so you can see as much as possible.

For a map of attractions, see page 127.

Suggested Itineraries

If You Have 1 Day

Enjoy a cup of coffee at one of the cafes along the Avenyn in the center of Gothenburg; then take the classical Padden boat ride, traveling through the moat and canal out to the harbor and the giant docks. Return for a stroll along the Avenyn; then take one of the summertime vintage trams to see part of the city ashore. Go to Liseberg amusement park in the evening.

If You Have 2 Days

For your first day, follow the suggestions above. On Day 2, take a boat trip to Elfsborg Fortress, leaving from the Stenpiren in the Gothenburg harbor and continuing under the Älvsborg Bridge to Elfsborg. In the afternoon visit the Göteborgs Konstmuseum and the Botanical Garden.

If You Have 3 Days

For the first 2 days, follow the itinerary suggested above. On Day 3, get up early to visit the fish auction at the harbor (begins at 7am); then go to the Feskekörka (Fish Church) nearby. Take tram no. 6 to Guldhedens Våttentorn (water tower) for a panoramic view of Gothenburg. Go to Götaplatsen to see the famed Poseiden fountain by Carl Milles. In the afternoon visit the Röhsska Museum of Arts and Crafts and stroll through the rose-filled Tradgärdsföreningen across from the Central Station.

If You Have 4–5 Days

For Days 1 to 3, follow the itinerary suggested above. On Day 4, take an excursion to Marstrand, north of the city. On Day 5, visit Nordstan, the biggest shopping center in Scandinavia. Spend the remaining part of the day exploring the southern archipelago, which you can do free with your Gothenburg Card (see "Getting Around," earlier in this chapter). The MS *Styrsö* and the steamboat *Bohuslän* depart from Skeppsbron/Stenpiren for trips around the archipelago.

THE TOP ATTRACTIONS

For a quick overview orientation, visit the 400-foot-tall **Guldhedens Vattentorn** (water tower), Syster Estrids Gata (☎ 031/82-00-09); to get there, take tram no. 6 or 7 from the center of the city, about a 10-minute ride. The elevator ride up the tower is free, and there's a cafeteria/snack bar on top. The tower is open October through March, Saturday through Thursday from noon to 10pm.

Early risers can visit the daily **fish auction** at the harbor, the largest fishing port in Scandinavia. The amusing auction begins at 7am sharp. You also can visit the **Feskekörka** (Fish Church), on Rosenlundsgatan, which is in the fish market. It's open Tuesday through Friday from 9am to 5pm and Saturday from 9am to 1pm.

For a look at Gothenburg, the traditional starting point is the cultural center, **Götaplatsen,** with its *Poseidon Fountain,* the work of Carl Milles. The trio of buildings here are the **Concert Hall,** the municipally owned **theater,** and the Göteborgs Konstmuseum.

Göteborgs Konstmuseum. Götaplatsen. ☎ **031/61-29-80.** Admission 45 SEK ($4.95) adults, 15 SEK ($1.65) children 7–16, free for children under 7. May–Aug, Mon–Fri 11am–4pm, Sat–Sun 11am–5pm; Sept–Apr, Tues and Thurs–Fri 11am–4pm, Wed 11am–9pm, Sat–Sun 11am–5pm. Tram: 4 or 5. Bus: 40.

Göteborgs Konstmuseum is the leading art museum of Gothenburg, with a good collection of modern art, notably of the French impressionists. Bonnard, Cézanne, van

Gogh, and even Picasso are represented, along with sculptures by Milles and Rodin. The gallery is noted for its collection of the works of 19th- and 20th-century Scandinavian artists (Zorn and Larsson of Dalarna, and Edvard Munch and Christian Krohg of Norway). Old masters also are represented, including Rembrandt and Rubens. The modern section includes work by Francis Bacon and Henry Moore.

Liseberg Park. Korsvägen. ☎ **031/40-01-00,** or 031/40-02-20 for daily programs and times. Admission 45 SEK ($4.95) adults, free for children under 7. June–Aug, Mon–Fri 3–11pm, Sat 11am–midnight, Sun 11am–10pm; Sept–Nov, Fri 5–11pm, Sat 11am–midnight, Sun 11am–10pm. Tram: 4 or 5 from the city.

Scandinavia's largest amusement park is more than 75 years old, and in terms of numbers of visitors, this is the number one tourist attraction in Sweden. It's a bit corny and doesn't have the class and the style of Copenhagen's Tivoli; nonetheless it is fun for the entire family. Some of Sweden's best performing artists entertain every summer at Stora Scenen, the park's main stage. The park's newest attraction is the Gasten Ghost Hotel filled with things that go bump in the night. Other adventure rides include the Källerado rapid river, a simulated white-water trip through the wilds of northern Sweden, and the HangOver, the most harrowing roller coaster in northern Europe, traveling at a frightening speed with all the usual bends and loops. The rocket launcher fires you 60 meters into the air; at the top you'll feel weightlessness before you come screaming back down. For the younger set there's a children's playground with a circus, a kiddie roller coaster, and a rabbit house where the Liseberg rabbits live. Like Disneyland, there also is a Fairy Tale Castle where knights, fair damsels, and other period figures amuse children, who are then taken on a Dragon Boat ride, evoking Sweden's Viking era. Many Gothenburgers like to come here in summer to eat or dine, as there are 18 fast-food places and ten restaurants, with food ranging from seafood in the harbor area to savory Italian pastas.

Röhsska Museum of Arts and Crafts. Vasagatan 37–39. ☎ **031/61-38-50.** Admission 25 SEK ($2.75) adults, 5 SEK (55¢) children 7–16, free for children under 7. May–Aug, Mon–Fri noon–4pm, Sat–Sun noon–5pm; Sept–Apr, Tues noon–9pm, Wed–Fri noon–4pm, Sat–Sun noon–5pm. Closed Aug 15–Sept 21. Tram: 1, 4, 5, 6, or 8. Bus: 40.

This museum houses a large collection of European furnishings, china, glass, pottery, and Asian artifacts plus permanent and temporary exhibits of modern handcrafts and industrial design. Among the exhibits are books, silver, and Chinese and Japanese art. The museum presents lecture series and guided tours.

Göteborg Maritime Center. Packhujkajem 8. ☎ **031/10-59-50.** www.gmtc.se/ index_ uk.htm. Admission 70 SEK ($7.70) adults, 35 SEK ($3.85) children 4–16, free for children under 4. July, daily 10am–9pm; May–June and Aug, daily 10am–6pm; Mar–Apr and Sept–Nov, daily 10am–4pm. Closed Dec–Feb. Tram: 5 to Lilla Bommen.

Located on the harbor, this museum is partly aboard the destroyer *Småland,* equipped with guns and torpedoes. In authentic settings, you can see lightships, steamships, and tugboats, among other watercraft. There are cafes at the center and on the quay.

East India House (Museum of Gothenburg). Norra Hamngatan 12. ☎ **031/61-27-70.** Admission 40 SEK ($4.40) adults, 10 SEK ($1.10) children 7–14, free for children under 7. June–Aug, daily 11am–4pm; Sept–May, Tues–Sun 11am–4pm. Tram: 1 or 9. Bus: 40, 58, or 60 to Brunnsparken.

This museum focuses on the history—archaeological, cultural, technical, and medical—of Gothenburg and its environs. There is an array of interesting permanent exhibits, including displays from the Viking era and unique artifacts found in the area.

Stadsbibliotek. Götaplatsen. ☎ **031/61-65-00.** Free admission. Mon–Thurs 10am–8pm, Fri 10am–6pm, Sat–Sun 11am–4pm. Tram: 1, 4, 5, or 6. Bus: 40.

Toward the end of the Avenyn is the public library, on the left at Götaplatsen. This is the main library of Gothenburg, the home of some 450,000 volumes in 50 languages, and a cafe. The library also has a listening room with recorded music, as well as a reading room with more than 100 foreign daily newspapers. One hall features continuously changing exhibits.

PARKS & GARDENS

Botaniska Trädgården (Botanical Garden). Carl Skottsbergsgata 22. ☎ 031/741-11-00. Free admission to garden; greenhouses 20 SEK ($2.20), free for children under 17. Garden, daily 9am–sunset. Greenhouses, May–Aug, daily 10am–5pm; Sept–Apr, daily 10am–4pm. Tram: 1, 2, or 7.

This park is the beauty oasis of Gothenburg, and is in fact the most dramatic, cultivated bit of nature in western Sweden. The botanic gardens were first opened to the public in 1923 and have been improved considerably over the years with better landscaping and more stunning plantings. Winding paths stretching for a few kilometers have been cut through the gardens and you can stroll along at leisure, absorbing the beauty of nature at every turn. There are plants and landscape scenes from around the world: You can wander into a bamboo grove evoking Southeast Asia, or explore a Japanese dale. In spring, the rhododendron valley bursts into bloom, one of the most stunning sights of Gothenburg. The splendid rock garden alone is worth the journey and features ponds, rugged rocks, cliffs, flowers, and a cascade.

Slottsskogen. Near Linnéplatsen. ☎ 031/61-18-90. Free admission. Daily 24 hours. Tram: 1 or 2 to Linnéplatsen.

With 274 acres, this is the largest park in Gothenburg. First laid out in 1874 in a naturally wooded area, today it has beautiful walks, animal enclosures, a saltwater pool, bird ponds, and an aviary, as well as a children's zoo (open May through August). A variety of events and entertainment take place here in summer. There's an outdoor cafe at the zoo, plus restaurants at Villa Bel Park and Björngårdsvillan.

Trädgårdsföreningen. Entrances on Slussgatan (across from the Central Station) and Södra Vägen. ☎ 031/61-18-83. Park, 15 SEK ($1.65) adults, free for children 16 and under, free for everyone Sept–Apr; Palm House, 20 SEK ($2.20) adults and children; Butterfly House, 35 SEK ($3.85) adults, 10 SEK ($1.10) children. May–Aug, daily 7am–9pm; Sept–Apr, daily 7am–6:30pm.

Located across the canal from the Central Station, this park boasts a large rosarium that flourishes with about 10,000 rose bushes of 4,000 different species. The park's centerpieces are the palm house, a greenhouse maintained at subtropical temperatures even in the depths of winter, and a butterfly house containing beautiful butterflies that flutter through a simulation of a natural habitat. The city of Gothenburg sometimes hosts exhibits, concerts (sometimes during the lunch hour), and children's theater pieces in the park.

ARCHITECTURAL HIGHLIGHTS

Drottning Kristinas Jaktslott (Queen Christina's Hunting Lodge). Otterhallegatan 16. ☎ 031/13-34-26. Free admission. Daily 11am–4pm. Tram: 2, 3, 4, or 7 to Lilla Torget.

The rounded walls of this stone-sided house—the oldest in Gothenburg—originally were conceived in the 1600s as part of an outpouring of civic pride (or civic savvy) when it was designated as a hideaway for Queen Christina during her occasional visits from Stockholm. Although the queen didn't use it very frequently, its stone and wood interior still evokes the austere majesty of this deeply religious, deeply troubled 17th-century monarch. Go to admire the architecture and don't expect a lot of exhibits (except for some Swedish antiques). In 1971, it was saved from demolition by the Ötterhallen Historical Preservation Society and the administration of the Gothenburg Historical Museum. There's a cafe that specializes in light snacks (try the piping-hot waffles) that begin at around 30 SEK ($3.30).

Kronhusbodarna. Kronhusgatan 1D. ☎ **031/711-08-32.** Tram: 1 or 7 to Brunnsparken.

One of the architectural showpieces of Gothenburg, Kronhusbodarna originally was built in the 1650s; it's the oldest non-ecclesiastical building in town. In the 1660s, it was pressed into service as the meeting place for the Swedish Parliament, which convened here hastily to welcome a visit from Charles X Gustav during his wars with Denmark. For many years, the building functioned as a warehouse and repair center for the Swedish military, stockpiling sailcloth and armaments. Today, its echoing interior accommodates a number of small-scale and rather sleepy artisans' studios. See "Shopping," below.

ESPECIALLY FOR KIDS

At **Liseberg amusement park** (see above), every day is children's day. The Liseberg Cirkus is a fun fair, and there are always comic characters to play with children. The pony merry-go-round, children's boats, and a fun-on-wheels merry-go-round all are free for tots.

Your children may want to stay at the amusement park's hotel, in the city center, a short walk from the park. **Hotel Liseberg Heden,** Sten Sturegatan S-411 38 Göteborg (☎ **031/750-69-109;** fax 031/750-69-30; www.liseberg.se), offers discounted summer rates. They include breakfast and coupons for free admission to the amusement park and many of its rides and shows. Between May and September, the discounted rate for double rooms is 850 SEK ($93.50). From October to April, doubles cost 840 SEK ($92.40) on Friday through Sunday, and 1,190 SEK ($130.90) Monday through Thursday. The hotel accepts major credit cards (AE, DC, MC, V). It was built in the 1930s as an army barracks and later functioned as a youth hostel. Today, after tons of improvements, it's a first-class, very comfortable hotel. To reach the 172-room hotel, take tram no. 4 or 5 to Berzeliegaten.

Naturhistoriska Museet I Göteborg, Slottsskogen (☎ **031/775-24-00**), displays stuffed animals from all over the world, including Sweden's only stuffed blue whale. It's open Tuesday to Friday 9am to 6pm, and Saturday and Sunday 11am to 5pm. Admission is 40 SEK ($4.40) for adults, 10 SEK ($1.10) for ages 7 to 20, free for children under 7. Tram: 1, 2, or 6. Bus: 51 or 54 to Linnéplatsen.

There's also a **children's zoo** at Slottsskogen from May to August (see "Parks & Gardens," above).

A restaurant that kids find especially intriguing is **Restaurang Räkan/Yellow Submarine** (see "Where to Dine" above), where seafood platters arrive in battery-powered boats at your table.

ORGANIZED TOURS

A sightseeing boat trip along the canals and out into the harbor will show you the old parts of central Gothenburg and take you under 20 bridges and out into the harbor. ✪ **Paddan Sightseeing Boats** (☎ **031/60-96-70**) offers 55-minute tours May through September 15, daily 10am to 5pm; September 12 to October 6, daily noon to 3pm. They leave from the terminal at Kungsportsplatsen in the city center. The fare is 75 SEK ($8.25) for adults, 50 SEK ($5.50) for children 4 to 15, and free for kids under 4. A family ticket (two adults and two children) costs 195 SEK ($21.45).

Nya Elfsborg (☎ **031/10-07-40**) is docked in the 17th-century fortress at the harbor's mouth. This boat takes you on a 90-minute tour from Lilla Bommen through the harbor, to and around Elfsborg Fortress, built in the 17th century to protect the Göta

Älv estuary and the western entrance to Sweden. It still bears traces of hard-fought sea battles against the Danes. Carvings on the prison walls tell tales of the threats and hopes of the 19th-century lifetime prisoners. A guide will be waiting for you at the cafeteria, museum, and souvenir shop. There are five departures per day from mid-May to the end of August. The fare is 75 SEK ($8.25) for adults, 45 SEK ($4.95) for children.

The **MS *Poseidon*** is available for an evening cruise of the archipelago. For information about available tours, check with the tourist office (see "Orientation," above), or **Bohus Line** (☎ 031/13-30-37), which provides excursion packages, brochures, tickets, and timetables. The tour costs 325 SEK ($35.75) for adults and 170 SEK ($18.70) for children 6–12. The 4-hour trip departs at 7pm.

For a guided 90-minute **bus tour** of Gothenburg, go to the tourist office or call ☎ 031/60-96-70 (see "Visitor Information," above) for details. City tours are offered daily from May to September. The fare is 125 SEK ($13.75) for adults, 85 SEK ($9.35) for children. Tours last 1½ hours. A combined 2-hour bus and boat tour costs 225 SEK ($24.75) for adults, 110 SEK ($12.10) for children.

6 Shopping

THE SHOPPING SCENE

Many residents of Copenhagen and Helsingør come to Gothenburg just for the day to buy Swedish merchandise. You can too, but you should shop at stores bearing the yellow-and-blue TAX-FREE SHOPPING sign. These stores are scattered throughout Gothenburg (see "Taxes," under "Fast Facts: Sweden," in chapter 3 for more information).

MAJOR SHOPPING DISTRICTS   Nordstan, with its 150 shops and stores, restaurants, hotel, patisseries, coffee shops, banks, travel agencies, and the post office, is the largest shopping mall in Scandinavia. Here you can find almost anything, from exclusive clothing boutiques to outlets for the major confectionery chains to bookshops. There's also a tourist information center. Most shops here are open Monday through Friday from 9:30am to 7pm and Saturday from 9:30am to 4pm.

Kungsgatan/Fredsgatan is Sweden's longest pedestrian mall (2 miles in length). The selection of shops is big and varied. Near these two streets you'll also find a number of smaller shopping centers, including Arkaden, Citypassagen, and Kompassen.

At **Grönsakstorget/Kungstorget,** little carts are put up daily with flowers, fruits, handcrafts, and jewelry, among other items. It's right in the city center, a throwback perhaps to the Middle Ages.

The often-mentioned **Avenyn,** with its many restaurants and cafes, also has a number of stores selling merchandise of interest to visitors.

Kronhusbodarna, Kronhusgatan 1D (☎ 031/711-08-32) (see "Architectural Highlights," above), houses a number of small-scale and rather sleepy studios for glassblowers, watch-makers, potters, and coppersmiths, some of whom sell their goods to passersby. They can be visited, if the artisans happen to show up (call ahead to make arrangements). Take tram no. 1 or 7 to Brunnsparken.

SHOPPING A TO Z
DEPARTMENT STORES
Bohusslöjds. Kungsportsavenyn 25. ☎ 031/16-00-72. Bus: 40.

This store has one of the best collections of Swedish handcrafts in Gothenburg. Amid a light-grained birch decor, you'll find wrought-iron chandeliers, unusual wallpaper, fabric by the yard, and other items such as hand-woven rugs, pine and birch-wood bowls, and assorted knickknacks, ideal as gifts or souvenirs.

C. J. Josephssons Glas & Porslin. Korsgatan 12 and Kyrkogatan 34. ☎ **031/17-56-15.** Tram: 1, 2, 3, 4, 5, or 7. Bus: 60.

This store has been selling Swedish glass since 1866 and has established an enviable reputation. The selection of Orrefors crystal and porcelain is stunning. There are signed original pieces by such well-known designers as Bertil Vallien and Goran Warff. There's a tourist tax-free shopping service plus full shipping service.

Nordiska Kompaniet (NK). Östra Hamngatan 42. ☎ **031/710-70-00.** Bus: 40.

Because this is a leading department store, shoppers are likely to come here first (also recommended in Stockholm; see "Shopping," in chapter 4). The store's packing specialists will take care in shipping your purchases home for you. Typical Swedish and Scandinavian articles are offered here—more than 200,000 items, ranging from Kosta Boda "sculpture" crystal, Orrefors crystal in all types and shapes, Rorstrand high-fired earthenware and fine porcelain, stainless steel, pewter items, dolls in national costumes, leather purses, Dalarna horses, Finnish carpeting, books about Sweden, Swedish records, and much, much more.

FASHION

Gillblad's. Kungsgatan 44. ☎ **031/10-88-46.** Tram: 1, 2, or 3.

This fashion outlet is known for its high-quality, well-made clothing for men and women. The inventory is tasteful, not flashy, and just the way its long-standing clients like it. It's especially noted for its collection of men's and women's suits for the office.

Hennes & Mauritz. Kungsgatan 55–57. ☎ **031/711-00-11.** Tram: 1, 2, or 3.

Established in the 1940s, this is a well-established clothing store for women that keeps an eye on what's happening in cutting-edge fashion capitals of other parts of the world. The venue and spirit here are trendy, with an emphasis on what might make a woman look as chic and youthful as possible for a very cool night out on the town. Despite its immediate sense of flair, garments are less expensive than you might suppose, with lots of cost-conscious bargains that are noted for having a very low profit markup. The same outfit maintains a menswear store a few storefronts away at no. 61 Kungsgatan (☎ 031/711-00-32).

Ströms. Kungsgatan 27–29. ☎ **031/17-71-00.** Tram: 1, 2, or 3.

This is the most visible emporium for clothing for men in Gothenburg, with a history at this location that goes back to 1886. Scattered over two floors of retail space, you'll find garments that range from the very formal to the very casual, and boutique-inspired subdivisions that contain ready-to-wear garments from the leading fashion houses of Europe. Despite the fact that most of its fame and reputation derives from its appeal to men, to a lesser extent it also sells garments for women and children.

HANDCRAFTS

Aside from some of the markets or streets already mentioned, the following establishment also specializes in handcrafts:

Lerverk. Västra Hamngatan 24–26. ☎ **031/13-13-49.** Tram: 1, 2, 3, 4, or 7 to Grönsakstorget.

This is a permanent exhibit center for 30 potters and glass-making craftspeople.

7 Gothenburg After Dark

To the Gothenburger in summer, there's nothing more exciting than sitting outdoors at a cafe along the Avenyn enjoying the short-lived season. Residents also like to take the whole family to the Liseberg amusement park (see "Seeing the Sights," earlier in this chapter). Although clubs are open in the summer, they're not well patronized until the cool weather sets in.

For a listing of entertainment events scheduled at the time of your visit, check the newspapers (*Göteborgs Posten* is best) or inquire at the tourist office. If Swedish dinner theater interests you, see Restaurant Gillestugan under "Where to Dine," above.

THE PERFORMING ARTS
THEATER

The Gothenburg Card (see "Getting Around," earlier in this chapter) allows you to buy two tickets for the price of one. Call the particular theater or the tourist office for program information. Performances also are announced in the newspapers.

Folkteatern. Olof Palmes Plats (by Järntorget). ☎ **031/20-38-20.** Tickets 80–140 SEK ($8.80–$15.40). Tram: 1, 3, or 4.

This theater stages productions of Swedish plays or foreign plays translated into Swedish. The season is from September to May, and performances are Tuesday to Friday at 7pm and Saturday at 6pm.

Stadsteatern. Götaplatsen. ☎ **031/61-50-50.** Tickets 120–160 SEK ($13.20–$17.60). Bus: 40.

This is one of the major theaters in Gothenburg, but invariably the plays are performed in Swedish. Ibsen in Swedish may be a bit hard to take without a knowledge of the language, but a musical may be understandable. The season runs from September to May. Performances usually are Tuesday through Friday at 7pm, Saturday at 6pm, and Sunday at 3pm.

OPERA & BALLET
Göteborgsoperan (Gothenburg Opera House). Packhuskajen. ☎ **031/10-80-00,** or 031/13-13-00 for ticket information. Ticket prices depend on the event.

This elegant new opera house was opened by the Swedish king in 1994 and features theater, opera, operettas, musicals, and ballet performances. It's situated right on a dock with views overlooking the water, and there are five bars and a cafe in the lobby. The main entrance (on Östra Hamngatan) leads to a foyer with a view of the harbor; here you'll find the box office and cloak room. Big productions can be staged here on a full scale. You'll have to check to see what performances might be scheduled at the time of your visit.

CLASSICAL MUSIC
Konserthuset. Götaplatsen. ☎ **031/16-70-00.** Tickets 150–450 SEK ($16.50–$49.50), but could range lower or higher depending on the performance. Bus: 40.

In the very center of Gothenburg, this is the major performance hall for classical music. In season (September through June), top world-class performers appear.

THE CLUB & MUSIC SCENE
NIGHTCLUBS

Bubbles. Avenyn 8. ☎ **031/10-58-20.** No cover. Tram: 1, 4, 5, or 6.

In stark contrast to the sprawling size of the Trädgåorn (see below), this nightclub and cocktail lounge is small scale and intimate. Outfitted in pale colors and attracting a clientele over 30, it's the most popular late-night venue in Gothenburg, sometimes attracting workers from restaurants around town who relax and chitchat here after a hard night's work. There's a small dance floor, but most visitors ignore it in favor of dialogues at the bar. Open daily 8pm to 5am.

Oakley's Country Club. Tredje Långgatan 16. ☎ **031/42-60-80.** Reservations recommended. Tram: 1, 3, 4, or 9.

Set within what originally was conceived as a fire station, and with a scarlet facade that stands out from its neighbors, the restaurant portion of this club opened in 1998 as a tongue-in-cheek parody of what you might find in the deserts of Nevada.

Beginning at 9pm, things get lively with reincarnations of Dale Evans about to break into song, cancan dancers belting out excerpts from *Annie Get Your Gun,* and a scantily clad trapeze artist who advises the menfolk in the audience how best to lasso a bedmate, a bride, or both. Expect a sense of camp and an interpretation of the American vernacular style that you might never, ever have expected east of the Atlantic. Menu items include sophisticated interpretations of New American cuisine, including chile-roasted crayfish, Mississippi alligator ribs, Caesar salads studded with crayfish, Annie's blackened salmon, Buffalo Bill's rib-eye steak, and the restaurant's own version of spare ribs. On the premises is a particularly elegant room for cigars and brandies. Main courses cost 98 to 249 SEK ($12.55 to $31.85), and the club is open daily 11am to 2pm and 6 to 11pm.

Park Lane Nightclub. In the Radisson SAS Park Avenue Hotel, Kungsportsavenyn 36–38. ☎ **031/20-60-58.** Cover 60–80 SEK ($6.60–$8.80); hotel guests enter free. Tram: 1, 4, 5, or 6. Bus: 40.

The leading nightclub along Sweden's west coast, the dinner-dance room here sometimes features international stars. Past celebrities have included Marlene Dietrich, Eartha Kitt, and the artist formerly known as Prince. The dance floor usually is packed. The international menu consists of light supper platters such as crab salad or toasted sandwiches. Beer begins at 50 SEK ($5.50). Open Wednesday through Sunday from 11pm to 3am.

Trädgoårn. Allegaten 8. ☎ **031/10-20-80.** Cover charge for disco 80–100 SEK ($8.80–$11); 2-course dinner and access to cabaret show 520 SEK ($57.20) per person. Main courses in restaurant 175–235 SEK ($19.25–$25.85). Restaurant, Mon–Fri 11:30am–3:30pm and Tues–Sat 6–10:30pm; cabaret, Wed–Sat beginning at 8pm; disco, Fri–Sat 11pm–5pm. Tram: 1, 3, or 5.

This is the largest and most comprehensive nightspot in Gothenburg, with a cavernous two-story interior that echoes on weekends with the simultaneous sounds of a restaurant, a cabaret, and a disco. No one under 25 is admitted to this cosmopolitan and urbane venue.

A DANCE CLUB

Valand. Vasagatan 41. ☎ **031/18-30-93.** Cover 80–100 SEK ($8.80–$11) for disco. Tram: 1, 4, 5, or 6. Bus: 40.

This combination restaurant and disco, one floor above street level in the center of town, is the biggest and best known in Gothenburg. As you enter there's a restaurant on your left and a large bar and dance floor on your right. There's also a small-stakes casino with blackjack and roulette. The minimum age for entry is 23. The club is open Thursday through Saturday from 8pm to 3am. For some memorable food, head for Lilla London, one floor below (see "Where to Dine," earlier in this chapter).

GAY GOTHENBURG

Greta. Drottninggaten 35. ☎ **031/13-69-49.** Reservations recommended Fri–Sat. Main courses 90–150 SEK ($9.90–$16.50). AE, MC, V. Daily 4pm–3am. Tram: 1, 2, or 3. INTERNATIONAL.

Named in honor of Greta Garbo, whose memorabilia adorns the walls here, this is the leading gay bar and restaurant in Gothenburg, with a clientele that includes all ages and all types of gay men and lesbians. Two animated bars rock and roll in ways that are completely independent from the on-site restaurant. Decor is a mixture of the kitschy old-fashioned and new wave, juxtapositioned in ways that are almost as interesting as the clientele. Menu items change at least every season, but might include fish and lime soup; lamb filet with mushrooms in a red wine sauce; breast of duck with potato croquettes; and a creamy chicken stew baked in phyllo pastry. Every Friday and Saturday night from 10pm till 3am, the place is transformed into a disco. The cover charge is 60 SEK ($6.60).

Leche. Vallgaten 30. No phone. Cover 60 SEK ($6.60). Tram: 1, 3, or 4.

It's tiny and it's open only one night a week, but during that brief interlude, it reigns as the premier women's bar of Gothenburg, attracting lesbians of all ages from miles around. Other nights of the week, gay women tend to congregate at the also-recommended Greta (see above). Open only Saturday 8pm to 3am.

8 Easy Excursions to the Bohuslän Coast & Halland

From Gothenburg's center, you can head north to explore the Bohuslän Coast or go south to visit Halland, the Swedish Riviera. These trips are best from June to early September, as they are far more enjoyable in fair weather than when winter winds are blowing.

THE BOHUSLÄN COAST

North of Gothenburg, the scenery of Bohuslän is dominated by the sea. Out in the archipelago, the waterways wind their way past myriad islands, sunken rocks, sounds, inlets, and waterside communities. Away from the coast, the countryside is varied, with wilderness areas, forests, mountains, and lakes offering wonderful opportunities for outdoor activities. You can cycle along carefully laid-out tracks, hike the Bohusleden Trail (tourist offices have maps), go fishing, play golf, or take out a canoe.

Many Swedes, including the late film actress Ingrid Bergman, have summer cottages in this chain of islands, which are linked by bridges or short ferry crossings. Train service is possible from Gothenburg through to Uddevalla (which is industrial) and on to Strömstad. Buses also cover the coast, but service is infrequent. It's best to take a **driving tour** of the coast, following the E6 motorway north from Gothenburg to one of the following destinations.

KUNGÄLV

If you're pressed for time, at least see Kungälv, 11 miles north of Gothenburg and reached by bus no. 301, 302, 303, or 330 from the Central Station. For information, contact **Kungälv Turistbyrå,** Fästningsholmen, S-442 81 Kungälv (☎ **0303/ 992-00**), usually open June through August, Monday through Saturday from 9am to 7pm and on Sunday from noon to 4pm; off-season, Monday through Friday from 9am to 6pm. The office also handles information for Marstrand (see the following).

The 1,000-year-old town of Kungälv, known by the Vikings as Kongahälla, has a panoramic position by the river of Nordre Älv. The well-preserved old town consists of **Gamla torget** (the old square), a church, and the cobbled streets of **Östra gatan** and **Vastra gatan,** where you'll find old wooden houses built centuries ago. An island in the river, **Fästningsholmen,** is an idyllic spot for a picnic.

On the E6 highway lie the ruins of the 14th-century **Bohus Fästning,** Fästningsholmen (☎ **0303/156-62**). This bastion played a leading role in the battles among Sweden, Norway, and Denmark to establish supremacy. Bohus Fästning (Bohus Castle and Fortress) was built by order of Norway's King Haakon V on Norwegian territory. After being ceded to Sweden in 1658, it was used as a prison. Climb the **tower** ("Father's Hat") for a panoramic view. Hours of operation are May 1 to June 26, daily from 10am to 7pm; June 27 to July 31, daily from 10am to 9pm; August 1 to 28, daily from 10am to 7pm; August 29 to September 25, daily from 11am to 4pm; closed off-season. Admission is 25 SEK ($2.75) for adults, 10 SEK ($1.10) for children 6 to 16, and free for children 5 and under.

WHERE TO STAY & DINE

Hotel Fars Hatt. Torget S-442 31 Kungälv. ☎ **0303/109-70.** Fax 0303/196-37. www. farshatt.se. E-mail: info@farshatt.se. 120 units. TV TEL. Mon–Thurs 1,040 SEK ($114.40) double; Sat–Sun 790 SEK ($86.90) double; all week long 1,140–1,440 SEK ($125.40–$158.40) suite. Rates include breakfast. AE, DC, MC, V. Free parking.

Established in the 17th century in the town center by the river, this site was used to refresh travelers with fish, game, and ale. Today, the tradition continues, albeit in a four-story building from the 1960s. An outdoor swimming pool, lakeside pier, a sauna, a solarium, conference rooms, a nearby golf course, jogging tracks, tennis courts, and airy dining rooms provide plenty to do. The restaurant menu offers a wide selection of Swedish and international dishes, and nonguests are welcome. The bedrooms are well furnished, each modern and recently renovated, with good beds and ample bathrooms.

MARSTRAND

This once-royal resort, frequented by the former Swedish king, Oscar II, is on a secluded island. Its little shops, art galleries, and pleasant walks are reminiscent of Nantucket, Massachusetts. Part of the fun of Marstrand is the ferry journey here; it lies 15½ miles west of Kungälv.

To reach the island, drive north along E6 from Gothenburg, exiting at the signs pointing to Marstrand. These lead you to the village of Koön, where you'll park your car. From the wharf at Koön, ferryboats depart every 20 minutes for Marstrand. No cars are allowed on either the ferryboats or the island. The round-trip costs 12 SEK ($1.30).

Another alternative is a bus, no. 312, which departs from Gothenburg's Central Station. Buses leave every hour year-round; no reservations are necessary. For 100 SEK ($11), you can purchase a combined bus and ferry ticket to the island. The bus stops first in the hamlet of Tjuvkil and then continues on to the wharf at Koön.

Young people from Gothenburg and its environs flock to Marstrand on weekends, filling up the clapboard-sided hotels. The resort, quiet all week, comes alive with the sounds of folk singers and the twang of guitars. The big event on Marstrand's calendar is the annual **international regatta,** which usually takes place the first 2 weeks in July.

The 17th-century **Carlsten Fortress** (☎ **0303/602-65**) towers over the island. After you climb up the hill, visit the chapel and then walk through the secret tunnel to the fortress, which dates from 1658 when Charles X Gustav decided that it should be built to protect the Swedish west-coast fleet. The bastions around the lower castle courtyard were constructed from 1689 to 1705, and then completed during the first half of the 19th century. Admission is 50 SEK ($5.50) for adults, 20 SEK ($2.20) for children 7 to 15, free for children 6 and under. It's open June through August, daily from noon to 4pm. Tours are conducted at noon, 1pm, 2pm, and 3pm.

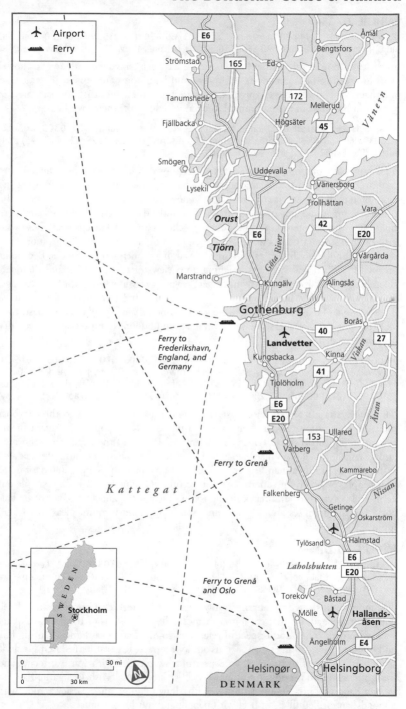

WHERE TO STAY

Batellet. Batellet S-440 30 Marstrand. ☎ **0303/600-10.** Fax 0303/60-607. 204 four-bed units, none with bathroom. 170 SEK ($18.70) per person. MC, V.

In the town center, this former bathing house has been converted into a youth hostel with four or five beds per room. All rooms and bathrooms are unisex. It attracts an international crowd. June through August are the busiest months. You can prepare your own breakfast in the communal kitchen. Guests make their own beds.

Grand Hotel Marstrand. Paradisparken, S-440 30 Marstrand. ☎ **0303/603-22.** Fax 0303/600-53. www.grandmarstrand.se. 28 units. A/C TV TEL. 1,595 SEK ($175.45) double; 1,795 SEK ($197.45) suite. AE, DC, MC, V.

This landmark building operates as a conventional hotel throughout the summer months, turning into a convention center when the cold wind blows in. Built at the close of the 19th century and frequently renovated and altered since, it used to be called "the grand old lady of Marstrand," back in the days when people spoke in these politically incorrect terms. Although today's clients are not as elegant as those who arrived with steamer trunks long ago, the Grand still holds its own. Renovations preserved the original architectural charm while adding modern conveniences. Bedrooms are well furnished and spacious, opening onto views of Paradise Park and the boat-filled harbor. Bathrooms are a winner here, each in classic white with brass fittings, and all with those old-fashioned bathtubs that grandpa and grandma used to bathe in. There's also a sauna with a view on the ground floor. Even if you're not a guest, consider patronizing the hotel's restaurant on the ground floor. Room service and laundry also are provided.

Villa Maritime. Hamngatan, S-440 30 Marstrand. ☎ **0303/610-25.** Fax 0303/616-20. www.villa-maritime.se. E-mail: receptionen@villa-maritime.se. 50 apts. June–Aug, 1,350 SEK ($148.50) 1 bdrm apt; 1,700 SEK ($187) 2 bdrm apt. Sept–May, 990–1,100 SEK ($108.90–$121) 1 bdrm apt; 1,280–1,440 SEK ($140.80–$158.40) 2 bdrm apt. AE, DC, MC, V.

This is Marstrand's largest and most visible hotel, located adjacent to the ferryboat piers. It's a favorite of Swedes who want to rent a fully equipped apartment in the busiest section of town. Originally built around 1900 and then radically renovated and enlarged in 1982, Villa Maritime has a red tile roof resembling an updated seafront hotel of Edwardian England. One-bedroom apartments are suitable for up to four people; two-bedroom apartments can accommodate up to six. Each is simple but comfortably furnished and has a sitting room, kitchenette, and (often) a private balcony. On the premises are a gym, sauna, solarium, laundry room, pleasant cocktail lounge, and bistro.

WHERE TO DINE

Restaurant Tenan. In the Grand Hotel, Paradisparken. ☎ **0303/603-22.** Reservations recommended. Main courses 200–330 SEK ($22–$36.30). AE, DC, MC, V. Daily noon–3pm and 6–10:30pm. INTERNATIONAL.

The most sophisticated restaurant in town lies on the street level of the Grand Hotel, within a trio of rooms that combines memorabilia and photos of the America's Cup Race with dark colors and respectful references to Sweden's royal family. During July and August, there's dining on a spacious outdoor terrace. Recommended items include platters of smoked fish with dill sauce; terrines of foie gras with warm brioches and fresh butter; seafood soups and piquant shellfish stews; anglerfish in a garlic-flavored saffron sauce; North Atlantic lobster with drawn butter and parsley; trout with almonds; and frilled fillets of beef with pepper and mushroom sauce.

LYSEKIL

This 200-year-old town, with its wooden houses and narrow alleyways, is a good base for exploring the coast. Today, it also contains a number of workshops for artisans, artists, and craftspeople who find the area a perfect retreat from the world.

Lysekil lies directly on the seashore, set against a backdrop of pink granite rocks. Fishing areas, as well as some of the best waters for diving in northern Europe, are found here. In summer there are occasional seal-watching trips, as well as sailing trips. Ask at the **tourist office** at Sodra Hamngatan 6 (☎ 0523/130-50), open Monday through Friday 9am to 5pm.

If you're driving, take Route E6 north from Gothenburg to Uddevalla, then head west along Route 161. An express bus from Gothenburg (no. 840) runs every 2 hours during the day.

The best sight in town is **Havets Hus,** Rosvikstorg (☎ 0523/165-30), a sea aquarium with a collection of animal and plant life from the Gullmaren and North Sea. The main attraction here is a tunnel aquarium showing a variety of different species such as cod, ray, halibut, lobster, shark, and much more. At this tunnel, massive fish swim over and around you. At a special pool, children can feel spiky starfish and slimy algae. Wave machines make some biotopes especially realistic. From February 7 to June 5 and August 24 to December 1, it is open daily 10am to 4pm. From June 6 to 20 and August 3 to 23, hours are daily from 10am to 6pm. From June 21 to August 2, it is open daily 10am to 8pm. Admission is 45 SEK ($4.95). The aquarium is a 5-minute walk from the tourist office, heading down toward the water.

The entire shoreline around Lysekil is today a nature reserve, with some 275 varieties of plant life. Sometimes in summer, guided "marine walks" and botanical tours are offered (ask at the tourist office; see above).

On the way north to Tanumshede (see below), we always continue north along the E6, but cut west near Rabbalshede to follow Route 163 to **Fjällbacka,** which, in our view, is one of the most perfect, picture-postcard, little fishing villages of Sweden. Houses are painted in bright shades with a wealth of gingerbread. Swedes call this *snickargladje,* although Americans are more familiar with the term *carpenter's Gothic.*

It was here that we traveled once to interview screen legend Ingrid Bergman, star of the classic *Casablanca* and other films. She'd invited us for lunch, which consisted of a loaf of freshly baked bread and a great big red beet. A lunch such as this isn't at all uncommon in Sweden in the summertime. Ms. Bergman's summer house was on one of the islands off the coast. In town, Swedes remember her fondly and the main square is called "Ingrid Bergman Square," with a statue of the screen goddess looking out over the water to her former home. Her ashes were scattered over the sea nearby.

If you should fall in love with the town, as you are likely to, consider an overnight stay at the 23-room **Stora Hotellet** (☎ 0525/310-03; fax 0525/310-93). Each room is decorated to depict a faraway place.

WHERE TO STAY & DINE

Hotel Lysekil. Rosvikstorg 1, S-453 30 Lysekil. ☎ **0523/66-55-30.** Fax 0523/155-20. www.hotel-lysekil.net. E-mail: info@hotel-lysekil.net. 990 SEK ($108.90) double; 1,290 SEK ($141.90) suite. Rates include breakfast. AE, DC, MC, V.

Built in a gable-roofed, traditional design, from brown bricks and copper, this is one of the most prominent hotels in town—a focal point for most of the town's business meetings, conventions, and corporate rendezvous. Bedrooms are smaller than one may hope, and are conservatively decorated with angular furniture and comfortable beds. Bathrooms also are small. On the premises is a pub with its own disco, a restaurant, and a conference room.

Fun Fact

Strömstad claims to have more hours of sunshine than anywhere else in Sweden.

Lysekil Havshotell. Turistgatan 13, S-453 30 Lysekil. ☎ **0523/797-50.** Fax 0523/142-04. www.strandflickorna.se. E-mail: info@strandflickorna.se. 15 units. TV TEL. 795–825 SEK ($87.45–$90.75) double; 995 SEK ($109.45) suite. AE, DC, MC, V. Free parking.

Set within a half mile west of the town center, this hotel originated as an upscale private home in 1900. Set behind a turn-of-the-century scarlet-and-white facade, within its own gardens, it has polite, well-rehearsed service, public rooms that evoke a bygone age, and comfortable bedrooms that were upgraded and renovated in 1993, with excellent mattresses and renewed beds. The staff here will prepare you a simple platter of food on request—virtually whenever you want it—but other than breakfast, meals are not served on a regular basis. Access from the center of Lysekil is particularly pleasant, as you can follow the seafront quays most of the way.

TANUMSHEDE

Back on the E6 heading north, the next destination of interest is Tanumshede, known for its collection of the greatest concentration of Bronze Age rock carvings in Scandinavia. If you're not driving, Tanumshede is reached by five express buses daily from Gothenburg; the trip takes 2 hours.

As you enter town, you can pay a visit first to **Tanum Turist,** Stora Oppen 5 (☎ **0525/204-00**), the local tourist bureau. Information regarding the best ways to visit the Bronze Age carvings is available here. The office is open from June through mid-August Monday through Saturday 10am to 6pm. Off-season hours are Monday through Thursday 8:30am to 4:30pm and Friday 8:30am to 3pm.

In 1994, the rock carvings of Tanum were included in the UNESCO World Heritage List. Just to the east of Tanumshede you can visit the ✪ **Vitlycke Museum** (☎ **0525/209-50**), which is open April to September daily 10am to 6pm; off-season Tuesday to Sunday 11am to 5pm. The museum charges 45 SEK ($4.95) for adults, 25 SEK ($2.75) for children 7 to 16 (free 6 and under). The museum documents the rock carvings and offers excursions to the rock carving faces, sometimes by moonlight. You also can obtain a map, "The Rock Carving Tour," which guides you easily among the rock carvings of northern Bohuslän, showing the way to Bohuslän's 10 most interesting rock-carving faces. Four are in Tanum and constitute the World Heritage area. Close to the museum, a Bronze Age farm is a full-scale reconstruction of a dwelling and farm from the era of the rock carvings. At a restaurant in the museum, the cuisine is inspired by Bronze Age raw materials such as meat and venison, fish and shellfish, parsley root, sorrel, and chickweed. Gooseberry ice cream rounds off this repast.

WHERE TO STAY & DINE

✪ **Tanums Gestgifveri.** Apoteksvägen 7, S-0457 00 Tanumshede. ☎ **0525/290-10.** Fax 0525/295-71. E-mail: tanumsgestgifveri@tninet.se. 30 units. TV. 1,080–1,500 SEK ($118.80–$165) double. Rate includes breakfast and dinner. AE, DC, MC, V. Closed Dec 24–Jan 30.

This hotel, one of the oldest continuously operating inns in the district, was established in 1613 in a forest about 6 miles inland from the sea. From the outside, it looks like a prosperous Swedish farmhouse, with rambling porches and painted in tones of pale ochre. Bedrooms are old-fashioned, cozy, and in most cases, accented to some degree with varnished paneling. Within a separate building, also constructed in the early 1600s but with many additions and improvements during the early 20th century, there's a well-managed restaurant that's classified as a Relais & Châteaux. Most residents of the hotel opt to dine here as well, but if you're just passing through, you should know that gastronomes go out of their way to visit this spot. For diners not residing within the hotel, main courses cost from 100 to 250 SEK ($11 to $27.50) each. Meals are served Tuesday to Sunday from noon to 3pm and 6 to 9pm. Specialties include a succulent version of fish stew served with rice and braised fresh vegetables, freshwater catfish with wine sauce, and sautéed anglerfish with garlic sauce.

STRÖMSTAD

Twenty miles north of Tanumshede, Strömstad knew greater glory in the 18th century when it was one of the most fashionable spas in Sweden. The town makes an excellent stopover for those heading farther north into the wilds of Sweden. Many Norwegians also pass through here because of ferry links to Sandefjord, Fredrikstad, and Halden in Norway. Strömstad also is the jumping-off point for those wishing to explore the Koster Islands, Sweden's most westerly inhabited islands.

Until 1658, Strömstad was part of Norway. Today, it is a fishing harbor and, in summer, a lively tourist center. Lying on the salty Skaggerrak on the borderline between Sweden and Norway, it's a place of rolling waves, cliffs warmed by the sun, and sandy beaches. A fish market is still held here at 7am Tuesday through Friday.

For information, head first for the tourist office, **Strömstad Tourist,** Torget. It's open June through August daily 8am to 8pm; off-season Monday through Friday 0.30am to 5pm. The office can help you arrange private rooms in the area, costing from 200 SEK ($22) per person, plus a 50 SEK ($5.50) booking fee. For more information, call ☎ **0526/62330.**

Strömstad is linked by rail to Gothenburg, a 3-hour journey. The E6 express bus between Gothenburg and Oslo also stops off here. Motorists should follow Route 176 off the E6 for a distance of 7½ miles.

Many visitors use Strömstad merely as a refueling stop for trips over to the **Koster Islands.** If you have time for only one island, make it **Nordkoster** (North Koster) which is a large nature reserve. You can explore the whole island on foot (cars are prohibited) in about 2 hours. **Sydkoster** (South Koster) is three times the size of North Koster and can be toured by bike. Before heading over there, ask at the Strömstad tourist office how to arrange rentals. The waters for both islands are the warmest in Sweden for summer swimming; or you can go bird- or seal-watching. The islands abound in wildflowers. From Strömstad, ferries leave from Laholmen and cost 80 SEK ($8.80) one way. The tourist office keeps a list of ferry schedules (subject to change because of weather conditions).

WHERE TO STAY & DINE

Hotel Laholmen. S-452 30 Strömstad. ☎ **0526/197-00.** Fax 0525/100-36. www.rica.no. E-mail: laholmen@top-stromstad.se. 123 units. MINIBAR TV TEL. Mid-June to Aug and Fri–Sat year-round, 1,100 SEK ($121) double; rest of year, 1,290 SEK ($141.90) double. Rates include breakfast. AE, DC, MC, V. Free parking.

This is the larger and better accessorized of Strömstad's two hotels, with a policy of remaining open year-round. Built in 1994, it has a design that follows parallel to the shoreline of a small peninsula jutting seaward from the center of town. Low and sprawling, and flanked on one side with a busy marina, the hotel has a streamlined, modern-looking decor and comfortable bedrooms that are monochromatic, well maintained, and cozy, with excellent beds but small bathrooms. Public areas have big windows, touches of varnished paneling, and a sense of spaciousness. There's no pool or health club on the premises, although the staff will direct you to nearby facilities. However, there is a big dining room serving good regional food (lots of fish), a disco, and an indoor-outdoor restaurant that operates only between June and early September.

Halland locals like pointing out that its inhabitants live longer and take less sick leave than other Swedes.

HALLAND: THE SWEDISH RIVIERA

Halland lies south of Gothenburg and, because of its white sandy beaches, is the fastest-growing tourist district in the country. During the summer months, the population of the region doubles.

Windsurfing is the major regional sport here, and Halland has produced many champions. Consistent, stable winds and shallow shoreline waters provide ideal conditions. Mellbystrand, Tylösand, Ringenäs, and Skrea beaches are those most favored by windsurfers.

In addition to the beaches, Halland's network of rivers and lakes gives the region its life and character. There are more than 900 bodies of water in the province and many of these inland lakes and rivers are ideal for canoeing and camping. Many places have public access areas with docks, swimming areas, and barbecues. Some lakes boast flowering water lilies or flowering meadows that extend down to the water's edge. Many salmon waters have been restored in recent years, and both salmon and trout make their way over the Atlantic to Halland's rivers. A number of lakes offer good perch and pike fishing.

Halland's mild winters and early springs help make it Sweden's most golf-intensive region. In all, there are 30 golf courses in the province. Try either the **Båstad Golf Club** at Boarp (☎ 0431/731-36), or at the **Bjäre Golf Club** at Solomonhög (☎ 0431/36-10-53), both located right outside the center of Båstad.

Our favorite places (either for bases or stopovers) include the following resorts:

KUNGSBACKA & TJOLÖHOLM

Once an important town in its own right, today Kungsbacka is merely a southern suburb of Gothenburg. However, it makes a good base for exploring one of the major attractions along the west coast of Sweden—the "English" castle of Tjolöholm, lying 7½ miles south of Kungsbacka.

In summer you can ask for information at the town's little tourist office (☎ 0300/345-95), in the center.

✪ **Tjolöholm Slott** at Fjärås (☎ 0300/544-200) lies on a beautiful peninsula in Kungsbackafjorden. It was built by a Scottish merchant, J. F. Dickson, at the turn of the century in a mock English style. Pronounced *chewla*-home, Tjolöholm came about through a design contest in the 1890s. In his late 20s, Lars Israel Wahman won the competition, and created this stunning, stately home.

Dickson was an avid horse breeder, but today the huge stables and indoor riding track have been converted into a cafe. A carriage museum on the site contains carriages but also a unique horse-drawn vacuum cleaner.

You also can explore the manor house, with its walls of Flanders marble and regal oak-paneled study by Liberty's of London. The bathrooms and boudoirs are fabulous, and the children's nursery was inspired by the designs of Charles Rennie Mackintosh. It's also fun to explore the grounds, which slope down to a sandy beach. The house is open June to August daily 11am to 4pm, and September and October Sunday 11am to 4pm only. A tour costs 45 SEK ($4.95).

Nearby you can explore the **Fjärås Bracka Open Air Museum** (☎ 0300/345-95), in the tiny village of Äskhult, rooted in the 17th and 18th centuries. In the 19th century, 35 people lived here; the last inhabitant died in 1964. Four buildings remain

A Cutting Tale

Regrettably, Dickson never saw the completion of his castle, Tjolöholm Slott. He cut himself as he opened a champagne bottle and fatally poisoned himself when he wrapped the lead cap around his wound.

on the sites where they originally were constructed. The oldest house dates from the 17th century. The houses have never been painted, and their gray timber walls give the place a special character. The site is open May to August daily 10am to 6pm; September only on Saturday and Sunday 10am to 6pm. Admission is free.

If you're not driving, you can reach Tjolöholm by public transportation. A local train goes from Gothenburg's Central Station to Kungsbacka in 20 minutes. Once at Kungsbacka, a bus runs to the house, departing Kungsbacka daily at 11am and returning in the afternoon. In July and August, a special SJ bus runs directly to Tjolöholm from Nils Ericsonplatsen in Gothenburg.

VARBERG

Twenty-eight miles south of Kungsbacka is the atmospheric old town of Varberg, which enjoyed fame in the 19th century as a bathing resort. Today, Varberg is one of Sweden's most popular coastal resorts, known for its nudist beaches. Within walking distance of the town center, you'll also find Apelviken Bay, where surfers flock from all over Europe to enjoy the waves.

Stop in at the **Varberg Tourist Office**, Brunnsparken (☎ 0340/887-70), for complete information about the town. From mid-June through mid-August, it's open Monday through Friday 9am to 6pm, Sunday 3 to 7pm. Off-season its hours are Monday through Friday 9am to 5pm.

From Gothenburg, regular trains run down the coast with frequent service to Varberg. Bus riders can take no. 732 from Gothenburg, then change to the no. 615 at Frillesås. Motorists can head south along E6 from Gothenburg.

Stena Line (☎ 0340/690-900) also offers ferry service year-round to Grenå in Denmark; a round-trip ticket costs 200 SEK ($22) and the sea journey takes 3 hours and 45 minutes.

All the ✪ **attractions of Varberg** can easily be explored on foot as most of them lie along the seafront. The major attraction is the 13th-century fortress, complete with moat, **Varbergs Fästning** (☎ 0340/185-20), set on a rocky promontory in the sea. It was home to the Swedish king, Magnus Erikkson. Important peace treaties with Denmark were signed here in 1343; but the fortress is best known for a suit of medieval clothing belonging to the **Bocksten Man,** a 600-year-old murder victim. The man was garroted, drowned, impaled, and then buried in a local bog until discovered by a Swedish farmer in 1936. His suit of ordinary clothing is the only known medieval clothing still in existence and consists of a cloak, a hood, shoes, and stockings. Thick, red ringlets cascade around his skull. Three stakes were thrust through his body. The idea, supposedly, was to ensure that his spirit never escaped to pursue his murderers.

The fortress also contains a **prison** from 1850; it was the first Swedish prison to be built with individual cells. Lifers were held here, with the last one departing in 1931. The museum is open Monday through Friday 10am to 4pm; Saturday and Sunday noon to 4pm. Admission is 20 SEK ($2.20) adults, 10 SEK ($1.10) children 6–16.

There isn't a great deal else worth pursuing in the other parts of the museum, which mostly features fishing exhibits and the like, except paintings by the Varberg School. The most famous artists of the 19th-century movement included Nils Kreuger, Karl Nordström, and Richard Bergh.

If you head down **Strandpromenaden** for about 5 minutes, you'll reach some well-known nudist beaches. **Kärringhålan** and **Skarpe** are reserved for nude bathing for women, whereas men bathe nude at **Goda Hopp.** This segregation of the sexes for the purposes of nudity is rather unusual in Sweden, where "mixed" nudity is more commonplace.

Where to Stay

Varbergs Stadthotell. Kungsgatan 24–26, S-432 41 Varberg. ☎ **800/528-1234** in the U.S., or 0340/161-00. Fax 0340/67-86-52. www.varbergsstadshotell.com. E-mail: info@varbergsstadshotell.com. 124 units. MINIBAR TV TEL. Late June to early Aug and Fri–Sat year-round, 1,205 SEK ($132.55) double; rest of year, 1,185–1,395 SEK ($130.35–$153.45) double. AE, DC, MC, V. Bus: 1 or 3.

This hotel, the grandest and most imposing building in town, was built in 1902 as a belle epoque replica of a French château that accepted socially prominent and well-heeled guests for overnight hotel stays. Set on the main square of town, it's hard to miss, partly because it also houses the town's best restaurant. (See "Where to Dine," below.) In 1997, all of its bedrooms were radically upgraded and renovated, generally with a contemporary look that's a lot more modern than the building's ornate exterior. One wing, however, to the right of the building as you face it, retains a greater emphasis on old-time grandeur, with some of the original antiques, higher ceilings, larger proportions, and better views over the town's main square. The bedrooms, which vary widely in size, all are well maintained, with good beds and ample bathrooms with fluffy towels and hair dryers. There's a health center and sauna on site, some rather grand reception areas, and a polite, hardworking staff.

Where to Dine

Café & Krog Stadt. In the Varbergs Stadthotell, Kungsgatan 24–26. ☎ **0340/161-00.** Reservations recommended. Fixed-price lunch 95 SEK ($10.45); main courses 200–290 SEK ($22–$31.90). AE, DC, MC, V. Daily noon–2pm and 7–10pm. Bus: 1 or 3. SWEDISH/CONTINENTAL.

Everything about this space evokes the grand age of dining. Built as part of a self-consciously upscale palace hotel in 1902, it has a high ceiling, a scattering of antiques, crystal chandeliers, formal service, and a pastel-and-gold color scheme that can be very soothing. Menu items include smoked chicken breast with tomato-and-basil sauce; shellfish with "vineyard" (white wine) sauce; cream of crayfish soup with sherry; sliced Serrano ham with wild mushrooms and lingonberry sauce; poached halibut with bouillabaisse sauce and fried potatoes; and fillets of reindeer with juniper berry sauce. The cooking is first rate, and the ingredients used are the finest in the area.

FALKENBERG

Known for its sandy beaches and salmon fishing, Falkenberg is the most attractive resort along the Swedish Riviera. It lies 18 miles south of Varberg, 16 miles north of Hamstad, and 58 miles south of Gothenburg. Sleepy all winter, the town comes alive in summer, as visitors flock here to enjoy some 6 miles of sandy beaches, the best of which include Skrea Strand, Ugglarp, Långasand, Boberg, and Rinsegård. Regardless of the beach you choose, you'll find the Kattegatt to be the best bathing water in Sweden.

Placed in the center of the long west coast of Sweden, Falkenberg is easily reached, enjoying frequent bus and train service from Gothenburg, as well as lying on the Gothenburg/Malmö rail line. Motorists leaving Varberg can continue southeast along E6 into Falkenberg.

Before exploring the area, you might head for the **Falkenbergs Turistbyrå,** Stortorget (☎ **0346/174-10**). The office is open mid-June through August, Monday through Saturday 9am to 5pm, Sunday 3 to 7pm. In September, it is open Monday

A Note for Shoppers

The oldest pottery still operating in Scandinavia, **Törngren's,** Krukmakareg 4 (☎ **0346/169-20**), dates from 1789. It may, in fact, be the oldest pottery in the north of Europe. The pottery is still on the original site, and continues to be run by the same family after seven generations. Open Monday to Friday 9:30am to 6pm, Saturday 9:30am to 2pm.

---

through Friday, 9am to 5pm and Saturday 10am to 2pm; October through May, Monday through Friday 9am to 5pm.

Named after the falcons that once were hunted here, Falkenberg is a well-preserved medieval town. Walk through its old town, lying to the west of the river, and you'll discover a warren of wooden cottages and narrow lanes paved with cobblestones. By the bridge over the Ätran River lie the ruins of a medieval fortress destroyed by an army of peasants in the 15th century. Close to the bridge stands **S:t Laurentii kyrka,** a church surrounded by cobblestone streets. The interior contains wall and ceiling paintings from the 1600s and 1700s. This church dates from the 12th century and was saved from demolition because it was put to secular use—as a shooting range, a movie house, and even a gym. In the 1920s, it was reconsecrated.

The major attraction is **Falkenbergs Museum,** Söderbron (☎ **0346/861-25**), which is housed in a four-story grain warehouse near the bridge. The museum displays artifacts removed from excavations in the area and surprisingly, a re-creation of life in the 1950s. There are mementos of dance bands of the era along with a stylized cafe, even a shoe repair shop of the time. It is open June through August, Tuesday through Friday 10am to 4pm and Saturday and Sunday noon to 4pm. Off-season hours are Tuesday through Friday and Sunday noon to 4pm. Admission is 20 SEK ($2.20).

The River Ätran runs through central Falkenberg and offers some of Sweden's best salmon fishing, although the waters today are overfished and catches are not what they used to be. The inventor of the mining safety lamp, Sir Humphrey Davy, came here in the 1820s to go fly-fishing. He popularized the glories of salmon fishing on the river and in time was followed by a parade of rich British sportsmen. If you'd like to try your luck, you can pick up a fishing license from the tourist bureau (see above) which entitles you to catch three fish per day; the license costs 95 SEK ($10.45).

Where to Stay & Dine

Grand Hotel Falkenberg. Hotellgatan 1, Box 224, S-311 23 Falkenberg. ☎ **0346/ 714-900.** Fax 0346/829-25. www.grandhotelfalkenberg.se. E-mail: info@strandbaden.elite.se. 71 units. MINIBAR TV TEL. Sun–Thurs 1,210 SEK ($133.10) double; Fri–Sat 900 SEK ($99). AE, DC, MC, V. Rates include breakfast. Free parking.

This grand, imposing hotel originally was built in 1931 in the center of town, adjacent to the lake. At the time, bedrooms occupied only the first and third floors, with a second floor that was devoted to reception space for parties and municipal functions. Since then, the second floor has been taken up by bedrooms. Each of these units is outfitted in pale colors, internationally modern furniture, and good beds, and has a modern-looking bathroom with ample towels.

Dining/Diversions: The white-walled in-house restaurant, set near the lobby on the hotel's ground floor, is open daily for lunch and dinner. It serves fixed-price menus for 90 SEK ($9.90), and main courses that range in price from 150 to 250 SEK ($16.50 to $27.50).

Amenities: Sauna, solarium, health club, disco, and a large, anonymous-looking gathering place that's transformed about every 2 weeks into a supper club with a live band.

Hotel Strandbaden. Havsbadsallén, S-311 42 Falkenberg. ☎ **0346/714-900.** Fax 0346/ 161-11. www.strandbaden.se. E-mail: info@strandbaden.se. 135 units. A/C MINIBAR TV TEL. Sun–Thurs 1,045–1,210 SEK ($114.95–$133.10) double, 1,285–1,485 SEK ($141.35–$163.35) suite. Fri–Sat 910–1,020 SEK ($100.10–$112.20) double, 1,045–1,190 SEK ($114.95–$130.90) suite. Rates include breakfast. AE, DC, MC, V. Free parking. Bus: 555 from Halmstad.

This hotel was built in the early 1990s on a low, rocky bluff directly above a sandy beach, overlooking a sea dotted with weathered rocky islets. On a total of three floors, it contains cozy, well-appointed, and modern public rooms, and conservatively deco-rated bedrooms that, although they don't have a lot of flair, are clean, well maintained, and comfortable with good beds and ample bathrooms. There's a restaurant and bar that's open daily for lunch and dinner. During the summer, most guests spend their days at the beach; the rest of the year, they swim free in the Klitterbad. Set only 10 yards from the hotel itself, it's the largest indoor saltwater pool in Sweden, with an echoing interior space that's worthy of an Olympic competition. Part of the Klitter-bad is devoted to sauna facilities, which also are free for hotel guests.

HALMSTAD

Once a grand walled town and a major stronghold of Danish power, Halmstad lies 90 miles south of Gothenburg and 25 miles south of Falkenberg, and is the golf capital of Sweden. Aside from the fabled Tylösand course, there are six other courses in town. In summer, Swedes and Danes (in the main) flock to its fabled strip of wide, white, sandy beach called Tylösand. Along with the adjacent Ringenäs and Frösakull beaches, this is one of the longest beaches in Scandinavia.

A longtime Swedish resort, Halmstad today is one of the fastest-growing towns in the country. Halmstad is forever linked to the memory of Christian IV, king of Den-mark (1588–1648). The king left his mark on the town. He spent a lot of time here and built Halmstad Castle, where in 1619 he entertained the Swedish king, Gustav Adolf II with 7 days of solid festivities.

Shortly after that meeting, a fire destroyed most of the town, but spared the castle. After the fire, Christian created a Renaissance town with a high street, Storgatan, and a grid of straight streets unlike the narrow, crooked ones of old. If you walk along Stor-gatan, you'll see many Renaissance-style merchants' houses from that rebuilding period. The Danes were driven out in 1645 and Halmstad returned to Sweden. Because the town had lost its military significance, the walls were torn down. All that remains is Norre Port, one of the great gateways.

Motorists can follow E6 southeast from Falkenburg. Halmstad lies on the major rail lines between Malmö and Gothenburg, so there is frequent service throughout the day.

The **Halmstads Turistbyrå,** Österskans, just by the Österbro Bridge (☎ 035/ 10-93-45), is open June through August, Monday through Friday 9am to 6pm, Sat-urday 10am to 1pm, and Sunday 1 to 3pm. Off-season hours are Monday through Friday 9am to 5pm.

Seeing the Sights

In the town center, **Stora Torg,** the market square, contains Europa and the Bull, a fountain designed by Carl Milles with mermen twisted around it. Flanking one side of the plaza is the **S:t Nikolai kykra,** Kyrkogatan (☎ 035/15-19-43), a 14th-century church. It and the castle were the only major structures to survive from the era of Christian IV. The church contains some of the finest stained-glass windows in Swe-den. The tall windows were created by Einar Forseth (1892–1988), who designed the golden mosaics in Stockholm's Stadhuset and the mosaic paving for England's Coven-try Cathedral. Erik Olson (1901–86), part of the fabled Halmstad Group, Sweden's first Surrealists, conceived the two smaller circular windows. The church is open daily from 8:30am to 6pm, charging no admission.

The town's major landmark is **Halmstad Slott,** which King Christian IV commissioned Hans van Steenwinckel, a Dutchman, to build in 1620, as part of Halmstad's defense system. Currently, it is the residence of the county governor and not open to the public, although you can see it from the outside and walk through the surrounding gardens 24 hours a day with no fee.

Along the river stands **Museet i Halmstad,** Tollsgatan (☎ **035/16-23-00**), which contains exhibits from local archaeological digs of only minor interest. Far more interesting here are the upper-floor rooms that contain home interiors from the 1600s through the 1800s. Here is an array of artifacts that includes everything from Gustavian harps to 1780s square pianos. On the top floor are paintings by the Halmstad Group, the fabled Surrealists of Sweden. From June 6 to August 16, the museum is open Monday through Friday from 10am to 4pm and on Saturday and Sunday from noon to 4pm. Off-season hours are daily 10am to 4pm and Saturday and Sunday noon to 4pm. Admission is 20 SEK ($2.20) adults and 10 SEK ($1.10) for children ages 7 to 15.

Two miles north of the town center, ✪ **Mjsellby Konstgård,** Mjallby (☎ **035/ 316-19**), also displays the art of the Halmstad Group. This group was composed of six artists, including the brothers Axel and Erik Olson and their cousin Waldemar Lorentzon, along with Esaias Thorén, Stellan Mörner, and Sven Jonson. They were post-Cubists who first worked here in 1929. In time, they developed a Nordic form of Surrealism that was deeply rooted in the landscapes of Halland. Many members of the group continued to produce until the 1980s. Set in the beautiful Halland countryside, the art center here was established by the daughter of Erik Olson. Along with permanent exhibitions from the Halmstad Group, the site also is host to temporary exhibitions, often by great masters such as Le Corbusier. To reach the center if you're not driving, take bus 350 to 351 and ask to be let off at the nearest stop (be warned: the museum is still half a mile away). From June 15 to September 30, hours are Tuesday through Sunday, 1 to 6pm; October to June 14, Tuesday through Sunday 1 to 5pm. Admission is 40 SEK ($4.40).

Where to Stay & Dine
Hotel Tylösand. P.O. Box 643, S-301 16 Halmstad. ☎ **035/305-00.** Fax 035/324-39. www.tylosand.se. E-mail: info@tylosand.se. 230 units. TV TEL. Sun–Thurs 1,340 SEK ($147.40) double; Fri–Sat 1,295 SEK ($142.45) double. AE, DC, MC, V. Free parking.

Hotel Tylösand, one of the most dramatically modern resorts in the region, occupies a parcel of rock-and-scrub-covered seafront land on a south-facing peninsula about 5½ miles west of Halmstad. In summer, the place is filled with families on holiday that enjoy the nearby beaches and wide-open landscapes. The rest of the year, management works hard to fill the place with corporate conventions and theme weekends during which guests participate in wine tastings and spa treatments, and recuperate from the stresses of everyday life. Bedrooms are airy, well furnished, and stylish, each decorated with a light touch and pale colors, plus good beds with adequate-size bathrooms. Throughout the premises, in both bedrooms and public areas, views extend over an eerie, sometimes surreal landscape that can be soothing, invigorating, isolated, and wild.

Dining/Diversions: The hotel contains a trio of restaurants ranging from an informal bistro to a formal modern area with light that floods in from a Nordic interpretation of a greenhouse. One of them features live dance music that's presented whenever there are enough guests in residence to justify the expense.

Amenities: The nearby beach, an indoor pool, sauna, spa and massage facilities, and a roster of organized activities that reminded us of life aboard a cruise ship.

Scandic Grand Hotel. Stationsgatan 44, S-302 45 Halmstad. ☎ **035/21-91-40.** Fax 035/ 14-96-20. 108 units. MINIBAR TV TEL. July to mid-Aug and Fri–Mon year-round, 895–995 SEK ($98.45–$109.45) double; rest of year, 1,235 SEK ($135.85) double;. Rates include breakfast. AE, DC, MC, V. Parking: 35 SEK ($3.85). Bus: 1.

Originally built in 1905, this hotel sports a mock-medieval blocky tower jutting skyward from its exposed corner. Set within a short walk from the railway station, traditionally it has attracted artists and business travelers to its well-upholstered, well-heeled interior. Accommodations were recently renovated and upgraded. Look for solid comfort, good beds, and a no-nonsense approach to the serious business of innkeeping, as reflected by the spick-and-span bathrooms with generous towels.

Dining/Diversions: The in-house restaurant serves well-prepared lunches and dinners every Monday through Friday. Otherwise, platters of food, sandwiches, and snacks are available at the hotel's bar.

Amenities: A computer center for use of hotel guests, a business center, a sauna, and a staff accustomed to acquiring goods and services for business clients of the hotel.

BÅSTAD

Jutting out on a peninsula surrounded by hills and a beautiful landscape, Båstad is the most fashionable international seaside resort in Sweden, lying 111 miles south of Gothenburg and 65 miles north of Malmö.

All the famous international tennis stars have played on the courts at Båstad. Swedish players of today have had much of their training here, inspired by the feats of Björn Borg. There are more than 50 courts in the district, in addition to the renowned Drivan Sports Centre. Tennis was played here as early as the 1880s and became firmly established in the 1920s. King Gustaf V took part in these championships for 15 years from 1930 onward under the pseudonym of "Mr. G," and Ludvig Nobel guaranteed financial backing for international tournaments.

Golf has established itself almost as much as tennis, and the Bjäre peninsula offers a choice of five courses. In 1929, Nobel purchased land at Boarp for Båstad's first golf course. The bay provides opportunities for regattas and different kinds of boating. Windsurfing is popular, as is skin diving. In summer, sea bathing also is popular along the coast.

The Bjäre peninsula, a traditional farming area, is known for its early potatoes, which are in demand all over Sweden for the midsummer table, to be served alongside a selection of pickled herring.

By car, take Route 115 from Båstad going immediately west. If you're not driving, you'll find speedy trains running frequently throughout the day between Gothenburg and Malmö. Six buses a day also arrive from Helsingborg, taking 1 hour.

For tourist information, **Båstad Turism,** Köpmangatan 1 at Stortorget (☎ **0431/ 750-45**), is open June 20 to August 7, Sunday through Friday from 10am to 6pm and Saturday from 10am to 2pm; off-season, Monday through Saturday from 10am to 4pm. You can book private rooms here from 150 SEK ($16.50) per person or rent bikes for 60 SEK ($6.60) per day. They also will provide information about booking tennis courts, renting sports equipment, or reserving a tee time for a round of golf.

Exploring the Area

The most interesting sights are not in Båstad itself but on the Bjäre peninsula (see below). However, before leaving the resort, you may want to call or visit **Mariakyrkan** (Saint Mary's), Köpmansgatan (☎ **0431/78706**). Open daily from 9am to 4pm, it's one of the landmark churches of Skåne. Saint Mary's was built between 1450 and

1500. Its tower was restored as recently as 1986, and the entire interior renewed in 1967. Inside are many treasures, including a sculpture of Saint Mary and Christ from about 1460 (found in the sanctuary). The altarpiece is from 1775, but the crucifix is medieval. The trumpet angel above the altar is from about the same time. The pulpit is from 1836, its hourglass from 1791. In the northern nave is a church clock from 1802 and various fresco paintings.

Båstad is noted for one of the principal attractions of southern Sweden, the ✪ **Norrvikens Trädgårdar** (Norrviken Gardens), Kattvik (☎ **0431/723-70**), 1½ miles west of the resort's center. Founded in 1906 by Rudolf Abelin, these gardens have been expanded and maintained according to his plans, embracing a number of styles. One is Italian baroque, with a pond framed with pyramid-shaped boxwood hedges and tall cypresses. A renaissance garden's boxwood patterns are reminiscent of the tapestry art of 15th-century Italy; in the flower garden, bulbs compete with annuals. There also are a Japanese garden, oriental terrace, rhododendron dell, a romantic garden, and a water garden.

At Villa Abelin, designed by the garden's founder, wisteria climbs the walls and blooms twice a year. The villa houses shops, exhibits, and information facilities. There also are a restaurant and a cafeteria on the grounds.

The gardens can be viewed from May 1 to September 6, daily from 10am to 5pm. Admission is 45 SEK ($4.95) for adults, 30 SEK ($3.30) for children under 12.

With the time you have remaining after exploring the gardens, you may want to turn your attention to the ✪ **Bjäre Peninsula,** the highlight of the entire region, where the widely varied scenery ranges from farm fields to cliff formations. Before exploring in depth, it's best to pick up a detailed map from the Båstad tourist office (see above).

The peninsula is devoted to sports, including windsurfing, tennis, golf, hiking trails, and mountain biking. It has white, sandy beaches reaching down to the sea. Riding paths and cycle roads also are set aside for these activities. You can play golf at five different 18-hole courses from early spring. The Båstad tourist office can provide more information.

If you don't have a car, public transport is provided by bus no. 525 leaving Båstad every hour Monday through Saturday. It traverses the center of the peninsula.

The Skaneleden walking trail runs the entire perimeter of the island and also is great for cycling. However, the terrain is quite hilly in places so you need to be in fabulous shape.

On the peninsula's western coast is the sleepy village of **Torekov,** a short drive from Kattvik. Here you'll find a bathing beach and pier where early-morning bathers can be seen walking down to the sea in bathing gowns and sandals.

From Torekov, you can take a boat to explore **Hallands Väderö,** an island off the west coast of Sweden. Old wooden fishing boats make the 15-minute crossing on the hour from June to August. From September to May, departures are every 2 hours. The cost is 70 SEK ($7.70) round-trip, with the last departure at 4:30pm daily. For more information, call **Bokningstelefon Halmstad** (☎ **035/10-50-70**).

One of Sweden's few remaining seal colonies exists on Hallands Väderö. "Seal safaris" come here to view, but not disturb, these animals. In addition to seals, the island is noted for its rich bird life, including guillemots, cormorants, eiders, and gulls.

Outdoor Activities

GOLF The region around Båstad is home to five separate golf courses. Two of them are amenable to accepting nonmembers who want to use the course during short-term visits to the region. They include the ✪ **Båstad Golf Club,** Boarp, S-269 21 Båstad (☎ **0431/731-36;** to reach it, follow the signs to Boarp and drive 2½ miles south of town), and the ✪ **Bjåre Golf Club,** Solomonhög 3086, S-269 93 Båstad (☎ 0431/ 36-10-53; follow the signs to Förslöv, driving 6 miles east of Båstad). Both charge greens fees of 235 to 350 SEK ($25.85 to $38.50) for 18 holes, depending on the season, and both have pro shops that will rent you clubs. Advance reservations for tee times are essential.

TENNIS   Båstad is irrevocably linked to the game of tennis, which it celebrates with fervor thanks to its role as the longtime home of the **Swedish Open.** If you want to improve your game, consider renting one of the 14 outdoor courts (available only between April and September) or one of the six indoor courts (available year-round) at the **Drivan Tennis Center,** Drivangårdens Vandrarhem (☎ 0431/685-00). Set about a half mile north of Båstad's town center, it's the site of a corps of tennis professionals and teachers, who give lessons for 250 SEK ($27.50) per hour. Both indoor and outdoor courts rent for 80 SEK ($8.80) per hour. And if you really want to immerse yourself in the spirit of the game, consider renting a bunk bed within the establishment's youth hostel, priced at 110 to 130 SEK ($12.10 to $14.30) per person. Functional-looking barrack-style bedrooms within the compound are designed for two to four occupants, and often are the temporary home of members of tennis teams from throughout Scandinavia. Originally established in 1929, this club built most of the tennis courts you see today around 1980.

Where to Stay

Hotel Buena Vista. Tarravägen 5, S-269 35 Båstad. ☎ **0431/760-00.** Fax 0431/791-00. www.buena.se. 30 units. TV TEL. Mon–Thurs 975 SEK ($107.25) double; Fri–Sun 895 SEK ($98.45) double. Rates include breakfast. AE, DC, MC, V. Free parking. Bus: 226.

The most historic and glamorous hotel in town occupies the venerable white walls of a mansion perched on a hilltop, a 3-minute walk uphill from the center of town. It was built in 1906 by John Francis Andersson, a late 19th-century immigrant from Småland who moved to Britain and then to the United States. When he opted to retire in Sweden, he built this elegant Italianate mansion.

Today, it's a site for small-scale conventions, wedding parties (there's a chapel with a vaulted ceiling on the premises), honeymooners, and regular tourists as well. Public areas have been restored to some of their original Edwardian-era opulence, with dark colors and lots of varnished hardwoods. Bedrooms, however, are relatively contemporary in their styling and in many cases a bit cramped, although mattresses are first rate. Bathrooms are tiled, relatively small, and simple, in many ways equivalent to what you'd expect in a modern roadside hotel.

Dining: Other than breakfast, meals are not served here regularly, but on an as-needed, catered basis. If you want dinner for groups of between two and several hundred people, on advance notice, the management will arrange for it at costs ranging from 150 to 400 SEK ($16.50 to $44) per head, depending on what you order.

Amenities: Room service for breakfast, concierge.

Hotel-Pension Enehall. Stationsterrassen 10, S-26900 Båstad. ☎ **0431/750-15.** Fax 0431/ 724-09. www.enehall.se. E-mail: enehall@enehall.se. 40 units. TV TEL. 660–800 SEK ($72.60–$88) double. Half-board 480 SEK ($52.80) per person. Rates include breakfast. AE, DC, MC, V. Free parking. Bus: 513.

On a slope of Hallandsåsen mountain, only a few minutes' walk from the sea, this cozy, intimate place caters mainly to Swedish families, and the occasional Dane or German. There are many personal touches here and the rooms, although small, are adequately equipped with good beds, tiny bathrooms, and minimal towels. The food is tasty; the service polite and efficient.

Hotel Riviera. Rivieravägen, S-269-39 Båstad. ☎ **0431/369-050.** Fax 0431/761-00. www.hotelriviera.nu. 50 units. TV TEL. 690 SEK ($75.90) double. Rates include breakfast. AE, DC, MC, V. Closed Sept–Apr. Free parking. Bus: 513.

Often a favorite venue for conferences, this is one of the better hotels in the area, and takes on a somewhat festive air in summer. Located by the sea, half a mile from the railroad station and 2 miles east of the town center, it offers views from many of its modern bedrooms, as well as its 300-seat restaurant. Both bedrooms and bathrooms are small, but comfortably furnished with good beds. The housekeeping is excellent. Many guests sit out in the gardens or on the terrace, whereas others prefer to play on the tennis courts. There's a large, cozy bar, plus a summer cafe on a sun-filled loggia. The kitchen serves a superb combination of Scandinavian and international food; in season there often is dancing to a live band.

Hotel Skansen. Kyrkogatan 2, S-269 21 Båstad. ☎ **0431/720-50.** Fax 0431/700-85. www.hotelskansen.se. 52 units. TV MINIBAR TEL. 830 SEK ($91.30) double. Rates include breakfast. AE, DC, MC, V. Free parking. Bus: 513; 5-minute walk.

Although it isn't as expensive as some of those within the chain, this hotel is associated with some of the most opulent and prestigious hotels in Sweden, including the Grand Hotel in Stockholm. It's also the most visible tennis venue in Sweden, surrounded with eight tennis courts that are the home every year to the Swedish Open. As such, it has housed, usually more than once, the most famous tennis stars in Sweden, including Björn Borg, Anders Järryd, and Henrik Holm. It originally was built as a warehouse for grain in 1877, a few minutes' walk from the marina and 50 yards from the beach. Today, it incorporates its original building (which today is listed as a national monument) with four more recent structures that surround eight tennis courts, some of which are equipped with stadiums for the above-mentioned tennis competitions. The interior has a beamed roof, pillars, and views over the sea. Renovated in 1997, bedrooms are airy, elegant, and traditionally outfitted with conservative furniture, including good beds with ample private bathrooms.

Dining: Regrettably, the in-house restaurant is open only between June and mid-September. Set within the oldest of the five buildings comprising the hotel, and outfitted in autumn tones of yellow and brown, it serves Swedish and international cuisine. The rest of the year, meals are served only to residents, and only by special arrangements. A cafe operates year-round, spilling over into the courtyard during warm weather.

Amenities: Beach facilities, conference facilities, eight tennis courts, health club, sauna, solarium within a 4-minute walk of the hotel.

Where to Dine

The preceding hotels all have good restaurants, although you should call in advance for a reservation. But if you're just passing through, consider dropping in at the **Solbackens Café & Wåffelbruk,** Italienska vägen (☎ **0431/70-200**). If the weather is fair, opt for a table on the terrace overlooking the water. This cafe is locally famous, known for serving Swedish waffles and other delights since 1907.

Centrecourten. Köpmansgatan 70b. ☎ **0431/75275.** Reservations recommended. Pizza 55–70 SEK ($6.05–$7.70); main courses 85–140 SEK ($9.35–$15.40). AE, M, V. Mon–Thurs 4–10pm, Fri 4–11:30pm, Sat noon–10:30pm, Sun noon–10pm. SWEDISH/INTERNATIONAL.

In a town as obsessed with tennis as Båstad, you'd expect at least one restaurant to be outfitted in a tennis-lovers theme. In this case, it consists of a cozy and small-scale dining room with photos of such stars as Björn Borg, a scattering of trophies, old-fashioned tennis memorabilia, and tennis racquets. Menu items include fresh fish, including mussels, lemon sole, and cod; breast of duck with bacon-flavored purée of potatoes; and brisket of beef with chanterelles and shallots. The food is no better than it should be, but the ingredients are fresh and the flavors often enticing, especially in the seafood selections.

Persson & Co. Köpmansgatan 75. ☎ **0431/75005.** Reservations recommended. Main courses 100–135 SEK ($11–$14.85). V. Wed–Sun 5–10pm. Bar stays open till 1am. SWEDISH.

Set close to both the bus station and Båstad's largest food market, this restaurant is known for an active bar area that's favored by the young-at-heart and the restless, a woodsy decor that may remind you of an English pub, and gargantuan portions. Menu items include a salmon tartare with capers and horseradish, at least three kinds of steaks, grilled halibut with a garlic-tomato sauce, and roasted filets of reindeer on a bed of wild mushrooms. Even if your taste buds don't always scream out hysterical praise here, the flavor combinations are most satisfying, and we like the chef's reliance on local ingredients whenever they are available to him.

Båstad After Dark
One of the most appealing places to hang out in Båstad is the bar at the already-recommended Persson & Co. Restaurant (see above). Here, according to a well-seasoned staff member, "It's not unlikely that you might form some kind of companionship bond with one of the locals." It's liveliest every Wednesday through Sunday from around 10pm till the 1am closing. Another active choice is **Pepe's Bodega,** Warmbadhuset Hamnen (☎ **0431/369169**), where spicy food and party-colored cocktails evoke a corner of either southern Spain, northern Mexico, or some undefined hideaway in a forgotten corner of South America. It's open Wednesday to Sunday for both food and an active bar life, from 5pm till 11pm for food, and until 1am for drinks.

ÄNGELHOLM
This is the major beach area for the city of Helsingborg. Its nearly 4 miles of golden sand attract a thriving summer business, as Helsingborg lies only 30 minutes away by train.

For information about the area, contact the **Ängelholms Turistbyrå,** Stortorget (☎ **0431/821-30**). It is open June through August, Monday through Friday 9am to 6pm, Saturday 9am to 4pm, and in July only, Sunday 11am to 3pm. Off-season times are Monday through Friday 9am to 4pm.

Frequent trains throughout the day link Båstad or Helsingborg with Ängelholm in less than 30 minutes. Buses also arrive frequently from Båstad. Motorists from Helsingborg in the south or Båstad in the north can travel the express highway, E6.

Seeing the Sights
The great botanist, Carolus Linnaeus, claimed that "Nowhere in Europe surpasses the place in charm, beauty, climate, and prosperity." A bit of an exaggeration, but Ängelholm and its surrounding area certainly are blessed with a varied and scenic landscape of coast and plain. The **Rönneå,** one of Sweden's loveliest rivers, rises in Lake Ringsjön and runs into the sea at Skälderviken Bay. The tourist office (see above) can provide details in summer about how to go for a canoe ride on this river.

Because of Ängelholm's position on this river, it was the cause of many bitter battles between Danes and Swedes. In 1658, following the peace of Roskilde, Ängelholm and the province of Skåne itself became firmly Swedish. The town was virtually destroyed twice in fierce fires in 1745 and 1802. The clay cuckoo, a ceramic pot, is the symbol of Ängelholm, which is very much a pottery town; potters have worked here since the 17th century. The pot is sold at dozens of stores throughout the town and is the best souvenir of a visit here.

The X-Philes

Ängelholm is big with UFO buffs. In 1946, Gösta Carlsson, a railway worker, claimed to have encountered tiny aliens from across the galaxy. Apparently, Carlsson was rather convincing; ever since the postwar era, European UFO conferences have been held here. The tourist board often runs tours to the site of the alleged landing from outer space.

Hantverksmuseum or the Ängelholm Craft Museum, Tingstorget (☎ 0431/ 875-03), is housed in Sweden's oldest prison, which dates from 1780. It depicts the history of ceramics in the area, and has exhibits of the work of well-known local artists. It is open May through August, Tuesday to Friday from 11am to 4pm and Saturday 10am to 2pm, and charges 10 SEK ($1.10) for admission. In September it is open Saturday and Sunday 11am to 4pm.

Where to Stay & Dine

Hotell Erikslund. Erikslund, S-262 96 Ängelholm. ☎ **0431/222-30.** Fax 0431/222-48. www.hotellerikslund.se. E-mail: reception@hotellerikslund.se. 140 units. TV TEL. Mid-June to late Aug and Fri–Sat year-round, 695 SEK ($76.45) double; rest of year, 945 SEK ($103.95) double. AE, DC, MC, V. Free parking. Bus: 506 from Ängelholm.

Set within rolling farmland, 4¼ miles south of Ängelholm, this hotel attracts lots of vacationing motorists (especially Germans) in summer during their explorations of the Swedish Riviera. It was built in 1991 in a vaguely Iberian format that includes sprawling, white-sided wings and a central tower that's capped with a gently sloping terracotta peaked roof. Grounds surrounding the property are lavishly planted with roses and perennials, encouraging walks in the natural grandeur of the surrounding region. Bedrooms are artfully simple, with glowing hardwood floors, outfitted with simple but tasteful furnishings, usually made from varnished birch and upholstery in such Nordic colors as pale blue and midnight blue, and stark white walls. Beds are firm, but the bathrooms are rather small. On the premises is a warm and cozy restaurant, Joel's, where twin dining rooms (one apple green, one white) serve Swedish and international cuisine. Although there's no golf course on the premises, about a dozen of them lie within a radius of about 20 miles. The staff at this hotel is familiar with the best of them, and can direct interested players. The hotel also has a spa.

6

Skåne (Including Helsingborg & Malmö)

In Sweden's southernmost corner, the province of Skåne offers varied scenery, large forests, and many waterways. The sea, with its ample, uncrowded beaches, is always within reach. And many of the larger towns have a continental aura, because of their proximity to other European countries.

Denmark and the rest of Europe now are easier to reach than ever before. In 2000, the Øresund Fixed Link between Denmark and Sweden was completed and opened to the public. A new artificial island was constructed halfway across the Øresund to connect 2 miles of immersed railway and motorway tunnels and a 4.8-mile bridge. Bridging the divide between Copenhagen and Malmö, this link will benefit culture, education, and research in both countries, as well as business and transportation. With three million people living within a 31-mile radius of the link, the region has the largest population concentration in the Nordic area.

Skåne's major urban cities are **Malmö, Helsingborg,** and the university and cathedral city of **Lund,** but many visit the little villages and undiscovered coastal towns in the summer months.

Skåne may not have fjords and snow-capped mountains, but it has about everything else: sandy beaches, sea resorts, and ports; medieval churches and ancient cities and towns; the finest castles (often surrounded by beautiful grounds and moats); some of the country's most stately cathedrals; and fertile plains, virgin forests, rolling hills, and thriving farms. Many poets, authors, and painters have found inspiration here.

The first settlers were deer hunters and fishers who moved from the south of Europe as the ice melted. Over thousands of years, their ancestors left many traces, from the Stone Age to the Viking Age and the early beginnings of Christianity. Once Skåne belonged to Denmark, but since 1658 it has been a firm part of the Swedish kingdom. There are no fewer than 300 small medieval parish churches in the province—all still in use. Castles and mansions, many founded 400 or 500 years ago, dot the landscape.

There are many beaches for swimming and sunbathing along Skåne's coast; in fact, like Halland (see chapter 5) it is known as the Swedish Riviera.

Skåne is easy to reach. You have a wide choice of flights, either to Malmö's Sturup Airport or to the Copenhagen airport from which

there are frequent Hovercraft connections directly to the center of Malmö. Hovercraft also run between downtown Copenhagen and Malmö; and every 15 or 20 minutes, day or night, connections are possible by car ferry from Helsingør, Denmark to Helsingborg, Sweden. If you're traveling by car, there are ferry routes from Denmark, Germany, and Poland.

1 Helsingborg

143 miles S of Gothenburg, 347 miles SW of Stockholm, 39 miles N of Malmö

At the narrowest point of the Øresund (Öresund in Swedish), 3 miles across the water that separates Sweden and Denmark, sits this industrial city and major port. Many people from Copenhagen who visit Kronborg Castle at Helsingør take a 25-minute ferry ride (which leaves every 20 minutes) across the sound for a look at Sweden.

Of course, what they see isn't "Sweden," but a modern city with an ancient history. In the Middle Ages, Helsingborg and Helsingør together controlled shipping along the sound. The city is mentioned in the 10th-century *Nial-Saga* (an ancient Viking document), and other documents also indicate that there was a town here in 1085. The city now has more than 100,000 inhabitants and the second busiest harbor in the country. This is the city that introduced pedestrian streets to Sweden, and it has long shore promenades along the sound.

The Goose of Honor

The tip of the Scandinavian peninsula was where Selma Lagerlöf's *The Wonderful Adventures of Nils* began. The story of the hero, who travels on the back of a wild goose, has been translated into all major languages. In reality, however, the web-footed, flat-billed, large-bodied geese of Skåne are tame and never travel far from home. No doubt they regret this on November 10 when Scanians celebrate this almost sacred bird with a gargantuan dinner—one enjoyed by everyone but the geese.

Helsingborg (Hålsingborg) recently rebuilt large, vacant-looking sections of its inner city into one of the most innovative urban centers in Sweden. The centerpiece of these restorations lies beside the harbor and includes an all-glass building, the **Knutpunkten,** on Järnvägsgatan. Contained within are the railroad, bus, and ferry-boat terminals, an array of shops similar to a North American mall, and a heliport. Many visitors say the sunlight-flooded railroad station is the cleanest, brightest, and most memorable they've ever seen. In addition, many dozens of trees and shrubs have transformed the center city into something like a verdant park, with trees between the lanes of traffic.

ESSENTIALS

GETTING THERE   By Ferry   Ferries from Helsingør, Denmark, leave the Danish harbor every 20 minutes day or night (trip time: 25 minutes). For information about ferryboats in Helsingborg call ☎ **042/18-61-00;** for information on the Danish side, call ☎ **33-15-15-15.** The cost of the ferryboat for pedestrians is 23 SEK ($2.55) each way or 40 SEK ($4.40) round-trip. The regular round-trip cost of the ferryboat for a car with up to five passengers is 510 SEK ($56.10) Sunday to Wednesday, or 445 SEK ($48.95) Thursday to Saturday. There's a reduction for drivers planning to return to Sweden the same day; in that event, the round-trip fare is 295 SEK ($32.45) for passage.

By Plane   The Ångelholm/Helsingborg airport lies 30 minutes from the center of the city, with regular connections to Stockholm's Arlanda airport. There are between seven and nine flights per day (flying time: 1 hour). For SAS reservations, call ☎ **0431/55-80-10.**

By Train   Trains run hourly during the day between Helsingborg and Malmö, taking 50 minutes. Trains arrive twice per day on the 7-hour trip from Stockholm, and they also leave Helsingborg twice per day for Stockholm. Trains between Gothenburg and Helsingborg depart and arrive twice a day (trip time: 2½ hours). Call ☎ **020/ 757575** for information.

By Bus   Three buses per day link Malmö and Helsingborg. Two leave in the morning and one in the afternoon, the trip taking 1 hour and 10 minutes. Buses leave twice per day from Gothenburg and arrive in Helsingborg in 3¼ hours. Buses to and from Stockholm leave once per day (trip time: 10 hours). Call ☎ **0200/21818** for more information.

By Car   From Malmö, head north on E6, taking 1 hour; from Gothenburg, drive south on E6 for 2½ hours; From Stockholm, take E4 south for 7½ hours until you reach Helsingborg.

Helsingborg

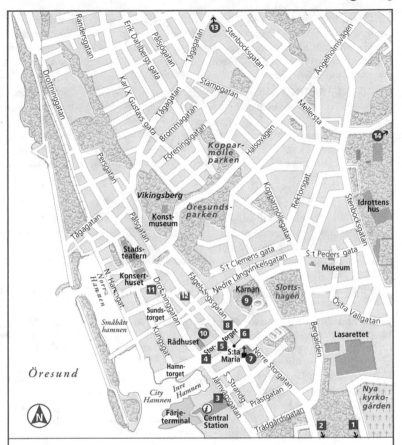

ATTRACTIONS ●

Fredriksdal Open-Air Museum
and Botanical Garden **14**
Kärnan (The Keep) **9**
Mairakyrkan (Church of St. Mary) **7**
Rådhuset (Town Hall) **10**
Sofiero Slott **13**

ACCOMMODATIONS ■

Hotel Helsingborg **6**
Hotel Högvakten **8**
Hotell Lìnnéa **3**
Hotell Viking **12**
Hotel Mollberg **4**
Hotel Nouveau **2**
Marina Plaza **11**
Radisson/SAS Grand Hotel
Helsingborg **5**
Scandic Partner Hotel Horisont **1**

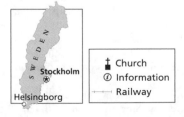

✝ Church
ⓘ Information
┼┼┼ Railway

VISITOR INFORMATION   The tourist office, **Helsingborg Turistbyrå,** Knut-punkten (☎ 042/10-43-50; www.helsingborg.se), is open May until September 15, Monday through Friday from 9am to 8pm and on Saturday and Sunday from 9am to 5pm; September 16 until April, Monday through Friday from 9am to 6pm and on Saturday from 10am to 2pm.

GETTING AROUND   Most of Helsingborg's sights are within walking distance; however, if your legs are tired and the weather less than perfect, you can always take a city bus, numbered 1 to 7. Most buses on their way north pass the Town Hall; those heading south go by Knutpunkten. You can buy tickets on board the buses, which cost 14 SEK ($1.55). Tickets are valid for transfer to another city bus line as long as you transfer within 1 hour from the time the ticket was stamped. For information, call ☎ 020/61-61-61.

SEEING THE SIGHTS

Built in 1897, the **Town Hall (Rådhuset),** Drottninggatan 7 (☎ 042/10-50-00), has handsome stained-glass windows depicting scenes from the town's history. Two memorial stones outside were presented by the Danes and the Norwegians to the Swedes for their assistance during World War II. There also is a sculpture relief representing the arrival of Danish refugees.

In the main town square, the **Stortorget** is a monument commemorating General Stenbock's victory at the Battle of Helsingborg in 1710 between Sweden and Denmark.

Fredriksdal Open-Air Museum and Botanical Garden. Hävertgatan. ☎ 042/104-540. Admission 30 SEK ($3.30), free for children 9 and under. Park, June–Aug, daily 10am–8pm; Sept–May, daily 11am–4pm. Manor, June–Sept, daily 11am–5pm; Oct–May, daily 10am–3pm. Bus: 2, 3, or 250.

This is among the largest and most complete open-air museums in Sweden, covering some 70 acres of rolling land within a 20-minute walk east of the town center. The park was built around a manor house constructed in 1787. After going through the main entrance, you can explore the rose garden, which has about 450 different types of roses, all part of one of Sweden's most remarkable botanical gardens. An open-air theater, part of the complex, was established in 1927. You also can wander through the French Park and the English Park.

Kärnan (The Keep). Kärngränden (off the Stortorget). ☎ 042/105-991. Admission 50 SEK ($5.50) adults, 5 SEK (55¢) children. Apr–May, Tues–Sun 9am–4pm; June–Aug, Tues–Sun 10am–7pm; Sept, daily 9am–3pm; Oct–Mar, daily 10am–2pm. Bus: 1 or 6.

One of the most important medieval monuments in Sweden, and the symbol of Helsingborg, Kärnan rises from the crest of a rocky ridge in the town center. This 100-foot-tall square tower originated mysteriously in the 11th century, but adopted its present form in the 1300s. Its name translates as "the keep," a moniker related to its original position as the most central tower (and prison) of the once-mighty Helsingborg Castle. The thickness of its walls (about 14 feet) make it the most solidly constructed building in the region. An object of bloody fighting between the Swedes and the Danes for generations, the castle and its fortifications were demolished in 1679. Of the once-mighty fortress, only Kärnan (which was restored and rebuilt in 1894) remains.

The easiest way to reach Kärnan is to board the elevator, which departs from the *terrasen* (terrace) of the town's main street, the Stortorget. For 5 SEK (65¢) per person, you'll be carried up the rocky hillside to the base of the tower. However, many visitors avoid the elevator, preferring instead to climb a winding set of flower-flanked steps as part of their exploration of the city. Once inside the tower, an additional 147 steps remain before you're rewarded with one of the most sweeping views in the district.

Mariakyrkan (Church of St. Mary). Södra Storgaten. ☎ **042/37-28-30.** Free admission. June–Aug, Mon–Sat 8am–6pm, Sun 9am–6pm; Sept–May, Mon–Sat 8am–4pm, Sun 9am–4pm. Bus: 1 or 6.

A short walk east from the harbor, this church was constructed in the 13th century but substantially rebuilt in the 15th century in a Danish Gothic style that evokes a basilica. Although the facade is plain, the interior is striking. Particularly noteworthy are the medieval altarpiece and its intricately carved Renaissance pulpit. If the sun is shining, the modern stained-glass windows are jewel-like.

Sofiero Slott. Sofierovägen. ☎ **042/137-400.** Admission 50 SEK ($5.50) adults, 10 SEK ($1.10) children. Daily 10am–6pm. Closed Oct to mid-Apr. Bus: 219 or 221.

One of the most famous buildings in southern Sweden, lying 3 miles north of Helsingborg, this castle was constructed in 1864–65 to be the summer residence of King Oscar II and his wife, Sofia. In 1905 it was bequeathed to their grandson, Gustav Adolph, and his wife, Margareta, who enlarged the site and created some of the most memorable gardens in the country. Their interests supposedly sparked a nationwide interest in landscape architecture, which continues stronger than ever throughout Sweden today. After his coronation, Gustav Adolph spent his last days here, eventually bequeathing Sofiero as a gift to the city of Helsingborg in 1973. In 1993, many of the original gardens were recreated in memory of their designer, Queen Margareta. Today, the most visited sites include the 1865 castle, which contains a cafe and restaurant; the rose garden; and the Rhododendron Ravine, with an estimated 10,000 rhododendrons, which are in their full glory in early June.

SHOPPING

In the center of Helsingborg you'll find a number of shopping possibilities, including **Väla Centrum,** which is one of the largest shopping centers in all of Scandinavia. To reach it, follow Hälsovägen and Ångelholmsvägen north about 3½ miles (it's signposted) or take bus 202 from Knutpunkten. Seemingly everything is here under one roof, including two large department stores and some 42 specialty shops, selling everything from shoes and clothing to flowers and tropical fish.

The best bookstore in town is **Bokman,** Järnvägsgatan 3 (☎ 042/13-75-75), with many English-language editions. The best center for class is **Duka Carl Anders,** Södergatan 22 (☎ 042/24-27-00), which carries the works of such prestigious manufacturers as Kosta Boda and Orrefors.

POTTERY

Northwest Scania is known as the pottery district of Sweden. The first Scanian pottery factory was founded in 1748 in Bosarp, 9¼ miles east of Helsingborg. The city of Helsingborg got its first factory in 1768 and another began manufacturing in 1832. Since then, the tradition has been redeveloped and revitalized, making the area famous far beyond the borders of Sweden.

At a point 4½ miles south of Helsingborg, you can visit **Raus Stenkarlsfabrik,** half a mile east of Råå (look for signs along Landskronavagen). It is open May through December, Monday through Friday 10am to 6pm, Saturday 10am to 4pm; off-season Saturday and Sunday 10am to 4pm. Call ☎ 042/26-01-30 for more information.

In Gantofta, 6.2 miles southeast of Helsingborg, lies **Jie-Keramik** (☎ 042/990-31), one of Scandinavia's leading manufacturers of hand-painted decorative ceramics, wall reliefs, wall clocks, figures, and other such items. You can visit a factory shop or patronize a cafe on site. From Helsingborg, drive south to Råå, then follow the signs to Gantofta. You also can take bus 209 from Knutpunkten in the center of Helsingborg. The outlet is open June through August, Monday through Friday 8am to 6pm, Saturday 8am to 4pm, Sunday 11am to 5pm. Off-season hours are Monday through Friday 10am to 5pm, Saturday 10am to 4pm, and Sunday noon to 4pm.

If you drive 12½ miles north of Helsingborg to Höganäs you'll find two famous stoneware factories. **Höganäs Saltglaserat** (☎ 042/33-83-33) has been manufacturing salt-glazed stoneware since 1835. Today the classic, salt-glazed Höganäs jars with their anchor symbol are still in production. Everything is made by hand and fired in coal-burning circular kilns from the turn of the century. The shop here is within the factory, so you can see the throwers in action and go inside the old kilns. Hours are June through August Monday through Friday 9am to 4pm; in December the shop is also open Saturday 10am to 1pm. The other outlet, **Höganäs Keramik** (☎ 042/33-20-75), is Scandinavia's largest stoneware manufacturer. In the Factory Shop, inaugurated in 1994, flawed goods from both Höganäs Keramik and Boda Nova are on sale at bargain prices. This outlet is open May to August Monday through Friday 9am to 6pm, Saturday and Sunday 10am to 5pm. Off-season hours are Monday through Friday 10am to 6pm, Saturday 10am to 4pm, and Sunday 11am to 4pm.

You also can visit **Gröna Gården,** Välluvsvågen 34 in Påarp (☎ 42/22-71-70), southeast of Helsingborg. Head toward Malmö, but exit at Barslov toward Påarp-Välluv. Here you will find an outlet offering many beautiful handcrafts in ceramic, glass, birch bark, forged metal, and wood. Handwoven fabrics, baskets, candles, wooden toys, and handmade jewelry are just some of the merchandise for sale. Hours are Tuesday through Friday 1 to 6pm, Saturday 10am to 1pm. In November and December, it also is open Sunday 1 to 4pm.

WHERE TO STAY
EXPENSIVE

Radisson/SAS Grand Hotel Helsingborg. Stortorget 8–12, Box 1104, S-251 11 Helsingborg. ☎ **800/333-3333** in the U.S., or 042/38-04-00. Fax 042/38-04-04. www.Radisson.com. 117 units. MINIBAR TV TEL. Mid-June to Aug and Fri–Sun year-round, 790–900 SEK ($86.90–$99) double; 1,090–1,900 SEK ($119.90–$209) suite. Rest of year, 1,400–1,600 SEK ($154–$176) double; 1,800–2,700 SEK ($198–$297) suite. Rates include breakfast. AE, DC, MC, V. Parking 115 SEK ($12.65). Bus: 7B or 1A.

In 1996, the premises of Helsingborg's grandest hotel—an imposing brick-fronted monument originally built in 1926—was radically upgraded. Since then, it has factored high on everybody's list of the most appealing hotels in southern Sweden, with a combination of high-ceilinged, richly paneled public areas and spacious, well-accessorized bedrooms with elaborate ceiling moldings, many decorative accessories of the old world, and lots of modern comforts and conveniences. These include roomy bedrooms with good mattresses and ample bathrooms with hair dryers. Some rooms are equipped with facilities for persons with disabilities; there also are no-smoking rooms.

Dining/Diversions: The most formal of the hotel's three restaurants is the Grand Séparée, serving Scandinavian delicacies against a backdrop of classical music. The Granderiet is an appealing bistro offering exotic and spicy dishes from around the world. The hotel's bar, Bakfickan, serves drinks and pub food such as salads, pastas, and burgers.

Amenities: Conference facilities, room service, an exercise room with sauna and solarium, concierge.

MODERATE

Hotel Helsingborg. Stortorget 20, S-252 23 Helsingborg. ☎ 042/12-09-45. Fax 042/21-54-61. www.hkchotels.se. E-mail: info.hotelhelsingborg@swedenhotels.se. 56 units. TV TEL. 995–1,225 SEK ($109.45–$134.75) double; 1,100–1,600 SEK ($121–$176) suite. Rates include breakfast. AE, DC, MC, V. Parking 90 SEK ($9.90). Bus: 7A, 7B, 1A, or 1B.

Of the three hotels that lie along this grand avenue, this one is closest to the city's medieval tourist attraction, the Kärnan. It has a heroic neoclassical frieze and three copper-sheathed towers, and occupies four floors of what used to be a bank headquarters, dating from 1901. The bedrooms are pleasantly modernized and flooded with sunlight. The rooms retain a certain Jugendstil (art nouveau) look, with strong colors, high ceilings, and many decorative touches. All rooms were upgraded and renovated in the early 1990s, with good beds and small though perfectly functional bathrooms. There's a lobby bar and a breakfast room. The lobby bar serves simple platters of light food and sandwiches 24 hours a day. A sauna is on the premises, along with boutiques at street level.

Hotel Mollberg. Stortorget 18, S-251 10 Helsingborg. ☎ **800/528-1234** in the U.S., or 042/12-02-70. Fax 042/14-96-18. www.hotelmollberg.se. 100 units. MINIBAR TV TEL. 790–1,290 SEK ($86.90–$141.90) double. Rates include breakfast. AE, DC, MC, V. Parking 85 SEK ($9.35). Bus: 7A, 7B, 1A, or 1B.

Hotel Mollberg often is called "Sweden's oldest continuously operated hotel and restaurant." Although a tavern has stood on this site since the 14th century, most of today's building was constructed in 1802 by the establishment's namesake, Peter Mollberg. Its elaborate wedding-cake exterior and high-ceilinged interior have long been hallmarks of the hotel A major renovation was carried out in 1986, with small restorations in 1994, 1996, and early 1998. The first-class rooms are all equipped with good beds, trouser presses, and hair dryers, among other amenities. Use of the solarium and sauna are included in the rates. The Mollberg has a dining room and a cocktail lounge. The Mollberg Brasserie offers light cuisine and is open Monday through Saturday from noon to 11pm.

Hotel Nouveau. Gasverksgatan 11. S-250 02 Helsingborg. ☎ 042/18-53-90. Fax 042/14-08-85. www.nouveauhotel.se. 79 units. TV TEL. Mid-June to mid-Aug and Fri–Sat year-round, 800 SEK ($88) double; rest of year, 1,295 SEK ($142.45) double. AE, DC, MC, V. Free parking. Bus: 7A or 1A.

In 1996, a somewhat nondescript and outmoded hotel from the 1960s was radically reconfigured and upgraded. The result is a tastefully decorated, brick hotel in shades of ochre with touches of marble. The decor throughout the hotel draws on upscale models from England and France and includes chintz curtains, varnished mahogany (often with wood inlays), and warm colors inspired by the tones of autumn. Rooms are nice and cozy, not overly large but well maintained, with tasteful fabrics, good beds, frequently renewed linen, and small but adequate bathrooms. Often a fresh flower is placed on your pillow at night, a thoughtful touch. There are conference facilities within the hotel, a worthwhile restaurant, and a well-trained staff whose best points include a sense of humor.

۞ Marina Plaza. Kungstorget 6, S-251 Helsingborg. ☎ **800/528-1234** in the U.S., or 042/19-21-00. Fax 042/14-96-16. www.marinaplazaelite.se. 190 units. MINIBAR TV TEL. 790–1,295 SEK ($86.90–$142.45) double; 1,995–2,700 SEK ($219.45–$297) suite. Midsummer discounts available. AE, DC, MC, V. Free parking. Bus: 41, 42, 43, or 44.

This is the most modern, most innovative, and most talked-about hotel in Helsingborg. Set adjacent to the city's transportation hub, the Knutpunkten, behind a light yellow facade studded with large glass windows; it contains an atrium-style lobby that overflows with trees, flowers, rock gardens, and fountains. A piano provides evening entertainment near the lobby's popular bar. Bedrooms line the inner walls of the hotel's atrium and are outfitted, as the hotel's name implies, with a color scheme of marine blue with nautical accessories. Rooms are moderate in size and each contains firm mattresses with adequately sized bathrooms equipped with hair dryers. The hotel contains two restaurants, the upscale Hamnkrogen and less formal Sailor's Pub, where Italian food is offered. There also is a disco, the Marina Nightclub. The hotel maintains a health club with a sauna and solarium.

Scandic Partner Hotel Horisont. Gustav Adolfs Gate 47, S-250 02 Helsingborg. ☎ 042/49-52-100. Fax 042/49-52-111. www.scandic-hotels.com. E-mail: horisont@scandic-hotels.com. 170 units. TV TEL. 710–1,473 SEK ($78.10–$162.05) double. Rates include breakfast. AE, DC, MC, V. Free parking. Bus: 7B or 1B.

Situated near a park at the edge of the commercial center of town, the angular and futuristic facade of this hotel was erected in 1985. The bedrooms are comfortably conservative, with plush upholstery, soundproof windows, and comfortable mattresses. On the premises is a warmly attractive bar lined with brick and touches of brass, and a high-ceilinged formal restaurant. Relaxation facilities include a center with saunas, whirlpools, and solariums. The hotel is about half a mile south of the ferryboat terminal.

INEXPENSIVE

Hotel Högvakten. Stortorget 14, P.O. Box 1074, SE-251 10 Helsingborg. ☎ 042/12-03-90. Fax 042/12-00-95. www.hotelhogvakten.com. 41 units. TV TEL. Mid-June to mid-Aug and Fri–Sun year-round, 675 SEK ($74.25) double; rest of year, 1,045 SEK ($114.95) double. Rates include breakfast. AE, DC, MC, V. Free parking. Bus: 7A, 7B, 1A, or 1B.

Set within a 5-minute walk from the ferryboat terminal, this hotel occupies the dignified premises of what was built as a private townhouse in 1914. Part of the appeal of its well-designed interior results from a radical renovation that was completed in 1996. Expect lots of autumn-inspired colors and comfortable, well-upholstered furnishings in both the public areas and the bedrooms. Bedrooms are bright and fresh and generally quite spacious. They were recently refurbished, and comfort and quality obviously were given priority when the beds and fabrics were chosen. Bathrooms are in state-of-the-art condition. No meals are served other than breakfast, although the polite and attentive staff is quick to help you select from the more than 30 restaurants in the area, many within easy walking distance from the hotel.

Hotell Linnéa. Prästgatan 4, S-252 24 Helsingborg. ☎ 042/21-46-60. Fax 042/14-16-55. www.hotel-linnea.se. E-mail: linnea@hotel-linea.se. 19 units. TV TEL. July–Aug and Fri–Sat year-round, 565–695 SEK ($62.15–$76.45) double; rest of year, 895 SEK ($98.45) double. Rates include breakfast. AE, DC, MC, V. Parking 90 SEK ($9.90). Bus: 7A or 7B.

Conveniently located a few yards from the point where ferryboats from Denmark pull in, this is a pleasant, small-scale hotel that occupies a pink-fronted, circa 1897 Italianate house whose scale and detailing might remind you of something from a historic New Orleans neighborhood. Bedrooms are appealingly outfitted with high-quality furnishings that include tasteful reproductions of 19th-century antiques, comfortable beds, and sometimes elaborate draperies. Bathrooms are small but adequate. No meals are served other than breakfast, but many reliable dining choices lie within a short walk from the hotel.

Hotell Viking. Fågelsångsgatan 1, S-252 20 Helsingborg. ☎ 042/14-44-20. Fax 042/18-43-20. www.hotellviking.se. E-mail: hotel.Viking@helsingborg.se. 41 units. MINIBAR TV TEL. Mid-June to July and Fri–Sun year-round, 765 SEK ($84.15) double; rest of year, 1,095 SEK ($120.45) double. Rates include breakfast. AE, DC, MC, V. Free parking. Bus: 7A, 7B, 1A, or 1B.

Set in the center of town, less than 2 blocks north of the Drottninggatan, this hotel looks more historic, cozier, and a bit more artfully cluttered than many of its more formal and streamlined competitors. It was built during the late 19th century as a row of shops, where usually the owners lived upstairs from their businesses. Today, after a radical mid-1990s remodeling, you'll find a carefully preserved sense of history, a pale color scheme of grays, beiges, and ochres, and a hands-on management style by the resident owners. Bedrooms are cozy, neat, and functional, with exceptionally firm mattresses. Bathrooms are a bit small, but adequately supplied with hair dryers and trouser presses. Breakfast is the only meal served, but the staff will be happy to direct you to the numerous nearby restaurants.

WHERE TO DINE

Anna Kock. Järnvägsgatan 23. ☎ **042/18-13-00.** Reservations recommended at lunch, required at dinner. Lunch platters 60 SEK ($6.60); main courses 85–195 SEK ($9.35–$21.45); 2-course fixed-price dinner 185 SEK ($20.35). AE, DC, MC, V. Tues–Fri 11am–2pm and 5:30–10pm, Sat noon–10:30pm. Bus: 3, 5, 7, 9, or 12. SWEDISH.

Decorated with a collection of modern Swedish watercolors and the kind of antique knickknacks you might find in a Swedish farmstead, this cozy restaurant contains only 11 tidy tables. Opened in 1989, it was named after "Anna the Cook," a locally famous chef to the region's early 20th-century bourgeoisie and aunt of the present owners, Claes and Susaan Andren. Menu items reflect the best of both modern and old-fashioned culinary techniques. Your meal might include Anna's pickled herring served with a Dutch blue cheese sauce, fillet of reindeer on a bed of morels and lingonberry sauce, breast of wild duck with kumquat sauce and rhubarb chutney, fried fillets of lemon sole with vermouth sauce and whitebait roe, or sautéed eggplant on a bed of mushrooms with pasta and tomato sauce. Lunches are simpler and less expensive than the carefully cultivated dinners that are the norm here.

Elinor. Kullagatan 53. ☎ **042/12-23-30.** Reservations required. Main courses 195–265 SEK ($21.45–$29.15); fixed-price lunch 230 SEK ($25.30); fixed-price dinner 300–400 SEK ($33–$44). AE, DC, MC, V. Mon–Sat 11:30am–2:30pm and 6–10:30pm. Closed July and lunch in early Aug. Bus: 1 or 6. SWEDISH/CONTINENTAL.

One of the best restaurants in town, Elinor is in a modest house built in the 1920s on a pleasant pedestrian walkway in the town center. There's a small bar for apéritifs and a well-upholstered dining room outfitted in soft shades of pastel. Future plans call for ownership to introduce a less expensive wine bar/annex to the already successful gourmet dining room. The menu changes frequently, always relying on seasonal ingredients. Though less influenced by nouvelle cuisine than in past years, the restaurant offers such well-prepared, tantalizing dishes as marinated herring with Swedish caviar and an onion and sour-cream sauce; fillet of reindeer with fresh morels; a ragoût of shrimp with chanterelles; and based on the seasons, unusual preparations of crayfish, lobster, turbot, salmon, trout, pheasant, duck, and partridge. Desserts often showcase the seasonal harvest of lingonberries, cloudberries, and blueberries.

۞ Oscar's Trapp. Terasstrapporna. ☎ **042/14-60-44.** Reservations recommended. Fixed-price menu 535 SEK ($58.85). AE, DC, MC, V. Mon–Sat 6–10pm. Closed July. Bus: 7A, 7B, 1, or 6. FRENCH/CONTINENTAL.

This is an appealingly upscale restaurant that's often confused with a busier, more bustling competitor (Restaurant Oscar), which is recommended separately, in the following review. Oscar's Trapp occupies the medieval, brick-built premises that sit directly at the base of Helsingborg's symbol and most visible tower, the Kärnan; it originally was designated as a jail. It's small and choice, with windows that overlook a view of the sea and no reminders of its once-punitive functions. It offers only a roster of impeccably prepared fixed-price menus, composed every day from market ingredients and traditional French recipes. Menu items might include carpaccio of tuna in a truffle-flavored vinaigrette, terrine of foie gras with sliced apples, and a delectable roasted rack of venison on a cake composed of parsley root and carrots, served with a lingonberry sauce.

✪ Restaurant Oscar. Sundstorget 7. ☎ **042/21-25-21.** Reservations recommended. Main courses 86–130 SEK ($9.45–$14.30); fixed-price lunch 79–210 SEK ($8.70–$23.10); fixed-price dinner 114–250 SEK ($12.55–$27.50). AE, DC, MC, V. Mon–Fri 11:30am–2pm; Mon–Sat 7:30–11pm. Bus: 7A, 7B, 1, or 6. SEAFOOD/GAME.

Overlooking a large parking lot near the ferryboat piers, in the center of town, this is the best-known and most frequently recommended seafood restaurant in town. Decorated like an upscale tavern, it contains a roster of nautical antiques and a sense of permanence that many diners find very appealing. Seafood is impeccably fresh, with a wide array of choices that range from the savory but unpretentious (fillets of cod fried in butter with capers, garlic, and boiled potatoes) to the rather grand (butterflied fillets of sole flambéed tableside with brandy and served with a ragoût of shrimp in lobster sauce). Other options include a worthwhile version of Marseillais bouillabaisse, which must be ordered a full day in advance, and a succulent version of Baltic-style fish stew, which usually is available any time. Also look for poached fillets of sole with a Chablis sauce and whitebait roe, and in autumn and winter, a roster of well-prepared venison dishes. Before or after your meal, check out the proudly displayed carcass of an 11-pound lobster—a zoological oddity that may remind you of a prop from a grade B horror flick—caught long ago in offshore waters.

HELSINGBORG AFTER DARK

Helsingborg has had its own city symphony orchestra since 1912. In 1932, its **Concert Hall** or Konserthuset opened at Drottninggatan 19 (☎ **042/17-65-00**). One of the finest examples of Swedish functionalism in the 1930s, today the hall is the venue for performances by the orchestra, made up of 50 musicians. The season opens in the middle of August with a 10-day Festspel, a festival with a different theme every year. Tickets are available at the **Helsingborg Stadsteater City Theatre,** Karl Johans Gata (☎ **042/10-68-10**), which dates from 1817. Today's city theater is one of the most modern in Europe; of course, performances are in Swedish.

In summer, when sunset is relatively late in the evening, there's a lot of emphasis placed on sitting in cafes and watching the city go by. An ideal site for this, open till long after the sun finally sets, is the **Ångfärjestationen,** Kungsgatan 1 (☎ **042/ 18-71-71**). Its venue includes an outdoor cafe and indoor pubs, restaurants, and a disco that rocks and rolls every Wednesday through Saturday regardless of the time of year and the length of the days. Something akin to a Biergarten you'd expect to find in Germany is **Dag & Natt,** Nordhamn (☎ **042/13-53-53**). Here a cocktail bar, a restaurant, a minicasino with small-stakes roulette tables, a disco, and a sweeping view over the straits between Sweden and Denmark keep things hopping. During summer, the area's space is expanded thanks to a colorful tent with temporary tables set up just for beer drinkers. Somewhat more attuned to hipsters, with a decor that includes crystal chandeliers and lots of original paintings (which often are rotated with works by other artists), is **Marina Nightclub,** Kungstorget 6 (☎ **042/19-21-00**). Set within the Hotel Marina Plaza, it admits only clients who can prove they're 24 or older. It's open Thursday through Saturday, from 10pm till around 3am.

An English-inspired pub that draws a busy and sometimes convivial crowd is **Telegrafen,** Norra Storgatan 14 (☎ **042/18-14-50**), where live music, especially jazz, is presented on either of two levels devoted to maintaining a cozy environment for drinking, dialoguing, and (sometimes) flirting. Jazz enthusiasts should consider an evening at one of the largest jazz venues in Sweden, **Jazzklubben,** Nedre Långvinkels-gatan 22 (☎ **042/18-49-00**). Keynote nights include Wednesday, Friday, and Saturday, when live Dixieland, blues, Celtic ballads, and progressive jazz are featured beginning around 8:30pm. Most other nights, based on a schedule that varies with the season and the whims of the staff, the place functions as a conventional bar.

2 Malmö

177 miles S of Gothenburg, 384 miles SW of Stockholm

Sweden's third-largest city, a busy port across the Øresund sound—now linked by bridge from Copenhagen—is the capital of Skåne and a good base for exploring the ancient castles and nearby manor. It's an old city, dating from the 13th century.

From early days, Malmö (pronounced mahl-*mer*) prospered because of its location on a sheltered bay. In the 16th century, when it was the second-largest city in Denmark, it vied with Copenhagen for economic and cultural leadership. Reminders of that age are **Malmöhus Castle** (see below), the **Town Hall,** and the **Stortorget,** plus several homes of rich burghers. Malmö has been a Swedish city since the end of a bloody war in 1658, when the Treaty of Roskilde incorporated the province of Skåne into Sweden.

ESSENTIALS

GETTING THERE By Plane Malmö's airport (☎ **040/613-11-00**) is at Sturup, 19 miles southeast of the city. It receives international flights from London, plus flights from cities within Sweden, including Gothenburg (50 minutes) and Stockholm (1 hour). Two airlines that serve the airport are **Malmö Aviation** (☎ **040/660-29-00**) and **SAS** (☎ **040/635-7200**). The airport's major international link to the world is Copenhagen Airport at Copenhagen, to which Malmö is connected by Hovercraft service.

By Train The Stockholm-Copenhagen express train has a branch service through to Malmö (☎ **040/202-000**). Service is frequent between Gothenburg and Malmö (3½ hours trip time). From Helsingborg to Malmö (45-minute trip time), trains leave hourly. From Stockholm, travel is 4½ hours aboard the high-speed X 2000 train; 6 to 7 hours aboard slower trains. There also is train service between Copenhagen and Malmö. Trains depart from the central railway stations of both cities at 20-minute intervals. The cost each way is 70 SEK ($7.70).

By Bus Two buses daily make the 4½-hour run from Gothenburg to Malmö. For bus information, call **Swebus** (☎ **0200/21818**).

By Hydrofoil Malmö and Copenhagen are linked by *Flygbåtana* (hydrofoil), with hourly service year-round from 5am to midnight, taking 45 minutes. Call ☎ **040/10-39-30** for information. The one-way cost is 80 SEK ($8.80). Should the Øresund freeze over, service is suspended.

By Car From Helsingborg, motorists can head southeast along the motorway 110, directly into the center of Malmö.

VISITOR INFORMATION The **Malmö Tourist Office,** Central Station Skeppsbron 2 (☎ **040/30-01-50;** www.malmo.se), is open Monday through Friday from 9am to 5pm and Saturday 10am to 2pm.

GETTING AROUND It's easy to walk around the city center, although you may need to rely on public transport if you're branching out to sights on the periphery. An

Malmö

ATTRACTIONS ●

Kommendanthuset
(Military Museum) **4**
Malmöhus Castle **6**
Malmö Museer **5**
Rooseum **15**
St. Petri
(St. Peter's Church) **10**
Teknik-Och Sjöfartsmuseet
(Museum of Technology
and Shipping) **3**
Vagnmusset
(Carriage Museum) **5**

ACCOMMODATIONS ■

Hotell Baltzar **13**
Hotell Royal **7**
Hotel Noble House **16**
Radisson SAS Hotel **12**
Residens Hotel **9**
Rica City Hotel **14**
Savoy Hotel **11**
Scandic Hotel Kramer **8**
Scandic Hotel Triangeln **1**
Theaterhotellet **2**

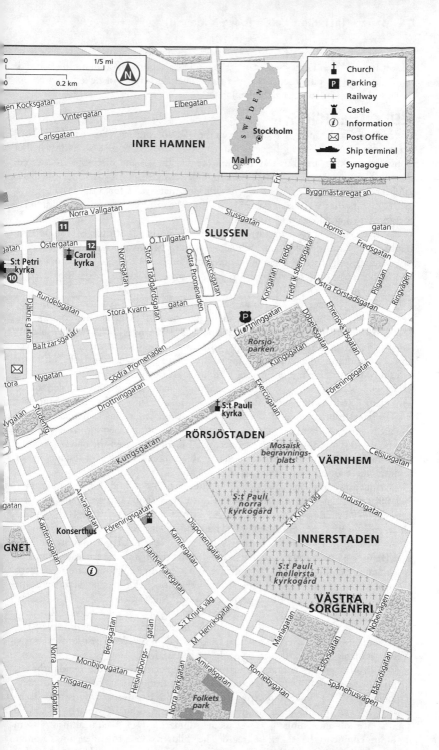

individual bus ticket costs 12 SEK ($1.30) and is valid for 1 hour. You also can purchase a 100 SEK ($11) magnetic card, which offers a slight reduction on the fare and can be used by several passengers at the same time. Both types of tickets are sold on the bus. (You must have exact change.)

SEEING THE SIGHTS

The **Malmö Card,** which is available from the Malmö Tourist Office, entitles visitors to free admission to most of the city's museums during the period of its validity. It also grants free parking, free bus travel within the city limits, and discounts in selected shops and restaurants. A card that's valid for 1 day costs 125 SEK ($13.75); one that's valid for 2 days goes for 150 SEK ($16.50); one that's valid for 3 days is 175 SEK ($19.25). An adult who has a Malmö card can be accompanied, with no additional charge, by two children up to 16 years old.

The Renaissance-era square surrounding the **fountain** on Stortorget is important architecturally, but the fountain itself is one of the most imaginative in Scandinavia, and includes a nightingale, the symbol of Malmö. Built in 1964, it commemorates the most important events in the city's history; for example, when the Swedes took the city back from the Danes in 1710.

Dominating Stortorget is the town hall or **Rådhuset,** which still retains its look of Renaissance splendor. It dates from 1546, but was restored by Helgo Zetterwall in the 1860s. It borders the east side of the square. It is especially impressive when illuminated at night. In the center of the square stands an equestrian statue of Carl X Gustav commemorating the return of Skåne to Sweden from Denmark in 1658. There are occasional tours of the interior; check with the tourist office (see above).

Nearby lies **Lilla Torg,** Malmö's most charming square, an attractive cobbled square with many fine half-timbered buildings dating from the 16th to the 18th centuries—it looks like a film set. In addition to its fountains and cafes, many handcraft shops also are found here. For many centuries this was the bustling open-air marketplace of Malmö, however, in the 20th century, a covered market replaced the open-air booths and stalls. Today, a modern market building also houses a number of restaurants. In summer, there are a lot of jewelry stalls.

Four major attractions are under the direction of Malmö Museer (☎ 040/ 341-000). Heading the list is **Malmöhus Castle,** on Malmöhusvägen, founded in the 15th century by Eric of Pomerania and rebuilt by Christian III in the 16th century. Once a prison (the earl of Bothwell, third husband of Mary Queen of Scots, was incarcerated here from 1568 to 1573), the castle now houses the **City Museum,** the **Natural History Museum,** the **Aquarium** and **Tropicarium,** and the **Art Museum.** The last contains a collection of old Scandinavian masters, especially those from southern Sweden, such as Carl Fredrik Hill (1849–1911), one of Sweden's best landscape painters and a forerunner of European modernism. Most interesting is the collection of Russian oil paintings from around 1900—the largest collection outside Russia. It also houses some modern art and good samples of Swedish furniture and textiles. The lyrical sketches in the foyer are by Carl Larsson, one of Sweden's best-known artists. West of Stortorget, the castle can be easily reached on foot.

Also in the group, across the street from the castle is **Kommendanthuset,** Malmöhusvägen, a military museum and a piece of history in its own right, displaying military artifacts and equipment. **Teknik-Och Sjöfartsmuseet** (Museum of Technology), on Malmöhusvägen, is near the Kommendanthuset. Ancient means of communication are exhibited, as well as the submarine *U-3.* Technical history from the steam engine to the jet can be traced. The children's department even has a pirate ship, and in summer an old-fashioned tramway is in operation. The **Vagnmusset**

(Carriage Museum), housed in the former military horse stable at Drottningtorget, displays carriages from the 18th century, coaches, and cycles.

We recommend buying a ticket costing 40 SEK ($4.40) for adults, 10 SEK ($1.10) for children 16 and under, which admits you to all sites mentioned above if visit on the same day. The museums are open daily from noon to 4pm.

Malmö's **S:t Petri** (St. Peter's Church), on Göran Olsgatan (☎ **040/35-90-40**), lies a block east of the Rådhus. Dark and a bit foreboding on the exterior, it is light and airy within. This Gothic church originated in the 14th century, when Malmö was under the control of the Hanseatic League, and was modeled on Marienkirche, a famous church in Lübeck, Germany. Other than the slender pillars and supporting ogive vaulting, the church's most stunning feature is its **Krämarkapellet**, or tradesmen's chapel, from the 1400s. Amazingly, the original artwork remains. At the Reformation, the artwork here was viewed as "redundant," and the chapel was sealed off, which in effect protected its paintings from the overzealous "restoration" of the reformers. Look for the impressive New Testament figures surrounded by decorative foliage on the vaulted ceiling. Also notice the tall retable from 1611 and an exquisitely carved black limestone and sandstone pulpit from 1599. The octagonal baptismal font from 1601, as well as the pulpit, were the work of master craftsman Daniel Tommisen. The church is open Monday through Friday 8am to 6pm, Saturday 9am to 6pm, and Sunday 10am to 6pm. Admission is free.

A final attraction, ✪ **Rooseum,** Gasverksgatan 22 (☎ **040/121-716**), is one of the country's most outstanding art museums, installed in what had been an electricity generating station at the turn of the century. In 1988, it was converted into this elegant museum, the brainchild of Fredrik Ross (1951–91), an art collector whose stated desire was to showcase modern art movements through a series of thematic exhibitions and shows. Although strongest on Nordic art, the exhibitions are international in scope. Hours are Tuesday through Sunday 11am to 5pm, and cost 40 SEK ($4.40).

A NEARBY MUSEUM

Svaneholm, between Malmö and Ystad, was founded in 1530 as a fortress, and later was partially converted into an Italian-style palace. Today, it houses a museum of paintings, furnishings, and tools dating primarily from the 18th and 19th centuries. The establishment is owned by the Svaneholm Castle Cooperative Society Ltd. For information, write Svaneholm Museum, S-274 00 Skurup (☎ **0411/400-12**).

Admission to the castle is 30 SEK ($3.30) for adults and 10 SEK ($1.10) for children. It's open April to June and September through December, Wednesday through Sunday from 11am to 4pm. The castle is closed completely in July and August. There is a restaurant on site (☎ **0411/450-40**) serving regional specialties. Reaching Svaneholm is difficult by public transportation; a train from Malmö stops at Skurup, but it's a walk of about 2 miles from there. Therefore, many visitors opt to go by taxi the rest of the way.

SHOPPING

Malmö's main pedestrian shopping street is **Södergatan,** which leads south of Stortorget toward the canal. Alternatively, if you haven't found what you are looking for in the specialty shops below, try **Hansa Companiet,** Stora Nygatan 50 (☎ **040/77-000**), Malmö's continental mart, a shopping complex with more than 40 shops, cafes, and restaurants. The latest fashions and items for the home are among the many specialties featured here. However, most foreign visitors come by to check out its selection of Swedish souvenirs and handcrafts.

CRYSTAL & GLASSWARE

Juvelerare Hugo Nilsson. Södra Tullgatan 2. ☎ **040/12-65-92.**

This shop, established in 1927, features some of the most famous names in Danish jewelry making, including Georg Jensen, Rauff, and Ole Lynggaard. Jewelry by Finnish designers such as Lapponia also is sold.

Silverbergs i Malmö. Baltzarsgatan 31. ☎ **040/740-80.**

This famous store reliably ships its stunning collection of glassware, crystal, furniture, and gifts all over the world.

FASHION

Mattssons Päls. Norra Vallgatan 98. ☎ **040/12-55-33.**

This is one of Sweden's leading furriers. Saga mink coats and jackets are the most luxurious buys, but Mattssons has a full range of fine furs at prices lower than in the United States. In the boutique are fur-lined poplins and accessories, all tax free for tourists. The store lies a 5-minute walk from the Central Station and the Copenhagen boats.

Röda Tråden. Adelgatan 5. ☎ **040/23-70-46.**

Here you'll find clothes designed by the well-known designer Maria Haid, plus handcrafts and souvenirs, along with unique ceramics, studio-designed glass, bronze and silver jewelry, and decorative tiles. On the top floor is an art gallery.

HANDCRAFTS

Ålgamark. Davidshallstorg 7. ☎ **040/97-49-60.**

An unusual collection of Nordic arts and crafts is sold at Ålgamark, where you'll find Viking jewelry (replicas in pewter, bronze, silver, and gold), along with handcrafts from Swedish Lapland. Traditional pendants, bracelets, and knives are also sold.

Form Design Centre. Lilla Torg. ☎ **040/10-36-10.**

Nearby, at 16th-century Lilla Torg, you can visit this museum-like exhibition space with boutiques selling upscale handcrafts, including Swedish textiles by the yard, woodcarvings, and all manner of other crafts.

WHERE TO STAY
EXPENSIVE

✪ **Hotel Noble House.** Gustav Adolfs Torg 47, S-211 39 Malmö. ☎ **040/664-30-00.** Fax 040/664-30-50. www.hkchotels.se. E-mail: noblehouse@hkchotels.se. 130 units. MINIBAR TV TEL. June 24–Aug 15 and Fri–Sat year-round, 995 SEK ($109.45) double; rest of year, 1,495 SEK ($164.45) double. Year-round, 1,850 SEK ($203.50) suite. Rates include breakfast. AE, DC, MC, V. Parking 95 SEK ($10.45). Closed Dec 22–26. Bus: 10, 11, 17, or 20.

Named after the best-selling novel by James Clavell (the former owner was a great fan), this is one of the most modern and up-to-date hotels in town, and certainly the most glamorous. The comfortable, pastel-colored rooms are decorated with copies of early 20th-century Swedish paintings. Because of the four-story hotel's convenient location in the town center, its quietest rooms face the interior courtyard.

Dining/Diversions: The hotel has a restaurant/bar that offers international and Swedish cuisine.

Amenities: An excellent concierge, room service, conference center, laundry service, and a solarium.

Radisson SAS Hotel. Östergatan 10, S-211 25 Malmö. ☎ **040/698-40-00.**
Fax 040/698-40-01. www.radissonsas.com. E-mail: guest@radissonsas.com. 224 units.
MINIBAR TV TEL. June 5–Aug 5, Mon–Thurs 1,090 SEK ($119.90) double; Aug 6–June 4,
Mon–Thurs 1,780 SEK ($195.80) double; Fri–Sun year-round, 980 SEK ($107.80) double.
Year-round, from 2,700 SEK ($297) suite. Rates include breakfast. AE, DC, MC, V. Parking 150
SEK ($16.50). Bus: 14 or 17.

Conscious of its role as one of the newest major hotels in Malmö, this hotel contains
tastefully decorated bedrooms, each with an elegant bathroom and such amenities as
video, hair dryer, trouser press, and radio. Built in 1988, the hotel rises seven floors
high and was designed to accommodate persons with disabilities. Although it's affiliated with Scandinavia's most visible airline, SAS, some visitors consider this hotel
bland, anonymous, and somewhat sterile.

    Dining/Diversions: A restaurant, **Thott's,** serves Scandinavian and continental
cuisine in a half-timbered house from the mid-16th century. There's also a bar.

    Amenities: Baby-sitting, express laundry, heated parking garage, sauna, business
center, room service.

Scandic Hotel Triangeln. Triangeln 2, S-200 10 Malmö. ☎ **040/693-47-00.**
Fax 040/693-47-11. www.scandic-hotels.com. 214 units. A/C MINIBAR TV TEL. June 24–Aug
7 and Fri–Sat year-round, 910 SEK ($100.10) double; rest of year, 1,704 SEK ($187.45)
double. Year-round, 2,300–4,100 SEK ($253–$451) suite. Rates include breakfast. AE, DC,
MC, V. Parking 90 SEK ($9.90). Bus: 14 or 17.

Malmö's most visible international luxury hotel rises 20 stories from a position in the
commercial heart of town. Built in 1989, it boasts sweeping views from virtually all
its bedrooms. The top three floors contain only suites and a well-designed health club.
Many of the clients here are business travelers who often are attending one of the
dozens of conventions that attract participants from throughout Europe. The bedrooms are tastefully and comfortably appointed with light colors, many electronic
amenities, and firm mattresses. The bathrooms are more than adequate.

    Dining/Diversions: One floor above lobby level is a restaurant, Upstairs, which
serves well-prepared but uncomplicated lunches. In the evening, it's upgraded to a
stylish international restaurant, called Figaro, where the prices are more expensive and
the ambience more formal and unhurried. The hotel also maintains a lobby bar/bistro.

    Amenities: Laundry and dry cleaning service, a fitness center with a sauna and
solarium, concierge, limited room service.

MODERATE

Hotell Baltzar. Södergatan 20, S-211 24 Malmö. ☎ **040/665-5700.** Fax 040/665-5710.
www.baltzar.hotel.se. 41 units. MINIBAR TV TEL. Mon–Thurs 1,080–1,600 SEK
($118.80–$176) double; Fri–Sun 830–1,350 SEK ($91.30–$148.50) double. Rates include
breakfast. AE, DC, MC, V. Parking 110 SEK ($12.10) per night. Bus: 10.

Around 1900, an entrepreneur who had made a fortune selling chocolate moved into
a private home whose turrets, towers, and fanciful ornamentation resembled a stone-
carved confection. Several decades later, when the home was transformed into an elegant and prestigious hotel, it was expanded into one of the (less ornate) neighboring
buildings, and its rooms were upgraded to comfortable and stylish-looking international standards. Today, you'll find a hotel with many charming corners and cubby-
holes. Grace notes include frescoed ceilings, substantial-looking antiques, and
elaborate draperies in some of the public areas. Furnishings and parquet floors in the
high-ceilinged bedrooms suggest a prosperous private home. Furnishings, including
good beds, are of a high standard. A location above an all-pedestrian street keeps
things relatively quiet inside. Breakfast is the only meal served, although room service
(sandwiches, salads, and drinks only) is available 24 hours a day.

Rica City Hotel. Stortorget 15 S-211 22 Malmö. ☎ **040/660-95-50.** Fax 040/660-95-59. www.malmocityhotels.se. 80 units. TV TEL. Mon–Thurs 1,370–1,410 SEK ($150.70–$155.10) double; Fri–Sun 800–900 SEK ($88–$99) double. Rates include breakfast. AE, DC, MC, V. Parking 60 SEK ($6.60). Bus: 14 or 17.

Built in 1912, this hotel lies on Malmö's main square, facing the town hall, a short walk from the railway station and the ferryboat terminals for Copenhagen-bound ships. In 1992, the guest rooms were rebuilt in a tasteful, modern format. The hotel is owned by the Salvation Army, which strictly forbids the consumption of alcohol on the premises. It's also part of a hotel chain (City Hotels) that operates four other Swedish hotels. The rooms are larger than you might expect, with good mattresses. Bathrooms tend to be cramped, but are well maintained. There's a sauna and solarium in the hotel's cellar. There's no restaurant (and certainly no bar) on the premises, but about a dozen restaurants are within walking distance.

Savoy Hotel. Norra Vallgatan 62, S-201 80 Malmö. ☎ **040/702-30.** Fax 040/97-85-51. www.elite.se. 109 units. MINIBAR TV TEL. June 19– Aug 9 and Fri–Sat year-round, 895 SEK ($98.45) double; rest of year, 1,350 SEK ($148.50) double. Year-round, 2,490 SEK ($273.90) suite. Rates include breakfast. AE, DC, MC, V. Parking 125 SEK ($13.75). Bus: 14 or 17.

This hotel has figured prominently in Malmö history; famous guests have included Dag Hammarskjöld, Liv Ullmann, Alan Alda, and Johnny ("Tarzan") Weissmuller. It boasts some of the most plushly decorated accommodations in Sweden. Rooms contain champagne-colored upholstery, cabriole-legged or Chippendale-style furniture, excellent beds, and all the extras of a deluxe hotel. Well-maintained bathrooms come in a wide variety of sizes, with hair dryers. In the hotel restaurant, you can order from an international menu, perhaps stopping for a before-dinner beer in the a British-style pub, the Bishop's Arms.

Scandic Hotel Kramer. Stortorget 7, S-201 21 Malmö. ☎ **040/20-88-00.** Fax 040/ 12-69-41. www.provobis.se/hotelkramer. 110 units. TV TEL. 900–1,695 SEK ($99–$186.45) double. Rates include breakfast. AE, DC, MC, V. Parking 150 SEK ($16.50). Bus: 14, 17, or 20.

At the side of the town's main square, this château-like twin-towered building is one of Malmö's landmark hotels. Built in 1875, it was renovated at the height of the art deco era. Between 1992 and 1994, the rooms were redecorated again with an old-fashioned sense of nostalgia, vaguely reminiscent of staterooms on a pre–Second World War ocean liner. Each has a firm mattress, a marble bathroom with dark paneling, curved walls, and kitschy, 1930s-style accessories. On the premises is Kramer's British Pub, an Anglophilic watering hole that serves whiskies, beers, and platters of food every day from 4pm to 1am.

Teaterhotellet. Rönngatan 3, S-211 47 Malmö. ☎ **040/665-58-00.** Fax 040/665-58-10. www.teaterhotellet.se. 45 units. TV TEL. Mon–Thurs 1,200 SEK ($132) double; Fri–Sun 750 SEK ($82.50) double. Rates include breakfast. AE, DC, MC, V. Free parking. Bus: 11.

The only negative aspect to this hotel derives from its banal-looking 1960s-era facade—no uglier than hundreds of other contemporaneous buildings throughout Scandinavia; neither is it particularly inviting or pleasing. Inside, however, you'll find a cozy, tasteful, and colorful venue that attracts many repeat clients. Appealing touches include tawny-colored marble floors, lots of elegant hardwood paneling, lacquered walls in tones of amber and beige, and in the bedrooms, spots of vibrant colors (especially jewel tones of red and green) that perk up even the grayest of Swedish winter days. Bedrooms were renovated in 1996 and have new furniture and mattresses, plus new bathrooms. The hotel's location, about a half mile south of the railway station, is near a verdant park and the Stadtstheater. Other than breakfast, no meals are served, but you usually can get someone to bring you a sandwich and coffee.

INEXPENSIVE

Hotell Royal. Norra Vallgatan 94, S-211 22 Malmö. ☎ **040/664-2500.** Fax 040/12-77-12. www.hotellroyal.com. E-mail: inforoyal@swedenhotels.se. 30 units. TV TEL. July and Fri–Sat year-round, 795–895 SEK ($87.45–$98.45) double; rest of year, 995–1,195 SEK ($109.45–$131.45) double. AE, DC, MC, V. Free parking on street 6pm–9am; otherwise, 12 SEK ($1.30) per hour 9am–6pm. Bus: 14 or 17.

This hotel, which occupies a desirable location adjacent to a canal, in the historic core of Malmö, is composed of three antique buildings surrounding an inner courtyard that's outfitted in summer with potted flowers and plastic tables and chairs. The most visible of the three buildings is a stately-looking, early 20th-century neoclassical townhouse; the oldest—which was closed for restoration at this writing—dates from the 1500s. Bedrooms inside are cozy, frilly, decorated in shades of white, turquoise, and peach, and comfortable. Bedrooms are rather small but inviting nonetheless, with good beds; most of the units have minibars. The bathrooms are a bit cramped. Your hosts are the Kilström brothers; they maintain a small conference center and work hard to keep their hotel shipshape. Breakfast is the only meal served.

Residens Hotel. Adelgatan 7, S-211 22 Malmö. ☎ **040/611-25-30.** Fax 040/30-09-60. www.elite.se/residens. 70 units. TV TEL. June to mid-Aug and Fri–Sat year-round, 750 SEK ($82.50) double; rest of year, 1,200 SEK ($132) double. Rates include breakfast. AE, DC, MC, V. Free parking. Bus: 14 or 17.

In 1987, a team of local investors enlarged the white-sided premises of a historic 1517 inn with the addition of a new brick-and-stone structure. The interconnected structures provide solid, comfortable, and upscale lodgings near the railroad station. Business travelers appreciate its many convention facilities. Except for specialized corners where an effort was made to duplicate a woodsy-looking men's club in London, many of the public areas are outfitted in a glossy, modern setup with lots of mirrors, touches of chrome, and polished marble floors. Guest rooms are more traditional-looking than the glossy public spaces, and larger than you may expect. They have hardwood floors or wall-to-wall carpeting, good beds, well-upholstered furnishings, and in some cases, Oriental carpets. The medium-size bathrooms are equipped with hair dryers and trouser presses. Windows are large and double-insulated against noise from the urban landscape outside. There's a bar on the premises, and a stylishly decorated lobby restaurant, but it's only open for lunch.

WHERE TO DINE
EXPENSIVE

✪ **Årstiderna I Kockska Huset.** Frans Suellsgatan 3. ☎ **040/23-09-10.** Reservations recommended. Main courses 150–265 SEK ($16.50–$29.15); fixed-price lunch 140–260 SEK ($15.40–$28.60); fixed-price dinner 295–450 SEK ($32.45–$49.50). AE, DC, MC, V. Mon–Fri 11:30am–midnight, Sat 5pm–1am. Bus: 14 or 17.

One of the most prestigious restaurants in Malmö lies on a shadowed medieval street within what was built in the 1480s as the home and political headquarters of the Danish-appointed governor of Malmö, Jürgen Kock. In its own richly Gothic way, it's the most unusual restaurant setting in town, with vaulted brick ceilings, severe-looking medieval detailing, and a conscious and deliberate lack of other kinds of adornment. Your hosts are Marie and Wilhelm Pieplow, who have created an environment where the prime ministers of both Sweden and Finland, as well as dozens of politicians, artists, and actors, have dined exceedingly well. Menu items change with the seasons; the establishment's name, årstiderna, translates from the Swedish as "The Four Seasons." Likely to be featured are butter-fried monkfish with parsley butter, salmon roe, and Norwegian lobster; orange-glazed wild duck with flap mushrooms and honey-rosemary sauce; fillet of venison in an herb crust with chanterelle mushrooms and juniper berry sauce; Swedish beefsteak with red wine and potato gratin; and a chocolate terrine with cloudberry sorbet and a compote of blackberries.

✪ Johan P. Saluhallen, Landbygatan. ☎ **040/97-18-18.** Reservations recommended. Main courses 170–225 SEK ($18.70–$24.75); 2-course fixed-price menu 210 SEK ($23.10); 3-course fixed-price menu 245 SEK ($26.95); 4-course fixed-price menu 495 SEK ($54.45); 5-course fixed-price menu 525 SEK ($57.75). Mon–Thurs 11:30am–10:30pm, Fri 7–11pm, S at 11:30am–5pm. Bus: 14 or 17. FISH/SEAFOOD.

Some of the most appealing seafood in Malmö is prepared and served within this artfully simple, mostly white dining room. The result is an almost pristine setting where the freshness of the seafood is the main draw. Menu items are prepared fresh every day, based on whatever is available at the nearby *Saluhallen* (marketplace). Examples include an award-winning version of fish soup that's inspired by the traditions of Provence; a leek and potato vichyssoise served with fresh mussels and a timbale of pike; baked monkfish with mustard-flavored spaetzle served with dried ham and braised cabbage in a tomato-flavored broth; and an old-fashioned version of chicken dumplings with mushroom risotto and sweet-and-sour tomato sauce. Dessert might include a mousse made with bitter white chocolate, served with dark chocolate madeleines and coffee sauce.

✪ Restaurant Kramer Gastronomie. In the Scandic Hotel Kramer, Stortorget 7. ☎ **040/20-88-06.** Reservations recommended. Main courses 155–240 SEK ($17.05–$26.40); 3-course fixed-price menu 285 SEK ($31.35); 7-course fixed-price menu 595 SEK ($65.45). AE, DC, MC, V. Mon–Fri 5–11pm, Sat 6–11pm. Bar stays open till 1am. Bus: 10. CONTINENTAL.

Accessed through the lobby of the also-recommended hotel, this restaurant serves the best food of any hotel dining room in Malmö. There's an upscale, woodsy-looking bar that's separated from the brown and off-white dining room with a leaded glass divider, and an attention to cuisine that brings a conservative, not particularly flashy clientele back again and again. The composition of the fixed-price menu changes every week, and it's relatively common for a group of business partners to spend three hours at table sampling the seven-course *menu dégustation*. The food is faultlessly fresh and handled beautifully by the kitchen staff, who believe in delicate seasonings and perfectly cooked dishes. The chef is dedicated to his job, personally shopping for market-fresh ingredients to inspire his imagination. Specific menu items include shots of shellfish bouillon served with parmesan chips and coriander salsa; scallops with grilled tuna and bacon; blackened filet of beef with pecorino cheese, lemon wedges, arugula, and a sauce made with a reduction of *court bouillon* and red wine; and chargrilled halibut with glazed turnips, truffle butter, and dill oil. Pastas here are upscale and esoteric, including a version with spinach, crayfish, fried filet of sole, and dill sauce.

MODERATE

Centiliter & Gram. Stortorget 17. ☎ **40/12-18-12.** Reservations recommended. Main courses 135–205 SEK ($14.85–$22.55). AE, DC, MC, V. Mon–Sat 11:30am–2pm; Mon–Wed 4:30pm–midnight, Thurs 4:30pm–1am, Fri–Sat 4:30pm–3am. Bus: 10. CONTINENTAL.

This is one of Malmö's hottest restaurants, with a hip clientele that includes lots of well-renowned painters and football (soccer) stars, as well as hordes of media and P.R. people. It occupies an artfully minimalist gray- and mauve-colored space whose focal point is a central, rectangular-shaped bar. Here, flirtations continue until late into the night, long after virtually everybody else has lost his or her interest in food. Menu items change with the seasons and whatever food fad happens to be in vogue in London, Stockholm, or Paris at the time. Stellar examples include a parcel of Italian goat cheese baked in phyllo pastry with a tomato and basil sauce; black mussels with white wine and cream sauce served with a tomato *bruschetta;* deliberately undercooked (i.e., "pink") duck breast with teriyaki sauce and an orange- and mango-flavored chutney; and grilled halibut and scallops with spicy Thai red curry, coconut milk, and jasmine-flavored rice. The establishment's name, incidentally, derives from wine (which is measured in centiliters) and food (which is measured in grams).

Kockska Krogen. Franss Suellsgatan 3. ☎ **040/703-20.** Reservations recommended. Main courses 170–260 SEK ($18.70–$28.60); fixed-price menus 295–425 SEK ($32.45–$46.75). AE, DC, MC, V. Mon–Fri 11:30am–midnight, Sat 5–11:30pm. Bus: 14 or 17. SWEDISH/FRENCH.

Kockska Krogen is named after a 16th-century Danish mayor who lived in the thick brick vaults of this building in the Old Town. During the Renaissance it was used as the city mint; to reach it, pass beneath an ornate fortified entrance. Stop for a beer in the pub near the entrance or proceed into the labyrinth of plaster-covered vaults that make up the many dining rooms. Each of the well-prepared specialties is named after a legendary person important in Malmö's history. You can order Dover sole with lobster and chestnuts, flambéed beef fillet, or honey-fried breast of duck, then follow your meal with one of 10 succulent desserts, such as rum-raisin ice cream in flambéed crepes.

Lemongrass. Grunbodgatan 9. ☎ **40/30-69-79.** Reservations recommended. Main courses 106–196 SEK ($11.65–$21.55); 7-course fixed-price menu 355 SEK ($39.05). AE, MC, V, Mon–Thurs 6pm–midnight, Fri–Sat 6pm–1am. Bus: 6 or 10. ASIAN.

This venue involves only one large, Spartan-looking room that's devoid of the artsy clutter of many Asian restaurants. Instead, on pale gray walls, you'll find clusters of exotic-looking orchids, as well as tufted bunches of the lemongrass for which the place was named. There's a bar where you can wait for your table, and a menu that contains food items from Japan (including sushi), China, and Thailand. A staff member will help you coordinate a meal from disparate culinary styles in ways that you might have expected only in Los Angeles, London, or New York.

Min Brors Krog (My Brother's Restaurant). S:t Pauli Kyrkogata 11. ☎ **040/305-303.** Reservations recommended. Main courses 95–165 SEK ($10.45–$18.15); 3-course fixed-price menu 198–225 SEK ($21.80–$24.75). Sun–Wed 6–10pm, Thurs–Sat 6–11pm. Closed Jan. AE, DC, MC, V. Bus: 11. CONTINENTAL.

This restaurant got its name from the owner's sister, who always recommended it to her friends as "my brother's restaurant." The name stuck and eventually became the establishment's legal moniker. It's more self-consciously "new age" than the other restaurants within this section, a fact that may or may not appeal to you, depending on your tastes. What you'll get is a compact-looking dining room outfitted in monochromes of gray and white, brightly patterned tablecloths, and a separate room that's devoted to a bar where cigar smokers are welcome. The food is consistently good and very fresh, and the dishes here have many local fans. Dishes are perfectly executed and well flavored. Menu items change with the whims of the chef, but might include duck consommé, oven-fried duck breast served with red wine and herb sauce; reindeer with juniper berry and herb sauce; and chocolate mousse served with raspberry sorbet.

Rådhuskällern. Kyrkogatan 5. ☎ **040/790-20.** Reservations recommended. 1-course fixed-price lunch 75 SEK ($8.25); main courses 160–210 SEK ($17.60–$23.10). AE, DC, MC, V. Mon–Fri 11:30am–2pm and 6–11pm, Sat 5–11pm. Bus: 14 or 17.

Even if your schedule doesn't allow you to dine here, you should at least drop in for a drink at the most atmospheric place in Malmö, the cellar of the town hall. Its severe exterior and labyrinth of underground vaults were built in 1546. Have a drink in the rustic pub or in the more formal crescent-shaped cocktail lounge before heading into the dark-vaulted dining room that, for centuries, stored gold, wine, furniture, and food. Full à la carte meals include a changing array of daily specials and such staples as halibut with lobster sauce, plank steak, fillet of veal, pepper steak, and roast duck. Although the cooking is first rate here, nothing on the menu overexcites the palate.

Wallman's Salonger. Generalsgatan 1. ☎ **040/749-45.** Reservations recommended. Main courses 200–250 SEK ($22–$27.50); 3-course fixed-price menu 399 SEK ($43.90). AE, DC, MC, V. Wed–Sat 7pm–2am. Closed May to mid-Aug. CONTINENTAL.

Large enough for 400 diners at a time and painted a heady shade of Bordeaux, this is the most entertaining restaurant in Malmö. One end of it contains a stage where the waitstaff—each a candidate for a job in the theater—will sing, dance, amuse, entertain, and generally be wonderful. Your meal will consist of a flavorful, but not particularly spectacular, assortment of steaks, soups, salads, seafood, veal, or pork dishes, but because most clients are gyrating on the dance floor before 11pm anyway, no one dwells on the nuances of the cuisine. You might hear a clone of a Broadway (NY) melody from one of the easy-to-look-at singers, but more likely possibilities include medleys of music from ABBA or Bon Jovi, as transmuted to a Nordic dance hall/supper club format where everybody has a good time.

INEXPENSIVE

Anno 1900. Norra Bultoftavagen 7. ☎ **040/18-47-47.** Reservations recommended. Fixed-price lunch 100 SEK ($11); main courses 120–190 SEK ($13.20–$20.90). AE, DC, MC, V. Mon–Fri 11:15am–2pm; Tues–Fri 6–11pm. Bus: 14 or 17. SWEDISH.

The name of this place gives a hint of what the decor inside will look like: lots of antique woodwork, lots of nostalgia, and accessories from the heyday of the Industrial Revolution. There's a garden in back that's open during warm weather if you want to escape the turn-of-the-century fussiness. Menu items derive from tried-and-true recipes that were developed and perfected at around the same era as the decor, with heavy emphasis on old-fashioned versions of cauliflower soup, halibut with horseradish sauce, chicken dumplings with noodles, roasted beef, steaks, *frikadeller* (meatballs), and fried herring. If you had a Swedish grandmother, this is the joint you would take her to.

Casa Mia. Södergatan 12. ☎ **040/23-05-00.** Reservations recommended. Pastas and pizzas 90–198 SEK ($9.90–$21.80); 1-course dagens (daily) menu 89–110 SEK ($9.80–$12.10). AE, DC, MC, V. Mon–Sat noon–11:30pm, Sun noon–10pm. Bus: 14 or 17. ITALIAN.

Suggestions of the gondola moorings of Venice ornament the front terrace of this Nordic version of a neighborhood trattoria. Troubadours stroll from table to crowded table singing Neapolitan ballads, and your waiter is likely to address you in Italian. You begin with a steaming bowl of *stracciatella alla romana* (egg and chicken soup), or the fish soup of the house, which could be followed by penne with shrimp, basil, cream, and tomatoes, or spaghetti with seafood. Later you might dig into saltimbocca alla romana (veal with ham), a portion of grilled scampi, escalope of veal stuffed with goose liver, or an array of grilled meats with aromatic herbs. There are more than 15 types of pizza on the menu, and pastries are offered for dessert. Okay, it's not as good as the food served in a typical trattoria in northern Italy, but at this Nordic outpost, the cuisine is a refreshing change of pace.

Restaurant B & B (Butik och Bar). Saluhallen, Landbygatan 52. ☎ **040/12-71-20.** Reservations recommended. Fixed-price lunch 65 SEK ($7.15); main courses 98–160 SEK ($10.80–$17.60). AE, DC, MC, V. Mon–Sat noon–10:30pm. Bus: 14 or 17. SWEDISH/INTERNATIONAL.

This well-managed and relatively inexpensive bistro is set within a corner of the Saluhallen (food market), which provides the very fresh ingredients that go into each of its menu items. The setting is artfully simple, with glowing hardwood floors, pristine-looking white walls, and a scattering of antiques that evoke the Sweden of long ago. Menu items are earthy, flavorful, unpretentious, and international, with occasional emphasis on Swedish staples such as creamy fish soup. Most of the others, however, are more exotic, including New Orleans versions of jambalaya, Cajun-inspired tagliatelle with blackened chicken and fiery sauces, teriyaki pork, roasted chicken with tiger prawns, and pasta with a salmon-flavored vodka sauce.

MALMÖ AFTER DARK

For serious after-dark pursuits, many locals, especially young people, head for nearby Copenhagen. However, there are several local amusements, as well; the best of which are previewed below.

From May to September, locals head for **Folkets Park** (People's Park), Amiralsgatan 35 (☎ 040/709-90), where sprawling amusement grounds and pleasure gardens, dancing pavilions, vaudeville performances, and open-air concerts all draw big crowds. Children will enjoy the playhouse, small zoo, reptile center, and the puppet theater. Restaurants also dot the grounds. Hours are daily from 3pm to midnight in summer, noon to 6pm in winter. Admission is free; however, some performances require an admission price of 50 to 110 SEK ($5.50 to $12.10). Take bus 11, 13, or 17 from the Gustav Adolfs Torg.

Dancing is the rage at the creatively designed **Nightclub Etage,** Stortorget 6 (☎ 040/23-20-60). Initially conceived as an upscale bar and restaurant in the late 1980s, this nightspot lowered its prices and began marketing to a mass audience in the early 1990s. Despite its lowered expectations, the bar has not seemed to suffer as a result. It's reached by climbing a circular staircase from an enclosed courtyard in the town's main square. Although satellite bars open and close regularly on other floors, the establishment's heart and soul is on the third floor, where a futuristic restaurant serves simple platters of food priced at 60 to 110 SEK ($6.60 to $12.10). The disco is just a few steps away. The complex is open Monday and Thursday through Saturday from 9pm to at least 3am, depending on the crowd. Cover for the disco ranges from 50 to 90 SEK ($5.50 to $9.90).

Plysch (pronounced "Plush") is a nightclub and cocktail bar located at Lillatorget 1 (☎ 040/12-76-70). When it was developed, its owners did everything they could to appoint it like a well-upholstered private apartment. The result is a labyrinth of medium-size rooms, each personalized and intimate to the point where you could imagine a host or hostess who's about to enter with the offer of yet another drink. Bars are strategically positioned here and there within the maze, and clients end up in conversational clusters on chairs, banquettes, window seats, or wherever. The only problem with this place is the limited hours—only two evenings per week (Friday and Saturday nights from 8pm to 3am). You can join the 30-and-older crowd that congregates here for a cover charge of 50 SEK ($5.50).

Many love affairs, some of which have seguéd into marriages, have gotten a boost at **Restaukang Stadt,** Hamburgsgatan 3 (☎ 040/12-22-21), where romantic dancing is the norm. Attendees tend to be over 35 and the recorded music is reminiscent of a '60s variety show. There's a restaurant on the premises serving platters of traditional Swedish food every Tuesday through Saturday between 8 and 11:30pm. Main courses cost from 100 to 165 SEK ($11 to $18.15). Music and bar activities are scheduled on Tuesday and Wednesday from 8pm to 1am, Thursday from 8pm to 2am, and Friday and Saturday from 8pm to 3am. The cover charge is 70 SEK ($7.70).

The largest nightclub in Malmö, **Club Privée,** Malmborgsgatan 7 (☎ **040/ 97-46-66**), contains five floors and tends to attract a slightly younger (20 to 25) clientele on Fridays than it does on Saturdays (20 to 30). Set near the Gustav Adolfs Torg, in the center of town, it has a decor that replicates an English pub—lots of Chesterfield sofas. There's a bar, and different music is played on each of the establishment's five floors. It's open only on Friday and Saturday nights from 11pm to 5am. The cover ranges from 60 to 70 SEK ($6.60 to $7.70), and a large beer costs 42 SEK ($4.60).

Nostalgic for Britain? The best replica of a British Pub is **The Bishop's Arms,** Norra Vallgatan 62 (☎ **040/702-30**), at the Savoy Hotel. Some of the best and coldest beer in town is served here, and there's always a congenial crowd.

Those seeking cultural activities after dark should get tickets to the Malmö Symphony Orchestra, which is renowned across Europe. It performs at the **Konserthus,** Föreningsgatan 35 (☎ **040/34-35-00**), and the **Musikhögskolan,** Ystadvägen 25 (☎ **040/19-22-00**). The tourist office distributes programs of other cultural events.

3 Lund

11 miles NE of Malmö, 187 miles S of Gothenburg, 374 miles SW of Stockholm

Lund probably was founded in 1020 by Canute the Great, ruler of the United Kingdom of England and Denmark, when this part of Sweden was a Danish possession. However, the city's 1,000-year anniversary was celebrated in 1990 because archaeological excavations show that a stave church was built here in 990. The city really made its mark when its cathedral was consecrated in 1145, after which Lund quickly became a center of religion, politics, culture, and commerce for all of Scandinavia.

The town has winding passageways, centuries-old buildings, and the richness of a university town. Lund University, founded in 1666, continues to play an active role in town life.

The most exciting time to be in Lund, as in Uppsala, is on Walpurgis Eve, April 30, when student revelries signal the advent of spring; but a visit to Lund at any time is a pleasure.

ESSENTIALS
GETTING THERE   By Train   Trains run hourly from Malmö (see above), only a 15-minute ride. Call ☎ **020/75-75-75.**

By Bus   Buses also arrive hourly from Malmö, but they take 30 minutes. Call ☎ **0200/21818.**

By Car   From Gothenburg, head south along E6; Malmö and Lund are linked by an express highway, only a 20-minute drive.

VISITOR INFORMATION   The tourist information office, **Lunds Turistbyrå,** at Kykogatan 11 (☎ **046/35-50-40**), is open June to August, Monday through Friday from 10am to 6pm and on Saturday and Sunday from 10am to 2pm; from September through May, Monday through Friday from 10am to 5pm and on Saturday 10am to 2pm.

SEEING THE SIGHTS
Botaniska Trädgården (Botanical Gardens). Östra Vallgatan 20. ☎ **046/222-73-20.** Free admission. Gardens, daily 6am–8pm; greenhouses, daily noon–3pm. Bus: 1, 2, 3, 4, 5, 6, or 7.

A block east of the cathedral, these gardens contain some 7,500 specimens of plants gathered from all over the world. On a hot summer day, this is the most pleasant place

Lund

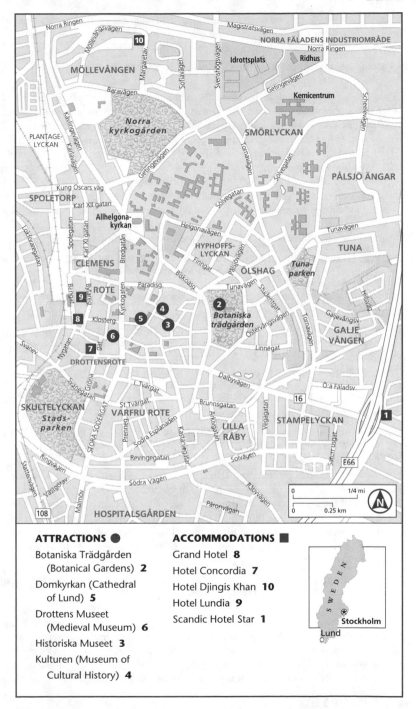

ATTRACTIONS ●

Botaniska Trädgården
(Botanical Gardens) **2**

Domkyrkan (Cathedral
of Lund) **5**

Drottens Museet
(Medieval Museum) **6**

Historiska Museet **3**

Kulturen (Museum of
Cultural History) **4**

ACCOMMODATIONS ■

Grand Hotel **8**

Hotel Concordia **7**

Hotel Djingis Khan **10**

Hotel Lundia **9**

Scandic Hotel Star **1**

to be in Lund. Clusters of students congregate here, stretching out beneath the trees, and families often use the grounds to enjoy a picnic lunch. Serious horticulturists should visit when the greenhouses are open (see hours above).

✪ **Domkyrkan (Cathedral of Lund).** Kyrkogatan. ☎ **046/35-87-00.** Free admission. Mon–Sat 8am–6pm, Sun 9am–6pm. Bus: 1, 2, 3, 4, 5, 6 or 7.

With this ancient cathedral, Romanesque architecture in Scandinavia reached its height; the eastern exterior of the church is one of the finest expressions of Romanesque architecture in northern Europe. The sandstone interior has sculptural details similar in quality and character to those in Lombardy and other parts of Italy. There also is a crypt with a high altar dedicated in 1123, and intricately carved choir stalls from about 1375.

A partly reconstructed 14th-century **astronomical clock** not only tells the time and the date, but stages a splashy tournament from the Middle Ages—complete with clashing knights and the blare of trumpets. And that's not all: The three wise men come out to pay homage to the Virgin and child. To see all this, time your visit to the cathedral for when the clock strikes noon (1pm on Sunday) or 3pm.

Drottens Museet (Medieval Museum). Kattesund 6. ☎ **046/14-13-28.** Admission 10 SEK ($1.10) adults, free for children. Tues–Fri 9am–noon and 1:30–4pm, Sat–Sun noon–4pm. Bus: 1, 2, 3, 4, 5, 6, or 7.

During the excavations for an inner-city office building that was completed in 1986, workers discovered the ruins of one of Sweden's earliest churches. A now-ruined Romanesque building that preceded the establishment of Lund itself by 100 years, it was built about 1,000 years ago. Recognizing its remnants as historically and aesthetically valuable, civic leaders ordered the construction of a series of large windows in the new building, allowing pedestrians on the sidewalk outside to see the ruins from above. While walking among the ruins, visitors can view an exhibition of mannequins dressed in medieval garb in scenes of everyday life. Also on display are some of the skeletons unearthed at the excavation site.

Historiska Museet. Kraftstorg 1. ☎ **046/222-79-44.** Admission 35 SEK ($3.85) adults, 15 SEK ($1.65) children 7–18, free for children under 7. Tues–Fri 11am–4pm, Sun 1–4pm. Closed Mon and Sat. Bus: 1, 2, 3, 4, 5, 6, or 7.

Founded in 1805, this is the second largest museum of archaeology in Sweden. Collections trace the development of the people of Skåne from antiquity to the Middle Ages. One of the skeletons displayed here is that of a young man dating from around 7000 B.C.; one of the oldest human skeletons found in northern Europe. Most collections from the Bronze Age came from tombs. During excavations in eastern Skåne, a large grave field was unearthed; the jewelry and weapons found are on display. The medieval exhibition is dominated by church art.

Kulturen (Museum of Cultural History). Tegnérsplatsen. ☎ **046/35-04-00.** Admission 40 SEK ($4.40) adults, free for children. June 15–Sept, daily 11am–5pm. Bus: 1, 2, 3, 4, 5, 6, or 7.

After leaving the cathedral, walk across the university grounds to Adelgatan, which the local citizens consider their most charming street. Here you'll find Kulturen, another of Sweden's open-air museums. This one contains reassembled sod-roofed farms and manor houses, a carriage museum, ceramics, peasant costumes, Viking artifacts, and old handcrafts, even a wooden church moved to this site from the glassworks district.

WHERE TO STAY

The tourist office (see above) can help you obtain housing in **private homes** for as little as 175 SEK ($19.25) per person per night.

○ Grand Hotel. Bantorget 1, S-221 04 Lund. ☎ **046/28-06-100.** Fax 046/28-06-150. www.grand.lundia.se. 84 units. MINIBAR TV TEL. June 7–Aug 8 and Fri–Sat year-round, 1,095 SEK ($120.45) double; 2,195 SEK ($241.45) suite. Rest of year, 1,795 SEK ($197.45) double; 3,950 SEK ($434.50) suite. Rates include breakfast. AE, DC, MC, V. Parking 80 SEK ($8.80). Bus: 1, 2, 3, 4, 5, 6, or 7.

This château-style hotel, the most prestigious in town, overlooks the fountains and flowers of a city park. Upstairs, each room has an old-fashioned decor and a few amenities, including cable TV. The more spacious rooms in the hotel's conical corner tower have better furnishings and open onto panoramic views of the town. The elegant restaurant offers fixed-price meals beginning at 200 SEK ($22). All the bedrooms have very firm and frequently replaced mattresses. The moderate-size bathrooms are equipped with hair dryers.

Hotel Concordia. Stålbrogatan 1, S-222-24 Lund. ☎ **046/13-50-50.** Fax 046/13-74-22. www.concordia.se. E-mail: info@concordia.se. 50 units. TV TEL. Sun–Thurs 1,495 SEK ($164.45) double; Fri–Sat 795 SEK ($87.45) double. Year-round, 1,500 SEK ($165) suite. Rates include breakfast. AE, DC, MC, V. Parking 50 SEK ($5.50). Bus: 1, 2, 3, 4, 5, 6, or 7.

Next door to the brick house where August Strindberg lived in 1897, this charming, ornate building was renovated a few years ago into a pleasant hotel. The modernized rooms are sedate, and a few are reserved for nonsmokers. Housekeeping here is among the finest in town, and bedrooms are moderate in size, with good beds. Although the bathrooms are a bit small, they are equipped with decent towels and hair dryers, and there's a sauna on the premises. The hotel is a 5-minute walk south of the railroad station.

Hotel Djingis Khan. Margarethevägen 7, S 222 40 Lund. ☎ **800/528-1234** in the U.S., or 046/14-00-60. Fax 046/14-36-26. www.bestwestern.com. 55 units. TV TEL. Sun–Thurs 1,295 SEK ($142.45) double; Fri–Sat 800 SEK ($88) double. Rates include breakfast. AE, DC, MC, V. Closed July. Free parking. Bus: 3 or 93.

Located within a 15-minute walk north of the town center, this hotel originally was built in the 1970s as employee housing for a local hospital, and then converted into this pleasant, well-managed hotel in the early 1990s. Two of its wings still contain private apartments, but the three-story bulk of its central core contains attractively modern bedrooms outfitted in a conservatively comfortable style, with good beds and small but adequate bathrooms. Affiliated with the Best Western chain of hotels, the Hotel Djingis Khan has far more style and charm than typical roadside U.S. Best Westerns: Public areas contain lots of English-inspired dark paneling, Chesterfield sofas, and an ambience that resembles a private men's club in London. The hotel's name, incidentally, derives from the most famous satirical comedy (*Ghenghis Khan*) ever produced in Lund. It was written in the 1950s by Hasse Alfredsson, and this hotel was named in its honor.

Hotel Lundia. Knut den Stores Gata 2, S-221 04. ☎ **046/280-65-00.** Fax 046/280-65-10. www.lundia.se. E-mail: hotel@lundi.se. 97 units. MINIBAR TV TEL. Late June to early Aug and Fri–Sat year-round, 895 SEK ($98.45) double; rest of year, 1,650 SEK ($181.50) double. Year-round, 2,500 SEK ($275) suite. Rates include breakfast. AE, DC, MC, V. Closed Dec 22–26. Parking 100 SEK ($11). Bus: 1, 2, 3, 4, 5, 6, or 7.

Operated by the same management as the Grand Hotel (see above), this is the most pleasantly situated and one of the most modern hotels in town. The interior has winding staircases, white marble sheathing, and big windows. Each bedroom has its own adequately sized tile bathroom, clothes press, and refrigerator, and is designed with Scandinavian fabrics and unusual lithographs. Most bedrooms are moderate in size, although singles are a bit cramped. Guests interested in a formal meal usually head for the dining room at the Grand, about a block away. Those interested in a less formal meal can patronize the in-house brasserie (see "Where to Dine," below). There's also a stylish nightclub located here.

✪ **Scandic Hotel Star.** Glimmervägen 5, PO Box 11026, SE-220 11 Lund. ☎ **046/ 211-20-00.** Fax 046/211-50-00. www.scandic-hotel.com. 196 units. TV TEL. Mid-June to mid-Aug and Fri–Sat year round 720 SEK ($79.20) double; rest of year, Sun–Thurs 1,445 SEK ($158.95) double. Year-round 2,380–2,800 SEK ($261.80–$308) suite. AE, DC, MC, V. Free parking. Bus: 3 or 7.

This hotel, a 20-minute walk from the town center, is the most comfortable in Lund. Built in 1991, it attracts lots of business conventions, as well as most of the rock stars and movie actors known throughout Sweden. Each of the hotel's double rooms is configured as a mini-suite, with a separate sitting area and traditional, conservative furnishings that would fit into a well-appointed upper-middle-class Swedish home. The public areas are more international and contemporary than the bedrooms, and have lots of potted or hanging plants, wicker furnishings, and varnished wood. The "relaxation center" has an exercise area, swimming pool, sauna, and solarium. The restaurant is open daily except Sunday for lunch and dinner. The well-upholstered bar area, which serves burgers and sandwiches every day, is especially busy on Sunday when the hotel's more formal dining room is closed.

WHERE TO DINE

Anna's Restaurant. Lilla Fiskaregatan 11. ☎ **046/13-04-24.** Reservations recommended. Main courses 110–185 SEK ($12.10–$20.35). AE, DC, MC, V. Mon–Sat 10am–11pm, Sun 10am–5pm. SWEDISH.

Some of the regular clients of this place compare it to a small, informal, and convivial tavern, the kind that's particularly appealing on cold winter nights. Set on two floors, one of which has a prominent and popular bar, it segues throughout the day from roles that swing from a simple bistro to a more elaborate restaurant as the evening progresses. Good-tasting menu items include dishes such as grilled salmon with lemon-butter and dill sauce; venison in port wine glaze; lobster soup; and savory steaks. In summer, consider a table on the outside terrace.

Brasserie Lundia. In the Hotel Lundia, Knut den Stores Gata 2. ☎ **046/280-65-22.** Reservations required Fri–Sat. Main courses 98–175 SEK ($10.80–$19.25). AE, DC, MC, V. Mon–Fri 11am–midnight, Sat noon–10pm, Sun 4–11pm. Bus: 1, 2, 3, 4, 5, 6, or 7. SWEDISH.

One of the most popular cafeterias in town, this brasserie is the only restaurant in Lund with its own in-house bakery. You'll find crisp salads, open-face sandwiches, and hot dishes as part of the full cafeteria meals. At night, the place becomes an à la carte restaurant with waitress service, serving steak tartare, fettuccine with salmon, tagliatelle Bolognese, grilled filet mignon, grilled pork cutlet with pepper sauce, deep-fried Camembert, and seven kinds of alcohol-rich after-dinner coffees. Although no one has ever accused the kitchen staff of being too experimental, everything is well prepared, and there's a good, relaxed service. The inviting decor features wood and russet-colored marble tables.

Gloria's Bar and Restaurant. S:t Petri Kyrkogata 9. ☎ **046/15-19-85.** Reservations recommended. Main courses 89–159 SEK ($9.80–$17.50). AE, MC, V. Mon–Fri 11:30am–10:30pm, Sat 12:30–11pm, Sun 1–10pm. Bus: 1, 2, 3, 4, 5, 6, or 7. AMERICAN.

The success of this American-inspired sports and Western bar would gladden the heart of any U.S.-born ideologue. On two floors of an old-fashioned building in the historic heart of town, it offers a crowded and likable bar in its cellar and an even larger bar upstairs. Scattered throughout the premises are photographs and posters of American sports heroes, baseball and football memorabilia, and artifacts from the Wild West. Draft beer costs 42 SEK ($5.40) for a foaming mug. Large portions of such rib-stickers as hamburgers, steaks, and an array of dishes inspired by the Cajun cuisine of Louisiana are sure to sate your hunger. All of these will be served to you by a staff appropriately clad in jeans, cowboy boots, and shirts emblazoned with Gloria's logo. Live music is performed between 9:30pm and 1am each Wednesday. Thursday night is a particular favorite because of its emphasis on rock 'n' roll.

Ø **Bar.** Mårtenstorget 9. ☎ **046/211-22-88.** Reservations recommended. Main courses 100–195 SEK ($11–$21.45). AE, DC, MC, V. Daily 11:30am–midnight. Bar until 1 or 2am. INTERNATIONAL.

One of the most interesting restaurants in Lund defines itself as a "laboratory for chefs" because of the experimental nature of a menu that changes virtually every week. The venue looks like it may have been designed by a Milanese post-modernist, with blue and ash-white walls and a strictly minimalist kind of angularity. It's usually mobbed with both diners and patrons of the convivial bar area. Here, you're likely to meet university students as well as their professors, all participating in animated dialogues. Menu items include a filet of elk with thyme sauce, served with apple and potato muffins; grilled halibut served with lemon oil, horseradish, and house-made pasta; and lime-flavored clam chowder with Vietnamese spring rolls.

Staket. Stora Södergatan 6. ☎ **046/211-93-67.** Reservations recommended. Main courses 125–160 SEK ($13.75–$17.60). AE, DC, MC, V. Mon–Fri 11am–11pm, Sat–Sun noon–11:30pm. Bus: 1, 2, 3, 4, 5, 6, or 7. SWEDISH/CONTINENTAL.

An old tavern that serves good food in an unspoiled atmosphere, this establishment occupies the cellar and the street level of a 15th-century building whose step-gabled brick facade is a historic landmark. Menu items include crabmeat cocktail, lobster or goulash soup, white fillet of pork, tournedos of beef, a mixed grill, marinated salmon, pickled herring, baked potatoes with black curry, and whitefish toast. Although both dining rooms are equally appealing, fondues (skewers of meat cooked at your table in pots of heated oil) are served only in the cellar.

LUND AFTER DARK

Most dance clubs in Lund tend to operate only on weekends, when the clientele includes many students from the nearby university. Examples include **Tetner's Restaurant,** Sandgatan 2 (☎ **046/131-333**), which opens a dance floor in the cellar every Saturday from 9pm till 2am. There's also a dance floor in the basement of the already recommended **Gloria's Restaurant,** every Friday and Saturday beginning at 10:30pm. Entrance is free. A final dance choice, also open only Friday and Saturday, is the **Palladium,** Stora Södergatan 13 (☎ **046/211-66-60**), which resembles a somewhat beery pub with a college-age clientele every other night of the week. Admission is free.

Lundia Nightcafé. Knut den Stores Gata 2. ☎ **046/280-65-22.** Cover 50 SEK ($5.50).

In the cellar of the Hotel Lundia (see "Where to Stay," above) are a small-stakes casino (blackjack and roulette), two different bars, a dance floor, and a modern cellar popular with students. Residents of the Hotel Lundia and guests and clients of diners from the Brasserie Lundia enter free, but everyone else pays the cover. Draft beer costs 45 SEK ($4.95). It's open from 11pm to 3am.

SIDE TRIPS FROM LUND

From Lund, you may want to make a side trip to **Dalby Church,** 5–240 12 Dalby (☎ **046/20-00-65**), in Dalby, 8 miles east of Lund. This starkly beautiful, well-preserved 11th-century former bishop's church built of stone is the oldest in Scandinavia; be sure to visit its crypt. Open daily from 9am to 4pm. Several buses a day (nos. 158 and 161) run between Lund center and Dalby.

About a 30-minute drive northeast of Lund (off Route 23) is the ✪ **Castle of Bosjökloster, Höör** (☎ 0413/250-48). Once a Benedictine convent founded around 1080, it was closed during the Reformation in the 16th century. The great courtyard is spectacular, with thousands of flowers and exotic shrubs, terraces, and a park with animals and birds. Indoors is the vaulted refectory and the stone hall where native arts and crafts, jewelry, and other Swedish goods are displayed. You can picnic on the grounds or enjoy lunch at a simple restaurant in the garden for 100 SEK ($11).

The entire complex is open daily from May 1 to September 30 8am to 8pm; the museum and exhibition hall inside the castle, daily 10am to 6pm. Admission is 40 SEK ($4.40) for adults, 25 SEK ($2.75) for senior citizens and students, 12 SEK ($1.30) for children 6 to 16, free for children under 6. In the park stands a 1,000-year-old oak tree. The castle lies 28 miles from Malmö and 18 miles from Lund. From Lund, there's a train link to Höör; after that, take bus no. R02 to Bösjokloster on Route 23, 3 miles south to Höör.

4 Ystad

34 miles E of Malmö, 28 miles W of Simrishamn

Ystad makes a good base for exploring the castles and manors of Skåne. An important port during the Middle Ages, Ystad retains its ancient look, with about 300 half-timbered houses, mazes of narrow lanes—even a watchman who sounds the hours of the night in the tower of St. Mary's Church.

Devotees of the silent screen know of Ystad as the birthplace of Valentino's "beautiful blond Viking" Anna Q. Nilsson, who was born here in 1890 and whose fame at one time was greater than that of Greta Garbo, a fellow Swede. Some of Nilsson's greatest films were *In the Heart of a Fool* (1921), *Ponjola* (1923) in which she played a boy, and *Midnight Lovers,* finished in 1925, the year of a horseback riding accident that ended her career. Today she is remembered mainly for appearing in a cameo role as one of the "waxworks" in the 1950 Gloria Swanson classic, *Sunset Boulevard.*

ESSENTIALS

GETTING THERE   By Train   There are good rail connections between Malmö and Ystad. From Monday to Friday trains run roughly on the hour between Malmö and Ystad, taking 1 hour. On Saturday, there are only four daily trains from Malmö, increasing to six on Sunday. For more information, call **020/75-75-75.**

By Bus   There are three daily buses Monday through Saturday from Malmö to Ystad, taking 1 hour. On Sunday, there is only one bus.

By Car   From Malmö, head east on Route 65. For more information, call ☎ **0200/21818.**

VISITOR INFORMATION   The tourist bureau, **Ystads Turistbyrå,** S:t Knuts Torg, (☎ 0411/577681; www.ystad.se), is at the bus station in the same building as the art museum (Konstmuseum). It's open mid-June through mid-August, Monday through Saturday 9am to 7pm, and Sunday 1 to 7pm; off-season, Monday through Friday 9am to 5pm.

SEEING THE SIGHTS

S:t Maria Kyrka. Stortorget. ☎ **0411/69-20-0.** Free admission. June to mid-Sept, daily 10am–6pm.

The focal point of the town is this church dating from the early 1200s. Every century that followed brought new additions and changes. Regrettably, many of its richest decorative features were removed in the 1880s because of changing tastes. However, some of the more interesting ones were brought back in a restoration program occurring 4 decades later. The chancel with the ambulatory is late Gothic, and the church spire dates from 1688. Inside, look for the baptismal chapel with a richly carved German altar from the 15th century. The font came from Lübeck, Germany in 1617 and the iron candelabra is a very early one from the 1300s. The early 17th-century baroque pulpit also is worth a look.

Museum of Modern Art (Ystads Konstmuseum). S:t Knuts Torg. ☎ **0411/77-285.** Admission 20 SEK ($2.20). Tues–Fri noon–5pm, Sat–Sun noon–4pm.

Permanent exhibits feature mainly Scandinavian and Danish art from the last 100 years, and there also is a small military museum. The Ystad Tourist Office is the same building as the museum.

City Museum (in the Grey Friars Monastery) (Stadsmuséet i Gråbrödraklostret). S:t Petri Kykoplan. ☎ **0411/577-286.** Admission 20 SEK ($2.20). Mon–Fri noon–5pm, Sat–Sun noon–4pm.

This is the only museum in Sweden residing in a medieval monastic house. Constructed in 1267, the building is a monument from the Danish era in the town of Ystad. Various antiquities in the museum trace the history of the area.

WHERE TO STAY

Hotel Continental. Hamngatan 13 S-271 00 Ystad. ☎ **0411/137-00.** Fax 0411/125-70. www.hotelcontinental-ystad.se. 52 units. TV TEL. June 21–Aug 4 and Fri–Sat year-round, 950 SEK ($104.50) double; rest of year, 1,090–1,200 SEK ($119.90–$132) double. AE, DC, MC, V. Parking 20 SEK ($2.20).

Belying the modern appointments, this hotel, dating from 1829, may be Skåne's oldest. The hotel is conveniently located opposite the train station and close to the ferry terminal. The attractively decorated bedrooms are furnished with tasteful, Italian-inspired decor and a number of modern amenities, including comfortable mattresses. A restoration added marble sheathing and crystal chandeliers to the lobby. The dining room is classically decorated, offering efficient and courteous service. The hotel owners take a personal interest in the welfare of their guests.

Hotel Tornväktaren. S:t Östergatan 33, S-271-34 Ystad. ☎ **0411/784-80.** Fax 0411/729-27. 9 units. TV TEL. 695 SEK ($76.45) double. Rates includes breakfast. AE, MC, V. Free parking.

Much of the charm of this simple bed-and-breakfast hotel derives from the hardworking presence of its owner, Ms. Inger Larsson. Her home is a turn-of-the-century stone-built structure with its own garden and red trim, set within a 10-minute walk from the railway station. Bedrooms are outfitted in pale pastels, with lots of homey touches that include frilly curtains, wall-to-wall carpeting, and lace doilies covering painted wooden furniture. Other than a filling morning breakfast, no meals are served.

Ystads Saltsjöbad. Saltsjöbadsgatan 6, S-271 39 Ystad. ☎ **0411/136-30.** Fax 0411/55-58-35. www.ystadssaltsjöbad.se. E-mail: info@ystadssaltsjöbad.se. 108 units. TV TEL. June 19–Aug 31, 990–1,090 SEK ($108.90–$119.90) double; Sept–June 18, 1,230–1,670 SEK ($135.30–$183.70) double. Mon–Thurs 2,070–2,300 SEK ($227.70–$253) suite; Fri–Sun 1,390–1,790 SEK ($152.90–$196.90) suite. AE, DC, MC, V. Free parking. Closed Dec 23–Jan 6.

Beautifully located on 10 acres of forested land beside the sea, close to Sweden's southernmost tip, this hotel was built in 1897 by one of the most famous opera stars of his day, Swedish-born Solomon Smith. Designed as a haven for the gilded-age aristocracy of northern Europe, it consists of three four-story buildings interconnected with big-windowed corridors, set close to the sands of an expansive beach. The bedrooms are comfortably furnished with a sense of turn-of-the-century nostalgia. About half of them were refurbished in the mid-1990s.

The clientele changes throughout the year. In summer, the hotel caters to individual clients who appreciate the beach; in winter, it's filled for the most part with corporate conventions. The neighborhood provides good opportunities for playing tennis and golf and there's a heated indoor pool with a water slide and a sauna. The hotel's Apotheket Restaurant serves good international cuisine and features a dance band several nights a week. There's also a cocktail bar and two cafes. The cafe with the outdoor terrace closes in winter.

WHERE TO DINE

Lottas Restaurang. Stortorget 11. ☎ **0411/788-00.** Reservations recommended. Main courses 130–175 SEK ($14.30–$19.25). AE, DC, MC, V. Mon–Sat 5–10:30pm. SWEDISH.

Whereas its fans praise it as one of the most popular and bustling restaurants in town, its detractors avoid it because of long delays in food service and the small, overworked staff. The food, however, is well prepared and served in a century-old building that once functioned as a private home. Within a brick-lined dining room, you'll be presented with a menu that reflects traditional Swedish cuisine and might include fried and creamed fillets of cod with dill-flavored boiled potatoes; pork schnitzels with asparagus and Béarnaise sauce; tenderloin of pork with mushrooms in cream sauce; and marinated breast of chicken with roasted potatoes. Among the desserts is a warm chocolate cake with ice cream.

Rådhuskällaren Ystad. Stortorget. ☎ **0411/185-10.** Main courses 85–150 SEK ($9.35–$16.50). AE, DC, MC, V. Mon–Sat 11:30am–2:30pm. SWEDISH.

One of the most reliable restaurants in Ystad occupies a series of vaulted cellars that were built as part of a monastery in the 1500s. Several hundred years later, the Rådhus (Town Hall) was reconstructed after a disastrous fire above the monastery's cellars. Today, amid small tables and romantic candlelight, you can enjoy such tasty dishes as shellfish soup with saffron, beef fillet stuffed with lobster, marinated and grilled tenderloin steak, grilled angler-fish with basil-cream sauce, saddle of lamb with fresh herbs, and roast reindeer with mushrooms and game sauce. The setting here usually is more crowded and hurried at lunchtime than it is at dinner.

✪ **Restaurant Bruggeriet.** Långgatan 20. ☎ **0411/69-9999.** Reservations recommended. Main courses 136–186 SEK ($14.95–$20.45). AE, DC, MC, V. Mon–Sat 11:30am–10:30pm, Sun 12:30–10pm. SWEDISH/INTERNATIONAL.

The most novel restaurant in Ystad occupies the site of what originally was built in 1749 as a warehouse for malt, a half-timbered brick building in the center of town. In 1996, a team of local entrepreneurs installed a series of large copper vats and transformed the site into a pleasant and cozy restaurant and brewery. Today, they specialize in two "tastes" of a beer that is marketed under the brand name *Ysta Färsköl*, which comes in both lager and dark versions. Depending on their size, they sell for 25 to 50 SEK ($3.20 to $6.40) per mug. The food seems carefully calibrated to taste best when consumed with either of the two beers. Examples include fried herring marinated in mustard and sour cream, served with mashed potatoes; grilled salmon with red wine sauce; marinated and baked Swedish lamb with garlic and herbs; tenderloin steak with brandy sauce; and a succulent version of barbecued ribs you might have expected in New Orleans.

Sandskogens Vardshus. Saltsjøvagen, Sandskogen. ☎ **0411/147-60.** Reservations recommended. Main courses 100–200 SEK ($11–$22); fixed-price lunch 85 SEK ($9.35); fixed-price dinner 195 SEK ($21.45). AE, DC, MC, V. Tues–Sun 11:30am–10pm. Closed Jan–Feb. SWEDISH.

Set about a mile east of Ystad's center, this structure originally was built in 1899 as a summer home for the town's mayor. It was converted to a restaurant in the 1930s, and has since provided local diners with well-prepared Swedish specialties that include marinated mussels; toast with whitebait roe, sour cream, and onions; fried brill with caramelized butter sauce; turbot with shrimp and Swedish caviar; gratin of lobster with lemon sole; and during certain seasons, a lingonberry or cloudberry parfait.

5 Simrishamn

391 miles S of Stockholm, 59 miles E of Malmö, 25 miles E of Ystad

One of the most idyllic towns along the Skåne coastline, Simrishamn features old half-timbered buildings, courtyards, and gardens. This seaport is the jumping-off point to the Danish island of Bornholm.

ESSENTIALS

GETTING THERE   By Train   Four trains a day, three on Saturday and Sunday, make the 45-minute run between Malmö and Simrishamn. For information, call ☎ **020/75-75-75.**

By Bus   Nine buses per day arrive from Kristianstad (four a day on Saturday and Sunday), and ten buses per day arrive from Ystad (three on Saturday and Sunday). From Lund, there are eight daily buses. Tickets can be purchased on board these buses. Call ☎ **0200/21818.**

By Car   From Ystad, our last stopover, continue east along Route 10.

VISITOR INFORMATION   For information about hotels, boardinghouses, summer cottages, and apartments, check with the tourist bureau. **Simrishamns Kommun Turistbyrå,** Tullhusgatan 2 (☎ **0414/160-60**), is open June through August, Monday through Friday 9am to 8pm, Saturday 11am to 8pm, and Sunday 12:30 to 8pm; September through May, Monday through Friday 9am to 5pm.

SEEING THE SIGHTS

Other than the charming little town itself, there isn't much to see after you've walked through the historic core. (The major attractions are in the environs; see the following.) The Old Town is a maze of fondant-colored tiny cottages that in some ways evoke a movie set. The chief attraction is **S:t Nicolai Kirke,** Storgatan (☎ **0414/41-24-80**). It's open daily 9am to 4pm, and charges no admission.

Originally constructed as a fisherman's chapel in the 12th century, the church literally dominates the town. It's built of chunky sandstone blocks, with a brick porch and step gables. Over the years there have been many additions. A nave was added in the 1300s, although the vault dates from the 1400s. Inside, look for the flamboyantly painted pulpit from the 1620s. The pews and votive ships on display are much later—from the 1800s. Outside you'll see two sculptures, both by Carl Milles. He called them *The Sisters* and *Angel with Trumpet.*

NEARBY ATTRACTIONS

Backakra. S-270 20 Loderup. ☎ **0411/52-66-11.** Admission 30 SEK ($3.30) adults, 15 SEK ($1.65) children. June 8–Aug 16, daily noon–5pm; May 16–June 7 and Aug 17–Sept 20, Sat–Sun noon–5pm. Closed Sept 21–May 15.

Located off the coastal road between Ystad and Simrishamn is the farm that Dag Hammarskjöld, the late United Nations secretary-general, purchased in 1957 and intended to make his home. Although he died in a plane crash before he could live there, the old farm has been restored according to his instructions. The rooms are filled with gifts to Mr. Hammarskjöld—everything from a Nepalese dagger to a lithograph by Picasso.

The site is 19 miles southwest of Simrishamn, and can be reached by the bus from Simrishamn marked YSTAD. Likewise, a bus from Ystad, marked SIMRISHAMN, also goes by the site. Scheduling your return might be difficult because of infrequent service—check in advance.

Other than the caretakers, the site is unoccupied most of the year, with the exception of any of the 18 members of the Swedish Academy, whose benefits and honors include use of the house for meditation and writing whenever they want.

✪ **Glimmingehus.** Hammenhög. ☎ **0414/320-89.** Admission 50 SEK ($5.50) adults, free for children. Daily 9am–6pm. Closed Nov–Mar. From Simrishamn follow Route 10 southwest for 6 miles to the village of Hammenhög and then follow signs.

Located 6 miles southwest of Simrishamn, this bleak castle was built between 1499 and 1505. It's the best-preserved medieval keep in Scandinavia, but the somewhat Gothic, step-gabled building is unfurnished. Visitors can order snacks or afternoon tea at a cafe on the premises. June through August, a guided tour in English leaves at 2pm every day. Lots of events take place in summer, including theatrical presentations, lectures, medieval meals with entertainment, and even a medieval festival in August.

✪ **Kivik Tomb.** Bredaror. No phone. Admission 15 SEK ($1.65). Daily 10am–6pm. Closed Sept–Apr. From Simrishamn follow Route 10 northwest to the village of Kivik, at which point the tomb is signposted.

Discovered in 1748, this remarkable find, Sweden's most amazing Bronze Age relic, is north of Simrishamn along the coast of Kivik. In a 1931 excavation, tomb furniture, bronze fragments, and some grave carvings were uncovered. A total of eight floodlit runic slabs depict pictures of horses, a sleigh, and what appears to be a fun-loving troupe of dancing seals. You can reach the site by car.

WHERE TO STAY

Hotel Kockska Gården. Storgatan 25, S-272 31 Simrishamn. ☎ **0414/41-17-55.** Fax 0414/117-55. 18 units. TV TEL. 700 SEK ($77) double. AE, MC, V. Free parking.

Like an unspoiled black-and-white, half-timbered coaching inn, this hotel is built around a large medieval courtyard in the town center. Its lounge combines the old and new, with a stone fireplace contrasting with balloon lamps. The bedrooms have been modernized, and the furnishings are up-to-date with tastefully coordinated colors and good beds. Bathrooms tend to be small. The only meal served is breakfast.

Hotel Svea. Strandvägen 3, S-272 31 Simrishamn. ☎ **0414/41-17-20.** Fax 0414/143-41. www.hotelsvea-simrishamn.com. 59 units. TV TEL. Mid-June to mid-Aug and Fri–Sun year-round, 890 SEK ($97.90) double; 1,050 SEK ($115.50) suite. Rest of year, 990 SEK ($108.90) double; 1,250 SEK ($137.50) suite. AE, DC, MC, V. Free parking.

Painted a shade of pale yellow, with a red tile roof that matches those of older buildings nearby, this is the best-recommended hotel in town, and site of a fine restaurant (Restaurant Svea), which is separately recommended in "Where to Dine" (see below). Although much of what you'll see today was rebuilt and radically renovated in 1986, the origins of this waterfront hotel in the town center date from around 1900. Many of its well-appointed, conservatively comfortable rooms overlook the yacht harbor.

The hotel's only suite, the Prince Eugen, is named after a member of the royal family of Sweden who stayed here shortly after the hotel was built.

WHERE TO DINE

Restaurant Svea. In the Hotel Svea. Strandvägen 3. ☎ **0414/41-17-20.** Reservations recommended. Fixed-price lunch 100 SEK ($11); main courses 105–195 SEK ($11.55–$21.45). AE, DC, MC, V. Mon–Fri noon–2pm and 6–9:30pm, Sat 7–10pm. SWEDISH/INTERNATIONAL.

The best restaurant in town lies within the pale yellow walls of the previously recommended hotel. Within a modern, mostly beige room whose windows overlook the harbor, the menu focuses on very fresh fish pulled from local waters; as well as beef, pork, chicken, and some exotic meats such as grilled fillets of ostrich, which the chef added to the menu mainly as a conversational oddity. Other menu items include strips of smoked duck breast in lemon sauce, a platter of artfully arranged herring prepared in at least three different ways, fillets of fried sole with white wine or tartar sauce, fish of the day prepared au gratin with shrimp and lobster sauce, medallions of pork with béarnaise sauce, and a succulent fillet of beef with salsa-style tomato sauce.

6 Kristianstad

45 miles N of Simrishamn, 59 miles NE of Malmö, 78 miles SE of Vaxjö

Called the "most Danish of Sweden's towns," Kristianstad actually was a part of Denmark for only 44 years. But its founder, Christian IV of Denmark, still makes his presence felt in many ways. In fact, the town, originally known as Christianstat, was issuing banknotes with a Danish king imprinted on them as late as 1898.

The city was founded in 1614 to defend the Danish kingdom against Swedish attacks. The fort laid out by Christian IV was northern Europe's most modern. The fortification period ended in 1847, and once the ramparts were leveled, Kristianstad expanded, building Parisian-style boulevards that earned for it the name "Little Paris." The only parts of the fortification still left are portions of the northernmost system surrounding what now is the residential district of Utanverken. After a century and a half without the restricting fortifications, Kristianstad has expanded to become the largest town in the county, just as Christian IV had hoped

ESSENTIALS

GETTING THERE   By Train   There is frequent rail service throughout the day from Malmö; the trip takes 1 hour and 15 minutes. Call ☎ **020/757575.**

By Bus   Local buses arrive several times a day from Ystad (trip time: 1 hour, 30 minutes) and also from Simrishamn (same trip time). Call ☎ **0200/21818.**

By Car   From Simrishamn, our last stopover, head northwest along Route 10 until you come to the junction with Route 118, at which point you go north into Kristianstad.

VISITOR INFORMATION   The **Kristianstads Turistbyrå** is at Stora Torg 291 (☎ **044/12-19-88;** www.kristianstadde). It is open in summer Monday through Friday 9am to 7pm, Saturday 9am to 3pm, and Sunday 2 to 6pm. Off-season hours are Monday through Friday 10am to 5pm, and the last Saturday of each month from 10am to 2pm.

SEEING THE SIGHTS

A Renaissance town created in 1614 by Christian IV, the "builder king" of Denmark, Kristianstad is eastern Skåne's most historic center. Thanks to a grid plan laid out by this long-ago king, it is still easy to find your way around the small city.

Those arriving at the train station are greeted by one of the city's major landmarks, **Trefaldighertskyrkan,** or the Holy Trinity Church, Västra Storgatan (☎ 044/ 20-64-00). It's open daily 9am to 4pm year-round. Built between 1617 and 1628, it is the most beautiful Renaissance church in Scandinavia. The grandiose exterior contains seven splendid spiraled gables; the high windows allow the light to flood inside. Inside, the vaulted design and slender granite pillars create an unusually beautiful architectural setting. Most of the church appointments date from the time of Christian IV, including the carved oak benches, the altarpiece, and the marble and alabaster pulpit, as well as the magnificent organ facade built in 1630.

Directly across from the church lies Storatorg, the major square of town, and the setting for the 19th-century **Rådhus** or Town Hall, located on Västra Storgatan. In a niche under the hands of the Town Hall clock stands a statue of Christian IV, a zinc copy of Bertel Thorvaldsen's bronze original that is in Christian IV's sepulcher in Denmark's Roskilde Cathedral. The current town hall replaced an older building in 1891 and is built in Christian IV's Renaissance style like structures in Copenhagen. Step through the arms-emblazoned portal and you'll be greeted by a bronze bust of Christian IV sculpted with exceptional skill by François Dieussart in 1643. The original stands in Rosenborg Palace in Copenhagen.

North of Storatorg is the **Länsmuseum,** Östra Boulevarden (☎ 044/13-52-45), sheltered in a structure that originally was intended as a royal palace for Christian IV in 1616. In time, however, it became an arsenal for Danish partisans during the bloody conflicts with Sweden. The building acquired its present look in the 1780s, becoming a regional museum in 1959. The art and handcraft collections here are worth seeing, especially the treasure trove of silver. The works of local artists also are displayed, and there is an array of some interesting textiles. The museum is open June through August, Monday through Friday 10am to 5pm (Wednesday until 8pm). Off-season hours are Monday through Friday noon to 5pm (Wednesday until 8pm). Admission is free.

A short walk east of Storatorg will take you to the **Filmmuseet** (Film Museum), at Östra Storgatan 53 (☎ 044/13-52-45). It's open Tuesday through Friday and Sunday from 1 to 4pm and closed on Monday and Saturday. Admission is free. Kristianstad was the cradle of the Swedish film industry. This unique museum is housed in the oldest film studio (1909) still standing in Sweden. Outside the door you're greeted by an early movie camera. On videotape inside you can view the flickering works of Sweden's first film directors.

When you tire of museums, head for **Tivoli Park,** which can be reached from the Film Museum by wandering down any of the roads to its right. Stroll beneath the avenues of horse chestnut trees and enjoy a drink at the Fornstugan Café. In the park is a theater built in the art nouveau style in 1906 by Axel Anderberg, who designed the Stockholm Opera. At the north end of the park is Barbacka Cultural Center, a lively home for the town's art gallery. There also is a cafeteria here.

Some residents claim that the best way to admire the topography around Kristianstad involves taking a boat ride on the nearby lakes and rivers. From early May to mid-September, a sightseeing steamer departs from Kristianstad for 2-hour tours of lakes Araslövs and Hammar, with time spent on the River Helge Å as well. Departures usually are daily at 11am, 2pm, and 6pm, and the cost per person is 75 SEK ($8.25). There's a cafeteria on board, and lots of deck space to enjoy the midsummer sunlight. For information and reservations, contact the tourist office (see above).

A NEARBY PALACE

Bäckaskog. S-290 34 Fjälkinge. ☎ **044/530-20.** Free admission. Apr–Sept, daily 9am–6pm; Oct–Mar, daily 10am–5pm. Closed Aug 16–May 14.

Nine miles north of Kristianstad, this country palace of King Charles XV stands in a 40-acre park, managed by the Swedish Forest Service. The castle, a National Trust building, originally was a monastery founded in the early 13th century. The chapel dates from 1230 but its tower is from 1640. There's a lot to see at Bäckaskog, including a biblical garden featuring trees, bushes, and herbs mentioned in the Bible or having some other religious connection.

There is a restaurant, plus 15 hotel rooms and 4 suites (all in a contemporary, rather than palatial, syle) that are open to guests all year. A double goes for 820 to 1,040 SEK ($90.20 to $114.40); suites range from 1,000 to 1,500 SEK ($110 to $165).

Exhibitions and sales of art and country furniture can be attended even when the castle is not open to visitors. The palace can be reached by taxi from Kristianstad; call **Taxi Allians** at ☎ **044/246246.** If you're driving from Kristiansand, go 9 miles north along E66 until you reach the turnoff for Fjälkinge, at which point Bäckaskog is signposted.

WHERE TO STAY

Hotel Turisten. Vestre Storgatan 17, S-291-32 Kristianstad. ☎ **044/12-61-50.** E-mail: info. turisten@swedenhotels.se. 33 units. TV TEL. June to mid-Aug, 550 SEK ($60.50) double; mid-Aug to May, 845 SEK ($92.95) double. Rates include breakfast. AE, DC, MC. V. Free parking.

Set near the heart of town, this hotel originally was built in the 1700s as the private home of the local judge. Today, it boasts some of the most elaborate brickwork in town, especially on its second floor where windows are gracefully arched and mullioned. Bedrooms are outfitted with more style and taste than you might have guessed from the hotel's relatively inexpensive rates. None is particularly large, but in view of their coziness and careful decorating, guests usually find that they're very comfortable, particularly the beds. Bathrooms are very small, however. Be aware that many staff members here don't speak English.

Quality Grand Hotel Kristianstad. Storgatan 15, Box 45, SE-291 32 Kristianstad. ☎ **044/10-36-00.** Fax 044/12-57-82. www.choicehotels.se. 148 units TV TEL. Mid-June to mid-Aug and Fri–Sun year-round, 750 SEK ($82.50) double; rest of year, 1,395–1,495 SEK ($153.45–$164.45) double. Year-round, 1,495–1,895 SEK ($164.45–$208.45) suite. Rates include breakfast. AE, DC, MC, V. Free parking. Bus: 11.

The largest and most centrally located hotel in Kristianstad rises from a position near the railway station, behind a conservative brick facade that was built in the early 1960s. In 1985, its size was doubled with a four-story new wing, and the interior was radically modernized to something akin to the best in town. Today, you'll find a busy series of conference rooms, and bedrooms that are conservatively outfitted in a style that's just a bit banal, but very comfortable with good beds and ample bathrooms.

Dining/Diversions: An in-house restaurant serves lunch and dinner daily. The bar is a scarlet-colored two-story space named Grands. A separate restaurant, open only on Thursday nights, offers disco and supper-club dance music for cheek-to-cheek dancing to a live orchestra.

Amenities: Conference rooms, sauna and health club/exercise areas. Computers are available for use by guests.

WHERE TO DINE

Jespers Mat & Vinhus. Södra Kaserngatan 6. ☎ **044/12-00-01.** Reservations recommended for dinner. 1-course fixed-price lunch 89 SEK ($9.80); main courses 160–250 SEK ($17.60–$27.50). AE, MC, V. Mon–Fri 11:30am–2pm; Tues–Sat 6–9pm (last order; bar stays open till 1am). SWEDISH/FRENCH.

Named after the owners, the Jespers family, this restaurant occupies the 700-year-old vaulted cellars that were used during the 1600s as a dormitory and storage depot for army troops. Today they're illuminated with soft lighting and flickering candles, and permeated with the scents of such menu items as lobster soup with chanterelles; homemade foie gras; filets of venison with wild mushrooms, and braised halibut with dill and wine sauce. This is one of the most inviting and attractively appealing restaurants in town, both in its welcome and in its cuisine. Food items are deftly handled by a skilled kitchen staff, and service is top rate.

Kalmar & the Southeast 7

Much of Southeast Sweden falls into the province of Småland, which includes the historic city of Kalmar and also the "Kingdom of Crystal" centered around Växjö. Many visitors make day trips down from Stockholm just to visit the famous glassworks such as Orrefors, but the province has so much more to offer than that. The province also is associated with elk, large forests, flowering meadows, and long stretches of *gädesgårdar,* characteristic local timber fences. There also are some 5,000 lakes teeming with fish.

Olaus Magnus wrote back in the 16th-century, "The forces of nature work in a more secretive and wonderful way on Lake Vättern than they do anywhere else." The city of Jönköping lies on the southern shores of Lake Vättern (not to be confused with the even larger lake of Vänern). The towns along this lake are just as appealing to tourists as Kalmar and the glassworks. The best centers are Granna, Vadstena, and Motala.

The area formed by Vättern actually touches four provinces, not just Småland. Land of myth and legend, the lake is one of the oldest cultural areas in the north of Europe. The water here is so pure that some 400,000 people use it as their drinking water supply. Despite the clarity of its water, the lake is notorious for its unpredictability; many a ship now lies at the bottom.

Finally, and if time remains, you can visit Örebro, beyond Motala and 37½ miles north of lake Vättern. Örebro is Sweden's sixth most populous city, lying on the shores of Lake Hjalmaren, the country's fourth largest lake.

1 Kalmar

181 miles NE of Malmö, 68 miles E of Växjö, 254 miles S of Stockholm, 211 miles E of Gothenburg

A coastal town opposite the Baltic island of Öland, historic Kalmar contains Sweden's best preserved Renaissance castle (see below). Today a thriving commercial center, Kalmar still retains many 17th-century buildings and sea captain's houses, many clustered around the Stortoget in the center of town. The first large-scale Swedish emigration to America, more than 3 centuries ago, originated in Kalmar (and ended up in Wilmington, Delaware).

Historically, the town is forever linked to the Kalmar Union, the treaty that three northern crowns signed here in 1397 linking Denmark,

Norway, and Sweden into an ill-fated but united kingdom. Queen Margrethe of Denmark headed the union, which was dissolved in 1523.

ESSENTIALS

GETTING THERE   By Plane   Kalmar Airport (☎ 0480/758810) receives two to four daily flights from Stockholm, taking 50 minutes. The airport is 3 miles west of the town center.

By Train   Seven trains a day make the 6½-hour run between Stockholm and Kalmar. Eight daily trains arrive from Malmö, taking 3 hours and 20 minutes. Call ☎ 020/75-75-75.

By Bus   Three to seven buses a day come from Stockholm on the 7-hour trip. From Gothenburg, there is one bus on both Friday and Saturday, taking 6 hours. For information call ☎ 0200/21818.

By Car   From Stockholm, take E66 south.

VISITOR INFORMATION   The Kalmar Tourist Office, **Turism I Kalmarbygåden,** is located at Latmagatan 6 (☎ 0480/153-50; www.kalmar.se/turism), near the railway station right in the town center. The office is open in summer, daily 9am to 7pm; September through May, Monday through Saturday 9am to 5pm.

CASTLES, CATHEDRALS & MORE

Still surrounded by parts of its old fortified walls, the 17th-century New Town is a warren of cobblestone streets and market squares. This town was created in 1647 after a devastating fire that caused the townspeople to move away from the old town to create this newer town on Kvarnholmen.

Domkyrkan (Kalmar Cathedral). Stortorget. ☎ **048/123-00.** Free admission. Daily 8am–4pm. Bus: 1, 2, 7, or 9.

From the marketplace, you can wander over to Stortorget to visit the town's 17th-century cathedral. **Kalmar Cathedral** is the only one in Sweden without a bishop, but it still is an impressive building. It was designed in 1160 by Nichodemus Tessin the Elder in the Italian Renaissance style. Tessin had visited Rome and had found inspiration there. The light, massive space of the interior is a reminder that the cathedral was built when Sweden was one of the great European powers. The altar was designed by Tessin the Younger, and it shimmers with gold. It's surrounded by a series of sculptures called *Faith* and *Mercy.*

Kalmar Konstmuseum. Slottsvägen 1D. ☎ **0480/41-14-15.** Admission 40 SEK ($4.40) adults, 30 SEK ($3.30) children. Fri–Mon and Wed 11am–5pm, Tues and Thurs 11am–8pm. Bus: 1, 2, 7, or 9.

The Kalmar Museum of Art contains works by Swedish painters Anders Zorn and Carl Larsson, along with other masterpieces from the 19th century up to the present day. Special and theme exhibitions also are held in the gallery. Sketches and finished works by important Swedish designers are displayed in the design gallery.

Kalmar Läns Museum (Kalmar County Museum). Skeppsbrogatan 51. ☎ **0480/563-00.** Admission 50 SEK ($5.50) adults, free for children 17 and under. June 15–Aug 15, daily 10am–6pm; off-season, Mon–Fri 10am–4pm, Sat–Sun 11am–4pm. Bus: 1, 2, 7, or 9.

The county museum's exhibits are in an old mill along the harbor. One of its most interesting exhibits is of the royal ship *Kronan,* which sank in the Baltic Sea off the island of Öland during a battle against the Danes and the Dutch in 1676. Only 42 of the 840 men aboard survived. The museum is responsible for excavation at the wreck site. Objects found by the marine archaeologists—glass bottles, tin plates, nautical

ATTRACTIONS ●
Domkyrkan (Kalmar Cathedral) **3**
Kalmar Konstmuseum **9**
Kalmar Läns Museum
 (Kalmar County Museum) **6**
Kalmar Slott (Kalmar Castle) **7**

ACCOMMODATIONS ■
Calmar Stadhotell **4**
First Hotel Witt **5**
Flyghotellet Törneby Herrgård **10**
Frimurare Hotellet **1**
Kalmarsund Hotell **2**
Romantik Slottshotellet **8**
Scandic Hotel Kalmar **10**

instruments, a seaman's chest, and many old coins—are on display. In another exhibit, the museum recreates the world of Jenny Nyström, a native of Kalmar who went to Paris and became a famous artist. Models, reproductions, and original paintings evoke her world and art. Outside the exhibits is a cafe.

✪ **Kalmar Slott (Kalmar Castle).** Slottsvägen. ☎ **0480/451-490.** Admission 70 SEK ($7.70) adults, 30 SEK ($3.30) for children 7–16, free for children 6 and under. Daily 10am–6pm. Bus: 1, 2, 7, or 9.

Founded in the 12th century, this strategically situated castle once was called the key to Sweden, and it's the principal sight in town. It was here that the Danish Queen Margrethe of Denmark launched the Kalmar Union, uniting the crowns of Denmark, Norway, and Sweden. In the 16th century, under order of King Gustavus Vasa and two of his sons, Erik XIV and Johan III, this moated medieval fortress was transformed into a Renaissance palace. Be sure to see the restored castle chapel as well as the prison for women, which was in use in the 18th and 19th centuries. English-language tours are conducted mid-June through mid-August, daily at 11am and 3pm. To get here, from the train station turn left on Tullbron.

SHOPPING

If you're searching for antiques, head for **Anderssons Antik,** Ölandsgatan 4 (☎ 0480/4741-62), or **Nostalgia Antik,** Esplanaden 6B (☎ 0480/188-09). For one of the best selections of ceramics and glassware, try **Noshörningen,** Olof Palmes gata 1 (☎ 0480/151-25). Another good selection is found at **Mats Nordell,** Milingsgatan 7 (☎ 0480/41-11-01). The town's best art gallery is **Arch Galleri,** Storgatan 57 (☎0480/42-05-80).

WHERE TO STAY

Kalmar offers an adequate range of accommodations, although many choose to stay on the island of Öland (see chapter 8).

The Kalmar Tourist Office (see above) can help you rent rooms in **private homes** for 270 SEK ($29.70) for a single and from 470 SEK ($51.70) for a double. Some of the private homes charge an additional 40 SEK ($4.40) for sheets, and perhaps 40 SEK ($4.40) for breakfast, if it's available at all—everything depends on the whim of the individual owner.

EXPENSIVE

✪ **Romantik Slottshotellet.** Slottsvägen 7, S-392 23 Kalmar. ☎ **0480/882-60.** Fax 0480/ 882-66. www.romantikhotels.com/kalmar. E-mail: romantikhotel@slottshotellet.se. 36 units. 1,325–1,450 SEK ($145.75–$159.50) double. Often weekend reductions. Rates include breakfast. AE, DC, MC, V. Free parking. Bus: 1, 2, 7, or 9.

In the center of Kalmar, close to the castle, this hotel wins as a traditional, nostalgic favorite. A gracious old house on a tranquil street, facing a waterfront park, it lies an easy walk from the train station. Each of the bedrooms has a different style of decoration and furnishing, with touches such as wallpapered walls, wooden floors, old-fashioned chandeliers, or brass or wood headboards reminiscent of a country house in England. Rooms vary widely in shape and style, but all are equipped with comfortable beds and average-size bathrooms. Everything is kept spotlessly clean. The hotel consists of both a main building from 1864 along with three annexes. Even the annexes have charming rooms. Breakfast is served in the pavilion, and on winter evenings tea and coffee are offered in the lounge. The hotel also offers facilities for those who want to cook their own meals. In summer, full restaurant service is offered on the terrace; otherwise only breakfast is served. There also is access to a sauna and solarium.

MODERATE

✪ **Calmar Stadhotell.** Stortorget 14, S-392 32 Kalmar. ☎ **0480/496-900.** Fax 0480/ 496-918. 143 units. MINIBAR TV TEL. June 6–Aug 2 and Fri–Sat year-round, 795 SEK ($87.45) double; rest of year, 1,190 SEK ($130.90) double. AE, DC, MC, V. Parking 95 SEK ($10.45). Bus: 1, 2, 7, or 9.

Located on the main square in the heart of the city, the Calmar Stadhotell was built in 1906. It still retains its romanticized architecture, with gables and a bell tower overlooking the cathedral, close to the train station. In 1999 a major renovation was completed, and the hotel now looks better than ever, with many of its original art nouveau touches still in place. Cut-glass chandeliers and even a library give the aura of a rich private home. Modular bathrooms with hair dryers are adjoined by large bedrooms (among the most spacious in town) with bedside controls; extremely good, firm mattresses; feather pillows and duvets; hardwood floors; and distinctive built-in furniture. Half the accommodations contain data ports, and some are no-smoking. Both Swedish and international dishes are served in the hotel's dining areas; and O'Keeffe's, the hotel pub, is among the most popular in town. There's also a nightclub open on weekends.

First Hotel Witt. Södra Långgatan 42. S-391 22 Kalmar. ☎ **0480/15250.** Fax 0480/ 15265. www.firsthotels.com. 112 units. TV TEL. Mid-June to Aug and Fri–Sun year-round, 799–899 SEK ($87.90–$98.90) double; rest of year, 1,299–1,499 SEK ($142.90–$164.90) double. Rates include breakfast. AE, DC, MC, V. Parking free on street, 95 SEK ($10.45) in hotel garage. Bus: 1, 2, or 3.

Although the foundations and some of the inner walls of this hotel date from the 1600s, most of what you'll see, both inside and out, dates from the 1970s, when what remained of the decrepit original was rebuilt and reconfigured. In 1997, bedrooms were renovated and furnished with conservatively dignified and very appealing furniture, new paint jobs, hardwood floors, and in some cases, good copies of oriental carpets. In addition to appealing to the average traveler—often couples or business people—the hotel designer planned some units especially for female travelers, families, persons with disabilities, and those with allergies. Rooms are generous in size, with attractive styling and excellent bathrooms containing hair dryers. Views usually extend out over Kalmar Sound, and the hotel's position in the heart of the old town is extremely convenient to virtually everything in the center. There's a well-conceived restaurant on the premises serving Swedish and international food, and a dark and cozy bar. There's also a sauna and solarium in the basement, and the largest and most attractive swimming pool of any hotel in Kalmar.

Kalmarsund Hotell. Fiskaregatan 5, S-392 32 Kalmar. ☎ **0480/181-00.** Fax 048/41-13-37. www.kalmarsundhotell.se. E-mail:infokalmarsund@swedenhotels.se. 85 units. MINIBAR TV TEL. Mon–Thurs 1,390–1,450 SEK ($152.90–$159.50) double; 1,775 SEK ($195.25) suite. Fri–Sun 790 SEK ($86.90) double; 990 SEK ($108.90) suite. Rates include breakfast. AE, DC, MC, V. Bus: 3.

Set in the heart of Kalmar, near the railway station, this hotel originated in 1982 when a 40-year-old complex of shops and offices was transformed into the well-maintained, well-managed hotel you see today. The staff here is responsible and motivated, and bedrooms are snug, modern, cozy, and nicely decorated with conservative modern furniture, including good beds. Bathrooms are functional and usually tiled. There's an attractive restaurant, Fiskarejatan Kroj, which is recommended separately (see below), and a bar. There's also a sauna, a health club with a bubbling whirlpool, and a series of convention facilities.

Scandic Hotel Kalmar. Dragonvagen 7, S-392 39 Kalmar. ☎ **0480/469-300.** Fax 0480/469-311. www.scandichotels.com. E-mail: kalmar@scandichotels.com. 148 units. TV TEL. June 25–Aug 8 and Fri–Sat year-round, 690 SEK ($75.90) double; rest of year, 1,375 SEK ($151.25) double. Rates include breakfast. AE, DC, MC, V. Free parking.

Comfortable, conservative, and well managed, this hotel is a low-rise two-story building erected in the 1970s and located about 1½ miles west of Kalmar's central core. The bedrooms are modern, clean, and outfitted with good beds. Although small, bathrooms are equipped with adequate shelf space and hair dryers.

INEXPENSIVE

Flyghotellet Törneby Herrgård. Flottiljvägen 9, S-392 41 Kalmar. ☎ **0480/200-24.** Fax 0480/202-24. 18 units. TV TEL. Sun–Thurs 1,095 SEK ($120.45) double; Fri–Sat 795 SEK ($87.45) double. Rates include breakfast. MC, V. Bus: 2.

This stately hotel lies on 3 acres of verdant parkland, near clear springs and streams, 3 miles west of Kalmar, a 1-minute drive from the airport. Although there has been an inn on this site since 1616, the elegantly symmetrical building you'll see today dates from the 1870s, when it was constructed as a manor house in a style similar to the classical ruins of Pompeii. Inside, Dagmar and Agneta Herlin have decorated their hotel and home with a roster of worthy antiques and color schemes that are almost universally pink-toned or salmon. There's a restaurant on the premises that's open to residents of the hotel at both lunch and dinner. Fixed-price menus cost from 160 and 220 SEK ($17.60 and $24.20); expect well-prepared, generous portions based on

French and Swedish traditions and lots of personal culinary flair. Bedrooms are cozy, well maintained, and charming.

Frimurare Hotellet. Larmtorget 2. S-392 Kalmar. ☎ **0480/15230.** Fax 0480/85887. www.frimurarehotell.et.gs2.com. E-mail: frimurarehotellet@kalmar.mail.telia.com. 34 units. MINIBAR TV TEL. June–Aug and Fri–Sat year-round, 770 SEK ($84.70) double; rest of year, 1,060 SEK ($116.60) double. Rates include breakfast. AE, DC, MC, V. Bus: 2.

One of the most visible and centrally located hotels in Kalmar, Frimurare Hotellet occupies a prominent site at the corner of the main square, in a richly detailed Italianate building that was constructed in 1875 as a headquarters for the local branch of the Freemasons. Today, after extensive renovations that were completed in the mid-1990s, the two lowest floors of the three-story building are devoted to a comfortable, cozy hotel; the uppermost, most stately floor is still the domain of the Freemasons, one of Kalmar's most active social and charitable organizations. Bedrooms are well maintained and in most cases, have high ceilings and appealingly formal furnishings, including firm mattresses. There's a copious breakfast buffet included in the room price and an in-house sauna.

WHERE TO DINE

Byttan Restaurant. Slottsvägen 1. ☎ **0480/163-60.** Reservations recommended in summer. Fixed-price lunch 65 SEK ($7.15); main courses 95–350 SEK ($10.45–$38.50). AE, DC, MC, V. June–Aug, daily 11am–midnight; Dec–May, daily 11am–2:30pm. Closed Sept–Nov. SWEDISH.

In the city park near the base of the castle, a 10-minute walk south of the town center, is one of the best spots for dining in Kalmar. From a terraced pavilion overlooking the water, you can sample one of the many soups Byttan Restaurant specializes in; they, too, are some of the best in town. Examples include cream of lobster and cream of mushroom. Main courses range from omelets to filet of beef with red wine sauce and forest mushrooms. Other dishes that might tantalize your palate include veal steak in a pepper-flavored cream sauce; sliced tenderloin of pork with red wine and herb sauce; and our all-time favorite here, salmon with a Riesling sauce (you also can order it with butter sauce). Guests may dine in the pavilion or in the vine-covered courtyard. The food is good and attractively prepared, and even if you don't come for a meal, the restaurant is a good place to have afternoon tea.

In 1994, the restaurant was enlarged with the addition of a bistro-inspired annex known as Däcket. Outfitted with wood paneling and shades of pale green, in summer it serves the same menu, during the same hours, as the main dining area. In winter, however, it features a simpler menu costing about 15% less than in the main dining area.

✪ **Kalmar Hamn Krog.** Skeppsbrogatan 30. ☎ **0480/411-020.** Reservations required. Main courses 240 SEK ($26.40); fixed-price lunch 70 SEK ($7.70); fixed-priced dinner 230 SEK ($25.30). AE, MC, V. Mon–Fri 11:30am–2pm; Mon–Sat 6–10pm. INTERNATIONAL.

Established in 1988, this quickly became the most stylish and gastronomically sophisticated restaurant in Kalmar, and it remains so today. Traditionally Kalmar Hamn Krog is the site of celebratory meals and anniversary parties—it's that special. The restaurant was built from scratch on an old pier where steamships used to deposit passengers from the neighboring island of Öland. Today, the interior is all blue and white. The kitchen slaves away to keep the restaurant's high-ranking position in Kalmar, and the products that go into the cuisine are the best in the city. Recommended dishes include pork filet with a port wine sauce or the grilled halibut with a dill and lemongrass stew. We also are especially fond of the filet of pike-perch in a sweet-and-sour curry sauce. One unusual specialty is the grilled steak with piña colada sauce. The latter gives the meat a scent of coconut-flavored rum and a hint of the tropics—most unusual in these northern climes. The wines are from Austria, the United States, and France, among other countries.

Restaurant Fiskarejatan Kroj. In the Kalmarsund Hotell, Fiskaregatan 5. ☎ **0480/ 181-00.** Reservations recommended. Main courses 100–250 SEK ($11–$27.50). AE, DC, MC, V. Mon–Sat 5–10pm. SEAFOOD.

This restaurant specializes in the freshest of Swedish seafood, usually hauled in that morning from the nearby Baltic. If you don't like fish, the chef usually prepares a limited array of veal, chicken, and beef dishes, each well seasoned and served in generous portions. Perfectly prepared examples include salmon with a balsamic and herb-flavored vinaigrette, baked cod with braised potatoes and dill, grilled turbot with a beurre-blanc (white butter) sauce, and North Atlantic lobster, when it's available. The intimate, wood-paneled space lined with temperature-controlled racks of wine makes for a cozy dining experience.

Salut. Storgatan 10. ☎ **0480/870-87.** Reservations recommended. Fixed-price lunch 54 SEK ($5.95); main courses 58–170 SEK ($6.40–$18.70). AE, DC, MC, V. Daily 11am–11pm. Bus 1, 7, or 9. SWEDISH/CONTINENTAL.

This is our favorite middle-bracket bistro in Kalmar, with enough variety to please any palate, reasonable prices, and a refreshing lack of pretensions. It consists of two separate dining rooms, one brick lined and designated for smokers and another with wallpaper and oil paintings that's reserved for nonsmokers. An attentive staff offers dishes that include at least a half-dozen kinds of pasta, including vegetarian pastas, seafood pastas, and one version with strips of grilled steak and gorgonzola sauce. Also look for grilled salmon with saffron sauce, grilled steaks with your choice of at least four different sauces, filets of sole with white wine sauce, and a dessert specialty of deep-fried camembert with hot cloudberry preserves. Meals are prepared with fresh ingredients whenever available, and no sauce or spice overwhelms the natural flavor. The food is consistently generous and well prepared.

KALMAR AFTER DARK

If a major cultural event is being staged, its likely venue is the local concert hall: **KalmarSalen,** Skeppsbrogatan 49 (☎ **0480/42 10 00**). Otherwise, most of the nighttime activity centers around **Lärmtorget 7** (☎ **0480/265-50**) or **UnderBar,** Lärmtorget 4 (☎ **0480/143-23**). Both are bars and offer no live entertainment.

2 Växjö

68 miles W of Kalmar, 275 miles S of Stockholm

Sweden's "Kingdom of Crystal" starts in Växjö, the central community for all of Småland. Some 16 factories here produce world-renowned Swedish crystal. The name Växjö comes from *Vägsjön,* or "lake where the roads meet." In addition to glassworks, this 14th-century city offers scenic lakes and forests, and traditional red-timbered cottages.

ESSENTIALS

GETTING THERE   By Plane   There are three daily flights between Stockholm and Växjö, arriving at the Växjö Airport, 5½ miles north of the center. For flight information, call ☎ **0470/759-210.**

By Train   There are train connections from Gothenburg, leaving at 8am daily and arriving in Växjö at 11:16am; from Malmö, leaving at 9am and arriving in Växjö at 3:16pm.

Trains arrive hourly throughout the day from Kalmar. Call ☎ **020/757575.**

By Bus   From Stockholm, buses leave on Friday and Saturday (take SJ Buss) at 2pm and arrive in Växjö at 8:55pm. Call ☎ **0200/21818.**

By Car   From Stockholm, take E4 south to Norrköping, then continue south along E66 to Kalmar. At Kalmar, head west on Route 25.

VISITOR INFORMATION   The **Växjö Tourist Information Office,** located at Kungsgatan 11 (☎ **0470/414-10**), is open mid-June to mid-August, Monday through Friday from 9am to 6pm and on Saturday from 10am to 2pm; Sunday 11am to 3pm; off-season, Monday through Friday from 9:30am to 4pm.

SEEING THE SIGHTS

In summer, between mid-June and late August, tours on Lake Helgåsjön are conducted aboard the century-old steamer **S/S *Angaren Thor,*** which reigns as one of the oldest wood-fired steamships in Scandinavia today. Don't expect state-of-the-art hardware aboard this ship, as part of the allure derives from old-fashioned brass fittings and a maritime dowdiness that is rapidly on the way to achieving high camp. A 2½-hour tour costs 100 SEK ($11); a 3½-hour tour, which usually includes some kind of food, goes for 220 SEK ($24.20). Other tours to more distant parts of the lake are arbitrarily scheduled, and are canceled and reactivated according to the weather, prior bookings, and the whim of the owners. For information and reservations, inquire at the local tourist office.

Småland Museum. Södra Järnvägsgatan 2. ☎ **0470/70-42-00.** Admission 40 SEK ($4.40) adults, free for those 19 and under. June–Aug, Tues–Fri 10am–5pm, Sat–Sun 11am–5pm; Sept–May, Tues–Fri 10am–5pm, Sat–Sun 11am–5pm. Bus: 4.

Established in 1792, this is the oldest provincial museum in Sweden. Located near the railroad station, it will give you a better sense of the area. Since 1996, the museum has been much improved and enlarged, with a new wing focusing on the history of Swedish glassmaking. You'll see tools and archives from the early days of the craft, with a special collection of more than 25,000 pieces. In a separate exhibit are displays of the finest artistic examples of Swedish glass produced over the centuries. In other areas of the museum you can view one of Sweden's largest coin collections, art exhibits, religious objects, weapons, and a special room housing an ethnological collection. Forestry and agricultural exhibits also are included.

Svenska Emigrantinstitutet (House of Emigrants). Museiparken. ☎ **0470/201-20.** Admission 40 SEK ($4.40). June–Aug, Mon–Fri 9am–6pm, Sat 11am–4pm, Sun 11am–4pm; Sept–May, Mon–Fri 9am–4pm, Sat–Sun 11am–4pm. Bus: 4.

This institution, founded in 1968, documents the 1.3 million Swedish people who left their homeland during the "America fever" years, the 1850s to the 1920s, and moved to the United States. The house contains exhibits on emigrant history as well as archives and a research library. A permanent exhibition, the *Dream of America,* presents insights into the background and consequences of the emigration. Minnesota Day is a folk festival held the second Sunday in August each year, drawing thousands of Swedes and Swedish-Americans.

Växjö Cathedral. Linnégatan. ☎ **0470/296-80.** Free admission. May–Sept, daily 8am–7pm; Oct–Apr, daily 8am–4pm. Bus: 4.

Legend has it that this cathedral stands on the spot where St. Sigfrid (Småland's missionary from York, England, in the 11th century) erected his little wooden church. The cathedral has copper-clad towers and a bright interior and its chimes are heard three times a day. Summer concerts are held in the cathedral on Thursday at 8pm.

Växjö

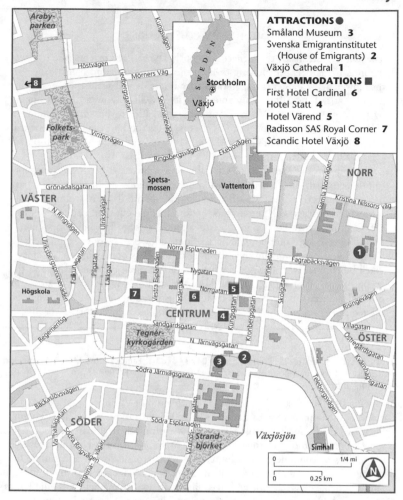

ATTRACTIONS ●
Småland Museum **3**
Svenska Emigrantinstitutet
(House of Emigrants) **2**
Växjö Cathedral **1**
ACCOMMODATIONS ■
First Hotel Cardinal **6**
Hotel Statt **4**
Hotel Värend **5**
Radisson SAS Royal Corner **7**
Scandic Hotel Växjö **8**

Adjacent to the cathedral is **Linnéparken** (LinnéPark), named for Carl von Linné (Carolus Linnaeus), the Swedish botanist who developed the scientific categories of plants. In the park, an arboretum displays 24 categories of perennials. There also are other flower gardens throughout and a playground for children. The cathedral is in the town center, by **Linnéparken.**

SHOPPING IN THE KINGDOM OF CRYSTAL

Between Kalmar and Växhö, within an hour's drive, are several glassworks, including **Orrefors** and **Kosta Boda.** Kosta Glassworks and Boda Glassworks have been the leading names in Swedish crystal since the 19th century. However, they have pooled their resources to become "Kosta Boda," and now operate as one empire, although many of their original glassworks still maintain a separate identity. Not only can you go on Sweden's grandest shopping trip, but you can see master glassblowers—among the world's finest—at work.

Buying Swedish Glass

The temperature inside the furnace is 2,066°F. The gatherer reaches into its flaming interior, gathers the glowing melt on the blowing iron and hands it over to the blower. The caramel-soft material sizzles as it is shaped against wet newsprint in the hands of the gaffer. Only an expert's touch will do now, a touch schooled by years of experience. When it's time for the gaffer to put the handle on a pitcher, he has to "see" how hot the glass is. If it's too hot, the attachment will run off or go through. If it's too cold, it will be impossible to attach. Hand-blown glass is a living craft, born in the hands of glass workers.

Shopping in the Kingdom of Crystal is one of Sweden's best tourism opportunities, especially if you keep the following points in mind: An average purchase can save you as much as 75% off stateside prices—and if you're willing to settle for seconds or glass with certain flaws, you can come out even better. Even if it is flawed, the glassware sold in the area is much superior to what you are likely to find in your local shopping mall back home. However, before heading here it's always best to do some advance scouting of the glass outlets in Stockholm, so you'll be familiar with the prices when you arrive. Seek out the red tags in the Växjö outlets; they signal that the glass has been greatly reduced in price for quick clearance. You can always look for special promotional deals that might be offered at any time of the year, depending on an outlet's inventory.

Åfors Glasbruk. Route 25, Eriksmala. ☎ **0471/41814.** Factory tours Mon–Fri 6am–3pm (you must call for an appointment first). Factory shop Mon–Fri 9am–6pm, Sat 9am–4pm, Sun noon–4pm.

At a point 18 miles west of Nybro and 31 miles south of Växjö, Åfors is a Kosta Boda glassworks, the domain of glass designers Bertil Vallien and his wife, Ulrica Hydman-Vallien, two of the most famous names in Swedish glass. It also is the showcase of Gunnel Sahlin, who often brings experiences of nature into the blowing room with her. She likes to combine contrasting elements, soft round forms, and simple lines, silky smooth surfaces and bright, brilliant color. Bertil Vallien is known for his stout Château Bohème glasses, rustic and masculine with a satisfying heft. His wife Ulrica's work is simple and clean, using strong colors. This place is especially popular with Christmas shoppers, as it is known for its ornaments.

✪ **Boda Glasbruk.** Storgatan (Hwy. 25). ☎ **0481/42410.** Free admission. Daily 9am–4pm. Bus: 218 from Lessebo, which has rail links to Växjö.

Although the Boda Glassworks (founded in 1864) long ago merged its administration with that of the Kosta Glassworks, this is the showroom for production of the Boda division of the conglomerate. Playful, even cheeky design is given free rein at Boda. Designers make wine glasses that dance, salad bowls that evoke the sweet smells of summer, and vases in which you can hear whispers of the jungle. The glass innovators here love to goad your senses and are never afraid to test the limits of their material. Sometimes glass might be combined with iron; at other times decorated with feathers! Located in the village of Boda, about 12 miles west of Nybro, it offers a discounted collection of seconds. Their flaws are almost imperceptible, but their prices are substantially lower than normal retail for more perfect pieces.

Bumps, discoloration, nicks, and bubbles are the most common faults in "seconds," but sometimes they are virtually unnoticeable except to a trained eye. Ask a factory if it's selling any discontinued styles. These products are invariably marked down for quick clearance. If you're a collector, you no doubt already know that a signed piece of art glass has value whereas an unsigned piece does not. Before leaving the store, make absolutely certain that the piece of glass you purchased (obviously not art glass) can go into the dishwasher. If it can't you'll have to wash the glass by hand. Detergents can cause glass to lose some of its luster.

If you're a light shopper, you can hand carry your purchases back on the plane, providing they are carefully wrapped. You also can have the store ship your glass home for you. On certain items, assuming you're getting a bargain, the cost of glass purchased in the "kingdom" can still be about 50% cheaper in Sweden than in the United States, even when shipping costs are added. As a rule, shipping costs equal about 30% of the marked price on the item. If your glass arrives broken, take a picture of the damaged merchandise and send it with a letter along with a copy of your receipt to the factory at which you made the purchase. All breakage is replaced.

Finally, count on visiting no more than six to eight outlets per day. Pick up a map at the tourist office in Växjö and devise your attack plan from that.

✪ **Kosta Glasbruk.** Hwy. 28. ☎ **0478/345-00.** Late June–early Aug, Mon–Fri 9am–6pm, Sat 9am–4pm, Sun 11am–4pm; off-season, Mon–Fri 9am–6pm, Sat 10am–4pm, Sun noon–4pm. Located between Eriksmala and the junction with Route 31, 12 miles east of Orrefors.

This main headquarters of the Kosta complex was founded in 1742 by two former generals, Anders Koskull and Georg Bogislaus Stael von Holstein, who at first brought in glass-blowing talent from Bohemia, then the reigning kingdom of crystal. Kosta pioneered the production of crystal, which must, by law, contain about one-fourth oxide. Here you can see the old Kosta Museum, with articles from the 18th and 19th centuries as well as exhibitions of contemporary glass. Despite Kosta's merger with the nearby Boda Glassworks, this original entity retains much of its separate identity. The best buys here are on items that have been discontinued. Artists here tell us they get their inspiration from about anything—the dew on a meadow, the morning mist on a lake, or a Swedish summer sky.

Målerås Glasbruk. Route 31, 9 miles NW of Orrefors. ☎ **0481/311-00.** Free admission. Mon–Fri 10am–6pm, Sat 10am–4pm, Sun 11am–4pm.

Set within a 10-minute drive from Orrefors (see below), this factory belongs to one of the few independent glassmakers still left in the glass district, the Målerås company. Much of their production revolves around the engravings of master artisan Mats Jonasson, whose trademark involves vivid images that are a bit less formal than those produced by competing (larger) manufacturers. Vivid images, such as a Dalmatian pup, his eyes glowing with mischief, are captured in the clearest of crystal, as well as images of flora and fauna. Especially intriguing here is the Black Magic collection, bowls in dramatic black glass with a sandblasted rim. The effect has been likened to one of Småland's deep forest ponds. After careful inspection of the seconds here, we could find no flaws, but the designer could—hence the reduced prices. Prices here are about half what you'd pay for similar purchases in Stockholm.

Orrefors Glasbruk. Rte. 31, Orrefors. ☎ **9481/341-995.** Free admission. June–July, Mon–Sat 9am–4pm, Sat 10am–4pm, Sun 11am–4pm; Aug–May, Mon–Fri 10am–noon and 1–4:30pm.

Orrefors, between Nybro and Lenhovda, 25 miles west of Kalmar, is one of the most famous names in Swedish glass. Guided tours are conducted Monday through Friday from 9:30am to 2:30pm any time someone shows up. During most of the year a visit incorporates tours of divisions that include glassblowers, cutters, and engravers of fine glass. In July, the cutters and engravers are on vacation, although demonstrations of glassblowing are still available. It's possible to purchase seconds (in most cases, hardly distinguishable from perfect pieces) and gift shipments can be arranged. Tax-free shopping also can be arranged in the factory's shop.

Although a handful of Orrefor subsidiaries (Sandvik and Strömbergshyttan) also offer tours of their factories, the most complete and comprehensive tours are presented by Orrefors. The best plan may be to tour Orrefors first, and then to inquire about specialized tours of the company's subsidiaries.

Studioglas Strömbergshyttan. Hovmantorp. ☎ **0478/310-75.** Free admission. Mon–Fri 9am–4pm, Sat 10am–4pm, Sun noon–4pm.

Lying 19 miles east of Växjö, reached along Route 25, is the domain of three master blowers: Håkan Gunnarsson, Leif Persson, and Mikael Axenbrandt. The trio started this studio in 1987 with a determination to experiment to the limits. The three glassblowers give their own creativity free rein in front of the furnace, creating dishes, vases, and decorative pieces with an utterly free approach to the glowing melt. Colors are brilliant and freely combined. Look also for Anna Örnberg's work, which has a youthful audacity, often a warm sense of humor, as her vases and small bowls are bursting with joy. For example, Anna puts pouting lips on fruit-colored fish vases that balance on their tail fins. The best days to visit are Monday and Wednesday, when you can see more artisans at work.

THE WORLD'S OLDEST WORKING PAPER MILL

Lessebo Papermill. Hwy. 25, Lessbro. ☎ **0771/110000.** Free admission. Mon–Fri 7am–4pm.

In the heart of the glassworks district, the small town of Lessebo on Route 25, lying 22 miles west of Orrefors, has as its major attraction this paper mill, the world's oldest working producer of handmade paper. In existence since 1693, the mill is open to the public so you can watch as paper passes through the various stages, from cotton pulp to individual sheets that are pressed and hung to dry. There's a gift shop where you can purchase handmade products, and tours are available in English, costing 150 SEK ($16.50) for anywhere from 1 to 30 persons. You should call in advance and make arrangements if you want a formal tour; however, most visitors just show up, collect the English-language pamphlets, stroll around the property, drop into the gift shop, and ask questions of the friendly, polite staff, most of whom speak English.

WHERE TO STAY

First Hotel Cardinal. Bäckgatan 10, S-352 30 Växjö. ☎ **0470/722800.** Fax 0470/722808. www.firsthotels.com. 70 units. TV TEL. July–Aug and Fri–Sat year-round, 695 SEK ($76.45) double; rest of year, 1,195–1,549 SEK ($131.45–$170.40) double. Rates include breakfast. AE, DC, MC, V. Parking 72 SEK ($7.90).

This appealing, traditionally decorated hotel rising four floors above the main street (Storgatan) of town provides four-star service to a clientele that includes lots of business travelers. In the late 1980s, the owners of this hotel radically renovated a turn-of-the-century apartment building and then restored the entire property in 1997. Bedrooms are well upholstered and decorated with more formality than you may have expected, in some cases with oriental carpets and under the eaves, a scattering of exposed timbers and beams. Beds are especially comfortable, often with hypoallergenic bedcoverings. Bathrooms are medium size and come equipped with hair dryers.

Dining: The formal and elegant Restaurant Cardinal is open only Monday through Friday. A fixed-price lunch costs 70 SEK ($7.70), whereas à la carte dinners average from around 200 SEK ($22) each.

Amenities: Exercise room, sauna, solarium, and conference facilities.

Hotel Statt. Kungsgatan 6, S-351 04 Växjö. ☎ **0470/134-00.** Fax 0470/448-37. www.scandichotels.com. 130 units. TV TEL. June 19–Aug 9 and Fri–Sun year-round, 750 SEK ($82.50) double; rest of year, 1,365 SEK ($150.15) double. Rates include breakfast. AE, DC, MC, V. Free parking. Bus: 4.

This venerable old hostelry has, after several restorations, become a choice place to stay, successfully combining the old and the new. Bedrooms have a bit of style and flair, often done with hardwood floors, superb mattresses, and a homelike feeling with oriental carpeting. Bathrooms are larger than average and often luxuriously appointed—some with a Jacuzzi, each with a hair dryer. The hotel's pleasant restaurant is outfitted like a rustic Swedish tavern, with strong, dark colors and a traditional menu of *husmanskost* (country cooking). Windows can be opened for gusts of fresh air. You might precede your meal with a pint of ale in O'Keeffe's pub or in a somewhat more formal cocktail bar. On the premises are an exercise room and sauna.

Hotell Värend. Kungsgatan 27, S-352 33 Växjö. ☎ **0470/104-85.** Fax 0470/362-61. www.ditthotell.com/varend. 30 units. TV TEL. July and Fri–Sat year-round, 495 SEK ($54.45) double; rest of year, 795 SEK ($87.45) double. Rates include breakfast. AE, DC, MC, V. Free parking.

Under the management of a hardworking family, the Wadsworths, this hotel emerged from the premises of what originally was built as a four-unit apartment house in the 1890s. Richly renovated and upgraded in 1996, but with very few of its original architectural adornments, the hotel lies just a 5-minute walk north of Växjö's main square, within a quiet residential neighborhood filled with private homes. Good-size bedrooms are clean, tasteful, simple, and well insulated against the harsh winters of central Sweden—safe havens for a cost-effective night or two. The beds are very comfortable and the bathrooms, though small, are beautifully maintained.

Radisson SAS Royal Corner. Liedbergsgatan 11, S-352 32 Växjö. ☎ **800/528-1234** in the U.S., or 0470/701000. Fax 0470/126-44. www.radissonsas.com. 154 units. TV TEL. Sun–Thurs 1,295–1,495 SEK ($142.45–$164.45) double; Fri–Sat 775 SEK ($85.25) double. All week long, 1,600 SEK ($176) suite. AE, DC, MC V. Free parking. Bus: 4.

In the town center, this first-class hotel rises six floors, taller than any other structure in town. The view from the upper floors offers panoramic vistas of Småland. Built in 1985 and well kept up, the hotel evokes a good American hotel with its standardized bedrooms, each outfitted in a functional style with Nordic pieces. Rooms are only slightly larger than average and all have good firm mattresses in the ample-size beds. Bathrooms are small but are beautifully maintained with shower stalls and hair dryers. Light meals are served in the hotel's cafe, and there is a nightclub-like first-class restaurant serving more formal Swedish regional specialties along with international dishes. There's a mini pool, along with a sauna and whirlpool.

Scandic Hotel Växjö. Hejaregatan 19, S-352 46 Växjö. ☎ **0470/736-000.** Fax 0470/ 736011. 106 units. TV TEL. Sun–Thurs 1,375 SEK ($151.25) double; Fri–Sat 680 SEK ($74.80) double. Rates include breakfast. AE, DC, MC, V. Free parking. Bus: 4.

One of the best-value hotels in Växjö, built in 1979, the Scandic offers well-furnished bedrooms, including some large enough for families. Each room is fitted in bright shades of blue, green, or pink and yellow, with good beds and small but well-maintained bathrooms. There's a restaurant and a self-service cafeteria, along with a small indoor swimming pool and a sauna. The hotel lies 2 miles west of the center of town on the road going to the airport.

WHERE TO DINE

Throughout the environs of Växjö and Orrefors, you'll find lots of separate and independent restaurant options, but one of the most enduring dining traditions involves an age-old method of cooking fish, potatoes, and sausages in the cooling chambers of the glassworks. Inaugurated during an era when fuel was conserved with something approaching religious zeal, the tradition, known as *Hyttsill,* developed into a slow-cooking method that made simple, hearty food particularly succulent, especially to hungry factory workers toiling in the cold.

This antique presentation is duplicated today as part of randomly scheduled evening entertainment provided by three of the region's biggest glassmakers. After the day's closing of some of the factories, usually around 3pm, trestle tables and simple chairs are carried onto the factory floor as a means of duplicating the simple communal meals of long ago. During the summer months, the large glassworks usually rotate the days and hours of their presentations.

Advance reservations are necessary, and per-person fees average 300 SEK ($33) for a full meal, with schnapps and beer an additional 30 to 40 SEK ($3.30 to $4.40) per glass. The meals invariably include such traditional glassmakers' dishes as herring with cream and onions, roasted or baked potatoes (traditionally these were baked in the hot ashes produced as a byproduct of the firing process); pork sausages, mustard, bread and butter, local cheeses, and cheesecake.

As part of the package, the organizers of these events usually include live musical entertainment and demonstrations of glassblowing. Be warned in advance that this is very much a movable feast. Even during the peak of midsummer, there's likely to be only about three of them scheduled during any week; during the winter, they might occur only once a month as a specially arranged group event that individuals can attend if they reserve a spot in advance. To be certain of getting a place, phone each of the glassworks individually, or phone any of the tourist offices within the area, for information and confirmations. For information and reservations for a meal served within the floor, call the **Kosta Glassworks** at ☎ **0478/34529;** the **Bergdala Glassworks** at ☎ **0478/31650;** or the **Orrefors Glassworks** at ☎ **0481/341995.**

Orrefors Inn. Hwy. 22, Orrefors. ☎ **0481/300-59.** Main courses 60–150 SEK ($6.60–$16.50); fixed-price menu 75 SEK ($8.25). AE, DC, MC, V. Mid-Oct to mid-Mar, Mon–Fri 10am–3:30pm, Sat 7am–4pm, Sun noon–4pm; mid-Mar to mid-Oct, Mon–Fri 9am–5pm, Sat 11am–5pm, Sun noon–4pm. SWEDISH.

Set in the center of the cluster of glass factories that have always dominated the economy of Orrefors, this historic inn was established in 1898 within four dining rooms of a wood-sided building that remains very similar to the original. You might imagine yourself in a rustic farmhouse, dining on a menu that's unrelentingly Swedish and in many ways authentic to the cuisine that many locals remember from childhood. Menu items include grilled salmon or steak served on a wooden platter; Swedish meatballs with brown sauce and roasted potatoes; and local moose steak with forest mushrooms and boiled potatoes. Don't expect the grand or experimental cuisine you might look for in Stockholm; instead, you'll get rib-sticking fare that can perk you up for a round of glass shopping at any of the nearby gift shops.

3 Jönköping

217 miles SW of Stockholm, 93 miles NE of Gothenburg, 124 miles NE of Helsingborg

At the southern rim of Lake Vättern, this is the lake's largest town. It once was famous for manufacturing matchsticks, and the original factory from the 1840s still stands, although the product is no longer made. However, a fascinating cultural area has been built up around the match museum. It's called the Tändsticksområdet, or "matchstick area."

Pronounced *yun-shurp-ing*, Jönköping is one of the oldest trading centers in Sweden, left over from the Middle Ages when it was granted its town charter in 1284. In the 19th century, the town was virtually synonymous with the matchstick used all over Europe and the local merchants became prosperous. However, in 1932, when demand had dwindled drastically, the local match tycoon, Ivar Kruger, shot himself rather than face bankruptcy. The end to the industry came shortly thereafter.

Today, a thriving town of some 52,000 people, Jönköping is a good base for exploring some of the more interesting points along the southern tier of Lake Vättern.

ESSENTIALS

GETTING THERE   By Train   At least two of the trains routed to Jönköping from Stockholm are direct and don't require any transfers en route. Otherwise, there's service from Stockholm every other hour throughout the day, with transfers required en route in the railway junction at Nässgö. Travel time from Stockholm by train, depending on transfers, takes about 3½ hours. From Kalmar, there usually are three trains per day to Jönköping, with two transfers required en route. Travel time ranges, depending on connections, from 4 to 5 hours. For information and timetables, call ☎ 020/757575.

By Bus   Bus transfers to Jönköping are preferable to train transfers, as they're more frequent and in most cases, more direct. There's at least one bus an hour arriving from Stockholm throughout the day, with no changes required en route. The trip takes about 3½ hours. For bus information and timetables, call ☎ 0200/21818.

By Car   From Växjö, continue along Route 30 northwest, directly into Jönköping.

VISITOR INFORMATION   The Jönköping Turistbyrån is at Djurlakartorget (☎ 036/10-50-50). Open June through October, Monday through Friday 8am to 7pm, Saturday 9am to 1pm. Otherwise, hours are Monday through Friday 8am to 5pm and Saturday 9am to 1pm. On the Web, try www.jonkoping.se.

MATCHES & MORE

Built in 1844, the town's largest match factory today is the home of **Tändsticksmuséet,** Västra Storgatan 18 (☎ 036/10-55-43). The museum documents the industry that made Jönköping famous—everything from match-making machines to matchbox labels. Before Jönköping entered the industry, matches were extremely dangerous. Phosphorous was used on the striking head, which was both poisonous to the factory workers and dangerous in the box when the match heads were rubbed against each other. But in 1855, Johan Edvard Lundström of Jönköping invented the safety match, which used red amorphous phosphorus on the striking surface of the box itself. This invention revolutionized the industry. A video is shown documenting the town's former industry. From May through August, hours are Monday through Friday from 10am to 5pm, Saturday and Sunday 11am to 3pm. From September through April, it is open Tuesday through Thursday noon to 4pm and Saturday and Sunday 11am to 3pm. Admission is 30 SEK ($3.30).

Another museum of note is **Jönköping Lans Museum,** Dag Hammarskjölds Plats (☎ **036/30-18-00**), the county museum that traces the history of Småland, often through archaeological digs. The history of the area is documented over the past 10,000 years. Exhibits extend into modern times as far as the invention of the sewing machine. There also is a collection of Swedish art, focusing mainly on the works of John Bauer, who became famous in Sweden for his Tolkienesque depictions of trolls and gnomes. Admission is 20 SEK ($2.20); free for ages 18 and under. Open daily 11am to 5pm.

Finally, **Friluftmuséet,** Stadsparken (☎ **036/105-428**), is an open-air museum in the town park. Interesting from an historical point of view, it exhibits numerous old Småland buildings—notably a cottage from the 17th century, and **Bäckabay Church,** whose oldest parts date from the 1580s. It is open only June through September, Monday through Friday 10am to 3pm and Saturday and Sunday 10am to 2pm, charging an admission of 45 SEK ($4.95).

WHERE TO STAY

Comfort Home Hotel Victoria. F. E. Elmgrens Gata 5, Box 173, S-551 13 Jönköping. ☎ **800/228-3323** in the U.S., or 036/71-28-00. Fax 035/71-50-50. www. victoriahome. com. E-mail: hotel@victoriahome.com. 90 units. TV TEL. Sun–Thurs 1,265–1,595 SEK ($139.15–$175.45) double; 1,995 SEK ($219.45) suite. Fri–Mon 695–895 SEK ($76.45–$98.45) double; 1,195 SEK ($131.45) suite. Rates include breakfast. AE, DC, MC, V. Parking 55 SEK ($6.05).

Set within the western sector of the town center, very close to the Västra Torget marketplace, this hotel evolved from the historic core of a once private, stately home that originally was built in 1885. In 1991, it was radically renovated and enlarged into a modern-day member of a nationwide chain. Despite this role as a member of a formula-based chain, it has an intelligent staff and really conveys a sense of intimacy. Some of the public areas retain their original architectural details, elaborate cove moldings, and rich panels; bedrooms tend to be conservatively and appealingly decorated, usually with off-white walls and rich, usually dark, upholstery. All of them have very good, sleep-friendly beds and ample-size bathrooms equipped with hair dryers. The hotel's centerpiece is its inner courtyard, which, since 1991, has been sheltered from the elements with a greenhouse-style glass canopy.

Dining: There's no restaurant on the premises, but management sets up a light supper buffet between 6 and 10pm every night that's free for guests, and which many guests substitute for a fuller meal in any of several nearby restaurants.

Amenities: Sauna and Jacuzzi. The staff will lend you a jogging outfit if you want to go jogging. There also are a series of convention facilities and conference rooms.

John Bauer Hotel. Södra Strandgatan 15, Box 2192, S-550 02 Jönköping. ☎ **800/528-1234** in the U.S., or 036/34-90-00. Fax 036/34-90-50. www.johnhbauer.se. E-mail: hotellet@johnbauer.se. 100 units. TV TEL. June–Aug and Fri–Sat year-round, 750 SEK ($82.50) double; rest of year, 1,210 SEK ($133.10) double. Rates include breakfast. AE, DC, MC, V. Parking: 70 SEK ($7.70).

One of the most famous and beloved artists to emerge from Jönköping was John Bauer (1882–1918), whose art nouveau–style illustrations for children's books are among the most famous in Sweden. This four-star hotel, which was built in the early 1980s, is named in his honor. It rises from a position in the center of town, in a design that's neither the most elegant, the most fashionable, nor necessarily the best decorated in Jönköping. But what you'll get is a homey, welcoming hotel, with a kind of kick-off-your-shoes-in-the-lobby-bar feeling, and a roster of bedrooms that aren't particularly cutting edge in their decor, but are cozy, clean, and warm with good beds and ample bathrooms. Staff members are welcoming, despite a sometimes disorganized feeling that might pervade some aspects of this hotel.

Dining: The Ester Kök & Bar provides competent cuisine in a glassed-in room evocative of a greenhouse. It's open for lunch Monday through Friday and for dinner every Monday through Saturday.

Amenities: Room service, concierge, sauna.

Provobis Stora Hotellet. Hotellplan, Box 23, S-551 12 Jönköping. ☎ **800/843-3311** in the U.S., or 036/10-00-00. Fax 036/71-93-20. www.provobis.se. 114 units. TV TEL. June–Aug and Fri–Sun year-round, 720 SEK ($79.20) double; rest of year, 1,375–1,495 SEK ($151.25–$164.45) double. Rates include breakfast. AE, DC, MC, V. Parking 60 SEK ($6.60).

This is one of the stateliest hotels in southeastern Sweden; its splendor emulates some of the architectural glory of a princely palace. Radically renovated in 1995, it's positioned in the heart of town, adjacent to an all-pedestrian street lined with shops, on the narrow isthmus that separates Lake Vättern from a smaller lake (the Munksjön). Inside, there is a curious blend of modern design that alternates with allegiance to the hotel's historic core. You'll find a modern-looking reception area that includes an ornate and neoclassical banqueting room known as the Hall of Mirrors. The largish bedrooms are clean, well maintained, and evocative of an upscale private home—one that's faithful to elegantly rustic farmhouse models. Each has a hardwood floor and either flowered or checked upholstery that deliberately evokes old-fashioned Sweden. The beds and mattresses are the city's finest; the ample-size bathrooms contain hair dryers and are well maintained. Our only complaints with this place are the sense of anonymity that results from its role as one of several members of a nationwide chain, and an oh-so-correct, regimented staff that doesn't have a clue about the history of the stately building where they work.

Dining/Diversions: There's a bistro-style restaurant, Emily's, on the premises, and a bar.

Amenities: Sauna and solarium, laundry service, pool table.

WHERE TO DINE

Borgmästaren. Borgmästeren Gränd 10. ☎ **036/16-14-40.** Reservations recommended. Fixed-price lunch 70 SEK ($7.70); main courses 98–178 SEK ($10.80–$19.60). AE, DC, MC, V. Mon–Thurs 10am–11pm, Fri–Sat 11am–midnight, Sun noon–6pm. SWEDISH.

One of the most appealingly conservative restaurants in town occupies a pair of dining rooms whose wood panels and rustic decor emulates that of a Swedish farmstead from the late 1800s. The old-fashioned menu items are wholesome, nutritious, and devoid of any nouveau influences from the faraway continent of Europe or the New World. Examples include filet steak Borgmästeren, served with a chanterelle and blue cheese sauce; filet of pork with peppercorns and herbs; salmon prepared and served at your table on a sizzling-hot stone; and different preparations of fish that include cod, herring, and whitefish. Expect a warm and cozy setting, and a polite and well-trained staff.

Gäddan & Gåsen. Barnarpsgatan 24. ☎ **036/12-00-99.** Reservations recommended. Fixed-price lunch 55 SEK ($6.05); main courses 100–180 SEK ($11–$19.80). AE, DC, MC, V. Daily 11am–3pm; Sun–Thurs 3–11pm, Fri–Sat 3pm–midnight. INTERNATIONAL.

This restaurant lies in the heart of town, in a circa-1950s building with thick walls and a rusticity that may remind you vaguely of something you'd find in Iberia. Its multilingual staff comes from virtually everywhere except Sweden, and is among the most cosmopolitan in town. Menu items include Provençal-style snails; onion or morel soup; tuna salads; prawn cocktails; Greek salad; T-bone steaks; tournedos of beef with red wine sauce and shallots; marinated filets of lamb with fines herbs; and shish kebabs. There also are pizzas and pastas. The fare is not particularly exciting, but is filling and hearty, even robust at times.

4 Along the Shores of Lake Vättern

Jönköping (see above) can serve as your gateway to Lake Vättern, especially if you're driving north from Småand. However, there are even more charming places along the lake, especially the towns of Gränna and Vadstena, as well as Motala.

This is Sweden's second largest lake (the similarly named Lake Vånern is much larger; see chapter 9).

Following the eastern shore, E4 is the most scenic route, providing panoramic vistas across the lake. The lake can be a sailor's nightmare at times, as it is known for its rough waters and often strong winds.

The sports-minded are attracted to the lake, especially for angling. The average depth of the lake is 128 feet and the deepest measured depth, south of Visingsö, is 422 feet. There are 28 different fish species remaining in this freshwater inland lake, which once was a sea bay. Some of these species have lived here since the Ice Age, including the famous Vättern alpine char. There also is an array of pike, perch, and pike-perch; along with grayling, salmon, and brown trout.

As a place for swimming, Lake Vättern has both a good and a bad reputation. Good because there aren't many inland lakes that can offer such long, Riviera-like beaches with water that is virtually drinkable; bad because of its great depth, and a temperature that one day can be suitable for swimming and the next day icy cold.

GRÄNNA

To reach this lakeside town, head north from Jönköping along E4. After a distance of 24½ miles, you reach Gränna, which lies at a point 174 miles southwest of Stockholm and 143 miles east of Gothenburg. The town of Tranås lies 25 miles from Gränna and is on the main rail route between Stockholm and Malmö. From Tranås, there are several buses that make the final run to Gränna.

You can head first for the Gränna-Visingsö Turistbyrå Brahegatan 48 (☎ 0390/410-10), open June through September, Monday through Friday 9am to 6pm, Saturday 10am to 2pm. The rest of the year, hours are Monday through Friday 10am to 4pm.

Gränna was founded in 1652 by Count Per Brahe, one of Sweden's first counts who had been governor of Finland. Nowadays it is mainly a summer town with boutiques, arts and crafts stalls, and a harbor area with camping, bathing, and restaurants. The town is known for its striped peppermint candy and for its devotion to hot-air ballooning. Per Brahe encouraged the planting of pear orchards in the environs, and pears from Gränna today are ranked as the finest in Scandinavia.

The **peppermint candy** industry is still going strong, and almost everyone who comes here picks up one or several as a souvenir. These red and white candy sticks, or *Polkargris,* were first made in 1859 by widow Amalia Eriksson. Today, they come in a wide assortment of flavors, shapes, and colors, including sugar-free.

SEEING THE SIGHTS

Grännaberger or Gränna Mountain can be reached either by car from the road between Gränna and Tranås or by climbing the steps that are found in a couple of places in town up to the top. Here, you find a splendid view and a fine area for

Lake Vättern

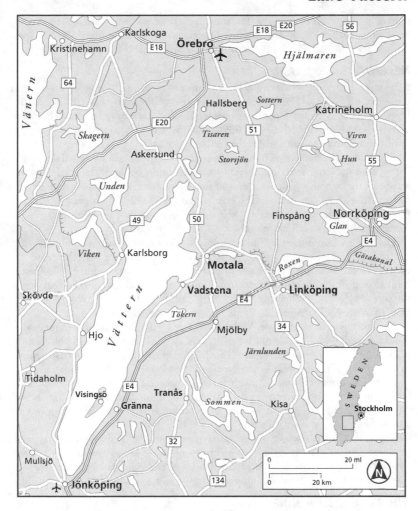

walking, plus a few buildings from the 17th century. If you're energetic, you can walk along a trail to **Skogstornet** (Forest Tower), from which the view of the area around Lake Vättern is panoramic. The Gränna area is a rich repository of Iron Age weapons, tools, menhirs (monoliths), and burial grounds, some 4,000 years old.

Gränna was the birthplace of the North Pole balloonist-explorer Salomon August Andrée, who made an ill-fated attempt in 1897 to cross the pole in the balloon *Ornen* (Eagle). The remains of the expedition were found in 1930 and can be seen in the **Andrée Museum,** Brahegatan 48 (☎ **0390/410-15**). With funding from Alfred Nobel and King Oscar, the flight north toward the pole lasted only 3 days. The balloon was forced to make a landing on ice. After 6 weeks of trekking, Andrée and his men died, either from the cold or trichinosis, contracted when they ate raw meat from a polar bear they'd speared. Their frozen but well-preserved bodies and their equipment were discovered by a Norwegian sailing ship, and the artifacts of that trip are on display at this museum. Museigården, a part of the museum, houses exhibits illustrating the history of the area. The museum is open mid-May through late August, daily from 10am to 5pm; late August through mid-May, daily from noon to 4pm. Admission is 40 SEK ($4.40) for adults and 20 SEK ($2.20) for children.

NEARBY VISINGÖ ISLAND

A 20-minute ferry trip will take you from Gränna to the island Visingsö, 4 miles across the water, for 50 SEK ($5.50) round-trip. Ferryboats leave every hour during the day in summer, and eight times per day in winter. Boats depart from the central harbor at Gränna; for information, call ☎ **0390/410-25.** There's a tourist office (summer information) near the point where the ferryboat docks.

The island can be traversed by car in 5 minutes, as it's long but very narrow. There are no road names or street numbers. In summer, some of the island residents meet arriving ferries with horse-drawn carriages for an excursion past the architectural highlights of the island (see below). The cost is 110 SEK ($12.10) per person for a 60-minute tour of the island, and 165 SEK ($18.15) per person for a 90-minute tour. There is no phone to call for information—it's all very casual.

This has been an important site since humans first set foot here some 6,000 years ago and large, Viking-era graves indicate how busy the area once was. On the southern part of the island are the remains of Sweden's oldest secular building, **Näs Castle,** built around 1150. According to the Icelandic sagas, it had a large treasury and was an important target in the fighting between the eastern and western parts of southern Sweden in the Middle Ages. The castle burned down in 1319.

The remains of another castle, **Visingsborg,** are by the harbor. This was the seat of the Brahe family whose progenitor, Per Brahe, Count of Visingsö, was a power in the Middle Ages in Sweden and Finland. Per Brahe also built the island's **parish church** in the 1680s, using the walls of the Stroja medieval church as the foundations. The tower and the door of the sacristy are from the old church; the door has old runic writing signifying that it was made in the 11th century. The church is baroque, unusual by Swedish standards. Also to be seen on Visingsö is Count Brahe's reconstructed 17th-century garden.

Kumlaby Church, whose oldest parts date from the 12th century, has well-preserved 15th-century murals. Visitors can climb the tower to a small roof balcony where they have a panoramic view of the island. The church is open only June through August, daily from 10:30am to 5:30pm. charging an admission of 15 SEK ($1.65).

WHERE TO STAY & DINE

Hotel Gyllene Uttern. On E4, S-563 00 Gränna. ☎ **0390/108-00.** Fax 0390/418-80. www.gylleneuttern.se. 45 units, 12 cabins. TV TEL. Sun–Thurs 1,190–1,290 SEK ($130.90–$141.90) double; Fri–Sat 890–990 SEK ($97.90–$108.90) double. All week long 1,650–1,750 SEK ($181.50–$192.50) suite; 800 SEK ($88) cabin. Rates include breakfast. AE, DC, MC, V. Free parking.

The "Golden Otter" is the honeymoon Shangri-la of Sweden, complete with a baroque wedding chapel in the basement. A step-gabled imitation castle built in 1937 overlooking Lake Vättern 2½ miles south of Gränna on the highway (E4) to Stockholm, Gyllene Uttern offers the best in food and lodgings in the area. The main dining room is highlighted by gilt-framed paintings (copies of great masters), medieval suits of armor, deeply set windows with views of the lake, and a bas-relief fireplace. Food is served to both guests and nonresidents. Fish from the lake is a specialty. A three-course fixed-price menu is served here Monday through Saturday noon to 9pm and Sunday noon to 8pm. Regional specialties are featured.

Although the dining room and public rooms are in the main building, it contains only nine guest rooms; the rest of the rooms are spread across the grounds in the annexes that were constructed in the 1960s. Throughout winter 1999, the hotel was closed for a massive renovation that upgraded all of its rooms. Note that the seven rooms in the main (circa 1937) building are the most nostalgic and old-fashioned (and will remain that way); the rooms within the two more modern annexes are more contemporary in their furnishing and decor. Cabins, each crafted from wood in a forest style, are available only in summer, and contain only the most basic (hot-plate style) of cooking equipment.

Hotell Västanå Slott. S-563-92 Gränna. ☎ **0390/107-00.** Fax 0390/418 75. 16 units, 12 with bathroom. 675 SEK ($74.25) double without bathroom; 950 SEK ($104.50) double with bathroom. MC, V. Closed mid-Oct to Apr. Free parking.

Although there are dozens of stately manors scattered throughout Sweden, this is one of the few that is open to the public. Formal and rigidly symmetrical, with a neoclassical design and a red tile roof, it originally was built in 1590 and by 1641 was the power base for what eventually became the Vasa family dynasty. Ironically, the building was rendered smaller (not larger) during two subsequent renovations. In 1770, parts of its original roof were demolished and rebuilt, and in 1928, the entire third floor was pulled down and the castle got the design and look one sees today. If you overnight here, realize in advance that to some extent you are invading the much-treasured precincts of what some still consider a private home. Bedrooms are high-ceilinged and spacious reminders of another era, with antiques, good carpets, and dramatic, sometimes allegorical paintings. Public rooms include suits of armor, frescoed ceilings, and historic mementos. No meals are served other than breakfast, but a nearby 18-hole golf course, where greens fees cost 220 SEK ($24.20), maintains a clubhouse where robust platters of food are served at both lunch and dinner every day. There's a tennis court within a short walk of the historic castle.

VADSTENA

The most important stopover on the Göta Canal trip is this medieval town full of narrow streets and old frame buildings on the eastern shores of Lake Vättern. The Middle Ages were Vadstena's great age of glory. The convent and church of St. Birgitta were known far and wide, and pilgrims thronged to see the saint's relics. King Gustav Vasa was a regular visitor in the 16th century, and built the famous Vadstena castle. In fact, there was a royal palace in Vadstena as early as the 13th century, when Birgitta was a lady-in-waiting before she went on to found the convent. Today there are still Sisters of St. Birgitta at Vadstena Convent. Vadstena is also known all over Sweden for its handmade lace—to see samples of this delicate product, walk along Stora Gatan, the main street.

Vadstena lies 159 miles southwest of Stockholm, 161 miles northeast of Gothenburg, and 37 miles north of Gränna. From the last stopover at Gränna, continue north along E4 until you reach the junction with Route 50, at which point you veer off the main highway and continue along 50 until you reach Vadstena. Bus 840 runs daily from Jönköping, and bus 855 departs from the Central Station in Stockholm, but only on Friday and Sunday. If you're driving here from Stockholm, take E4 southwest; at the junction of Route 206, head northwest.

The tourist bureau, **Vadstena Turistbyrå,** is located at Rådhustorget, S-592 80 Vadstena (☎ **0143/151-25;** www.vadstena.se). June through August it's open Monday through Friday 10am to 7pm, Saturday 10am to 5pm, and Sunday 3 to 7pm. In September, it's open Monday through Friday 10am to 6pm, and Saturday 10am to 2pm. From October to May, it's open Monday through Friday only, 9am to 3pm.

SEEING THE SIGHTS

Vadstena Abbey. Grasgatan 31. ☎ **0143/29850.** Free admission. May and Sept, daily 9am–5pm; June and Aug, daily 9am–7pm; July, daily 9am–8pm, Oct–Apr, Mon–Sat 9am–4pm, Sun 10am–1pm.

Built between the mid-14th and the 15th centuries to specifications outlined by its founder, St. Birgitta (Bridget) of Sweden, this Gothic church is rich in medieval art. Parts of the abbey date from 1250. The abbey housed the nuns of St. Birgitta's order until their expulsion in 1595.

The New Monastery and Church, built in 1973, show the same traditional simplicity of style St. Birgitta prescribed for her order. The view through the huge windows is the only decoration in this otherwise stark church. The nuns, who returned to Sweden in 1963, will show the church and their guest house to interested visitors at times convenient to their own schedule. It's a 3-minute walk from Stora Torget.

Vadstena Castle. Slottsvägen. ☎ **0143/31570.** Admission 50 SEK ($5.50) adults, 150 SEK ($16.50) children 7–15, free for children 6 and under. June–Aug, daily 11am–7pm, Sept–May, Mon–Fri 11am–4pm.

Founded in 1545 by Gustavus Vasa, king of Sweden, but not completed until 1620, this is one of the most splendid Renaissance Vasa castles, erected during a period of national expansion. It dominates the town from its moated position on the lake, just behind the old courthouse in the southern part of town. Vadstena was last inhabited by royalty in 1715, and was restored in the 19th century. Since 1899, the greater part of the castle has been used for provincial archives. In 1998, the Swedish federal government began a massive renovation of the castle ramparts, at vast expense, which probably will be completed during the lifetime of this book. The castle will remain open throughout the renovations.

WHERE TO STAY

Kungs Starby Hotell & Restaurang. Ödeshögsvägen, S-592 30 Vadstena. ☎ **0143/ 751-00.** Fax 0143/751-70. www.sdbergs.com. E-mail: starby@sdbergs.com. 61 units. TV TEL. July and Fri–Sat year-round, 880 SEK ($96.80) double; rest of year, 1,155 SEK ($127.05) double. Rates include breakfast. AE, DC, MC, V. Free parking.

As an estate, this place dates from the 1200s, when it was known for the fertility of its soil and its feudal prestige. In 1520, Swedish king Gustav Vasa added it to his roster of houses and castles, thereby beginning a fashion for members of the royal family and members of their entourage (including the legendary courtesan Hedwig Eleanora) to drop in for rest and relaxation. The building as you see it today, which lies about a half mile south of the town center, dates mostly from the late 1800s, except for modern, circa-1984 wings that contain most of the establishment's bedrooms. Each of these is furnished with contemporary furniture, pastel colors, and sleek, functional styling with good beds and small bathrooms. Regrettably, the experience you'll have here will be a bit more staid and conservative than the building's racy origins would suppose. Some of the big attractions are the indoor swimming pool, the health club, and the restaurant, which is recommended separately below.

Vadstena Klosterhotellet. Klosterområdet, S-592 30 Vadstena. ☎ **0143/315-30.** Fax 0143/136-48. 29 units. TV TEL. 1,200–1,305 SEK ($132–$143.55) double. Rates include breakfast. AE, DC, MC, V. Free parking.

What once was the premier religious stronghold in Sweden has been transformed into a hotel and conference center that welcomes individuals (and occasional church and civil groups) into its sprawling and echoing medieval premises. Set adjacent to the abbey church, about 700 yards from Vadstena Castle, it's contained within one wing of an L-shaped building that was constructed in the 12th century as a convent. The remainder of the building—which includes 59 nuns' cells and the longest triple-barrel vault (190 feet long) in northern Sweden—can be explored without hindrance. As such, you'll get the feeling of living in a compact and discreetly modernized subdivision of a vast and once-mighty compound that included lodgings for monks, nuns, and various church hierarchies.

Accommodations, which are slated for a discreet renovation early in 1999, are severely dignified and deliberately Spartan-looking, with dark-stained copies of furniture inspired by medieval models, stark white walls, and a vague and anything-but-plush sense of their original function as lodgings for penitents. They are nonetheless comfortable, with high ceilings; good mattresses; and simple, small, but adequate bathrooms. Rooms that overlook the lake are at the high end of the price spectrum; units overlooking the town and forest are at the low end. Breakfast is served on the ground floor amid the stonework of what originally was built as the nun's refectory. A short walk away, within what used to be the monastery associated with the compound, is a full-fledged restaurant. Open daily for lunch and dinner, with hours that vary according to the season, it serves main courses costing from 150 to 200 SEK ($16.50 to $22); and fixed-price menus that range from 75 to 85 SEK ($8.25 to $9.35).

WHERE TO DINE

Rådhuskällaren. Rådhustorget. ☎ **0143/121-70.** Reservations recommended. Main courses 65–160 SEK ($7.15–$17.60). DC, MC, V. Mid-May to Aug, daily noon–10pm; Sept to mid-May, Wed–Thurs 6–11pm, Fri–Sat noon–2am, Sun noon–5pm. SWEDISH.

A meal here affords the opportunity to visit the interior of the oldest courthouse and town hall in Sweden, as the restaurant lies within its early 14th-century cellar, beneath vaulted ceilings, above medieval flagstone floors. Menu items are rib-sticking, substantial fare designed to ward off the cold of a Swedish winter. Examples include such staples as roasted beef with horseradish sauce; fried filets of codfish with dill sauce and boiled potatoes; tenderloin of pork with mushrooms in cream and béarnaise sauce; poached filet of lemon sole with an asparagus and leek ragoût; and halibut steak with horseradish sauce. Dessert might be a slice of warm chocolate cake with elder flower ice cream.

Valven. Storgatan 18. ☎ **0143/123-40.** Reservations recommended. Main courses on bistro menu 45–139 SEK ($4.95–$15.30); main courses on "restaurant menu" 178–220 SEK ($19.60–$24.20). Daily noon–3pm and 6–10:30pm. AE, DC, MC, V. SWEDISH/INTERNATIONAL.

Set beside Vadstena's busiest commercial thoroughfare, this restaurant occupies a series of vaulted stone rooms that originally were built in the 15th century by the local church. Today, the place is warmly illuminated, partially by candlelight, and maintained as its showcase restaurant by the also recommended Kungs Starby Hotel, which lies within a five-minute walk to the south. Regardless of where you sit within this place, a staff member will hand you two different menus, the simpler of which contains dishes such as cheese platters, steaks, salads, and sandwiches, and grilled chicken with herb sauce. The more elaborate menu offers a more upscale and finely honed cuisine, including grilled turbot with saffron sauce; tournedos with pepper sauce, smoked filet of reindeer, and bouillabaisse. Dessert might include a gratin of chocolate with forest berries and house-made ice cream.

MOTALA

On the eastern shore of Lake Vättern, a stone's throw from the Göta Canal, Motala is called the "bicycle town," as it contains 31 miles of designated bicycle paths, which many local residents use year-round. Every June sees the running of the world's largest bicycle exercise race around Lake Vättern. The town lies 130 miles southwest of Stockholm, 293 miles northeast of Helsingborg, and 163 miles northeast of Gothenburg.

From Vadstena, continue north along Route 8, with Lake Vättern on your right, and you'll come to Motala after a drive of 8 miles. If you're not driving, you can take bus 16, which runs along the eastern side of Lake Vättern.

Before reaching Stockholm, Göta Canal cruises go through Motala. And before reaching the canal, waters of the lake go through a flight of five locks, a dramatic sight that makes Motala one of the highlights of the Göta Canal cruises. Motala was designed by Baltzar von Platen, one of the waterway's creators, and he remains a popular local hero. His grave beside his statue lies on the canal sidewalk.

For information about Motala and the surrounding area, call at the **Motala Turist-byrå,** Fokes Hus, Repslagaregatan 1 (☎ 0141/22-52-54; www.motala-tourism.se), open June to August daily 10am to 6pm. Off-season hours are daily 10am to 5pm.

SEEING THE SIGHTS

The fan-shaped layout of Motala was the creation of Baltzar von Platen. The town is rather bland but makes an excellent center for exploring nearby attractions. A pleasant way to enjoy the canal and its surroundings is to go cycling along the old towpath. Bikes can be rented at the tourist office kiosk down by the harbor from June to mid-August, daily 8am to 8pm, for 60 SEK ($6.60) per day.

Also intriguing is to take a boat trip along the canal to Borensburg, 12½ miles east of Motala. In summer, these 5-hour boat trips leave Motala at 10:30am, and cost 200 SEK ($22) round-trip.

Just 2 miles east of town is **Varamon Beach,** its half mile of golden sand making it one of Scandinavia's largest inland bathing beaches. It has the warmest waters in Lake Vättern (which isn't saying much), and often is thick with milk-white bodies soaking up the summer sun. It's also a venue for windsurfing. Locals like to call Varamon their "Riviera of Lake Vättern."

Motala has some museums, but all are of only minor interest. The best is the **Motala Motor Museum** (☎ 0141/588-88), lying at the edge of the harbor. Cars of various eras are intriguingly exhibited—for example, parked outside an Esso Station. Music of the car's era blares from radio sets. All the vintage cars displayed in the showrooms are kept in shiny mint condition. Hours are May through September, daily 10am to 8pm, costing 40 SEK ($4.40) for admission; from October to April, Monday through Friday 8am to 3pm, Saturday and Sunday 11am to 5pm.

Also of interest is the **Canal and Maritime Museum,** just up from the motor museum (☎ 0141/202-050). This museum presents the creation and importance of the Göta Canal, which is known as the country's greatest historical structure. Exhibits detail the canal's construction and demonstrate how a lock is operated. Hours are May, Monday through Friday 9am to 4pm; June and August, Monday through Friday 8am to 6pm; and July daily 8am to 8pm. Admission is 20 SEK ($2.20).

WHERE TO STAY

Palace Hotel. Kungsgatan 1, S-591 30 Motala. ☎ **0141/21-66-60.** Fax 0141/572-21. www.palacemotala.se. 55 units. MINIBAR TV TEL. Mid-June to Aug and Fri–Sat year-round, 850 SEK ($93.50) double; rest of year, 1,040 SEK ($114.40) double. Rates include breakfast. AE, DC, MC, V. Free parking.

Set within the heart of Motala and favored by business travelers from Germany, France, the United Kingdom, and the United States, this three-story hotel is a pleasant, well-managed place that originally was built in 1964. Throughout, you'll find a bland but comfortable kind of international modernity, especially within the bedrooms. Here, amid wall-to-wall carpets, sometimes frilly curtains, well-padded beds, and a writing table, you'll find a place where even older members of your management team would feel comfortable. The more expensive rooms are labeled business class and are larger and more comfortable. There's no full-fledged restaurant, but a pub serves drinks and simple platters of food. There's also a solarium for sunbathing even in darkest midwinter.

Stadshotellet Motala. Stora Torget, Box 19, S-591 21 Motala. ☎ **0141/21-64-00.** Fax 0141/21-46-05. www.stadshotelletmotala.se. 78 units. MINIBAR TV TEL. Mid-June to mid-Aug and Fri–Sat year-round, 850 SEK ($93.50) double; rest of year, 1,150 SEK ($126.50) double. Rates include breakfast. AE, DC, MC, V. Parking 6 SEK (65¢) per hour 9am–6pm; otherwise free.

The most highly recommended and most prestigious hotel in town originally was built in 1880 in a location adjacent to the town's main square (Stora Torget) and enlarged in 1923. Rising four floors, with access to a pleasant garden that's centered around a circular reflecting pool, it offers a traditional, consciously upscale decor that includes dozens of yards of fabric sewn into the most elaborate draperies in town, and a mostly Chippendale or Queen Anne decor in the public areas. Throughout, there's a sense of plush, well-heeled bourgeoisie taste, and such architectural adornments as ceiling friezes showing cherubs cavorting across vineyards, surrounded by formal, usually neoclassical moldings. Bedrooms have high ceilings, formal furnishings, plush carpets, firm mattresses, and small but very clean bathrooms. There's a bar, several conference rooms, and a sauna on the premises. The hotel's dining room, Restaurant Stadshotellet Motala, is recommended separately in "Where to Dine."

WHERE TO DINE

Restaurant Hallen. Prästgatan 8. ☎ **0141/21-91-00.** Reservations recommended. Fixed-price lunch 75 SEK ($8.25); main courses 139–159 SEK ($15.30–$17.50). AE, DC, MC, V. Mon–Fri 11am–2pm; Tues–Thurs 6–11pm, Fri–Sat 6pm–3am. SWEDISH.

The most authentically Swedish restaurant in Motala occupies an ochre-colored, green-roofed building that originally was constructed in the 1830s as a food market and general store. Today, it does a more active business as a luncheon stopover (when as many as 100 guests cram in) than it does at nighttime, when management reduces the seating capacity by about half. Within a decor inspired by a Swedish farmstead from the turn of the century, you can order heaping portions of traditional, well-prepared, and flavorful cuisine that includes whitebait roe with chopped onions and egg yolks, shrimp cocktail with toast, Italian prosciutto wrapped around slices of Gorgonzola cheese, filet of flounder with lobster sauce, baked salmon with mashed potatoes and lemon, filet of pork with chanterelle sauce, and loin of beef with a gratin of Gorgonzola. There is a disco on Friday and Saturday after 10pm.

Restaurant Stadshotellet Motala. Stora Torget. ☎ **0141/216-400.** Reservations recommended. Fixed-price lunch 60 SEK ($6.60); main courses 130–200 SEK ($14.30–$22). AE, DC, MC, V. Daily 11am–10:30pm. SWEDISH/CONTINENTAL.

This is the most formal, most intricate, and most elaborate restaurant in Motala, with an antique setting within the oldest (circa 1880) section of the town's most formal hotel. Beneath high ceilings and elaborate cove moldings, in a Queen Anne-style setting, you'll find well-prepared food that's often based on local ingredients. These include venison, pheasant, and grouse (in season); and a year-round local delicacy consisting of freshwater char from nearby lakes, poached with herbs and served with boiled potatoes and hollandaise sauce. The menu changes frequently, but includes whitefish roe with chopped onions, sour cream, and chopped egg yolks; smoked salmon with horseradish sauce and shrimp; and tournedos of beef with tomato-garlic sauce. Look for lots of private wedding and anniversary parties conducted within the private function rooms of this restaurant, and a sense of local municipal politics within the nerve center of this very small town.

ÖREBRO

Our final destination, Örebro, doesn't open onto Lake Vättern, but lies 37½ miles north of the lake, strategically located on the main route from southwest Sweden to the capital city of Stockholm. Sweden's sixth most populous city, it opens on the shores of Lake Hjälmaren, the fourth largest lake in the country.

Its castle (see below) is one of the most famous in Sweden, and it also lies at the River Svartån, which is studded with water lilies in summer. To the immediate west of the center is Lake Tysslingen, which is best reached by a leisurely bike ride. Many birders come here to view the lake in the spring when thousands upon thousands of whooper swans temporarily settle on the way to Finland from their winter retreats.

Motorists departing our last stopover at Motala can continue north along Route 50 until they reach the junction with E3, an express highway that will carry them north into the center of Örebro.

You also can visit Örebro directly on a main east-west train from Stockholm (trip time: 3 hours). For information about the town, contact **Destination Örebro,** Slottet (in the castle; ☎ 019/21-21-21). It is open June through August, Monday through Friday 9am to 7pm, Saturday and Sunday 10am to 5pm. Off-season hours are Monday through Friday 9am to 5pm, Saturday and Sunday 11am to 3pm.

EXPLORING THE AREA

If you'd like to follow our suggestion and take a bike ride out to **Lake Tysslingen,** you can rent a bike at **Servicecentralen,** Hamnplan (☎ 019/21-19-09), for 45 to 60 SEK ($6.60) per day. The tourist office (see above) can provide information about boat tours of **Lake Hjälmaren** on either M/S *Linna* or M/S *Gustav Lagerfbjelke.* A 3-hour boat cruise costs 250 SEK ($27.50) round-trip.

The town's major attraction is **Örebro Slott** (☎ 019/21-21-21), which for more than 700 years has kept a watchful eye on everyone crossing the bridge over the River Svartån. The oldest part of the castle, a defense tower, was erected in the latter half of the 13th century. The tower was added to in the 14th century to make an even larger stronghold. Toward the end of the 16th century, one of the most impressive Renaissance castles in Sweden grew up here. The castle lies on an island in the Svartån, dominating the town. Over the years, the castle has been restored, and restored again. Today, it has a grand romantic exterior, although not much remains inside. There is no original furniture, and much of the interior is used for county offices. Nevertheless, tour guides valiantly struggle to recreate the romance and lore of the slott. The beamed Rikssalen, or Parliament Hall, remodeled in 1927, has several portraits, notably that of Karl XI and his family. Surprisingly, all pop-eyed because of the arsenic used to whiten their faces. Also on site the newly organized Slottsmuseet functions as a county museum, displaying the saga of the county since the days of the Stone Age. From May through September only, guided tours in English are conducted daily at 2pm, costing 50 SEK ($5.50) per person.

Beautifully situated on the banks of the Svartån in the center of Örebro is the little, wooden, open-air village of **Wadköping.** The village consists of a collection of ancient buildings from Örebro and the surrounding countryside. Opened in 1965, it contains 18th-century timbered structures in the traditional barn red, and lovely, bright 19th-century wooden houses that all have been moved to this site in the city park, Stadsparfken. Nowadays, Wadköping is thriving with a cafe, craftspeople at work, shops, some minor museums, exhibitions, a theater, and puppet shows. The entire area can be visited May through August, Tuesday through Sunday 11am to 6pm, September through April, Tuesday through Sunday 11am to 4pm. Admission is free.

The major church of town is **S:t Nicolai Kyrka,** Stortorget (☎ **019/12-40-25**), dating from 1260 and standing on the main square of Örebro. It was extensively restored in the 1860s, so little of its former medieval character remains. The church is a frequent venue for temporary art exhibitions. It was here in 1810 that Jean Baptiste Bernadotte, Napoléon's marshal, was elected successor to the Swedish throne.

SHOPPING

If you're interested in Swedish handcrafts, the finest outlet along Lake Vättern is **Konsthantverkarna,** Järntorgsgatan 2 (☎ **019/10-79-05**), a shop in central Örebro run by professional craft workers. No junk is allowed here, and the crafts are not only well made but have much charm—ideal for gifts and souvenirs.

WHERE TO STAY & DINE

Rica City Hotel Örebro. Kungsgatan 24, S-702 24 Örebro. ☎ **019/601-4200.** Fax 019/601-4209. www.rica.cityhotels.se. 104 units. MINIBAR TV TEL. July to mid-Aug and Fri–Sat year-round, 610 SEK ($67.10) double; rest of year, 1,130 SEK ($124.30) double. Rates include breakfast. AE, DC, MC, V. Parking 45 SEK ($4.95) per day in nearby public garage.

Set in the town center, behind an angular, brick-and-stucco facade, this six-story hotel was built in 1986 and has done a thriving trade with business travelers ever since. A member of a well-respected nationwide chain, it offers cozy, pastel-colored bedrooms with comfortable mattresses and flowery prints, a sauna, and a cheerful, cooperative staff. You can get a drink at the reception area of the hotel, but other than breakfast, no meals are served.

Scandic Hotel Grand Örebro City. Fabriksgatan 21-23, Box 8112, S-700 08 Örebro. ☎ **019/767-4300.** Fax 0191/767-4311. www.scandic-hotels.com. E-mail:orebrogrand@ scandic-hotels.com. 221 units. TV TEL. Mid-June to mid-Aug and Fri–Sat year-round, 740–810 SEK ($81.40–$89.10) double; rest of year, 1,440–1,590 SEK ($158.40–$174.90) double. Suites 1,645–2,231 SEK ($180.95–$245.40) year-round. Rates include breakfast. AE, DC, MC, V. Parking 95 SEK ($10.45).

Erected in the mid-1980s in a seven-story format in the center of town, this hotel provides clean, well-maintained accommodations within a setting that's deeply immersed in the international and modern format that's widespread across the world. Despite an upscale decor that includes lots of hardwood panels, marble floors, and a dramatic modern staircase within the lobby, there are touches that will quickly remind you of the charming aspects of Sweden, most visible of which is a well-trained staff. Bedrooms contain aspects that evoke a living room in a comfortably contemporary modern home, partly because of the occasional sofa and, in some cases, reproductions of Turkish or Persian carpets.

Dining/Diversions: There's a cozy bar outfitted in tones of peach, russet, and natural woods; and a well-recommended restaurant, Coupol, a mix between an upscale Paris bistro and a farmhouse restaurant in Tuscany.

Amenities: Two saunas, a Jacuzzi, and a small gym, all clustered into a "Relax-Center" on the hotel's seventh (uppermost) floor.

8

The Baltic Islands: Öland & Gotland

Two of the most rewarding destinations in all of Scandinavia lie in the Baltic Sea: the islands of Öland and Gotland, each with a long history and each popular in summer when the Swedes themselves flock here for sunshine and beaches. And flock they do; although some 60,000 people live on Gotland year-round, in summer that number can reach almost a million.

Called the "island of sun and winds," Öland is known for its luxuriant vegetation. There are plants here from Iberia, the Alps, and eastern Europe that survived the Ice Age and the warmer post-glacial period. Many are found in no other Scandinavian country, and there is a profusion of orchids, some 30 species in all. Öland also is a land from prehistoric times. Remains from 4,000-year-old burial chambers can be seen here, as well as many runic stones from the Viking era.

Today, the inhabitants of Öland make their living mainly through agriculture, fishing, food production, industry, and tourism. This flat, rural Baltic island is covered in windmills and connected to southern Sweden by one of the longest bridges in Europe. Its best center is Borgholm, the capital, a small resort with a recreational harbor on the west coast of the island. Shallow, crystal-clear waters make Öland's beaches as family friendly as the weather: This is Sweden's sunniest province.

Two hundred years ago a British visitor called Ölanders "the Italians of the north," suggesting a more extroverted streak than mainland Swedes. After a visit you can decide that for yourself.

As fascinating as Öland is, we recommend Gotland, particularly its ancient capital of Visby, if you have time to visit only one island.

Because the climate is milder on Gotland than in the rest of Sweden, the scenery here offers a wide variety of flora and fauna. Vast, white beaches and midsummer waters much warmer than you might expect, are the big lure in summer, although many visitors, especially foreigners, come to take in its unique landscape of statuesque limestone formations, cliffs, forests, heaths, and meadows.

In Gotland, some 1,000 farms dating from the Viking era and medieval epoch, are still in use today. Off the coast of Gotland lie several other islands, each different. Farthest to the north is Gotska Sandön, a place of myths and legends and the stronghold of Sweden's last pirates. Just a stone's throw off the north coast lies Fårö, familiar to many as a once-favorite retreat of Olof Palme, Ingmar Bergman, and other political and cultural personalities. To the west, the twin

Lilla and Stora Karlsö islands are famed for their huge colonies of guillemots and other sea birds.

If you don't have time to absorb the island itself, try at least for a look at Visby, which in 1995 was put on UNESCO's World Heritage list. Visby, of course, is the capital of Gotland and is surrounded by well-preserved medieval walls. Some 2,000 citizens live within these walls today. Once a Viking trading station, Visby, in the 12th century, developed into a leading commercial center for trade across the Baltic Sea. In time it became one of the most important cities of the Hanseatic League. Churches were founded and the city grew and prospered as 13 ruined churches, two monasteries, a cathedral, and 200 buildings resting on medieval foundations attest today. Within the walls are several shops, restaurants, pubs, and clubs, many of which are open year-round.

1 Öland

25 miles E of Kalmar, 291 miles S of Stockholm

More Swedes emigrated from Öland to the United States during the 19th century than from any other province in Sweden. Ultimately, the Baltic island would lose a quarter of its population. Many émigrés, however, returned here to retire. Little wonder, considering how beautiful it is, with its sandy beaches, its treeless steppe (*Alvaret*) covered with wildflowers, its bird life, and its profusion of windmills silhouetted against the summer sky.

One of Europe's longest bridges, nearly 4 miles long, connects Kalmar with Öland. At 87½ miles long and 10 miles wide, this is Sweden's second largest island, but its smallest province. Beaches run along both coasts, and there is only one town, Borgholm, a summer retreat. The royal summer residence is at Solliden. To rent a summer house on the beach, get in touch with the tourist office (see below).

ESSENTIALS

GETTING THERE   By Bus   Buses run from the Kalmar terminal to Borgholm on Öland in less than an hour; take no. 101 or 106. Call ☎ **0200/21818.**

By Car   From Kalmar, take the bridge over the sound, then turn left onto Route 136 to reach Borgholm.

VISITOR INFORMATION   Go to the **Ölands Tourist AB,** Färjestaden (☎ **0485/ 89000**), at the Öland end of the famous 4-mile bridge. It's open June 27 through July, Monday through Saturday from 9am to 7pm and on Sunday from 10am to 6pm; May through June 26 and in August, Monday through Friday from 9am to 6pm, on Saturday from 10am to 5pm, and on Sunday from 10am to 4pm; and September through April, Monday through Friday from 9am to 5pm.

OUTDOOR ACTIVITIES

BIKING   Öland is great cycling country. Although there are those who bike the entire 80-mile stretch of the island, others are less ambitious. Whatever your cycling plans, you'll find seemingly endless cycle tracks along flat roads.

Bike rentals are available near the point where the ferryboat will deposit you from the Swedish mainland, at **Färjestaden Cykelaffär,** Storegatan 67 (☎ **0485/300-74**), for 80 SEK ($8.80) per day.

GOLFING   **Ekerum Golf Course,** Ekerum, S-387-92 Borgholm (☎ **0485/800-00**), is 10 miles south of Borgholm, surrounded by the rolling lushness of an isolated region near the island's center. This course was created in 1991 as part of the also recommended Sunwing Ekerem Hotel. It's open throughout the winter, even when a light dusting of snow complicates the par scores a bit. Focusing on driving ranges that lie between verdant forests and rolling fields, it charges greens fees of between 230 and 290 SEK ($25.30 and $31.90) per day, depending on the season you want to play. You can pick and choose from an 18-hole course and a 9-hole course that lies immediately adjacent.

SEEING THE SIGHTS
A PREHISTORIC VILLAGE

✪ **Eketorp Ring-Fort.** Degerhamn. ☎ **0485/66-20-00.** Admission 45 SEK ($4.95) adults, free for children 15 and under. May 1–June 19, daily 10am–5pm; June 20–Aug 2, daily 10am–6pm; Aug 3–Sept 15, daily 10am–5pm. Unless you have a car, getting here is tricky, although 4 buses a day (no. 112) come here from the Mörbylånga bus station. 2 buses make the run on Sat and only 1 on Sun. Check with the tourist office (see above) for bus timetables.

One of Öland's more interesting attractions is this prehistoric fortified village that has been excavated and reconstructed so that visitors can see how people lived in this area centuries ago. The site is unique in Scandinavia, representing the only rebuilt prehistoric fort. It's on the island's extreme southern tip, 22 miles south of Mörbylånga, rising starkly from a treeless landscape of steppe-like, nonfrozen tundra.

Eketorp is one of 15 known prehistoric forts on the island. Excavations have shown three phases of settlement here from A.D. 300 to 1300. Today, a large selection of the massive wall that encircled this ring-fort has been reconstructed, along with Iron Age houses within the walls. You can see dwellings, cattle byres, and storehouses reconstructed using ancient crafts and materials, as well as species of livestock. Objects found in the excavations include simple tools, skillfully crafted jewelry, and weapons. The best of these finds are exhibited in a museum inside the fort wall.

IN BORGHOLM

The actual capital, **Borgholm,** merits only a passing visit. It is extremely overcrowded during the month of July when tourists, mainly the Swedes themselves, overrun its bars, cafes, and pizzerias. At that time it takes on a carnival atmosphere, later settling down for a long winter's nap.

Just to the north of the town center of Borgholm you can visit the ruins of **Blårör,** the island's largest Bronze Age cairn, although there isn't much to see here today. When it was discovered in 1849, the tomb in its center had already been plundered by grave robbers. In 1920 four more tombs were discovered but they too had been plundered. What remains are a few sunken granite stones. This site is mainly for serious archaeologists.

Borgholms Slott. Borgholm ☎ **0480/88083.** Admission 40 SEK ($4.40) adults, free for children. May to Aug, daily 10am–6pm. To get there you can walk through a nature reserve signposted from the center of Borgholm. By car, take the first exit south of Route 136.

This attraction, one of Sweden's most important historical monuments, lies just to the southwest of the center of Borgholm at the top of the sheer, steep face of the Landborg Cliffs. In the Middle Ages, this was one of the major royal castles of Sweden, center of intrigue and endless battles. Subject to frequent attacks, it guarded the sound and was Sweden's southernmost outpost against Denmark. The castle was partially destroyed during the Kalmar War (1611–1613). King Karl X Gustav ordered that the castle be restored and turned into a baroque palace, but building was interrupted in 1709 because of a cash shortage. In 1806 fire reduced the palace to its present ruins. Remains of the original fortified circular tower can still be seen in the northwest corner of the inner courtyard.

Öland

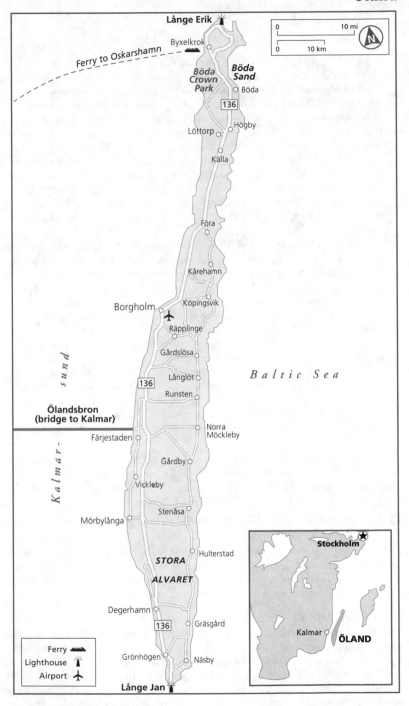

Länge Erik

0   10 mi
0   10 km

Byxelkrok

Ferry to Oskarshamn

Böda
Crown
Park

Böda
Sand

Böda

136

Högby

Löttorp

Källa

Föra

Kårehamn

Köpingsvik

Borgholm

Räpplinge

Gårdslösa

Långlöt

136

Runsten

B a l t i c   S e a

s u n d

Ölandsbron
(bridge to Kalmar)

Norra
Möckleby

Färjestaden

K a l m a r -

Gårdby

Vickleby

Stenåsa

Mörbylånga

Hulterstad

STORA

ALVARET

Degerhamn

136

Gräsgård

Grönhögen

Näsby

Länge Jan

Stockholm

Kalmar

ÖLAND

Ferry
Lighthouse
Airport

The Blue Maiden

Lying off the west coast of Öland rises one of the most remote and "forgotten" islands of the Baltic, **Blå Jungfrun,** whose name translates as "the Blue Maiden." It rises high above the Kalmar Straits, 423 feet above the sea bed and 280 feet above sea level. Uninhabited and home only to colonies of birds and wildlife, it's noteworthy for its bare, windswept cliffs, slabs of red granite, and thousands of rocky outcroppings. More of a rock spur than an island, it measures less than ¾ mile long, and ½ mile wide, covering an area of about 163 acres. Designated as a national park, the island has two separate harbors, both of which lie near the northern tip: Lervik to the east and Sikhamn to the west. The direction and intensity of the wind at the time of your arrival will determine which of the two the crew of your ferryboat will use for a landing. Seas surrounding the island are tricky: Even a light wind can make it difficult to approach the island's rocky coastline.

Olaus Magnus, a famous Swedish bishop, mentioned Blå Jungfrun as long ago as 1555. Carl von Linné (Linnaeus) was the first to describe the island in detail, having visited it in 1745 during his "Journey to Öland and Gothland."

Later, the forest and plant life suffered the impact of drought and the foolish mistake of introducing rabbits, which caused much damage to vegetation. Quarrying in 1904 brought more ecological disasters, especially when the largest of the great caves on the island were blown up. After World War I forces mobilized to save the island; industrialist Torsten Kreuger donated enough money for the island to be purchased and turned over to Sweden as a national park.

Once on the island, you can observe how the granite dome was covered by sediment some 500 million years ago and how the island took shape about one million years ago during the Quaternary Ice Age. The larger boulder fields in the south of the island always draw much interest, as do the lichens and bird life.

Lying only a short walk south is the royal family's Italian-style villa, which they often use as their residence in summer. This white palace was built by Queen Victoria of Sweden from 1903 to 1906 as a summer retreat. Their home is off-limits, but you can wander through Solliden Park (see the following), the gardens of the villa.

✪ **Solliden Park.** Borgholm. ☎ **0485/153-55.** 40 SEK ($4.40) adults, free for children under 10. May 15–Sept 15, daily 1–6pm.

Queen Victoria also commissioned the landscaping of Solliden's extensive gardens and parkland, which many devotees rate as some of the loveliest in Sweden. Exhibitions about Swedish royalty are housed in a new pavilion, which also contains a gift shop. On site is a creperie selling ice cream, crepes, and drinks.

IN CENTRAL ÖLAND

To explore Central Öland, you can travel east from Borgholm (bus 102 runs here) following signs to Räpplinge. This brings you to Storlinge Kvarna, a row of seven windmills. Less than a mile south, you arrive at **Gärdslösa,** the island's best preserved medieval church. Inside is a pulpit made in 1666 along with paintings from the 1200s.

Your major stopover will be a mile or two south in the village of **Himmelsberga,** which is preserved as an open-air museum with farms built along both sides of the narrow village road. The heart of the museum consists of three large farms with buildings dating from the 18th and 19th centuries. You can see furnishings, farm equipment,

You're sure to see the island's black guillemot, as well as rare birds such as the water pipit and the velvet scoter. Even the white-tailed sea eagle often can be viewed.

The "labyrinth," the only ancient monument on the island, was first mentioned by von Linné, who called it "Trojeborg." An intricate maze of paths, it lies on a level area of rock on the southern slope of the island.

The best way to view the attractions of the Blue Maiden involves signing up for one of the summer (June through August only) tours of the island, conducted by Hans Arvidsson, a local fisherman. To reach him, call ☎ 0485/240-05. During that period, excursions depart every day from the piers at Byxelkrok at 9pm, return to Öland around 3:30pm, and cost 130 SEK ($14.30) per adult, 70 SEK ($7.70) for children under 12. There is a lecture and guidance associated with the tour, and several hours of unstructured time for wandering over the island's surface, examining the flora and fauna.

An alternative method of reaching the Blue Maiden involves departures from Oskarshamn, on the Swedish mainland. From the harborfront at Oskarshamn, the M.S. *Soltust* departs every day of the week, except Saturday and Monday, at 9am, with a return scheduled for 3pm. Transit takes about 90 minutes each way, allowing about 3 hours to explore, on foot, the hiking trails that crisscross the island. A kiosk on the island dispenses maps and local information about how best to appreciate this sparsely inhabited island's charms. Round-trip transit costs 170 SEK ($18.70) per person. For information and reservations, call ☎ 0491/19777, or the tourist office of Iskarshamn at ☎ 0491/88188. To contact the local branch (in Kalmar) of the Swedish National Park Service, the organization that oversees the hiking trails on the Blue Maiden, call ☎ 0480/82195.

---

carriages, and sleighs common to that period in Öland's history. In the Cottage Café, you can order freshly baked cakes to be consumed under the shade of walnut and maple trees in a garden. The gallery offers a constantly changing array of art and handcraft shows. The site is open May 15 to September 15, daily 10am to 6pm. During the summer there are activities ranging from open-air theater productions to concerts with jazz and folk music. For more information call ☎ 0485/56-10-22.

IN SOUTH ÖLAND

Stora Alvaret, a giant limestone plain, dominates the southern part of the island. This great plateau is almost entirely devoid of trees, covering an area 23 miles long and 9 miles wide. The thin soil in places gives way to bare limestone outcrops, creating the impression of a barren landscape. Yet the area is teeming with life and is, in fact, the last refuge for a number of unique plant and animal species. You'll see everything from colorful orchids to soaring skylarks in the spring, from rock-roses to golden plovers in summer, from rose hips to cranes in the autumn. **Vickleby** is the most attractive village stopover.

Capellagården. Vickleby. ☎ 0485/361-93. June 1–Aug 12, 10am–6pm, but call first. Reached on Route 136 between Fårjestaden to the north and Mörbylånga to the south.

Vickleby is the site of a craft college founded in the late 1950s by Carl Malmsten. Today, the college is a training school for cabinet making, woodworking, ceramics, textiles, design, and horticulture. It also has one of Sweden's largest herb gardens, containing a wide variety of unusual plants. During the summer, the college stages exhibitions and sales in the old Vickleby school.

Ottenby Naturum. Otenby Nature Reserve. ☎ **0485/66-10-93.** Admission 50 SEK ($5.50). July 4–Aug 1, daily 10am–7pm; Apr 4–July 3 and Aug 2–Nov 1, 10am–4pm. From Borgholm follow Route 136 all the way south to the southern tip of the island where you'll see Ottenby Naturum signposted with hiking trails leading you into the reserve.

At the southern tip of Öland sits this exhibition of nature and culture, one of the best bird watching sites anywhere in Sweden. An ornithological station here pursues research. The surrounding area was an ancient park and the hunting ground of kings. In the 16th century, King Johan III stocked the park with fallow deer, and the strain still thrives here today. The park also is the breeding ground for the rare golden oriole. At Ottenby you can also see the coast-to-coast wall built by King Karl X Gustaf in 1650 to fence off the deer and to improve hunting.

IN NORTH ÖLAND

From Borgholm Route 136 head north to a more varied landscape than in the south. At Föra, a village 12½ miles to the north, stands **Die Kirche von Föra,** with its well-preserved defensive tower. In the Middle Ages, churches doubled as fortresses. If it's open, look inside the interior, which still has a medieval aura, with a cross dating from the 15th century.

North of the village of Sodvik, you come to **Lilla Horns Iovangar** (Little Horn Forest Meadows), which are abundantly flowering meadows best viewed in the late spring.

Before you reach the village of Källa, you'll spot **Källa kyrka,** which stands lonely and deserted today after its last parishioners departed in 1888. In a setting of flowery meadows, this church from the Middle Ages has drystone walls; however, its furnishings are long gone. On site are ancient burial tombs. The church was last "modernized" in the 14th century, and it was frequently attacked during Baltic sea wars.

Continuing north you arrive at the village of Högby, site of **Högby kyrka och kyrkstallare,** a religious shrine from the Middle Ages, now in ruins.

After leaving Högby, your last major village will be Böda before you reach the island's largest greenbelt, the stunningly beautiful **Böda kronopark.** Before going all the way to the northern tip of the kronopark, you can make a slight 6-mile detour west from Böda on Route 136 to see the Skäftekarr Museum.

One of Öland's newest attractions, the **Skäftekarr Museum,** Lottorp (☎ **0485/ 22-111**), opened in 1998 on the site of the archaeological excavations of an Iron Age village. On the premises is an exhibition showing what farm life was like in the 6th century A.D., and a reconstruction of several of the village's grave sites. The site also contains nearly a dozen well-preserved foundations of stone buildings, each attributed to five separate farms established between A.D. 300 and 700. Know in advance that you'll be visiting a site still in the process of being excavated and enlarged. On site is an unusual botanical garden planted by a local gardener during the mid–19th century. It boasts 100 or so different trees and bushes and is ideal for country rambles. Midsummer festivities, including musical events and lectures, are staged at this park. Adjacent to the park is a 1½-mile path that's ideal for walks. The path follows a "cultural route," passing the ancient settlements from the Iron Age. Also here is a cafe, built in 1860, in which you can order a complete meal or light refreshments. The site is open year-round Monday through Friday from 10am to 4pm. From May 1 to September 15 hours are extended daily from 10am to 6pm. Admission costs 40 SEK ($4.40) for adults and 20 SEK ($2.20) for children 6 to 15. Children under 6 enter free.

This northern "crown" over Öland is shaped like a bird's head, the beak facing east. Here are the island's best beaches, lying for the most part on the eastern coastline. The beaches start at Böda Sand. The best and most frequented stretch runs for a mile north of Kyckesand. One section is signposted and reserved for nudists.

Finally, you reach the island's most scenic part, **Trollskogen** or Trolls Forest. This storm-swept forest with ivy-covered trunks is at the very northeastern tip of Öland. Part of Böda Crown Park, it is like a setting from a child's fairy tale. You expect to see the wicked witch emerge at any time from the gnarled trunks of the ancient oaks. This forest offers some of the island's most dramatic walks.

SHOPPING ON ÖLAND

The items you haul back from Öland probably will involve either durable clothing suitable for nature walks in the rugged outdoors, or examples of local handcrafts and pottery made by arts-oriented refugees from urban life. One of the most appealing outlets for ceramics and pottery is **Lolla & Mary,** Hamnen, very close to the piers of Färjestaden (☎ 0485/318-81), where the idiosyncratic and painstakingly crafted ceramics of a team of local artisans are displayed and sold. Nearby, at **Atelje Ölandss-nipan,** Hamnplanen, Färjestaden (☎ 0485/319-95), some of the most artfully crafted miniature ship models in Sweden are displayed, each authentic to one or another of the many vessels that have sought shelter in Öland's harbor.

Celebrity hunters may appreciate the art gallery that devotes a good percentage of its time and efforts to a well-known resident of Stockholm; artist, singer, and actor Lasse Åberg. His paintings usually are on display in the hamlet of Högby, adjacent to the village church, at the **Gallieriet l Högny,** Huvudgatan, Högby (☎ 070/556-54-34). An interesting collection of antiques is stockpiled and sold at **Antikgården,** Salomonstorp, in the hamlet of Köpingsvik (☎ 0485/727-83). And if you happen to be driving near the northern tip of the island, consider a visit to yet another ceramics studio, **Glömminge Krukmarkeri** (☎ 0485/372-26), which lies in the heart of the hamlet of Glömminge, 6 miles north of the point where the bridge from the Swedish mainland first deposits you on Öland.

WHERE TO STAY

Ekerum Golf & Conference Center. Ekerum, S 387 92 Borgholm. ☎ **0485/80080** or 0485/80000. Fax 0485/80010. www.ekerum.com. 72 2-bedroom apts with kitchens (sleeps 4). TV TEL. 1,990 SEK ($218.90) double occupancy, for 1–2 nights, plus a 350 SEK ($38.50) obligatory clean-up fee. Discounts available for stays of 3 or more nights. AE, DC, MC, V. Closed Oct 23–Mar. Free parking. Bus: 101.

Set 9 miles south of Borgholm, this hotel was built in 1991 at the same time as the adjacent Ekerum golf courses, the best on the island. The hotel is designed as an avant-garde complex of buildings, the older of which have red roofs, ochre-colored walls, and a sense of a former use as farmhouses. The newer buildings are white-sided post-modern structures, the largest of which is a three-story gabled building with prominent bay windows and a design that seems to have been inspired by the early 20th century. Accommodations are clean, conservative, and tasteful, each with a wood-burning stove and comfortable, unfrilly furniture where a golf enthusiast might feel at home after time on the links. A restaurant and a bar are on the premises.

Guntorps Herrgård. Guntorpsgatan, 387-36 Borgholm. ☎ **0485/13-000.** Fax 0485/13-319. www. guntorp.oland.com. E-mail: ulf@guntorp.oland.com. 20 units. TV TEL. 895 SEK ($98.45) double. Rate includes breakfast. AE, DC, MC. Closed 2 weeks at Christmas. Free parking.

Set about a half mile southeast of Borgholm's center, the premises of this hotel were built in 1918 as the family home of the merchants and politicians who controlled the island's commerce around the turn of the century. New wings were added to the stately building in 1986; shortly thereafter, a restaurant, open only for dinner every night from 6 to 9:30pm, was added as well. Today, you'll find clean, well-maintained, and rather simple bedrooms; a small conference and convention facility; and a heated outdoor swimming pool set within the rear garden.

○ **Halltops Gästgiveri.** Högstrum, S-387 92 Borgholm. ☎ **0485/850-00.** Fax 0485/850-01. www.checkpoint-oland.com/halltops/. E-mail: halltorps.gastgiveri@mailbox.calypso.net. 36 units. TV TEL. 1,050 SEK ($115.50) double. AE, DC, MC, V. Free parking. From Borgholm, take bus no. 101 or 106.

Set near the geographic center of the island, 6 miles south of Borgholm, this tasteful and reliable hotel occupies one of the oldest manor houses of Öland, a yellow-sided complex of steep-roofed buildings whose origins date from the 17th century. Launched as a hotel in 1975, and renovated and massively enlarged in 1991, it has a tranquil, farmland setting, with a view across the Kalmarsund and the Halltorp Forest. Once it was a royal farming estate, and between the end of World War I and the early 1970s, it functioned as a home for the elderly before its limestone walls were massively reinforced and it was transformed into an inn. Bedrooms are cozy and intimate, often with beamed ceilings, and each outfitted with an artfully old-fashioned allure that's the result of serious efforts on the part of a team of decorators. About two-thirds are within a newly built annex; the remaining dozen or so are within the original manor house. Each is named after a region of Sweden, with a decor that's inspired by traditional models from that region. Unlike many other hotels on the island, this one remains open all year.

Dining: The in-house restaurant is recommended separately (see "Where to Dine," below).

Amenities: The hotel has a sun terrace overlooking the island's west coast, two saunas, and conference facilities.

Hotel Borgholm. Trädgårdsgatan 15, S-387 31 Borgholm. ☎ **0485/770-60.** Fax 0485/124-66. www.hotellborgholm.com. E-mail: info@hotellborgholm.com. 24 units. TV TEL. 890 SEK ($97.90) double. Rate includes breakfast. AE, DC, MC, V. Free parking.

This establishment has been in the restaurant business far longer (since 1850) than it has been a hotel. But in the 1950s, the site was enlarged with a pleasant and airy set of bedrooms that have been renovated several times since then. The hotel is convenient to everything in Borgholm—it's only about 50 yards from the Storegatan, the town's main street—and remains open throughout the winter for the many Swedish and European business travelers who make it their home during their time in Borgholm. Bedrooms are high-ceilinged and tastefully decorated in a monochromatic style, with a heavy emphasis on bordeaux with white trim and conservative furnishings. On the premises is the separately recommended restaurant and a cocktail lounge.

Hotel Skansen. S-386 21 Färjestaden. ☎ **0485/30530.** Fax 0485/34804. www. Stefan-noren.se/skansen. 25 units. TV TEL. Selected weekends July to mid-Aug and Sun–Thurs year-round, 840 SEK ($92.40) double; Fri–Sat 600 SEK ($66) double. Rate includes breakfast. AE, DC, MC, V. Free parking. Bus: 101.

Positioned among trees, forests, and fields, 21 miles south of Borgholm, this hotel is targeted by ecologists, nature lovers, and anyone who's interested in getting away from the pressures of urban life. It's composed of three separate buildings, each with an old-fashioned ochre-colored exterior that might remind you of an antique inn, and a tile roof. The oldest of the buildings dates from 1811; the entire compound was tastefully renovated in 1991. Inside, you'll find a cocktail lounge and a well-managed restaurant where fixed-price lunches cost from 60 SEK ($6.60) and à la carte dinners begin at 210 SEK ($23.10) per person. Public areas tastefully combine modern furnishings, some of them upholstered in black leather, Persian carpets, and hardwood floors. Bedrooms are simple but comfortable, and outfitted with angular modern furniture with emphasis on white walls and varnished hardwoods.

Strand Hotell. Villagatan 4, S-387 88 Borgholm. ☎ **0485/888-88.** Fax 0485/124-27. www.strand.borgholm.se. E-mail: info@strand.borgholm.se. 1,390 SEK ($152.90) double. Apts with kitchens available only on selected weeks in summer for 5,500–11,250 SEK ($605–$1,237.50) per week, double occupancy. Rates include breakfast. AE, DC, MC, V. Free parking. Bus: 101.

This is the largest, splashiest, and most glittery hotel on Öland, the closest thing there to a seafront resort in Atlantic City, New Jersey. Built in 1952 and massively enlarged in 1973, it was renovated in 1991 into a venue that's much, much better accessorized. Most accommodations are within a slope-sided, four-story building whose sides taper into a lopsided pyramid as they rise, a design that creates large, sun-flooded terraces for many of the rooms inside. Each is outfitted with pale colors and uncontroversial modern furniture, usually made from blond laminated woods such as birch. Many of them overlook an upscale marina, part of which is owned by the hotel, and which once won an award as the best privately owned yacht harbor in Sweden. About 16 of the units with kitchens are privately owned and used as vacation homes by urbanites. These are rented out by the week (selected weeks only) during some periods when the owners are out of town.

Dining/Diversions: On the premises are two year-round restaurants serving a standard Swedish and international fare. Two additional restaurants are created out of otherwise unused space in summer, and disco dancing also is offered in the summer months.

Amenities: Indoor swimming pool, sauna, solarium, fitness room, room service, concierge.

WHERE TO DINE

✪ **Halltops Gästgiveri.** In the Sunwing Ekerum Hotel Högstrum, Borgholm. ☎ **0485/850 00.** Reservations recommended. Main courses 175–225 SEK ($19.25–$24.75); fixed-price menu 285 SEK ($31.35). AE, DC, MC, V. Daily noon–10pm. From Borgholm, take bus 101 or 106. SWEDISH.

Set within the previously recommended inn (see "Where to Stay," above), this is one of the most nostalgic and appealing restaurants in Öland. The dining rooms evoke old-fashioned Sweden, but in a way that's charming and with none of the drawbacks of that less mechanized, less convenient age. Menu items usually are seasoned with herbs and vegetables from nearby suppliers, which arrive ultra-fresh at frequent intervals. Two particularly appealing specialties include fillets of cod brought in by local fishers, fried and served with parsley-flavored butter, and fillets of island lamb with thyme sauce and au gratin potatoes. Unlike many competing restaurants on the island, this one is open year-round.

✪ **Restaurant Bakfickan.** In the Hotel Borgholm, Trädgårdsgatan 15. ☎ **0485/77060.** Reservations recommended. Main courses 100–400 SEK ($11–$44). June–Aug, daily 6–10pm; Sept–May, Tues–Sat noon–2pm. AE, DC, MC, V. INTERNATIONAL.

The dining room of the Hotel Borgholm doesn't look particularly fancy or glamorous. In fact, it's a modern, somewhat nondescript room with pastel walls and tables that are just a bit overcrowded. But according to local gastronomes, the decor is merely an uncontroversial foil for the best restaurant venue on Öland, with food that's at the top of the A-list for its international flair, subtle flavors, and panache. The culinary force behind its excellence is German-born Karin Fransson, an entrepreneur who is widely recognized as the most sophisticated chef and culinary mentor on the island. Marvelous things are done here to local lamb and fish (especially codfish). A typical meal might include garlic-fried mussels from local waters; smoked and baked salmon served cold with a compote of tomatoes, a timbale of avocados, and a lime-basil sauce; or roasted Öland lamb wrapped in bacon and served with a potato and parsnip strudel and marinated peppers.

ÖLAND AFTER DARK

Both of the island's most popular pubs lie in Borgholm and tend to attract clients from throughout the island. A local favorite is **Pubben,** Storgatan 18 (☎ 0485/124-15). Open nightly at 5pm, it stocks nearly 50 brands of whisky, enough to make you feel you've wandered into a single-malt pub in Scotland. Its biggest competitor is **Rooky Bar,** Södralanggatan (☎ 0485/77758). Set a short distance from the harbor, it features some kind of live musician (usually a pianist or a guitar player), who appears most nights after 8pm. It's open nightly from 6pm to 2am.

2 Gotland & Visby °

136 miles S of Stockholm, 93 miles S of Nynäshamn, 55 miles E of the Swedish mainland

In the middle of the Baltic Sea sits the ancient home of the Goths, the island of Gotland, about 75 miles long and 35 miles wide. Swedes go to Gotland—Sweden's most popular tourist island—for sunny holidays by the sea, whereas North Americans tend to be more interested in the old walled city of Visby. But an investment of a little extra time will reveal that Gotland—with its cliffs, unusual rock formations, bathing beaches, and rolling countryside—is rich territory. Buses traverse the island, as do organized tours out of Visby.

From the end of the 12th century and during the 13th, the walled city of Visby rose to the zenith of its power as the seat of the powerful Hanseatic merchants and the trade center of northern Europe. During its heyday, 17 churches were built, stepgabled houses were erected of stone, and the townspeople lived in relative luxury. Visby eventually was ransacked by the Danes, however, and fell into a decline. Sometime late in the 19th century, when Visby was recognized as a treasure house of medieval art and became the number-one spot in Scandinavia for experiencing the charm of the Middle Ages, it became a major tourist attraction.

ESSENTIALS

GETTING THERE   By Plane   Visitors can fly **SAS** to Gotland from Stockholm; there are three daily flights, which take about 30 minutes. For information and schedules, call ☎ 020/727-000. There is bus service between Visby and the airport between June and August only. Buses run about four times a day at times that coincide with the arrival of flights.

By Boat   Those who want to take the boat to Gotland must first go to Nynäshamn; by bus from Stockholm it's about a 1-hour ride. The car-ferry to Visby leaves at midnight and takes about 5 hours. In summer there also are day connections. You can make reservations through your travel agent or directly with the ferry service, **Destination Gotland,** for cabin or car space. It's wise to book deck space if you plan to travel on a weekend. Call ☎ 0498/201-020 in Stockholm.

Gotland

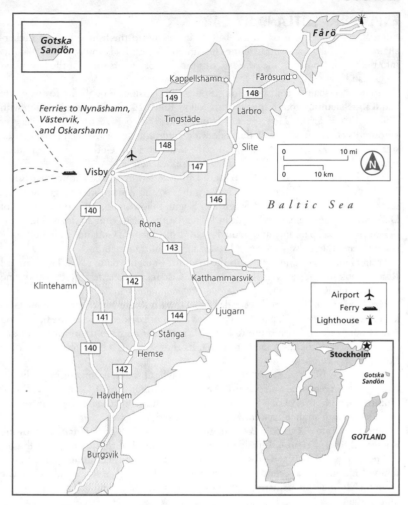

VISITOR INFORMATION   In Visby, contact the tourist bureau, **Gotlands Turist Service,** Österväg 1 (☎ **0498/24-70-65**), open May through August, Monday through Friday from 7am to 7pm and Saturday and Sunday from 7am to 6pm; and September through April, Monday through Friday from 8am to 5pm and Saturday and Sunday from 10am to 4pm.

A SPECIAL EVENT   During the annual ✪ **Medieval Week** in August, for 8 days Visby once again becomes a Hanseatic town. At the harbor, Strandgatan swarms with people in medieval dress, many of them tending market stalls. You meet the blacksmith, barber, cobbler, and trader. Musicians play the hurdy-gurdy, the fiddle, and the flute; jesters play the fool. Toward nightfall a kingly procession comes into the square. The program has more than 100 such events during the festival, along with medieval mystery plays, masses, choral and instrumental music, tournaments, and displays of horses, as well as archery competitions, fire-eaters, belly dancers, and walking tours of the medieval town.

EXPLORING GOTLAND BY CAR

From Visby, drive north on Route 149, heading toward the fishing port of **Licker-shamn**. Look for a narrow trail along the cliffs. This path leads you to a rock that juts into the water. Known as the *Maiden,* this promontory offers some of the best views on Gotland.

From Lickershamn, continue along Route 149, passing through the towns of **Ire** and **Kappelshamn**. From Kappelshamn, follow Route 149 south to the junction with Route 148 in **Lärbro**. Here, go north on Route 148 to **Fårösund**. The village of Fårösund sits on the shores of the mile-wide Fårösund channel, which separates the small island of **Fårö** (sheep island) from the main island of Gotland. You can take a ferry to Fårö to visit some of the island's superb beaches.

From Fårösund, take Route 148 back to Lärbro. A few miles past Lärbro, take Route 146 southwest toward **Slite**. Follow it down the coast to **Aurungs**. Here, go west on a secondary road heading toward **Siggur**. In Siggur, follow signs south to the village of **Dalhem**. The most remarkable sight in Dalhem is the village church, situated just outside town. Its wall paintings and stained glass are the finest on Gotland. Train buffs may enjoy visiting the Railway Museum located in the old train station.

From Dalhem, continue south on the road that brought you to town. Head toward **Roma**. Look for the ruins of Roma Abbey, a Cistercian monastery destroyed during the Protestant Reformation.

Head west from Roma on a secondary road toward Route 140 that runs along Gotland's western coast. You'll pass through the villages of **Bander** and **Sojvide** before you reach Route 140. Follow it south to Burgsvik, a popular port and resort town. Just east of **Burgsvik**, visit the small hamlet of **Öja.** Its church boasts a triumphal cross dating from the 13th century.

After visiting Öja, return to Burgsvik. Here you head south, passing through the villages of **Bottarvegården** and **Vamlingbo**. At the southern tip of Gotland you'll find **Hoburgen,** with its towering lighthouse. Along with the lighthouse, you'll encounter cliffs, many with strange rock formations, and a series of caves.

Return to Burgsvik to connect with Route 140. Turn off after **Fidenäs**, following Route 142 toward **Hemse**. Outside Hemse, take Route 144 to **Ljugarn**, a small port and resort town on Gotland's east coast. You can visit the small customs museum. Just south of Ljugarn, on a secondary road, is a series of Bronze Age stone sculptures. The seven rock formations, depicting ancient ships, form the largest group of stone settings on the island.

Follow Route 143 northwest from Ljugarn and return to Visby.

SEEING THE SIGHTS
IN VISBY

Visby is a good town for walkers, but you may want to take one of the organized tours that are offered in season. Because so many of the sights, particularly the ruins of the 13th- and 14th-century churches, are better appreciated with some background, we recommend the tours that take 2 hours each and cost 75 SEK ($9.60) per participant. They're offered only in summer, between mid-June and mid-August. Between mid-June and mid-July, English-language tours are conducted every Monday, Wednesday, Thursday, and Saturday at 11:30am. Between mid-July and mid-August they're conducted on the same days, with an additional tour beginning at 2:30pm.

In town, you can walk about, observing houses from the Middle Ages, ruined fortifications, and churches. Notable among these is the **Burmeisterska Huset,** the home of the burmeister or the leading German merchant, at Strandgatan 9.

Visby

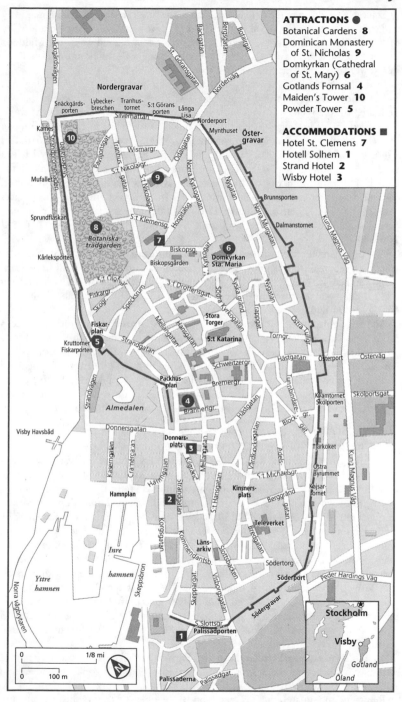

ATTRACTIONS ●
Botanical Gardens **8**
Dominican Monastery
  of St. Nicholas **9**
Domkyrkan (Cathedral
  of St. Mary) **6**
Gotlands Fornsal **4**
Maiden's Tower **10**
Powder Tower **5**

ACCOMMODATIONS ■
Hotel St. Clemens **7**
Hotell Solhem **1**
Strand Hotel **2**
Wisby Hotel **3**

You can walk down to the old **Hanseatic harbor** (not the same harbor in use today) and stroll through the **Botanical Gardens,** which have earned for Visby the title "City of Roses." You'll pass two of the most famous towers in the old wall—the **Maiden's Tower** (a peasant girl was buried alive here for helping a Danish king) and the **Powder Tower** (the oldest fortification in Visby).

In the heyday of its power and glory, little Visby boasted 17 churches. Only one today, **Domkyrkan** (Cathedral of St. Mary), is in use. Found at Kyrkberget, it was dedicated in 1225 and was built with funds collected by German merchant ships. Pope Clement VI in Avignon gave his permission to build the so-called Swertingska chapel in 1349. The church was damaged in four serious fires: 1400, 1586, 1610, and 1744. It attained its status as a cathedral in 1572. The only original fixture left is a sandstone font from the 1200s. The landmark of Visby is the two towers of the church. The tower at the western front is square, whereas two slimmer ones appear on the east. In the interior, one of the curiosities is the fringe of grotesque angels' faces beneath the pulpit. Hours are Monday through Friday and Sunday from 8am to 9pm, Saturday 8am to 6:30pm. Free admission. For more information, call ☎ **0498/ 206-800.**

Also of interest are the ruins of the former **Dominican Monastery of St. Nicholas** just down the road from Domkyrkan. The church has a rose window cut from a single big stone—it's more than 10 feet in diameter. Work began on the monastery in 1230, but it was destroyed by Lübeck forces in 1525. For more information, call ☎ **0498/206-800.**

Another sightseeing recommendation is **Gotlands Fornsal,** the Historical Museum of Gotland, Strandgatan 14 (☎ **0498/29-27-00**), on a medieval street noted for its step-gabled houses. The museum contains some of the most interesting artifacts discovered on Gotland, including carved stones dating from A.D. 400, art from medieval and later periods, plus furniture and household items. It's open May 15 to August, daily from 11am to 6pm; September to May 14, Tuesday through Sunday from noon to 4pm. Admission is 40 SEK ($4.40) for adults, free for children 16 and under.

ON THE ISLAND

At the **Turistbyrå,** Österväg 1 (☎ **0498/24-70-65**), ask what island tours are scheduled during your visit; these daily tours (different every day) are the best way to get a quick overview of Gotland. The price can be as low as 50 SEK ($5.50) for a brief walking tour or as high as 360 SEK ($39.60) for a complete tour of the island by van.

One thing you can be sure of is that each tour will visit the **Lummelunda Grottan,** Lummelunds Bruk (☎ **0498/273050**), a karst cave formed of limestone bedrock by a subterranean stream. The explored part of the stream cave stretches for 2.6 miles and contains stalactite and stalagmite formations, fossil remains, and subterranean waters. The part of the cave with some of the biggest and most beautiful chambers is open to visitors. It's located 8 miles north of Visby along Route 149. A bus departs from Österport Visby June 19 to August 14, daily at 2pm. The cave is open May to June 25, daily from 9am to 4pm; June 26 to August 14, daily from 9am to 6pm; August 15 to September 14, daily from 9am to 4pm (closed at other times). Visits on your own cost 45 SEK ($4.95) for adults, 30 SEK ($3.30) for children 5 to 15, free for children 4 and under.

One tour goes to **northern Gotland and Fårö.** A bus takes you to the ferry port of Fårösund, with a 10-minute ferry ride over the strait followed by an excursion around Fårö (Sheep Island) so that you can see dwarf forests and moors.

Returning to Gotland, the bus takes you to the open-air cultural history museum at **Bunge,** which documents the old peasant culture. That's followed by a tour of the

Planning Ahead

For all its attractions, Visby doesn't have enough hotels. Because accommodations are packed in summer, you need to reserve in advance. If at all possible, try to telephone for reservations from Stockholm.

Blase Limestone Museum in Fleringe, which has two lime kilns (now restored) from the turn of the century. The tours take place in summer, on Tuesday and Thursday from 8:30am to 5:30pm.

Another tour takes you to the southern tip of the island to see the legendary "old man of **Hoburgen**," a rock formation known as a chalk stack. The tour also includes the Iron Age village of **Gervide** as well as two 17th-century farms. The bus travels along the windswept shoreline of the west coast.

SHOPPING

The most memorable goods available for acquisition on Gotland are produced on the island, usually by individual craftspeople working in highly detailed, small-scale productions. One store at which you can find such products is **Yllet,** S:t Hansgatan 19, Visby (☎ **0498/21-40-44**), where clothing made from wool produced by thousands of local sheep is sold in the form of sweaters, scarves, hats, gloves, coats, and winter wear for men, women, and children. Colors here tend to be natural and soft, usually deriving from the untinted, unbleached fibers originally produced by the sheep themselves. Also, don't overlook the gift shop that's showcased within the island's historical museum, **Gotlands Fornsal,** Strandgatan 14, Visby (☎ **0498/29-27-00**); where reproductions of some of the museum's art objects are for sale, as well as handcrafts and textiles made on the island.

Gotland is home to dozens of independent artists, most of whom work out of their own houses or studios manufacturing ceramics, textiles, woodcarvings, or examples of metalwork. Their merchandise tends to be marketed by cooperatives, loosely organized networks that publicize and display the works of artists whose work is judged by a panel as representative of good-quality expressions of the local art and handcraft scene. Objects are displayed and can be purchased at two separate agencies: **Galerie & Butik Gotland Konsthantverkare,** Hästgatan (☎ **0498/21-03-49**), and **Galerie Kvinnfolki,** Donnersplats 2 (☎ **0498/21-00-51**). Kvinnfolki limits its merchandise to items crafted only by women, which includes jam made from local berries, textiles, children's clothing, and a line of cosmetics made on the island from all-natural oils, emollients, and pigments.

WHERE TO STAY

If you should arrive without reservations, contact the **Gotland Resort** (☎ **0498/20-12-60**). The English-speaking staff will try to arrange for rooms in a hotel or private home in or near Visby. The average rate for an accommodation in a private home is 500 SEK ($55) per person, per night.

IN VISBY

✪ **Hotel St. Clemens.** Smedjegatan 3, S-621 55 Visby. ☎ **0498/21-90-00.** Fax 0498/27-94-43. www.clemenshotell.se. E-mail: info@clemenshotell.se. 32 units. TV TEL. 840–980 SEK ($92.40–$107.80) double. Additional bed 180 SEK ($19.80) extra. Rates include breakfast. DC, MC, V. Free parking.

This 18th-century building in the town center has been successfully transformed into a well-run little hotel. It's decorated tastefully in a modern style, with light pastels used effectively. It's open all year, and the staff is helpful and efficient. In spite of the hotel's age, all of its bedrooms have modern shower and toilet facilities with adequate shelf space and fluffy towels. All renovations were carried out with great care so as not to ruin the architecture. No two rooms are identical; your choices range from the smallest single in the shoemaker's old house with a view over church ruins to a four-bed unit with a sloping ceiling and the greenery of the botanical gardens framing the window. Even the old stable offers rooms especially for guests with allergies—no smoking, of course. In these rooms the toilets are accessible to wheelchairs. A comfortable, cozy atmosphere permeates the whole place, a series of five antique buildings connected by two pleasant gardens. Breakfast is the only meal served but it's a generous buffet.

Hotell Solhem. Solhemsgatan 3, S-621 58 Visby. ☎ **0498/27-90-70.** Fax 0498/21-95-23. www.strandhotel.net/solhem. E-mail: solhem@strandhotel.net. 94 units. TV TEL. 790–1,240 SEK ($86.90–$136.40) double. Rates include breakfast. Closed Sat–Sun Jan–Feb. AE, DC, MC, V. Free parking.

One of the newest, most recently renovated hotels in Visby was built in 1987 on a hilly slope overlooking the harbor, a few blocks north of the center. In 1998, its size was doubled thanks to a new addition, designed to match the hotel's existing core with ochre-colored walls, prominent gables, a terra-cotta roof, and a vague sense of the seafaring life of the early 19th century. Bedrooms are comfortable, cozy, and warm, with simple but tasteful furniture. There's a sauna on site, but no restaurant on the premises other than a room devoted to breakfasts.

Strand Hotel. Strandgatan 34, S-621 56 Visby. ☎ **800/528-1234** in the U.S., or 0498/ 25-88-00. Fax 0498/27-81-11. www.strandhotel.com. E-mail: strand.hotel@gotlandica.se. 112 units. TV TEL. 1,290–1,390 SEK ($141.90–$152.90) double. Rates include breakfast. AE, MC, V. Free parking.

This popular four-story hotel, a Best Western, was built in 1982 on the waterfront a short walk from the harbor. Groups of people are always congregating in the lobby, and the comfortable bedrooms are tastefully modern. Mattresses are replaced as the need arises, and the bathrooms are well maintained with up-to-date plumbing and good towels. Breakfast is the only meal served. Facilities include a sauna and an indoor pool.

✪ Wisby Hotel. Strandgatan 6, S-621 21 Visby. ☎ **0498/25-75-00.** Fax 0498/21-13-20. www.wisbyhotell.se. E-mail: info@wisbyhotell.se. 133 units. MINIBAR TV TEL. July and Fri–Sat year-round, 960–1,470 SEK ($105.60–$161.70) double; rest of year, 1,410 SEK ($155.10) double. Year-round, 1,950 SEK ($214.50) suite. Rates include breakfast. AE, DC, MC, V. Free parking.

When this hotel was radically restored and upgraded in the early 1990s, it became the best and most glamorous on the island. Set close to the harbor front in the town center, its historic core includes medieval foundations and the type of solid stonework you'll see elsewhere in Visby. Radiating outward from the core are newer additions that span several centuries. The best feature of the hotel, which makes it the finest place to stay off-season, is a winter garden, a bold combination of steel, glass, and Gotland sandstone. You can relax in a leather armchair with a drink and admire the greenery and the changing Nordic light. On the premises are a restaurant, a bistro, two bars, and a conscientious staff. Room service is daily from 7am to 11pm; saunas, massage, and babysitting services are also available. The bedrooms are conservatively elegant, and some have reproductions of 18th-century furniture. The bathrooms are a bit small, but adequate. Housekeeping is excellent.

A NEARBY HOTEL

Toftagården Hotell & Restaurang. Tofta. S-621 98 Visby. ☎ **0498/29-70-00.** Fax 0498/
26-56-66. E-mail: info@toftgarden.se. 30 units, 5 cottages. TV. 875–1,325 SEK ($96.25–
$145.75) double. Rates include breakfast. AE, DC, MC, V. Free parking.

Set adjacent to the island's coast, 12½ miles south of Visby, and separated from the
beach only by a windbreak of trees, this cozy, family-managed hotel grew up and
developed from a core that was established shortly after World War II. Much improved
and enlarged since then, its most visible section was built in the 1980s as a gable-
fronted replica of a large private house. Both the conventional bedrooms and the quin-
tet of cottages are cozy, comfortably outfitted with simple furnishings and good beds.
The variation in prices derives from the fact that a handful of them were renovated less
recently than the more expensive ones and have older, slightly more worn upholstery
and furniture.

Part of the allure of this place derives from its well-managed restaurant, which serves
specialties from Gotland and the rest of Sweden every day from noon to 8pm (until
10pm during July and August). Main courses cost from 135 to 155 SEK ($17.30 to
$19.85); specialties include roasted Gotland lamb and different preparations of salmon.

WHERE TO DINE

Burmeister. Strandgatan 6, Visby. ☎ **0498/21-03-73.** Reservations required. Main courses
140–200 SEK ($15.40–$22); pizzas 85–110 SEK ($9.35–$12.10). AE, DC, MC, V. June 15–Aug
15, daily noon–4pm and 6–10:30pm. Disco, mid–June to mid–Aug, Tues–Wed 10pm–2am;
year-round, Fri–Sat 10pm–2am. ITALIAN.

This large restaurant in the town center offers dining indoors or under shady fruit trees
in the garden of a 16th-century house originally built for the wealthiest citizen of Visby.
Diners can look out on the surrounding medieval buildings from many of the tables.
The cuisine is rather standard international, never achieving any glory but not disap-
pointing, either. The place is incredibly popular in summer, and long lines form—so
they must be doing something right. Pizza is the most popular menu choice. After
10pm in summer the restaurant becomes a disco; the cover charge is 80 SEK ($8.80).

Gutekällaren. Stortorget 3, Visby. ☎ **0498/21-00-43.** Main courses 105–195 SEK
($11.55–$21.45). AE, DC, MC, V. Daily 6–11pm. SWEDISH.

This restaurant and bar in the town center originally was built as a tavern in the early
1600s on older foundations. It was enlarged in 1789 and today is one of the oldest
buildings (if not the oldest) in Visby. It offers fresh fish and meat dishes, including
some vegetarian specialties. You might begin with a fish soup made with lobster and
shrimp, then follow with fillet of sole Waleska or roast lamb chops. The dessert specialty in summer is a parfait made of local berries. Cookery here is solid and reliable,
with fresh ingredients. The ambience is sober, however, for this fun-loving island of
summer fun. But once the dining is out of the way, the place livens up considerably
(see "Visby After Dark," below).

Munkkällaren. Lilla Torggränd 2, Visby. ☎ **0498/27-14-00.** Reservations required in summer. Main courses 90–168 SEK ($9.90–$18.50). AE, DC, MC, V. Restaurant, daily 6–11pm;
pubs, daily 6pm–2am. SWEDISH/INTERNATIONAL.

This restaurant, although not the most expensive in town, is one of the best. You'll re-
cognize it in the center of Visby by its brown wooden facade. The dining room, which
is only a few steps from the street, is sheathed in white stone, parts of which date from
1100. In summer, the management opens the doors to two more pubs in the compound. Glasses of beer cost 45 SEK ($4.95). The main pub, Munken, offers platters

of good tasting and flavorful *husmanskost* (Swedish home cooking), including *frikadeller* (meatballs). In the restaurant you might begin with escargots in creamy garlic sauce or toast with Swedish caviar. Specialties include shellfish stew, salmon-stuffed sole with spinach and a saffron sauce, and venison in port-wine sauce. Live music often is performed in the courtyard, beginning around 8pm. After the music stops on Saturday and Sunday, a disco opens every night from 11pm to 2am. Admission to the disco is 60 SEK ($6.60).

VISBY AFTER DARK

There's a lot more energy expended on star gazing, wave watching, and ecology in Gotland than on bar-hopping and nocturnal flirting. But if you want to heat it up after dark, there's a limited offering nonetheless. The island's premier venue for folks over 40 who enjoy dancing "very tight" (ballroom style) occurs every Saturday night at the **Borgen Bar,** Hästgatan 24 (☎ **0498/24-79-55**), which contains a restaurant, a dance floor, and recordings that are selected as a means of encouraging patrons to dance (the music ranges from the big band era to more modern, supper club selections). A more hipster-ish alternative where dancers are less inclined to wrap themselves romantically in each other's arms is the **Munkkälleren,** which was recommended previously as a restaurant, and derives at least some of its business from its role as a bar and late-night, weekend-only disco. An equivalent venue is offered at **Gutekälleren,** another previously recommended restaurant, whose interior becomes a disco either 2 or 4 nights a week, beginning around 10pm, for high-energy dancers mostly aged 35 and under. If you happen to be a bit older than 35, you'll still feel comfortable hanging out at the establishment's bar, soaking up aquavit and local color.

SOUTHERN GOTLAND

As charming as Visby is, many savvy Swedes prefer to stay in southern Gotland in the hamlet of Burgsvik, 56 miles south of Visby. This is a popular port and resort town. If you have a car you may want to check it out.

WHERE TO STAY

Pensionat Holmhällar. Vamlingbo, S-620-10 Burgsvik. ☎ **0498/498030.** Fax 0498/ 49-80-56. 50 units. 600 SEK ($66) double. Half board 475 SEK ($52.25) per person. No credit cards. Free parking.

The origins of this hotel date from 1940, when it was built as a barracks and administrative center by the Swedish army as they pondered the political role they should take vis-à-vis the growing menace of Nazi Germany. In 1949, it was enlarged and adapted into a resort hotel, and further enlarged throughout the course of the 1960s and 1970s. Today, it incorporates three separate buildings and 16 simple cottages within an area of natural beauty, 200 yards from one of the best beaches on the southern region of Gotland. Bedrooms are a step up from army barracks in comfort, but they are small with rather thin mattresses. Bathrooms also are rather cramped. The clientele tends to be interested in nature, ecology, beach life, and an utter lack of distractions from the outside world. There's a restaurant on the premises that maintains impossibly early hours (dinner is served only from 5 to 7:30pm) and specializes in family-style set menus priced at 75 SEK ($8.25) each. There's a sauna on the premises (summer only) as well.

Know in advance that this place is much more appealing in summer than in winter: Between October and March, services and access to most of this hotel are radically curtailed. All dining and drinking facilities are closed, and only a handful of outlying cottages are available for rent. These cost 250 SEK ($27.50) for a double without bathroom; and 350 SEK ($38.50) for a double with bathroom. In addition, no linens or towels are provided off-season, so you'll have to bring your own.

Värdshuset Björklunda. S-620 10 Burgsvik. ☎ **0498/49-71-90.** Fax 0498/49-78-50. 20 units. TV. 619–750 SEK ($68.10–$82.50) double. Rates include breakfast. AE, DC, MC, V. Free parking.

Originating more than a century ago as an unpretentious farmhouse, this hotel developed during the 1970s into a well-respected inn that's directed today by charming and hardworking members of the Jacobson family. Set near a small beach, within a forest, and beside the main highway leading south into Burgsvik, the inn draws a loyal clientele into its restaurant between June and August, when it's open daily from noon to 8:30pm (last order).

Within a cozy, traditionally decorated dining room, you can order culinary specialties from Gotland and to a lesser extent, from the rest of Sweden as well. Examples include smoked fillets of lamb, barbecued lamb (a treat available only on Saturday nights), and fresh salmon served with saffron sauce. Main courses cost from 75 to 140 SEK ($8.25 to $15.40); fixed-price menus (lunch only) 65 SEK ($7.15). Menu service is curtailed and presented on an "as needed" basis the rest of the year, so if you arrive between October and April, it's likely that your meal will be served *en famille* with the Jacobsons, without the fanfare of a commercial restaurant, but with some of the warmth and conviviality of a smoothly functioning private home. Bedrooms are simple and modern, a function of a radical renovation that was completed in 1995. Although fairly comfortable, rooms are extremely small. Bathrooms also are a bit cramped.

9

The Göta Canal & Lake Vänern

Connecting Gothenburg and Stockholm with a direct inland water route, the Göta Canal makes for an unforgettable journey with 65 locks between the North Sea and the Baltic. The canal is called "Sweden's blue ribbon," and it runs through the province of Västergötland between Lake Vänern and Lake Vättern (often confused because of the similarity in their names).

The shifting scenery along the entire length of the canal makes it among the most beautiful panoramas in Europe. It's preferable to see it by water, but you also can drive or cycle along the canal.

The history of the canal dates from 1810, when the former naval officer Baltzar von Platen, assisted by some 60,000 soldiers, began what was to be a 22-year project. The first of the locks was built in Forsvik in 1813 and is still in use today.

Toward the end of the 19th century, the canal's importance as a transport artery began to diminish. Gradually, however, the idea of using it for leisure activities began to catch on, and today 4,000 boats a year use the canal, in addition to a significant number of passenger vessels and even canoes.

The towpaths are almost as busy as the canal itself. Where oxen once could be seen giving barges and sailing craft a much-needed tow, you now find walkers and cyclists making their way through the leafy countryside.

One of the highlights of any trip along the Göta Canal is to take in views of Lake Vänern, an island sea that has existed since 6500 B.C.; although back then it covered a much larger area than today. It is the largest lake in Sweden and the third largest lake in Europe, encompassing 1,322 square miles. It is 90 miles long and 50 miles wide at one point.

The present-day Lake Vänern took shape during the Iron Age around 300 B.C. Some 20 tributaries of varying size feed water into the lake, although that water is discharged through just one outflow, the River Göta. The amount of water being discharged is just over 500,000 liters per second, which in effect means the water in the lake is changed every ninth year. The lake boasts about 20,000 small islands and rocks, forming the world's largest freshwater archipelago.

1 The Göta Canal

A fascinating summer boat trip and one of Sweden's major attractions is the 4-day
✪ **Göta Canal cruise,** which covers 350 miles from Gothenburg (Göteborg) in the
west to Stockholm in the east (or vice versa). The Göta Canal is composed of a series
of artificial canals, lakes, and rivers connected by a series of 65 locks (the highest is
more than 300 feet above sea level), and the 4-day cruise makes four or five stops along
the way. Day trips and longer cruises also are offered.

The canal was begun in the early 19th century for the purpose of transporting goods
across Sweden, thereby avoiding expensive tolls levied by Denmark on ships entering
and leaving the Baltic Sea. However, soon after the canal was completed, Denmark
waived its shipping tolls, and the railway between Stockholm and Gothenburg was created, thereby allowing for the cheaper and faster shipment of goods across Sweden.
Thus the canal became more of a tourist attraction than a means of transportation.

Boats depart Gothenburg heading east along the Göta älv River. About 30 minutes
outside Gothenburg, you'll see the 14th-century **Bohus Fortress.** This bastion played
a leading role in the battles among Sweden, Norway, and Denmark to establish
supremacy. Bohus Castle and Fortress (Bohus Fästning) was built by order of Norway's
Haakon V on Norwegian territory. After the territory was ceded to Sweden in 1658,
Bohus Fortress was used as a prison. Climb the tower, **"Father's Hat,"** for a panoramic
view. Farther down the river, the boat will pass the town of **Kungälv;** known by the
Vikings as Konghälla, its traditions are 1,000 years old.

As the boat proceeds eastward on the Göta's clear water, the landscape becomes
wilder. About 5 hours into the journey you reach the town of **Trollhättan,** home of
one of Europe's largest power stations. The once-renowned Trollhättan Falls, now
almost dry, can be seen at their full capacity only in July. Today, most of the water is
diverted through a series of underground channels to the power station.

After passing through a series of locks, boats enter **Lake Vänern,** Sweden's largest
lake, with a surface area of more than 1,322 square miles. The trip across Lake Vänern
takes about 8 hours. Along the way you'll pass **Lidköping,** home of the famous
Rörstrand porcelain. Lidköping received its charter in 1446. North of Lidköping, on
the island of Kållandsö, stands **Läckö Slott,** a castle dating from 1298. Originally
home of the bishops of Skara, the castle was given to King Gustavus Vasa in 1528, and
later presented to Sweden's great hero, Gen. Magnus Gabriel de la Gardie.

Having crossed Lake Vänern, the boats once again enter the canal. A series of locks,
including the canal's oldest at Forsvik, carry the steamers through to Sweden's second-
largest lake, **Lake Vättern** (see chapter 7). This lake is famous for its beauty and
translucent water. At some points visibility reaches a depth of 50 feet.

Along the eastern shore of Lake Vättern sits the medieval town of **Vadstena,** the
most important stopover on the Göta Canal trip. Within the town are old narrow
streets and frame buildings. It's known throughout Sweden for its delicate handmade
lace, which you can see by walking along Stora Gatan, the main street. Also of interest
is the **Klosterkyrkan (Abbey Church).** Built between the mid-14th and the 15th centuries to specifications outlined by its founder, St. Birgitta (Bridget) of Sweden, this
Gothic church is rich in medieval art. Parts of the abbey date from 1250; the abbey
had sheltered the nuns of St. Birgitta's Order until they were expelled in 1595.

Another important sight is **Vadstena Castle.** Construction began under Gustavus
Vasa, king of Sweden in 1545, but was not completed until 1620. This splendid
Renaissance Vasa castle, erected during a period of national expansion, dominates the
town from its moated position on the lake, just behind the old courthouse in the

The Göta Canal

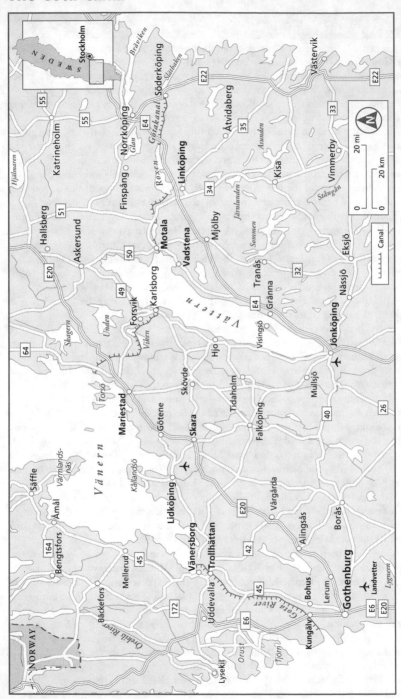

southern part of town. Royalty has not lived in the castle since 1715, but it was restored in the 19th century.

Boats bound for Stockholm depart Lake Vättern and pass through two small lakes, Boren and Roxen. Just south of Lake Roxen you'll find the university town of **Linköping,** site of a battle between Roman Catholic King Sigismund of Poland and Duke Charles of Södermanland (later Charles IX). Charles won the battle and established Linköping as part of Sweden, rather than a province of Rome. In the town's main square stands the Folkung Fountain, one of sculptor Carl Milles's most popular works. Northwest of the main square you'll find the cathedral, a not always harmonious blend of Romanesque and Gothic architecture.

From Linköping, boats enter Lake Roxen and continue their journey northeast by canal to **Slätbaken,** a fjord that stretches to the sea. Steamers then continue along the coast to Stockholm.

The **Göta Canal Steamship Company** offers turn-of-the-century steamers, including its 1874 *Juno,* which claims to be the world's oldest passenger vessel offering overnight accommodations. The line also operates the 1912 *Wilhelm Tham* and the newer—that is, 1931—*Diana.* Officers, staff, and crew are Swedish. Passengers can walk, jog, or bike along the canal path, and there are organized shore excursions at many stops along the way.

For bookings, contact **Scantours** (☎ 800/223-7226). The 4-day cruises range from $775 to $1,325 per person, double occupancy; 6-day cruises from $1,225 to $1,650. Discounts are given for early reservations.

2 Trollhättan

43 miles N of Gothenburg, 272 miles SW of Stockholm

Once early inhabitants learned how to harness the power of the Göta River, they began to build sawmills along its banks. By the early 16th century a small community had been established. The building of the Göta Canal in the 18th and 19th centuries gave Trollhättan its first major thrust toward the future. Hundreds of laborers moved in to build the canal and its locks, and houses sprang up on the islands and banks of the river as the community grew.

In time, cheap electricity obtained directly from the power stations at the falls attracted business companies that in time led to major industries (including Saab). Today, companies such as Saab have put Trollhättan on the Nordic map, as well as employing a good percentage of its 50,000 inhabitants.

ESSENTIALS

GETTING THERE   By Train   About 20 trains roll into Trollhättan every day from Gothenburg, each of them direct, and each taking about 55 minutes. For information about train service into Trollhättan, call ☎ 020/75-75-75.

By Bus   Likewise, about 15 buses arrive every day in Trollhättan from Gothenburg, taking abut the same amount of time. For schedules and information, call ☎ 0200/21818.

By Car   From Gothenburg, head north on Route 45.

VISITOR INFORMATION   For facts on the area, go to the **Trollhättan Tourist Office,** Åkersjövägen 10 (☎ 0520/49-76-54; www.trollhattan.se). It is open June through August, Monday through Saturday 9am to 5pm, September through May, Monday through Friday 10am to 4pm.

Lake Vänern

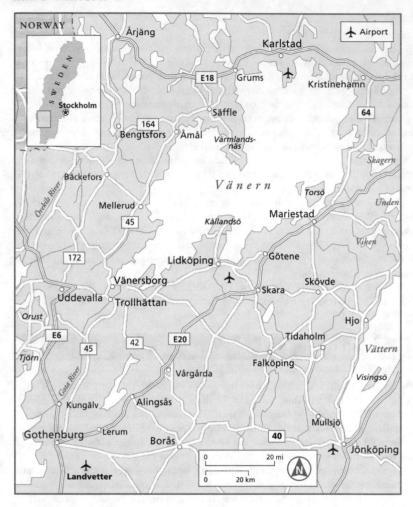

SEEING THE SIGHTS

In Trollhättan, the Göta River takes a mighty leap, a spectacular sight that has attracted visitors to the town for centuries. The best view spots for observing these waterfalls include Kopparklinten, Nyckelbergeet, and Spikön Island. Trollhättan's *Fallensdagar* (Fall Days) is the best-known event in town and occurs during 3 days in July (dates vary annually). The Göta River and the waterfalls are celebrated in this nearly 40-year-old festival. Outdoor stages are used for entertainment and the town's pubs, restaurants, and clubs do a lively business.

The Göta River has the highest flow of any Swedish river, and stretches for 56½ miles. The waterfalls at Trollhättan, with a drop of 104 feet, once were an obstacle difficult to overcome; however, they have since been harnessed. Today, you can see the water flow into the gorge at a rate of 300,000 feet per second—but only at certain times, such as Fall Days in July.

A nearby attraction, about 1¼ miles south of town, is **Kanalmuseet,** Slussområdet (☎ **0520/47-22-06**), which lies at the top of a 104-foot "staircase" created by the locks. It tells the story of the Trollhättan Canal in pictures, models, and tools. An on-site cinema shows historic footage of the locks throughout their history. It is open only between June and August 20, daily from 11am to 7pm. Admission is 10 SEK ($1.10) per person. To reach it from the center of town, follow the signposts pointing to "Slussarna" ("The Locks").

One of the most exciting things to do is to take a walk along the falls. The promenade is called **Schleusenpromenade,** and a walk along this pathway will reveal ruins of the failed canals of the 18th century. In the Gamle Dal'n Park area, locks from the early and mid-19th century remain. Information boards tell of the huge obstacle the falls once presented before they were tamed, and how the unique industrial landscape you see today came about.

If you stroll south on the promenade, you reach the **Energihuset Insikten** (☎ **0520/888-83**), which answers your questions about energy and power in the area with slide shows, computers, energy cycles, water pumps, and many more hands-on exhibits. This 1910 building housing the institute contains 13 massive generators. There is no admission fee, and hours are daily 10am to 6pm from June 8 to August 23. From April 4 to June 7 and from August 24 to October 25, it is open only Saturday and Sunday noon to 4pm.

If you cross the canal and head into Trollhättan's industrial hinterland, you'll come to the **Saab Bilmuseum,** Åkerssjövägen, Nohans Industriområde (☎ **0520/843-44**), where you can experience more than 50 years of innovative car engineering. From two-stroke to turbo, the history of Saab is presented dramatically. The museum displays an example of every model of Saab ever built, and designs for those to come in the future. Open June 8 to August 16 daily 10am to 6pm; otherwise Monday through Friday 10am to noon and 1 to 5pm. Admission is 30 SEK ($3.30).

SHOPPING

The best place for arts and crafts is **Handkraft Trollhättan,** Magasinsgatan 1 (☎ **0520/42-92-42**), a year-round shop with high-quality arts and crafts made by local artisans.

WHERE TO STAY

Hotel Swania. Storgatan 49, S 461 27 Trollhättan. ☎ **0520/890 100.** Fax 0520/397-02. www.swania_scandic-hotels.com. 195 units. MINIBAR TV TEL. Sun–Thurs 1,444 SEK ($158.85) double; 2,000 SEK ($220) minisuite for 2. Fri–Sat 835 SEK ($91.85) double; 1,045 SEK ($114.95) minisuite for 2. Rates include breakfast. AE, DC, MC, V. Free parking.

The grandest, most attractive hotel in town is this redbrick monument whose roof and ornate detailing date from 1916. Frequent renovations since then, most recently in 1998, have brought it up to modern-day standards while retaining the monumental staircases, high ceilings, and in some cases, elaborate cove moldings of its original construction. It sits directly beside the Göta Canal, in the heart of town, and as such often is the rendezvous point for various public service organizations and charities. Bedrooms are traditional, conservative, and comfortable; not at all experimental or prone to decorative risk taking. However, they are among the most reliable and biggest in town, and certainly have the best beds. Bathrooms are well maintained and equipped with hair dryers.

Dining/Diversions: The hotel's most formal dining venue is The Terrace, open daily for lunch and dinner. Less elaborate is the Brasserie, a crowded, busily decorated enclave with oil paintings, local memorabilia, and an active bar trade that's reminiscent of an informal restaurant in France. There's a swimming pool and a sauna in the hotel's basement. There's also a disco (Club Swania) that's open only on Saturday night from 7pm to 2am. Residents of the hotel enter free; nonresidents pay a cover charge of 60 SEK ($6.60).

Amenities: Room service, concierge, dry cleaning/laundry.

Hotel Trollhättan. Polhemsgatan 6, S-461 30 Trollhättan. ☎ **0520/125-65.** Fax 0520/154-71. www.hoteltrollhattan.se. 50 units. TV TEL. Mid-June to Aug and Fri–Sun year-round, 725 SEK ($79.75) double; rest of year, 825 SEK ($90.75) double. Rates include breakfast. AE, DC, MC, V. Free parking.

Near the town's main square (Drottningtorget), this hotel originated in the 1950s as a small guest house above the post office. Today, after a renovation and enlargement in the late 1980s, the hotel has two additional floors (although the town's main post office still occupies the establishment's ground floor). Inside, you'll find an efficiently decorated, functional, and practical refuge that's favored by business travelers and out-of-town relatives of local homeowners during occasions such as weddings and anniversaries. Bedrooms have hardwood floors, big windows, good beds, small bathrooms, and relentlessly functional furnishings.

Kung Oscar Hotel. Drottninggatan 17, S-461 32 Trollhättan. ☎ **0520/47-04-70.** Fax 0520/47-04-71. www.kungoscar.se. 55 units. MINIBAR TV TEL. Sun–Thurs 1,130 SEK ($124.30) double; Fri–Sat 800 SEK ($88) double. Rates include breakfast. AE, DC, MC, V. Free parking. Bus: 11.

Set in the center of town, near Trollhättan's community center, this five-story hotel originated in the 1950s as an apartment house. In the late 1980s it was adapted and upgraded into a hotel that looks rather plush, at least from the inside. The strongest points are the bedrooms, which are appealingly and rather formally decorated in pleasing tones of soft gray and beige. A small cafe on site serves light food such as salads and sandwiches. A sauna, small-scale swimming pool, and solarium provide opportunities to relax.

3 Vänersborg

9 miles north of Trollhättan, 53 miles N of Gothenburg

The famed poet, Birger Sjöberg, may have exaggerated a bit in calling Vänersborg "Little Paris," but it is, nonetheless, one of the most idyllic stopovers along the Göta Canal.

Vänersborg grew from its roots in Brätte, a medieval trade center next to Vassbotten. The glory days of Brätte were the early 1600s. (In 1944 the former region was excavated by archaeologists.) It took a great many workers in Brätte to unload the Vänern ships and reload the goods onto horse-drawn carriages. In time it became difficult for ships to enter the bay, as the bottom was silting up. More land was needed for expansion, and Vänersborg grew up as a result of this. It was granted its town charter in 1644 and became the county seat in 1679.

When the Trollhättan Canal was built, shipping became a major source of income. Light industry, administration, and schools later would become part of Vänersborg's profile. In 1834, a fire leveled the town, turning it into a heap of smoking ash in just 14 hours. Only a handful of buildings survived. Afterward, the new city plan design included a wide fire-break street that was laid to avoid another catastrophe.

ESSENTIALS

GETTING THERE **By Train** Between six and eight trains arrive from Stockholm every day; depending on the train, the trip takes between 3 and 4½ hours. Most require you to change trains in Herrlgungå en route. About 10 nonstop trains arrive from Gothenburg daily and take about an hour. For information, call ☎ 020/ 75-75-75.

By Bus At least two buses arrive from Stockholm every day, a travel time of 6 hours, as well as a handful of buses from Gothenburg (travel time about 90 minutes). For bus information affecting Vänersborg and the towns around it, call ☎ 0200/21818.

By Car From Trollhättan, our last stopover, continue north along Route 45 into Vänersborg.

VISITOR INFORMATION The **tourist office** in Vänersborg is one of the few in Sweden that changes its address according to the season. Between June and August, it's at Kungsgatan 15 (☎ 0521/27-14-00; www.vanersborg.se), where it operates every day from 11:30am to 4pm. The rest of the year, it operates from a base at Sundsgatan 6B (same phone), from Monday to Friday 8am to 5pm. For written inquiries, address your correspondence to P.O. Box 77, S-462 40 Vänersborg, Sweden.

SEEING THE SIGHTS

Torget, laid out in 1860, became the town's market area. It is still the center of town, and a good place from which to start exploring. The chief attraction in town is the **Vänersborg Museet,** Plantaget (☎ 0521/600-62), which displays objects from around the world. The West African bird collection is its most famous exhibit. Its exhibits have hardly changed since the late 19th century, and it remains appropriately gloomy. A reconstruction of Birger Sjöberg's home can be seen. He, of course, was the city's great poet and troubadour, who called Vänersborg "Little Paris." It includes many of his personal belongings and authentic pieces from the turn of the 20th century. Other collections are devoted to natural history, agriculture, and a history of music. The museum is open June through August, Tuesday through Thursday and Saturday and Sunday noon to 4pm. Off-season hours are Tuesday through Thursday and Saturday and Sunday noon to 4pm. Admission is 20 SEK ($2.20).

Anyone who is interested in handcrafts, particularly doll-making, may appreciate the exhibits within the **Vänersborg Doll Studio & Museum,** Residensgatan 2 (☎ 0521/615-71). It's open year-round Tuesday through Friday from 10am to 1pm and 2 to 6pm, and Saturday from 10am to 1pm. It's housed in the oldest wooden structure still standing in Vänersborg—the building was built in the 1790s—but the dolls go back only to the 1890s. You can view Birgitta Pererson's own prize-winning dolls, and her work is available for purchase in the on-site shop, along with a full range of doll-making materials. Entrance is 20 SEK ($2.20).

East of town, you can visit the twin bluffs of **Halleberg** and **Hunneberg,** which are 500 million years old. Halleberg and Hunneberg have been used as hunting grounds since the 1500s. Traditionally, this was Swedish elk country, but disease has reduced the stock to around 120 animals. However, there is still a great deal of other wildlife, including deer, hare, and foxes. King Oscar II began the tradition of holding the royal elk hunt here, and hunting rights are still held by the Swedish king. Today, the "elk safaris" hunt with cameras rather than guns. Ask at the tourist office in Vänersborg if you'd like to frame some Swedish elk.

You also can visit the **Naturskola Nature Center** at Hunneberg (☎ 0521/ 22-37-70), a center that explores the history, flora, and fauna of the twin bluffs. It is open Monday through Friday from 10am to 4pm, Saturday 10am to 2pm, and Sunday 10am to 3pm. There's a cafe on site and plenty of information available about the wildlife still living in the surrounding hills.

SHOPPING

At ✪ **Konsthantverkarna i Vänersborg,** Edsgatan 5 (☎ **0521/107-47**), more than 20 craftspeople and artisans present their work for sale under one roof. This is one of the best places to shop for handcrafts along Lake Vänern. It is open daily except Sunday in midsummer.

WHERE TO STAY

✪ **Ronnums Herrgård.** S-468 30 Vargön. ☎ **0521/223270.** Fax 0521/22-06-60. www. softwarehotels.se/ronnum/. 61 units. Mid-June to mid-Aug and Fri–Sat year-round, 1,040 SEK ($114.40) double; 1,350 SEK ($148.50) suite. Rest of year, 1,235 SEK ($135.85) double; 1,730 SEK ($190.30) suite. AE, DC, MC, V. Free parking. From Vänersborg, drive south for 3 miles, following the signs to Vargön.

This much-renovated 18th-century manor house is a particularly charming, small-scale place to stay. Sheathed with yellow clapboards and a red roof, it lies within its own park, with window views that sweep out over the surrounding forest and the low hills nearby. Bedrooms are outfitted with pastel colors and furniture that's more contemporary than what you'll find within the main house. With the exception of the sauna and a pair of tennis courts, there are very few amenities on site. There is a bar and a cozy restaurant where, amid 19th-century Swedish antiques, lunch is served Monday through Friday from 11:30am to 1:30pm, and dinner every Monday through Saturday from 6 to 9:30pm. Dinner specialties include platters of Swedish herring, Swedish caviar, venison with Swedish chanterelles, and a roster of dessert parfaits whose composition changes virtually every evening.

Scandic Hotel Vänersborg. Nabbensberg, S-462 40 Vänersborg. ☎ **0521/621-20.** Fax 0521/609-23. www.scandic.com. E-mail: vanersborg.rec@scandichotels.se. 119 units. TV TEL. June 19–Aug 10 and Fri–Sat year-round, 640 SEK ($70.40) double; rest of year, 1,307 SEK ($143.75) double. Rates include breakfast. AE, DC, MC, V. Free parking.

Adjacent to the Göta Canal, a mile south of the center of Vänersborg, this four-story hotel was built in 1977 and renovated in the mid-1990s. Inside, you'll find intensely colorful public areas that include a bar and a restaurant as well as convention facilities, a gym, a sauna, and an indoor pool. Bedrooms are angular and modern looking, with somewhat spartan lines that are softened by ample use of wood-veneered panels, and spaces that seem a bit larger than they are thanks to large mirrors. This member of the Scandic chain benefits from a cooperative and well-trained staff. Mattresses are frequently replaced and bathrooms, though small, are spotless and contain hair dryers.

WHERE TO DINE

Motorists may consider driving outside of town to Ronnums Herrgård for some of the most elegant dining in the area (see "Where to Stay," above).

Koppragrillen. Sundsgatan 11. ☎ **0521/181-51.** Reservations recommended. Main courses 85–260 SEK ($9.35–$28.60). AE, DC, MC, V. Mon–Fri 11am–11pm, Sat–Sun noon–11pm. INTERNATIONAL.

Set in a 1960s-era building in the center of town, within a dining room cozily outfitted in a conservative rustic style, this is one of the very few independent restaurants that remains open every day for both lunch and dinner. Menu specialties feature a well-seasoned roster of dishes that include halibut with fresh tomatoes and banana-flavored butter sauce, boiled venison with horseradish sauce, fillet of beef with Madeira sauce, and grilled veal or chateaubriand with Béarnaise sauce.

4 Lidköping

87 miles NE of Gothenburg, 34 miles NE of Vänersborg

Lidköping really is two towns, divided by the River Lidan. During the Middle Ages, the Old Town (east bank) developed at the river's only fjord as a commercial center with busy river traffic. It received its town charter in 1446. Then, in the 1670s, the Earl of Läckö began systematic construction of a new town on the west bank of the river. The straight streets and rectangular blocks used in laying out the town have been mostly preserved to the present. Notably, the great square, still used as the marketplace for the town and surrounding country, was surprisingly modern for the period.

Since the Middle Ages, Lidköping's economy has been based on trade and handcrafts. Given its location between the old main road from Götaälvdalen (the Göta River valley) and the shipping lanes on Lake Vänern, it was inevitable that it would develop into a commercial center for the area.

ESSENTIALS

GETTING THERE   By Train   Trains arrive in Lidköping at frequent intervals from both Stockholm (between two and four times a day, depending on the day of the week), and Gothenburg (eight per day Monday through Friday and between two and three per day on weekends, depending on the season). Transits from Stockholm require a change of equipment in the town of Hallsberg, and a total travel time of around 2½ hours. Alternatively, you can travel by train from Stockholm to the town of Skövde, then continue by bus for an additional 45 minutes to Lidköping. Buses are more or less timed to coincide with the arrival of trains. Travel time from Gothenburg requires 2 hours, and sometimes a change of equipment in the railway junction of Herrljunga en route. For rail information in Lidköping, call ☎ 020/75-75-75.

By Bus   Bus travel to Lidköping from both Stockholm and Gothenburg is less convenient than the equivalent trip by train. There are two buses per day from Stockholm, each taking 4 hours for the trip, and about two per day from Gothenburg, requiring about 2 to 2½ hours. For information, call ☎ 0200/21818.

By Car   From Vänersborg, continue northeast along Route 44 into Lidköping.

VISITOR INFORMATION   For information, go to the **Turistbyrån i Lidköping,** Bangatan 3 (☎ 0510/77-05-00; www.lidkoping.se/tourist). It's open June to mid-August, Monday through Saturday 9am to 7pm, Sunday 2 to 7pm. The rest of the year, hours are Monday through Friday 9am to 5pm.

SEEING THE SIGHTS

The open-air markets that trace their origins from 1680 are still held in the market square in the new town, although in a somewhat modified condition from the early days. Trade goods today consist of such foodstuff as vegetables, cheese, fruit, baskets, clothing, pottery goods, and "necessary commodities." The market usually is held on Wednesday and Saturday, as well as on the 6 weekdays before Christmas Day. From May through August hours are 7am to 2pm, 8am to 2pm in other months.

Gamla Rådhuset (or Town Hall), located in the center of town at Nya Stadens Torg, now is synonymous with Lidköping. The building originally was the hunting lodge of the Earl of Läckö and was moved from Kålland to become the town hall here. Today, it houses a cafe, a handcrafts center, and the Tourist Bureau.

The town's claim to fame is the **Rörstrands Fabriksbod,** Fabriksgatan (☎ 0510/823-46). Sweden's oldest and most prestigious ceramics works, founded in 1726, is known for is beautiful china and stoneware. It lies in the heart of a bleak industrial

A Time-Honored Tradition

One market tradition has been maintained from the days when farm animals and fresh meat (now banned) were a part of the goods offered for sale or trade: On each market day, traders collect around the square and wait for the Town Hall clock to strike. The custom is that no one enters the square before the clock has chimed six or seven strokes.

area near the lake. Far more interesting than the on-site Porslinsmuseum is the number of designs for sale. It is open Monday through Friday 10am to 6pm, Saturday 10am to 2pm, Sunday noon to 4pm. Normally you can visit on your own; however, in June and August guided tours are offered for 15 SEK ($1.65).

Among the museums, **Vänermuseet**, Frammnäsvägen 2 (☎ **0510/77-00-65**), is devoted to the Lake Vänern region. One project that has attracted much attention is the charting of wrecks on the bottom of Lake Vänern. Artifacts removed from the wrecks are on display. One of the high points of the exhibition here is glass artist Bertil Vallien's 3-meter-long glass boat, which hovers like a compass needle pointing north to Lake Vänern, Sweden's largest lake and the third largest in Europe. Other exhibitions focus on the countryside and cultural history of the lakeside region. There is room for children to play, too. Kids can take the helm of the cargo boat *Dahlia* in a full gale, or punt across the channel in the museum's own ferryboat. In 1998, a new exhibition of Sweden's oldest meteorite and ancient fossils opened. You also can purchase handcrafts in the museum shop or have lunch in the on-site Näcken restaurant. The museum is open Tuesday through Friday 10am to 5pm, Saturday and Sunday noon to 5pm. Admission is 20 SEK ($2.20) for adults, 10 SEK ($1.10) for children.

A PALATIAL EXCURSION

✪ **Läckö Slott.** ☎ **0510/103-20.** Admission 70 SEK ($7.70) adults, 35 SEK ($3.85) children 7–15, free for children 6 and under. May–Sept, daily 10am–6pm. Closed off-season. From Lidköping, drive immediately north of the town along a small secondary road. There is no route number, so follow signs to Läckö. Go all the way to the end of the road (14 miles).

Only the royal palace in Stockholm is larger than this 13th-century castle on an island in Lake Vänern. The castle was at the apex of its glory when magnus Gabriel de la Gardie, a contemporary of Queen Christina, made it the cultural center of Västergötland province. In 1682, Karl XI confiscated the castle in hopes of curtailing the power of the nobility. By 1830 all of its furnishings had been auctioned off, but many of the original antiques have since been reclaimed and brought back to the Renaissance palace. A walk through the castle grounds is one of the highlights of a visit here. Off the courtyard in the old castle storeroom, an on-site restaurant has been established. Each year the castle stages a different exhibit; these can range from medieval jousting to contemporary art. During June, July, and August, visitors can either promenade through the place on their own, or take a guided tour (loosely scheduled for whenever people show up) in Swedish and English that's included in the price of admission. During May and September, the site is open the same hours, but the departure times of the tours are more rigidly defined, and guests must participate in one of them.

WHERE TO STAY

Edward Hotel. Skaragatan 7, S-531 32 Lidköping. ☎ **0510/79000.** Fax 0510/790099. www.edwardhotel.se. E-mail: info@edwardhotel.se. 59 units. MINIBAR TV TEL. July to mid-Aug and Fri–Sat year-round, 795 SEK ($87.45) double; rest of year, 1,395 SEK ($153.45) double. Rates include breakfast. AE, DC, MC V. Free parking.

Rising from a position near the river in the heart of town, this three-story hotel was constructed in 1984 in a solidly built design that any engineer could tell you will resist the fiercest storm and the most frigid Swedish winter. Public areas are floored with slabs of marble, and have the kind of contemporary detail that you might associate with an airport check-in desk. Bedrooms are outfitted in tones of beige and autumn-inspired colors, with built-in headboards and a sense of modern, no-nonsense efficiency. One of the best aspects is the mechanized beds whose heads and feet can be raised or lowered according to a sleeper's wishes. Bathrooms are snug but adequate, with good shelf space. On the premises are a billiard room and a sauna, a bar, and a cozy brasserie, one of the most popular in town, recommended separately in "Where to Dine" (see below).

Hotell Läckö. Gamla Stadens Torg 5, S-531 32 Lidköping. ☎ **0510/230-00.** Fax 0510/ 621-91. 19 units, 17 with bathroom. TV TEL. Sun–Thurs 795 SEK ($87.45) double with bathroom; Fri–Sat 590 SEK ($64.90) double with bathroom. Rates include breakfast. AE, MC, V. Free parking.

This is one of the less sophisticated hotels of Lidköping, with a staff that doesn't speak a lot of English, and an old-fashioned setup that you'll either find charming or not, depending on your tastes and levels of indulgence. It's housed within a once-stately building that originally was built as a hotel around 1900, and which retains some, but not all, of its original architectural adornments. Each of the bedrooms is outfitted with a different, usually pastel, color scheme, and many retain some of the older furniture that was in place when the hotel originally opened. Although the hotel is old-fashioned, beds are modern, and all the doubles have a small private bathroom. Two singles are rented without a bathroom. No meals are served other than breakfast and there's no bar on the premises, but overall you might appreciate the cozy and old-fashioned atmosphere, which is in direct contrast to glossier, newer, more internationally conscious hotels.

Hotel Stadt Lidköping. Gamla Stadens Torg 1, S-531 02 Lidköping. ☎ **800/528-1234** in the U.S., or 0510/220-85. Fax 0510/215-32. www.hotelstadtlidkoping.se. E-mail: hotel @stadtlidkoping.se. 44 units. Sun–Thurs 1,200 SEK ($132) double; Fri–Sat 750 SEK ($82.50) double. AE, DC, MC, V. Free parking.

Long a traditional favorite, this Best Western hotel has been considerably improved and upgraded over the years. Built in a classic townhouse style, it is separated from the nearby riverbank by a row of linden trees. The hotel has been sedately modernized without losing its antique appeal. The medium-size bedrooms are well furnished, with good beds and ample-size bathrooms that are well maintained. We've found it to be the most active place in town at night, with a restaurant, nightclub, and O'Keeffe's Pub. Registration is near an amusingly abstract statue of a baby elephant in the lobby. Guests also will find a sauna for relaxing.

WHERE TO DINE

Eddie's Brasserie. In the Edward Hotel, Skaragatan 7. ☎ **0510/79000.** Reservations recommended. Main courses 90–150 SEK ($9.90–$16.50); fixed-price menu 65 SEK ($7.15). AE, DC, MC, V. Mon–Fri 11:30am–2pm; Mon–Thurs 6–11pm, Fri–Sat 8–11pm. SWEDISH/ INTERNATIONAL.

Set on the street level of the previously recommended hotel, within an angular and contemporary room outfitted with wood paneling and shades of pale green and yellow, this is one of the most animated and bustling restaurants in town. Menu items include a roster of traditional Swedish specialties, as well as more innovative and daring items from other parts of Europe and the world. Examples include shrimp and black roe in puff pastry; boiled chopped egg with anchovies and onions, served with Swedish brown bread; grilled salmon with garlic-braised prawns, lime-flavored yogurt, and chili oil; and a substantial-looking fillet of beef with Provençal-style mushrooms.

5 Skara

80 miles NE of Gothenburg, 217 miles SW of Stockholm, 15½ miles SE of Lidköping

This highly recommended stopover lies between Karlstad and Gothenburg in the province of Västergötland, the ancient western country of the once-dreaded Goths. Skara, which is in the heart of the province, is reached by Europe Hwy. 3 and makes a good center for exploring some of the district's major sights, such as Läckö Castle and Varnhem Abbey.

Both an educational center and a cathedral town, Skara was an ancient religious center even before Christianity came to Sweden. With its wooden buildings and green squares, it remains unspoiled.

There is an excellent outdoor swimming pool here, and a small children's pool.

ESSENTIALS

GETTING THERE   By Train   Lidköping doesn't have a railway junction of its own; consequently, rail passengers from everywhere, including the half dozen trains arriving here from Gothenburg every day, disembark in the town of Skövde, 16 miles to the east of Skara. From there, they take a bus marked LIDKÖPING, at a cost of 40 SEK ($4.40) each way to reach Skara. For information, call ☎ 020/75-75-75.

By Bus   There also are about five express buses every day making the 2-hour trip from Gothenburg. Each deposits its passengers in the heart of town. For bus information, call ☎ 0200/21818.

By Car   From Lidköping, follow Route 47 directly southeast into Skara.

VISITOR INFORMATION   For information about Skara and its surrounding area, head for the **Skara Turistbyrå,** Skolgatan 1 (☎ 0511/325-80; www.turistbyraskara.se). Between early June and late August it's open Monday through Friday from 9am to 7pm, and Saturday and Sunday from 10am to 2pm. The rest of the year it's open Monday through Friday 9am to 1pm and 2 to 5pm.

SEEING THE SIGHTS

Skara Domkyrkan Sancta Maria. Järnvägatan. ☎ **0511/20-179.** Free admission. Mon–Sat 10am–4pm, Sun 9:30am–1:30pm.

Classic in its purity of line, the twin-spired **Sancta Maria,** in the center of town, was founded in 1150, and then extensively restored in the 19th century. Inside, look for the magnificent stained-glass windows by Bo Beskow. Excavations beneath the cathedral have revealed remains of the only known Swedish medieval crypt. One of the cathedral's treasures is a funeral chalice dating from 1065, the property of a bishop.

Lansbibliotek. Prubbatorget. ☎ **0511/320-60.** Free admission. Mon–Thurs 11am–8pm, Fri 11am–6pm, Sat 10am–2pm.

North of the cathedral, next door to the diocesan library (Gamla Bibliotek), from the 1850s, is a library combining the treasures of the diocese and the region. Some 300,000 books, among them 3,000 handwritten works, are contained in the library. Outstanding among them is the *Skara Missal,* the oldest preserved book written in Sweden, dating from 1150. The collections of the combined library facilities are used in connection with research of local history and genealogy. There also are books that can be borrowed and many magazines and newspapers for use by visitors.

Västergötland Museum. Stadträgården. ☎ **0511/26000.** Admission 30 SEK ($3.30) adults, free for ages 18 and under. Mon–Tues and Thurs–Fri 10am–5pm, Wed 10am–9pm, Sat–Sun noon–5pm.

Angling Along Göta Älv

The southwestern parts of Lake Vänern and the valley of the River Göta have been called an angler's El Dorado. Fishers can troll for salmon and trout on Lake Vänern, or fly-fish on the River Göta. These are well-stocked trout waters in an area where spinning and fly-fishing are permitted for the price of a daily permit. The area also provides waters filled with pike, perch, and different members of the carp family.

Lake Vänern alone has some 30 different species of fish. The bay of Vänersborg offers the best variety of good fishing locations. During recent years about 35,000 young salmon and trout have been released annually into the lake to keep the stock plentiful. The ultimate goal is to make Lake Vänern the best angling lake in Europe.

Another good fishing spot is the plateau Hallsjön near Vargön and beautiful lake Hallsjön, which is well stocked with rainbow trout. The local district council of Vänersborg leases the lake from the crown. Between May and September they release 4 tons of rainbow trout into the lake. When available, char and brown trout are released. Both spinning and fly-fishing are allowed. With a bit of luck you may encounter a Swedish elk on the shores of the lake while you're fishing. Fireplaces are provided along the lake for grilling food or enjoying a log fire, and there are wind shelters as well. The plateau of Hunneberg contains several lakes, notably Igelsjön and Kvarnsjön, which are restocked with rainbow trout every year. The other lakes contain good stocks of pike and perch.

Fishing licenses can be obtained at **Fiske-Shopen,** Strandgatan 29 (☎ **0520/ 361-15**), in Trollhättan, and at **Vargöns Järnhandel,** Lövvägen (☎ **0521/ 22-01-30**), in Vänersborg.

One of Sweden's most impressive provincial museums lies in Skara's town park; its collection is rich in artifacts, such as ecclesiastical woodcarvings and medieval stone art, from the surrounding district. Near the main buildings of the museum is the **Old Village.** These wooden buildings from the 16th to the 19th century were torn down in the province and reassembled on this site. A megalithic grave known as a **stone cist** also has been brought here, and there are such workers' facilities as a smithy, a carpenter's workshop, and a windmill. Also nearby is a **Museum of Veterinary History** and the **Kråk Manor House,** a fully furnished 18th-century dwelling, where meals and refreshments are served in the old cellar. The **Agricultural Museum** is housed in a large cowshed from the village of Karleby, where the development of agriculture in Västergötland is shown from the first permanent farmers in the Neolithic period up to the present.

Skara Sommerland. Skovde. ☎ **0511/640-00.** Admission 170 SEK ($18.70) for anyone 3 feet or more in height. Mid-May to late Aug, daily 10am–7pm; Sept, Sat–Sun 10am–7pm. Closed Oct to mid-May. Drive 5 miles east of town, following the signs to Skovde.

Scandinavia's largest leisure park for children offers a wealth of activities, including lots of swimming pools and water slides in Aqualand, gold panning, a water-ski lake, bumper boats, canoes, archery, trampolines, a mini-zoo, and pony riding, among other attractions—70 in all.

NEARBY ATTRACTIONS

Varnhem Kloster Kyrka. S-532 73 Varnhem. ☎ **0511/603-170.** Admission 20 SEK ($2.20) adults, 5 SEK (55¢) ages 7–15, free for children 6 and under. Apr, daily 10am–4pm; May–Aug, daily 9am–6pm; Sept, daily noon–4pm. Drive east of Skara on Route 49 for 9 miles.

This former Cistercian monastery was completed in 1260 after the previous abbey had burned. Angry Danes razed it again in the mid-16th century, but it was restored by Christina's friend, Count Magnus Gabriel de la Gardie, who is buried here. Designed as a cross-vaulted, three-aisled basilica, the medieval abbey also contains the grave of Birger Jarl, founder of Stockholm.

Habo Kyrka. Habo. ☎ **036/42082.** Free admission. May–Aug, Mon–Sat 8am–8pm and Sun 10am–8pm; Oct–Feb, Mon–Sat 9am–4pm, Sun 10am–4pm; Sept and Mar–Apr, Mon–Sat 9am–6pm, Sun 10am–6pm. Situated 62 miles southeast of Skara on the southern edge of Lake Vättern. From Skara, follow signs to Falköping, then signs to Jönköping.

This church stands outside the village of Habo, 12 miles north of Jönköping, near Lake Vättern. (It's close enough to Varnhem to be visited on the same day.) Habo Kyrka is an old, barn-red frame church. From 1721 to 1723 it was enlarged to its present structure. The sandstone altar was consecrated about 1347, and the baptismal font is from the 13th century.

WHERE TO STAY

Hotel Stadskällaren. Skaraborgsgatan 15, S-532 22 Skara. ☎ **051/11-34-10.** Fax 051/11-21-48. www.hotelstadskallaren.se. 32 units. TV TEL. Mon–Thurs 850 SEK ($93.50) double; Fri–Sun 540 SEK ($59.40) double. Rates include breakfast. AE, DC, MC, V. Free parking.

Of the three hotels in Skara, this is the oldest, most historic, and most charming. Constructed around 1900 as a hotel, it occupies a site in the city center, behind an old-fashioned gable-sided building with white walls and green shutters. Inside, you'll find a blandly international contemporary decor, and bedrooms painted in shades of pale blue. Each has a high ceiling, some original modern paintings, and a somewhat cramped arrangement that includes a writing table, a comfortable chair for reading, and a small-screen TV. Beds have firm mattresses and the bathrooms, although small, are adequate for the job and have spotless maintenance. There's a restaurant on the premises, which is separately recommended in "Where to Dine," below.

Skara Stadshotell. Järnvägsgatan 5, S-532 30 Skara. ☎ **0511/13000.** Fax 0511/21384. www.skarastadshotell.se. E-mail: skara.stadt@skara.mail.telia.com. 75 units. TV TEL. Midsummer and Sat–Sun year-round, 530–790 SEK ($58.30–$86.90) double; rest of year, 1,195 SEK ($131.45) double. AE, DC, MC, V. Free parking.

In the heart of town, a block from the cathedral, this longtime favorite is built like a small French château. It is one of the best of the Stads hotels in the area, with a ballroom and dining room that often reflect the social events that take place here. Its generally large bedrooms are impressive and decorated in a contemporary style with comfortable beds and good-size bathrooms with hair dryers. The cuisine is among the town's finest, and in summer guests like to dine outside on the terrace. There is a bar with frosty mugs of beer, and the town's best swimming pool.

WHERE TO DINE

Restaurant Stadskällaren. Skaraborgsgatan 15. ☎ **051/11-34-10.** Main courses 80–160 SEK ($8.80–$17.60). Daily 6–8pm. AE, DC, MC, V. SWEDISH.

Associated with the previously recommended hotel, this restaurant occupies a pale blue, simply decorated dining room whose main visual allure derives from a collection of unusual modern paintings by Swedish and Italian artists. Menu items are thoughtfully prepared and served in generous portions. They might include pheasant soup, well-seasoned versions of Angus beef, and veal schnitzels in a morel-flavored cream sauce.

6 Mariestad

25 miles NE of Lidköping, 198 miles SW of Stockholm, 112 miles NE of Gothenburg

Called the "pearl of Lake Vänern," Mariestad is known for its many well-preserved old structures in its Gamla Stan (or Old Town). Despite several widespread town fires, many old structures still remain, including one building from the 17th century. The town lies on the eastern shore of Lake Vänern and is one of the best stopovers for those sailing the Göta Canal. It takes its name from Maria von Pfaltz, the first wife of Duke Karl (later Karl IX).

This lakeside town is lovelier and less industrialized than Lidköping. Take along a camera, as its medieval quarter and its harbor area have many scenic views. The town contains a wide array of architectural styles, including Gustavian, Carolean, classical, and art nouveau. It's been called a "living museum" of architecture.

ESSENTIALS

GETTING THERE   By Train   There's about one train per hour arriving in Mariestad from Stockholm, usually with a change in Töreboda Skövde en route. Depending on the train, transit takes from 2½ to 3 hours. There also are two or three trains per day between Mariestad and Lidköping, a trip of about an hour, on a not particularly busy rail line that runs perpendicular to the busier main east-to-west rail routings. For information, call ☎ 020/75-75-75.

By Bus   Bus travel to Mariestad from Stockholm is less convenient than equivalent transit by train. There are two buses per day from Stockholm, each requiring between 3½ and 4 hours for the trip, and one or two from Lidköping, taking less than an hour. For information, call ☎ 0200/21818.

By Car   From Lidköping (discussed above), continue northeast along Route 44 until you come to the junction with the express highway, E3, which will carry you into Mariestad.

VISITOR INFORMATION   The **Mariestad Turistbyrå,** Hamnplan (☎ 0501/ 100-01; www.mariestad.se), is open June through August, Monday through Friday 8am to 7pm, Saturday and Sunday 9am to 6pm. From September to May, hours are Monday through Friday 8am to 4pm.

SEEING THE SIGHTS

If time is limited, head first for the Old Town where you can walk medieval streets and see some of the old buildings; the most interesting of these lie along Kyrkogatan.

At Kyrkogatan 21 is the **first general hospital** in Mariestad, built in 1760, the third such hospital in Sweden. At Kyrkogatan 31, you'll see a **timbered cottage** called Aron's House, a burger's house from the 17th century, which survived the fire of 1693.

The town's most important monument is **Mariestad Domkyrka** (cathedral), Kyrkogatan (no phone), open daily June 15 through August 7am to 9pm. The rest of the year it is open daily 7am to 4pm. This cathedral was built between 1593 and 1625 because of religious controversies between Duke Karl and his brother, King Johan III. In 1580 Värmland and the northern part of Västergötland had been detached from the diocese of Skara and given a superintendent of their own, residing at Mariestad. The duke had the new cathedral built according to plans made by Dutchman Willelm Boy for the church of Santa Clara in Stockholm, thereby freely copying his brother's most important building in the Swedish capital. The nave gives a remarkable impression of unbroken unity following the traditions of the late Middle Ages. Vigorous vaults span a considerable width without supporting pillars. The present-day appearance of the cathedral was brought about by a restoration beginning in 1903 by the architect Folke Zetterval, who gave the spire its present height.

Other than the cathedral, the major attraction here is the **cruise** up to Lake Vänern to the start of the Göta Canal's main stretch at Sjotorp, 12 miles from Mariestad. Between Karlsborg and Sjotorp there are 21 locks. The most scenic section stretches up to Lyrestad, lying east of Sjotorp and 12 miles north of Mariestad on the motorway, E20. For information on lake and canal cruises for day trips, contact the tourist bureau (see above). Cruises cost 200 SEK ($22), last 5 to 6 hours, and are conducted between June and late August only. Most of them begin at Sjotorp. For information, call ☎ **0501/514-70.**

Other attractions in and around the town include the **Vadsbo Museum,** Marieholm (☎ **0501/632-14**), located in the wings of the county governor's residence in the town center. The building originally was constructed as the governor's house in the 18th century. Exhibits include artifacts from the city history, a carriage collection, and temporary thematic and art exhibitions. In 1998, a small industry museum opened here as well. Admission is 20 SEK ($2.20) adults, 10 SEK ($1.10) for children. It is open June through August, Tuesday through Sunday 1 to 5pm. Off-season hours are only Wednesday and Sunday 1 to 7pm.

The **Canal Museum (Kanalmuseet)** at Sjotorp, 12 miles from Mariestad, lies along the harbor at Hamn (☎ **0501/514-34**), and houses exhibitions showing the building of the Göta Canal and the operations of the Sjotorp shipyard. There also is a large collection of engine history, a ship and shipwreck exhibition, as well as various thematic shows. It is open daily June through August only, charging 20 SEK ($2.20) for adults, 5 SEK (55¢) for children. To reach Sjotorp, head north of Mariestad along Route 64.

Lugnås Rocks, on Lungnåsberget Hill, south of Mariestad (take E3 going south from Mariestad and look for signs at the hamlet of Lugnås), once was the site of a major milestone manufacturing industry begun way back in the 12th century. One of the old caves is open for guided tours Sunday from noon to 4pm in May, June, and August. In July, tours are conducted daily from 11am to 4pm. Admission is 25 SEK ($2.75). For information about this attraction, inquire at the Mariestad tourist bureau.

WHERE TO STAY

Bergs Hotell. Kyrkogatan 18, S-542 30 Mariestad. ☎ **0501/103-24.** 5 units, none with bathroom. 500 SEK ($55) double. Rates include breakfast. AE, DC, MC, V. Free parking.

Part of the allure of this 300-year-old hotel derives from its position in the oldest part of town, in a neighborhood composed only of equivalently antique houses. Set behind a one-story pink facade that from the back side reveals itself as a two-story structure, it's the domain of the kindhearted landlady, Elisabeth Åkerlind. No meals are served other than breakfast, but the cobble-covered courtyard in back, punctuated as it is with pear trees and flowers, is a charming place to read or write. Bedrooms are outfitted in a style similar to a Swedish beach house, with painted furniture, cozy, somewhat cramped dimensions, and very few grace notes other than a sense of antique Swedish charm and many other generations who have gone before you to this place.

Stadshotelleet. Nya Torget, S-54238 Mariestad. ☎ **0501/138-00.** Fax 0501/77470. 29 units. TV TEL. Sun–Thurs 1,100 SEK ($121) double; Fri–Sat 770 SEK ($84.70) double. AE, DC, MC, V. Free parking.

The most substantial hotel in town appeals to overnight visitors through its call to nostalgia and antique charm, part of which derives from its construction more than a century ago. A three-story building from the 1880s, its salmon-colored stone rises above the town's main square. Public rooms are high-ceilinged with some of their original detailing, and bedrooms—painted blue with dark pink carpeting—are just dowdy enough to appeal to everyone's sense of old-fashioned virtue. There's a bar on the premises, a health club, a sauna, and a restaurant that only serves lunch. More substantial meals, including dinners, are featured within the separately recommended Restaurant S:t Michel, which lies within a 3-minute walk.

WHERE TO DINE

S:t Michel. Kungsgatan 1. ☎ **0501/199-00.** Reservations recommended. Fixed-price lunch 75 SEK ($8.25); main courses 125–159 SEK ($13.75–$17.50). AE, DC, MC, V. Daily 11am–2pm and 6:30–11pm. SWEDISH/INTERNATIONAL.

Although it's set within separate premises, this restaurant is associated with the Stadhotellet, which often steers its residents here. Cozy and well maintained, it serves good food that arrives in generous portions with a bit of culinary flair. Examples include fillets "black and white" that mix pork cutlets with béarnaise sauce and beef fillets with wine sauce on the same platter. Tournedos are served with your choice of three different sauces, and you also can order flambéed pepper steak or grilled fillets of sole stuffed with lobster.

Telegrafen. Kungsgatan 5. ☎ **0501/18050.** Fixed-price lunch 55 SEK ($6.05); dinner main courses 119–155 SEK ($13.10–$17.05). AE, DC, MC, V. Mon–Fri 11am–3pm; Tues–Sat 5–10pm. SWEDISH/FRENCH.

One of the town's newest restaurants occupies a pair of high-ceilinged rooms whose terra-cotta color scheme and postmodern design may remind you of a hip and trendy restaurant in Los Angeles or London. Menues are radically different at lunch and dinner, with lunches consisting exclusively of a brisk, fixed-price affair where at least 15 varieties of main-course salads, as well as a limited selection of meats and fish, are offered and consumed by most of the office workers of the town. Dinners are more formal and more elaborate, with more cadenced service, and menu items that include well-prepared French variations of such local ingredients as chicken, duck, beef, and fish from local freshwater streams. There's a disco on the premises, two bars, and an active nightlife venue that has at one time or another welcomed virtually every hipster or hipster wannabe in the region. The disco opens Wednesday through Saturday at 10pm. Entrance usually is free, but if there's a live band, entrance costs between 75 and 100 SEK ($8.25 and $11), depending on who is playing. The bars are a singles-bar smörgåsbord in this otherwise rather staid community.

10 Värmland & Dalarna

Two provinces in the heart of Sweden's southern region represent the soul of this Scandinavian nation. In the province of Dalarna lies Lake Siljan; and Värmland, farther south, opens onto Lake Vänern, the third largest inland sea in Europe.

In one of her most famous works, *The Saga of Gösta Berling*, Nobel Prize winner and native Swede Selma Lagerlöf lyrically described Värmland life in the early 19th century. Today, the province in parts remains much as she saw it.

Karlstad, on the shores of Lake Vänern, makes an ideal stopover for exploring the province of Värmland. Among its chef waterways are the Göta River and the Göta Canal. A smaller body of water, Lake Vättern, lies to the east of Vänern.

Sometimes described as Sweden in miniature, Värmland is a land of mountains, rolling hill country, islands, and rivers. Värmland is also a province of festivals, music, art, literature, and handcrafts. Visitors can enjoy boating, fishing, skiing, hiking, folklore, and historic sights.

Forests still cover a large part of Värmland, and the 170-mile-long Klarälven River carries logs to the industrial areas around Lake Vänern.

Dalarna is the most traditional of all the provinces, complete with maypole dancing, fiddlers' music, folk costumes, and handcrafts (including the Dala horse, Sweden's most popular souvenir). *Dalarna* means "valleys," and sometimes you'll see it referred to as Dalecarlia, the Anglicized form of the name.

Lake Siljan, maybe the most beautiful lake in Europe, is ringed with resort villages and towns. Leksand, Tällberg, and Rättvik attract visitors during summer with sports, folklore, and a week of music. In winter, people come here for skiing.

Any time is good for a visit to Dalarna, but during midsummer, June 23 to June 26, the Dalecarlians celebrate the custom of maypole dancing. At that time they race through the forest gathering birch bows and nosegays of wildflowers with which they cover the maypole. Then the pole is raised and, under the midsummer-lit sky, they dance around it until dawn; a good, respectable pagan custom.

The quickest and easiest way to reach these provinces is by train from the Central Station in Stockholm, a 4½-hour trip. All the following towns have good rail connections with each other. Motorists from Oslo can stop over in Dalarna before venturing on to the Swedish capital. Similarly, visitors to Gothenburg can head north to both Värmland and Dalarna before seeing Stockholm.

If you drive, however, you can see more of the scenery, including a spectacular section between Vadstena and Jönköping, where it winds along the eastern shore of Lake Vättern. If you want to see the area in a hurry, and are dependent on public transportation, you can fly to Mora and use it as a center for exploring Dalarna, or fly from Stockholm to Karlstad and use that city as a base for exploring the Värmland district. Both Karlstad and Mora also have good rail connections from Stockholm. Many visitors see a "nutshell" version of central Sweden by taking the Göta Canal trip (see chapter 9).

1 Karlstad

154 miles NE of Gothenburg, 186 miles W of Stockholm

The capital of Värmland, this port city is at the mouth of the Klarälven River. Karlstad has many attractions for visitors, plus many moderately priced restaurants and comfortable hotels. Because of its location, it has long been a center for trade and transport, and is a good starting point for many of the tourist routes of Värmland.

A trading center called Thingwalla first stood on the site of the city, but in 1584 Duke Charles (later Sweden's King Charles IX) founded Karlstad. Here you can see Sweden's longest stone bridge, East Bridge, built in the 18th century. The oldest quarter, **Almen,** on Älvgatan, was saved from a disastrous fire in 1865. You can visit this area today and see the old grammar school and the Bishop's house.

ESSENTIALS

GETTING THERE   By Plane   Nine flights on Linjeflyg, a division of SAS, connect Stockholm and Karlstad daily, the "jump" taking 45 minutes. The airport lies less than a mile southwest of Karlstadt's center. For flight information, call ☎ **054/45-55-010.**

By Train   Six trains per day run between Gothenburg and Karlstadt, 10 trains per day arrive from Stockholm, and 3 trains per day come from Oslo. All take about 3 hours. For rail information, call ☎ **020/75-75-75.**

By Bus   Three buses per day arrive from Gothenburg, taking 4 hours; four weekly from Stockholm, taking 4½ hours; and two weekly from Oslo, taking 4½ hours. Check locally for bus schedules, which change from month to month. For general information, call ☎ **0200/21818.**

By Car   From Stockholm, take E18 west all the way, and from Gothenburg head north along the E6 expressway, turning northeast at the junction of Route 45, which runs all the way to Karlstad.

VISITOR INFORMATION   Karlstad and most of the region around it are represented by the **Vum]rmlands Tourist Bureau,** in the city's new conference center, Tage Erlander Gatan (☎ **054/22-25-50;** www.varmland.org). It's open June 16 to August 14, Monday through Saturday from 9am to 6pm and on Sunday from 1 to 6pm; the rest of the year, Monday through Friday from 9am to 5pm.

SEEING THE SIGHTS

One of the most appealing ways to get an overview of the geography around Karlstad involves taking a short-term cruise. The **Sola** is a small-scale lake cruiser with oversized windows and an on-board cafe. Its home port is Karlstad's **Imre Hamn (Inner Harbor),** where it embarks on between two and five cruises a day, depending on the schedule, between mid-June and late August. Tours average 90 minutes in length, and incorporate views of the city and the several islands situated near the entrance to its harbor. They cost 75 SEK ($8.25) for adults and 35 SEK ($3.85) for children aged

Värmland

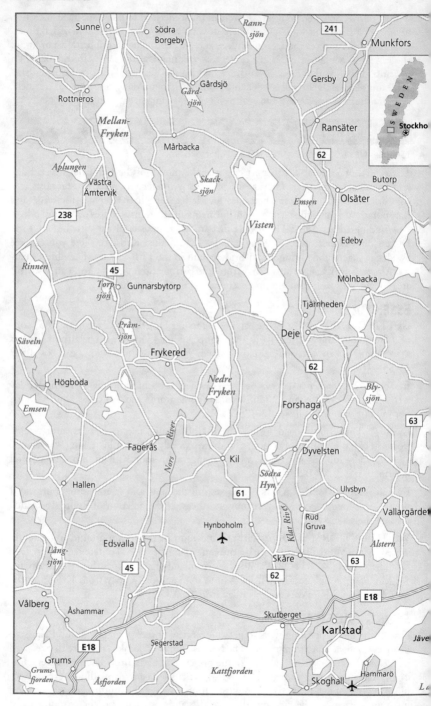

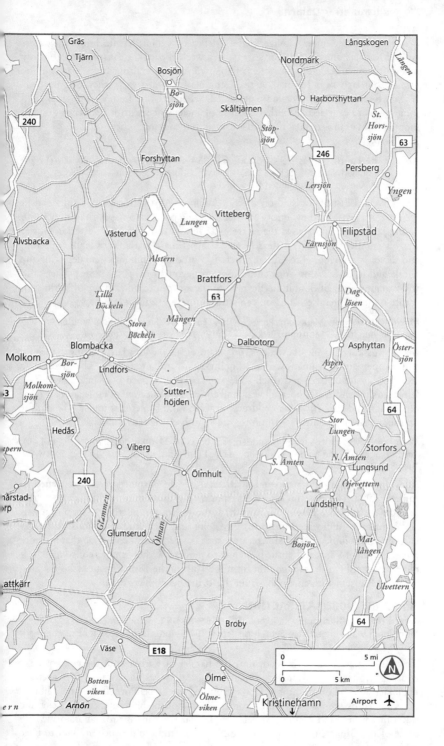

Gräs
Tjärn
Bosjön
Bo-
sjön
Skåltjärnen
240
Forshyttan
Stöp-
sjön
246
Vitteberg
Lungen
Västerud
Alstern
Brattfors
63
Lilla
Böckeln
Mången
Stora
Böckeln
Dalbotorp
Blombacka
Molkom
Bor-
sjön
Lindfors
Molkom-
sjön
Sutter-
höjden
3
Hedås
spern
Viberg
240
Ölmhult
härstad-
rp
Glumserud
Glemmen
Ölman
attkärr

Långskogen
Nordmark
Lången
Harborshyttan
St.
Hors-
sjön
63
Persberg
Lersjön
Yngen
Filipstad
Färnsjön
Dag-
lösen
Asphyttan
Öster-
sjön
Aspen
64
Stor
Lungen
Storfors
N. Ämten
Lungsund
S. Ämten
Öjevettern
Lundsberg
Bosjön
Mat-
lången
Ulvettern

Broby
64
Väse
E18
Ölme
Botten-
viken
Arnön
Ölme-
viken
Kristinehamn
e r n

0   5 mi
0   5 km
N
Airport ✈

269

6 to 12 (free 5 and under). Longer cruises that carry you farther afield from the waters around Karlstad are scheduled at least twice a week aboard the *Polstjärnan,* the only steam-driven cruiser left in the waters of Lake Vänern. Specializing in the waters of the mini-archipelago near Karlstad, with a length of 3 hours each, they cost 85 SEK ($9.35) for adults; free for children under 12. Schedules vary from week to week, and sometimes are canceled altogether because of inclement weather. For schedules and more information, contact Karlstad's tourist information office, or dial ☎ 054/22-25-50.

Alster's Herrgård. Alsters Herrgårdsväg. ☎ **054/834-081.** Admission 20 SEK ($2.20) adults self-guided tour, 25 SEK ($2.75) adults conducted tour, free for children. Daily 11am–6pm. Closed Sept–Apr. Bus: 14, 15, or 17.

Lying 5 miles east of Karlstad on the Stockholm road, this manor is maintained in memory of Gustaf Fröding, one of Sweden's leading poets who was born here in 1860. Squire Jan Fröding purchased the estate in 1837 and transformed its exterior. Gustaf was his grandchild. Today, Alster's Manor is an affiliate of the Värmlands Museum, and serves as a memorial to Gustaf. There is a Fröding exhibition here depicting the family and its possessions—one entire room is devoted to Gustaf's sisters. There also is a changing array of exhibitions devoted to the art, music, and culture of Värmland. A cafe is on the premises, and you can stroll through Fröding Grove.

Mariebergsskogen. Mariebergs Park. ☎ **054/15-92-00.** Free admission. Amusement section May–Aug, daily 11am–6pm. Park daily 8am–11pm.

Mariebergsskogen is one of Sweden's top pleasure parks, with a fair, dancing, a theater, and an open-air museum, as well as an animal park and a restaurant. The Tivoli-style section, the site of rides and small-scale amusements, is open only in summer. The Children's Petting Zoo is open all year, and contains a collection of tame animals (rabbits, goats, and lambs), which children can watch and sometimes touch. The park is on the southern outskirts, a 15-minute walk south of the town center.

Värmlands Museum. Sandgrundsudden. ☎ **054/14-31-00.** Admission 40 SEK ($4.40), free for ages 19 and under. June–Aug, daily 11am–5pm (until 9pm Thurs); Sept–May, Tues–Sun 11am–5pm.

After this museum outgrew its old quarters, a greatly expanded version reopened in summer 1998. The museum is the best repository of the history of Värmland; you can see how the province developed, from its early settlers and pilgrims to its mill towns and industries. Audiovisual programs give color and shape to the exhibits. Although changing exhibitions are staged here, there also is a permanent collection that includes the evolution of Värmland music from folk to modern. Other exhibits concern archaeology, textiles, Finnish immigration from the 16th to the 18th centuries, and the evolution of Karlstad with an emphasis on the 19th and 20th centuries.

A NEARBY NOBEL ATTRACTION

Alfred Nobel's Björkborn. Karlskoga. ☎ **0586/833-11.** Admission 60 SEK ($6.60), free for children 9 and under. May–Sept, Mon–Fri 10:30am–4pm. Take E18 35 miles east of Karlstad to the town of Karlskoga.

Thirty-five miles east of Karlstad, near the hamlet of Karlskoga at the edge of Lake Möckeln, you'll find a white-sided manor house that was the home of the inventor, manufacturer, and philanthropist who established the Nobel Prize. It contains a library that's valued by scholars and which contains many of the philosophical and scientific tracts that were read by Alfred Nobel himself. You also can visit the laboratory where some of the armaments that later made Nobel's fortune, and which are said to have

ATTRACTIONS ●
Alster's Herrgård **9**
Mariebergsskogen **1**
Värmlands Museum **7**

ACCOMMODATIONS ■
Elite Stadshotellet **4**
First Hotel Plaza **6**
Gösta Berling **5**
Scandic Hotel Winn **3**
Scandic Klarälven **8**
Wåxnäs Hotel-Konferens **2**

caused him an overwhelming sense of guilt, were developed. There's a cafe on site, and a staff that is proud of the site's role as the only Nobel-related museum in the world.

SHOPPING

Connoisseurs seek out Värmland antiques at **Blandorama,** Östra Kanalgatan 2 (☎ 054/18-07-16), and **Britts Antiklynd,** Vikengatan 17-B (☎ 054/18-84-51). The best center for arts, crafts, and gifts is **Katrin Lööf Keramik,** Strandvägen 20 (☎ 054/21-00-55). Local jewelry is sold at **Isaksson Porfyr,** Kasernhojden 23 (☎ 054/15-19-00), and cut glass is offered by **Evys Presenter o. Alternativbokhandel,** Östra Torggatan 19 (☎ 054/15-21-95).

WHERE TO STAY
EXPENSIVE

Elite Stadshotellet. Kungsgatan 22, S-651 08 Karlstad. ☎ **800/528-1234** in the U.S. Fax 054/293-031. www.bestwestern.se/karlstad. E-mail: stadshotellet.karlstad@elite.se. 139 units. TV TEL. Sun–Thurs 1,395 SEK ($153.45) double; Fri–Sat 725 SEK ($79.75) double. All week long 1,800–2,700 SEK ($198–$297) suite. Rates include breakfast. AE, DC, MC, V. Parking 90 SEK ($9.90).

This hotel, with a yellow-and-white imperial neo-baroque facade, is one of the most impressive 19th-century hotels in all of Scandinavia. The bedrooms range from sedately modern to the more old-fashioned, but all are well maintained with firm mattresses and ample bathrooms supplied with generous towels and hair dryers. The hotel is a 5-minute walk north from the rail station.

Dining/Diversions: The gourmet restaurant, Matsalom, serves first-class food at lunch. You can lunch amid elaborately carved turn-of-the-century walls beneath a ceiling embellished with sea serpents. Only the British-inspired pub, Bishops Arms, serves dinner, costing from 100 to 175 SEK ($11 to $19.25).

Amenities: Room service, laundry/dry cleaning, concierge, separate saunas and solariums for men and women.

First Hotel Plaza. Västra Torggatan 2, SE-652 25 Karlstad. ☎ **054/100-200.** Fax 054/ 100-224. www.firsthotels.se. E-mail: Per.lindstrom@firsthotels.se. 121 units. TV TEL. June–Aug 15 and Sat–Sun year-round, 750 SEK ($82.50) double; rest of year, 1,438 SEK ($158.20) double. Year-round, 2,900 SEK ($319) suite. AE, DC, MC, V. Parking 70 SEK ($7.70).

This exclusive business and leisure hotel was awarded four stars by the Société Suisse des Hôteliers. Since it was built in 1984, the First Hotel Plaza has been considerably upgraded and improved. The rooms are elegantly decorated and generally spacious, with good, firm beds and medium-size bathrooms equipped with hair dryers. The most expensive rooms are the business units, which have more work space, including a large desk. These units also come with robes and a minibar.

Dining/Diversions: The Plaza Garden, a popular brasserie, is located in the atrium and serves international cuisine. But the prestige restaurant is the Vivaldi, with its superb menu and well-stocked wine cellar in a gracious 19th-century setting (see "Where to Dine," below). Guests can round off the evening at the popular club, New York.

Amenities: Clad in elegant marble, a relaxation center offers a whirlpool, solarium, sauna, and steam bath along with sweeping views of the city. Room service, laundry/dry cleaning, concierge.

✪ **Scandic Hotel Winn.** Norra Strandgatan 9–11, S-652 24 Karlstad. ☎ **054/77-64-700.** Fax 054/77-64-711. E-mail: karlstad-winn.res@scandic-hotels.se. 198 units. TV TEL. June 20–Aug 5, 725 SEK ($79.75) double; Aug 6–June 19, 1,681 SEK ($184.90) double. Year-round, 2,500 SEK ($275) suite. Rates include breakfast. AE, DC, MC, V. Parking 95 SEK ($10.45).

Although this establishment is part of a chain, it has charm and grace and is at the very top of Karlstad choices. It's also the most up to date in town. Built on the shores of the Klarälven River in the heart of Karlstad, it attracts both business travelers and vacationers. The bedrooms are most often spacious with extremely firm beds and ample-size bathrooms with hair dryers. Each has carpeting, video movies, radio, trouser press, and traditional furnishings that are replaced when they start to show wear and tear. Several of the bedrooms also contain a minibar. In 1998, the owners doubled the size of this hotel by buying the building next door and joining it to the hotel's existing core.

Dining/Diversions: Café Artist is a well-frequented place known for its good food (see "Where to Dine," following). There's also a piano bar.

Amenities: Solarium, sauna, room service, laundry/dry cleaning, concierge.

MODERATE

✪ **Gösta Berling.** Drottninggatan 1, S-652 24 Karlstad. ☎ **054/15-01-90.** Fax 054/ 15-28-26. www.stay.nu. E-mail: gostaberling@swedenhotel.se. 75 units. TV TEL. 1,100 SEK ($121) double. Closed Sat–Sun. Parking 80 SEK ($8.80).

Named after the hero in Selma Lagerlöf's celebrated novel, this weekday hotel lies at the beginning of the biggest shopping street in Karlstad. Although it's relatively bland, it generally is recognized for offering the best value in town. There are few public rooms to speak of, other than an unpretentious breakfast room, but the welcome is warm and the comfort good. The cozy and carpeted bedrooms are frequently reno-vated. All have good beds with firm mattresses and small though spotlessly maintained bathrooms. Some units are no-smoking. The hotel also has a sauna.

Scandic Klarälven. Sandbäcksgatan 6, S-653 40 Karlstad. ☎ **054/77-645-00.** Fax 054/ 77-645-11. www.scandic-hotels.com. E-mail: klaralven@scandic-hotels.com. 143 units. TV TEL. June 30–Aug 5 and Fri–Sat year-round, 600–710 SEK ($66–$78.10) double; rest of year, 1,375–1,444 SEK ($151.25–$158.85) double. Rates include breakfast. AE, DC, MC, V. Free parking.

Part of a chain, this comfortable, well-designed hotel is a well-recommended, middle-bracket place favored by business travelers from throughout Sweden. Set about a half mile north of the Karlstad's commercial core, on a grassy strip of land midway between the Klarälven River and the E18 highway, this low-slung hotel was built around 1970 and renovated in the mid-1990s. Bedrooms contain unremarkable furniture with con-temporary, international styling, and monochromatic color schemes, plus firm mat-tresses and spotless bathrooms. The rooms at the cheaper end of the above-mentioned spectrum have only one double bed, and actually are a bit smaller than comfort allows. It's better to opt for one of the slightly more expensive rooms, because they are a lot bigger and more comfortable. On the premises are conference facilities; a bar; a bistro-style restaurant with exposed wine racks, hardwood floors, and international cuisine; a sauna; and a swimming pool.

INEXPENSIVE

Wåxnäs Hotel-Konferens. Ventilgatan 1, S-654 45 Karlstad. ☎ **054/56-00-80.** Fax 054/ 56-88-19. www.stekhuset.com. E-mail: hotwax@karlstad.mail.telia.com. 40 units. MINIBAR TV TEL. Mid-June to mid-Aug and Fri–Sat year-round, 680 SEK ($74.80) double; rest of year, 990 SEK ($108.90) double. Rates include breakfast. Free parking. Bus: 33 or 35.

The best-known aspect of this well-managed hotel involves its restaurant, Stek Huset, which is one of the finest in the district (see "Where to Dine," below). The hotel itself was built almost as an afterthought to the restaurant in the 1970s, on a quiet triangle of land that abuts the E18 highway, about a mile west of Karlstad's center. The two-story hotel offers clean, internationally modern bedrooms outfitted with angular, motel-style furniture that's comfortable but not particularly plush. The owners are a Swedish-Greek team headed by members of the Apostolidi family. There's a sauna and solarium on the premises and, under separate management, a bowling alley. The site of the hotel, incidentally, was famous throughout the 18th and 19th centuries as the biggest marketplace for horse trading in central Sweden.

WHERE TO DINE

Café Artist. In the Scandic Hotel Winn, Norra Strandgatan 9–11. ☎ **054/77-64-700.** Reservations recommended for dinner on weekends. Lunch buffet 79 SEK ($8.70) per person; dinner main courses 100–219 SEK ($11–$24.10). AE, DC, MC, V. Mon–Fri 11:30am–11pm, Sat 5pm–11:30pm, Sun 6–10:30pm. SWEDISH/FRENCH.

Karlstad's best restaurant occupies the street level of the Scandic Hotel Winn (see "Where to Stay," above), although its culinary finesse is more obvious at nighttime than at lunch. The setting contains lots of 19th century pinewood antiques and lots of carefully finished paneling, which overall creates a cozy glow of old-fashioned well being. The only option at lunchtime is a copious buffet attended by many of the town's office workers, who select from a generous medley of fish, meats, soups, salads, and vegetarian dishes. Evening meals are more elaborate, with well-choreographed ser-vice and menu items that include well-prepared olive-and-feta-stuffed chicken with herbs, garlic, and potato pie and filet of lamb with sage and alpine char with a white wine sauce. A dessert favorite is homemade vanilla ice cream with a compote of warm cloudberries.

Plaza Vivaldi. In the First Hotel Plaza, Vastra Torggatan 2. ☎ **054/10-02-00.** Reservations recommended. Main courses 120–250 SEK ($13.20–$27.50). AE, DC, MC, V. Daily noon–2pm and 6–11pm. SWEDISH.

One of the best restaurants in Karlstad is on the lobby level of the First Hotel Plaza (see "Where to Stay," above). Its decor combines modern with antique and traditional. Specialties of the chef are likely to include lime- and ginger-marinated salmon flavored with coriander, noisettes of reindeer with chanterelles, filet of veal in a creamy morel sauce, breast of pheasant with white wine sauce and grapes, and filet of monkfish. The chefs are highly skilled and they've got imagination, but they never go too far. Their dishes are perfectly balanced and technically superb in every way.

Skogen Terrassen. Mariebergsskogen. ☎ **0541/15-20-80.** Reservations recommended. Smörgåsbord 250 SEK ($27.50). AE, MC, V. June–Aug, Mon–Sat 11:30am–2pm; off-season, Mon–Sat 11am–6pm. SWEDISH.

The allure here is the copious smörgåsbord buffet. You can eat either on a rustic terrace with a view of the spruces ringing the lake and the nearby amusement park, or in the spacious dining hall with its high wooden ceilings and antiques. You are presented with a lavish array of Swedish delicacies, including herring, shrimp, fish, salads, and meat, as well as homemade desserts.

✪ Stek Huset. In the Wåxnäs Hotel-Konferens, Ventilgatan 1. ☎ **054/56-00-80.** Reservations recommended at lunch, required at dinner. Fixed-price lunches 75–200 SEK ($8.25–$22); main courses 75–300 SEK ($8.25–$33). AE, DC, MC, V. Bus: 33 or 35. INTERNATIONAL.

Set on the lobby level of the Wåxnäs Hotel-Konferens (see "Where to Stay," above), this is one of the most famous and best-recommended restaurants in Karlstad, attracting diners from as far away as Jönköping. The setting is blue, dark red, and woodsy, with artfully illuminated tables and lots of drama associated with steaks and fish that frequently are flambéed at the table. The menu focuses on fish and on beefsteaks from both Sweden and Ireland. Two of the best-recommended dishes are a version of pepper steak that clients drive long distances to try, and a signature dish of deboned sole, grilled and served au gratin with creamed mushrooms and shrimp. A dessert that absolutely never fails to please clients is fresh raspberries with hot sabayon sauce and ice cream. A long list of wines from virtually everywhere is available to accompany your meal.

Värdshuset Alstern. Morgonvägen 4. ☎ **0541/83-49-00.** Reservations recommended. 1-course fixed-price lunch 125 SEK ($13.75); main courses 140–220 SEK ($15.40–$24.20). AE, MC, V. Mon–Fri 11:30am–2pm, Sat–Sun 1–5pm. Closed Jan and 3 weeks in July. FRENCH/SWEDISH.

Two miles north of Karlstad near Route 63 on a hillside above Lake Alstern, this place makes a fine luncheon excursion. It occupies a 1920s Dutch-gabled building. Depending on the season, you can enjoy game specialties such as elk with hand-picked berries and wild mushrooms, along with lighter offerings such as fresh fish dishes, well-flavored meats, and vegetables prepared just right.

KARLSTAD AFTER DARK

There's more fun in the summer, of course. Karlstad's biggest entertainment complex, to which famous artists often come, is **Jäger,** Västra Torggatan 8 (☎ **054/10-10-66**). Here you'll find three bars, two dance floors, and two open-air summer restaurants. **Restaurant Sandgrund,** Sandgrundsudden (☎ **054/21-16-70**), is Värmland's best-known dance restaurant. Lots of people frequent this place, and it's easy to make new acquaintances. A pub and disco on two floors, **Trollet & Jacop's,** Kungsgatan 18 (☎ 054/ 21-95-95), draws a lively, young crowd. One of the town's best pubs is **Bishops Arms,** in the Stadshotellet, Kungsgatan 22 (☎ 054/29-30-00). This is a classic pub opening on the Klarälven, and offering a wide range of beers.

2 Sunne

236 miles W of Stockholm, 38 miles NW of Karlstad, 179 miles NE of Gothenburg

Lying on Lake Fryken, Sunne is the center for tourism in Fryksdalen (Fryken Valley). The "land of legend," as Fryksdalen is known, is associated with the writings of Selma Lagerlöf. In fact, Sunne was the prototype for the village of Bro in *The Saga of Gösta Berling,* her most famous work. From Sunne, you can take boat trips on Lake Fryken, or play golf on a nine-hole course.

In winter, Sunne often attracts skiers, as it has Värmland's highest lift capacity and the most modern cross-country stadium in Europe. Its slalom facility has a ski school, ski rentals, a ski shop, sports services, a restaurant, and a lodge. There are 10 descents that vary in difficulty; four of them are lit when twilight falls. Akka Stadium is the name of Sunne's ski stadium, and there are several cross-country trails starting from here. For information about skiing in the area, call **Ski Sunne** at ☎ 0565/602-80.

ESSENTIALS

GETTING THERE   By Train   Four or five trains arrive daily on the 4½-hour trip from Stockholm, and from Gothenburg there are another four or five trains a day, which take 3⅔ hours. You always have to change trains in Kil, and sometimes in Hallsberg, depending on the train. From Oslo there are two trains per day, requiring a change in Kil; trip time is 3 to 4 hours. For more information, call ☎ 020/75-75-75.

By Bus   If you're traveling from Stockholm, take the train. The bus trip is too complicated and has too many transfers. From Gothenburg, one bus a day arrives Monday through Friday on the 7¼-hour trip; transfer in Karlstad. Call ☎ 0200/21818 for schedules.

By Car   Drive north along 61 or 45 from Karlstad.

VISITOR INFORMATION   For information, the **Sunne Turistbyrå,** Mejerigatan 2 (☎ 0565/135-30), is open June 20 to August 5, Monday through Saturday from 9am to 7pm and on Sunday from 1 to 6pm; August 6 to June 19, Monday through Friday from 9am to 5pm.

SEEING THE SIGHTS

Sundsbergs Gård. Ekebyvagen. ☎ **0565/103-63.** Free admission. June 25–Aug 10, Tues–Sun noon–4pm. Closed Aug 11–June 24.

In the center of Sunne, this museum depicts various exhibits that illustrate domestic life over a 300-year period at a Värmland manor house. From the kitchen to the drawing room, exhibits are labeled to indicate what particular century or time period they represent. This summer-only museum is close to the landmark Hotel Selma Lagerlöf.

NEARBY LITERARY ATTRACTIONS

✪ **Mårbacka Minnesgård.** Mårbacka. ☎ **0565/310-27.** Admission 50 SEK ($5.50) adults, 25 SEK ($2.75) children. May to mid-Sept, daily 10am–4:30pm; off-season, Sat only at 2pm (guided tour).

On the other side of the water, 6 miles southeast of Sunne and 36 miles north of Karlstad, Mårbacka is the former home of Selma Lagerlöf (1858–1940), who won the Nobel Prize for literature. The pillared building is kept much as she left it at the time of her death. The estate is filled with her furnishings and mementos. It was disguised as Lövdala in her masterpiece *The Saga of Gösta Berling*.

✪ Rottneros Herrgårde. Rottneros. ☎ **0565/602-95.** Admission 60 SEK ($6.60). Mid-May to early June and late Aug, Mon–Fri 10am–4pm, Sat–Sun 10am–6pm; mid- to late June, Mon–Fri 10am–5pm, Sat–Sun 10am–5pm; July to late Aug, daily 10am–6pm. Take Route 45, 2½ miles south from Sunne.

This major attraction sits on the western shore of Lake Fryken and is one of the most famous fairyland settings in Sweden. Rotteros Manor, a site developed during the 13th century, provided the inspiration for the mythical manor house of Ekeby, which appears in Selma Lagerlöf's saga. Although the interior of the building is private, there's a manicured park and a world-class sculpture garden surrounding the building. Set amid verdant landscaping are more than 100 pieces of sculpture crafted by such artists as Carl Milles. The foremost sculptors of each of the neighboring Scandinavian countries also are represented: Kai Nielsen of Denmark, Gustav Vigeland of Norway, and Wäinö Aaltonen of Finland. On the grounds is a cafeteria and licensed restaurant.

SHOPPING

Sunne is known for its long-standing tradition of arts and crafts. The landscape, nature, and translucent colors have "conspired" to spark creativity in local artisans, or so it is said. One of the most interesting centers for purchases of arts and crafts is **Art By,** By 109 (☎ **0565/140-45**), lying 2½ miles north of Sunne. Auction bargains are available on occasion, and there is a beautiful selection of furniture in this old country store atmosphere. At the cafe you can see works by modern artists and craftspeople and enjoy home cooking, including home-baked bread.

WHERE TO STAY & DINE

Broby Gåstgivaregård. Långgatan 25, S-686 24 Sunne. ☎ **0565/133-70.** Fax 0565/125-53. www.brobx.nu. 36 units, 26 with bathroom. 715 SEK ($78.65) double with bathroom; annex, 400 SEK ($44) double without bathroom. Rates include breakfast. AE, DC, MC, V. Free parking.

Cozy, family managed, and completely unpretentious, this is a reliable, small-scale inn whose two sections date from 1900 and the mid-1960s, respectively. The more appealing of the two sections is the older—an ochre-sided, many-gabled building. All bedrooms contain private bathrooms, furniture inspired by the building's original age, and cheerful color schemes of blue and yellow. Less appealing are the bedrooms within the annex, none of which has a private bathroom, and in which sheets and towels are not provided. (Rented by backpackers, students, and bare-boned budgeteers, they're as simple as anything we want to recommend in this guidebook.) On the premises is a restaurant serving Swedish-style lunches and dinners Monday through Saturday. The food is good and hearty and worth a visit even if you're not staying here.

Hotel FrykenStrand. By 80, S-686 93 Sunne. ☎ **0565/133-00.** Fax 0565/71-16-91. www.frykenstrand.se. E-mail: gast@frykenstrand.se. 62 units. TV TEL. Mid-June to mid-Aug and Fri–Sun year-round, daily 350–400 SEK ($38.50–$44) double; rest of year, 750 SEK ($82.50) double. Rates include breakfast. AE, DC, MC, V. Free parking. From Sunne, follow the signs to Torsby.

Set on well-kept lawns 2 miles north of the center of Sunne, a few feet uphill from the waters of Lake Frykken, this is a three-story hotel whose two sections were built in the early 1960s and the early 1980s. During clement weather, many of the hotel's social activities take place on masonry terraces that flank its edges. The sunny and very clean interior offers big-windowed views, especially from the hotel's dining room, out over the surrounding lake and landscapes. Accommodations are comfortable, plushly upholstered with pastel-colored accessories, and outfitted like cozy nests—not overly large, but appealing and sleep inducing. The hotel contains a conventional sauna that's open year-round. More whimsical is the floating, wood-fired sauna that operates from a tiny hut built atop a raft in the lake. Participants dive directly into the waters after working up a sweat inside. The hotel restaurant is appealingly polite and friendly, with an emphasis on old-fashioned and traditional Swedish specialties. From June to August, it's open daily for lunch and dinner; the rest of the year, it's open only when business warrants it, so call before driving out here to dine. Main courses cost from 95 to 170 SEK ($10.45 to $18.70); a fixed-price lunch from a buffet that emphasizes different kinds of salads costs 55 SEK ($6.05).

✪ **Hotel Selma Lag & Spa Selma Lagerlöf.** Ekebyvågen, S-686 28 Sunne. ☎ **0565/ 166-00.** Fax 0565/166-20. www.selmaspa.se. E-mail: slhotspa.alphascope.net. 340 units. MINIBAR TV TEL. Hotel: mid-June to mid-Aug, 495 SEK ($54.45) per person double. Late Aug–early June, 395 SEK ($43.45) per person double. Year-round, 1,000 SEK ($110) per person suite. Rates include breakfast. Spa: mid-June to mid-Aug, 685 SEK ($75.35) per person double; 985 SEK ($108.35) per person suite. Rates include half-board. Mid-Aug to mid-June, 2,790 SEK ($306.90) double; 3,790 SEK ($416.90) suite. Rates include full board. AE, DC, MC, V. Free parking.

Completed in 1992, this is the only full-service spa in a Swedish hotel. Owned by a conglomerate of Danish and Swedish banks, it was launched in 1982 with the construction of a consciously old-fashioned core ("the hotel") designed like a stately Swedish manor house. Ten years later, a nine-story tower ("the spa") was built 300 yards away, with modern bedrooms with balconies, convention facilities, and a full array of spa treatments. Most visitors check into the spa for a minimum of 3 days for a series of stress-reducing and health-promoting regimes. Sports enthusiasts appreciate the many opportunities in the surrounding region for skiing and hiking.

Bedrooms, with excellent mattresses and ample bathrooms complete with hair dryers, in both the spa and the hotel are the best and most up-to-date in Värmland. In the spa section, the bedrooms are sold only on a full-board basis in winter or a half-board in summer. The spa section contains 184 rooms. In the hotel, breakfast-only guests are accepted. Guests at the hotel must pay for extra activities, whereas spa guests get some activities such as daily aerobics classes free. However, all spa treatments require supplemental food. Note that meals in the spa are diet conscious and fat free, whereas the hotel restaurant serves a sophisticated fare of Swedish regional specialties, some from Värmland, and top rate international dishes—mainly continental—as well.

The hotel and spa lie at the edge of Lake Fryken, about a 5-minute drive south of the center of Sunne. Each of the separate buildings has its own reception staff, restaurant, and bars. The nightlife facilities in the older section usually are more animated and fun.

3 Filipstad

167 miles W of Stockholm, 192 miles NE of Gothenburg

The tourist center for the Bergslag (mining) area of Värmland, Filipstad was founded in 1611. It is almost certain that iron ore was mined in this region even before the black death of the 14th century, and documentary evidence establishes it as being a thriving business in 1413. The main mine products were iron and manganese ore; but silver, copper, lead, and zinc ore also were found. Even gold occasionally has been unearthed.

Today, the Filipstad Bergslag smelting houses have vanished and only two mines remain in operation, but visitors can see the old open mine shafts, ruins of ironworks, and grand manor houses where the ironmasters once lived. Other industries here include the making of Wasa Crispbread (knäckebröd) and tourism. Canoeing is a favorite summer activity, whereas downhill and cross-country skiing lure winter visitors.

Filipstad's main claim to fame (for Americans) is native son and inventor John Ericsson, who was born in nearby Långbanshyttan. (See box below.)

Ericsson's brother was Baron Nils Ericsson, a noted construction engineer in Sweden who is known for having planned and built Sweden's first main railway.

Another well-known Filipstad figure is poet Nils Ferlin, whose realistic statue sits on a park bench in the center of town.

ESSENTIALS

GETTING THERE   By Train   You can't take the train to Filipstad. The nearest station is at Kristinehamn, from which you can make bus connections to Filipstad. For rail information, call ☎ **020/75-75-75.**

By Bus   Daily connections are possible from Karlstad. Call ☎ **0200/21818** for schedules. The bus ride from Karlstad to Filipstad, a distance of 37 miles, takes about 40 minutes.

By Car   Follow Route 61 through Arvika to Kil. Drive through Forshaga to Route 63 to Molkom and Filipstad.

VISITOR INFORMATION   The **Filipstads Turistbyrå,** S-682 27 Filipstad (☎ **0590/715-60;** www.varmland.org), is open daily from 10am to 8pm (closes at 4pm in winter).

SEEING THE SIGHTS

A visit to Filipstad wouldn't be complete without an excursion to the little settlement of **Långbans Gruvby,** Hyttbacken (☎ **0590/221-81**), lying 12 miles northeast of the center. Mining on this site was carried out from the middle of the 16th century until 1972. The Långban mines were especially known in the 19th century for producing manganese, and during the last decades of their activity they were primary sources of dolomite. More than 300 different kinds of minerals have been found here. Långban today is a well-preserved mining village with mine holes, shaft towers, a smelting house, workmen's houses, and a manor house. In 1803, the Swedish-American inventor John Ericsson was born in a wing of the old managing director's residence. The site is open to all daily noon to 5pm, charging no admission. For information about it, call ☎ **0590/220-45.**

Half a mile from the town center, **Storbrohhyttan Hembygådsgården,** Munkeberg (☎ **0590/140-28**), is a restored blast furnace and ironworks that have been made into a mining museum with a wealth of artifacts. On site is a cafe and crafts center, Tullhuset, that's open Monday through Friday year-round from noon to 7pm. An employee at Tullhuset shows newcomers the blast furnace lying a few steps away. The cost of the visit is 65 SEK ($7.15).

The artisans of Filipstad sell and exhibit their handcrafts at **Kjortelgården,** Hantverksgatan 17 (☎ **0590/153-50**). There also is a simple cafe on site.

Lesjöfors Museum. Lesjöfors. ☎ **0590/31122.** Admission 40 SEK ($4.40). June–Aug, Mon–Fri 10am–4pm, Sat–Sun 2–5pm; Sept–May, Thurs–Sat 2–5pm. Take Route 64 north of town 22 miles.

This evocative museum illustrates 3 centuries of Värmland history. You'll find yourself transferred to different epochs, feeling the spirit of Lesjöfors from the beginning of the century. The museum not only presents the history of the steelworks that once were

The Swede Who Helped Defeat the South

He may not have figured in *Gone With the Wind*, but John Ericsson, the famous Swedish inventor, helped the North win the war against the Confederacy. Born near Filipstad on July 31, 1803, Ericsson joined the Swedish army in 1820. Eventually he migrated to England, where he failed in a competition to create a new locomotive for the Liverpool and Manchester Railway when his "Novelty" developed engine trouble.

Disappointed, he moved to America, where he gained fame for his inventions, above all, the marine propeller. His fame was cemented when his warship, the Yankee *Monitor,* defeated the Confederate *Merrimac* on May 9, 1862. This defeat saved the northern fleet and led to the Union naval forces quickly taking command of the sea, closing off Confederate ports by blockade.

Ericsson also invented the steam fire engine and the hot-air (or caloric) engine, and made several improvements in steam boilers. Even though this son of Filipstad lived abroad for much of his life, he placed his inventions at the disposal of the Swedish navy.

After a successful life as an inventor, John Ericsson died on March 8, 1889, in the United States. As he had requested to be buried at Filipstad on his native ground, his remains were transported to Sweden on the American armed cruiser *Baltimore.* He arrived back home with full honors and a magnificent hearse bearing his body. All the residents of Filipstad turned out to welcome home their now-famous native son.

On July 31, 1895, the John Ericsson Mausoleum was consecrated on the anniversary of Ericsson's birth. Once more, the town honored its great son, and the streets were decorated with flags, flowers, and several triumphal arches. The mausoleum lies at **Östra Kyrkogården** (☎ **0590/715-60**) today, and often is visited by Americans (at least Yankees), among others. Every year since 1929, the John Ericsson Society places a wreath of flowers, in the shape of a propeller, at this mausoleum.

Every July 31, Filipstad stages a mock naval battle between the *Merrimac,* the armored vessel of the Confederates and the smaller *Monitor,* the more easily maneuvered gunboat of Ericsson's. The *Monitor* always wins, of course.

in the town, but also re-creates the society, organizations, sports, and housing of the workers who lived here. You'll see authentic environments, even the waiting room of the former factory. In the foundry hall you can view exhibits of some of the steel products once created here. (Artist Larseric Vänerlöf shaped an impressive sculpture from some of the different molds left behind when the factory shut down.) One section recreates in minute detail a kitchen from the 1950s.

WHERE TO STAY & DINE

✪ **Hennickehammars Herrgård.** Lake Hemtjärn, S-682 00 Filipstad. ☎ **0590/608500.** Fax 0590/608505. 54 units. TV TEL. Fri–Sat 1,100 SEK ($121) double; Sun–Thurs 1,250 SEK ($137.50) double. AE, DC, MC, V. Free parking.

Built in 1722 as the home of a wealthy landowner, this hotel, with its elegant detailing and symmetrical facade, is a comfortable country spot loaded with personality and charm. On lawns close to the edge of Lake Hemtjarn, 2½ miles south of Filipstad, rooms are either in one of several outbuildings or in the main manor house itself. Guests can swim in the lake, rent horses at a nearby riding school, play tennis, or enjoy golf at a course about 9 miles away. Each unit is stylishly comfortable, thanks to a renovation that brought new mattresses and improved the bathrooms.

The best dining in and around Filipstad is found at the hotel restaurant, which is open to the general public daily from noon to 2pm and 7 to 9pm. A fixed-price, three-course evening meal costs 325 SEK ($35.75). From Monday through Friday a lunch buffet is served for 155 SEK ($17.05); however, on Saturday and Sunday a more elaborate Swedish smörgåsbord is offered at 195 SEK ($21.45) per person.

Hotel John. John Ericssonsgatan 8, S-682 00 Filipstad. ☎ **0590/125-30.** Fax 0590/106-68. www.swedenhotel.se. 47 units. TV TEL. Mid-June to mid-Aug and Fri–Sat year-round, 670 SEK ($73.70) double; rest of year, 980 SEK ($107.80) double. Rates include breakfast. AE, DC, MC, V. Free parking.

Set near the center of town, close to the junction of highways 64 and 65, this low-slung, two-story, white-walled hotel dates from 1974, when it was designed to cater to both roadside traffic and corporate conventions. Inside, you'll find a tavern-style restaurant, a bar, a sauna, a gym, wood-floored bedrooms with double-glazed windows, and decor that's equivalent to that within dozens of middle-bracket hotels throughout the western hemisphere. Bedrooms, although rather motel standard, are comfortable and fine for an overnight stopover. Bathrooms are a bit tiny.

4 Falun

303 miles NE of Gothenburg, 142 miles NW of Stockholm

An exploration of the Dalarna region begins in Falun, the old capital of Dalarna; it lies on both sides of the Falu River. This town is noted for its copper mines; the income generated from copper has supported many Swedish kings. Just 6½ miles northeast, you can visit the home of the famed Swedish painter Carl Larsson.

ESSENTIALS

GETTING THERE   By Train   There is frequent service during the day from Stockholm (trip time: 3 hours) and from Gothenburg (trip time: 6 hours). For schedules, call ☎ **020/75-75-75.**

By Bus   Buses operated by **Swebus** (☎ **0200/21818**) run between Stockholm and Falun either once or twice every Friday, Saturday, and Sunday, depending on the season. Coming from Gothenburg, although the distance is greater, buses arrive twice a day every day of the week, making frequent stops along the way. The second bus company that services Falun is **Masexpressen** (☎ **08/107766**), which operates additional buses into Falun from Stockholm and other points within Sweden.

By Car   If you're driving to Falun from Stockholm, take the E18 expressway northwest to the junction with Route 70. From here, continue to the junction with Route 60, where you head northwest. Falun is signposted.

VISITOR INFORMATION   The Falun Tourist Office, Trotzgatan 10–12 (☎ **023/830-50**) is open from mid-August to mid-June, every Monday through Friday from 9am to 6pm, and Saturday from 10am to 2pm. During summer, from mid-June to mid-August, it's open Monday through Friday from 9am to 9pm, Saturday from 10am to 5pm, and Sunday from 11am to 5pm. For more information on Falun, refer to the town's Web site at **www.welcom.falun.se.**

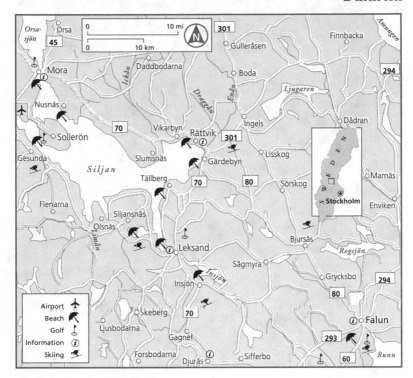

Dalarna

Airport ✈
Beach 🏖
Golf ⛳
Information ⓘ
Skiing 🎿

SEEING THE SIGHTS

Go first to the market square, Stora Torget, to see the **Kristine Church** (☎ 023/ 279-10), a copper-roofed structure dating from the mid-17th century (the tower itself dates from 1865). It's open daily from 10am to 4pm and admission is free.

Lugnet. S-79131 Falun ☎ 023/83500. Admission 40 SEK ($4.10) for a day's use of all the facilities (except massage). Sports hall, daily 8am–9pm.

This is one of Sweden's largest and most comprehensive sports complexes. Its main fame derives from its selection in 1974 as the site for the cross-country skiing World's Championship. Today, it contains a large-scale hotel (the below-recommended Scandic), a ski jump, an ice hockey rink, and a sports hall that's the centerpiece for all the other facilities (including miles of cross-country ski tracks and a campground), and the site of an indoor pool, a sauna, and a steam bath.

Bjursås Ski Center. S-791 71, Falun. ☎ 023/51153. Day pass 195 SEK ($21.45). Bjursberget is about 13 miles north of the center of Falun; follow the signs pointing to Råttuik.

This ski center has six mechanized ski lifts, 10 downhill slopes, and a restaurant or two. It does not, however, resemble a full-fledged ski resort like Gstaad or Chamonix. Don't expect much more than a big parking lot and lots of snow, ice, and midwinter darkness, with illuminated ski trails and a sense of family fun and Scandinavian thrift. Equipment can be rented on site.

Carl Larsson-gården. Carl Larssons Väg 12, Sundborn. ☎ 023/600-53. Admission 65 SEK ($7.15) adults, 25 SEK ($2.75) children 7–15, free for children 6 and under. May–Sept, daily 10am–5pm; Oct–Apr, by appointment only (call ☎ 023/60069 for reservations). Bus: 64 from Falun.

Falun

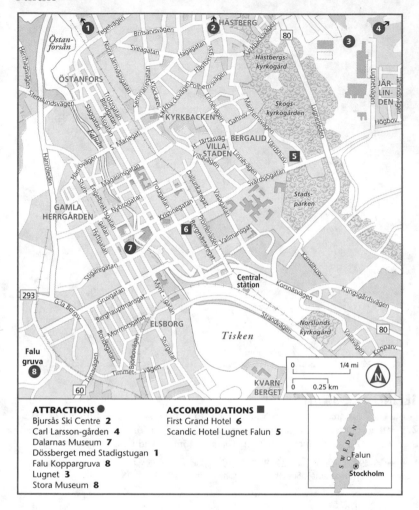

ATTRACTIONS ●
Bjursås Ski Centre **2**
Carl Larsson-gården **4**
Dalarnas Museum **7**
Dössberget med Stadigstugan **1**
Falu Koppargruva **8**
Lugnet **3**
Stora Museum **8**

ACCOMMODATIONS ■
First Grand Hotel **6**
Scandic Hotel Lugnet Falun **5**

A 20-minute trip from Falun will take you to a small village, Sundborn, site of Lilla Hyttnas, Carl Larsson's home (now known as Carl Larsson-gården). Larsson became Sweden's most admired artist during his lifetime (1853–1919). Through Larsson's watercolor paintings of his own house, it has become known throughout Sweden. In the United States, reproductions of Larsson's watercolors, mainly of his wife, Karin, and their children, appear frequently on prints, calendars, and greeting cards. There are guided tours throughout the day, and English-language tours sometimes are available.

While at the home of the artist, you can also ask about viewing **Carl Larssons porträttsambling** (a portrait collection donated by Larsson), displayed in the Congregation House next to the local church. The pictures, painted between 1905 and 1918, depict well-known local residents representing many different occupations. One of the best known portraits is that of a carpenter, Hans Arnbon, of whom Larsson said: "Before the Devil can get his slippers on, Arnbon is standing there at his lathe or his bench." To reach the garden, take bus no. 64 from Falun to Sundborn, which is 5 minutes away from Carl Larsson-gården.

Portrait of the Artist

Admired though Carl Larsson was during his lifetime, he still could hold a grudge. When his erstwhile friend, the playwright August Strindberg, published a vicious attack on Larsson, the artist took a knife and stalked Strindberg through the streets of Stockholm.

⭐ **Dalarnas Museum.** Stirgaregatan 2–4. ☎ **023/76-55-00.** Admission 40 SEK ($4.40) adults, 20 SEK ($2.20) ages 7–18, free for children 6 and under. Mon–Fri 10am–5pm, weekends noon–5pm.

This is Dalarna's most intriguing folk art museum. It's especially rich in genuine, old, colorful folk costumes and their accessories, and also exhibits the best collections of peasant wall paintings. The music section is especially interesting, and you can hear recordings of fiddlers and young girls blowing the traditional small alp-horns. The Falun group of graphic artists is well known in the Swedish art world, and the six artists who made up that elite group in the early decades of the 20th century are displayed here. Of these, Axel Fridell is the finest. A faithful reconstruction of Swedish writer Selma Lagerlöf's study with its original furnishings has been installed in the museum.

Dössberget med Stadigstugan. Bjursås. ☎ **23/507-37.** Free admission. Daily noon–6pm. 12½ miles northwest of Falun follow the direction to Rättvik to the signpost leading into Bjursås.

The typical paintings of Dalarna, which were produced mainly from the 1780s to the 1860s, occupy a significant place in the cultural history of the province. Artists would paint on either canvas or paper, often working on a painting in sections. Then they would join those sections together to form a large painting that was intended to fill a generous space, such as a large wall in a dining room in a manor house. One of the most acclaimed peasant painters was Mats Persson Stadig from Bjursås, who lived here from 1786 to 1862. His home and paintings are on view at Stadigstugan, as well as at the Dalarnas Museum (see above). Old homestead buildings housing the local history museum are located on the mountain of Dössberget. If time is limited, visit only Stadigstugan, as it has the most interesting collection.

Stadigstugan actually is the outbuilding of a blandly modern restaurant, Dössberget, which is named after the nearby mountain and serves lunch and dinner daily from June to August, usually from noon to 9pm (off-season it closes around 6pm). Main courses cost from 150 to 250 SEK ($16.50 to $27.50).

⭐ **Falu Koppargruva.** Gruvplatsen. ☎ **023/158-25.** Admission 60 SEK ($6.60) adults, 30 SEK ($3.30) children 17 and under. May–Aug, daily 10am–4pm; Mar–Apr and Sept–Nov 15, Sat–Sun 12:30–4pm. Closed Nov 16–Feb 28.

This copper mine, now in the town center, was the world's largest producer of copper during the 17th century; it supplied the raw material used for the roof of the Palace of Versailles. After a visit to the mine in 1734, Carl von Linné called it, "Sweden's greatest wonder, but as terrible as Hell itself." Since 1970, when the mine was opened to the public, more than one million visitors have taken the elevator 180 feet below the surface of the earth and into the mine. Guides take you through old chambers and winding passages dating from the Middle Ages. In one section of the mine you'll see a shaft divided by a timber wall that's more than 650 feet high; this may be the world's tallest wooden structure. Today the only industrial product of the mine is pigment used for producing the Sweden's signature red paint (Falu Rödfärg), which is used not only on virtually all Swedish barns, but on thousands upon thousands of private homes and even commercial and public buildings. Buildings painted this shade of barn red have become virtual symbols of Sweden.

Stora Museum. Vid Falu Gruva. ☎ **023/71-14-75.** Admission 60 SEK ($6.60). May–Aug, daily 10am–4:30pm; off-season, daily 12:30–4:30pm.

This museum is devoted to the technical and industrial past of the area, visualizing the history of its copper mountain. Most interesting here is a model room with Christopher Polhem's clever inventions. Polhem (1661–1751) was the father of Swedish mechanics, and loved using devices such as mechanical alphabets. Entering this museum is like a step into the 18th century; the tiled stoves, antiques, decorative molded plaster, and chandeliers all are of the era—either the genuine article or an exact replica. In the coin cabinet, the entire history of minting copper coins is documented. Various methods of producing iron are described in pictures and models.

WHERE TO STAY & DINE

First Grand Hotel. Trotzgatan 9–11, S-791 71 Falun. ☎ **023/7948-80.** Fax 023/14143. www.firsthotels.se. 152 units. TV TEL. Sun–Thurs 1,249 SEK ($137.40) double; Fri–Sat 699 SEK ($76.90) double. All week long 2,195 SEK ($241.45) suite. Rates include breakfast. AE, DC, MC, V. Parking 80 SEK ($8.80). Bus: 701 or 704.

This buff-colored hotel 100 yards south of the landmark Falun Church was built in the late 19th century; a modern addition was constructed in 1974. The whole complex was renovated in the 1980s so that the bedrooms, featuring a tasteful modern or Chippendale-inspired decor, are among the best decorated in town. Some 23 bedrooms have a minibar and all have comfortable beds. On the premises you'll find a small indoor pool, sauna, and restaurant.

Scandic Hotel Lugnet Falun. Svärdsjögatan 51, S-791 31 Falun. ☎ **023/669-2200.** Fax 023/669-2211. E-mail: lugnet@scandic-hotels.com. 153 units. MINIBAR TV TEL. July–Aug and Fri–Sat year-round, 680 SEK ($74.80) double; rest of year, 1,375 SEK ($151.25) double, 200 SEK ($22) supplement suite. Rates include breakfast. AE, DC, MC, V. Free parking.

Rising a dozen floors above a forested landscape, less than a 10-minute walk from the center of Falun, this hotel is one of the tallest buildings in town. As if that weren't enough, its pale green facade and futuristic detailing also make it one of the most unusual. Built in the early 1990s, with vertical rows of bay windows, it has well-crafted public areas outfitted in natural materials that include lots of stone and wood, and contemporary bedrooms. Although it has a chain hotel feel, the rooms are nonetheless well designed and furnished with especially good beds. The bathrooms are ample for the job, with a good supply of shelf space. The majority of the bedrooms are no-smoking, and there also is an "environmental floor," where 97% of the waste of the room is recycled. Expect tour bus groups and a hardworking, sometimes slightly harassed staff (especially when hordes of newcomers check in collectively).

Dining/Diversions: There's a bistro-style restaurant and a bar on the premises.

Amenities: Health club with sauna, bowling alley, swimming pool, and three auditorium-style conference rooms with space for between 90 and 250 people; limited room service that operates during conventional lunch and dinner hours.

5 Leksand

30 miles W of Falun, 11 miles S of Rättvik, 166 miles NW of Stockholm

Leksands Noret, as it's called, is a doorway to Lake Siljan, and no less an authority than Hans Christian Andersen found the setting idyllic. Leksand in its present form dates from the early 1900's, when it was reconstructed following a fire that razed the community. However, some type of settlement has existed on this site since pagan times.

Sweden's Best White-Water Rafting

The best way to profit from the meltdown of Sweden's winter snows involves floating downstream atop the surging waters of the Klarälven River, a scenic stream that originates in the high altitudes of Norway, and which eventually flows through Värmland. Whitewater enthusiasts gravitate to its northern stretches; aficionados of calmer waters move to points near its southern terminus. One of the most respected outfitters for excursions along any length of this historic river is **Vildmark in Värmland,** P.O. Box 209, Torsby SE 68525 (☎ **0560/14040;** www.vildmark.se). Established in 1980, and known throughout the region for the quality of its guides, it offers canoe excursions along the northern lengths of the river between April and October, providing canoes, instruction, and all the equipment and excitement you'll need. More unusual than the whitewater aspects of this place is what the company promotes along the calmer southern stretches, where as many as 6 million logs were floated downstream every year until the practice was halted for the most part in 1991. You'll be taught how to lash together a log raft, equivalent to what Huckleberry Finn might have built for treks along the Mississippi. On a raft lashed together with hemp rope, without metal fasteners or wire of any kind, you'll float downstream, past panoramic vistas, as part of treks that last between 1 and 7 days. Participants sleep either aboard their rafts, which consist of three layers of log stacked atop one another, or in tents along the shore. Rafts are suitable for between two and six passengers, and eventually are disassembled and sent to paper mills to be turned into pulp. A 4-day experience covering about 30 downstream miles costs 1,660 SEK ($182.60) per adult; a 7-day jaunt covering twice that distance costs 1,900 SEK ($218.90) per person.

Less structured trips are offered by a competitor in Värmland, in a location 93 miles north of Karlstad. Here, you can contact **Branäs Sport,** Branäs Fritidsanläggin, S-680 20 Sysslebäck (☎ **564/352-09**), an operation that devotes much of its time to the rental of cross-country skis, but also conducts white-water rafting on several nearby streams and rivers at prices roughly equivalent to those at the more carefully organized Fänforsens, recommended above.

Many of the old traditions of the province still flourish here. Women occasionally don the traditional dress for church on Sunday, and in June and July the long "church boats" from Viking times may cross the lake carrying parishioners to church. These same boats compete in a church-boat race on the first Sunday in July. Since World War II, a miracle play, *The Road to Heaven,* has been presented here in open-air performances, providing an insight into the customs and folklore of Dalarna. The play runs for 10 days at the end of July.

ESSENTIALS

GETTING THERE   By Plane   You can fly from Stockholm on **Skyways** (☎ **0250/301-75**); the nearest airport is **Dala-Airport** (☎ **0243/645-00**), in Borlänge, 31 miles south, from which there is frequent bus and train service to Leksand. Car rentals are available at the airport.

By Train   There's a direct train from Stockholm to Mora that stops in Leksand (travel time: 3½ hours). For reservations and information, call ☎ **020/75-75-75.**

By Boat Another way to reach Leksand is by boat, the ✪ *Gustaf Wasa;* call ☎ 010/252-32-92 for information and reservations. Every Monday at 3pm it makes one long trip from Mora to Leksand (through Rättvik). The round-trip fare is 120 SEK ($13.20) for adults, 60 SEK ($6.60) for children. Tickets are sold on board.

By Car From Falun, our last stopover, head north on Route 80 to Bjursås, then go west on a secondary road toward Sågmyra. Follow the signs into Leksand.

VISITOR INFORMATION Contact the **Leksands Turistbyrå,** Norsgatan 23 (☎ 0247/803-00; www.stab.se), open June 15 to August 10, Monday through Friday from 9am to 8pm, Saturday from 10am to 8pm, and Sunday from 11am to 8pm; August 11 to 18, Monday through Friday from 9am to 6pm, Saturday from 10am to 6pm, and Sunday from 11am to 6pm; and August 19 to June 14, Monday through Friday from 9am to 5pm and Saturday from 10am to 1pm.

A SPECIAL EVENT Sweden's biggest music festival, **Music at Lake Siljan,** takes place during the first week of July. There are some 100 concerts covering a wide range of music at venues in both Leksand and Rättvik. Folk music, "the meeting of the fiddlers," predominates. For information, contact **Music at Lake Siljan,** Box 28, S-795 21 Rättvik (☎ 0248/102-90).

ENJOYING THE OUTDOORS

A sports-oriented and health-conscious town, Leksand provides ample opportunity for outdoor sports. The town's tourist office can provide information on local swimming, cross-country skiing, curling, ice skating, tennis, and boat rides on Lake Siljan, all of which are available in or near the town center, depending on the season and weather conditions. There are downhill skiing facilities at **Granberget,** about 13 miles to the southwest. Granberget is neither the biggest nor best ski facility in Sweden. On the premises are five mechanized lifts and one restaurant, and no hotels at all. A 1-day ski pass costs 130 SEK ($14.30). For information, call or write **Ski Leksand Granberget,** S-79330 Leksand (☎ 0247/22330; fax 0247/22306).

SEEING THE SIGHTS

Leksands Kyrka. Norsgatan, near the lake. ☎ 0247/807-00. Free admission to the church; tour 50 SEK ($5.50) per person. Mid-June to early Aug, guided tours (in Swedish and English) Mon–Sat 10am–1pm and 2–5pm, Sun 1–5pm.

Leksand's "Parish Church" was founded in the 13th century. It has retained its present form since 1715, and is still one of the largest rural churches in Sweden. During renovations in 1971, a burial site was found that dates from the period when the Vikings were being converted to Christianity.

Hembygdsgårdar. Norsgatan. ☎ 0247/802-45. Admission 20 SEK ($2.20) adults, free for children. Mid-June to mid-Aug, Mon–Fri noon–4pm, Sat–Sun noon–5pm.

This open-air summer museum is near the parish church. Situated in a cluster of 18th- and 19th-century buildings that are themselves part of the museum's collections, it features depictions by 18th- and 19th-century peasants of Christ and his Apostles in Dalarna dress.

WHERE TO STAY

During the summer you may find it fun to rent a *stuga* (log cabin) with four beds for 2,600 to 4,000 SEK ($286 to $440) per week. You can use it as a base for exploring all of Dalarna. The **Leksands Turistbyrå,** Box 52, S-793 22 Leksand (☎ 0247/803-00), will book you into one. You also can inquire about renting a room in a private home.

Masesgården. Grytnäs 61, S-793 92 Leksand. ☎ **0247/122-31.** Fax 0247/122-51. www. masesgarden.se. E-mail: info@masesgarden.se. 34 units, 23 with bathroom. 4,150 SEK ($456.50) per person, per week, in double without bathroom; 4,750 SEK ($522.50) per person, per week, in double with bathroom. Rates include all meals and 30 hours of supervised sports activities. AE, DC, MC, V. Free parking.

This is one of the most sports- and fitness-conscious hotels in Sweden, with a reputation for educating guests about new eating and exercise habits, and an ongoing theme of preventing disease and depression through proper diet and exercise. Most clients check in for a week at a time, interpreting the many supervised aerobic and sports regimes as a kind of non-conventional spa program where clients of every age actually exercise rather than simply indulging in the "pampering." Set beside an inlet of the sea, with a view of Leksand across the fjord, it's designed in a sprawling compound of low-slung buildings that reminded us of a university athletic compound. Bedrooms are soothing, more plush than you might imagine, and decorated with a whimsical, often charming assortment of knickknacks.

Dining: All food served is vegetarian, fresh, and arranged in an ongoing series of buffets. Meal hours are daily 8:30 to 9:30am; 12:30 to 1:30pm; and 5:30 to 6:30pm. The feel is family style and communal, and wait staff are viewed as "helpers" rather than as conventional employees. There's lots of chitchat among the various tables, and lots of socializing among the guests, most of whom are women ages 20 to 50. This establishment's restaurant is open to nonresidents, but only if they phone in advance and there is room in the limited-capacity dining room.

Amenities: A daily program similar to what you may find aboard a cruise ship lists a series of lectures (astrological reincarnation and modern lifestyles are ongoing favorite topics) and physical disciplines such as tai chi. Different theme weeks stress such individual subjects as meditation and modern yoga, and Reiki healing through applied massage. Aerobics, some conducted in a swimming pool, and weight training, as well as lectures stressing the linkage between a healthy body and a healthy soul, also are offered. Although classes are conducted in Swedish, most staff members speak English and translate progressively for anyone who needs it. Participation is not for the faint-hearted; be prepared to sweat and reevaluate your lifestyle in ways that may not always be completely comfortable.

Moskogen Motel. Insjövägen 50, S-793 00 Leksand. ☎ **0247/146-00.** Fax 0247/144-30. 52 units, all with shower only. TV TEL. 820 SEK ($90.20) double; 1,050 SEK ($115.50) suite. Rates include breakfast. DC, MC, V. Free parking. Bus: 58.

Termed "a self-service holiday village," this motel, with its red-painted, wood-sided huts, makes a good base for excursions around the Lake Siljan area. The bedrooms are well furnished and comfortable, and each is equipped with a tiny kitchen, TV, shower, toilet, a good bed, and phone. A restaurant on the premises serves light lunches and dinners. Facilities include a Jacuzzi, sauna, solarium, gym room, an outdoor pool, and tennis courts. The Moskogen is a mile west of the railway station.

WHERE TO DINE

Bosporen. Torget 1. ☎ **0247/132-80.** Main courses 70–200 SEK ($7.70–$22). AE, DC, MC, V. Daily noon–11pm. SWEDISH/TURKISH.

This restaurant, 400 yards west of the railroad station, was given its Istanbul-derived name by its Turkish-born owners (who maintain longer and more reliable hours than any other place in town). The chefs are equally at home in both the Swedish and Turkish kitchens. Shish kebabs and Turkish salads are featured, but from Sweden you also can order fried Baltic herring, sautéed trout, fresh salmon, or plank steak. The cooking is fair, and even a bit exotic in a town not fabled for its restaurants.

6　Tällberg

8 miles N of Leksand, 174 miles NW of Stockholm, 322 miles NE of Gothenburg

This lakeside village, charmingly in tune with the spirit and tradition of Dalarna, is our favorite spot in the whole province, and the area of choice for nature lovers in both summer and winter. Skiing, curling, skating, and sleigh rides are popular sports, and swimming and boating lure summer visitors. Tällberg's beauty was discovered after artists and other cultural celebrities built summer houses in the village.

ESSENTIALS

GETTING THERE　By Train　Trains from Gothenburg require about 7 hours, with a change in Börlange. There are direct trains daily from Stockholm, but with many stopovers, the trip time is about 3½ hours. Trains also make the 10-minute run between Leksand and Tällberg. Call ☎ 020/75-75-75 for information.

By Bus　There is no direct bus service from Stockholm or Gothenburg. Bus passengers get off at either Leksand or Rättvik, where local bus connections can be made. Call ☎ 0200/21818 for information.

By Car　Take the E18 expressway northwest from Stockholm, then turn onto Route 70 toward Börlange and drive all the way to Tällberg, a 3-hour drive.

VISITOR INFORMATION　For information, the Leksand Tourist Office handles queries (see above).

SEEING THE SIGHTS

For information on outdoor activities, ask the advice of the staff at any of the town's hotels. Of particular merit is the staff within the **Hotel Långbers,** S-79370 Tallberg (☎ 0247/50290). Most indoor sports in Tällberg are guided by the staff at the **Feel House** (C.Q.) (☎ 0247/89386), which lies within a sports compound adjacent to the Hotel Dalecarlia (☎ 0247/89100). Rebuilt in 1997, it contains an indoor pool, weight lifting and exercise facilities, sauna and massage facilities, and a staff that knows virtually everything about sports within the Lake Siljan region.

One worthwhile attraction in the center of Tällberg is the **Holen Gustaf Ancarcronas,** Holen (☎ 0247/500-33), a collection of nine wood-sided buildings that were restored and, in some cases, hauled into position from other parts of Dalarna under the guidance of collector and local resident Gustaf Ancarcronas between 1910 and 1911. Ancarcronas (1869–1933) amassed a considerable collection of folk artifacts during his lifetime, many of which are on display within the compound. It's open only for a limited part of each summer, from mid-June to early August, daily from noon to 4pm. Admission and a guided tour costs 20 SEK ($2.20).

Another attraction is **Fråsgården,** Ytterboda (☎ 0247/602-60), a family farm estate dating from the 18th century, which today is configured as an open-air museum with a significant collection of Dalarna folk costumes. It maintains the same hours and same admission price as the above-mentioned Holen Gustaf Ancarcronas. During the seasons when both monuments are closed, you can get information about them by calling ☎ 0247/802-45. To reach Fråsgården from Tällberg, a distance of 3 miles to the south, follow the signs to Leksand, then the signs to Ytterboda.

WHERE TO STAY

The **Hotel Klockargården** (see "Where to Dine," below), also rents bedrooms.

Akerblads i Tällberg. Sjögattu 2, S-793 70 Tällberg. ☎ **0247/508-00.** Fax 0247/506-52. www.akerblads-tallberg.se. E-mail: info@akerblads-tallberg.se. 65 units. TV TEL. 1,190 SEK ($130.90) double; 1,490 SEK ($163.90) mini-suite. MC, V. Free parking.

An old-fashioned family hotel since 1910, this establishment is 1¼ miles south of Tällberg station at the crossroads leading down to Lake Siljan. The core of the house is still the wooden storehouse in the courtyard, but there has been much rebuilding over the years, including an addition of minisuites with complete bathrooms (which include tubs instead of just shower stalls) and minibars. All rooms at the hotel are done in an attractive Dala style (generally folkloric and typical of the 18th-century farms in the area) with comfortable beds and small bathrooms. A massage pool, sauna, solarium, and tennis court are some of the features. During the winter you can take advantage of a sleigh ride, and then warm up with a log fire and hot mulled wine. For the less snowy weather, bicycles are available at no charge. The hotel restaurant is known for its home-style cooking, buffets, and homemade bread. There's also a replica of an old pub where you can get a drink or a cheap pub lunch.

Green Hotel. S-793 70 Tällberg. ☎ **0247/502-50.** Fax 0247/501-30. www.greenhotel.se. 101 units. TEL. 850 SEK ($93.50) double. Rates include breakfast. MC, V. Free parking.

This hotel, whose wide array of rooms ranges from small to VIP size, is located on a lawn sloping down toward the lake half a mile west of the railroad station. The staff wears regional costumes, and the lounge has a notable art collection. On the premises are five saunas and a swimming pool whose surface is covered every Saturday night with a glass top and converted to a dance floor. Open all year, the hotel offers an array of summer and winter sports. A few of the more luxurious bedrooms have their own fireplaces and private saunas, and some contain a TV. The hotel has a restaurant and bar, where the Swedish dinners average 225 SEK ($24.75).

☺ Hotel Dalecarlia. S-793 70 Tällberg. ☎ **0247/891-00.** Fax 0247/50240. www. dalecarlia.se. 80 units. MINIBAR TV TEL. 1,190 SEK ($130.90) double. Rates include breakfast. AE, DC, MC, V. Free parking.

This is the largest, most substantial, and most prestigious hotel in Tällberg, with an historic, woodsy-looking core that was built in 1910, and a state-of-the-art enlargement that was added in 1991. Set on sloping land near Lake Siljan, it evokes an alpine hotel in Switzerland thanks to lots of varnished panels and a cozy, elegantly rustic public area that has lots of comfy chairs for reading, gossiping, or whatever. Bedrooms are outfitted in tones of pale blue or green, with comfortable mattresses and medium-size tiled bathrooms. Although much of its business derives from its appeal to the Scandinavian companies who hold conventions within its meeting rooms, it also offers many of the diversions and outdoor activities of a lakeside resort.

Dining/Diversions: The hotel's dining room is a large, woodsy-looking affair with big windows overlooking the lake and attentive service from a uniformed staff. There's also a bar.

Amenities: Health club with exercise area and Jacuzzis, sauna, an indoor swimming pool, aerobics, and massage service; room service available daily from 7am to 11pm.

Siljansgården. Sjögattu 36, S-793 70 Tällberg. ☎ **0247/247-500-40.** Fax 0247/ 247-500-13. www.siljan-dalarna.com/fi/siljansgarden. E-mail: post@siljansgarden.w.se. 50 units, 12 cottages. May–Aug, 400–850 SEK ($44–$93.50) double; Sept–Apr, 600–900 SEK ($66–$99) double. Cottages (May–Sept only) 300–700 SEK ($33–$77). Rates include breakfast. DC, MC, V. Free parking.

Originally built in 1915, this rustic, timber-sided hotel stands on 12 acres on the shores of the lake a mile west of the railroad station. On the grounds is a bathing beach, a tennis court, a rowboat, a minigolf course, and sauna. The hotel bedrooms are simply furnished but comfortable. In addition, 12 rustic summer cottages are suitable for up to four occupants, making them a family favorite. As they're not heated, they are available only in summer. A restaurant in the main building is licensed for beer and wine only, and serves a one-course lunch and a three-course dinner. In spite of the winter snows, the hotel is open all year. Cottage renters need to bring their own sleeping bags, but sheets can be rented.

WHERE TO DINE

Restaurant at the Hotel Klockargården. Siljansvägen 6, S-793 70 Tällberg. ☎ **0247/502-60.** Fax 0247/502-16. Reservations recommended. June 21–Aug 15, daily 6–10pm. Rest of year, open only at selected holidays (Christmas, school holidays). SWEDISH.

Some aspects of this place may remind you of a chalet in Switzerland, thanks to blackened wooden siding, steep roofs designed to shed snowfalls, and an artfully maintained rusticity. The hotel that contains it is composed of about a half dozen 18th- and 19th-century wood-sided buildings, some of which were already here as part of a farmstead; others of which were hauled in from other parts of Dalarna. The compound as you'll see it today was rebuilt, following old-fashioned aesthetics, in 1959.

Frankly, we value this place mostly for its restaurant, where local specialties include fried elk steak with juniper berry sauce, platters of fried whitefish with parsley-butter sauce, salmon from nearby Lake Siljan prepared in any of at least three different ways, and such conventional dishes as roasted chicken with dill, and fried steaks with garlic and wine sauce. The most appealing moment here is during the weekend smörgåsbords, when the agrarian bounty of central Sweden makes itself visible on groaning buffet tables in a style that originated about a century ago.

The hotel also rents 40 well-maintained bedrooms, each of which is decorated with handwoven textiles and woodcarvings created by local artisans. With breakfast included, doubles rent for 450 to 550 SEK ($49.50 to $60.50); and minisuites, double occupancy, for 750 SEK ($82.50). Each has a TV and telephone.

7 Rättvik

13 miles NE of Leksand, 171 miles NW of Stockholm

Rättvik, which has some of the best hotels in the district, is one of the most popular resorts bordering Lake Siljan. In summer, conducted tours begin here and go around Lake Siljan. Culture and tradition have long been associated with Rättvik; you'll find peasant costumes, folk dancing, Dalarna paintings, arts and crafts, fiddle music, and "church boats," flamboyantly painted boats in which entire congregations floated for Sunday services. The old style of architecture is still prevalent, and you'll find many timber houses. Carpenters and painters from Rättvik are known for their craftsmanship.

ESSENTIALS

GETTING THERE   By Train   You can reach Rättvik by rail. The Stockholm train to Mora stops in Leksand, where you can catch another train for the short trip to Rättvik. Train information in Stockholm is available at the **Central Station** (☎ **020/75-75-75**).

By Bus   Buses to Rättvik operate Friday through Sunday from Stockholm. There also is a bus connection between Leksand. For schedules, call ☎ **0200/21818.**

By Car   From Leksand, head north on Route 70 into Rättvik.

VISITOR INFORMATION   The **Rättvik Tourist Office** is in the train station (☎ **0248/702-00;** www.siljan-dalarnia.com). It's open June 15 to August 10, Monday through Friday from 9am to 8pm, Saturday from 10am to 8pm, and Sunday from 11am to 8pm; August 11 to 18, Monday through Friday from 9am to 6pm, Saturday from 10am to 6pm, and Sunday from 11am to 6pm; August 18 to June 14, Monday through Friday from 9am to 5pm and Saturday from 10am to 1pm.

SEEING THE SIGHTS

In central Sweden, the old saying "you can't see the forest for the trees" often holds true—literally! For an antidote to that, and a sweeping view that stretches for many miles, drive 3 miles east of town along the road leading to Falun. Here, soaring more than 80 feet skyward, is a red-sided wooden tower, originally built in 1897, called the **Vidablick,** Hantverksbyn (☎ **0248/302-50**). Be warned in advance that there's no elevator and the stairs are steep. Admission is 20 SEK ($2.20) for adults, 5 SEK (55¢) for children. On the premises are a coffee shop and a souvenir stand. The complex is open only from June 1 to August 15, daily from 10am to 9pm.

Gammelgården (☎ **0248/514-45**) is an antique Dalarna farmstead whose pastures and architecture evoke the 19th century. The hours are erratic—basically it's open whenever a farm resident is able to conduct a tour—so it's important to phone in advance. Upon prior notification, visits can be arranged throughout the year, but regular scheduling is most likely between mid-June and mid-August, when hours are Monday through Saturday from 11am to 6pm and Sunday from noon to 6pm. Admission is 20 SEK ($2.20). To reach Gammelgården from the center of Rättvik, drive 1 mile north of town along route 70, following the signs pointing to Mora.

If you're interested in art, you can visit the artists' village (established by the Swedish artist Sören Erikson) at **Rättviks Hantverksby,** Gårdebyn (☎ **0248/302-50**).

WHERE TO STAY

Hotel Gärdebygården. S-795 00 Rättvik. ☎ **0248/30250.** Fax 0248/30660. E-mail: Vidablick@hantverksbyn.se. 87 units. TV TEL. 795 SEK ($87.45) double. Rates include breakfast. MC, V. Free parking. Bus: 58 or 70.

This good value, located off Storgaten in the town center, was launched in 1906 and last renovated in 1995. A big breakfast is served every day—it's almost like a Swedish smörgåsbord—and a Dalarna fiddler appears 2 nights a week. Some nights are devoted to communal singalongs. Within a short walk of the lake, the hotel has expanded into a pair of outlying buildings. The bedrooms are comfortably and sedately furnished with conservative furniture and good, firm beds, but the bathrooms are small. Some units open onto a view of the lake. Cross-country ski trails and jogging paths are a short distance away.

Hotel Lerdalshöjden. S-795 00 Rättvik. ☎ **0248/511-50.** Fax 0248/511-77. 95 units. TV TEL. 853 SEK ($93.85) double; year-round 1,400 SEK ($154) suite. Rates include breakfast. DC, MC, V. Free parking. Bus: 58 or 70.

Near the top of a hill overlooking Rättvik, a 10-minute walk north from the lake, this building is a 1988 stylish rebirth of a turn-of-the-century hotel that had deteriorated. The only remaining part of the original is the Lerdalshöjden Restaurant, which retains the original walls and feeling of the old place (see "Where to Dine," below). The bedrooms are well furnished and maintained, and are decorated with modern accessories and amenities. The hotel has a sauna with a view over the lake, plus an exercise room.

WHERE TO DINE

Lerdalshöjden. In the Lerdalshöjden Hotel, Rättvik. ☎ **0248/111-50.** Reservations recommended. Main courses 135–210 SEK ($14.85–$23.10). DC, MC, V. Daily noon–2pm and 6–9pm. Closed: Aug 16–June 14. SWEDISH.

Near the top of a hill overlooking Rättvik, a 10-minute walk north from the lake, this restaurant is the only original section remaining from the 1988 remodeling of a turn-of-the-century hotel. It has long been a favorite with locals from the nearby lake district. They like the good, traditional Swedish home-style cooking, which is based on fresh fish and beef dishes. Try, for example, steak tartare with bleak roe or fried ptarmigan with red currant sauce.

8 Mora

28 miles W of Rättvik, 204 miles NW of Stockholm

In Upper Dalarna, between Lake Orsa and Lake Siljan, the provincial town of Mora is our final major stopover in the province. Summer travelers find this business and residential center a good base for exploring the district.

Mora was the village where Gustavus Vasa rallied the peasants in Sweden's 16th-century war against Danish rule. Every year in March this event is commemorated by the 50-mile Vasa Race.

ESSENTIALS

GETTING THERE   By Plane   You can fly from Stockholm on **Skyways Air** (☎ 08/595-13-500); there is Sunday to Friday service, and the flight time is 40 minutes. The airport (☎ 0250/301-75) is about 4 miles from the center; taxis meet arriving flights.

By Train   There's direct rail service daily from Stockholm (trip time: 4 hours). For information and schedules, call ☎ 020/75-75-75.

By Bus   There are weekend buses leaving from Stockholm's Central Station for the 4¼-hour trip. Contact **Swebus Vasatrafik** at ☎ 0200/21818.

By Boat   The *Gustaf Wasa* (see "Essentials" in the "Leksand" section, above) travels between Mora and Leksand. The boat departs Leksand in the afternoon and it leaves Mora at 3pm on Monday. The round-trip cost is 120 SEK ($13.20) for adults and 60 SEK ($6.60) for children. Call ☎ 010/252-32-92 for information and reservations.

By Car   From Rättvik, continue around Lake Siljan on Route 70 to Mora.

VISITOR INFORMATION   Contact the **Mora Turistbyrå,** Angbåtskajen (☎ 0250/265-50; www.siltan-dalarna.com). It's open June 15 to August 10, Monday through Friday from 9am to 8pm, Saturday from 10am to 8pm, and Sunday from 11am to 8pm; August 11 to 18, Monday through Friday from 9am to 6pm, Saturday from 10am to 6pm, Sunday 11am to 6pm; August 19 to June 14, Monday through Friday from 9am to 5pm, Saturday from 10am to 1pm.

SEEING THE SIGHTS

Mora is home to a **Santa complex** (☎ 0250/212-00), which features Santa's house and factory. Visitors can meet Santa and see his helpers making and wrapping presents for children all over the world, and children can enroll in Santa School and participate in troll and treasure hunts.

Mora also was the hometown of Anders Zorn (1860–1920), Sweden's most famous painter, and all of the town's top sights are associated with him. The first, **Lisselby,** is an area near the Zorn Museum made up of old houses that now are used as arts and crafts studios and boutiques. At **Balder-Lisselby** (no phone), a craft center, you can watch handcrafts being made Monday through Saturday between 9am and 6pm, except at lunchtime.

Zornmuseet (Zorn Museum). Vasagatan 36. ☎ **0250/165-60.** Admission 35 SEK ($3.85) adults, 15 SEK ($1.65) children. Mid-May to Aug, Mon–Sat 9am–5pm, Sun 11am–5pm; Sept to mid-May, Mon–Sat noon–5pm, Sun 1–5pm.

This museum displays not only a wide array of the artist's own works (among them, *Midnight*), but paintings from his private collection—including works by Prince Eugen and Carl Larsson, also of Dalarna. Works by major foreign artists (sculptures by Kai Nielsen of Denmark and etchings by Rembrandt) also are exhibited, as well as rural art and handcrafts of Dalarna.

Zornsgården. Vasagatan 36. ☎ **0250/165-60.** Admission 45 SEK ($4.95) adults, 15 SEK ($1.65) children. Mid-June to Aug, Mon–Sat 10am–5pm, Sun 11am–5pm; Sept to mid-June, Mon–Sat noon–5pm, Sun 1–5pm. Full tours of the house are conducted by guides at noon, 1pm, 2pm, and 3pm.

The artist's former home, adjoining the museum, has been left just as it was when Mrs. Zorn died in 1942. Its chief attraction, aside from the paintings displayed, is Zorn's personally designed Great Hall on the top floor.

NEARBY SHOPPING IN NUSNÄS

In Nusnäs, about 6 miles southeast of Mora, you can watch the famous Dalarna horse (*dalahäst*) being made. You're free to walk around the workshops watching the craftspeople at work, and the finished products can be purchased at a shop on the premises. They also sell wooden shoes and other craft items. **Nils Olsson Hemslöjd** (☎ **0250/ 372-00**) is open June to mid-August, Monday through Friday from 8am to 6pm and Saturday and Sunday from 9am to 5pm; and mid-August to May, Monday through Friday from 8am to 5pm and Saturday from 10am to 2pm. To find Nusnäs, take the signposted main road east from Mora, turning off to the right at Farnas. From Mora, bus no. 108 also runs to Nusnäs.

WHERE TO STAY

First Mora Hotel. Strandgatan 12, S-792 00 Mora. ☎ **800/528-1234** in the U.S. and Canada, or 0250/717-50. Fax 0250/189-81. www.firsthotels.com. 141 units. MINIBAR TV TEL. 1,048–1,389 SEK ($115.30–$152.80) double. Rates include breakfast. AE, DC, MC, V. Parking 90 SEK ($9.90) in the garage, free outdoors.

Situated in the center of town across from the lakefront, a minute's walk from the tourist bureau, the Mora Hotel has been renovated over the years to include sun terraces and glassed-in verandas. The interior is tasteful with bright colors. All accommodations have comfortable furniture, good beds, nonalcoholic minibars, and ample bathrooms. On the premises is an indoor pool, along with several dining facilities. The best is the Terrassen (see "Where to Dine," below). On Friday and Saturday the hotel's disco charges 70 SEK ($7.70) admission for visitors, but it's free for hotel guests.

Hotel Moraparken. Box 294, S-792 25 Mora. ☎ **0250/178-00.** Fax 0250/185-83. www. moraparken.se. 75 units. TV TEL. Mid-June to mid-Aug and Fri–Sun year-round, 620 SEK ($68.20) double; rest of year, 800 SEK ($88) double. Rates include breakfast. AE, DC, MC, V. Free parking.

Although it lies within a 2-minute drive from the center of Mora, you'll get the impression that you're deep in the Swedish wilderness here, thanks to this hotel's location within a forested park, midway between a pond and the banks of the river Västerdal. Laid out in a low-slung, rustic design with a steeply peaked roof and lots of exposed wood, it was built in 1976 as a restaurant, and expanded in 1982 into the sports-conscious establishment you see today. Accommodations are woodsy, simple, and uncomplicated, and although comfortable, far from being particularly plush. This seems to suit the participants in the many conventions held here, who enjoy rowing boats and canoes and swimming in the nearby pond, hiking in the surrounding forest, and attending meals in one of two restaurants. One of these is used at breakfast and lunch; the other at dinner and during the supper dances held here throughout the year. On the premises is an indoor pool, a sauna, and a gym. The reception desk is closed, with most of the staff off duty, every night between 10pm and 7am.

WHERE TO DINE

Terrassen. In the First Hotel Mora, Strandgatan 12. ☎ **0250/717-50.** Reservations recommended. Main courses 175–300 SEK ($19.25–$33). AE, DC, MC, V. Mon–Sat 11:30am–11pm. SWEDISH.

One of the finest dining rooms in the area, this is a good bet for a meal even if you aren't staying at the hotel. Fresh produce is used whenever possible, and fresh fish and Swedish beef dishes are featured. You might begin with herring or enjoy a freshly made salad. Service is polite and efficient.

The Bothnian Coast

North of Stockholm, Sweden's east coast opens onto Bottenhavet, or the Gulf of Bothnia. Russia made many incursions here in the 18th century, devastating the land and often burning the towns. Many other towns were destroyed by natural fires, then quickly rebuilt with much broader streets to prevent the spread of fires. However, a lot of the old wooden houses remain in such towns as Gävle and Hudiksvall.

Just south of the Arctic Circle, the geographical position of the area suggests a climate that can be daunting; the winters certainly are harsh, with temperatures often falling below freezing. However, the summer months, with their 24-hour-a-day sunshine, can be idyllic (if you disregard the mosquitoes). Most of the population in the area is concentrated in certain areas, such as in the two coastal cities of Umeå and Skellefteå. The activity of these cities contrasts with the utter tranquility of the countryside west of the coastline, where there may be as few as four inhabitants per square kilometer. At times you'll feel you have the sparsely populated interior all to yourself.

The chief attraction of the Bothnian Coast is the stretch known as the High Coast or Höga Kusten, a 90-mile land mass of jagged coastline and rocky hills lying between Härnösand and Örnsköldsvik. The land is a combination of thousands of small lakes, wild rivers, and unspoiled coastlines; as well as vast forests of pine and spruce, high mountains, and low farmlands. In summertime, the islands and shallow sandy beaches are popular places for excursions, and many Swedes maintain summer homes in the area. The brand-new E4 expressway takes you right along the coast to all the towns recommended in this chapter.

1 Gävle

112 miles NW of Stockholm, 68 miles NW of Uppsala

The capital of the province of Gästrikland, Gävle has a population of 85,000 and is a major port for the shipment of ore and timber from the nearby mining regions. It can be your gateway to the Bothnian Coast.

Pronounced *Yerv*-le, it is the southernmost town of Norrland, a region making up two-thirds of the land mass of Sweden.

An old city, Gävle was granted its town charter in 1446, although you'd never know it today in this modern city of broad squares, wide avenues, and rather monumental buildings (at least by the standards of northern Sweden).

The Bothnian Coast

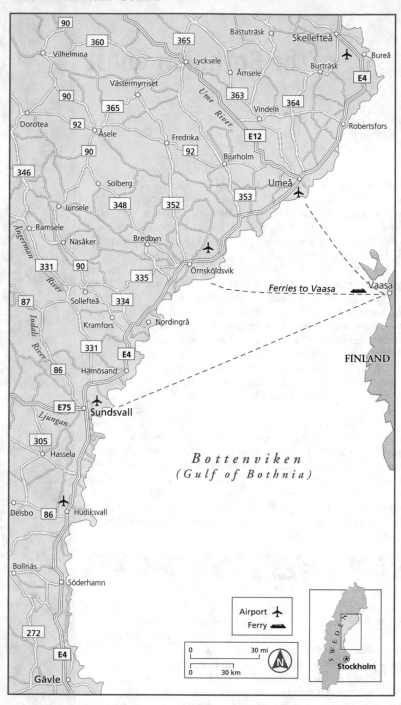

90

360

365

Bastuträsk

Skellefteå

Vilhelmina

Lycksele

Åmsele

Burträsk

Bureå

E4

Västermyrriset

363

Vindeln

364

90

365

92

Fredrika

E12

Dorotea

Åsele

92

Robertsfors

90

Bjurholm

346

Solberg

Umeå

Junsele

348

352

353

Ramsele

Näsåker

Bredbyn

331

90

Örnsköldsvik

335

Ferries to Vaasa

Vaasa

87

Sollefteå

334

FINLAND

Kramfors

Nordingrå

331

E4

86

Härnösand

E75

Sundsvall

305

Hassela

B o t t e n v i k e n
(G u l f   o f   B o t h n i a)

Delsbo

86

Hudiksvall

Bollnäs

Söderhamn

Airport ✈
Ferry ⛴

0   30 mi
0   30 km

N

SWEDEN

Stockholm

272

E4

Gävle

Insider's Tip

In summer, stop at the tourist office's open-air cafe (Norra Kyrkogatan 14; ☎ 026/14-74-30) in Berggrenska Gården. It serves delicious homemade bread, so it's worth a visit even if you don't have questions for the tourist office.

A fire swept across Gävle in 1869, virtually destroying the city. The place you see before you is the result of replanning in the wake of the disaster.

ESSENTIALS

GETTING THERE   By Train   Gävle is on a major rail line between Stockholm and the north (trip time is only 2 hours). For schedules, call ☎ 020/75-75-75. Trains from Stockholm go through Uppsala, the university city.

By Bus   There also is bus service between Uppsala and Gävle. For information, call ☎ 0200/21818.

By Car   From Uppsala, continue northwest into Gävle.

VISITOR INFORMATION   The Gävle Tourist Office is at Norra Kyrkogatan 14 (☎ 026/14-74-30), open June through August daily 9am to 6pm. Off-season hours are Monday through Friday 9am to 4pm.

SEEING THE SIGHTS

If it's a summery, sunny day, consider a boat tour to the little island of **Limön,** which is part of an archipelago. For 30 SEK ($3.30) per ticket, the tourist office will book you on the tour. Limön has a nature trail and a mass grave and memorial to 19th-century sailors who went down at sea here. Boats depart from the quay at Södra Skeppsbron. Call ☎ 026/14-74-30 for information and bookings.

The major attraction here is **Gamla Gefle,** a tiny section of old Gävle that escaped the disastrous fire in 1869 that destroyed most of the town. There really isn't a lot left of it, so you can imagine just how raging the fire must have been. You can still walk along some of the old cobblestone streets, especially Nedre Bergsgränd, Bergsgränd, and Övre Bergsgatan, which will give you some idea of what ancient Gävle must have looked like. In summer, these streets can be a delight, as homeowners fill their window boxes with flowers, especially geraniums. Most of the old wooden cottages are painted in pastels. Gamla Gefle lies south of the modern city.

Joe Hill Garden. At Nedre Bergsgatan 28, Gamla Gefle. ☎ 026/61-34-25. Free admission. June–Aug, daily 10am–3pm.

This curiosity in Old Town was the birthplace of Johan Emanuel Hägglund in 1879. Changing his name to Joe Hill, he emigrated to the United States in 1902. In time, he became a working-class hero and a U.S. union organizer. His speeches became rallying cries to his comrades in the Industrial Workers of the World (Wobblies) and he even wrote folk songs that inspired underpaid laborers. However, in 1915, company bosses in Salt Lake City framed him for murder to remove him from the scene as an effective labor organizer. A jury found him guilty and he was executed. The scheme later was revealed, but the actual court process of exoneration never took place. The museum here is devoted to his legacy, including personal mementos. You can even see the last telegram that came in announcing his execution.

✪ **Gävleborg County Museum.** Länsmuséet Gävleborg, Södra Strandgatan 20 (the other side of Gamla Gefle, on a canal). ☎ 026/65-56-00. Admission 25 SEK ($2.75). Tues and Thurs–Fri 10am–4pm, Wed 10am–9pm, Sat–Sun 1–5pm.

This very intriguing provincial museum is one of northern Sweden's best; its collection is a virtual textbook of Swedish art from the 17th century to the 1990s. Some of the country's best-known painters are represented: Alexander Roslin, Marcus Larsson, Ernst Josephsson, Carl Larsson, Sigrid Hjérten, Peter Tillberg, Lena Cronqvist, Peter Dahl, Ernst Billgren, Ebba Matz, and Bianca Maria Barmen, among others. The collection is continually enlarged with new works.

The museum is rich in other exhibits as well, including some artifacts that date from the Stone Age and the Viking era. Some of the space is devoted to the 19th century, the glory days of Gävle when large ships sailed far up the river carrying cargo from all over the world. Exhibitions include pictures of the fire that destroyed Gävle, ships, and the recreation of the interior of a middle-class family house.

Gunnar Cyrén, the internationally known designer of glassware, lives in Gävle. The museum has the largest collection of objects by this craftsman. You can see sets of his glass, his art glassware, and even utility goods he designed in plastic and stainless steel. Look for the set of glass he designed especially for the 90th anniversary of the Nobel Prize awards in 1991.

WHERE TO STAY

Hotell Gävle. Staketgatan 44, S-803 11 Gävle. ☎ **026/-66-51-00.** Fax 026/51-75-10. E-mail: infogavle@swedenhotels.se. 50 units. TV TEL. Mid-June to mid-Aug and Fri–Sat year-round, 525–630 SEK ($57.75–$69.30) double; rest of year, 895–995 SEK ($98.45–$109.45) double. Rates include breakfast. AE, DC, MC, V. Free parking.

One of the least pretentious hotels in town occupies a simple, brick-fronted building that's less than a 5-minute walk from the railway station. Inside, you'll find a family-managed hotel that maintains lobby hours from 6am to 11pm Sunday through Thursday, and Friday through Sunday 24 hours a day. (If you plan on arriving after the lobby is locked, someone will tell you the security code for the front door and make a key available to you if you phone in advance with details of your arrival time.) Bedrooms are artfully outfitted in tones of off-white and brown, accented with touches of mahogany and walnut, always with comfortable mattresses and modern but small bathrooms. There's no restaurant on the premises, but sandwiches are available, and every Monday through Thursday management places a large heated urn containing some kind of nutritious soup in the lobby. There's also a sauna on the premises and a wholesome breakfast buffet. During the lifetime of the present edition of this guide, management plans to replace all the carpeting within the bedrooms with hardwood floors.

Hotel Winn. Norra Slottsgatan 9, P.O. Box 1417, S-801 38 Gävle. ☎ **026/17-70-00.** Fax 026/10-59-60. E-mail: info@winngavle.softwarehotels.se. 200 units. TV TEL. Mid-June to mid-Aug and Fri–Sat year-round, 790 SEK ($86.90) double; rest of year, 1,290 SEK ($141.90) double. Year-round, 1,340 SEK ($147.40) suite. Rates include breakfast. AE, DC, MC, V. Parking 75 SEK ($8.25).

This is one of the most modern and comfortable hotels in town, and it lies across the street from the town's main square. Designed with buff-colored brick and big windows, it's clean, well managed, and a popular choice for many of the region's business travelers. Inside, the lavish use of autumn tones warms and softens the glossy look of the marble and stone that sheathe many of the floors and walls of the public areas. Bedrooms are calm, quiet, comfortable, and soothing.

Dining/Diversions: Café Artist is a premier dining venue within Gävle, serving lunch and dinner every day to the accompaniment of a piano positioned in the nearby bar and cocktail lounge.

Gävle

ATTRACTIONS ●
Gävleborg County Museum **4**
Joe Hill Garden **5**

ACCOMMODATIONS ■
Hotell Gävle **2**
Hotel Winn **1**
Provobis Grand Central Hotel **3**

Amenities: The hotel maintains a "health complex" in its cellar that includes an indoor swimming pool, saunas, and tanning beds. There's also an especially attractive conference and convention center on the premises.

Provobis Grand Central Hotel. Nygatan 45, P.O. Box 317, S-801 04 Gävle. ☎ **026/12-90-60.** Fax 026/12-44-99. www.provobis.se/hotels. E-mail: grand.central.hotel@provobis.se. 220 units. MINIBAR TV TEL. Mid-June to mid-Aug and Fri–Sat year-round, 780–980 SEK ($8.80) double; 2,650 SEK ($291.50) suite. Rest of year, 1,345–1,675 SEK ($147.95–$184.25) double; 2,650 SEK ($291.50) suite. Rates include breakfast. AE, DC, MC, V. Parking 90 SEK ($9.90).

This hotel was built in a smaller version in 1896, about the time that the railway tracks first connected Gävle with the rest of Europe. It was configured from the beginning as a site convenient to the railway station, and was designed in a brassy, belle epoque motif reminiscent of a resort along the southern coast of England. In the 1960s it was massively expanded with new wings. Today, regardless of their position within the various wings of this hotel, bedrooms deliberately emulate the old-fashioned, nostalgic decor that was part of the establishment from the beginning. Expect modern comforts combined with heavy doses of turn-of-the-century details in the forms of reproduction Victorian era sofas, leather armchairs, busy patterns, and rich, dark colors. The bathrooms are small but perfectly efficient and have ample shelf space.

Dining/Diversions: The more formal of the hotel's two restaurants is the Skeppet Cellar restaurant, site of many of Gävle's business reunions. More animated, but open

| **Fun Fact** |

Coffee is virtually the national drink of Sweden, in the same way a good "cuppa" (cup of tea) is the drink of England. As the home of the famous Gevalia coffee (the most northerly coffee-roasting plant in the world), Gävle is known to coffee drinkers everywhere.

only from 8pm until midnight every Thursday and Saturday, is the Trädgården supper club, where live and recorded music provide the opportunity for ballroom dancing 2 nights per week. There's also a bar and cocktail lounge on the premises.

Amenities: A sauna, a health club, and a concierge staff devoted to procuring whatever you need during your stay here.

WHERE TO DINE

Captain Zet's. Norra Kopmangatan 12B. ☎ **026/10-60-65.** Reservations recommended. Main courses 65–140 SEK ($7.15–$15.40). MC, V. Daily 11am–11pm. INTERNATIONAL.

This is a highly appealing restaurant whose maritime decor evokes the heady seafaring days of Gävle's supremacy as a trading center and seaport. Its name derives from the first initials of the three partners (Zirre, Eva, and Tommy) who established it and run it today. Surrounded by collections of old photographs and scaled-down model ships, you can order well-prepared platters whose portions are generous and flavorful. Worthy starters include a savory portion of grilled Cypriot cheese with Mediterranean herbs, a shrimp cocktail presented in a dish shaped like a boat, or a bowl of steaming lobster soup. Main courses might include halibut with snow peas and shrimp, marinated pork chops with chanterelles and gratin of potatoes, filet mignon with Madeira sauce, or salmon steak with spinach and lemon-flavored butter sauce.

Matilda's. Timmermansgatan 23. ☎ **026/62-53-49.** Reservations required. Main courses 125–175 SEK ($13.75–$19.25). AE, DC, MC, V. Mon–Thurs 5–11pm, Fri–Sat 5–midnight, Sun 2–9pm. INTERNATIONAL.

The most celebrated restaurant in Gävle occupies two small rooms of a 1950s-era building in the town center, each of which is outfitted in tones of green and white with touches of red. Its food is served to 13 tables at a time, only in the evening, when artfully positioned spotlights illuminate an open kitchen whose activities seem more intense and more theatrical than at any other eatery in town. Menu items change with the season and the whim of the chef, but are likely to include carpaccio of beef with olive oil, fresh basil, and grated Parmesan; a savory pie stuffed with Swedish cheddar and roe caviar; cream of shrimp soup with herbs; filet of beef with garlic-flavored cream sauce; veal filet "saltimbocca"; and filets of sea bass fried in butter and served with an herb-flavored cream sauce. Don't underestimate the desirability of a table at this place: Reservations at Matilda's are more sought after than at any other restaurant in the region, so competition is intense—especially on weekends.

2 Söderhamn

155 miles NW of Stockholm, 44 miles NW of Gävle

An industrial port city of some 32,000 people, Söderhamn lies at the center of an archipelago of 500 islands. Storjungfrun is the largest island; the entire stretch of islands—from Furuvik in the south to Gnarpsbaden in the north—is called Jungfrukusten, or "Virgin Coast."

There used to be many fishing villages on these islands, but today only Skärså has an active fishing industry. The other islands now are devoted to leisure activities centered on summer cottages and pleasure boats. Depending heavily on the weather, the tourist boat M/S *Strömskär* provides trips through the islands of Söderhamn's archipelago. For information about possible trips, call ☎ 026/12-77-66.

Söderhamn once was more important than it is today. Founded in 1620, it owed its early development to the achievements of Gustav II Adolf, who in 1617 won a longstanding war with the Russians. He established firm possession of a large portion of the Swedish coast. Söderhamn was ideal for development, as it stood in a safe place at the head of a 7-mile-long fjord.

Like Gävle, Söderhamn has suffered its share of fires. The most devastating, which destroyed virtually everything, came in 1876. After the debris was cleared, Söderhamn bounced back as a totally new town, with a grid pattern and ample parks.

ESSENTIALS

GETTING THERE   By Train   There are about five trains per day from Stockholm. En route, each of the trains stops in both Uppsala and Gävle, picking up passengers for the continuation of the ride northward. The trip from Stockholm to Söderhamn takes 2 to 3 hours. From Uppsala it takes 1½ to 2 hours. For railway information, call ☎ 020/75-75-75.

By Bus   Buses from Stockholm and Uppsala to Söderhamn are less convenient, less frequent, and slower than equivalent transits by train. Transit from Gävle takes about an hour. For bus schedule and information, call ☎ 0200/21818.

By Car   From Gävle, continue along the coastal road, E4, into Söderhamn.

VISITOR INFORMATION   The **Söderhamn Tourist Office,** Resecentrum (☎ 0270/753-53), is open June to early August, Monday through Friday 9am to 7pm, Saturday and Sunday noon to 5pm. At other times, it's open Monday through Friday 9am to 4pm.

SEEING THE SIGHTS

Söderhamn is a good city for long, refreshing walks, as it is a green oasis with extensive parks and flower gardens. In all, there are 100 plant species growing in various settings around town.

Oskarsborg Tower. Östra Berget. Free admission. Mid-June to mid-August, daily 9am–9pm. Follow the signs from the station along the rail tracks.

For the best appreciation of the layout of the town, head for the Oskarsborg tower, which was inaugurated in 1895 by Gabriel Schöning, and has become the symbol of Söderhamn. The tower itself is 75 feet high and 211 feet above sea level. From its top you can see one of the most panoramic views in the north of Sweden. In summer, a cafe is open here.

Söderhamn Museum. Oxtorgsgatan. ☎ 0270/157-91. Admission 20 SEK ($2.20). July–early Aug, daily noon–5pm.

Söderhamn's major museum, which traces the regional history of the area, is housed in a former rifle manufacturing workshop. You learn of Söderhamn's former role as a munitions center, when it manufactured weapons to help Sweden turn back the Russian tide and dominate northern Europe. You also can see, among other exhibits, relics from one of the town's earliest churches (no longer existing).

OUTDOOR PURSUITS

Of course, you didn't come this far north to confine yourself to museum visits, with all the great outdoors awaiting you. The tourist office (see above) is particularly helpful in supplying information about what to see and do with Mother Nature.

The forests around Söderhamn stretch for miles and miles. There are forest paths, nature reserves, and areas for rambling where you can find tranquillity. One good example is the **Mostigen Path,** which stretches for 10½ miles east of the town center. Look for the signs adjacent to the tourist office.

Söderhamn Golf Course, Nygatan 5B (☎ 0270/281-300), is beautifully situated on the coast, lying about 5 miles from the center of Söderhamn. It is an 18-hole, par-72 course in a particularly scenic woodland. There also is a driving range, golf shop, and clubhouse with changing rooms and a restaurant. Greens fees range from 180 to 220 SEK ($19.80 to $24.20) for 18 holes of golf, depending on the day of the week.

Fishing is popular at the mouth of the Ljusnan River, where there is a good chance of catching salmon, sea trout, and whitefish. Ten-kilo (22-pound) "monsters" are not unheard of. The fishing waters extend over a stretch of about 5 miles between the Ljusne power station and the sea. The fishing season spans the entire year, but spring and autumn are the best periods. Fishing permits can be obtained from a vending machine at the clubhouse in Ljusne. You also can rent fishing cottages in the district. Call the above-mentioned tourist office for more information.

WHERE TO STAY

First Hotel Statt. Oxtorgsgatan 17, P.O. Box 64, SE-826 22 Söderhamn. ☎ 0270/414-10. Fax 0270/135-24. www.firsthotels.com. E-mail: info@firsthotels.se. 78 units. TV TEL. Mid-June to mid-Aug and Fri–Sat year-round, 748 SEK ($82.30) double; rest of year, 1,048–1,448 SEK ($115.30–$159.30) double. Year-round, 1,635 SEK ($179.85) suite. AE, DC, MC, V. Rates include breakfast. Free parking.

This hotel represents one of the most unconventional pairings of new and old architecture we've seen in this part of Sweden. Its original core dates from 1880, when a dignified-looking two-story house was erected in a position about 500 yards west of the Rådhus (town hall). In modern times, a series of enlargements and annexes were superimposed onto the hotel's original framework—not always with aesthetic success. The final result is a clean, respectable hotel with lots of exposed hardwood on the floors, dramatic draperies, and an overriding sense of well-maintained, no-nonsense modernity. Bedrooms are clean and, though somewhat banal in their decor and furnishings, are warm and cozy.

Dining/Diversions: On the premises are a wood-toned bar and the Stadtsrestaurang restaurant, recommended separately below.

Amenities: Sauna, solarium, conference rooms.

WHERE TO DINE

Stadtsrestaurang. In the First Hotel Statt, Oxtorgsgatan 17. ☎ 0270/414-10. Reservations recommended. Fixed-price lunches 65–100 SEK ($7.15–$11); dinner main courses 150–210 SEK ($16.50–$23.10). AE, DC, MC, V. Mon–Sat 11am–2pm and 6–11pm. INTERNATIONAL.

This restaurant is managed independently from the chain-member hotel that contains it and, as such, feels a bit more personal. The setting is correct, proper, and well laid out, with a decor that includes white linens, hardwood floors, and a sense of conservative well being. Menu items include lots of fresh fish, usually grilled and served simply with lemon butter or hollandaise sauce, veal and chicken dishes, Swedish caviar spread on chunks of rough-textured rye bread, and chicken with a dill-flavored cream sauce. The cuisine, although flavorful, isn't very imaginative.

3 Hudiksvall

186 miles NW of Stockholm, 32 miles NW of Söderhamn, 80 miles N of Gävle

With a population of 20,000, Hudiksvall is much smaller than Söderhamn, but many visitors find it more charming. It is the oldest town in Sweden north of Gävle, dating from 1582. Originally it grew up around Lillfjärden Bay at the mouth of the Hornån River, but in the early 1600s when the sea receded, Hudiksvall was forced to move closer to the water. Even today one is always conscious of the sea. The harbor itself is right in the town center, and locals have always survived by fishing and trade.

The town's heritage is visible in the typical fishers' cottages along the Strömmingssundet Sound, the well-preserved wooden buildings of the Fiskarstan, and the area of town around Lilla Kyrkogatan.

Historically, Hudiksvall has been subject to attack, especially in the wars between Sweden and Russia. It came under particular assault in 1721 when virtually half the building here were razed to the ground.

Despite Hudiksvall's long history, the town also is very modern, with a lot of amenities and stores for such a small place. This is because it serves as the commercial center for the whole of northern Hälsingland, and people who live in remote wildernesses drive for miles and miles to come into town and shop.

In Sweden, Hudiksvall once was known as Glada Hudik or "Lively Hudiksvall," a phrase coined in the mid-19th century, in the heyday of the pleasure-seeking timber barons of the district. Today its charming streets and beautiful old buildings are still lively in summer.

ESSENTIALS

GETTING THERE   By Train   Depending on the season and the route you take, there are between four and eight trains per day between Gävle and Hudiksval, and between six and seven per day from Stockholm and from Södermalm, both of which follow the same rail lines. Travel time from Södermalm is around 40 minutes; from Gävle between 60 and 75 minutes; and from Stockholm, between 2½ and 3 hours. For rail schedules and fares, call ☎ 020/75-75-75.

By Bus   Bus travel from Stockholm and Gävle to Hudiksval is less convenient, and slower, than rail travel; but in some instances, especially on weekends, it's a bit cheaper. For bus schedules and fares from all points of Sweden into Hudiksval, call ☎ 0200/21818.

By Car   From Söderhamn, our last stopover, follow E4 northwest.

VISITOR INFORMATION   The **Hudiksvalls Turistbyrå**, Möljen (☎ 0650/191-00), is open mid-June to mid-August, Monday through Friday 9am to 7pm, Saturday 10am to 6pm, and Sunday noon to 6pm. Otherwise, hours are Monday through Friday 9am to 4pm.

SEEING THE SIGHTS

As an old town, Hudiksvall has a proud architectural heritage. As you're walking around town, examples worth seeking out include **Hantverksgården,** Störgutan 44, with its unique terraces overlooking Hudiksvallsfjärden Bay, and the **Hudiksvall Theatre,** on Västra Tullgatan (☎ 0650/10813), formerly a spa.

Lillfjärden is an oasis in the heart of Hudiksvall. This former inlet from the sea was the site of the town's first harbor. Today, it is a lake with a diverse bird life, an ideal place for a lovely walk.

The best place to go on a summer day is the small old harbor called Möljen, where locals head to soak up the precious (and fleeting) sunshine. Old fishers' cottages and storefronts line this harbor. Here you'll find an assortment of shops, handcraft studios, and other retail outlets occupying what formerly were warehouses.

Bigger than Möljen, and also an interesting district to explore, is **Fiskarstan,** or Fisher's Town, which is reached by going down Storgatan behind the First Hotel Statt. Here you will find the best examples of late 18th- and 19th-century architecture— sometimes called "imperial architecture." Buildings here are wood paneled, and the cobblestone streets are narrow. Fishermen and their families lived here in close proximity during the bitter winters. As you walk along the streets in summer, you'll note that the current residents plant window boxes with brightly colored flowers.

If you'd like to learn something about the artistic and cultural history of the area, head for the **Halsingland Museum,** Storgatan 31 (☎ **0650/196-00**). It's open Tuesday through Friday 9am to 4pm (Wednesday until 8pm), and Saturday and Sunday 11am to 3pm, charging an admission of 20 SEK ($2.20). Housed in a former bank, the museum displays finds from various archaeological digs in the area. Excavations uncovered an Iron Age burial site and a Malsta runic stone that was inscribed with upright strokes. Local medieval wood carving also is displayed, most of the work by Haaken Gulleson, who was the most distinguished artisan in this form. Boats, ship models, and fishing equipment reveal how the locals earned their livelihood. On the second floor is a display of peasant art collections including sledges, textiles, chests, and clocks, along with folkloric costumes. Middle-class interiors from the late 18th and 19th centuries are recreated. The paintings of John Sten hold particular interest. This local son dabbled in an extremely decorative and fanciful style.

EXPLORING THE ARCHIPELAGO

The archipelago around Hudiksvall is one of the most beautiful along the coast of northern Sweden. At the turn of the century there were more than 50 fishing villages and harbors in the Hudiksvall archipelago. Today, only a few full-time fishermen make their living here. Most of the old fishing villages now are filled in the summer with Swedes, often from Stockholm, who use fishers' cottages as summer homes.

In the northern part of the archipelago, the Hornslandet peninsula protrudes into the sea like a giant breakwater. There are two fishing villages on the peninsula— **Hölick** and **Kuggörarna.** You can bathe in the sea, fish in excellent waters, enjoy a variety of hikes, or visit an ancient cave. This is a naturalist's paradise with many unique species of flora and fauna. Several areas now come under the protection of nature reserves.

The tourist office (see above) serves as a clearinghouse for all tours. Contact them for maps as well as the most up-to-date, thorough information available for regional excursions.

OUTDOOR PURSUITS

The area around Hudiksvall offers many excellent footpaths for **hiking.** A network of forest roads gives access to the paths at several points, so you can choose any length of walk you wish. You can camp along the way in the meager shelters provided (basically just sheds to protect you from heavy downpours). In theory, trails are open to winter hikers, although violent storms sometimes make hiking impossible. Maps and route descriptions are available at the tourist office (see above).

Sjuvallsleden Path is a hilly path passing some of the highest peaks in Hälsingland (the province in which both Söderhamn and Hudiksvall lie). The path is 18 miles long and starts at the Ofärne activity center in Forsa, a small town lying immediately west of Hudiksvall. It takes you past seven traditional hill farms south of the Dellen lakes, finishing in Delsbo, a town northwest of Hudiksvall. Another path from Hudiksvall connects with it at Ofärne so you can walk all the way from Hudiksvall to the settlement at Delsbo, a distance of some 30 miles.

The **Kolarstigen Path** is 20 miles long and fairly hilly; it takes you through the woods north of North Dellen lake, between Sörgimma and Hallboviken, passing six hill routes en route. Finally, **Kajvallsleden Path** is 27 miles long, running between Delsbo and Ljusdal. It connects Sjuvallsleden and Ljusnanleden, which together constitute a footpath some 80 miles long, though undulating in places.

The majesty of the surrounding lakes and waterways make them worthy places to go canoeing. Although other sites are closer to town, the best equipped of the lot is **Svågadalens,** Vildmarkscenter, Bjuråker (☎ **0653/310-22** or 070/687-79-56). Located in the isolated hamlet of Bjuråker, 40 miles northwest of Hudiksvall, they rent canoes during the summer months for 250 SEK ($27.50) per day, plus the cost of any transportation for you and the canoe to the surrounding lakes and rivers. The staff there is well versed in recommending venues and itineraries that cover the surrounding lakes. For a fee of between 100 and 150 SEK ($11 and $16.50), they'll even meet you at prearranged times to transport you across land as a means of allowing you to explore more than one body of water during any given day or week. An equivalent rental outfit that's not as well rounded, but closer to Hudiksvall, is **Ankarmons Camping,** Iggesund (☎ **0650/20505**), which lies 6 miles south of Hudiksvall, and charges 150 SEK ($16.50) for a day's canoe rental.

Seven different **fishing** areas offer the keen fisher a variety of waters, from lakes and rivers to stocked streams. You may fish freely in the sea without a permit, as long as you use a rod and line. Perch, pike, whitefish, salmon, grayling, Baltic herring, and sea trout are among your possible catches. You need a permit, however, to fish in local lakes and rivers. The tourist office has all the necessary information about fishing in the waters around Hudiksvall. Fishing permits also are on sale here; they range in price from 45 to 60 SEK ($6.60) each, depending on where you want to fish and what species are in season at the time.

SHOPPING

Many artists and craftspeople live and work in and around Hudiksvall, particularly on the shores of the beautiful Dellen lakes. Local crafts include woodcarving from the local pine and spruces, ceramics, leather items, and tinwork. The hotels recommended in this chapter each maintain small-scale kiosks providing a representative sampling of these goods. The tourist office (see above) will give you further details of galleries and exhibitions that may be open at the time of your visit.

WHERE TO STAY

First Hotel Statt. Storgatan 36, P.O. Box 55, S-824 22 Hudiksvaal. ☎ **0650/150-60.** Fax 0650/960-95. www.firsthotels.com. E-mail: info@firsthotels.se. 106 units. TV TEL. Mid-June to mid-Aug and Fri–Sat year-round, 748 SEK ($82.30) double; rest of year, 1,048–1,448 SEK ($115.30–$159.30) double. Year-round, 1,635 SEK ($179.85) suite. AE, DC, MC, V. Parking 50 SEK ($5.50).

Set about a half mile north of the city's railway station, this is the grandest, most stately hotel in town. It originally was built in the early 1800s as a neoclassical villa, but in 1993, a team of entrepreneurs radically upgraded and enlarged its symmetrical, ochre-colored original core. Today, amid lawns and gardens, you'll find a gracefully integrated combination of new and old architecture wherein the high ceilings and airiness of the original have been preserved, albeit with modern interior lines and lots of new marble floors and streamlined walls. Bedrooms within the establishment's original core are smaller, a bit less elegant, and cheaper than those within the newer sections. Each contains modern furniture that's well maintained, cozy, and appropriate to this hotel's role as a site for corporate conventions. Most rooms have views overlooking the sea. Bathrooms are rather small, containing showers but no tubs.

Dining/Entertainment: Live orchestras sometimes play in the hotel's restaurant, attracting a crowd of dance enthusiasts, especially on Saturday nights. First Hotel Statt Cuisine is a combination of international dishes and regional specialties using market-fresh ingredients deftly handled by a kitchen staff trained on the continent. There's also a bar.

Amenities: An indoor pool, a sauna, an exercise room, and a "relax center" where you can recover from the rigors of the sauna. There also are facilities for conventions and group meetings.

✪ **Hotell Hudik.** Norra Kyrkogatan 11, S-824 00 Hudiksvall. ☎ **0650/5410-00.** Fax 0650/541-050. 53 units. MINIBAR TV TEL. Mid-June to early Aug and Fri–Sat year-round, 695 SEK ($76.45) double; rest of year, 1,075 SEK ($118.25) double. AE, DC, MC, V. Free parking.

The most appealing hotel in town wins approval with its personal service and thoughtful extras. Originally built of red brick around 1960, it was enlarged in 1980. Today, in its location in the town center near the hospital and the police station, it offers cozy bedrooms that are tastefully decorated and furnished and spotlessly maintained. Rooms occasionally have themes, such as the Sailor's Room with a nautical decor. Bathrooms have hair dryers and adequate shelf space. No meals are served other than breakfast, but there's a sauna on site, an outdoor swimming pool, an indoor Jacuzzi for use year-round, and a handful of conference rooms.

WHERE TO DINE

Restaurant Cardinal. Storgatan 24. ☎ **0650/10505.** Reservations recommended. Fixed-price lunches (11am–2pm) 65–89 SEK ($7.15–$9.80); dinner main courses 112–150 SEK ($12.30–$16.50). AE, DC, MC, V. Daily 11am–10pm. INTERNATIONAL.

On first glance, you may think you've entered an informal and sometimes boisterous Irish pub where the focus is exclusively on the bar trade. But don't be fooled, as this place takes its food and service seriously—often to the point where hotel receptionists throughout Hudiksvall recommend it as the most appealing restaurant in town. Within a dark-green and dark-red decor inspired by the pubs of Ireland, you can order a medley of perfectly prepared fresh fish, chicken, steak, and pork dishes that are offered in combinations such as "black and white" filets (pork and filet steak served on the same platter with béarnaise, truffles, and mushroom sauce), smoked salmon stuffed with shrimp in a mayonnaise sauce, and filet Oscar (filets of pork with crabmeat, lemon, and béarnaise sauce).

4 Sundsvall

242 miles NW of Stockholm, 151 miles NW of Oslo

A fire on Midsummer's Day in 1888 that ravaged old Sundsvall and left 9,000 residents homeless induced wealthy timber barons from the region's forests and sawmills to rebuild the town in stone to ensure that it would never again burn to the ground. Today, this capital of the tiny province of Medelpad is known as "Stone City," and the buildings in the heart of Sundsvall appear just as they did at the end of the 19th century.

Thanks to a location between the great rivers Ljungan and Indalsälv, and through the rise of forestry in the 19th century, Sundsvall has long been a commercial center and one of the most important industrial areas in the north of Sweden. It has an enormous production of wood pulp, its chief commodity. It first received its town charter in 1624, a grant from Gustavus Adolphus, and its first major disaster occurred in 1721 when invading Russian troops burned it to the ground. Sundsvall then languished in obscurity until the 19th century when timber barons moved in and launched it on the road to prosperity.

Just north of Sundsvall, Timrå is a coastal town known for its site at the river delta of Indalsälven. The delta was formed 200 years ago when an adventurous local legend, Wild Hussen, drained Ragundasjön lake and in the process altered the course of the river. The delta area offers a wide variety of flora, fish, and bird life. Timrå also is the site of the Sundsvall-Härnösand Airport-Milanda. A combined population of 115,000 makes the Sundsvall/Timrå region northern Sweden's most densely populated.

ESSENTIALS

GETTING THERE   By Plane   SAS (☎ **020/727-000**) is the only carrier flying into Sundsvall; from Stockholm, there are nine nonstop flights a day, each taking about an hour. Planes land at the Sundsvall-Härnösand Airport-Midlanda. From the center of Sundsvall, at the bus station on Esplanaden (☎ **020/51-15-13** for information), buses (each of which is marked "Flygplats") depart for the airport at intervals that coincide with the arrival and departure of flights.

By Train   There are about four trains a day from Gävle (a 2½-hour ride) and about seven trains a day from Stockholm (a 5-hour ride). For rail schedules, call ☎ **020/ 75-75-75.**

By Bus   From both Gävle and Stockholm, there are four to five buses a day; their itineraries are a bit slower and less convenient than the trains'. For bus information, call ☎ **0200/21818.**

By Car   From Hudiksvall, continue northwest along E4.

VISITOR INFORMATION   Contact **Sundsvall Turism,** Hamnplan 4 (☎ **060/ 19-29-00**), open mid-June to mid-August, Monday through Friday 9am to 8pm and Saturday and Sunday 10am to 8pm. Off-season hours are Monday through Friday 11am to 5pm.

SEEING THE SIGHTS

You'll have plenty of space for walking around Sundsvall and seeing the stone structures. A broad major avenue, **Esplanaden,** cuts the grid of streets in two sections. **Esplanaden** itself is crossed by **Storgatan,** the broadest street in the city. The center square, **Storatorget,** is the most interesting part of the city. It's home to impromptu art exhibitions and is the site of a fresh fruit and vegetable market every Monday through Saturday, beginning at 9:30am.

At Storatorget, look at the **Gran Building** on the north site of the square. It is named for Peter Gran, a much-traveled apothecary. The entrance to the building is adorned with the town and county coats-of-arms. In the building, **Edvall's,** a jewelry shop, is the only fully intact shop interior in the town dating from the 1890s. Make sure to admire the magnificent hand-painted glass ceiling.

The town hall, or **Stadshuset,** stands on the south side of Storatorget. Built of stone in 1862, it was in need of only repair following the great fire that destroyed the town. The roof is ornamented by two groups of figures that symbolize the activities originally housed in the structure: police, jail, hotel, and rooms for celebrations. One of the groups depicts justice, blindfolded, with her scales and sword.

The town's best park, **Vängåvan,** lies northwest of Esplanaden. Its name, "gift from a friend," originated when two friends donated the land to the town in 1873. The park

Sundsvall

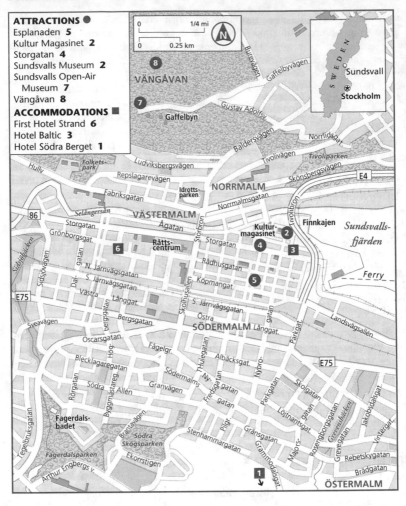

ATTRACTIONS ●
Esplanaden **5**
Kultur Magasinet **2**
Storgatan **4**
Sundsvalls Museum **2**
Sundsvalls Open-Air
  Museum **7**
Vängåvan **8**
ACCOMMODATIONS ■
First Hotel Strand **6**
Hotel Baltic **3**
Hotel Södra Berget **1**

is dominated by a large fountain decorated with sculptures to represent the foundations of Sundsvall: commerce, shipping, industry, craftsmanship, knowledge, and wis-
dom. At the base of the fountain stand three bears holding the crests of Sundsvall, the
county of Västernorrland, and Sweden.

✪ **Kultur Magasinet.** Storgatan 29, down by the harbor. ☎ **060/19-18-00.** Free admission. Mon–Thurs 10am–7pm, Fri 10am–6pm, Sat–Sun 11am–4pm.

This "culture warehouse," which includes the museum below, is housed in a quartet
of four restored 19th-century warehouses. Once, these warehouses were used to store
flour, sugar, spices, coffee, dried fruit, and other products for the winter months when
the townspeople were unable to use the frozen waterways to buy these staples. Following its restoration, Kultur Magasinet became one of Sweden's most popular tourist
attractions, drawing some 700,000 visitors annually.

The complex includes a children's cultural center, the town library, and the Café
Skonerten, where you'll smell the aroma of newly baked buns and cakes. The center

also is the venue for theater, lecture, debates, and speeches from writers and artists. Music—everything from folksingers to orchestras—dominates the agenda.

Sundsvalls Museum. Inside Kultur Magasinet (see above). ☎ **060/19-18-03.** Free admission. Mon–Thurs 10am–7pm, Fri 10am–6pm, Sat–Sun 11am–4pm.

This widely varied, major museum, with both permanent and temporary exhibits, is devoted to local history, handcrafts, and much more. Temporary shows tend to focus on art and photography. The museum's art collection includes works from Swedish artists of the 19th century including Leander Engström, Arne Jones, Max Book, Birgitta Muhr, and Anders Boquist. In one section, "Sawmill Workers and Gentlemen," the Sundsvall's great timber era is recreated through models, portraits, and photographs. Another exhibit, "Sun Mountain Water," describes nature in Medelpad. The "Högom Chieftain" is the name of an exhibit devoted to Norrland's richest burial site from the time of the great migrations around A.D. 500. The "Town Which Transformed Itself" depicts the period between 1886 and 1891 when central Sundsvall emerged from a wooden town destroyed by fire to a European stone city with wide boulevards and richly decorated buildings. The museum also contains a reconstruction of Carl Frisendahl's Paris studio (he was a sculptor, drawer, and painter from Näsåker on the Ångerman River), and a large donation of his sculptures, sketches, and paintings.

IN NORRA & SÖDRA STADSBERGET

Sundsvall is situated in a valley between two town hills, Norra and Södra Stadsberget. Norra is the lower of the two, 87 feet above sea level, with views of the town far out to sea. Here you'll find the **Sundsvall Open-Air Museum** (Frilftsmuseum), Norra Stadsberget (☎ **060/61-17-48**), which is open June through August, Monday through Friday 9am to 6pm, Saturday noon to 4pm, and Sunday 11am to 4pm. Off-season hours are Monday through Friday 9am to 4pm. Admission is free. The museum is housed in one of several old farm buildings gracing the hillside. For the children there is a farm zoo with domestic animals. More interesting for adults is the **Grankotten (Fir Cone) Restaurant,** with an outdoor summer terrace.

The hill to the south, **Södra Berget,** has developed into a center for **outdoor activities** in both summer and winter. There is an extensive system of trails, including Sweden's longest illuminated trail, stretching for 2½ miles. The Tarzan and Bear Trails, with tunnels, lianas, and a rope bridge, offer fun for the whole family. The centerpiece of the mountain is a world-class slalom slope and a gigantic track system, the latter used by such international champions as Vladimir Smirnov. There also are open resting cabins, cots, and cozy windbreaks in the middle of the woods. For more information, call the hotel **Södra Berget** (☎ **060/67-10-00**) or **Sidsjobacken** (☎ **060/61-09-26**), a site that helps administer the ski trails and rents ski equipment. A 1-day ski pass for unlimited use of these facilities costs 100 SEK ($11).

A TRIP TO THE ISLAND OF ALNÖ

Alnö is a summer retreat with inviting beaches (and very cold waters!). Of these, **Tranviken,** on the southern tip, is the best and most popular. The island also is known for its geology; its bedrock is volcanic, with a rock type, nepheline syenite, that has been found only here and in South Africa. Alnö is connected by bridge to the Swedish mainland and lies 4½ miles east of Sundsval. Bus no. 1 makes hourly runs between Sundsval and the island's biggest hamlet, Wi, which is in the center.

Alnö Gamle Kyrka (☎ **060/55-60-60**) in Wi is by far the island's most interesting site, thanks to its origins in the 11th century. The church usually can be visited in summer daily from 9am to 7pm. Other than that, the allure of Alnö derives from its rural charm and summer holiday ambience. It is drab and melancholy, and very insular throughout the winter. The **Alnö Rural Community Center** is open June through August from 10am to 6pm daily, presenting the Sawmill Era in its museum, along with a collection of rock samples. At the southern end of Alnö, not far from Tranviken, is the old fishing village of **Spikarna,** which has no charm beyond that of wandering its streets. From Wi, catch the bus marked SPIKARNA.

SHOPPING

About a dozen craftspeople run **Myrstacken** at Nybrogatan 8 (☎ 060/61-06-74), Sundsvall, selling their own work and that of others. Here you will find any number of handmade gifts, including stoneware and pottery, wooden trays and bowls, handwoven carpets and tablecloths, and specially designed jewelry.

At **Skvaderboden,** on Norra Berget (☎ 060/61-17-48), Sundsvall, you'll find, among other articles, handmade wooden replicas of that curious, imaginary beast, the skvader. This animal is said to be a cross between a hare and a wood-grouse cock.

Trollska galeriet, Nybrogatan 5, Sundsvall (☎ 060/12-15-00), specializes in trolls. Rolf Lidberg's good-natured trolls are portrayed on postcards, posters, and clothing. Russian handcrafts also are available here.

Norrland's largest shopping center, and the focal point for thousands of shoppers who drive here from throughout the region, is the **IKEA-huset,** which lies in the hamlet of Birsta, 3 miles north of Sundsval. To reach it from Sundsval, drive north along Route E4, following the signs to Haparanda. The largest of more than 40 merchants within the complex is housewares and furniture giant IKEA (☎ 060/14-42-00), whose warehouse-sized premises function as Sweden's unofficial ambassador to designers, decorators, and average consumers around the world.

WHERE TO STAY

First Hotel Strand. Strandgatan 10, P.O. Box 459, S-851 06 Sundsvall. ☎ 060/12-18-00. Fax 060/61-92-02. 203 units. MINIBAR TV TEL. Mid-June to mid-Aug and Fri–Sat year-round, 775 SEK ($85.25) double; 1,195–1,695 SEK ($131.45–$186.45) suite. Rest of year, 945–1,295 SEK ($103.95–$142.45) double; 1,695–2,195 SEK ($186.45–$241.45) suite. AE, DC, MC, V. Free parking.

Built of russet-colored bricks in the mid-1970s and set in the center of town within a pair of five- and six-story buildings, this hotel is a well-respected, well-planned member of a nationwide chain. Bedrooms are universally comfortable and well designed. The best rooms are categorized as business-class rooms, and are outfitted with hardwood floors and color schemes of dark blue and white. The less expensive rooms, although comfortable and well maintained, are less dramatic, and have pastel-colored decor and more conventional-looking accessories.

Dining/Diversions: The Seaport Bar and Restaurant is one of the most appealing places to unwind in town, thanks to well-prepared food, stiff drinks, and a venue that's preferred by many of the businesspersons of town for after-work libations.

Amenities: There's a small indoor pool, a sauna, and convention facilities; and a well-trained staff that's alert to most of the resources of the town and region.

Hotel Baltic. Sjögatan 5, S-852 34 Sundsvall. ☎ 060/15-59-35. Fax 060/12-45-60. www.baltichotell.com. E-mail: info.baltic@swedenhotels.se. 73 units. MINIBAR TV TEL. Mid-June to early Aug and Fri–Sat year-round, 695 SEK ($76.45) double; 1,095 SEK ($120.45) suite. Rest of year, 1,100 SEK ($121) double; 1,700 SEK ($187) suite. AC,DC, MC, V. Rates include breakfast. Free parking.

Despite many updates, enlargements, and renovations since it originally was built around the turn of the century, this hotel still retains vague hints of its original detailing and architectural adornments. And although some aspects of the place may not particularly appeal to you (such as claustrophobically narrow upstairs hallways and an occasional sense of banal modernism), others (such as sections of the original masonry facade, and third-floor bedrooms where the ceilings slope inward like those in a romantic garret) are charming. Furnishings are comfortable, albeit standardized, and well maintained. You may feel a bit cramped in the small rooms, but the mattresses are especially good.

Dining/Diversions: The Skeppsbrokällaren, a replica of a British pub, with lots of exposed wood and checkerboard-patterned floor ties, serves steaming platters of rib-sticking food and strong drinks.

Amenities: A sauna, and a series of meeting and convention facilities.

Hotel Södra Berget. P.O. Box 858, S-851 24 Sundsvall. ☎ **800/528-1234** in the U.S., or 060/67-10-00. Fax 060/67-10-10. E-mail: sale@sodra-berget.se. 182 units. MINIBAR TV TEL. Mid-June to mid-Aug and Fri–Sat year-round, 850 SEK ($93.50) double; 1,190 SEK ($130.90) suite. Rest of year, 1,440 SEK ($158.40) double; 1,650 SEK ($181.50) suite. AE, DC, MC, V. Free parking. Follow the Nybrogatan, and then the Gramn Ödalsgatan for 2½ miles south of the town center.

Named after the mountaintop on which it sits, this is one of the most modern hotels in town, and certainly possesses the most panoramic views. Built in 1985 with four floors and renovated on a large scale in 1990, it's perched at a higher elevation than any other structure in town. Bedrooms are comfortable, with contemporary furniture and monochromatic color schemes of gray and blue. The suites, each of which has its own sauna, and rates not much higher than those of the conventional bedrooms, are particularly recommended. Much of the hotel's business derives from participants in corporate conventions who come here for the most complete and comprehensive facilities along the Bothnian coast.

Dining/Diversions: The more formal and appealing of the hotel's two restaurants is the Lille Matsalan (little dining room), site of daily lunches and dinners served, for the most part, to individual clients. Participants in the many conventions held here usually are steered toward the larger and somewhat more anonymous Stora Matsalan. Drinks are served in the sky bar on the hotel's uppermost (fourth) floor.

Amenities: The hotel has the most complete spa and massage facilities in town, with a battery of hydrotherapy and massage techniques, and big-windowed views sweeping out over the mountain and town. There's no swimming pool on-site, although a pair of Jacuzzis fill in the breach. A network of hiking and jogging trails (15½ miles) begins and ends at the hotel.

WHERE TO DINE

Jops. Trädsgårdsgatan 35. ☎ **060/12-19-66.** Reservations recommended. Fixed-price lunch 65 SEK ($7.15); dinner main courses 100–208 SEK ($11–$22.90). AE, DC, MC, V. Mon–Thurs 11am–11pm, Fri 11am–1am, Sat 2pm–2am. INTERNATIONAL.

This is the most fun, amusing restaurant in Sundsvall, with a clientele that swears by its sense of whimsy and a decor that looks like a testimonial to pop art. Album covers decorate the ceiling; old-fashioned Swedish landscapes and framed cartoons cover the wood-paneled walls; and throughout you'll find the kind of kitsch that, if you have any sense of humor at all, at least will make you smile. The menu nicely combines Swedish cuisine with touches of the Orient and the New World. Examples include toast smeared with Swedish caviar, stir-fried prawns with ginger and garlic, potato skins stuffed with sirloin chunks and au gratin of cheese, and herb-laden kebabs with mushrooms and peppers. The burgers are the best in town.

SUNDSVALL AFTER DARK

Although the city seems to hibernate in the cold winter months, summer is a time to enjoy the outdoors. A lot of people still dance the fox-trot, and bands have double-barreled names like Thor-Leifs or Sven-Ingvars. If you don't know the steps, you'll probably meet some Swedes who will teach you. From May to August only, there is dancing at **Sundsvall Folkets Park** (☎ **060/17-17-90**). In winter, the disco scene prevails. It's best experienced at **Gustaf II Adolf,** Storgatan 25-27 (☎ **060/ 17-23-20**), or at **Oscar, Vängåvanb** (☎ **060/12-98-11**).

5 Härnösand

341 miles NW of Stockholm, 31 miles N of Sundsvall

Founded in 1582, Härnösand is the oldest town in the administrative district of Västernorrland. A center of education, with some important industries, Härnösand lies in the province of Ångerman River. Like other towns along this coast, it's had its share of disasters, including two major fires, one in 1710 and another in 1714, plus a ransacking invasion by imperialistic Russians in 1721. It is the best base for exploring Ångermanland, that area of Sweden that most resembles Norway, with its jagged coastlines and long fjords stretching inland, and also the High Coast or Höga Kusten (see below).

Härnösand is built on islands connected by bridges. Lubbe Nordstrom, author of such books as *Lort Sverige* and *Petter Svenska,* called it "close to heaven as it is so beautiful." A bit of an exaggeration, but the setting is one of the most scenic in Sweden.

ESSENTIALS

GETTING THERE   By Train   There are about four trains a day running to Härnösand from Sundsvall, each taking between 45 and 60 minutes. However, because of circuitous rail lines, it's faster and more convenient to take the bus. For railway information, call ☎ **020/75-75-75.**

By Bus   There are between 9 and 10 buses a day, each taking about 40 minutes, for the transit between Härnösand and Sundsvall. Because many folks who work in Sundsvall opt to live in Härnösand, they're usually filled with commuters just before and after the beginning of the work day. For bus information, call ☎ **0200/21818.**

By Car   Continue north from Sundsvall along E4.

VISITOR INFORMATION   The **Härnösand Tourist Office** is at Järnvägsgatan 2 (☎ **0611/881-40**), open June through August daily 8am to 8pm, September through May, Monday through Friday 10am to 4pm.

SEEING THE SIGHTS

The town center is on the island of Härnön, and its main square, **Stora Torget,** is the most beautiful in the north of Sweden. The setting is magnificent, with the yellow residence of the governor, an impressive bank building, and a beautiful art hall. In the middle of the square stands the sculpture *Evolution,* the work of Hagbard Sollös, a Norwegian artist.

From here you can stroll through the narrow lanes in **Östanbäcken,** the Old Town. Along the way, despite the fires that have swept through here, you can still see some 18th-century houses. Most of the shops and restaurants of Hörnosänd lie in and around Stora Torget.

A particularly appealing sightseeing option is aboard the sturdy decks of the **M/S Adalen III,** which carries supplies among many of the communities along the High

Coast of this part of Sweden. A popular and panoramic choice is possible every Wednesday between May and August, when it sails between Härnosänd, on the Bothnian coast, past the rocky inlets of the High Coast and up the Angerman River to the historic town of Sollefteå. Although the distance is less than 70 miles, it takes 8 hours to make the trip. The cost of the boat ride, one way, is 160 SEK ($17.60). At the end of the trip, you'll have to take a bus from Sollefteå back to Härnosänd, a 90-minute trip, priced at 56 SEK ($6.15) per person.

A shorter trip departs from Hårnosänd twice every Tuesday between May and September, for the hamlet of Vida, a 12-mile distance north along the High Coast. Round-trip transit, which includes a brief stopover in Vida, takes 4 hours and incorporates sweeping views over the savagely eroded coastline as part of the experience. Round-trip passage costs 120 SEK ($13.20) per person.

Tickets for both excursions are available from the **tourist office** (☎ 0611/881-40) and the M/S *Adalen III,* whose number is likely to change seasonally. It's usually best to call the tourist office directly.

Just a couple of miles from the center of Härnosänd you'll find **Smitingens havsbad,** one of the best places for outdoor swimming in Norrland. However, the waters are icy cold, even in the middle of summer. The sandy beach is generously long and suitable for children. In the area are some comfortable rocks warmed by the sun, which you can lie on (like a seal) to warm up. There is a cafe here as well.

The chief attraction in the main part of town is the neoclassical **Domkyrkan,** Västra Kyrkogatan (☎ 0611/24525), the smallest cathedral in Sweden. An old stone church stood here in 1593 and remained intact through the fires of 1710 and 1714. However, when the Russians ransacked the town in 1721, it was badly damaged by fire. Using the walls that remained, rebuilding, from 1842 to 1846, gave birth to the present-day cathedral. Today, a dozen pillars support two side galleries. The baroque altar from 1728 was built by Jacob Saverberg. Above the entrance rises the powerful front of the organ, which the famous organ builder Johan Cahman built in 1731. In the vestry is a solid iron door from 1765, a leftover from the original church. Hours are daily 10am to 4pm; admission is free.

From the center, signs direct you to the **Lansmuseet Murberget** (☎ 0611/88600), about a mile north of the town center, which incorporates two museums into one administrative whole. The larger and more appealing of the museums is the **Murberget Open-Air Museum,** the largest of its kind in Sweden outside of Stockholm's Skansen. If you don't have a car of your own, bus nos. 2 and 52 run here every hour in summer between May and August. More than 80 buildings have been moved from various country locations to the bucolic, peaceful grounds here. Examples include traditional Ångermanland farmhouses and an antique Murberg church, a building that's often the site of local weddings. The open-air museum is open May through August, daily from 11am to 5pm. Entrance is free, but a guided tour of the premises, which departs virtually whenever you decide you want it, costs 60 SEK ($6.60) per person.

The other of the two subdivisions is the **Lansmuseet Västernorrland** (☎ 0611/886-00), an indoor, year-round county museum devoted to the history of the area. Inaugurated in 1994, this museum contains, among other exhibitions, one of Sweden's largest collections of old weapons including hunting, folk, and military weapons, some dating from the 17th century. Flintlock guns, spears, accessories, hunting traps, and tools—it's all here.

On site, local craftspeople also demonstrate traditional crafts; everything from embroidery to the forging of iron. It's open daily, year-round, from 11am to 5pm. Entrance is free.

WHERE TO STAY

Stadt Hotellet. Skeppsbron 9, S-871 30 Härnösand. ☎ **0611/105-10.** Fax 0611/228-11. 95 units. TV TEL. Mid-June to mid-Aug and Fri–Sat year-round, 748 SEK ($82.30) double; rest of year, 1,298 SEK ($142.80) double. AE, DC, MC, V. Rates include breakfast. Free parking.

Few hotels along the Bothnian coast blend as gracefully as this one does with the surrounding houses. Part of this is because of its original construction many years ago as a compound of houses that share a communal rear courtyard. Even after a section of it was modernized in the 1960s, about a dozen of the rooms retained their high-ceilinged, big-windowed original configurations, and as such are a bit more charming and nostalgic than their more modern counterparts. (The old-fashioned rooms are those numbered 230 to 234 and those numbered 330 to 341.) Regardless of your room assignment, you'll find moderately sized bedrooms with particularly excellent mattresses, plus small but well-organized bathrooms. The hotel, the largest in town, contains an attractive and cozy pub (the Sneezing Duck), a sauna and small exercise room, and a well-recommended restaurant, Johan III, named in honor of the Swedish monarch who founded the town.

WHERE TO DINE

The Highlander. Nybrogatan 5. ☎ **0611/511170.** Main courses 100–145 SEK ($11–$15.95). MC, V. Mon–Fri 11am–2pm; Tues–Sat 6–11pm. SCOTTISH/INTERNATIONAL.

Praised by virtually every hotel receptionist in town for the quality and large portions of food, this pub and bistro celebrates the aesthetics and conviviality of Scotland. (Note the green-and-red, tartan-patterned carpeting and an array of at least 20 different brands of single-malt whiskies.) The cuisine is consistently excellent and uses first-rate ingredients. Menu items include Highland steaks with a whisky-flavored pepper sauce; fried salmon with a cream sauce and herbs; and savory hamburgers served with coleslaw, red onions, and English cheddar. What's the most popular single-malt scotch served within this paean to Scotland? Oban, a whisky from the Western Highlands.

CONTINUING ALONG HÖGA KUSTEN (THE HIGH COAST)

One of the most scenic and panoramic stretches of nature in all Sweden lies on the Bothnian coast between Härnösand and Örnsköldsvik. Along this stretch of Route 4, known as the High Coast, rolling mountains and luxuriant valleys seem to plunge into the gulf itself.

The coastline also is the setting for the Höga Kusten Bridge, the longest bridge in Sweden and the seventh longest in the world. Built over the Ångermanälv River, it was inaugurated at Christmas in 1997. Its two towers, called pylons, are Sweden's tallest constructions at 585 feet.

The coast presents a scenic panorama at every turn, from sheer cliffs rising above the turbulent waters to craggy outcroppings of rock. Occasionally you'll see a tranquil sandy cove. Dozens of islands, some hardly large enough to land on, lie off the coast. Many islands are much larger and provide a setting for pine forests. In summer, many Swedes like to walk the entire distance of the coast along **Höga Kusten leden,** which extends 80 miles from the new bridge just north of Härnösand to Varvsberget in Örnsköldsvik.

Depending on the time of the year of your visit, the tourist office (see "Visitor Information," above) will advise you on the best way of seeing the most scenic islands in the chain, using a combination of boat and bus. (These schedules are constantly being changed.) The loveliest islands in the archipelago include **Högbonden, Ulvön,** and **Trysunda.**

Just a 10-minute boat ride from the mainland, **Högbonden** has only nature to entertain you. Its sole building is a lighthouse at the highest point on the island, surveying a rocky plateau. The lighthouse has been turned into a youth hostel. To reach the island, go to Bönhamn, where the M/F *Högbonden* sails from mid-June to mid-August every 2 hours daily from 10am to 6pm. For information, call ☎ 0614/ 179-54. A return ticket costs 60 SEK ($6.60).

Ulvön Island really is two islands: Norra Ulvön and uninhabited Södra Ulvön. Ulvön was once the site of a large fishing village, but over decades its settlers have mostly deserted it, leaving behind about 40 hearty souls. The main hamlet is Ulvöhamn, where you'll see many fishers' cottages and boat houses. Walk its narrow village street and duck in to look at the old fisherman's chapel before going to the **Café Måsen,** the major meeting place of town and the summer rendezvous point for boaters in the area. If you have time, take in the panoramic view from Lotsberget Hill. To reach the island, go to Docksta, from which the M/S *Kusttrafik* (☎ 0613/105-50) departs for Ulvön daily at 10:15am, June through August, arriving in Ulvöhamn in about an hour. The cost of a return ticket is 135 SEK ($14.85).

Boats departing from Ulvön also reach the island of **Trysunda** in about an hour, pulling into a narrow U-shaped harbor, site of the island's tiny village. This is the best-preserved fishing village in Ångermanland, and it's nestled among the cliffs far out to sea. The village contains about 40 red and white fishers' cottages right on the water-front, along with a fishers' chapel from the 1600s. Many Swedes come here to bathe on the rocks in summer. The little island also is crisscrossed with many hiking trails. The M/F *Ulvön* sails from Ulvöhamn daily, costing 85 SEK ($9.35) one way. For schedules, call ☎ 070/651-92-65.

6 Umeå

435 miles N of Stockholm, 341 miles N of Gävle, 186 miles N of Sundsvall

With a population of 100,000 and an average age of 35, Umeå is a city of knowledge and culture with a multiethnic population. Some 50 native tongues, from Albanian to Wolof, are spoken here.

Norrland University's 20,000 students are what make the city so youthful. Stylish and wide boulevards and a fast-flowing river make for a dramatic cityscape.

It wasn't easy for Swedish kings to convert the Ume delta fishermen into city dwellers. The first town privileges (the town's charter) were granted in 1588, but few people settled there at first. It wasn't until 1622 that King Gustav II Adolf succeeded in getting people to live at Umeå and pursue trade.

The 18th century saw Umeå suffering from war and unrest, and plundered by Russian soldiers. In 1809, Umeå became the center for military operations when Sweden was drawn into the Napoleonic wars, during which it lost Finland and suffered greatly. It wasn't until the 1830s that business picked up as shipping, trade, and shipbuilding flourished. Timber barons moved in, and the mouth of the Ume River, Umeå, became a major port. After Umeå was laid to waste by a devastating fire in 1888, a new city of well-ordered buildings and tree-lined avenues with fire breaks was built.

ESSENTIALS

GETTING THERE   By Plane   Access by air to Umeå is controlled by two airlines, the more visible of which is **SAS.** Less frequent service is offered by Norway-based **Braathens.** Between the two airlines, there are at least a dozen flights a day winging in from such places as Stockholm, Oslo, and Malmö. For information about flights on either airline, call ☎ 020/727-000.

By Train   A night train, whose compartments come with showers and breakfast, takes travelers from Stockholm to Umeå at least twice daily. Trip time is 9 hours. For schedules, call ☎ 020/75-75-75.

By Bus   Bus transit from Stockholm is faster and more efficient than equivalent transits by train, because the roads heading north to Umeå are shorter than the somewhat more circuitous rail lines. Trip time is around 7½ to 8 hours, depending on road conditions. For schedules and information, call ☎ 0200/21818.

By Car   From Härnösand continue north along E4.

VISITOR INFORMATION   Umeå Turistbyrå, Renmarkstorget 15 (☎ 090/ 16-16-16), is open mid-June to mid-August, Monday through Friday 8am to 8pm, Saturday 10am to 5pm, and 11am to 5pm. Off-season hours are Monday through Friday 9am to 6pm and Saturday 11am to 2pm.

SEEING THE SIGHTS

Umeå is called the "city of birch trees." Hundreds of these trees were planted along every boulevard following the fire of 1888 that destroyed the town. They are at their colorful best in autumn when university students return by the thousands, enlivening the city after a sleepy summer. Theater, opera, concerts, and other cultural attractions also return, bringing the city renewed vigor.

East of the tourist bureau, **Rådhuseplanaden** (Town Hall Esplanade) is a wide-open area with the city hall, constructed of red brick, lying to the south. There are not many old wooden mansions left, except in the district along and east of Östra Kyrkogatan where you will find a rich concentration of antique houses. The redbrick neo-Gothic church on the Storgatan is from 1894. To the east of the church is **Döbelns Park,** named for Georg Carl von Döbeln, the commander who, on October 8, 1809, officially disbanded the Swedish/Finnish army when Finland fell to Russian control.

The town's major museum complex is called **Gamlia** (☎ 090/16-52-27), and can easily occupy the better part of your day. This sprawling area lies ½ mile northeast of the town center and can be reached by driving or walking. Admission is free to all the museums.

The town's original museum, ✪ **Friluftsmuseet,** is still going strong. It consists of about 20 regional buildings in an open-air setting, with the oldest dating from the 1600s. Attractions include a grain-drying kiln, a windmill, a smokehouse for meats, an octagonal chapel still used for weddings, two threshing floors, a school, and a farmhouse. Guides dressed in folkloric clothing will show you around and answer questions. In an on-site bakery, the traditional unleavened bread of the north, *tunnbröd,* is prepared for you to sample. The place still seems like an active farm with its collection of barnyard animals.

Most of the main museum collection is found in the ✪ **Västerbottens Museum** (☎ 090/17-18-00), a repository of the history of the province. The exhibits go back to prehistoric times. A ski found here has been dated to 5200 B.C., making it the oldest in the world. Exhibits also trace the history of the region during the Industrial Revolution. Some exhibitions offer glimpses into reindeer breeding and Lapp or Sami culture. A scaled-down model, 12½ feet long, of Umeå's riverfront shows what a portion of the city looked like before the disastrous fire of 1888. It is open June to mid-August, Monday through Friday 10am to 5pm, and Saturday and Sunday noon to 5pm. Off-season times are Tuesday through Friday 10am to 4pm, Saturday noon to 4pm, and Sunday noon to 5pm.

Linked to the Västerbottens Museum is the **Bilmuseum,** or Picture Museum (☎ 090/17-18-00), which is run by the university. This is the venue for temporary exhibitions. Among its permanent collection, it houses the university art collection, including works by two of the most famous artists of Sweden, Carl Larsson and Anders Zorn. The museum is open mid-June to mid-August, daily noon to 5pm; off-season Tuesday through Saturday noon to 4pm and Sunday noon to 5pm.

WHERE TO STAY

First Hotel Grand. Storgatan 46, S-903 26 Umeå. ☎ **090/77-88-70.** Fax 090/13-30-55. www.firsthotels.se. E-mail: info@firsthotels.se. 85 units. TV TEL. Mid-June to mid-Aug and Fri–Sat year-round, 690–790 SEK ($75.90–$86.90) double; 995 SEK ($109.45) suite. Rest of year, 1,145–1,245 SEK ($125.95–$136.95) double; 1,345 SEK ($147.95) suite. Rates include breakfast. AE, DC, MC, V. Free parking.

Although its original premises have been massively improved and expanded over the years, most recently in 1998 when all its bedrooms were renovated, the origins of this hotel are almost 100 years old. At that time, it was the first stone-built public building in town, erected in the aftermath of a disastrous fire that had destroyed almost everything in Umeå. Since 1995, it has been a member of the nationwide First Hotel chain, which carefully preserves the bedrooms' original high-ceilinged configuration, despite well-planned overlays of modern carpeting and contemporary furnishings. Bathrooms are partially tiled; rooms, although not as comfortable as those within the town's premier hotel, the Provobis Umeå, are nonetheless very comfortable with excellent beds.

Dining/Diversions: In the cellar is an Italian concept restaurant, **Primo & Ciao Ciao,** a lighthearted and whimsical affair incorporating everything from pizza and pastas to veal and chicken parmigiana.

Amenities: Sauna with an adjoining cluster of chaise lounges for relaxing.

Provobis Umeå Plaza. Storgatan 40, P.O. Box 3133, S-903 04 Umeå. ☎ **090/17-70-00.** Fax 090/17-70-50. www.provobis.se/hotels. E-mail: umea.plaza@provobis.se. 196 units. MINIBAR TV TEL. Mid-June to Aug 9 and Fri–Sat year-round, 740 SEK ($81.40) double; rest of year, 1,295 SEK ($142.45) double. Rates include breakfast. AE, DC, MC, V. Parking 85 SEK ($9.35).

The most stylish and best-accessorized hotel in Umeå rises 14 white-and-pale-green floors from a position in the center of town. Built in 1992 with a flair unmatched by any other hotel in the region, it offers well-maintained green-and-russet-colored bedrooms that are outfitted in an internationally inspired contemporary design. Each has well-upholstered furniture, comfortable mattresses, plus tiled bathrooms with hair dryers. The staff here is particularly well trained, with insights into many of the diversions and services available within the region.

Dining/Diversions: Adjacent to the lobby, there's both a brasserie and a more formal à la carte restaurant, both of which are recommended in "Where to Dine." There's also a cocktail lounge.

Amenities: The hotel contains Umeå's most appealing sauna, which is a compound of wood-sheathed rooms on the hotel's panoramic top floor, with a view from your super-heated cubicle out over the frigid landscapes of northern Sweden.

Strand Hotel. Vestra Strandgatan 11, S-903 26 Umeå. ☎ **090-70-40-00.** Fax 090/70-40-90. E-mail: strand@lindfors.se. 44 units. TV TEL. Mid-June to mid-Aug and Fri–Sat year-round, 645 SEK ($70.95) double; rest of year, 995 SEK ($109.45) double. Rates include breakfast. AE, DC, MC, V. Free parking.

Set in the town center and separated from the banks of the river by a parking lot and a waterfront boulevard, this is a boxy-looking, efficiently designed, not particularly frilly hotel that's favored by a clientele of (usually male) business travelers from other parts of Sweden. Some aspects of it, particularly its weather-tight windows, angular conservatism, and aura of no-nonsense durability, resemble a YMCA headquarters in some medium-size American city. Bedrooms have white walls, wall-to-wall carpeting, good mattresses, solid furniture crafted from hardwoods and hardwood veneers, and tiled, modern bathrooms that give off lots of hot water. On the premises are a sauna and a staff that's well versed in the various resources available within the district.

There's no restaurant, but management lays out a free evening buffet containing the ingredients for a light supper every night between 6 and around 7:30pm.

WHERE TO DINE

Brasserie Rop/Restaurant Whispers. In the Provobis Umeå Plaza, Storgatan 40. ☎ 090/ **17-70-00.** Reservations recommended evenings only. Rop Brasserie, fixed-price lunch 65 SEK ($7.15); main courses 70–150 SEK ($7.70–$16.50). Whispers, main courses 150–250 SEK ($16.50–$27.50). AE, DC, MC, V. Rop Brasserie, daily 11am–2pm and 5–11pm; Whispers, daily 5–11:30pm. SWEDISH/INTERNATIONAL.

Which of these two restaurants you select may depend on whether you're in the mood for convivial, sometimes raucous, dialogue or for contemplative, hushed silence. Both lie near the lobby of Umeå's best hotel, but whereas Rop (which is Swedish for "speaking in a loud voice") offers just that, Whispers, as the name implies, is much quieter and more decorous. Rop contains close-spaced tables like a French brasserie's and serves sandwiches, burgers, pastas, pizzas, chicken fajitas, grilled fish, salads, and steaks. Whispers, part of whose space is within a glassed-in greenhouse with a view of the midwinter ice that clogs the nearby river, specializes in more elaborate, finely tuned cuisine. Much of this is based on local ingredients, including very fresh elk meat, moose, reindeer, salmon, and perch; often cooked with Arctic berries (including juniper berries, cloudberries, and whortleberries), herbs, and wine.

✪ **Il Fratello.** Nygatan 22. ☎ **090/12-95-51.** Reservations recommended. Main courses 95–220 SEK ($10.45–$24.20); fixed-price menus 180–380 SEK ($19.80–$41.80). AE, DC, MC, V. Mon–Sat 5–11pm. ITALIAN.

Much of the success of this restaurant derives from the long-term residence of its owner, Jörgen Berggren, in Sicily and in Naples, where he developed an abiding interest in the flavors and presentations of high-quality Italian cuisine. Today, Il Fratello is the most appealing and stylish independent restaurant in Umeå. Within a woodsy-looking interior outfitted in dark, warm colors, with access to a wine cellar that sometimes is the venue for pre-dinner wine tasting for groups of eight or more, you'll enjoy Italian cuisine of impressive quality and diversity. Antipasti selections are rich and varied, with all the Parma ham, mortadella, fresh-made mozzarella, and marinated fish and vegetables you'd expect. Pastas are homemade, and when combined with local shellfish and seafood, usually are terrific. A particularly successful starter is mozzarella baked in puff pastry with sun-dried tomatoes and Parma ham, saltimbocca (veal with ham) in a lemon sauce, and an involtini of turbot with salmon and shellfish.

UMEÅ AFTER DARK

Don't think that just because you're in the far north of Sweden that folks here won't want to get down and party. If you have any nocturnal energy at all, you'll probably discover that the frigid air and long nights add an intensity to nightclubbing that simply doesn't exist in more clement climes to the south.

The town's most visible and largest nightlife compound is **Blå Kök o Bar (Blue Avenue),** Rådhusesplanaden (☎ **090/13-23-00**). Within its multistory premises you'll find a disco, two separate restaurants, a pub, and a stage for the presentation of live music. It's open every night from 5pm till 3am. Dinner service, where main courses cost from 49 to 169 SEK ($5.40 to $18.60), is a little earlier in the evening, with most of the musical pizzazz beginning around 9pm. There's a cover charge of between 40 and 60 SEK ($4.40 and $6.60) Saturday night between 9pm and midnight only. Although the venue caters to youthful enthusiasts most nights of the week, the slightly older crowd will feel more comfortable here on Thursdays, when live music stresses golden disco from the '70s and '80s, as opposed to the heavy metal and techno music that's the norm on other nights.

7 Skellefteå

508 miles N of Stockholm, 81 miles N of Umeå

This pleasant coastal town on the north coast of Sweden and between the banks of the Ume and Skellefte rivers is an industrial port. Its chief industry is the refining of metal ores from the nearby mining area of Boliden.

The town was founded on a religious edict issued in 1324 by King Magnus Eriksson, inviting all those "who believe in Christ or want to" to find a settlement here. Many Christians heeded the call, and by the end of the 1700s they had constructed the monumental **Skellefteå Church,** hailed as the largest and most beautiful building in the north of Sweden.

ESSENTIALS

GETTING THERE   By Train & Bus   Skellefteå does not have a railway station of its own; consequently, the trains rushing northward from southern Sweden pull into the station within the hamlet of Bastu Trask, 30 miles from the center of Skellefteå. And whereas that makes rail transit from Stockholm feasible (there's a day train and a night train, each taking 16 hours to reach Bastu Trask from Stockholm), it makes rail transit from Umeå relatively inconvenient. Consequently, if you're looking for the easiest access to Skellefteå from Umeå, you'll find that any of the five or six **buses** (2 hours each way) are by far the faster and more convenient mode of access. For information about rail connections into Skellefteå, call ☎ **020/75-75-75.** For bus connections into Skellefteå, call ☎ **0910/10-507.**

By Car   From Umeå continue north along the E4 with the coast on your right.

VISITOR INFORMATION   The **tourist office** at Kanalgatan 56 (☎ **0910/ 73-60-20**) is open late June to early August, Monday through Friday 10am to 7pm, Saturday and Sunday 10am to 3pm. Off-season times are Monday and Thursday 8am to 5pm, Friday 8am to 4pm.

SEEING THE SIGHTS

Finished in 1799 on a plan that corresponds to the shape of a Greek cross, ✪ **Skellefteå Kyrko (Skellefteå Church), Kyrkogatan 5** (☎ **0910/73-55-10**), is open daily throughout the year from noon to 7pm. Noteworthy for its temple-like porticoes and its cupola with a lantern, this building grew up on the site of a church from the Middle Ages, of which only the 15th-century vestry is preserved. Its most valuable treasure is a collection of medieval wood carvings. The six statues before the altar depict the Virgin and child, saints Erik and Katarina, St. Anne with Virgin and child, St. Michael, and St Olof. The pulpit dates from 1648. Be sure to seek out the church's chief treasure, the **Virgin of Skellefteå,** a walnut carving, probably German, that is 8 centuries old. It can be found near the altar and is one of the few remaining Romanesque images of the Virgin of Sweden.

The church, which is within an easy walk of the center, is part of the parish village of **Bonnstan.** These parish villages were commonplace in the provinces of Norbotten and Västerbotten in the north of Sweden. They consisted of a kyrkstad, as this one does, which is a series of simple wooden houses clustered around the church.

On Kyrkstand, you'll see five long rows of weather-beaten log houses with wooden shutters. These wooden houses are carefully preserved in their natural state by government authorities, and it's illegal to install electricity in them or modernize them in any way.

Sweden's Parish Villages

After breaking with the Catholic Church in 1527, the Swedish clergy mandated that parishioners had to attend church to learn Lutheran fundamentals. Anyone residing within 6 miles of the church had to attend services every Sunday; those 6 to 12 miles from the church had to attend every other week; and those between 12 and 18 miles away had to attend every 3 weeks. Wooden houses were erected for anyone who lived farther away and could not get home by nightfall, particularly in the dark months of winter. They retired here after services and then returned home on Monday morning. Many people still live full-time in these old houses, especially in summer, and sometimes they are rented out to visitors.

You also can visit **Nordanå** (☎ **0910/73-55-10**), an open-air museum reached by walking along Strandgatan. The largest building here houses the Skellefteå Museum in an old school. There's a cafe on site, as well as a series of temporary exhibitions. The permanent collection includes displays of prehistoric relics, old coins, and a history of the industrial development of the area. The most intriguing exhibit is a collection of jewelry from the Bronze Age.

The open-air museum itself consists of about a dozen buildings—from a Lapp storage hut to shops selling handcrafts—moved to this site. One bakery demonstrates how bread was made the old-fashioned way, and the staff will sell you samples. Admission is free; the site is open in summer Monday through Friday 10am to 5pm, Saturday and Sunday noon to 4pm.

WHERE TO STAY

First Hotel Statt. Stationsgatan 8, P.O. Box 1, S-931 21 Skellefteå. ☎ **0910/141-40.** Fax 0910/126-28. www.firsthotels.com. E-mail: info@firsthotels.se. 91 units. MINIBAR TV TEL. Mid-June to mid-Aug and Fri–Sat year-round, 748 SEK ($82.30) double; rest of year, 1,249 SEK ($137.40) double. Rates include breakfast. AE, DC, MC, V. Parking 60 SEK ($6.60).

Built in 1995 adjacent to a river (the Skellefte Älv) that runs through the center of town, this is a well-managed, stylish, four-story hotel that's proud of its design by well-known architect Anders Tengbom. About 75% of the bedrooms were renovated within 2 years of its original construction, during a process that upgraded the rooms into a version more comfortable than they were originally. Decorated in warm, sunny colors to counterbalance the often dark days you'll find here, the bedrooms are quite spacious, with lovely wooden floors. Bathrooms, although small, are well equipped with either a shower or bathtub, trouser presses, and hair dryers. Some accommodations, designed for women, are called "First Lady" rooms, with such extra touches as a peephole in the door, an iron, a tea maker, a full-length mirror, a make-up mirror, a beauty kit, and extra skirt hangers. On the premises is a sauna, a restaurant that's open daily for dinner (but not for lunch), and a staff that's willing to reserve rental cars and secretarial/business services.

Scandic Hotel. Kanalgatan 75, S-931 78 Skellefteå. ☎ **0910/75-24-00.** Fax 0910/77-84-11. 131 units. MINIBAR TV TEL. Mid-June to mid-Aug and Fri–Sat year-round, 680 SEK ($80.80) double; 1,175 SEK ($129.25) suite. Rest of year, 1,444 SEK ($158.85) double; 1,650 SEK ($181.50) suite. AE, DC, MC, V. Free parking.

One of the largest and most modern hotels in town lies a 3-minute walk from the city's main square behind a modern, slope-roofed facade that looks capable of resisting the fiercest of Arctic blasts. Bedrooms are cozy, well upholstered, and contemporary looking, with a big-city stylishness that's a pleasant contrast to the masses of potted plants that fill up the atrium-style lobby. Bedrooms are a bit small, although each is provided with a generous working desk. Firm beds make the place more alluring, as do details such as trouser presses and hair dryers. Some units also contain an iron. The bathrooms are small, but tidy.

WHERE TO DINE

✪ **Restaurant Kriti.** Kanalgatan 51. ☎ **0910/77-95-35.** Reservations recommended. Pizzas 78–96 SEK ($8.60–$10.55); main courses 165–220 SEK ($18.15–$24.20). AE, DC, MC, V. Mon–Thurs 11am–2pm and 4:30–10pm, Fri 11am–2pm and 4:30–11pm, Sat 1–11pm. GREEK.

This restaurant is much acclaimed and celebrated in this part of Sweden, not only because its food is excellent, but because it's the only Greek restaurant in the entire northern tier of Sweden. As such, it does a busy trade with Nordics who arrive with fond memories of their past vacations along the Mediterranean, and who leave as ardent fans of the souvlaki, moussaka, calamari, lamb chops, and grilled salmon or whitefish that this place serves up with style. There is a selection of pizzas available, as well as stuffed vine leaves and a roster of salads (including a tasty version with shrimp) that work well as starters. Don't expect photographs of the Acropolis or any of the Greek aesthetic clichés. The establishment's most obvious concession to the Greek aesthetic derives from the music, which incorporates everything from bouzouki to popular Greek singers emulating Melina Mercouri.

12 Swedish Lapland

Swedish Lapland, or Norrland, as the Swedes call it, is Europe's last wilderness—9,400 square kilometers of more or less untouched nature. Norrland covers roughly half the area of Sweden, and one-quarter of the country lies north of the Arctic Circle. This wild, undisturbed domain of the midnight sun is a land of high mountains and plateaus, endless forests and vast swamplands, crystal-blue lakes and majestic mountains; glaciers, waterfalls, rushing rivers, and forests.

Like the Grand Canyon and the Galapagos Islands, Lapland, whose natural wonders include a population of brown bear and alpine flora, is listed as a World Heritage site. It has been occupied by the Samis since prehistoric times. Most still make their living from their reindeer herds.

The territory can be reached easily. Fast electric trains take you from Stockholm to Narvik in Norway, with stops at Kiruna and Abisko. The express train, *Nordpilen,* takes a day and a night to travel from Stockholm to far north of the Arctic Circle. Once here you'll find mail-coach buses connecting the other villages and settlements in the north.

It's much quicker to fly, of course, and there are airports at Umea, Lulea, and Kiruna. The last, for example, is reached by air in 4 hours from Stockholm. Those with more time may want to drive here. From Stockholm, just stay on E4, the longest road in Europe. From Stockholm to the Finnish border town of Haparanda, you'll ride along about 700 miles of good surface.

Various towns in Lapland can serve as a center from which to explore the Laponian area. Under these individual town listings we'll also preview individual national parks to visit in Laponia.

1 Enjoying the Great Outdoors

In the north of Sweden you'll find wilderness outside of every town, as well as forests, wild rivers, unspoiled coastlines, thousands of tranquil lakes, high mountains, and low farmlands. The town you stop over in may be dull, but getting to the town is part of the fun, as your trip will take you through unspoiled wilderness along roads that range from an express highway to the smallest logging road that winds its way deep into the forests.

Many visitors come north just to explore the national parks of Sweden. The most spectacular of the lot is **Muddus Nationalpark** (see "Gällivare," below), some 121,000 acres in all. Also from Gällivare, you also can reach other national parks, including Stora Sjöfallet and Padjelanta. These parks combine to form Europe's largest national

park, a land mass of 3,245 square miles. Others come to explore the highest mountain in Sweden, **Kebnekaise,** at 6,965 feet (see "Kiruna," below).

Abisko is the best center for exploring **Abisko National Park,** where the mountains tower as high as 3,900 feet. Abisko also is one of the best centers for watching the midnight sun, and it's the start of the longest marked hiking trail in the world, the **Kungsleden,** or "Royal Trail," which stretches from Abisko to Hemavan, a distance of 210 miles.

As one of the last great wildernesses of Europe, Lapland offers a wide array of outdoor activities. You can play golf at the most northerly courses in the world, go on horseback riding trips, experience white-water rafting along rapids, or even go canoeing. In winter, dog and reindeer teams can take you on an adventure through the wilderness. Lapland has the best grayling fishing in Europe, and you can hunt for small game and elk.

Fishing trips, golfing jaunts, horseback riding, and especially dog and reindeer sledding should be arranged in advance through a tour group before you go to Sweden. It is not usually possible to just show up on the doorstep and book into these activities. For general information and bookings once you are in Sweden, most questions can be answered by calling **Destination Kiruna,** Mommagatan 3, in Kiruna (☎ **0980/ 171-81**).

Bug Off!

Mosquitoes arrive with the warm weather at the end of June and disappear at the end of August. The best way to protect yourself is to wear thick, preferably bright, clothing; avoid large stretches of water; and use mosquito repellent on exposed skin. Treat bites with Salubrin, Alsolsprit, or something similar.

Although Destination Kiruna can book you on last-minute sporting activities once you are in Sweden, it is better to book in advance. Contact **Lynx Ski Travel** (☎ 800/422-5969 in the U.S.); or **Norvista** (☎ 800/526-4927 in the U.S. or 800/461-8651 in Canada).

GOLFING   If you want to set up some golfing adventure in north Sweden, this too should be arranged in advance. Of course, golf will be heavily dependent on the weather, and it's not always possible to play golf even in the summer. A potential golfer also will be plagued with mosquitoes on the golf courses. For information about a golf vacation, contact **Idrefjällen Golfklubb,** P.O. Box 32, S-790 91 Idre (☎ **0253/202-75**).

HIKING & CAMPING   Swedish Lapland is a paradise for hikers and campers (if you don't mind the mosquitoes in summer). Before you go, get in touch with the **Svenska Turistföreningen (Swedish Touring Club),** Stureplan 4c (Box 25), S-101 20 Stockholm (☎ **08/463-21-00**), which maintains mountain hotels and has built bridges, marked hiking routes, and even introduced regular boat services on some lakes.

There are hundreds of miles of marked hiking and skiing tracks (March, April, and even May are recommended for skiing; hiking is best in the warm summer months). Some 90 mountain hotels or Lapp-type huts (called *fjällstugor* and *kåtor,* respectively) are available, with beds and bedding, cooking utensils, and firewood. Huts can be used for only 1 or 2 nights. The club also sponsors mountain stations (*fjällstationer*).

You must be in good physical condition and have suitable equipment before you set out, because most of the area is uninhabited. Neophytes are advised to join one of the tours offered by the Swedish Touring Club (contact the club for more details).

SKIING   In spite of the bitter cold, many come here to ski in winter. At least snow is guaranteed here, unlike at some alpine resorts of Switzerland and Austria. Kiruna, Gällivare, and Arvidsjaur offer some of the best possible conditions for cross-country skiing. Local tourist offices will offer constantly changing advice about how to hook up with many of these activities, which naturally depend a great deal on weather conditions.

2 Luleå: The Gateway to Lapland

578 miles N of Stockholm

Our tour north begins in Luleå on the way to Lapland. This port city on Sweden's east coast at the northern end of the Gulf of Bothnia is 70 miles south of the Arctic Circle. Luleå is the largest town in Norrbotten; boats depart from its piers for some 300 offshore islets and skerries known for their flora and fauna.

Luleå has a surprisingly mild climate—its average annual temperature is only 3° to 5° lower than that of Malmö, on the southern tip of Sweden.

A port for shipping iron ore in summer, Luleå's harbor is frozen over until May. Fire has destroyed most of the Old Town. The state-owned ironworks here has led to a dramatic growth in population.

Establishing a city this far north was laden with difficulties. Gustavus Adolphus may have founded the city in 1621, but it wasn't until 1940 that development really took hold. Today, as the seat of the University of Luleå, the town has a population of 70,000 and is liveliest when the students are here in winter, although most foreigners (except businesspeople) see it only in summer.

ESSENTIALS

GETTING THERE   By Plane   SAS runs 12 flights each weekday between Stockholm and Luleå (10 on Saturday and Sunday), which take 1¼ hours. There are 11 flights each weekday between Gothenburg and Luleå (7 on Saturday and Sunday), taking 2¼ hours. For information and schedules, call ☎ **020/727-000.**

By Train   Six trains arrive daily from Stockholm (travel time 15 hours); an additional six come from Gothenburg (travel time 19 hours). Trains from Stockholm to Kiruna usually deposit passengers bound for Luleå at the railway junction at Boden, 6 miles northwest of Luleå. Here they board one of three connecting trains a day going between Boden and Luleå. Train traffic from Gothenburg to Luleå also necessitates a transfer in Boden. For more information, phone **020/75-75-75.**

By Bus   A bus runs between Stockholm and Luleå on Friday and Sunday, taking 14 hours. For further information, call **Swebus** at ☎ **0200/21818.**

Northern Lights & the Midnight Sun

If you visit Lapland/Norrbotten (the remote northeastern province of Sweden) in the winter, at dusk you will see the northern lights, a sparkling display of colors.

The northern lights are shimmering lights with surging colors in the sky, a natural phenomenon that can amaze the observer just as much as the most lavish fireworks display. They often can be seen during the dark season, from early in the evening until midnight. The northern lights occur in the Arctic region and are seen more clearly and more frequently the farther north you travel.

The source of energy for the northern lights is the sun and the solar winds. Solar wind plasma is constantly emitted by the sun at a velocity of 248 miles per second. Some of the energy absorbed by the earth's magnetic field accelerates the ions and electrons. The electrons are steered toward the polar regions and, at a few hundred miles from the earth, the electrons collide with atmospheric atoms and molecules. On collision, a small amount of the electrons' kinetic energy is transformed into visible light.

You also experience the midnight sun above the Arctic Circle. By midnight sun we mean that it is possible to see more than half of the sun when it is directly north. At midsummer, it can be seen south of the Arctic Circle thanks to the refraction of light in the atmosphere. From a high hill with a good view to the north, the midnight sun can still be seen quite far to the south. The farther north you go, the longer this phenomenon lasts: In the far north it's from the end of May to the end of July.

· The light at night is milder and softer than the harsh, blinding sunshine of the day and creates an impression that time is somehow standing still. There are many activities and events connected with the midnight sun, including trips to the mountains, bike races, and fishing contests at night. Local tourist offices will have more information about these events.

By Car   From Stockholm, take the E4 expressway north to Uppsala and continue northward along the coast until you reach Luleå.

VISITOR INFORMATION   Contact the **Luleå Tourist Office** at Storgatan 43B Luleå (☎ **0920/29-35-00**), open in summer Monday through Friday from 9am to 7pm and Saturday and Sunday from 10am to 4pm; off-season Monday through Friday from 10am to 6pm and Saturday from 10am to 2pm.

SEEING THE SIGHTS

Some of the most evocative and historic architecture in Luleå lies 6 miles north of the modern city in ✪ **Gammelstad** (Old Town), the town's original medieval core, and a once-thriving trading center. Its demise as a viable commercial center began when the nearby harbor became clogged with silt and was rendered unnavigable. In 1649, a new city, modern-day Luleå, was established, and the Old Town—except the church described below—fell into decline and disrepair. Today it serves as a reminder of another era, and the site of the region's most famous church, **Gammelstads Kyrka,** also known as Neder Lulea Kyrka (no phone). Built in 1492, the church is surrounded by clusters of nearly identical red-sided huts, many of which date from the 18th and 19th centuries. The church rented these to families and citizens traveling to Luleå from the surrounding region as temporary homes during holy days. In 1996, UNESCO declared the church and the cluster of huts around it a world heritage site.

Gammelstad's other important site is the **Hägnan Museum** (also known as the Gammelstads Friluftsmuseum), 95400 Gammelstad (☎ **0920/293809**). Consisting of about a dozen historic buildings hauled in from throughout Norbotten, it's open between April and October, daily from 10am to 5 or 6pm, depending on the season. Entrance is free. To reach Gammelstad from modern-day Luleå, take bus no. 8 or 9 from Luleå's center.

Adjacent to Gammelstad Bay, you'll find some of the richest bird life in Sweden. Ornithologists have counted 285 different species of birds during the spring migrations. The best way to experience this cornucopia of bird life involves following a well-marked hiking trail for 4½ miles south of Gammelstad. Signs will point from Gammelstad to the Gammelstads Vikens Naturreservat. For information about the trail, call either the Luleå Tourist Office (see above) or Michael Öhmann, head of the local park service, at ☎ **0920/16308.** The trail, consisting of well-trod earth, gravel, and boardwalks, traverses mostly marshy, usually forested terrain teeming with bird life. En route, you'll find barbecue pits for picnics and an unstaffed, unsupervised 30-foot tower (Kömpmannholmen, no phone) that's useful for spying on bird nests in the upper branches of nearby trees. The trail ends in Luleå's suburb of Pörson, site of the local university, and site of a small-scale museum, **Teknykens Hus,** Pörson, 97187 Luleå (☎ **0920/72200**). Conceived as a tribute to the industries that bring employment and prosperity to Norbotten, it's open Tuesday through Friday from 9am to noon, and Saturday and Sunday from noon to 4pm. Entrance fee of 30 SEK ($3.30) is levied only between April and October. From Pörson, after your visit to the museum, take bus no. 15 or 16 back to Luleå. Hiking along the above-mentioned trail is not recommended in winter, as heavy snowfalls obliterate the signs and the path, and it's unsafe for all but the most experienced of local residents in top physical condition.

Norrbottens Museum. Storgatan 2. ☎ **0920/24-35-00.** Free admission. June–Aug, Mon–Tues and Thurs–Fri 10am–4pm, Wed 10am–8pm, Sat–Sun noon–4pm. Off-season, Mon–Fri noon–4pm. Bus: 1, 2, 4, 5, 8, or 9.

Close to the city center at Hermelin Park, Norrbottens Museum presents a comprehensive look at Norrbotten's history over the centuries, showing how people lived in

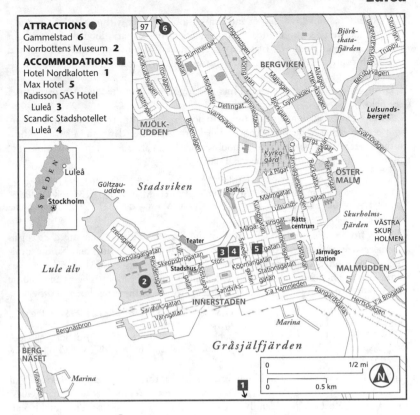

ATTRACTIONS ●
Gammelstad **6**
Norrbottens Museum **2**
ACCOMMODATIONS ■
Hotel Nordkalotten **1**
Max Hotel **5**
Radisson SAS Hotel
    Luleå **3**
Scandic Stadshotellet
    Luleå **4**

these northern regions in bygone days. The museum possesses the world's most complete collection of Lapp artifacts.

WHERE TO STAY

○ **Hotel Nordkalotten.** Lulviksvägen 1, S-972 54 Luleå. ☎ **0920/20-00-00.** Fax 0920/199-09. www.nordkalotten.com. 172 units. TV TEL. Mid-June to mid-Aug and Fri–Sat year-round, 780 SEK ($85.80) double; 1,000 SEK ($110) suite. Rest of year, 1,150 SEK ($126.50) double; 1,350 SEK ($148.50) suite. AE, DC, MC, V. Free parking. From Luleå's center, follow the signs to the airport.

Set 3 miles south of the town center, this is the most architecturally interesting hotel in the region, with some of the most charming grace notes. It originated in 1979, when the city of Luleå established a tourist information center on its premises. In 1984, the hotel was acquired by an independent entrepreneur who was lucky enough to secure thousands of first-growth pine logs (many between 600 and 1,000 years old) that had been culled from forests in Finland and Russia. To create the comfortable hotel you'll see today, he hired well-known Finnish architect Esko Lehmola to arrange the logs into the structural beams and walls of the hotel's reception area, sauna, and convention center. The result, which could never be duplicated today simply because the raw materials are no longer available, is a hotel where the growth rings of the wood reveal the fabric of hundreds of years of forest life—direction of sunlight, climate changes, and rainfall—a source of endless fascination for foresters and botanists.

Most unusual of all is a dining and convention room set within what's shaped like an enormous teepee, also crafted from the ancient trees, that's flooded with sunlight from wraparound windows. Bedrooms are outfitted in soothing tones of beige and gray, with conservatively contemporary furnishings, very comfortable beds, and wall-to-wall carpeting.

Dining: The hotel's lunch and dinner restaurants are described in "Where to Dine" (see below).

Amenities: Local companies compete to book space within the teepee for their corporate meetings. Other, more conventional, space is offered within a small auditorium. There's an indoor swimming pool whose waters are a few steps from a blazing, stone-sided fireplace, and an octagonal sauna.

Max Hotel. Storgatan 59, S-951 31 Luleå. ☎ **0920/22-02-20.** Fax 0920/94-790. www. maxhotel.se. E-mail: mail@maxhotel.se. 83 units. TV TEL. Mon–Thurs 1,275 SEK ($140.25) double; Fri–Sun 680 SEK ($74.80) double. AE, DC, MC, V. Parking 85 SEK ($9.35). Closed June 30–Aug 8. Bus: 1, 2, 4, 5, 8, or 9.

The bus from the airport stops in front of the Max, on Luleå's main street, except in summer when the hotel is closed. Designed tastefully with clean lines and Nordic furniture, the Max offers comfortable accommodations in a much-restored older hotel. Free coffee, tea, and hot chocolate are offered day and night in the lobby. There's an in-house sauna, but for dining, guests usually are directed to one of the other hotels nearby.

Radisson SAS Hotel Luleå. Storgatan 17,S-971 28 Luleå. ☎ **800/2221-2350** in the U.S., or 0920/940-00. Fax 0920/20-10-12. www.radisson.com. 211 units. TV TEL. Mon–Thurs 1,395–1,595 SEK ($153.45–$175.45) double; Fri–Sun 890 SEK ($97.90) double. All week long, 2,995 SEK ($329.45) suite. Rates include breakfast. AE, DC, MC, V. Parking 95 SEK ($10.45). Bus 1, 2, 4, 5, 8, or 9.

Built in 1979 and most recently renovated in 1990, this hotel has six stories, two of which are buried underground. It lies on Luleå's main street in the town center. Guest rooms are comfortable but blandly international in style and decor. The hotel has an indoor swimming pool, a solarium, saunas, and billiard tables.

Hotel Luleå's restaurant, the Cook's Inn, specializes in charcoal-grilled meats. The Cleo disco, in the cellar, is open Thursday through Saturday from 9pm to 3am, year-round. The admission fee is 80 SEK ($8.80). Its most popular nights are Thursday and Saturday, when a live dance band is featured.

Scandi Stadshotellet Luleå. Storgatan 15, S-951 31 Luleå. ☎ **0920/67-000.** Fax 0920/ 670-92. www.provobis.se. E-mail: gunnel.lindstrom@provobis.se. 135 units. TV TEL. 1,561–1,726 SEK ($171.70–$189.85) double; 2,400 SEK ($264) suite. Rates include breakfast. AE, DC, MC, V. Parking 80 SEK ($8.80). Bus: 1, 2, 4, 5, 8, or 9.

The stately, ornate, brick-and-stone building is the oldest (1900), grandest, and most traditional hotel in town. It's in the center of the city, next to the waterfront. The modernized public area has kept a few old-fashioned details from the original building. Guest rooms are comfortable and well furnished. There's a lounge, a bar, and a restaurant.

WHERE TO DINE

The Restaurants at the Hotel Nordkalotten. Lulviksvägen 1. ☎ **0920/20-00-00.** Reservations recommended. Fixed-price lunch 120 SEK ($13.20); lunch main courses 140–160 SEK ($15.40–$17.60); dinner main courses 145–189 SEK ($15.95–$20.80). AE, DC, MC, V. Daily 11am–2pm and 6–10pm. From Luleå's center, follow the signs to the airport and drive 3 miles south of town. SWEDISH/LAPPISH.

Some clients come for a meal at this hotel just to see what hundreds of thousands of kronors' worth of exotic and very old timber can produce. (For more on this, refer to the recommendation of the hotel that contains it, above.) Once you get here, however, you'll also find well-prepared cuisine, a polite and friendly welcome, and flavors that are unique to Sweden's far north. Lunch usually is served in the teepee-shaped building that's the hotel's trademark; dinner, traditionally, is within the Renhagen (Reindeer) Restaurant, where log walls, a flagstone-built fireplace, and flickering candles create a soothing but dramatic ambience. Menu items include liberal use of elk, reindeer, salmon, forest mushrooms and berries, and freshwater char. Presentations are elegant, in some cases emulating the upscale restaurants of Stockholm.

3 Arvidsjaur

434 miles N of Stockholm, 69 miles S of the Arctic Circle, 106 miles SW of Luleå

A modern community, Arvidsjaur nevertheless has an old Lappish center with well-preserved, cone-shaped huts where reindeer are rounded up and marked in June and July. The city lies in a belt of coniferous forests bordering on the highland region, these forests alone would merit a visit.

Excellent skiing, an untouched wilderness with an abundance of wildlife, and good fishing at the Pite and Skellefte rivers are a few of this region's temptations.

ESSENTIALS

GETTING THERE   By Plane   Arvidsjaur can be reached by air from Stockholm, with daily departures in both directions. Flight time is 2 hours, 5 minutes. For information and bookings, call **SAS ☎ 020/727-000.**

By Train   Arvidsjaur has rail links with Stockholm. Train schedules change depending on the time of year, so you should call for information at **020/75-75-75.** Arvidsjaur is on the inland railway, a line that stretches for nearly 800 miles, running between Kristinehamn in Värmland to Gällivare in Lapland. There are rail connections to the Northern Mainline from Stockholm up to the Finnish border.

By Bus   Weekend buses from Stockholm, with a change in Skellefteå (see chapter 11) can be booked through **Nyman & Schultz Travel Agency** by calling ☎ **0960/471-30.** For other bus connections in the area, including to Arjeplog, call ☎ **0960/103-07.**

By Car   Most motorists take the eastern coastal road of Sweden, E4, which runs through Umeå to Skellefteå. At Skellefteå, head inland and northwest along Route 94 into Arvidsjaur.

VISITOR INFORMATION   The **Arvidsjaur Tourist Bureau,** at Garvaregatan 4 (☎ **0960/175-00**), is open June 15 to August 16 daily 8:30am to 6:30pm. Otherwise, hours are Monday through Friday 9 to 11:30am and 12:30 to 5pm.

SEEING THE SIGHTS

Places of interest in town include **Lapp Town** (☎ **0960/125-25**), in the center, with the world's largest preserved Lapp church village and more than 800 Lapp wooden huts and lodgings. From June 15 to August 15 daily guided tours are offered at 3pm. Hours are noon to 5pm, and the fee is 25 SEK ($2.75). Children up to 12 are admitted free.

You can visit also the **Glommersträsk Historical Museum** (☎ **0960/202-91**), a local heritage center. The farming estate here is from the 1700s, consisting of 12 buildings that contain a large collection of practical objects from the early colonization of the Lapp region. These include the region's first schoolroom from the 1840s, as well as a smithy. There is an on-site retail shop for handcrafts. Admission is 10 SEK ($1.10). It is open June 2 to August 29, Monday through Friday 10am to 5pm and Saturday noon to 4pm.

The Lapps (Sami) in Sweden

The Lapps (or Sami), of whom 15,000 to 17,000 live in Sweden, have inhabited the area since ancient times. The area of Lapp settlement (known as Sapmi) extends over the entire Scandinavian Arctic region and stretches along the mountain districts on both sides of the Swedish-Norwegian border down to the northernmost part of Dalarna.

Many Lapps maintain links to their ancient culture, whereas others have completely assimilated. Some 2,500 still lead the nomadic life of their ancestors, herding reindeer and wearing traditional multicolored dress.

The language of the Lapps belongs to the Finno-Ugric group. A large part of Lapp literature has been published in northern Sami, which is spoken by approximately 75% of Lapps. As with all Arctic societies, oral literature has always played a prominent role. Among Lapps, this oral tradition takes the form of *yoiking,* a type of singing. (Once governments tried to suppress this, but now yoiking is enjoying a renaissance.) One of the classic works of Lapp literature is Johan Turi's *Tale of the Lapps,* first published in 1910.

Handcrafts are important in the Lapp economy. Several craft designers have developed new forms of decorative art, producing a revival in Lapp handcraft tradition.

Many members of the Sami community feel that the term *Lapp* has negative connotations; it's gradually being replaced by the indigenous minority's own name for itself, *sábme,* or other dialect variations. Sami seems to be the most favored English translation of Lapp, and the word is used increasingly.

EXPLORING THE AREA

Directly south of Arvidsjaur lies the exquisite low-mountains preservation region of **Vittjåkk-Akkanålke,** a forest reserve with hiking paths cut through its wild and beautiful reaches. The paths are 1, 2, or 3 miles in length. Also contained within the nature preserve is **Lake Stenträsket,** which is known for its char fishing. In summer, you can rent boats to tour the lake. The summit of Akkanålke can be reached by car, offering a panoramic lookout perch.

If you're adventurous, you can ride the **Piteälv River Rapids** (☎ 0960/175-00) at a point about 32 miles north of Arvidsjaur. The Pite River (its English name) is one of Sweden's four extensively developed major waterways, tracing its headwaters to the Sulitelma Glacier on the Norwegian border. At the Troll Rapids, the river turns into frothing rapids and then a cascade near Trollholmen. From July 4 to August 8 organized tours are offered, departing Arvidsjaur daily at 10am, 12:30pm, and 3pm. Families are charged 790 SEK ($86.90), adults 300 SEK ($33), and children up to 15 150 SEK ($16.50). The river-rafting jaunt is a 2-hour trip. To reach the region by car, take Route 45 north from Arvidsjaur until you come to the signpost leading to the rapids.

Lappish souvenirs and handcrafts are available at **Anna-Lisas Souvenirbutik,** Stationsgatan 3 (☎ 0960/106-33), and **Hantvershuset Ekorren,** Auktsjaur (☎ 0960/400-00).

WHERE TO STAY & DINE

Laponia Hotel. Storgatan 45, S-933 33 Arvidsjaur. ☎ **0960/555-00.** Fax 0960/555-99. www.laponia-gielas.se. E-mail: laponia@laponia-gielas.se. 115 units. TV TEL. Mid-June to mid-Aug and Fri–Sat year-round, 740 SEK ($81.40) double; rest of year, 1,105 SEK ($121.55) double. Rates include breakfast. AE, DC, MC, V. Free parking.

The best-recommended and most substantial hotel in town was built in 1957 and has been renovated many times since, most recently in 1996. The interior contains an indoor swimming pool, a bar, a restaurant that's open daily from 11:30am to 10pm, a disco, two saunas, and conference rooms that reflect the urban tastes of big-city Stockholm. Bedrooms are comfortable, uncontroversial, outfitted the way you'd expect in an upscale motel, and filled with light from big windows. The food at the hotel here is the best in town. You can savor both regional specialties of Lapland and international dishes.

EASY EXCURSIONS FROM ARVIDSJAUR

Arjeplog sits on the edge of high mountain country on a peninsula between the great lakes of Uddjaur and Hornavan. The highlands in this region are studded with excellent fishing waters (you can practically catch whitefish from the roadside). The church at Arjeplog was built in 1767, and contains a bridal crown (made from flowers and tree branches from the forest); legend says that it once was stolen by the Lapps but was found again up in the mountains. This city was colonized in the 16th century when silver mining started in Nasafjäll on the Norwegian border. Reindeer at that time carried the silver to Piteä for shipment. In **Aldorfstrom,** the silver village, you can still see some of the buildings from the old purifying plant. Today, lead ore is mined in the "underwater mine" at Laisvall.

Guided visits to the area stop at **Galtispouda,** a mountain range outside Arjeplog, which offers a panoramic outlook over the surrounding lakes and mountains. The Arvidsjaur tourist board (see above) organizes excursions to the area in July, departing from the tourist office Monday, Wednesday, and Friday at 8:30am, with a return at 4pm. The cost is 310 SEK ($34.10) for adults, and 275 SEK ($30.25) for ages 6 to 16 (5 and under free). Visiting the silver museum at Arjeplog is another 30 SEK ($3.30). To reach both Arjeplog and Galtispouda by car, drive northwest along Route 95.

4 Tärnaby & Hemavan

223 miles NE of Umeå, 204 miles W of Luleå, 273 miles N of Östersund, 626 miles N of Stockholm

Tärnaby was the birthplace of Ingmar Stenmark, double Olympic gold medalist and Sweden's greatest skier. Not surprisingly, Tärnaby also is the center of Sweden's most accessible alpine region, offering beautiful mountains and a chain of lakes. Hikers can strike out for Artfjället, Norra Storfjället, Mortsfjället, and Atoklinton, perhaps with hired guides. And Laxfjället, with its fine ski hills and gentle slopes, is nearby on the Blå Vägen (European Road 79).

Hemaven is the largest tourist resort in the area. Many paths lead toward Norra Storfjället, a small mountain visible from Hemavan. A delta formed by the River Ume is particularly rich in bird life.

The greatest trail is the **Kungsleden** (Royal Trail), running from Hemavan to Abisko for a distance of 210 miles. This is one of the most fascinating trails in Europe.

ESSENTIALS

GETTING THERE   By Plane   Most visitors use the airport at Umeå rather than the one at Arvisjaur because of the higher frequency of flights. You can call **SAS** for flight information at Umeå (☎ **020/727-000**) to see which flight is more convenient for you.

By Train   Two trains depart daily from Stockholm for the far northern rail junction of Storuman. Trains from Gothenburg headed for Storuman also are routed through Stockholm. From Storuman, it's necessary to go the rest of the way by bus (1½ hours or more, depending on the weather). Call ☎ **020/75-75-75** for rail schedules.

By Bus   From the rail junction at Storuman, there are three or four buses per day making the 78-mile run to Tärnaby. From the airport at Umeå, there are three or four buses a day, but it takes 5 hours. For schedules, call ☎ **020/21818.**

By Car   Take E4 north to Stockholm, transferring onto Route E75 at the junction to Östersund. From here, take Route 88 north to Storuman, then head northwest on E37 to Tärnaby. From Arvidsjaur, head southwest along Route 45 until you reach the junction with E12 heading west.

VISITOR INFORMATION   For information, **Turistinformation,** in the town center (☎ **0954/104-50**), is open mid-June to mid-August, daily from 9am to 8pm; off-season, Monday through Friday from 9am to 5pm.

EXPLORING THE AREA

Tärnaby and Hemavan may be tiny mountain villages, but they are visited because they mark the end of the ✪ **Kungsleden Trail,** one of the great hiking trails of Europe. The villages themselves are almost devoid of attractions, but come as a welcome relief for those nearing the end of the trail. Most hikers begin their odyssey at Abisko (see "Abisko," below), and end their journeys at Hemavan. However, you may prefer to go against the flow by starting at Hemavan, and ending at Abisko. For more information, see "Abisko," later in this chapter.

Instead of staying at Hemavan, you can stay at Tärnaby, the little village nearby. It is much more attractive, with meadows whose midsummer wildflowers run up to the edge of the dark forests that surround the town.

At the eastern edge of the village, on the road coming in from Storuman, is the **Samigården** (no phone), a tiny museum devoted to Sami history. It usually is open from late June to mid-August daily from 10am to 4pm, charging 10 SEK ($1.30) for admission. At the museum, you'll get a preview of old-time customs and traditions. For example, you'll learn that in olden days hunters killed bears and brought them to the village, where they cut open the animal's gall bladder and drank the liquid fresh from the kill.

The tourist office (see above) is staffed by helpful people who have the latest information on hiking and fishing in the area. Because conditions are constantly changing, depending on the weather and the season it is wise to inquire locally here before heading out into the wilderness on your own without advice.

The town's most popular walk, which is signposted from the center, is across a series of meadows to **Laxfjället mountain.** From the base of that mountain, you can look back for a panoramic view of Tärnaby. If the day is warm and sunny, you can follow the signs to the "beach" at **Lake Laisan.** Locals go swimming here in July, but if you're from Florida, the waters might always feel too cold for you.

WHERE TO STAY & DINE

Laisalidens Fjällhotell. S-920 64 Tärnaby. ☎ **0954/21100.** Fax 0954/211-63. E-mail: laisalidens@tninet.se. 16 units. TV TEL. 750 SEK ($82.50) double. Rate includes breakfast. MC, V. Free parking. Bus: Vlå Vägen from Umeå. From the center of Tärnaby follow Route 73 west for 12½ miles until you come to the hotel.

This is the best hotel in the region, and has a particularly accommodating staff. Its steep, sloping roof is designed to shed the winter's heavy snowfalls and the dark, woodsy facade looks like a modern chalet. With windows opening onto views of the lake, this traditionally decorated mountain hotel offers pleasant but functional-looking bedrooms that are kept immaculately clean. The hotel arranges fishing trips as well as motorboat excursions to the nearby lakes. Built in 1953 and renovated in 1992, the hotel lies 12½ miles west of Tärnaby, gloriously isolated amid trees and tundra. Bathrooms are very tiny with a shower stalls, toilets, and basic sinks. Simple Swedish food is served three times daily.

Tärnaby Fjällhotell. Östra Strandvägen 16, S-920 64 Tärnaby. ☎ **0954/104-20.** Fax 0954/106-27. E-mail: hotell@tarnaby.hotell.se. 36 units. TV TEL. Winter, 880 SEK ($96.80) double; 2,685 SEK ($295.35) weekly for apt with kitchen for 2. Summer, 565 SEK ($62.15) double; 2,225 SEK ($244.75) weekly for apt with kitchen for 2. Rates include breakfast for residents of the hotel, but not for residents of the apts. AE, DC, MC, V. Free parking.

This is the larger of the two hotels in the town center. Built in 1956 and renovated in 1988, its rooms are comfortable and well maintained, with pastel colors and contemporary furnishings. The hotel offers a sauna, table tennis, a drying-off room for after-ski comfort, and several lounges. In addition to the regular bedrooms, the hotel rents 30 apartments on a weekly basis, each a stripped-down, woodsy-looking affair that does not incorporate any of the basic cleaning or daily maintenance service that is routinely provided in the conventional bedrooms. On the premises is a cozy, wood-sheathed restaurant serving lunch and dinner every day, with full meals priced at 180 SEK ($19.80) each.

5 Jokkmokk

123 miles NW of Luleå, 740 miles N of Stockholm, 127 miles S of Kiruna

This community on the Luleå River, just north of the Arctic Circle, has been a Sami trading and cultural center since the 17th century. With a population of 3,400 hearty souls, Jokkmokk (which means "bend in the river") is the largest settlement in the *kommun* (municipality). Bus routes link Jokkmokk with other villages in the area.

Who comes to Jokkmokk? Other than the summer tourists, visitors are mostly business travelers involved in some aspect of the timber industry or the hydroelectric power industry. Jokkmokk and the 12 hydroelectric plants that lie nearby produce as much as 25% of all the electricity used in Sweden. Most residents of the town were born here, except for a very limited number of urban refugees from Stockholm.

ESSENTIALS

GETTING THERE   By Plane   The nearest airport is in Luleå, 123 miles away (see "Getting There" in the "Luleå" section, above, or call **SAS** at ☎ **020/727-000**). From Luleå, you can take a bus the final leg of the journey.

By Train   There is one train per day from Stockholm to Jokkmokk, but you must change trains at Östersund. For rail information and schedules, call ☎ **020/75-75-75.**

By Bus   There is one scheduled bus per day from Luleå to Jokkmokk, which is timed to meet the plane's arrival. For information, call ☎ **0200/21818.**

By Car   From Luleå, take Route 97 northwest.

VISITOR INFORMATION   Contact the **Jokkmokk Turistbyrå,** at Stortorget 4 (☎ **0971/121-40**), open mid-June to mid-August, daily from 8am to 5pm; mid-August to mid-June, Monday through Friday from 8:30am to 4pm.

SEEING THE SIGHTS

The Lapps (Sami) hold an ✪ **annual market** here in early February, when they sell their local handcrafts. "The Great Winter Market" is a 400-year-old tradition. Held on the first weekend (Thursday through Sunday) of each February, it attracts some 30,000 people, not just to buy and sell, but also for the special experience of the place. If you're planning to come, you'll need to make hotel reservations a year in advance.

Salmon fishing is possible in the town's central lake, and although locals jump in the river in summer to take a dip, we suggest you watch from the sidelines unless you're a polar bear.

A Quick Stop

If you're traveling from Luleå on Route 97 toward Jokkmokk, consider stopping at Boden. Founded in 1809, this is Sweden's oldest garrison town. After losing Finland to Russia, and fearful of a Russian invasion, Sweden built this fortress to protect its interior region. Visit the Garrionmuseet (Garrison Museum), which has exhibits on military history as well as many uniforms and weapons used throughout Sweden's history.

Karl IX decreed that the winter meeting place of the Jokkmokk Sami would be the site of a market and church. The first church, built in 1607, was known as the **Lapp Church.** A nearby hill, known as **Storknabben,** has a cafe from which, if the weather is clear, the midnight sun can be seen for about 20 days in midsummer.

Because Jokkmokk is the center of Sami culture in this area, an important establishment is the national Swedish Mountain and Sami Museum ✪ **Ájtte,** Kyrkogatan (☎ **0971/170-70**), in the center of town. This museum (whose Sami name translates to "storage hut") is one of the largest of its kind; its exhibits integrate nature and the cultures of the Swedish mountain region. A new part of the museum is the **Alpine Garden,** which lies close to the museum on Lappstavägen. If you want to learn about the natural environment and the flora of the north of Sweden, this is the place to go. The mountain flora is easily accessible and beautifully arranged. There's also a restaurant and a gift shop. Museum admission is 40 SEK ($4.40) for adults, free for children 16 and under. The museum is open year-round; in summer, Monday through Friday from 9am to 7pm and Saturday and Sunday from 11am to 6pm; off-season it closes at 4pm.

A JOURNEY BACK IN TIME
Vuollerim. Murjeksvägen 31. ☎ **0976/101-65.** Admission 50 SEK ($5.50). June–Aug, Mon–Fri 9am–6pm; Sept–May, Mon–Fri 9am–4pm. Take Route 97 toward Boden and Luleå 28 miles southeast of Jokkmokk.

This 6,000-year-old winter settlement at the mouth of the Luleå River was created and used by a group of Stone Age people. They eventually abandoned this site, probably in search of better hunting grounds. They lived by hunting, fishing, and gathering berries and plants. Their abandoned site remained untouched until 1983 when researchers from Umeå found this unique settlement, perhaps the best preserved in northern Europe. The Stone Age dwellings were equipped with a prehistoric heating system, and this winter village was populated by four to eight family groups. Diggings in the area have increased knowledge of the prehistory of northern Sweden. Visitors can see a full-size replica of the dwelling, and a cafe on site is surrounded by an exhibition of objects found during the excavations. A slide display offers a journey through thousands of years. The museum with other Stone Age exhibits can be visited.

OUTDOOR & ADVENTURE
Exploring conditions are optimal from mid-June to mid-August; you (and, unfortunately, the mosquitoes) will find the area most accessible at this time. The best way to tackle the region is to first consult the tourist office (see above). They will help you with maps and advice about how to see some of the best of the surrounding wilderness, and advise visitors about local conditions.

You can **hike** to the mighty **Muddus Fall** in the deep ravine of the Muddus River. Trips are conducted June 2 to August 24, daily from 9am to 5pm; they last about 8 hours and cover a distance of some 8 miles. The price, including food, guide, and transportation, is 550 SEK ($60.50) for adults, 200 SEK ($22) for ages 7 to 15, and 150 SEK ($16.50) for those 6 and under. For more information, call ☎ 0971/122-20.

At nearby **Lake Talvatissjön** you can catch Arctic char and rainbow trout (if you're lucky). Visit the tourist office for a *fiskekort* (fishing permit). Prices were not available at press time, but they'll probably be around $10. At the lake is a cleaning table for the fish, and a fireplace or grill in case you'd like to cook your catch.

Jokkmokk also offers **white-water rafting** at **Pärläven,** a river just to the west of town. Call **Äventyarna** at ☎ 0971/12696 for information. The cost of a white-water adventure is 350 SEK ($38.50), with safety equipment provided. All details, including the place to meet, are arranged over the phone.

SHOPPING

At **Jokkmoks Tenn,** Sigurd Åhman (☎ 0971/554-20), you will find the best collection of Sami traditional handcrafts. A workshop here is carried on as a family business. The best buys are in pewter objects and Lapp jewelry. If you'd like a selection of tough and durable clothing for winter, head for **Polstjärnan Atelje,** Hantverkaregatan 9 (☎ 0971/126-73). At **Jokkmokks Stencenter,** Talvatis (☎ 0971/122-35), rocks and minerals from the surrounding region are turned into beautiful jewelry and other items. Some of their offerings include mylonite, which is warm and colorful in red-black shades; unakite, in pink and green with flower patterns; quartzite, with various patterns and colors; gabbro, which is black with golden flakes of pyrite, and hornfels in a soft brown, almost beige color. You can tour through the workshop here Monday through Friday in July from 10am to 3pm; at other times by appointment.

WHERE TO STAY

✪ **Hotel Jokkmokk.** Box 85, Solgatan 24, S-262 23 Jokkmokk. ☎ **0971/777-00.** Fax 0971/556-25. 75 units. TV TEL. Mid-June to mid-Aug and Fri–Sat year-round, 775 SEK ($85.25) double; rest of year, 1,329 SEK ($146.20) double. Rates include breakfast. AE, DC, MC, V. Free parking.

The largest and best-appointed hotel in town was built in the mid-1980s just north of the edge of Lake Talvatis, near the town center. Designed in a modern format that includes simple, boxy lines and lots of varnished hardwoods, it offers clean, well-organized, and comfortable shelter against the sometimes savage climate, and all the well-upholstered comforts of a big-city hotel. (Part of that feeling derives from the fact that some of its staff and managers are urban refugees from the Swedish capital, who moved here to get closer to the great outdoors.) Bedrooms have big windows overlooking the lake, the forest, and in some cases, the lakeside road. All have comfortable beds, fresh colors inspired by a Scandinavian springtime, and bathrooms with plenty of very welcome hot water. Six of the units are designated as "ladies' rooms"—especially

---

Chillin' in Jokkmokk

Jokkmokk is one of the coldest places in Sweden in winter, with temperatures plunging below −30°F for days at a time. In the winter, the cold weather forces the Lapp Church to inter corpses in wall vaults until the spring thaw will permit burial in the ground.

feminine bedrooms adorned with pastels and florals. The hotel contains an indoor swimming pool, a sauna with an exercise area, a bar, and the best restaurant in town, which is recommended separately in "Where to Dine" (see below).

Hotell Gästis. Harrevägen 1, S-96 231 Jokkmokk. ☎ **0971/100-12.** Fax 0971/100-44. 20 units. TV TEL. 500–795 SEK ($55–$87.45) double. Rates include breakfast. AE, DC, MC, V. Free parking.

This landmark hotel, dating from 1932, is in the exact center of the town, about 200 yards from the rail station. In some respects it has the qualities of a frontier-country hotel. On offer are well-maintained bedrooms with modern furnishings and good beds. Floors are either carpeted or covered in vinyl. The restaurant has won many awards and serves well-prepared meals, including continental dishes and *husmanskost* (good home cooking). Entertainment and dancing are presented once a week. The sauna is free for all hotel guests.

WHERE TO DINE

The Restaurant in the Hotel Jokkmokk. Solgatan 24. ☎ **0971/553-20.** Reservations recommended. Main courses 145–185 SEK ($15.95–$20.35). AE, DC, MC, V. Daily 5–11pm. SWEDISH/LAPPISH.

There's not a great variety of restaurant options in Jokkmokk, but you'll find the best evening dining in town in this well-managed hotel dining room. Within a carpeted room with laminated ceiling beams and a sweeping row of windows overlooking the lake, you'll enjoy rich and flavorful specialties whose ingredients are found in the surrounding Lappish terrain. Specialties include a "Jokkmokk pan" that consists of a mixture of cubed reindeer filet, mushrooms, onions, and potatoes, bound together in an herb-flavored cream sauce and served in a copper chafing dish brought directly to the table. Other unusual choices include local freshwater char with saffron sauce and mashed potatoes or filet of elk with forest mushroom sauce.

6 Kvikkjokk

689 miles N of Stockholm, 60 miles W of Gällivare, 107 miles W of Luleå, 74 miles NW of Jokkmokk

Kvikkjokk was a silver-ore center in the 17th century, and many historical relics from that period can be seen in the area today. Today, this mountain village is known as one of Lapland's most beautiful resorts, and serves as the gateway to **Sarek National Park,** the largest wilderness area in Europe and one of the most representative of the highland regions. It's virtually inaccessible, almost entirely without trails, huts, or bridges. Nevertheless, the flora and fauna are fascinating, and the park as a whole is a richly rewarding experience for the dedicated outdoor adventurer.

ESSENTIALS

GETTING THERE   By Train & Bus   Take the train to Jokkmokk (see above), from which you must change to a bus to Kvikkjokk. For rail information and schedules, call ☎ **020/75-75-75.** There are two buses per day running between Jokkmokk and Kvikkjokk, a distance of 74 miles. Unfortunately, the buses don't always connect with train arrivals from Stockholm. For schedules, call ☎ **0200/21818.**

By Car   Take E4 north from Stockholm to Luleå, then head northwest along Route 97 through Boden to Jokkmok. To get there from Jokkmokk, drive north on Route 45. After passing the town of Vaikijaur, turn west on a secondary road, following the signs to Klubbudden. Continue west on this road, passing through the towns of Tjåmotis, Njavve, and Arrenjarka until you reach Kvikkjokk.

VISITOR INFORMATION   The tourist office at Jokkmokk (see above) can provide data about the area.

EXPLORING THE WILDERNESS

The ✪ **Sarek National Park,** between the Stora and Lilla Luleälv, covers an area of 750 square miles, with about 100 glaciers and 87 mountains rising more than 5,900 feet (8 are more than 6,500 feet). The most visited valley, **Rapadel,** opens onto Lake Laidaure. In winter, sled dogs pull people through this valley.

In 1909, Sweden established this nature reserve in the wilderness so that it could be preserved for future generations. To take a mountain walk through the entire park would take at least a week; most visitors stay only a day or two. Although rugged and beautiful, Sarek is considered extremely difficult for even the most experienced of hikers. There is absolutely nothing here to aid the visitor—no designated hiking trails, no tourist facilities, no cabins or mountain huts, and no bridges over rivers (whose undertows, incidentally, are very dangerous). Mosquitoes can be downright treacherous, covering your eyes, nose, and ears. You should explore the park only if you hire an experienced guide. Contact a local hotel such as **Kvikkjokk Fjällstation,** below, for a recommendation.

Kvikkjokk, at the end of Route 805, is the starting or finishing point for many hikers using the **Kungsleden Trail.** Call the **Svenska Turistforeningen** at ☎ 08/463-21-00 for information and also see "Abisko," below. One- or two-day outings can be made in various directions. Local guides also can lead you on an interesting boat trip (inquire at the hotel listed below). The boat will take you to a fascinating delta where the Tarra and Karnajokk rivers meet. The area also is good for canoeing.

WHERE TO STAY & DINE

Kvikkjokk Fjällstation. S-962 02 Kvikkjokk. ☎ **0971/210-22.** 18 units, none with bathroom. 200 SEK ($22) per person. AE, MC, V. Closed Sept 15–Mar 15. Free parking.

Originally established in 1907 by the Swedish Touring Club, and enlarged with an annex in the 1960s, this mountain chalet offers simple, no-frills accommodations for hikers, hill-walkers, and rock-climbers. It's also the headquarters for a network of guides who operate canoe and hiking trips into the vast wilderness areas that fan out on all sides. Accommodations are functional, woodsy, and basic, and include eight double rooms, eight four-bed rooms, and two cabins with four beds each. There's a sauna, a plain restaurant, and access to canoe rentals and a variety of guided tours that depart at frequent intervals. The chalet is open only in summer. For information about the Kvikkmokk Fjällstation out of season, call the **tourist information office** in Jokkmokk (80 miles away) at ☎ **0971/121-40.**

7 Gällivare

60 miles N of the Arctic Circle, 744 miles N of Stockholm

As a city that is one of the most important sources of iron ore in Europe, Gällivare has a grim, industrial look to much of its landscape. Traditionally, it has been a rather dour mining town, despite its location at the center of some of the great unspoiled wonders of Europe. Not until the recent advent of the Dundret Hotel's (see "Where to Stay & Dine," below) high-energy marketing efforts had this town been involved with resort-style sports.

This is a land of contrasts, from high mountain peaks to deep mines. We like to visit Gällivare mainly to explore some of the national parks, which range from a primeval forest at Muddus to panoramic scenery at Stora Sjöfjället. If you come in winter, the northern lights and may persuade you to extend your visit.

ESSENTIALS

GETTING THERE   By Plane   There are two direct flights per day from Stockholm. There also are several commuter planes daily through Umeå to the Lapland Airport at Gällivare. Call **SAS** (☎ 020/727-000) for information and schedules.

By Train   The night train from Stockholm leaves about midday, allowing you to wake up in Gällivare in the morning in time for breakfast. For information and schedules, call ☎ 020/75-75-75.

By Bus   The **Regional Express** has convenient daily runs that link Gällivare with Luleå, Ostersund, and Narvik in Norway. For information and schedules, call ☎ 0200/21818.

By Car   From Jokkmokk, continue northeast along Route 45.

VISITOR INFORMATION   Tourist Information, Storgaan 16 (☎ 0970/166-60), is open June to mid-August, daily 9am to 8pm; the rest of the year, Monday through Friday 9am to 4pm.

FROM MOUNTAINS TO MINES

Many visitors, especially those from Stockholm, come for the winter skiing. Often national ski teams from abroad come here for training, as the town itself lies only a 10-minute drive from the ski slopes and trails. Snow is virtually guaranteed here earlier than anywhere else in Sweden from late October to late April. In fact, the ski season is Sweden's longest—200 days of the year.

The Dundret Hotel (see "Where to Stay & Dine," below) owns all the lifts, and controls access to the slopes and other ski-related infrastructures in town. Lift tickets cost 145 SEK ($18.55) per day or 365 SEK ($46.70) for 3 days. (Note that these prices are inexpensive when compared to the alpine resorts farther south.)

If you follow Route 45 5 miles south of Gällivare, you'll arrive at **Dundret,** or Thunder Mountain. Many visitors come here to witness the spectacle of the midnight sun, best viewed from June 2 to July 12 at a cafe table on the summit, which is open daily in summer from 9pm to 1am. The ✪ **panoramic view** takes in the iron ore mountain of Malmberget to the north and the peak of another mountain, Kebnekaise, to the northwest. You also can see the national parks of Sarek and Padjelanta to the west. Even the valley of the Lule River with the mountains of Norway in the backdrop can be viewed on a clear night.

Many visitors come here to take **mine tours,** which can be booked at the tourist office. There are two different tours, both offered only from June to August. One goes to an underground iron ore mine Monday through Friday at 10am and 2pm, and costs 180 SEK ($19.80); the other visits a copper mine Monday through Friday at 2pm, and costs 160 SEK ($17.60). The latter tour always takes in **Kåkstan,** which is the shanty town in Malmberget, dating from 1888 when jobs were plentiful and wages high, but housing was scarce. As a result, the town of Malmberget came into being, with dwellings of every shape and size.

The iron mine tour of **Gruvtur** takes 3 hours and also visits the Gruvmuseet (mining museum), which displays artifacts from 250 years of mining. You also can visit various production sites and go underground to the ore face. The copper mine tour lasts 3½ hours, beginning at the shanty town and going on to an open-cast mine at Aitik. This is the largest copper mine still operating in Europe, and it's also Sweden's largest gold mine, producing 2 tons of gold annually.

EXPLORING THE NATIONAL PARKS

Many visitors come to Gällivare in the summer to explore the national parks. Various little unmarked roads (open in summer only) west of Gällivare will take you through the parks; but the best way to visit them is to ask the tourist office to pinpoint a tour route for you (a wonderful service) that takes your time and stamina into account. They also can give you up-to-date road conditions, supply maps, answer questions, and advise you on the best ways to experience the parks.

If you plan serious hiking, write (they don't accept calls) the **National Council on Mountain Safety,** Fjällsäkerhetsrådet at Naturvardsverket, S-171 85, Solna.

MUDDUS NATIONAL PARK

Muddus, south of Gällivare, is one of Sweden's most spectacular parks. Fortunately, it also is the park most often recommended to beginners or less experienced hikers. It's always best to check locally before starting out on any exploration deep into the wilderness, but some general guidelines are as follows: During May and early June the ground at Muddus is most often boggy and wet because of rapid snow melt. Conditions are best in July and early August, but keep in mind that summers are short, and the weather conditions changeable. It can be hot and sunny at Muddus one hour and raining the next. By mid-August snow could be falling.

Essentially, Muddus consists of marshland and forest (mostly pine) in the area between Gällivare and Jokkmokk. It's worth exploring some of its 121,000 acres, which house bears, moose, otters, wolverines, and many bird species. In summer, you may spot grazing reindeer or perhaps a whooper swan. The Muddusjokk River flows through the park, providing a panoramic 140-foot waterfall. Trails also cross the park; they're well marked and lead visitors to the most scenic spots.

If you have time only to sample the park's beauty, and don't plan extensive in-depth penetration of the forest, you can explore the western edges of Muddus, which skirt Route 45 as it goes north from Gällivare. The best approach is to leave Route 45 at Liggadammen. Even if you don't have a car, there are several buses per day in summer running from Gällivare to Liggadammen. Once here you'll see a trail leading to Skaite. You can follow this trail for a couple of hours, and once at Skaite, you can take an extensive hiking trail that stretches for 31 miles. This well-marked trail has cabins along the way plus a campsite by Muddus Falls, which is the most beautiful part of this national park.

STORA SJÖFÄLLET & PADJELANTA

Stora Sjöfället, along with Padjelanta National Park (see below), comprise 3,245 miles, making it Europe's largest national park. Padjelanta demands more mountain hiking experience than Stora Sjöfället. The forests here contain many of the same species as the alpine area, but there also are blue hare, moose, fox, ermines, squirrels, otters, martens, and lynx. The most common fish are trout, alpine char, grayling, burbot, and whitefish. Reindeer breeding is carried on throughout the year in both parks, with about 125 reindeer breeders owning a total of 25,000 animals. During spring, summer, and autumn, most Lapps live in these mountains at about seven settlements, which include Ritjem and Kutjaure.

Lake Virihaure in Padjelanta National Park often is called Sweden's most beautiful lake. Both parks contain marked hiking trails, and overnight accommodations are available in cabins—mainly Lapp huts and cottages. Good hiking equipment, including a tent, is advisable if you're planning a long hike through either park. Huts are just basic cabins with a roof and four walls—you'll have to bring a sleeping bag. They generally have summer-only toilets. Cottages vary, but may have beds (you provide your own sleeping bag) and cooking facilities. They also have toilets (but a shower is rare). Hikers usually just crash at huts, but cottages should be reserved. You should call the **Swedish Touring Club** (☎ 08/463-21-00) before you go.

You can **fish** in Padjelanta with a permit (contact any tourist office), but not in Stora Sjöfället.

WHERE TO STAY & DINE

✪ **Dundret.** P.O. Box 82, S-982 21 Gällivare. ☎ **0970/145-60.** Fax 0970/148-28. 35 units; 90 self-catering cottages with kitchen. TV TEL. Year-round 1,140 SEK ($125.40) double. Rate includes breakfast. 990–1,140 SEK ($108.90–$125.40) 4-bed cottage, with linens. Breakfast 70 SEK ($7.70) extra per person. A 1-time final cleaning fee costs 400 SEK ($44), regardless of the length of your stay in a cottage. AE, DC, MC, V. From Gällivare's center, drive 2 miles north, following the signs of Jokkmokk.

Although Gällivare contains about a half dozen other hotels and guest houses, this is the only one that caters to ecology lovers, sports enthusiasts, and anyone interested in direct, firsthand exposure to Lapland's great outdoors. It dates from the 1920s, when some mountain huts on nearby peaks were the site of ski competitions for national athletic groups, but the main building as you'll see it today was constructed in the 1950s, with frequent improvements and enlargements ever since. Known fondly by the staff as Björn Fälten (the Bear Trap), it's the longest log-built building in Europe, with all the idiosyncratic and rustic touches you'd expect.

Since it was founded, many of the developments at this resort have involved the construction and maintenance of 90 cottages, each of them built of wood and outfitted in a rustic style appropriate to the far north. Each has a kitchen, holds up to four people, and receives a minimum of time and attention from the staff once the occupants have checked in. Preferable are the conventional hotel rooms; each receives daily maid service and is outfitted in a cozy, modern style that includes views over the surrounding wilderness; lots of heat and warmth; and comfortable chairs, beds, and small sofas. Bathrooms in both cottages and hotel rooms are very compact, but they are well kept with up-to-date plumbing.

Dining/Diversions: We like the main restaurant, Björn Fälen. Set within the hotel's main building, it's open daily for lunch and dinner and is the most comprehensive and formal restaurant at the resort. The Snow Brasserie (a hamburger joint where you can get something to eat without even removing your skis) and the Snow Bistro (a rustic, wood-sheathed site for informal meals on the slopes, adjacent to a roaring fireplace) are busy throughout the winter. After-ski conviviality is a feature within any of several bars on the premises, one of which specializes in Scottish single malts. The Restaurant Idet serves only pizzas and platters of Swedish game, especially elk, moose, and salmon. "Number Five," a mountainside chalet that was built in 1937 as a lookout post for the Swedish army, now functions as a daytime cafe (October through May only) for skiers. The hotel's main building contains a disco for late-night dancing throughout the year.

Amenities: The resort's first chair lift, inaugurated in 1955, was the first in Sweden. Rebuilt in 1978 and supplemented with another since then, both lead to at least a dozen well-maintained downhill slopes of varying degrees of difficulty. Six of these are illuminated for use throughout the long, dark winter. There's also a small-scale ski jump, a health and fitness center with a limited array of spa facilities, and a very attractive log-sided room that contains a heated indoor pool; facilities for snowboarding; and Snowland, a child-care and entertainment facility designed to interest and amuse young children, presumably while their parents take time out for themselves. (A regular sight here are snow bears inspired by the characters at Disney who ride with young children in motorized sleighs.) Kiosks and sports shops rent and sell ski equipment and accessories. The staff is adept at arranging snow-scooter safaris, ice-fishing, dog team trips, junkets on sleighs pulled by reindeer, overnight stays in a Lapp tent, and outdoor barbecues, regardless of the season. They also can arrange for visits to remote mountain streams where you can catch graylings. The schools of graylings found in this part of Sweden are the largest concentration of this type of fish in Europe.

8 Kiruna

120 miles N of Jokkmokk, 818 miles N of Stockholm

Covering more than 3,000 square miles, Kiruna is the largest (in terms of geography) city in the world. Its extensive boundaries incorporate both Kebnekaise Mountain and Lake Torneträsk. This northernmost town in Sweden lies at about the same latitude as Greenland. The midnight sun can be seen here from mid-May to mid-July.

ESSENTIALS

GETTING THERE   **By Plane**   **SAS** (☎ 020/727-000) flies three times daily from Stockholm (flight time: 95 minutes).

By Train   Two or three trains per day make the 16-hour trip to Gällivare, a major rail junction. From here, you can change trains to Kiruna, a trip of 1½ hours. For schedules and information, phone ☎ 020/75-75-75.

By Bus   There's also daily bus service between Gällivare and Kiruna. Contact **Länstrafiken** at ☎ 0926/756-80.

By Car   From Gällivare, continue northwest along E10.

VISITOR INFORMATION   Contact the **Kiruna Turistbyrå,** Lars Janssons Vagen 17 (☎ 0980/188-80), open June 15 to August 20, daily from 9am to 6pm; August 21 to June 14, Monday through Friday from 9am to 4pm.

SEEING THE SIGHTS

Kiruna, which emerged at the turn of the century, owes its location to the nearby deposits of iron ore. Guided tours of the mines are offered year-round (children 9 and under are not permitted on these tours). Visitors are taken through an underground network of tunnels and chambers. For details on the tours, contact **LKAB Mining Company,** LKAB, S 981 86 Kiruna (☎ 980/710 16).

Southeast of the railroad station, the tower of the **Stadshus** (☎ 0980/70-496) dominates Kiruna. The building was designed by Arthur von Schmalensee and inaugurated in 1963. A carillon of 23 bells rings out at noon and 6pm daily. This cast-iron tower was designed by Bror Markland; note the unusual door handles of reindeer horn and birch. The interior draws upon materials from around the world: a mosaic floor from Italy, walls of handmade brick from The Netherlands, and pine from the American Northwest. Note also the hand-knotted hanging entitled *Magic Drum from Rautas,* a stunning work by artist Sven Xet Erixon. The upper part of the hanging depicts the midnight sun. Inside there's an art collection and some Sami handcraft exhibits. It's open June through August, Monday through Friday from 9am to 6pm and Saturday and Sunday from 10am to 6pm; September through May, Monday through Friday from 9am to 5pm.

A short walk up the road will take you to the ✪ **Kiruna Kyrka** (☎ 0980/101-40), open in summer daily from 8am to 10pm (in July, from 9am to 5pm). This church was constructed like a stylized Sami tent in 1912 (indeed, the dark timber interior does evoke a Lapp hut), an origami design of rafters and wood beams. Gustaf Wickman designed this unusual church, which has a free-standing bell tower supported by 12 props. Christian Eriksson designed the gilt bronze statues standing sentinel around the roofline. They represent such states of mind as shyness, arrogance, trust, melancholy, and love. Above the main door of the church is a relief depicting groups of Lapps beneath the clouds of heaven. This, too, is Eriksson's creation. The altarpiece by Prince Eugen evokes Paradise as a Tuscan landscape, a rather inappropriate image for this part of the world. Eriksson also created the cross depicting Lapps praying and, at its base, a metal sculpture entitled "St George and the Dragon."

You also can visit **Hjalmar Lundbohmsgården** (☎ 0980/701-10), the official museum of the city of Kiruna. It's situated in a manor house built in 1899 by the city's founder and owner of most of the region's iron mines, Hjalmar Lundbohm. Many of the museum's exhibits deal with the city's origins in the late 19th century, the economic conditions in Europe that made its growth possible, and the personality of the entrepreneur who persuaded thousands of Swedes to move north to work in the mines. It's open June through August, daily from 10am to 6pm; off-season, you must phone ahead for opening hours, which could be any day of the week between the hours of noon and 6pm. Admission is 30 SEK ($3.30) for adults, and free for children.

VISITING SWEDEN'S HIGHEST MOUNTAIN

Fifty miles away from the commercial center of town, the highest mountain in Sweden, **Kebnekaise Mountain,** rises 6,965 feet above sea level. To reach the mountain (a trip best made in late June to mid-August; from mid-August to September, whether you can make the trip depends entirely on weather conditions), take a bus to **Aroksjokk** village from the bus stop in Kiruna's center (no phone). Ask for schedules at the train station next door where there is usually somebody on duty, or check with the Kiruna Tourist Office. From **Aroksjokk** village, a motorboat will take you to the Lapp village of **Nikkaluokta.** From here, it's a 13-mile hike (including another short boat trip) to the foot of the mountain. The trail is signposted at various points and runs along streams, and through meadows and pinewoods. Some of the Sami in the village of Nikkaluokta will offer you their services as a guide on the hike; negotiate the fee depending on the time of the year and the number of your party. You do not have to seek them out; once you arrive at Nikkaluokta, they will come to you, eager to assist. The Samis also can arrange overnight stays and hikes or boating trips. The Swedish Touring Club has a mountain station at Kebnekaise, and the station guide here can arrange group hikes to the summit (requiring about 4 hours for the ascent). It's a fairly easy climb for those in good physical shape; no mountaineering equipment is necessary. *Note:* It also is possible to ski on Kebnekaise mountain in winter; it's best to consult the tourist board for more information.

SHOPPING

About 2½ miles north of Kiruna along highway E10 is a showcase of Lappish artifacts, **Mattarahkka** (☎ 0980/191-91). Established in 1993, it's a log house capped proudly with the red, blue, yellow, and green Sami flag. The site includes workshops where visitors can watch traditional Sami products (knives, leather knapsacks, hats, gloves, and tunics) being made. Many of the items are for sale. The interior includes a simple cafe. The site is open from late June to August daily from 10am to 6pm; off-season, Monday through Friday from noon to 6pm.

WHERE TO STAY

Jukkasjärvi Wärdshus och Hembygdsgård at Jukkasjärvi also rents accommodations (see "Where to Dine," below).

Hotel Kebne. Konduktogrsatan 7, S-981 34 Kiruna. ☎ **0980/123-80.** Fax 0980/681-81. 54 units. TV TEL. June 15–Aug 15, 595 SEK ($65.45) double. Aug 16–June 14, Sun–Thurs 1,075 SEK ($118.25) double; Fri–Sat 595 SEK ($65.45) double. Rates include breakfast. AE, DC, MC, V. Free parking.

Located next to the police station on the main road passing through Kiruna (airport buses stop at the door), this hotel consists of two separate buildings, both constructed around 1911 and radically renovated in 1984 and 1987, respectively. The bedrooms are modern and comfortable, each decorated in a bland international style, with room service available until 11pm. The hotel also operates one of the best restaurants in Kiruna. Open only for breakfast and dinner, there's a two-course, fixed-price menu for 129 SEK ($14.20), which some visitors tout as the best evening bargain in town.

Scandic Hotel Ferrum. Lars Janssongatan 15, S-981 21 Kiruna. ☎ **0980/39-86-00.** Fax 0980/39-86-11. E-mail: ferrum@scandic-hotels.se. 170 units. TV TEL. June 17–Aug 14, 790 SEK ($86.90) double. Aug 15–June 16, Sun–Thurs 1,740 SEK ($191.40) double; Fri–Sat 790 SEK ($86.90) double. Rates include breakfast. AE, DC, MC, V. Closed Dec 23–26. Parking 75 SEK ($8.25).

Run by the Scandic chain, this hotel is named after the iron ore (*ferrum*) for which Kiruna is famous. The six-story hotel was built in 1967 and is one of the tallest buildings in town. Functional and standardized in design, it's one of your best bets for lodging and food. It has two well-run restaurants, Reenstiern and Mommas, a steakhouse, plus a cocktail bar and a small casino. The bedrooms are modern, monochromatic, and comfortably furnished with excellent beds. Rooms are available for people with disabilities and for guests with allergies. The hotel's top floor has conference rooms, a sauna, solarium, and exercise room.

Vinter Hotell Palatset. P.O. Box 18, Järnvägsgatan 18, S-981 21 Kiruna. ☎ **0980/ 677-70.** Fax 0980/130-50. www.kiruna.se/~vinterp. E-mail: vinterp@kiruna.se. 20 units. TV TEL. Mid-June to mid-Aug and Fri–Sat year-round, 590–790 SEK ($64.90–$86.90) double; rest of year, 890–1,290 SEK ($97.90–$141.90) double. Rates include breakfast. AE, DC, MC, V. Free parking.

This hotel occupies what originally was built in 1904 as a private home for a prosperous entrepreneur in the iron-ore industry. Radically renovated and upgraded in 1989 and 1990, it includes the main, much-improved house, a 1950s-era annex containing four of the hotel's 20 rooms, a sauna/solarium complex, and a bar with an open fireplace. There's also a dining room, frequented mostly by other residents of the hotel, that serves rib-sticking Swedish food. Bedrooms are high-ceilinged, dignified looking, and outfitted with hardwood floors, comfortable modern furniture, and good beds. Bathrooms are quite small.

WHERE TO DINE

☉ Jukkasjärvi Wärdshus och Hembygdsgård. Jukkasjärvi, Marknadsvägen 63, S-981 91 Kiruna. ☎ **0980/668-42.** Reservations recommended. Fixed-price lunch 95 SEK ($10.45); main courses 175–235 SEK ($19.25–$25.85). AE, DC, MC, V. SWEDISH.

Set 10 miles east of the center of Kiruna, this is the best independent restaurant in the district, and the one that's frequently cited as a culinary beacon within the rest of Swedish Lapland. Set within what was built in the 1850s as a clapboard-sided retirement home for aging and ailing Lapps, it contains room for 80 diners at a time, and a venue that takes far northern cuisine very, very seriously. Menu items include a devoted use of local ingredients, and include Arctic char with apple cider sauce, filet of reindeer with Arctic shiitake mushrooms, fresh-caught Arctic salmon with lemon sauce, and a succulent filet of beef with garlic-flavored yogurt sauce. Expect wild berries (especially cloudberries), herring (many varieties), dried and smoked meats, reindeer in season, and mushrooms from the fields along with salted fish.

On the premises is a separate building that's responsible for renting about 45 cottages, each with a kitchen; no maid or maintenance service is associated with the rental. They rent, year-round, for 500 SEK ($55) per day, for between one and four occupants.

Holiday on Ice

Since the late 1980s, the most unusual, and most impermanent, hotel in Sweden is recreated early every winter on the frozen steppes near the iron mines of Jukkasjärvi, 125 miles north of the Arctic Circle. Here, the architect Yngve Bergqvist, financed by a group of friends who (not surprisingly) developed the original concept over bottles of vodka in an overheated sauna, uses jackhammers, bulldozers, and chainsaws to fashion a 14-room hotel out of 4,000 tons of densely packed snow and ice. The basic design is that of an igloo, but with endless amounts of whimsical sculptural detail thrown in as part of the novelty. Like Conrad Hilton's worst nightmare, the resulting "hotel" will inevitably buckle, collapse, and then vanish during the spring thaws. Despite its temporary state, during the long and frigid darkness of north Sweden's midwinter, it attracts a steady stream of engineers, theatrical designers, sociologists, and the merely curious, who avail themselves of timely activities in Sweden's far north: dogsled and snowmobile rides, cross-country skiing, and shimmering views of the aurora borealis. On the premises are an enormous reception hall, a multimedia theater, two saunas, and an ice chapel appropriate for simple meditation, weddings, and baptisms.

Available for occupancy (temperatures permitting) between mid-December and sometime in March, the hotel resembles an Arctic cross between an Arabian casbah and a medieval cathedral. Minarets are formed by dribbling water for about a week onto what eventually becomes a slender and soaring pillar of ice. Domes are formed igloo-style out of ice blocks arranged in a curved-roof circle. Reception halls boast rambling vaults supported by futuristic-looking columns of translucent ice, and sometimes whimsical sculptures whose sense of the absurd heightens a venue that visitors describe as surreal. Some of these are angled in ways that amplify the weak midwinter daylight that filters through panes of (what else?) chainsawed ice.

Purists quickly embrace the structure as the perfect marriage of architecture with the environment; sensualists usually admire it hastily before heading off to warmer climes and other, more conventional hotels.

What's the most frequently asked question on the lips of virtually everyone who shows up? "Is it comfortable?" The answer is not particularly; although a

9 Abisko

55 miles NW of Kiruna, 911 miles N of Stockholm

Any resort north of the Arctic Circle is a curiosity; Abisko, on the southern shore of Lake Torneträsk, encompasses a scenic valley, a lake, and an island. An elevator takes passengers to Mount Nuolja (Njulla). Nearby is the protected Abisko National Park, containing remarkable flora, including orchids.

ESSENTIALS

GETTING THERE   By Train & Bus   You can get a train to Kiruna (see above). From here, there are both bus and rail links into Abisko. For train information, call ☎ 0200/21818. For bus information, call ☎ 020/640-640.

By Car   From Kiruna, continue northwest on E10 into Abisko.

VISITOR INFORMATION   Contact the tourist office in Kiruna (see above).

stay probably will enhance your appreciation for the (warm and modern) comforts of conventional housing. Upon arrival, guests are issued thermal jumpsuits of "beaver nylon" whose air-lock cuffs are designed to help the wearer survive temperatures as low as −8°F. Beds are fashioned from blocks of chiseled ice lavishly draped, Eskimo-style, with reindeer skins. Guests keep warm with insulated body bags that were developed for walks on the moon. Other than a temporary escape into the hotel's sauna, be prepared for big chills: Room temperatures remain cold enough to keep the walls from melting. Some claim that this exposure will bolster your immune system so that it can better fight infections when you return to your usual environment.

The interior decor is, as you'd expect, hyperglacial, and loaded with insights into what the world might look like if an atomic war drove civilization underground to confront its stark and frigid destiny. Most rooms resemble a setting from a scary 1950s sci-fi flick, sometimes with an icy version of a pair of skin-draped Adirondack chairs pulled up to the surreal glow of an electric fireplace that emits light but, rather distressingly, no heat. Throughout there's an endearing decorative reliance on whatever bas-reliefs and curios its artisans may have decided to chisel into the ice.

There's lots of standing up at the long countertop crafted from ice that doubles as a bar. What should you drink? Swedish vodka, of course, that's dyed a (frigid) shade of blue and served in cups crafted from ice. Vodka never gets any colder than this.

Interested in this holiday on ice? Contact ✪ **The Ice Hotel,** Jukkas AB, Marknadsvägen 63, S-981 91 Jukkasjärvi, Sweden (☎ **980/668-00;** fax 980/668-90). Doubles cost from 1,700 SEK ($187) per day, including breakfast. Heated cabins, located near the ice palace, are available for 1,480 to 1,680 SEK ($162.80 to $184.80) per night, double. Toilets are available in a heated building next door.

From Kiruna, head east immediately along Route E10 until you come to a signpost marked JUKKASJÄRVI and follow this tiny road northeast for about 1½ miles.

EXPLORING THE AREA

✪ **Abisko National Park** (☎ 0980/40-200), established in 1903, is situated around the Abiskojokk River, including the mouth of the river where it flows into Lake Torneträsk. This is a typical alpine valley with a rich variety of flora and fauna. The highest mountain is Slåttatjåkka, 3,900 feet above sea level. Slightly shorter Njulla, which rises 3,800 feet, has a cable car. The name "Abisko" is a Lapp word meaning "ocean forest." The park's proximity to the Atlantic gives it a maritime character, with milder winters and cooler summers than the more continentally influenced areas east of the Scandes or Caledonian Mountains.

Abisko is more easily accessible than **Vadvetjåkka National Park,** the other, smaller park in the area. Three sides of Vadvetjåkka Park are bounded by water that is difficult to wade through, and the fourth side is rough terrain with treacherously slippery slope bogs and steep precipices complete with rock slides. Established in 1920, it lies northwest of Lake Torneträsk, with its northern limits at the Norwegian border. It's composed of mountain precipices and large tracts of bog and delta. It also has rich flora, along with impressive brook ravines. Its highest mountain is Vadvetjåkka, with a southern peak at 3,650 feet above sea level.

Abisko is one of the best centers for watching the **midnight sun,** which can be seen from June 13 to July 4. It's also the start of the longest marked trail in the world, the Kungsleden.

The ✪ **Kungsleden (Royal Trail)** may just prove to be the hike of a lifetime; this approximately 210-mile trail journeys through Abisko National Park to Riksgränsen on the Norwegian frontier cutting through Sweden's highest mountain (Kebnekaise) on the way. Properly fortified and with adequate camping equipment, including a sleeping bag and food, you can set out to walk these trails, which tend to be well maintained and clearly marked. Cabins and rest stops (local guides refer to them as "fell stations") are spaced a day's hike (8 to 13 miles) apart, so you'll have adequate areas to rest between bouts of trekking and hill climbing. These huts provide barely adequate shelter from the wind, rain, snow, and hail in case the weather turns turbulent, as it so often does in this part of the world. At most of the stops you cook your own food and clean up before leaving. Most lack running water, although there are some summer-only toilets. At certain points, the trail crosses lakes and rivers, where boats will be found for that purpose. The trail actually follows the old nomadic paths of the Lapps. Those with less time or energy will find the trail broken up into several smaller segments.

The trail is long but relatively easy to walk along. All the streams en route are traversed by bridges. In places where the ground is marshy, it has been overlaid with wooden planks. In summer, you'll often encounter locals who operate boat services on some of the lakes you'll encounter along the way. Often, they'll rent you a rowboat or canoe from a makeshift kiosk or collapsible tent that's dismantled and hauled away after the first frost.

During the summer, the trail is not as isolated as you may think. It is in fact the busiest hiking trail in Sweden, and adventurers from all over the world can be seen traversing it. The trail is most crowded in July, when the weather usually is most reliable.

For maps and more information about this adventure, contact the local tourist office or the **Svenska Turistförening,** the Swedish Tourist Club, P.O. Box 25, S101 20 Stockholm (☎ 08/463-21-00).

WHERE TO STAY & DINE

Abisko Touriststation. S-98107 24 Abisko. ☎ **0980/402-00.** Fax 0980/401-40. www. stfabosko.com. E-mail: info@abisko.stfturist.se. 77 units, 3 with bathroom; 56 cabin apt. 770 SEK ($84.70) double without bathroom; 910–1,030 SEK ($100.10–$113.30) double with bathroom. Rates include breakfast. Cabin apt 975 SEK ($107.25) per night or 5,425 SEK ($596.75) per week up to 6 occupants. AE, MC, V. Free parking.

Owned by the Swedish Touring Club since 1910, this big, modern hotel about 500 yards from the bus station offers accommodations in the main building, the annex, and within 28 cabins. Each cabin is made up of two apartments suitable for up to six occupants, and each unit features a kitchen and private bathroom. From the hotel you can see the lake and the mountains. The staff is helpful in providing information about excursions. The rooms are basic but reasonably comfortable, and some offer exceptional views.

Northernmost Golf in the World

Here's how to achieve one-upmanship on your golfing pals back home: You can play at the northernmost golf course in the world. The **Arctic Golf Course** has only nine holes, occupying a terrain of mostly thin-soiled tundra with a scattering of birchwood forest. It is open only from mid-June to mid-August. During that limited period, golfers play 24 hours per day, the course lit by the Midnight Sun. For more information, contact Björkliden Arctic Golf Club, Kvarnbacksvägen 28, Bromma S-168 74 (☎ 08/28-94-30). Bromma is a suburb of Stockholm.

CROSSING THE BORDER TO NORWAY

Because Abisko is close to the Norwegian border, you may want to cross into Norway (don't forget your passport!) after your tour of Swedish Lapland. If so, just take E10 west across the border toward Narvik. From Kiruna, trains and buses go to the hamlet of Rigsgrånsen, the last settlement in Sweden, before continuing for the final, short leg to Narvik. Schedules depend entirely on the weather; for buses call ☎ 0200/21818; for trains ☎ 020/75-75-75. However, if you'd like to return to Stockholm, follow E10 east toward the coast, then head south on E4 to the capital city.

Appendix: Sweden in Depth

Roughly the size of California, Sweden has some 174,000 square miles of land mass, bordering Finland to its northeast and Norway to its west. As the northern end creeps over the Arctic Circle, the southern third of Sweden juts into the Baltic Sea. This southern tier is the site of most of the population; much of the north is uninhabited, and occupies one of the last great wildernesses of Europe.

Known for its warm summers and bitterly cold winters, Sweden is a land of lakes and forests, mountains and meadows. Because of generally poor soil and a rocky landscape, Swedes have turned to mining, steel production, and forestry to spur their economy.

Swedes are known for their almost mystical love of nature. Although they travel in winter to escape the cold, they are known as their own greatest tourists when the all-too-brief summer arrives. Many Swedes have second homes in remote parts of the country.

Many visitors heading for history- and monument-rich France or Italy mistakenly think Sweden lacks attractions. This is not the case. Sweden possesses 1,140 historic fortresses, 2,500 open-air runic stones, 25,000 protected Iron Age graveyards, and 10 royal castles around the Stockholm area alone.

As in parts of the American West, you'll encounter one thing in Sweden that is not always available in Europe: the wide-open yonder. Space characterizes Sweden's vast forests, mountains, and national parks. Sometimes you can travel for miles without encountering another soul.

Stockholm is, of course, the major target of nearly all visitors. More than 7 centuries old, it is a regal place, filled with everything from the winding cobbled streets of its medieval district to the marble, glass, and granite of its high-rises in the commercial center. It is a city of serenity, of beautiful buildings, countless shopping opportunities, and sightseeing galore. And no other European capital has such a dramatic landscape as Stockholm's 24,000 islands, skerries, and islets. It is a city designed to delight.

As many other world capitals decay and seem long past their prime, Stockholm grows better with age. No longer as provincial as it was even 15 years ago, today Stockholm is lively, vibrant, and filled with nightlife and great restaurants; along with a sophisticated, savvy population enjoying one of the world's highest standards of living.

But Sweden only begins in Stockholm. At least two other major cities merit exploration: Gothenburg and Malmö. Gothenburg enjoys a dramatic landscape along Sweden's craggy western coastline; this major seaport is filled with tree-lined boulevards, restaurants, museums, endless shopping, elegant buildings, and nightclubs. North of Gothenburg you encounter sleepy fishing harbors in rocky coves and offshore islands where city folk come in summer to retreat.

Southwestern Malmö boasts one of northern Europe's most attractive medieval centers, and also is a good base for exploring the ancient university city of Lund nearby, with its mass of students, a revered 12th-century Romanesque cathedral, medieval streets, and numerous museums.

However grand the cities may be, any native Swede will tell you that the countryside is the chief reason to visit. Our favorite destinations, the folkloric provinces of Dalarna and Värmland, form Sweden's heartland. Filled with forests and vast lakes, this is the landscape of the country's greatest literature. Some towns, especially around Lake Siljan, still look as they did in the Middle Ages. Folk dances and music festivals keep the summer lively.

The ancient province of Skåne in the southwest is called the château country because of all the French-like castles that still dot its landscape of undulating fields and curving, rocky coastline. In spring, black windmills and white churches pose against a background of yellow rape, crimson poppies, and lush green meadows.

For sheer scenic drama, nothing equals Lapland, that remote and isolated region of Europe in the north, home to the Lapps (or Sami) and their reindeer herds. It's a domain of truly awesome proportions. Birch-clad valleys and sprawling woodlands of pine give way to waterfalls, roaring river rapids, mountain plateaus, and fens covered with moss. The numerous rivers of the region snake down from the mountains to spill out into the Gulf of Bothnia, and the locals have long ago accepted and adapted to the hearty lifestyle imposed on them by the weather. Unspoiled nature under the midnight sun is a potent attraction.

Finally, there is the island of Gotland in the Baltic, which knew its heyday in Viking times. This land of beaches, spas, and sailing has a warmer climate than the rest of Sweden. Some 100 churches and chapels still remain on the island, and its capital of Visby is one of the oldest cities of Sweden. Its Old Town wall stretches for 2 miles and is capped by 44 towers, a sight evocative of the Middle Ages with its crenellated turrets and long, thin, arched windows.

Sweden is a country where you can enjoy history and urban pleasures, but the nation's heart and soul can be found in its vast landscapes. From a summer wilderness fragrant with fields of orchids and traversed by wild elk, to the dark wintry landscape dotted by husky sleds and paraskiing, Sweden provides a stunning vacation experience.

1 Sweden Today

Sweden is one of the most paradoxical nations on earth. An essentially conservative country, it is nonetheless a leader in social welfare, prison reform, and equal opportunity for women.

Despite trouble maintaining its once bustling economy, Sweden has long enjoyed some of the highest wages and the best standard of living in Europe. There may be trouble in paradise, but compared with the rest of the world, Sweden is better off than most other nations.

This is a land where the urbane and the untamed are said to live harmoniously. With a population density of only 48 people per square mile, there's ample space for all of Sweden's 8.3 million residents. About 85% of Sweden's citizens live in the southern half of the country. The north is populated by Sweden's two chief minority groups: the Sami (Lapp) and the Finnish-speaking people of the northeast. Among the cities, Stockholm is the political capital, with a population of 1,435,000; Gothenburg, the automobile manufacturing center, has 704,000; and Malmö, the port city, has 458,000.

Once home to an ethnically homogenous society, Sweden has experienced a vast wave of immigration in the past several years. Today, more than 10% of Sweden's residents are immigrants or the children of immigrant parents. Most of this influx is from other Scandinavian countries. Because of Sweden's strong stance on human rights, it also has become a major destination for political and social refugees from Africa and the Middle East. A vast number of immigrants seeking asylum come from the former Yugoslavia.

Sweden's government is a constitutional monarchy supported by a parliamentary government. The royal family functions primarily in a ceremonial capacity. The actual ruling body is a one-chamber parliament, whose members are popularly elected for 3-year terms. The present government is headed by a Social Democrat, Goeran Persson. Because of Sweden's location in the Baltic, it has been active in promoting peace among the warring Baltic states. The country is an active member of the United Nations and was admitted as a full member to the European Union in 1995.

Like other European countries, Sweden's policy of cradle-to-grave welfare has been threatened in recent years. The main topic of debate in the Social Democrat–dominated parliament is how to sustain Sweden's generous welfare system while putting a halt to ever-increasing taxes, currently at 59%. At this time, the state provides health insurance along with many generous family benefits, including an allowance for care providers, 15 months paid parental leave after the birth of a child (divided between both parents), tax-free child allowances, and education stipends for children. When a Swede reaches retirement at age 65, he or she is entitled to a hefty pension that rises with inflation.

Education plays an important role in Sweden. Schools are run by various municipalities, providing free tuition, books, and lunches. Although attendance is mandatory for only 9 years, 90% of Swedes pursue some form of higher education. Adult education and university study are funded by the state.

Sweden's high level of education coincides with its high-tech industrial economy. Although in years past Sweden's economy was based on agriculture, in the latter half of the 20th century industry has become predominant, employing nearly 80% of all Swedish workers. More than 50% of Sweden's exports are composed of heavy machinery including cars, trucks, and telecommunications equipment. Companies such as Saab and Volvo (recently bought by Ford Motor Co.) produce vehicles familiar throughout the world. Despite Sweden's industrial milieu, the country still manages to produce some 80% of its own food.

Although such a highly industrialized nation depends on its factories, Sweden has enacted stringent environmental policies. The task of monitoring the country's environment is the responsibility of local governments. Each of Sweden's 286 municipalities has the right to limit pollutant emissions in its own sector.

The environment has always played an integral role in the lives of Swedes. Sweden has 20 national parks; although these wilderness areas are not regulated by law, Sweden's policy of free access entitles citizens to unlimited admission at no charge.

Another important element is Sweden's strong focus on culture. Over the past 25 years, Swedes have turned their attention to music. Today, young people are purchasing more recorded music and attending more live concerts than they were even a decade ago. Book reading is on the rise (more than 9,000 titles are published in Sweden every year, and Swedes traditionally have had a literacy rate of over 99%), museum attendance has increased, and there's greater interest in the media. The average Swede spends 6 hours per day immersed in some form of mass media (newspapers, magazines, television, radio, and so forth).

Increasingly, Sweden is being pressed to drop its neutrality and to join an expanding NATO. Although it firmly resists that pressure, Sweden has, nonetheless, taken part in Bosnian peacekeeping. Although Sweden has been a member of the European Union since 1995, polls today indicate that it would reject membership if a new election were held.

There is a certain nostalgia sweeping Sweden today, a desire to return to the way life used to be when Sweden was one of the three or four richest countries in the world.

As Sweden moves into the 21st century, its problems continue. For example, businesses can't grow because it's too expensive to hire people. Observers have noted that young Swedes are starting to think internationally, and some of them are leaving Sweden to take positions elsewhere in the global economy. "The people leaving are the very people that Sweden needs the most," one Swedish businessman lamented to the press.

2 The Natural Environment

Sweden stretches about 990 miles from north to south, but it's sparsely populated, with a disproportionate amount of territory lying above the Arctic Circle. Sweden is one of the countries located farthest from the equator. From north to south, Sweden lies at roughly the same latitude as Alaska. Forests cover more than half the land; Sweden is a heavily industrialized nation and less than 10% of its land is used for agriculture.

Sweden can be divided into three main regions: the mountainous northern zone of Norrland; Svealand, the lake-filled, hilly region of central Sweden; and Götaland, the broad plateau in southern Sweden, home of most of the country's agricultural enterprises.

Sweden has more than 100,000 lakes, including Vänern, the largest in western Europe. About 9% of the countryside is covered by lakes, which play an important role in transporting goods from the Baltic ports to cities throughout Sweden and the rest of Scandinavia. Canals link many of these lakes to the sea. The most important of these is the Göta Canal. Constructed in the 19th century, this 370-mile-long canal links Gothenburg in the west to Stockholm in the east. Some 121 miles of canals were constructed to connect the various lakes and rivers that make up this waterway.

Sweden's rivers tend to be short and to empty into one of the numerous lakes. They're used for short-haul transportation, linking the network of lakes, but especially for providing hydroelectric power to fuel the many factories scattered throughout the countryside. The most important rivers are the Pite, the Lule, and the Indal.

Sweden's expansive seacoast is more than 1,550 miles long. The west is bounded by the Kattegat and the Skagerrak, and the east by the Gulf of Bothnia and the Baltic Sea. Numerous small islands and reefs dot the eastern and southwestern coasts. If all the inlets and islands were included, the coastline of Sweden would measure 4,650 miles. Öland and Gotland, Sweden's largest, most populated islands, are situated in the Baltic Sea, off the eastern coast.

❓ Did You Know?

- Sweden ranks second after Finland in coffee consumption per capita worldwide. In 1993, the Swedes consumed 76.8 million kilograms of roast coffee, an average of roughly three to five cups per person, per day.
- Counting all the inlets, promontories, and islands, Sweden has a coastal strip 4,650 miles long—one-fifth of the earth's circumference.
- A survey showed that a large percentage of Americans confuse Sweden and Switzerland.
- Half the couples living together in Sweden are unmarried.
- Sweden has contributed two words to international gastronomy: *smörgåsbord* (smorgasbord in English) and *Absolut.*
- The world's longest smörgåsbord was prepared in Sweden, stretching for 798 yards.
- James Joyce, F. Scott Fitzgerald, George Orwell, Marcel Proust, and Aldous Huxley *did not* win Sweden's Nobel Prize for literature.
- Sweden is one of the five nations that established colonies in North America.

Sweden is a center for alpine activities including skiing, hiking, and glacier walking; most of which take place in the mountainous regions of Norrland. This far-northern area is home to many of the country's highest peaks, including its highest mountain, Kebnekaise, at 6,946 feet.

The flora of Sweden varies with the region. There are five rather disparate zones, each supporting a distinct array of plant life: the tundra in the north, coniferous forests below the timber line, central Sweden's birch forests, coniferous forests in the south, and the beech and oak zones found in the southern regions.

Animal life also differs depending on the region. The countryside teems with bears, elk, reindeer, fox, wolves, and otters. Numerous game birds also make their home in Sweden's expansive forests.

3 History 101

Dateline

- **829** Christianity is introduced by St. Anskar.
- **1008** Pagan Viking king Olaf Skottkonung converts to Christianity.
- **1130–56** King Sverker unites the lands of Svear and Gotar, the heart of today's modern nation.
- **1160** King Eric IX presides over a Christian country and becomes patron saint of Sweden.
- **1248** Birger Jarl abolishes serfdom and founds Stockholm.

continues

THE VIKINGS Although documented by little other than legend, the Viking age (roughly A.D. 700 to 1000) is the epoch that has most captured the attention of the world. Up to then, Sweden had been relatively isolated, although travelers from the south brought some artifacts from different civilizations.

The base of Viking power at the time was the coastal regions around and to the north of what today is Stockholm. Either as plunderers, merchants, or slave traders—perhaps a combination of all three—Swedish Vikings maintained contact with the East, both Russia and Constantinople, and with parts of western Europe, including Britain and Ireland. Swedish Vikings joined their brother Vikings in Norway and Denmark in pillaging, trading with, or conquering parts of Ireland and the British Isles, their favorite targets.

CHRISTIANITY & THE MIDDLE AGES

With the aid of missions sent from Britain and northern Germany, Christianity gradually made headway, having been introduced in 829 by St. Anskar, a Frankish missionary. It did not become widespread, however, until the 11th century. In 1008 Olaf Skottkonung, the ruler of a powerful kingdom in northern Sweden, converted to Christianity, but later in the century the religion came into confusion, with civil wars and a pagan reaction against the converting missionaries.

Ruling from 1130 to 1156, King Sverker united the lands of Svear and Gotar, which later became the heart of modern Sweden. A strong centralized government developed under this king.

Christianity finally became almost universally accepted under Eric IX, who ruled until 1160. He led a crusade to Finland and later became the patron saint of Sweden. By 1164 his son, Charles VII, had founded the first archbishopric at Uppsala. The increasing influence of this new religion led to the death of the Viking slave trade, and many Vikings turned to agriculture as the basis of their economy. A landowning aristocracy eventually arose.

Sweden's ties with the Hanseatic ports of Germany grew stronger, and trade with other Baltic ports flourished at the city of Visby on the island of Gotland. Sweden traded in copper, pelts, iron, and butter, among other products.

Sweden's greatest medieval statesman was Birger Jarl, who ruled from 1248 to 1266; during his reign, he abolished serfdom and founded Stockholm. When his son, Magnus Ladulås, became king in 1275, he granted extensive power to the Catholic Church and founded a hereditary aristocracy.

AN INTRANORDIC UNION

Magnus VII of Norway (1316–1374) was only 3 years old when he was elected to the Swedish throne, but his election signaled a recognition of the benefits of increased cooperation within the Nordic world. During his reign there emerged distinct social classes, including the aristocracy; the Catholic clergy (which owned more than 20% of the land); peasant farmers and laborers; and a commercial class of landowners, foresters, mine-owners, and merchants. The fortunes and power of this last group were based on trade links

- **1319** Magnus VII of Norway unites Sweden with Norway.
- **1350** Black Death sweeps across Sweden.
- **1389** Margaretha rules Sweden, Norway, and Denmark by the Union of Kalmar.
- **1523** Gustavus Vasa founds the Vasa Dynasty.
- **1598** Sigismund deposed after brief union of thrones of Sweden and Poland.
- **1600–11** Karl IX leads Sweden into ill-fated wars with Denmark, Russia, and Poland.
- **1611** Gustavus II Adolphus ascends to the throne; presides over ascension of Sweden as a great European power.
- **1648** Treaty of Westphalia grants Sweden the possessions of Stettin, Bremen, and West Pomerania.
- **1654** Queen Christina abdicates the Swedish throne.
- **1655–97** Long reign of Charles XI renews Sweden's strength.
- **1718** Killed in battle, Charles XII, leader of the Great Northern War, presides over demise of Swedish empire.
- **1746–92** Gustavus III revives the absolute power of the monarchy.
- **1809** Napoléon names Jean Bernadotte as heir to the throne of Sweden.
- **1889** The Social Democratic Party is formed.
- **1905** Sweden grants independence to Norway.
- **1909** Suffrage for all men is achieved.
- **1921** Suffrage for women and an 8-hour workday are established.
- **1940** Sweden declares its neutrality in World War II.
- **1946** Sweden joins the United Nations.

continues

- **1953** Dag Hammarskjöld becomes secretary-general of the United Nations.
- **1973** Karl XVI Gustaf ascends the throne.
- **1986** Olof Palme, prime minister and leader of the Social Democrats, is assassinated.
- **1992** Sweden faces currency crisis.
- **1994** Refugees and the welfare system strain Sweden's budget.
- **1995** Along with Finland and Austria, Sweden is granted full membership in the European Union.
- **1996** Social Democrat Goeran Persson, Sweden's finance minister, is elected prime minister.
- **1997** World headlines link Sweden to past sterilization programs and Nazi gold.
- **1998** Social Democrats remain in power on pledge to continue huge welfare programs.
- **2000** The $3 billion Øresund bridge links Denmark and Sweden for the first time.

with a well-organized handful of trading cities (the Hanseatic League) scattered throughout Germany and along the Baltic coastline. As trade increased, these cities (especially Visby, on the island of Gotland) and their residents flourished, and the power of the Hanseatic League grew.

In 1350, the Black Death arrived in Sweden, decimating the population. This proved to be the greatest catastrophe experienced by the Western world up to that time. Having been imported from Asia, and having wrought havoc in China and Turkistan, it is thought to have spread to Sweden through trade with Britain. The plague seriously hindered Sweden's development, although the country didn't suffer as much as nations such as England.

In 1389, the Swedish aristocracy, fearing the growing power of the Germans within the Hanseatic League, negotiated for an intra-Nordic union with Denmark and the remaining medieval fiefdoms in Norway and Finland. The birth process of this experimental union began in the Swedish city of Kalmar, which gave its name in 1397 to the brief but farsighted Union of Kalmar. A leading figure in its development was the Danish queen Margaretha, who was already queen of Denmark and Norway when the aristocracy of Sweden offered her the throne in 1389. Despite the ideals of the union, it collapsed after about 40 years because of a revolt by merchants, miners, and peasants in defense of Sweden's trade links with the Hanseatic League, coupled with power struggles between Danish and Swedish nobles.

Although the union was a failure, one of its legacies was the establishment—partly as a compromise among different political factions—of a Riksdag (parliament) made up of representatives from various towns and regions; the peasant classes also had some limited representation.

Queen Margaretha's heir (her nephew, Eric of Pomerania; 1382–1459) became the crowned head of three countries (Norway, Denmark, and Sweden). He spent most of his reign fighting with the Hanseatic League. Deposed in 1439, he was replaced by Christopher of Bavaria, whose early death in 1448 led to a major conflict and the eventual dissolution of the Kalmar Union. The Danish king, Christian II, invaded Stockholm in 1520, massacred the leaders who opposed him, and established an unpopular reign; there was much civil disobedience until the emergence of the Vasa dynasty, which expelled the Danes.

THE VASA DYNASTY In May 1520, a Swedish nobleman, Gustavus Vasa, returned from captivity in Denmark and immediately began to plan for the military expulsion of the Danes from Sweden. In 1523 he captured Stockholm from its Danish rulers, won official recognition for Swedish independence, and was elected king of Sweden.

In a power struggle with the Catholic church, he confiscated most church-held lands (vastly increasing the power of the state overnight) and established Lutheranism as the national religion. He commissioned a complete translation of the Bible and other religious works into Swedish, and forcefully put down local uprisings in the Swedish provinces. He established the right of succession for his offspring and decreed that his son, Eric XIV, would follow him as king (which he did in 1543).

Although at first Eric was a wise ruler, his eventual downfall was in part due to his growing conflicts with Swedish noblemen and a marriage to his unpopular mistress, Karin Mansdotter. (Previously, he had unsuccessfully negotiated marriage with the English queen, Elizabeth I.) Eric eventually went insane before being replaced by Johan III.

The next 50 years were marked by Danish plots to regain control of Sweden and Swedish plots to conquer Poland, Estonia, and the Baltic trade routes leading to Russia. A dynastic link to the royal families of Poland led to the ascension of Sigismund (son of the Swedish king Johan III) in Warsaw. When his father died, Sigismund became king of both Sweden and Poland simultaneously. His Catholicism, however, was opposed by Sweden, which expelled him in 1598. He was followed by Karl (Charles) IX (1566–1632), who led Sweden into a dangerous and expensive series of wars with Denmark, Russia, and its former ally, Poland.

By 1611, as Sweden was fighting simply to survive, Gustavus II Adolphus (1594–1632) ascended the throne. Viewed today as a brilliant politician and military leader, he was one of the century's most stalwart Protestants at a time when political alliances often were formed along religious lines. After organizing an army composed mainly of farmers and field hands (financed by money from the Falun copper mines), he secured Sweden's safety, and with his armies penetrated as far south as Bavaria. He died fighting against the Hapsburg emperor's Catholic army near the city of Lützen in 1632.

When he died, his heir and only child, Christina (1626–89), was 6 years old. During her childhood, power was held by the respected Swedish statesman Axel Oxenstierna, who continued the Thirty Years' War in Germany for another 16 years. It finally concluded with the Treaty of Westphalia in 1648. Christina, who did not want to pursue war and had converted to Catholicism (against the advice of her counselors), abdicated the throne in 1654 in favor of her cousin, Charles X Gustav (1622–60).

Ten years after his rise to power, Charles X expelled the Danes from many of Sweden's southern provinces, establishing the Swedish borders along the approximate lines of today. He also invaded and conquered Poland (1655–56), but his territorial ambitions were thwarted by a national uprising. He later defeated the Danes (1657–58), and at the time of his death Sweden was ringed by enemies. Charles X was succeeded by Charles XI (1655–97), whose reign was fiscally traumatic. The endless wars with Denmark (and other kingdoms in northern Germany) continued. However, an even greater problem was the growing power of wealthy Swedish nobles, who had amassed (usually through outright purchase from the cash-poor monarchy) an estimated 72% of Sweden's land. In a bitter and acrimonious process, Charles redistributed the land into approximately equal shares held by the monarchy, the nobles, and Sweden's independent farmers. The position of small landowners has remained secure in Sweden ever since, although the absolute monarch gained increased power. With Charles's new-found wealth, he greatly strengthened the country's military power.

Charles XII (1682–1718) came to the throne at the age of 4 with his mother, the queen, as regent. Denmark, Poland, and Russia allied themselves against Sweden in the Great Northern War, which broke out in 1700. Charles invaded Russia but was defeated; he escaped to Turkey, where he remained a prisoner for

4 years. In 1714, he returned to Sweden to continue fighting, but was killed in 1718. Charles XII presided over the collapse of the Swedish empire.

Under Frederick I (1676–1751) Sweden regained some of its former prestige. The chancellor, Count Arvid Horn (1664–1742), had real power. He formed an alliance with England, Prussia, and France against Russia. The Hattar (Hats) and Mossorna (Caps) were the two opposing parties in the Riksdag then, and the Hats began a war with Russia in 1741. The conflict continued through the reign of the next king, Adolphus Frederick (1710–71). Although he initiated many reforms, encouraged the arts, and transformed the architectural landscape of Stockholm, Gustavus III (1746–92) revived the absolute power of the monarchy, perhaps as a reaction against the changes effected by the French Revolution. He was assassinated by a group of fanatical noblemen while attending a ball at the Opera.

THE 19TH CENTURY   The next king was Gustavus IV (1778–1837). Because he hated Napoléon, Gustavus IV led Sweden into the Third Coalition against France (1805–07). For his efforts, he lost Stralsund and Swedish Pomerania; in the wars against Russia and Denmark, Sweden lost Finland in 1808. The next year, following an uprising, Gustavus IV was overthrown and died in exile.

A new constitution was written in 1808, granting the Riksdag equal power with the king. Under these provisions, Charles XIII (1748–1818), the uncle of the deposed king, became the new monarch.

Napoléon arranged for his aide, Jean Bernadotte (1763–1844), to become heir to the Swedish throne. Bernadotte won a war with Denmark, forcing that country to cede Norway to Sweden (1814). Upon the death of Charles, Bernadotte became king of Sweden and Norway, ruling as Charles XIV. During his reign, Sweden adopted a policy of neutrality, and the royal line that he established is still on the throne today. Charles XIV was succeeded by his son, Oscar I (1799–1859), who introduced many reforms, including freedom of worship and of the press.

The Industrial Revolution of the 19th century changed the face of Sweden. The Social Democratic Party was launched in 1889, leading to a universal suffrage movement. All males acquired the right to vote in 1909.

THE 20TH CENTURY   Norway declared its independence in 1905 and Sweden accepted the secession. Sweden adhered to a policy of neutrality during World War I, although many Swedes were sympathetic to the German cause. Many Swedish volunteers enlisted in the White Army during the Russian Revolution of 1917.

In 1921, women gained the right to vote, and an 8-hour workday was established. The Social Democratic Party continued to grow in power, and after 1932 a welfare state was instituted.

Although Sweden offered weapons and volunteers to Finland during its Winter War against the Soviet Union in 1939, it declared its neutrality during World War II. Sweden evoked long-lived resentment from its neighbor, Norway, whose cities were leveled by the Nazi troops that had been granted free passage across Swedish territory. Under heavy Allied threats against Sweden in 1943 and 1944, Nazi troop transports through the country eventually were halted. Throughout the war, Sweden accepted many impoverished and homeless refugees. The rescue attempts of Hungarian Jews led by Swedish businessman and diplomat Raoul Wallenberg have been recounted in books and films.

Sweden joined the United Nations in 1946 but refused to join NATO in 1949. Rather more disturbing was Sweden's decision to return to the Soviet

There's Something About the Swedes

The Swedes are responsible for inventing much that has changed modern life, including the safety match, alternating current, the milk separator, the refrigerator, the vacuum cleaner, and the ball bearing. And of course, there's the zipper (which has led to all sorts of interesting situations all over the world).

Union many German and Baltic refugees who had opposed Russia during the war. They were presumably killed on Stalin's orders.

Dag Hammarskjöld, as secretary-general of the United Nations in 1953, did much to help Sweden regain the international respect that it had lost because of its wartime policies. In 1961, toward the end of his second 5-year term, he was killed in an airplane crash.

Sweden continued to institute social reforms in the 1950s and 1960s, including the establishment of a national health service.

At only 27 years, Karl XVI Gustaf became king of Sweden in 1973, following the death of his grandfather, Gustaf VI Adolf (the king's father had been killed in an airplane crash when the king was still a child). In 1976, he married Silvia Sommerlath, who was born in Germany. King Karl XVI Gustaf and Queen Silvia have three children.

The Social Democrats ruled until 1976, when they were toppled by a Center/Liberal/Moderate coalition. The Social Democrats returned in 1982, but lost their majority in 1985 and had to rely on Communist support to enact legislation.

The leader of their party since 1969, Olof Palme was prime minister until his assassination outside a movie theater in Stockholm in 1986. A pacifist, he was a staunch critic of the United States, especially during the Vietnam War. In spite of an arrest, the murder has not been satisfactorily resolved.

Following the assassination of Olaf Palme, vice-prime minister Ingvar Carlsson was shoehorned into power, in accordance with provisions within the Social Democratic Party's bylaws. There he remained as an honest but dull caretaker until the end of Palme's elected term, devoted to promoting the party platforms of bountiful social benefits coupled with staggeringly high taxes.

In the early 1990s, Sweden faced some of the most troubling economic problems in recent memory, foremost of which was slow economic growth. Inflation was severe. In 1992, the government, then led by Conservative Prime Minister Carl Bildt, experienced a currency crisis that made headlines around the world. In September 1994, the Social Democrats, again spearheaded by Ingvar Carlsson, were returned to office after a brief interim of Conservative rule. The election brought the proportion of women in the Swedish Parliament to 41%, the highest in the world.

In 1995, Sweden, along with Finland and Austria, was granted full membership in the European Union, thereby providing a context for much-needed economic growth. In 1996, Prime Minister Carlsson, citing advanced age and a growing distaste for public life (in which he was the butt of many jokes that compared his appearance to that of an old shoe), retired midway through the elected term of his party.

Following well-established Parliamentary procedures, fellow Social Democrat Goeran Persson took his place. A highly capable former finance minister, Persson appealed to Swedes with a platform that advocated cutting taxes and curtailing government spending. Despite personal talent, Persson has been judged as a capable but remote administrator whose most visible drawback is a chilly, somewhat arrogant personal style that has provoked murmurs of discontent among some members of the Swedish electorate.

Just as its own image of itself as one of the most progressive nations on earth was being questioned, a chilling chapter from Sweden's past was revealed in 1997. Sweden had as many as 60,000 of its citizens sterilized, some involuntarily, from 1935 to 1976. The ideas behind the sterilization program had similarities to Nazi ideas of racial superiority. Singled out were those judged to be inferior, flawed by bad eyesight, mental retardation, and otherwise "undesirable" racial characteristics. The state wanted to prevent these genetic characteristics from being passed on. This law wasn't overturned until 1976. The respected newspaper *Dagens Nyheter* stirred national debate and worldwide headlines when it ran a series of articles about the former program, and at press time, Sweden had decided to pay reparations to those affected by the program.

As if this weren't bad enough, Sweden's once-lustrous reputation received more battering in 1997 with revelations of wartime iron exports that fed Hitler's military machine and of postwar Swedish hoarding of German gold, much of it looted from Nazi victims, which it received in payment for the metal.

In an election in September 1998, Social Democrats, still led by Goeran Persson, remained in power on a pledge to increase spending on the country's huge welfare program. The party secretary of the Moderates, Gunner Hokmark, found little comfort in the election, claiming, "It puts Swedes in a left lock that is stronger than any other country of Europe."

The government presently spends 46% of the gross national product on welfare, more than any other industrialized country. The income taxes required to support this public outlay take 59% of the pay of people. Employers pay up to 41% of employee remuneration into social security and pension plans. The former Communist Party now is called the Left Party, and it has steadily been growing in approval with voters.

In May of 2000, Sweden, for the first time in its history, became physically linked with the continent by the Øresund Bridge. Both Queen Margrethe of Denmark and King Carl Gustaf of Sweden inaugurated the span that links the Scandinavian peninsula with Europe. Construction on the 10-mile motor and railway link began in 1995.

The bridge gives the island of Zealand (the eastern part of Denmark) and Scania (the southern part of Sweden) a shared bridge, serving some 3.5 million inhabitants in the area.

The Øresund region, which encompasses parts of both Sweden and Denmark, is the largest domestic market in Northern Europe—larger than Stockholm and equal in size to Berlin, Hamburg, and Amsterdam combined. Built at a cost of $3 billion, it is the largest combined rail and road tunnel in the world. The price of a one-way fare in a passenger car is $30.

In theory, a vehicle now can travel in roughly a straight line from the Arctic coast of Norway to the Mediterranean shores of Spain. For centuries, it has been a dream to link the continent from its northern tip to its southern toe. The "Øresund Fixed Link" spans the icy Øresund Sound between the cities of Copenhagen and Malmö.

4 Famous Swedes

Ingmar Bergman (b. 1918)   Sweden's greatest film director made his debut in 1938 as an amateur director at a theater in Stockholm. His first feature film, *Crisis,* was released in 1945, but it wasn't until the 1950s that he became world famous. He made such highly acclaimed films as *The Seventh Seal, Wild Strawberries,* and *Cries and Whispers,* all hailed as classics. In three decades he directed more than 40 films, each dealing with a universal theme such as human isolation.

Ingrid Bergman (1916–82)   One of the world's finest stage and screen actresses always predicted that in spite of her impressive achievements, her obituaries would carry the headlines "Star of Casablanca Dies." And so they did. An unknown, she left Sweden for Hollywood to make *Intermezzo,* which was followed by such great films as *Gaslight* (her first Oscar), *For Whom the Bell Tolls, Notorious,* and *Anastasia.* She embodied virtue in such films as the *Bells of St. Mary's* and *Joan of Arc,* which led to a massive outcry against her when she left her Swedish husband and child to marry the Italian film director Roberto Rossellini. She was even condemned in the U.S. Senate. Sixteen years later she made a powerful comeback; *Murder on the Orient Express* brought her a third and final Oscar.

Baron Jons Jakob Berzelius (1779–1848)   Born in Vaversunda Sorgård in Sweden, Berzelius studied chemistry and medicine, graduating from Uppsala in 1802. He was named a member of the Royal Academy of Sciences in 1808, becoming secretary for life there in 1818. In 1835, King Charles XIV made him a baron. His many books on chemistry include *Theory of Chemical Proportions and Chemical Action of Electricity* in 1844. He was one of the fathers of modern chemistry, developing a system of chemical symbols and atomic weights of the elements.

Björn Borg (b. 1956)   At 17 years of age, this world-famous tennis player was on world-class circuits. Beginning in 1976, he won five consecutive Wimbledon singles titles. With his long hair, headband, and superbly elastic legs, he personified an era in tennis. Borg was to help Sweden win the first Davis Cup Trophy against the former Czechoslovakia in 1975, making him a national hero in his homeland. With 62 singles titles to his name, Borg is remembered for his sheer athleticism on the court and his ice-cool temperament under pressure.

Charles XII (1682–1718)   The oldest son of Charles XI of Sweden and Ulrika Eleanora of Denmark, this king is one of the most famous ever to emerge from Sweden. Following his father on the throne, he became an absolute monarch in 1697 at the age of 15. In 1700, the Great Northern War broke out as Sweden faced Denmark, Poland, and Russia. He crushed the forces of Peter the Great in 1701, but eventually lost to the Russian army in 1709, and was forced into exile in Turkey. Returning to Sweden in 1714, he invaded Norway 4 years later, where he was fatally shot in the head.

Queen Christina (1626–89)   Christina became queen of Sweden at the age of 6, when she ruled under regents. Ironically, she is best remembered for two events: her abdication in 1654 and a Greta Garbo film, *Queen Christina.* Born in a palace in Stockholm on December 8, 1626, she was the daughter of King Gustavus II Adolphus and Maria Eleanora of Brandenburg. Taught philosophy by Descartes, Christina established a school system in Sweden, helped bring about the first Swedish newspaper, and improved industry. Her favorite residence was Riario Palace in Rome where she lived with her lover, Decio Cardinal Azzolino, to whom she left everything in her will. She was buried at St. Peter's in Rome. The Vatican Library holds her entire collection of books.

Stefan Bengt Edberg (b. 1966)   Today a well-paid spokesperson for Adidas, in 1988, Edberg became the first Swede since Borg to win the Wimbledon singles title. He went on to win again in 1990 and followed that by winning the

U.S. Open in 1991 and again in 1992. He lives in England and France, and remains one of the world's most admired tennis players.

John Ericsson (1803–89)   Sweden's most famous inventor played a decisive role in the Civil War in the United States. He was born in Långbanshyttan, Sweden on July 31, 1801, and by 1820 had joined the Swedish Army. Ericsson's marine propeller, by 1843, had shown itself superior to the paddle wheel. His warship, *Monitor,* on May 9, 1862, defeated the Confederacy's *Merrimac,* saving the Yankee fleet and earning the inventor world renown. Although he moved to the United States and played a part in its turbulent history, he specified that he be buried on Swedish soil. After Ericsson's death in the United States on March 8, 1889, his body was transported to Sweden on the American armored cruiser *Baltimore* with full honors.

Greta Garbo (1905–90)   One of the "fabulous faces" of the 20th century, Garbo was a screen actress of legendary charm who, after coming to MGM in 1925, launched a career that was to include such screen classics as *Anna Christie* (her first talkie), *Grand Hotel, Camille,* and *Ninotchka.* She played opposite some of the biggest male stars in film history—often with her lover John Gilbert. ("I would rather spend an hour with Fleka than a lifetime with any other woman," he said of her.) Born Greta Gustafsson on September 18, 1905, in the city slums of Stockholm at Blekingegatan 32 (now a restaurant), she got her start as a *Tvålflicka* ("soap lather girl") in a barbershop, and later modeled hats at PUB Department store. In Hollywood she abdicated as screen queen in 1941. "They dug my grave. I play no more bad womens." Her most famous address was a seven-room apartment overlooking the East River in New York where she lived under the pseudonym "Miss Harriet Brown."

Dag Hammarskjöld (1905–61)   In 1936, Hammarskjöld became undersecretary in the Ministry of Finance and later president of the board controlling the Bank of Sweden. After serving as minister of state, he was named secretary-general of the United Nations where he presided over bitter Cold War disputes. He was unanimously re-elected for another 5 years in 1957. He met crisis after crisis, notably over the Suez Canal. His sending United Nations troops to the Belgian Congo was bitterly denounced by the Soviet Union, which demanded his resignation; he refused. He was posthumously awarded the Nobel Peace Prize.

John Hanson (1721–83)   A colonial Swede, this "first president of the United States" was born in Mulberry Grove, Maryland, and in time became a plantation owner with some 100 black slaves. In 1781, when Maryland became the last of 13 colonies to ratify the Articles of Confederation, the Continental Congress unanimously elected John Hanson the first president of the United States in a Congress assembled for a 12-month term—8 years before George Washington was elected. During his 1-year term (1781–82), he established the Department of State, War, Navy, and Treasury and set up a national judiciary, a national bank, and a post office; and formed a cabinet. He died in his sleep a year after leaving office. Virtually unknown, ignored, or forgotten by most Americans, he is still remembered in Maryland on April 14, John Hanson Day, and by lobbyists who want to make that date a national holiday. A life-size statue of Hanson stands in the rotunda of the Capitol building in Washington.

Charles John (1763–1844)   Born as Jean Bernadotte in Paul, France, he launched his military career by joining the French army in 1790. Meeting and becoming friends with Napoléon in 1797, Bernadotte later became his bitter enemy. He married Napoléon's ex-fiancée, Desirée Clary, in 1798 (the Marlon Brando film *Desirée* was based on these events). In 1803, Bernadotte became minister to the United States, and in 1810 he was asked to become prince of Sweden to replace Charles XIII upon his death. Charles John allied with Russia, Great Britain, and Prussia to take Norway from Denmark and to fight Napoléon. The Danes were defeated in 1813 in the Battle of Leipzig, and Charles John took control of Norway.

Selma Lagerlöf (1858–1940)   The towering woman writer of her country, the novelist was called "specifically Swedish and undeniably universal" by Paul Valery. Her works, including *The Saga of Gösta Berling* and *The Wonderful Adventures of Nils,* have been translated into 40 languages. In 1909 she won the Nobel Prize for literature, and in 1914 was made the first female member of the Swedish Academy. At 75 she published her last collection of short stories and was at work on a novel when she died at her beloved Mårbacka, outside Karlstad (open to the public).

Jenny Lind (1820–87)   "The Swedish Nightingale" was born the daughter of a lace manufacturer in Stockholm and went from there to captivate the hearts of the world with her music. She also captured the heart of Hans Christian Andersen (but didn't want it). Launched in opera in 1837, she appeared in France and England before her 2-year triumphant tour of the United States, at which time she was engaged to P. T. Barnum. Settling in England after her 1852 marriage to Otto Goldschmidt, she appeared in oratorios and concerts there, eventually becoming a professor of music. Her last public appearance was at Düsseldorf, Germany, on January 20, 1870, singing an oratorio composed by her husband. She died on November 2, 1887 at Malvern, England.

Astrid Lindgren (b. 1907)   This children's book writer has enjoyed international fame as the creator of Pippi Longstocking (Pippi Långssstrump). Her works have been published around the world in various languages, and it's estimated that she has sold 6 million copies. She conceived of this red-haired, rambunctious heroine in 1944 as a present to her daughter. In 1949, a Hamburg-based publisher acquired continental rights and launched Lindgren and Pippi into international stardom. Her writings have earned her a position as one of Sweden's most honored writers, and she remains the most widely read Swedish-born author in the world. In 1993, she won the UNESCO International Book Award.

Carolus Linnaeus (or Carl von Linné) (1707–78)   The great Swedish botanist compiled *Species Plantarum* (Plant Species), a definitive catalogue of plants, in 1753. Nicknamed "the little botanist" at the age of 8, he began the modern system of botanical nomenclature. Linnaeus was born at South Rashult, Sweden, on May 23, 1707. At Uppsala University, he was given a chair of botany in 1742. The Linnaeus Garden at Uppsala is open to the public. Here he received a "Patent of Nobility" and the new name Carl von Linné. After suffering an apoplectic attack, he died on January 20, 1778, and was buried at the University of Uppsala Cathedral.

Volvo Versus ABBA

In the late 1970s, money generated by ABBA was second only to that of Volvo in terms of total exports from Sweden.

Ikea Style

One of the most famous manufacturers of household furniture and housewares in the world is Ikea, a company founded after World War II whose stores are sprawling warehouses filled with a cornucopia of modern furniture and household accessories that show the good life *à la Suèdoise*. Their trademark style involves ample amounts of birch trim and birch veneer, sometimes accented with black, always presented in a "less is more" format that shows the virtues of thrift, simple lines, and efficiency. From the core of two megastores, set to the north and south of Stockholm, respectively, a series of other outlets have sprung up around the world. Vital to the organization's self-image is the presence of a cafeteria serving all-Swedish food. They provide cost-conscious refreshments and pick-me-ups that fortify shoppers (and those who merely crave *frikadeller* [meatballs]), at budget prices.

Carl Milles (1875–1955)   The most distinguished Swedish sculptor of the 20th century was born in Uppsala and studied in Paris where he won recognition. He was greatly influenced by Rodin and sculpted in an impressionistic style, mainly in clay, wood, and stone. He worked in Sweden until 1930, but from then on lived in the United States where he became an American citizen and executed many notable commissions, including "Meeting of the Water" in St. Louis. His later works, exhibited from Chicago to New York, had a simplified quality that was both expressive and dramatic.

Alfred Nobel (1833–96)   This 19th-century Swedish industrialist and creator of prizes that bear his name was the inventor of dynamite which, although used in war, has played an important role in the industrial development of the world. He studied explosives and in 1867 was given a British patent for dynamite. He constructed and perfected detonators and amassed a great fortune, amounting to $9.2 million upon his death, which he stipulated go as prizes "to those who have conferred the greatest benefit on mankind."

Olof Palme (1927–86)   The former prime minister of Sweden ironically became better known upon his death. Leaving a cinema with his wife, he was mysteriously gunned down on a street. A controversial leader, Palme was a leader of the so-called Socialist International, consisting of Social Democratic Parties, and was particularly active in the Third World. His vehement attacks on the United States at the time of the Vietnam War led to acrid exchanges with Washington. To the end, he was a great champion of the welfare society.

August Strindberg (1849–1912)   Son of a steamship agent and a former waitress, Strindberg had an unhappy childhood as related in his autobiography *The Son of a Servant* in 1889. But in time he was to become the country's greatest playwright, exerting a profound influence on international drama. A freelance journalist and later a librarian, he tried many professions before publishing his widely acclaimed novel *The Red Room,* written in 1879. Between stormy marriages, he wrote many plays, including *The Father* (1887) and *Miss Julie* (1888). He died of cancer on May 14, 1912, in Stockholm and was ignored in death as in life by the Swedish Academy.

Emanuel Swedenborg (1688–1772)   Son of a bishop in Skåra, who was a major religious figure in Sweden, Swedenborg became a scientist, philosopher,

Swedish Yankees

Waves of Swedes came to the United States in the 19th century and rushed to embrace Americanisms and the English language. Perhaps because they blend in so well, the descendants of those immigrants are among the least noticeable, least self-asserting national group in the country today. Despite their assimilation, Swedish immigrants have had an influence as profound as that of any other national group.

The Swedes first settled in North America in 1638, when the colony of New Sweden was established at the mouth of the Delaware River. The settlement was captured by the Dutch 17 years later, and the settlers evacuated to New Amsterdam, the town that became New York. Famous Swedes who left their mark included Capt. Jonas Bronck, whose homestead still bears a version of his name—the Bronx. Later, during the American Revolution, came such ideologues as Count Axel von Fersen (who reportedly had a tryst or two with Marie Antoinette) and John Mårtensson (John Morton), one of the signers of the Declaration of Independence. Sweden, lacking a base in the New World and eager to undermine Britain (one of its most powerful maritime rivals), was the first country to sign a trade agreement with the fledgling United States.

Fascination with the New World overcame Sweden's population in earnest in 1846, and waves of Swedes set out to seek health, wealth, religious freedom, and a land of their own. During a 5-year period beginning in 1868, five annual crops failed in Sweden, leading to the migration of at least 100,000 people. Between 1846 and 1873, a total of 1.5 million Swedes emigrated to North America—a figure that's especially impressive considering that Sweden's entire population was only around 4 million. The drain on the country's human resources was disastrous. Of all European countries, only Ireland lost a larger proportion of its population to emigration.

It's noteworthy that Sweden's high literacy rate, which endured despite the famine that affected many immigrants, helped Swedes to assimilate in the New World. In some regions of the Midwest, Swedes tended to settle together, but there were never any urban ghettos inhabited mainly by Swedes.

The first, and among the best-publicized, group of Swedish immigrants was a 1,500-member religious sect known as Jansonists (Erikjansare) whose leader, Erik Jansson, founded a colony in Illinois known as Bishop's Hill. Conceived as a utopia where all goods and property would be shared in common, it attracted national journalistic attention until an enraged disciple, furious at the refusal of the group's leader to allow his wife to leave the community, shot Jansson. Jansson's disciples, who believed he was immortal and would soon be resurrected, scattered throughout the Midwest and eventually established their own farms.

and theologian. He studied in Uppsala and went to England to pursue his interest in natural sciences. Influenced by Descartes, he published many philosophical and psychological works in the 1720s and 1730s, in which he saw the world as subject to mechanical laws. He was concerned with the source and structure of matter, concluding finally that the soul is material, as reported in his *Regnum Animale.* His theological insights had great influence on Dostoyevsky, Emerson, Balzac, Ezra Pound, and others; many congregations in the United States take Swedenborg's writings as their doctrinal basis. His *Journal of Dreams* is still widely read.

Mai Zetterling (1926–94)   One of Europe's busiest female film directors, Zetterling died while filming *The Woman Who Cleaned the World,* which she had written. Born in Vasteras to a working-class family, she first became famous as an actress in the film *Torment* (1947), written by Ingmar Bergman. She appeared opposite such stars as Danny Kaye in *Knock on Wood* (1954) and Peter Sellers in *Only Two Can Play* (1961). In the 1960s and 1970s, she turned to directing such films as *Night Games* (1966) and *Of Seals and Men* (1979). She also wrote short stories, novels, and children's books.

Anders Zorn (1860–1920)   A member of the Association of Artists, founded in the 19th century. His famous works include *Midsummer Nights' Dance* and *Young Girls Bathing.* His works can be seen in Dalarna, Stockholm, and Chicago.

5 The Swedish Chef

The fame of the *smörgåsbord* (smörgåsbord) is justly deserved. Using a vast array of dishes—everything from Baltic herring to smoked reindeer—the smörgåsbord can be eaten either as hors d'oeuvres or as a meal in itself.

One cardinal rule of the smörgåsbord: Don't mix fish and meat dishes. It is customary to begin with *sill* (herring), prepared in many ways. Herring usually is followed by other treats from the sea (jellied eel, smoked fish, and raw pickled salmon); then diners proceed to the cold meat dishes, such as baked ham or liver paste, which are accompanied by vegetable salads. Hot dishes, often Swedish meatballs, come next, and are backed up by cheese and crackers, and sometimes a fresh fruit salad.

The smörgåsbord is not served as often in Sweden as many visitors seem to believe, as it requires time-consuming preparation. Many Swedish families reserve it for special occasions. In lieu of the 40-dish smörgåsbord, some restaurants have taken to serving a plate of *assietter* (hors d'oeuvres). One of the tricks for enjoying smörgåsbord is timing. It's best to go early, when dishes are fresh. Late arrivals may be more fashionable, but the food often is stale.

The average times for meals in Sweden are generally from 8 to 11am for the standard continental breakfast, noon to 2:30pm for lunch, and as early as 5:30pm for dinner to around 8 or 8:30pm (many restaurants in Stockholm are open to midnight—but don't count on this in the small villages).

A Swedish breakfast at your hotel might consist of cheese, ham, sausage, egg, bread, and perhaps *filmjölk,* a kind of sour-milk yogurt. **Smörgas,** the famous Swedish open-face sandwich, like the Danish *smørrebrød* and Norwegian *smørbrød,* is a slice of buttered bread with something on top. It is eaten for breakfast or any time during the day, and you'll find it at varying prices, depending on what you order and where you order it.

Unless you decide to have smörgåsbord (never served in the evening) at lunch, you'll find that the Swedes do not go in for lavish spreads in the middle of the day. The usual luncheon order consists of one course, as you'll observe on menus, especially in larger towns. Dinner menus are for complete meals, with appetizer, main course and side dishes, and dessert included.

Generally Swedish chefs tend to be far more expert with **fish dishes** (freshwater pike and salmon are star choices) than with meat courses. The Swedes go stark raving mad at the sight of *kraftor* (crayfish), in season from mid-August to mid-September. This succulent, dill-flavored delicacy is eaten with the fingers, and much of the fun is the elaborate ritual surrounding its consumption.

A platter of thin **pancakes,** served with lingonberries (comparable to cranberries), is the traditional Thursday-night dinner in Sweden. It often is preceded by yellow split-pea soup seasoned with pork. It's good any night of the week—but somehow better on Thursday.

The Swedish cuisine used to be deficient in fresh vegetables and fruits, relying heavily on the tin can, but this is no longer true. Potatoes are the staff of life, but fresh salads have long peppered the landscape, especially in big cities.

The calorie-laden Swedish pastry—the mainstay of the konditori (cafeteria)—is tempting and fatal to weight-watchers.

DRINKS **Kaffe** (coffee) is the universal drink in Sweden, although tea (taken straight) and milk also are popular. The water is perfectly safe to drink all over Sweden. Those who want a reprieve from alcohol might find the fruit-flavored **Pommac** a good soft-drink beverage, but Coca-Cola is ubiquitous.

The state monopoly, Systembolaget, controls the sale of alcoholic beverages. Licensed restaurants may sell alcohol after noon only (1pm on Sunday).

Schnapps or aquavit, served icy cold, is a superb Swedish drink, often used to accompany smörgåsbord. The run-of-the-mill Swedish **beer** (pilsner) has only a small amount of alcohol. All restaurants serve *lättol* (light beer) and *folköl,* a somewhat stronger brew. Swedish vodka, or **brännvin,** is made from corn and potatoes and flavored with different spices. All brännvin is served ice cold in schnapps glasses. Keep in mind that aquavit is much stronger than it looks, and Sweden has strictly enforced rules about drinking and driving. Most Swedes seem to drink their liquor straight. But mixed drinks, especially in urban areas, are now more commonplace. Either way, the drink prices are sky-high.

6 Recommended Books

BIOGRAPHY *Swedes in North America (1638–1988),* by Sten Carlsson (Streiffert & Co., 1988), traces the lives of some of the 2% of the North American population that has some sort of Swedish background—from Greta Garbo to Charles Lindbergh.

Alfred Nobel, by Kenne Fant (Arcade, 1993), traces the life of this Swedish industrialist and chemist, the inventor of dynamite. The book reveals that this shy pacifist believed the creation of weapons for massive annihilation would make war impossible. Excerpts from his heretofore unpublished letters to his coquettish Austrian mistress also are included.

Garbo: Her Story, by Antoni Gronowicz (Simon & Schuster, 1990), is a controversial, unauthorized memoir based on a long and intimate friendship, going behind the fabulous face, with many candid details of this most reluctant of movie legends.

Sunday's Children, by Ingmar Bergman (Arcade, 1994), set in the summer of 1926, is an autobiographical novel in which the Swedish director returns to the scene of his childhood.

FILM *Ingmar Bergman: The Cinema As Mistress,* by Philip Mosley (Marion Boyars, 1981), is a critical study of Bergman's oeuvre dating from his earliest work as a writer and director in the late 1940s up to *Autumn Sonata.*

Swedish Cinema, from Ingeborg Holm to Fanny and Alexander, by Peter Cowie (Swedish Institute, 1985), covers the complete history of Swedish films, from the emergence of the silent era to the rise of Ingmar Bergman, up to the most recent wave.

HISTORY & MYTHOLOGY The Vikings are the subject of numerous works, including *The Vikings,* by Johannes Brönsted (Penguin, 1983), and *Viking Ways: On the Viking Age in Sweden,* by Maj Odelberg (Swedish Institute, 1986).

Scandinavian Folk & Fairy Tales, edited by Claire Booss (Avenel, 1994), is an extraordinary collection filled with elves, dwarfs, trolls, goblins, and other spirits of the house and barnyard.

LITERATURE & THEATER *A History of Swedish Literature,* by Ingemar Algulin (Swedish Institute, 1989), is the best overview on the subject—from the runic inscriptions of the Viking age up to modern fiction.

Three Plays: Father, Miss Julie, Easter, by August Strindberg (Penguin, many editions), provides an insight into the world of this strange Swedish genius who wrote a number of highly arresting dramas, of which these are some of the best known.

Index

See also Accommodations and Restaurant indexes below.

General Index

ACCOMMODATIONS

Accommodations Index

RESTAURANTS

Restaurant Index

Restaurant Index

FROMMER'S® COMPLETE TRAVEL GUIDES

Alaska
Amsterdam
Argentina & Chile
Arizona
Atlanta
Australia
Austria
Bahamas
Barcelona, Madrid & Seville
Beijing
Belgium, Holland &
  Luxembourg
Bermuda
Boston
British Columbia & the
  Canadian Rockies
Budapest & the Best of Hungary
California
Canada
Cancún, Cozumel & the
  Yucatán
Cape Cod, Nantucket &
  Martha's Vineyard
Caribbean
Caribbean Cruises & Ports
  of Call
Caribbean Ports of Call
Carolinas & Georgia
Chicago
China
Colorado
Costa Rica
Denmark
Denver, Boulder & Colorado
  Springs
England
Europe

European Cruises & Ports of Call
Florida
France
Germany
Greece
Greek Islands
Hawaii
Hong Kong
Honolulu, Waikiki & Oahu
Ireland
Israel
Italy
Jamaica
Japan
Las Vegas
London
Los Angeles
Maryland & Delaware
Maui
Mexico
Montana & Wyoming
Montréal & Québec City
Munich & the Bavarian Alps
Nashville & Memphis
Nepal
New England
New Mexico
New Orleans
New York City
New Zealand
Nova Scotia, New Brunswick &
  Prince Edward Island
Oregon
Paris
Philadelphia & the Amish
  Country
Portugal

Prague & the Best of the Czech
  Republic
Provence & the Riviera
Puerto Rico
Rome
San Antonio & Austin
San Diego
San Francisco
Santa Fe, Taos & Albuquerque
Scandinavia
Scotland
Seattle & Portland
Shanghai
Singapore & Malaysia
South Africa
Southeast Asia
South Florida
South Pacific
Spain
Sweden
Switzerland
Texas
Thailand
Tokyo
Toronto
Tuscany & Umbria
USA
Utah
Vancouver & Victoria
Vermont, New Hampshire
  & Maine
Vienna & the Danube Valley
Virgin Islands
Virginia
Walt Disney World & Orlando
Washington, D.C.
Washington State

FROMMER'S® DOLLAR-A-DAY GUIDES

Australia from $50 a Day
California from $70 a Day
Caribbean from $70 a Day
England from $70 a Day
Europe from $70 a Day

Florida from $70 a Day
Hawaii from $70 a Day
Ireland from $60 a Day
Italy from $70 a Day
London from $85 a Day

New York from $80 a Day
Paris from $80 a Day
San Francisco from $60 a Day
Washington, D.C.,
  from $70 a Day

FROMMER'S® PORTABLE GUIDES

Acapulco, Ixtapa &
  Zihuatanejo
Alaska Cruises & Ports
  of Call
Amsterdam
Australia's Great Barrier Reef
Bahamas
Baja & Los Cabos
Berlin
Boston
California Wine Country
Charleston & Savannah
Chicago

Dublin
Hawaii: The Big Island
Hong Kong
Houston
Las Vegas
London
Los Angeles
Maine Coast
Maui
Miami
New Orleans
New York City
Paris

Phoenix & Scottsdale
Portland
Puerto Rico
Puerto Vallarta, Manzanillo &
  Guadalajara
San Diego
San Francisco
Seattle
Sydney
Tampa & St. Petersburg
Vancouver
Venice
Washington, D.C.

FROMMER'S® NATIONAL PARK GUIDES

Family Vacations in the
  National Parks
Grand Canyon

National Parks of the American
  West
Rocky Mountain
Yellowstone & Grand Teton

Yosemite & Sequoia/
  Kings Canyon
Zion & Bryce Canyon

FROMMER'S® MEMORABLE WALKS

Chicago	New York	San Francisco
London	Paris	Washington, D.C.

FROMMER'S® GREAT OUTDOOR GUIDES

Arizona & New Mexico	Northern California	Southern New England
New England	Southern California & Baja	Vermont & New Hampshire

FROMMER'S® BORN TO SHOP GUIDES

Born to Shop: France	Born to Shop: Italy	Born to Shop: New York
Born to Shop: Hong Kong, Shanghai & Beijing	Born to Shop: London	Born to Shop: Paris

FROMMER'S® IRREVERENT GUIDES

Amsterdam	Los Angeles	Seattle & Portland
Boston	Manhattan	Vancouver
Chicago	New Orleans	Walt Disney World
Las Vegas	Paris	Washington, D.C.
London	San Francisco	

FROMMER'S® BEST-LOVED DRIVING TOURS

America	France	New England
Britain	Germany	Scotland
California	Ireland	Spain
Florida	Italy	Western Europe

THE UNOFFICIAL GUIDES®

Bed & Breakfasts in California	Golf Vacations in the Eastern U.S.	New Orleans
Bed & Breakfasts in New England	The Great Smoky & Blue Ridge Mountains	New York City
Bed & Breakfasts in the Northwest	Inside Disney	Paris
Bed & Breakfasts in Southeast	Hawaii	San Francisco
Beyond Disney	Las Vegas	Skiing in the West
Branson, Missouri	London	Southeast with Kids
California with Kids	Mid-Atlantic with Kids	Walt Disney World
Chicago	Mini Las Vegas	Walt Disney World for Grown-ups
Cruises	Mini-Mickey	Walt Disney World for Kids
Disneyland	New England with Kids	Washington, D.C.
Florida with Kids		World's Best Diving Vacations

SPECIAL-INTEREST TITLES

Frommer's Britain's Best Bed & Breakfasts and Country Inns	Hanging Out in Europe
Frommer's France's Best Bed & Breakfasts and Country Inns	Hanging Out in France
	Hanging Out in Ireland
	Hanging Out in Italy
Frommer's Italy's Best Bed & Breakfasts and Country Inns	Hanging Out in Spain
Frommer's Caribbean Hideaways	Israel Past & Present
Frommer's Adventure Guide to Australia & New Zealand	Frommer's The Moon
	Frommer's New York City with Kids
Frommer's Adventure Guide to Central America	The New York Times' Guide to Unforgettable Weekends
Frommer's Adventure Guide to India & Pakistan	Places Rated Almanac
Frommer's Adventure Guide to South America	Retirement Places Rated
Frommer's Adventure Guide to Southeast Asia	Frommer's Road Atlas Britain
Frommer's Adventure Guide to Southern Africa	Frommer's Road Atlas Europe
Frommer's Gay & Lesbian Europe	Frommer's Washington, D.C., with Kids
Frommer's Exploring America by RV	Frommer's What the Airlines Never Tell You
Hanging Out in England	

Let Us Hear From You!

)ear Frommer's Reader,

ou are our greatest resource in keeping our guides relevant, timely, and lively. Ve'd love to hear from you about your travel experiences—good or bad. Want to ecommend a great restaurant or a hotel off the beaten path—or register a complaint? ny thoughts on how to improve the guide itself?

lease use this page to share your thoughts with me and mail it to the address below.)r if you like, send a FAX or e-mail me at frommersfeedback@hungryminds.com. nd so that we can thank you—and keep you up on the latest developments in ravel—we invite you to sign up for a free daily Frommer's e-mail travel update. Just rite your e-mail address on the back of this page. Also, if you'd like to take a moment) answer a few questions about yourself to help us improve our guides, please com- lete the following quick survey. (We'll keep that information confidential.)

hanks for your insights.

ours sincerely,

Michael Spring

Iichael Spring, *Publisher*

Iame (Optional) _____

ddress_____

_____

.ity_____State_____ZIP_____

.ame of Frommer's Travel Guide _____

.omments_____

_____

_____

_____

_____

_____

_____

_____

_____

_____

Please tell us a little about yourself so that we can serve you and the Frommer's community better. We will keep this information confidential.

Age: ( )18-24; ( )25-39; ( )40-49; ( )50-55; ( )Over 55

Income: ( )Under $25,000; ( )$25,000-$50,000; ( )$50,000-$100,000; ( )Over $100,000

I am: ( )Single, never married; ( )Married, with children; ( )Married, without children; ( )Divorced; ( )Widowed

Number of people in my household: ( )1; ( )2; ( )3; ( )4; ( )5 or more

Number of people in my household under 18: ( )1; ( )2; ( )3; ( )4; ( )5 or more

I am ( )a student; ( )employed full-time; ( )employed part-time; ( )not employed at this time ( )retired; ( )other

I took ( )0; ( )1; ( )2; ( )3; ( )4 or more leisure trips in the past 12 months

My last vacation was ( )a weekend; ( )1 week; ( )2 weeks; ( )3 or more weeks

My last vacation was to ( )the U.S.; ( )Canada; ( )Mexico; ( )Europe; ( )Asia; ( )South America; ( )Central America; ( )The Caribbean; ( )Africa; ( )Middle East; ( )Australia/New Zealand

( )I would; ( )would not buy a Frommer's Travel Guide for business travel

I access the Internet ( )at home; ( )at work; ( )both; ( )I do not use the Internet

I used the Internet to do research for my last trip. ( )Yes; ( )No

I used the Internet to book accommodations or air travel on my last trip. ( )Yes; ( )No

My favorite travel site is ( )frommers.com; ( )travelocity.com; ( )expedia.com;

other_____

I use Frommer's Travel Guides ( )always; ( )sometimes; ( )seldom

I usually buy ( )1; ( )2; ( )more than 2 guides when I travel

Other guides I use include _____

What's the most important thing we could do to improve Frommer's Travel Guides?

_____

_____

_____

_____

Yes, please send me a daily e-mail travel update. My e-mail address is

_____

Mail to: Michael Spring, Publisher and Vice President, Frommer's Travel Guides
909 Third Ave., New York, NY 10022   FAX: 212.884.5432